Oswald Joseph Reichel

A Complete Manual Of Canon Law

Volume 2, Church Discipline

Oswald Joseph Reichel

A Complete Manual Of Canon Law
Volume 2, Church Discipline

ISBN/EAN: 9783741110207

Manufactured in Europe, USA, Canada, Australia, Japa

Cover: Foto ©Lupo / pixelio.de

Manufactured and distributed by brebook publishing software (www.brebook.com)

Oswald Joseph Reichel

A Complete Manual Of Canon Law

Catholic Standard Library

A COMPLETE

MANUAL OF CANON LAW

BY OSWALD J. REICHEL, B.C.L., M.A., F.S.A.
Some time Vice-Principal of Cuddesdon College

MANUALS OF CANON LAW

A Series of Short Manuals in which not only the law is laid down, but references given to authorities for every statement, so that readers may be able to verify the law for themselves.

1s. each Part.

Part I. THE CANON LAW OF THE SACRAMENTS. The Sacraments generally, the Nature and Essentials of a Sacrament, Signs and their Uses.

Part II. OF BAPTISM. Containing Baptism, Confirmation, the Position and Duties of Laymen.

Parts III., IV., and V. OF THE EUCHARIST. Containing the Law of the Sacrifice, of Communion, &c.

Parts VI. and VII. THE CANON LAW OF PENANCE. Containing the Ministry and Discipline of Reconciliation, Extreme Unction, &c.

Parts VIII. and IX. THE CANON LAW OF ORDER.

Parts X. and XI. THE LAW OF MATRIMONY.

Parts XII. and XIII. OF ECCLESIASTICAL SACRAMENTS, &c.

Parts XIV., XV., and XVI. OF DISCIPLINE GENERALLY AND THE LAW OF EXCESSES.

Parts XVII. and XVIII. LAW OF DISCIPLINE OF THE RELIGIOUS LIFE AND OF RELIGIOUS ORDERS.

Parts XIX.-XX. OF ECCLESIASTICAL SEVERITY AND SPIRITUAL COURTS.

Parts XXI.-XXII. CANONICAL PROCEDURE AND ACTS IN JUDGMENT.

Parts XXIII., XXIV., and XXV. ACTS IN JUDGMENT, CONCLUSION OF A CAUSE, INDICES AND TITLES.

Also in Volumes, demy 8vo, 12s. each net.

Vol. I. THE SACRAMENTS.
" II. CHURCH DISCIPLINE.
" III. CHURCH GOVERNMENT. [*In the Press.*
" IV. THE PAROCHIAL SYSTEM. [*In the Press.*

Any Parts or Vols. may be had separately, post free, at the published price.

"That it is the work of a scholar of very wide reading, the mass of evidence, historical and liturgical, with which the pages are almost overcrowded, amply proves."—*Tablet.*
"It is of the highest value to one entering upon the study of its subject, and likely also to prove of great service to advanced canonists for purposes of reference."—*Scotsman.*
"It is difficult to conceive a work more acceptable to Churchmen. It is a most learned work—learned, indeed, beyond the dreams of the most pedantic."—*Law Times.*
"Written in a style clear and precise. By his accurate and methodical researches the author has rendered a true service to careful studies."—*La Civiltà Cattolica.*
"Supplies a very urgent need which is very widely felt now that the study of Canon Law is being revived in the English Church."—*Church Times.*

By the Same Author, Papers Read before the Exeter Diocesan Society.

SOLEMN MASS AT ROME IN THE NINTH CENTURY. Second Edition, with a Sketch Plan of Basilica. 8vo, 1s.

THE ORIGIN OF ENGLISH LITURGICAL VESTMENTS PRESCRIBED FOR USE IN THE THIRTEENTH CENTURY. With Six Illustrations. 8vo, 1s. 6d.

JOHN HODGES, BEDFORD STREET, STRAND, LONDON

A COMPLETE MANUAL OF
CANON LAW

BY

OSWALD J. REICHEL, M.A., B.C.L., F.S.A.
AUTHOR OF
"THE SEE OF ROME IN THE MIDDLE AGES," ETC.

Ἐγώ εἰμι ἡ θύρα· δι' ἐμοῦ ἐάν τις εἰσέλθῃ, σωθήσεται· Ὁ φιλῶν τὴν ψυχὴν αὐτοῦ, ἀπολέσει αὐτήν· καὶ ὁ μισῶν τὴν ψυχὴν αὐτοῦ ἐν τῷ κόσμῳ τούτῳ, εἰς ζωὴν αἰώνιον φυλάξει αὐτήν.—JOHN x. 9; xii. 25.

VOLUME II
CHURCH DISCIPLINE

JOHN HODGES
BEDFORD STREET, STRAND, LONDON
1896

PREFACE.

On the 20th day of June 1894 the most blessed Bishop of old Rome, Leo XIII., addressed an encyclical letter to the rulers and nations of the world, in which, "drawn," as he informs them, "to follow the example of our Redeemer and Master Jesus Christ, Who, when about to return to heaven, implored of God, His Father, in earnest prayer, that His disciples and followers should be of one mind and of one heart," and breathing the Spirit of his divine Master, he most earnestly invited them to unity.

He then laid it down that the true union between Christians "consists in [1] a unity of faith, and [2] a unity of government," adding further [3] that this union can no otherwise be brought about than by acknowledging "the primacy of the Roman pontiff," and appealed to the oldest traditions to verify this statement.

To this encyclical Anthimos, the Bishop of the most holy Apostolic and patriarchal throne of Constantinople, together with twelve other Orthodox Catholic bishops, made reply in the month of August 1895, by a patriarchal and synodic encyclical letter addressed to all the bishops and clergy, and all the religious and Orthodox community under their united charge, in which, after saying how great is their yearning for the reunion of the Churches, they make the following among other statements:—

"3. Agreeably, therefore, to this sacred desire, our Orthodox Church of Christ is always ready to receive any proposal for reunion, provided only the Bishop of Rome once and for all shake off the chain of his many and divers 'privily brought in' [2 Pet. ii. 1] anti-evangelical innovations—the same which also provoked the sorrowful division of the Churches of East and West, and return to the ground of the holy Seven Ecumenical Councils, which, compacted as they were by the Holy Ghost of representatives of all the holy Churches of God, for the determination of the right doctrine of the faith against those affecting heresy, have universal and eternal validity in the Church of Christ."

The encyclical then proceeds to draw attention to the innovations referred to, in which the following passages are prominent:—

"7. The One Holy Catholic and Apostolic Church of the Seven Ecumenical Councils believed and taught, agreeably to the evangelic statements, that the Holy Ghost proceedeth from the Father; but in the West, from the ninth century onwards, the sacred Creed . . . began to be falsified, and the idea that the Holy Ghost proceedeth also from the Son to be wilfully propagated. Assuredly Pope Leo XIII. cannot be ignorant of the fact that his orthodox predecessor and namesake . . . Leo III., in 809, synodically disclaimed this anti-evangelical and wholly unlawful addition, 'and from the Son.'

"8. The One Holy Catholic and Apostolic Church of the Seven Ecumenical Councils baptized with three immersions in the water, and Pope Pelagius calls the trine immersion an ordinance of the Lord; and in the thirteenth century baptism by three immersions still prevailed in the West; . . . but in later times sprinkling and affusion were 'privily brought in.'

"10. The One Holy Catholic and Apostolic Church of the Seven Ecumenical Councils received that the precious gifts are hallowed after the prayer of the invocation of the Holy Ghost by the blessing of the priest, as the ancient rituals of Rome and the Gauls bear witness. Howbeit, afterwards the

Papal Church innovated in this by wilfully laying down that the hallowing of the precious gifts takes place along with the enunciation of the words of the Lord, 'Take, eat, this is My body,' and, 'Drink ye all of it, for this is My blood.'

"12. The One Holy Catholic and Apostolic Church of the Seven Ecumenical Councils, walking in the inspired teaching of Holy Scripture and the original Apostolic traditions, prays and invokes the mercy of God for the pardon and repose of those that have fallen asleep in the Lord (Heb. xi. 40; 2 Tim. i. 8; 2 Macc. xii. 44, 45). But the Papal Church, from the twelfth century onwards, invented and heaped together in the person of the Pope, as the possessor of privilege, a multitude of innovations touching a purgatorial fire, touching a superabundance of merits on the part of the saints, and the distribution of them to them that need, and the like.

"13. The One Holy Catholic and Apostolic Church of the Seven Ecumenical Councils teaches that the supernatural taking of human nature by the only begotten Son and Word of God, 'of the Holy Ghost and the Virgin Mary,' is alone pure and immaculate, but the Papal Church again innovated scarcely forty years ago by teaching a new-fangled doctrine of an immaculate conception of the Theotokos and ever-Virgin Mary—a doctrine unknown to the ancient Church.

"14. . . . When we revert to the Fathers, and the Ecumenical Councils of the Church of the first nine centuries, we reach the assurance that never was the Bishop of Rome regarded as the supreme authority and infallible head of the Church, and that every bishop is head and president of his own particular Church, subject only to the synodic constitutions and decisions of the Church at large, as alone infallible, the Bishop of Rome being in no wise excepted from this rule; . . . while the sole Eternal, Divine, and Immortal Head of the Church is our Lord Jesus Christ, for 'He is the head of the body the Church' (Col. i. 18)."

Comparing these two encyclicals, we might almost be disposed to say that the prospect of reunion is hopeless. But again the words of the venerable Pontiff of old Rome occur:—

"We are well aware . . . that there are those who consider that we are far too sanguine, and look for things that are rather to be wished for than expected. But we unhesitatingly place all our hope and confidence in the Saviour of mankind, Jesus Christ, well remembering what great things have been achieved in times past by the folly of the Cross and its preaching, to the astonishment and confusion of the 'wisdom of the world.'"

Surely, as we read these words, we cannot help feeling that they have about them the true ring of the Master's teaching, and that if all the bishops of Christendom were pervaded by the same spirit, that which now seems so unlikely, considering the obstacles to be cleared away, would promptly come to pass!

2. The writer has ventured to place extracts from these two encyclicals side by side, in order that it may be seen what are the principal points which at present keep asunder the two largest sections of the Christian world. Others, such as the use of unleavened bread, and the withholding the cup from the laity by the Roman Church, are, indeed, mentioned in the Eastern encyclical; but if it were clearly understood that they were merely points of discipline peculiar to the Roman Church, it is probable that they would not be found insuperable barriers to reunion.

At present, however, the fact has to be faced that the Western Church has, by its own authority, inserted the words, "and from the Son" in the Creed, which to the Easterns savours of heresy. Considering that the Roman Church is hardly likely to proclaim its fallibility by striking them out, and that we have it on the authority of Christ Himself that "when the Paraclete is come, whom I will send to you from the Father, even the Spirit of truth, which proceedeth from the Father" (John xv. 26), is it permissible to hazard the opinion that the East might admit words such as, *and has been sent forth from the Father by the Son,* after the clause, "which proceedeth from the Father," provided they were inserted in the Creed by Ecumenical authority?

3. Such kindly criticism has been bestowed upon the previous volume of this work that the author feels diffident in making any remarks upon what some have suggested as possible amendments. One point, however, does deserve attention.

It is matter of common knowledge that a large number of Roman canonical writers, from the thirteenth century downwards, have stated that the essential form in consecrating the Eucharist is the repetition of Christ's words of institution. Still it is believed that no authority can be quoted from the first ten centuries in support of this view; and the unanimous opinion of the Easterns, alike in ancient and in modern times, is opposed to it. It is, moreover, believed to be a fact that the Liturgy of Addai and Mari, in its oldest form, before it was tampered with to bring it into accord with the prepossessions of modern Westerns, does not even contain the words of institution, and some of the ablest writers of the Roman Church, for instance Le Brun, reject the current view of the Roman canonists. Under such circumstances it seemed safer to express a view which has been always held by all, rather than a mediæval theory which owes its rise to Scholasticism, and with which those who are not versed in Scholasticism seem to desire to have nothing to do.

It has also been suggested that separate chapters might with advantage have been given to confirmation and annealing, instead of, as at present, the one being included in baptism, the other in penance. In itself this is a small thing. Without denying that such a course has advantages, if it is desired to accentuate the fact of there being seven sacraments, and neither more nor fewer, yet the disadvantages seemed to the writer to outweigh the advantages. Early Christian writers who speak of baptism and its effects in such glowing terms understand thereby baptism as a whole, *i.e.*, the great liturgical rite, which included three sacraments in the Scholastic sense of the term—viz., the sacrament of exorcism, the sacrament of the washing, and the sacrament of the chrism or laying on of hands. To apply their elaborate language and the blessings they attach to baptism to the administration of one of these parts only to the exclusion of the two others, is surely to introduce confusion, and appears to have supplied the anvil upon which the modern heresy denying the sacramental efficacy of baptism is based.

And here, again, it should be remembered that the Eastern Church knows nothing of Scholasticism, and has never passed through this phase of thought. The West has; and although, as a system generally taught and received, Scholasticism has passed away, yet it has not done so without leaving many traces behind it. "O God, whose *property* is ever to have mercy" is a phrase which to a non-Scholastic mind has no meaning. The reduction of matter and form to certain irreducible *minima* are, again, conceptions which we owe to Scholasticism. The doctrine of intention as now taught is another Scholastic product. Accordingly, the great Roman Church, which in formulating the doctrine of the Immaculate Conception of the ever-Virgin Mary, has carried the application of logic to spiritual matters further than any other Church has dared to do, finds it necessary first to teach its future theologians the Scholastic philosophy, that into minds moulded by that teaching may be poured the Western theology built up on Scholasticism. It is suggested that this carrying of the Scholastic philosophy, with all that it practically involves, into the sphere of theology may have more to answer for than any other set of facts in estranging the East from the West. As the triumph of logic, Scholasticism is no doubt a magnificent system; but who shall venture to assert that by applying the laws of the human mind in its present state of existence, to superphenomenal realities you can obtain a knowledge of eternal truth? Surely, to assert this is to make the human mind the measure of all things, and to reduce God, who is immeasurable, to the standard of human ideas and human conceptions! Out of itself, the human mind can only elaborate that which, like itself, is human. The true knowledge of God must therefore be a matter of revelation, not of logic. "Touching the Almighty, we cannot find Him out" (Job xxxvii. 23).

At the Norwich Church Congress, Mr. J. W. Birkbeck told a story as to how he was once nonplussed by a Kieff monk asking him, "Do you always use incense in your churches?" Upon his replying, "No, not always—only sometimes," the monk retorted, "Did I not tell you that yours is a Popish Church? For you know that it was the Papists who invented low masses, with no music or incense, and that just about the time when they were inventing their new clause, 'and from the Son,' for the Creed."

This story he told, not as an example of a serious hindrance to unity, nor yet of theological learning, but of the sort of misunderstanding which constantly arises in the East from discussing matters from totally different points of view. Have not quite as great misunderstandings occurred in the West from a similar cause?

4. In this, as in the previous volume, the author has endeavoured to confine the statements in the text strictly within the limits of the authorities cited or referred to in the notes. To have expanded these statements into what some would prefer to call whole truths, might to others have seemed to be corrupting them into untruths; and, at any rate, the expansions of modern text-writers carry with them no general authority. The authorities cited date from various times, and come from

different parts of the Church. It cannot, therefore, even be said that the laws they lay down are, or ever were at any one time, obligatory on the whole Church. Those who framed them did so for the benefit of the particular patriarchate or province over which they bore rule; and inasmuch as they presided over people of various races, and of varying moral and intellectual perceptions, rules which were wanted in one part of the Church might often not be wanted in another. Yet, as they all were acting under the Divine Spirit's guidance, and all acknowledged Christ as the only source of life, of holiness, and of truth, this threefold acknowledgment forms the underlying basis of all the canons they drew up.

If this fact is once fully realised, it will be seen that canon law is not, what it is so often treated as being, a branch of ordinary law having ecclesiastical authority, and the spiritual counterpart of the Roman civil law. This view of it grew up in ages when spiritual and temporal authority were united in the person of the Pontiff, and the spiritual was too often treated as a branch of the temporal. But the canon law of the whole Church is a great deal more than this. It is no less than the record of the Spirit's work, fulfilling itself in time by means of legislative enactments. Regarded thus, the study of canon law, instead of being a dry study of technical restrictions, pieced together by legal experts on the principles of the Roman law, will be found to be a study of the Spirit's work in the Church in times past, and of a manifestation of spiritual life, light, and truth, seeking to express itself in every age in the most perfect way. It is from this platform that the author has endeavoured to approach his subject. He will be well content should his endeavour stimulate others to work on similar lines, and thus, however remotely, contribute to the greater glory of God.

A LA RONDE, NEAR LYMPSTONE, DEVON,
    Feast of St. George, 1896.

CONTENTS.

CHAPTER I.

DISCIPLINE GENERALLY.

	PAGE
1. THE NATURE AND OBJECT OF DISCIPLINE	1
The Nature of Discipline	1
The Power of the Keys	2
Subject-Matter of this Power	3
2. VARIOUS KINDS OF DISCIPLINE	4
Remedial Discipline	4
Penal Discipline	5
Effect of the Novatian Schism	7
Subsequent Modifications in the Western Church	8
3. VARIOUS MODES OF ADMINISTERING DISCIPLINE	9
Non-Sacramental	10
Sacramental	11
Public	12
4. SOLEMN DISCIPLINE	16
The Class excluded from Church	17
The Classes admitted within the Church	18
Regulations prescribed in Solemn Discipline	20
Lent the proper Season for	21
Solemn Restoration the Termination	22
5. THE FOUNDATION OF DISCIPLINE—VOWS	24
A Vow Defined	24
Public and Private Vows	25
Parts of a Public Vow	25
Simple Vows	26
Solemn Vows	28
6. PRIVILEGES, DISPENSATIONS, AND LICENSES	29
Privileges defined	30
Dispensations	31

	PAGE
Conditions of a Dispensation	31
By whom Granted	31
Allowed and Forbidden Dispensations	33
No Dispensation without Good Cause	36

CHAPTER II.

THE DISCIPLINE OF ORDINARY LIFE—EXCESSES.

1. THE SUBJECT-MATTER OF DISCIPLINE	39
Excesses defined by the Church	39
Vary according to the Degree of the Vow	40
Threefold Obligations of the Baptismal Vow	43
2. CRIMES AGAINST GOD	45
Apostasy	45
Blasphemy	47
Heresy	48
Schism	50
Simony	54
Sacrilege	58
3. CRIMES AGAINST FELLOW-MEN	63
Murder	63
Strife and Conspiracy	66
Robbery and Arson	66
Deceit and Falsehood	67
Usury	69
4. CRIMES AGAINST BODILY HOLINESS	71
Gluttony and Drunkenness	71
Incontinence, Concubinage, and Fornication	73
Adultery, Incest, and Sacrilege	74
Unnatural Crimes	75
5. EXCESSES OF THE CLERICAL LIFE	77

CHAPTER III.

DISCIPLINE OF THE RELIGIOUS LIFE.

1. THE RELIGIOUS LIFE	80
Definition and Forms of	80
The Solitary Religious Life	80

Contents.

	PAGE
The Life of Associated Asceticism.	81
The Religious Life in Common	84
Extension of the Common Life to Clergy	84
2. GILDS, CONFRATERNITIES, SOCIETIES, CONGREGATIONS	87
Gilds and Confraternities	87
Congregations	91
3. RELIGIOUS SOCIETIES.	92
The Religious Household	92
Development of the Abbot's Position	93
Obedientials	98
4. ADMISSION TO THE RELIGIOUS LIFE.	99
Dedication of Children	100
Voluntary Adoption of	101
Necessary Conditions for	102
Form of Profession	103
Distinction from Order	104
5. DUTIES OF THE RELIGIOUS LIFE	106
Poverty	108
Temperance	110
Dress	111
Chastity	112
Obedience	113
6. COMMUNITIES OF RELIGIOUS WOMEN	114
Canonesses	115
Minikins	116
Dedication of Girls	117
Veiling of Nuns	118

CHAPTER IV.

RELIGIOUS ORDERS.

1. ORIGIN OF RELIGIOUS ORDERS	120
2. CONTEMPLATIVE ORDERS OF LAYMEN	121
Rule of St. Benedict	121
The Reformed Benedictines or Black Monks	122
The Cluniacs	124
The Camaldunians	124
The Cistercians or White Monks	124
The Carthusians	125

	PAGE
3. CONTEMPLATIVE ORDERS OF CLERGY	126
Canons Regular of St. Augustin	126
Praemonstrants	127
Gilbertines	128
4. ORDERS OF ACTIVE CHARITY	128
Individual Congregations	128
Hospitallers	129
Templars	129
5. MENDICANT ORDERS	130
Dominicans	130
Franciscans	131
Carmelites	132
Austin Friars	133
6. LATER MISSIONARY ORDERS	133

CHAPTER V.

ECCLESIASTICAL SEVERITY.

1. CENSURES, PENANCES, AND PENALTIES	135
2. REMEDIAL SEVERITY, CENSURES	138
Suspension	139
Excommunication	140
Solemn Excommunication, the Anathema	142
Excommunications Passed and to be Passed	143
General Effects of	145
Effects of, on one in Orders	146
Restrictions upon	147
Of General Observance	148
3. THE INTERDICT	149
Local and Personal	150
Complete and Partial	151
4. CORRECTIVE SEVERITY, PENANCES	152
Penance defined	152
Three Kinds of	153
5. VINDICTIVE SEVERITY—PENALTIES	155
Temporal Penalties	156
Spiritual Penalties	158
Censure indirectly Penal—Suspension	160

Contents. xvii

	PAGE
Deprivation	165
Deposition and Degradation	167
6. RELAXATION OF CENSURES—RECONCILIATION	169
Absolution	169
Who may Give	170
Precautionary	171
Absolution with Reincidence	171

CHAPTER VI.
SPIRITUAL COURTS.

1. DISCIPLINARY PROCEDURE	174
2. ORIGIN OF COURTS CHRISTIAN	175
Procedure in Early Times	175
Origin of Judicial Courts	176
Constitution of	179
Spiritual Courts in the Empire	181
Spiritual Courts in this Country	182
Extra-Judicial Courts	185
Judicial Courts	187
3. JURISDICTION OF SPIRITUAL COURTS IN THIS COUNTRY	189
Matters excluded	192
Matters included	194
Spiritual Causes	195
Mixed Causes	197
Temporal Causes	201
Legal Recognition of	201
Legal Restraints upon	204
Encroachments of Post-Mediaeval Legislation	205
Abolition of Civil Disabilities	207
Remaining Jurisdiction	208
4. SPIRITUAL JUDGES	210
Judges Ordinary	211
Qualifications	211
Disabilities	212
Suspect Judges	214
Duties of	215

VOL. II.   *b*

		PAGE
5. DELEGATES OR SURROGATES	. . . . .	218
Qualifications.	. . . . . .	219
Limits of Commission	. . . . .	220
6. PLAINTIFFS AND DEFENDANTS	. . . .	222
Disqualified Persons	. . . . .	222
Compellable Persons	. . . . .	223
7. PROCTORS AND ADVOCATES	. . . .	224
Proctors Judicial or Extra-Judicial	. . .	225
Their Appointment and Powers	. . . .	225
Commencement and Termination of Office	. .	228
Advocates, their Duties and Qualifications	. .	230

CHAPTER VII.

CANONICAL PROCEDURE.

1. SPIRITUAL CAUSES	. . . .	233
2. VARIOUS MODES OF PROCEDURE	. . . .	236
Causes of Office	. . . . . .	236
Causes of Instance .	. . . . . .	237
3. ACTION	. . . .	239
Two Kinds of	. . . . . .	239
Presence of the Criminal Element in	. . .	240
Distinguishing Features of	. . . .	241
4. ACCUSATION	. . . . . .	242
Essential Features of	. . . . .	242
Restraints on .	. . . . . .	243
Effects of	. . . .	246
Disuse of	. . . .	247
5. DENUNCIATION OR PRESENTMENT	. . .	248
Paternal	. . . .	249
Canonical	. . . .	250
Judicial .	. . . .	250
How Made	. . . .	251
Superior's Duty in Regard to	. . . .	253
6. INQUISITION	. . . . . .	254
General .	. . . .	255
Particular	. . . .	255
Privileges of a Necessary Promoter	. . .	257
7. CANONICAL PURGATION	. . . . .	258

CHAPTER VIII.

ACTS IN JUDGMENT.

1. THE PROCESS AND ITS PARTS	262
2. THE INTRODUCTION OF A CAUSE	264
The Petition or Libel	265
Citation	268
Various Kinds of	270
Service of	272
Effect of Service	273
Appearance or Non-Appearance	274
Appearance under Protest	275
Dilatory Exceptions	276
Reconvention or Counter-Claim	276
Settlement before Contestation	277
Change and Enlargement of Libel	279
Terms	279
3. THE INSTANCE OF A CAUSE—THE SUIT	280
Contestation	281
Effects of Contestation	282
Oath of Calumny	282
Personal Decree	284
Order of Investigation	285
Exceptions	286
4. PROOF	289
Definition of	289
Full and Half Proof	290
Evidence of Fact	291
Confession	292
Proof by Witnesses	293
Proper Witnesses	294
Number of Witnesses	296
Refutation of Witnesses	298
Proof by Instruments	298
Publication of Depositions	300

CHAPTER IX.

CONCLUSION OF A CAUSE.

	PAGE
1. THE JUDGE'S OFFICE	302
Three Meanings of the Conclusion of a Cause	302
Extent of the Judge's Duty	303
2. PRESUMPTIONS	305
Legal	306
Personal—Ordeal	307
3. SENTENCES AND MATTERS JUDICIALLY SETTLED	308
Final and Interlocutory Sentences	308
Valid Sentences	309
Exercise of the Judge's Office	311
Sentences of Law and of the Judge	312
Matters Judicially Settled	315
4. EXECUTION	318
Exceptions of Fraud and Nullity	319
Costs	320
Contumacy	320
5. APPEALS	322
Origin and Definition of	323
Judicial and Extra-Judicial	324
Interlocutory and Final	327
Effects of	328
Time for Appealing	330
The Four Fatal Terms	331
Regularity of	332
Abolition of Appeals to the Pope in this Country	333

SHORT MANUALS OF CANON LAW.

I.

DISCIPLINE GENERALLY.

The Nature and Object of Discipline.

1. The one object for which the Church exists upon earth is the glory of God through the salvation and sanctification of mankind. To attain this object it is necessary that those who are "dead in trespasses and sins" should have a new life infused and maintained in them, for which purpose the sacraments have been committed to the Church; but it is no less necessary that they should be restored to that unity among themselves which sin and its consequences have broken, so that as a united body of righteous men their light may shine before the world. To effect this restoration, discipline is requisite. The acceptance of the Christian faith (¹) or right belief leads men to desire the sacraments. The effort to observe Christ's commandments or the practice of holiness (²) brings them to submit to discipline.

2. By discipline is understood the power of producing actions in accordance with the faith, and restraining departures from Christ's rule of truth or holiness by spiritual coercion or severity (³). Discipline may therefore be said to be the divinely appointed instrument whereby such as have been placed in the

---

(1). Acts xxiv. 24; Gal. i. 23; Jude 3, 20; Heb. xi. 6: χωρὶς δὲ πίστεως ἀδύνατον εὐαρεστῆσαι. Clem. Strom. v. 13: The Lord says, I am the Door of the sheep [1 John x. 1–3, 7]; men must then be saved by learning the truth in Christ.

(2). Heb. xii. 14: χωρὶς ἁγιασμοῦ οὐδεὶς ὄψεται τὸν Κύριον.

(3). Cavagnis iii. 83.

way of salvation are carried forward to perfection by enduring hardship (⁴), and such as have deviated from the precepts of the Gospel and the commandments of life are brought back to righteousness through repentance and satisfaction (⁵). The power of exercising or prescribing discipline was committed to the Church by Christ Himself, who received all judgment from the Father (⁶), and is ordinarily called the power of binding and loosing, or the power of the keys. It involves two things: (1) the key of judgment or interpretation, whereby the unchanging truth of Christ is explained in the varying terminology of

(4). Justin 1 Apol. 40; Hippolyt. x. 30: Whatever sufferings thou didst undergo while being a man, these He gave to thee because thou wast of mortal mould. . . . And provided thou obeyest His solemn injunctions, and becomest a faithful follower of Him that is good, thou shalt in the world to come resemble Him. Cyprian de Vest. Virg. c. 1: Discipline, the safeguard of hope, the bond of faith, the guide of the way of salvation, the stimulus and nourishment of good dispositions, the teacher of virtue, causes us to abide alway in Christ, and to live continually for God, and to attain to the heavenly promises and divine rewards. . . . The Holy Spirit says in the Psalms, Keep discipline, &c. [Kiss the Son, &c.. Ps. II. 12], but unto the ungodly saith God, Why dost thou preach My laws and takest My commandment to thy mouth, whereas thou hatest discipline? [Ps. L. 17]. And again, He that casteth away discipline is miserable [Wisd. III. 11], . . . for whom the Lord loveth He correcteth [Prov. III. 11]. Ep. 48 (Oxf. 52), 2: Neither can those remain in God's Church who have not maintained its divine and ecclesiastical discipline, either in the conversation of their life or the peace of their character. Ep. 61 (Oxf. 4): We do not depart from the traditions of the Gospel, but with constancy . . . maintain the discipline of the Church.

(5). Cyprian Ep. 7 (Oxf. 11), 7; 14 (Oxf. 20), 1; 22 (Oxf. 27); 24 (Oxf. 28), 2; 27 (Oxf. 34); 30 (Oxf. 2): Maintain the ever-guarded rule of discipline; 39 (Oxf. 43), 2; 51 (Oxf. 55), 3; 54 (Oxf. 59), 1 and 2: Ecclesiastical discipline is not to be forsaken, nor priestly censure to be relaxed because we are disturbed with reproaches.

(6). John v. 22, 27; Tertullian Scorpiac. c. 10: For though you think heaven still shut, remember that the Lord left here to Peter, and through him to the Church, the keys of it, which every one who has been here put to the question, and also made confession, will carry with him. Pacian, Ep. 1 ad Sempron.: If bishops have inherited from the apostles the power of washing and anointing with chrism, they have inherited also the power of binding and loosing.

different ages, races, and people, and the abiding law of holiness is applied to the varying circumstances of times and places, some things being pronounced allowed, other things forbidden (7); and (2) the key of coercion or restraint (8), whereby effect is given to what the key of judgment has locked or unlocked (9).

3. The power of the keys, *i.e.*, of interpretation and coercion, extends to the whole sphere of faith and morals, because Christ came not only to be the Life, but also the Truth, and the Way to the Father. When it is applied to persons, the private life of those living in the world, the community life of those pursuing the counsels of perfection, it is termed personal discipline, either ordinary personal discipline or religious discipline. When it is applied to things—the liturgical worship

---

(7). Among the Jews, if a rabbi were asked whether the law allowed such or such conduct, if he replied in the affirmative he was said to loose, otherwise, to bind. So one part of the Church's binding or loosing is to determine whether certain actions are allowed or not; in other words, to interpret. See *Order*, note 134.

(8). Augustin ap. Gratian Caus. XXIII. Qu. VI. c. 1.: Schismatics say, Whom did Christ compel? I answer, Paul. Let them see in this case Christ first compelling, then teaching; first striking, then comforting. It is, however, wonderful that he who was first brought to the Gospel by bodily suffering laboured therein more abundantly than all who were called by a word, and whom greater fear first brought to charity, in him perfect charity should have cast out fear. Why, then, should the Church not compel her lost sons to return, if those lost sons have compelled others to be lost? Yea, even those who were not compelled to go astray but only led astray, if by fear-inspiring but health-giving lives such are brought home to her bosom, does not pious mother Church receive them with kindness, having more joy over them than over such as never wandered away? Pelagius *Ibid.* 1 Dist. XVII. § 4; Devoti Lib. III. Tit. L

(9). Augustin ap. Gratian Caus. XXXII. Qu. 1. c. 8: Without doubt remission of sins is given by the keys of the kingdom of heaven. Odo's Can. 2, A.D. 943: We admonish kings and princes to be obedient to their archbishops and bishops, because the keys of the kingdom of heaven are given to them. Gratian 1 Dist. XX. Pars. II. § 1: With the one key power was given to him [Peter] to discern between disease and disease, with the other power to cast out from or admit to the Church. Lynd. 266, 336, 352, 248.

of the Church, sacred places, seasons, and times—it is termed liturgical discipline. For the present we confine ourselves to personal discipline.

Discipline—Remedial, Penal, and Vindictive.

4. It has been already seen that the object of the sacraments is to bring men into and to keep them in communion with God, through the ministrations of the Church, which is the Body of Christ. Similarly, the end of discipline is to keep those who are members of the Church in full corporate communion with each other, not only as righteous men, but as righteous men illuminating the world. Accordingly, personal discipline is of two kinds: (1) remedial, for the purpose of advancing personal holiness and bringing back wanderers to the fold; (2) penal, for the purpose of vindicating the Church's claim to holiness before the world, and securing public satisfaction for crimes and offences which obscure its light. The former is called censure or correction, the latter punishment or vengeance ([10]).

5. The aim of remedial discipline is primarily the soul's health and the reform of an offender, so that every member of Christ's body may be presented before God pure and spotless ([11]). In it, therefore, no more harshness should be employed for the purpose of correction than is really necessary ([12]);

---

(10). 2 Cor. x. 6. The term ultio is used by Hieronym. ap. Gratian I. Dist. XCIII. c. 23; Leo *Ibid.* Caus. I. Qu. VII. c. 18; Gelasius, A.D. 494, *Ibid.* Caus. II. Qu. VII. c. 47; Gregory *Ibid.* c. 46; Const. 9 Edmund, A.D. 1236; Decret. Lib. III. Tit. XLI. c. 10, and Tit. XLIV. c. 1 and Lib. IV. Tit. III. c. 3; Lynd. 247.

(11). Col. I. 28; Lynd. 129: Understand that proceedings are taken for the soul's health when the aim is not to inflict the canonical penalty according to the quality of the crime or offence, but only that the offender may be amended from his crime.

(12). Cyprian Ep. 64 (Oxf. 3), 3: We desire to overcome the wrongdoings of individuals by clemency and patience rather than to punish them by our priestly (*i.e.*, episcopal) power. *Id.* Ep. 11 (Oxf. 17), 2: In smaller sins which are not committed against God, penance may be performed in a set time. Gregory IV. ap. Gratian I. Dist. XLV. c. 4: Rulers

hence one great part of remedial discipline is warning or monition ([13]).

6. Penal discipline is exercised primarily for the good of others and to vindicate the holiness of the Church before the world, but it is also exercised secondarily for the good of the offender ([14]). Hence it may be employed without warning whenever the good of others requires it; but unless the good of others requires it, it should not be resorted to without threefold warning ([15]). The good of others is held to require it: (1) when crime is manifest and notorious ([16]); (2) when by a canon of Churches must be dealt with patiently, and corrected rather than condemned forthwith.

([13]). S. Matt. XVIII. 15–17: Moreover, if thy brother shall trespass against thee, go and tell him his fault between him and thee alone; if he shall hear thee, thou hast gained thy brother. But if he will not hear thee, then take with thee one or two more, that in the mouth of two or three witnesses every word may be established. And if he shall neglect to hear them, tell it unto the Church. Ambros. ap. Gratian Caus. XXIII. Qu. IV. c. 26; Augustin *Ibid.* c. 24; Baedae Poenit. v. 7, A.D. 750, in H. & S. III. 331. Alexander III. to Archbishop of Canterbury in Decret. Lib. III. Tit. II. c. 4: We enjoin you carefully to warn clergy. . . . If within forty days they refuse to comply, suspend them till they come to satisfaction. Concil. Ebor. A.D. 1195, Can. 19; Concil. Westminster A.D. 1200, Can. 7: That prelates do not excommunicate their subjects without canonical warning. Concil. Lat. IV. A.D. 1215, Can. 47 in Decret. Lib. v. Tit. XXXIX. c. 48; Honorius III. *Ibid.* Lib. III. Tit. l. c. 16, and Lib. v. Tit. XXXIX. c. 48, and Tit. l. c. 2; Lynd. 69. 120, 206, 240 says that the archbishop cannot proceed to punish in a case when he cannot monish unless monition has been given by some one else.

([14]). So Augustin ap. Gratian Caus. XXIV. Qu. III. c. 17, says that even the anathema may, if God so will, turn to, and prove to be most healthy correction. *Ibid.* Qu. IV. c. 51.

([15]). Gregory ap. Gratian I. Dist. LXXXVI. c. 24, and Gregory VII. *Ibid.* I. Dist. XCVI. c. 10, allowed it to be good in certain cases without warning, but Alexander III. in Decret. Lib. II. Tit. XXVIII. c. 26, held otherwise. Concil. Lat. IV. A.D. 1215, Can. 47, *Ibid.* Lib. v. Tit. XXXIX. c. 48; Const. 26 Langton, A.D. 1222; Concil. Lugdun. A.D. 1245, in Sext. Lib. v. Tit. XL. c. 3, says that an excommunication without previous warning does not hold good. Concil. Lugdun. II. A.D. 1274, *Ibid.* c. 9.

([16]). Const. 26 Langton, A.D. 1222: We decree that sentence be pronounced against none without canonical warning, unless when the excess is manifest. See *Spiritual Judicatures*, note 122 to § 7.

of the Church a particular crime is directed to be punished without warning ([17]); (3) when it is an open act of contempt of the judge ([18]); and (4) when it is an offence for which an *ipso facto* or *ipso jure* sentence has been already prescribed, and is not merely directed to be prescribed ([19]). The means of coercion used to enforce discipline either penal or remedial which are purely spiritual are termed severity ([20]) or austerity ([21]); those which are temporal, or which involve temporal consequences, animadversion ([22]). Animadversion, when administered solely by way of warning to others and regardless of the welfare of the offender, is called vindictive punishment.

7. In the early days of the Church, when the holiness of the body before the world was accounted of primary importance, penal discipline played a more important part than it has done since ([23]). Yet even then no uniform method of severity

(17). Concil. Lat. IV. A.D. 1215, Can. 8 in Decret. Lib. v. Tit. 1. c. 24; Const. 18 Otho, A.D. 1237; Const. 5 Peckham, A.D. 1279: Our will is that the rehearsal [of Const. 18 Otho] be looked upon as a monition. Const. 21 Peckham, A.D. 1281: We ordain that without any admonition they fall under the punishments aforesaid.

(18). Decret. Lib. II. Tit. XXVI. c. 16, and Lib. III. Tit. XXXIX. c. 25; Lynd. 349.

(19). Gregory ap. Gratian Caus. v. Qu. 1. c. 2, pronounced a general sentence of excommunication on an unknown person. Concil. Westminster A.D. 1200, Can. 7; Const. 1 Langton, A.D. 1222.

(20). Cyprian Ep. 29 (Oxf. 36), 1; Ep. 30, 2; Ep. 54 (Oxf. 59), 1; Augustin ap. Gratian I. Dist. XLIV. c. 1: Severity must be exercised towards the sins of few. Syn. Rom. A.D. 680, Can. 3; Concil. Cabilon. II. A.D. 813, *Ibid*. Caus. XVI. Qu. VII. c. 28; Ayliffe 157, says that censure is confined to excommunication, suspension, and interdict, whereas severity includes every other form of ecclesiastical punishment. Decret. Lib. v. Tit. XL. c. 20.

(21). Leo *Ibid*. I. Dist. LXXXVI. c. 1, calls it *austerior disciplina;* Hieronym. *Ibid*. I. Dist. XLV. c. 16, *austeritas*.

(22). Nicolaus, A.D. 864, ap. Gratian Caus. VI. Qu. III. c. 3, mentions together correction and animadversion. Decret. Lib. v. Tit. XXXVII. c. 12; Const. 19 Othobon, A.D. 1268; Lynd. 322; Ayliffe 157.

(23). Thus, in Acts v., Ananias and Sapphira were not merely excommunicated but were struck dead. In 1 Tim. I. 20, St. Paul says that he has delivered Hymenæus and Alexander over to Satan, that they may learn not to speak slanderously ($\beta\lambda\alpha\sigma\phi\eta\mu\epsilon\hat{\iota}\nu$). Conf. 2 Tim. IV. 15. In 1

existed for the treatment of those guilty of the greater crimes, such as idolatry, murder, adultery '(24). A second baptism being impossible (25), such offenders were in some places excluded from the Church altogether, and without hope of return (26); in others they were allowed to be readmitted, after a long period of penance, by the imposition of hands (27); in others only at the hour of death (28). In the Roman Church, at least since the beginning of the third century, they were treated with considerable leniency (29).

8. After the great schism of Novatus in the middle of the third century, the question of the treatment of offenders continued to be a vexed one until it was settled by the Nicene

Cor. v. 3–5, St. Paul, spiritually present with the Corinthians, in consistory delivers the incestuous man to Satan for the destruction of the flesh ($\epsilon\dot{\iota}s$ $\delta\lambda\epsilon\theta\rho o\nu$ $\tau\hat{\eta}s$ $\sigma\alpha\rho\kappa\dot{o}s$). In 1 Cor. IV. 21 he threatens to come with a rod, and (2 Cor. XIII. 2) declares that he will not spare, but (2 Cor. X. 6) will punish every kind of disobedience.

(24). Cyprian Ep. 51 (Oxf. 55), 21 : Subject to maintaining the bond of concord, every bishop disposes and directs his own acts.

(25). Heb. VI. 4. See *Penance*, note 13.

(26). Concil. Elib. A.D. 305, Can. 1, 6, 7 : Let them not even at the close receive Communion. Concil. Sardic. A.D. 341, Can. 1, forbids the viaticum to be given to simoniacal bishops. Concil. Valentin. A.D. 374, Can. 3.

(27). Euseb. VI. 43 quotes the rule : That Novatus and those who adopt his uncharitable and inhuman opinion be alienated from the Church, but that brethren who have incurred any calamity should be treated and healed with the remedies of repentance. Ambros. ap. Gratian Caus. XXXIII. Qu. III. Dist. 1. c. 50 : No one can do penance profitably unless he hopes for indulgence. But they say that Communion ought not to be restored to the lapsed. . . . Yet God has excepted no crime, who has forgiven all sins. Cyprian *Ibid*. c. 57 ; Isidor. *Ibid*. I. Dist. 1. c. 28.

(28). Cyprian Ep. 52 (Oxf. 56), 2 : It was decided in the council that penitents in peril of sickness should be assisted [with the viaticum]. Concil. Nic. A.D. 325, Can. 13 : Respecting the dying, let the old canonical rule be observed, so that if any one is at the point of death he be not deprived of the last and most necessary viaticum. Theodori Poenit. I. VIII. 5 and I. IX. 7, following Julius ap. Gratian Caus. XXVI. Qu. VI. c. 12, declares a priest guilty of souls who refuses penance to the dying. Devoti Inst. Lib. II. Tit. II. § 87.

(29). Tertullian de Pudic. c. 1, A.D. 202, complains of Zephyrinus allowing restoration after adultery.

rule ([30]), which provided that any one guilty of denying the faith (which was the greatest crime of all) should be excluded from participating in the offering of the Church for a period of twelve years, during which he should pass through a course of regular discipline, and at its close be replaced in his original position if found deserving. When the sin was private and known only through the offender's confession, or if otherwise the bishop thought fit, the time might be abbreviated ([31]).

9. In the Western Church custom or law had, before the sixth century, (1) habitually fixed the period of exclusion from offering at seven years, unless special circumstances aggravated the offence and called for a longer period ([32]), and (2) had regularly indulged the offender by admitting him to Communion before his time of exclusion from offering had expired ([33]). It then further (3) allowed the severer bodily penances, even for manifest crimes, to be commuted into pilgrimages, almsgiving, and other works of mercy; and (4) finally, in conformity with Roman law, practically protected offenders from penal consequences by making the accuser

(30). Can. 11 : As to those who have transgressed without necessity, or without loss of estate, or without danger, or the like, . . . the Synod has decreed : . . . As many of them as do sincerely repent shall pass three years among the hearers ; for seven years they shall be kneelers, and for two years they shall share with the people [of God] in prayer without [participating in] the offering. Concil. Aurel. II. A.D. 533, Can. 20.

(31). Concil. Nic. A.D. 325, Can. 12 ; Rabanus, A.D. 829, ap. Gratian I. Dist. 1. c. 34 : Those who are taken or convicted publicly of perjury [similarly, Cap. 26 Theodulf, A.D. 877, ap. Gratian Caus. XXII. Qu. l. c. 17], theft, fornication, and such like crimes, ought, according to the ancient canons, to forfeit their place ; . . . but those who make confession of such sins secretly committed by them before God's eye, in the presence of His priest . . . to these the hope of pardon may be promised by the mercy of God . . . if by fasting and almsgiving and watching and prayer they seek to make amends.

(32). Isidor. ap. Gratian Caus. XXXIII. Qu. II. c. 11 : The rule of the canons which orders the restitution of a penitent to his former state after seven years . . . the ancient fathers did not frame after their own fancy, but according to a ruling of divine judgment. *Ibid.* Qu. III. Dist. VII. and Caus. XXII. Qu. l. c. 17. and I. Dist. 1. c. 28.

(33). See *The Eucharist*, note 254.

liable to the penalty himself if he failed to substantiate his accusation. The effect of these provisions was to abolish vindictive discipline almost entirely as an ecclesiastical institution, leaving the infliction of ordinary pains and penalties to civil tribunals. Such discipline as is now and has long been enforced in spiritual courts—except in countries where the spiritual authorities have themselves the temporal government also—is only quasi-penal, and not vindictive, *i.e.*, even when imposed in the public interest, as in the case of contumacious heretics and criminal clergy, it is declared to be administered for the soul's health, and its rigour is mitigated accordingly.

Varieties of Discipline.

10. There are several ways in which discipline, whether penal or remedial, may be exercised, but all of them may be distinguished as being either public or private ([34]). When it is exercised publicly in the face of the Church, it is said to be discipline of the outer tribunal or the contentious forum; when privately, to be discipline of the inner tribunal or non-contentious forum. Of public discipline, again, there are two kinds ([35]): (1) that which is exercised openly for the good of

---

([34]). Hieronym. ap. Gratian Caus. xi. Qu. iii. c. 21: In two ways a man may be delivered to Satan, viz., (1) publicly, when the offence is manifest to the Church; (2) privately, when it is not so manifest. Concil. Camaracen. Tit. xiv. c. 1 ap. Labbé Tom. xx. 1411: A two-fold ecclesiastical forum has been established by Christ by the name of the Keys: one of the sacrament of penance, which regards the conscience, in which the guilty one is not bound or loosed except upon his own confession; the other of jurisdiction and external government, in which the guilty one is convicted and judged, not only on his own confession but by witnesses. Morinus de Poenit. Adm. Lib. vii. c. 1. sec. 1 considers two tribunals distinguished about the year 700 A.D. Van Espen considers both tribunals were identical up to the twelfth century. Du Pin derives the outer tribunal from the prince's authority. Lynd. 127, 129, 135, 164, 327, 337: He who confesses is condemned in foro contentioso, but absolved in foro poenitentiae.

([35]). Lynd. 339: Penance is called public in a double sense. In one sense that is called public which is solemn, and in this sense a clerk may not do public penance (Gratian 1 Dist. l. c. 65). In another sense that is

the Church, leaving it to work its own effect on the individual, which is called simply public discipline or the hoe of ecclesiastical discipline ([36]); (2) that which is exercised openly for the good of the offender when the public prayers of the Church on his behalf are combined with it. The latter is called solemn discipline. Again, discipline of the inner tribunal is sometimes received non-sacramentally, in the court of the soul, after confession to God only, by a humble submission to the visitations wherewith He afflicts in this life; at other times sacramentally, in the court of penance ([37]). We have, therefore, to distinguish four distinct varieties of discipline, viz., (1) non-sacramental, in the court of the soul; (2) sacramental, in the court of penance; (3) public, for the good of the Church; and (4) solemn, for the good of the individual as well.

11. The private fulfilment of a Christian man's duties and his unseen shortcomings in his efforts to live a Christian life, are matters which do not directly fall within the cognisance of the Christian community unless attention is drawn to them by the individual's own confession ([38]). They do, however, in-

called public which is done publicly, and such penance a clerk can do (Gratian 1 Dist. xxviii. c. 9). Gregory *Ibid.* Caus. xxxiii. Qu. iii. Dist. vi. c. 2, and Decret. Lib. v. Tit. xxxviii. c. 7.

(36). Const. Mepham A.D. 1328: It concerns prelates ... to root out by the sword of the Spirit and the hoe of ecclesiastical discipline all hurtful vices.

(37). The Franciscan Elbel Theol. Decal. Pars. v. p. 253 divides as above; also Ferraris Bibl. *verb.* Forum; but the latter says the forum internum, or forum conscientiae, consists of two divisions—one sacramental, the other non-sacramental. Lynd. 339 says there are three kinds of penance, (1) solemn, (2) public, (3) private; but, p. 327: There are three kinds of confession, (1) in the court of the soul before God, (2) in the court of penance before His representative, (3) before a judge in the contentious court. In the first kind of confession a hidden sin is not exposed, because it is already known to God; in the last a sin is not exposed with a view to pardon; in the intermediate kind a sin is exposed, and with a view to pardon. *Ibid.* 236.

(38). Col. iii. 3: Your life is hid with Christ in God. Innocent iii. in Decret. Lib. v. Tit. iii. c. 33: The Church does not sit in [public] judgment on secret things. Const. 9 Peckham A.D. 1281; Lynd. 187, 203, 236, 327.

directly fall within its cognisance, because whatever lowers the holiness of one member lowers the holiness of the whole body. Hence the Church is careful to point out that, when mortal sin has been committed, its ill effects are not ordinarily got rid of without spiritual assistance and penitential hardship ([39]). Still, wherever there is true repentance, there is undoubtedly God's forgiveness on confession being made to Him only in the court of the soul ([40]), and the effects of sin may be purged by cheerful submission to divine chastisement ([41]).

12. For those who require spiritual assistance the tribunal of penance is provided by the Church, in which God's mercy is obtained for the offender by the prayers of others, and the remedial discipline necessary to undo the effects of sin is indicated by the confessor. An ordinary confessor has, however, only a commission from the Church to reconcile privately, and that within the limits of his commission, after a course of private discipline, but at the hour of death he may reconcile one who is undergoing public or solemn discipline ([42]).

([39]). Origen Hom. II. c. 6 in Psalm XXXVII. (II. 688): They who have sinned, if indeed they conceal and keep the sin close, are urged internally. . . . Only carefully look out for the person to whom you ought to confess your sin. Augustin Serm. 392: Let no one say, I do penance in secret before God. It is enough that God, who will pardon me, knows that I repent in secret. Then it were said in vain, What things ye shall loose upon earth shall be loosed in heaven. Dunstan Can. 56, A.D. 963: The necessary assistance of a man of God is very effectual for the cure of sin in penance, even as the recovery of a sick man is on a good physician. See *Penance*, note 23.

([40]). See *Penance*, § 15.

([41]). Heb. XII. 6; Ps. XCIV. 12; 1 Cor. XI. 32. See *Penance*, § 19.

([42]). Concil. Nic. A.D. 325, Can. 13 ap. Gratian Caus. XXVI. Qu. VI. c. 9; Concil. Carthag. II. Can. 4, A.D. 390, *Ibid.* c. 5: If any one is in danger and desires to be reconciled to the divine altars, if the bishop is absent let the presbyter forthwith consult him, and by his command reconcile the penitent in danger. Leo *Ibid.* c. 10; Coelestin *Ibid.* c. 13; Concil. Brac. II. A.D. 572, *Ibid.* c. 5; Theodori Poenit. I. VIII. 5 in H. & S. III. 184; Concil. Ebor. A.D. 1195, Can. 17; Const. 16 Edmund, A.D. 1236: At the hour of death absolution is to be denied to none but upon a condition that they present themselves to the apostolic presence if they recover. Const. 26 Othobon, A.D. 1268; Const. 17 Peckham, A.D. 1281:

13. When offences are manifest ([43]), so that scandal ([44]) arises from them and the light of the Church in the world is thereby obscured, the necessity arises for the exercise of the discipline of the outer tribunal. Yet since the publicity of the outer tribunal under the existing circumstances of the Church leads to serious social and civil consequences, whereas the Church is before all things the kingdom of righteousness, justice, and mercy, the exercise of public discipline is hemmed in by strict rules of procedure ([45]). In the outer tribunal offences, if denied, are required to be established by evidence in a regular way ([46]), whereas in the inner tribunal the offender's

At the point of death any priest may absolve them upon condition that, if they recover, they do within three months make confession to their proper bishop.

(43). Concil. Carthag. II. Can. 3, A.D. 390, ap. Gratian Caus. XXVI. Qu. VI. c. 1 ; Concil. Carthag. III. Can. 32, A.D. 397, *Ibid.* c. 14 : Whatever penitent's crime is public and notorious, so that it disturbs the whole Church, let the [bishop's] hand be laid on him before the apse. Augustin *Ibid.* Caus. XXIII. Qu. IV. c. 19 ; Calixtus II. A.D. 1139, in Decret. Lib. v. Tit. XXXVIII. c. 1 : Manifest crimes may not be purged by secret correction. *Ibid.* Tit. IX. c. 11, and Tit. IX. c. 2, and Tit. XVIII. c. 5 ; Lynd. 336.

(44). Lynd. 112 defines scandal as "dictum vel factum minus rectum vel signum cujus occasione aliquis trahitur ad consensum alicujus peccati et praebet alicui occasionem offensionis vel ruinae."

(45). Evaristus ap. Gratian Caus. XXX. Qu. v. c. 10 : We ought to condemn no one without a true and rigorous proof. For the apostle saith : Who art thou, O man, that judgest another ? To his own Master he standeth or falleth. Let not, therefore, hearsay crimes move any one, nor let any one ever believe current rumours without certain proof ; but let him first diligently inquire into what he hears, lest he do anything precipitately. Lynd. 233 : If a presbyter knows of the sin of another, and that is a hidden sin, and he is applied to in private [to give the communion], he ought to refuse it. But if [the offender] publicly comes for it, he ought to give it for three reasons : (1) because he who inflicts a public punishment for a private sin is a revealer of confession or a betrayer of crime ; (2) because every Christian has a right to receive the Eucharist, unless he is in mortal sin ; (3) because the Spirit bloweth where it listeth ; and (4) because it would cause scandal to refuse it.

(46). Augustin *Ibid.* Caus. II. Qu. II. c. 1 : We cannot give sentence against any one unless he is either convicted or spontaneously confesses. *Ibid.* Caus. XV. Qu. V. c. 1 : If he has either spontaneously confessed or

Discipline Generally. 13

uncorroborated statements are proof, and he is at once accuser and accused (⁴⁷). The outer tribunal, moreover, as being the tribunal of Christ's visible kingdom upon earth, requires to be presided over by the bishop or one deputed to represent him, such as an archdeacon or spiritual judge (⁴⁸). The inner tribunal, being the tribunal of the Church as an intercessory body with heaven, requires one to preside over it who has the capacity of effectually interceding for the offender, a presbyter or bishop (⁴⁹).

14. Ordinary public discipline, which is administered by the bishop (⁵⁰) or a spiritual judge in the interests of the people, is

been proved guilty by lawful witnesses, let him be visited with canonical sentence. Gregory *Ibid.* I. Dist. LXXIV. c. 2 : No innocent man should be unjustly deprived of the ministry of his order.

(47). Const. 1 Peckham, A.D. 1281 : We lay the stress of the proof upon the oath of him that is to receive the sacrament, who is to take care of what concerns his salvation. Lynd. 233 : The mere assertion must be believed of him who says he has confessed ; 332.

(48). Leo Epist. 108 (al. 83) : The Mediator between God and man, Christ Jesus, hath given this power to the presidents of His Church, that they should both impose penance on those who confess, and should admit the same, when purified by wholesome satisfaction, through the gate of reconciliation to the communion of the sacraments. Theodori Poenit. I. IV. 5 in H. & S. III. 180 : If one kill a clerk, he is in the bishop's judgment. Concil. Chelsea A.D. 787, Can. 3 ; Athelstan's Law 7, A D. 925 : Let him who swears a false oath never be thought worthy . . . to lie in consecrated ground, unless he have the bishop's testimony . . . that he hath made satisfaction. Cnut's Law 25, A.D. 1018 : Till he desist and make deep satisfaction, as the bishop enjoins. Concil. Ebor. A.D. 1195, Can. 7 : If they repent of their perjury, let them be sent to the archbishop or bishop, or the general confessor of the diocese. Concil. Winton A.D. 1071, Can. 11 : That only bishops give sentence for gross crimes. Const. 4 Thorsby, A.D. 1363, enumerates thirty-seven gross crimes reserved for the bishop's judgment. Lynd. 340.

(49). Ordinary presbyters have no jurisdiction of the outer tribunal, and only jurisdiction of the inner tribunal excepting the reserved cases. See *Duties of Order*, § 20, and *Penance*, § 5. Conf. Gratian Caus. XXVI. Qu. VI. c. 4 ; Caus. XV. Qu. v. c. 2. Nevertheless, Const. 35 Edmund, A.D. 1236, authorised parish priests [*i.e.*, not parochial incumbents, but their coadjutors] to censure the detainers of tithes.

(50). Concil. Clovesho, A.D. 787, Can. 3 : Let the bishop separate the

confined to crimes which are open and manifest, or else to those which have become manifest by being judicially established before a contentious tribunal (⁵¹). Offences which are believed only to exist are directed to be tolerantly borne with until they are clearly brought home (⁵²). Of sins of thought or intention incestuous, coerce soothsayers, fortune-tellers, enchanters, diviners, wizards, and such as are guilty of sacrilege, and suppress all vices.

(51). Origen Hom. 21 in Lib. Jesu Nave c. I. (II. 447): Unless sin is evident, we may cast no one out of the Church, lest in rooting up tares we should root up wheat also. Innocent, A.D. 405, ap. Gratian Caus. XXXII. Qu. v. c. 23: Non habent latentia crimina vindictam. Julian *Ibid*. Caus. XXIV. Qu. III. c. 18: The crimes of all which have become generally manifest, the guilty parties refusing to admit them . . . must be burnt out and cured. Urban II. *Ibid*. I. Dist. XXXII. c. 11: We speak of things which are manifest. Secret things God knows and judges. Decret. Lib. v. Tit. l. c. 17 directs inquisitors to disclose all except hidden crimes. Lucius III. in Decret. Lib. III. Tit. II. c. 7: Notorious crime is one thing, secret crime another. Notorious is said to be that for which a presbyter is canonically condemned, secret that which is tolerated by the Church. Lynd. 56; Morin de Poenit. v. 8; Devoti Lib. II. Tit. II. § 72.

(52). Ambros. ap. Gratian Caus. II. Qu. I. c. 17: Christ did not eject Judas, although He knew he was a thief. *Id. Ibid.* c. 31: If any one has not power to cast forth one whom he knows to be guilty, or is not able to prove him guilty, he is without blame; for no judge may condemn without an accuser. Augustin Ep. 137, *Ibid.* c. 12: Therefore I have not ventured to suppress or remove the name of that presbyter from the number of his colleagues, lest I should seem to affront the divine power under whose examination the matter now rests, if I anticipated divine judgment by my own. *Id.* de Poenit. c. 3, *Ibid.* Caus. XI. Qu. III. c. 75: Although many things may be true, yet no judge dare believe them unless they are established by certain proofs. *Id. Ibid.* Caus. XXIII. Qu. IV. c. 1: The evil must be tolerated for the sake of peace, nor must there be any corporal separation from them. *Id. Ibid.* c. 2: Do ye who are good tolerate the bad, for Christ tolerated Judas. Concil. Afric. *Ibid.* Caus. VI. Qu. II. c. 3; Gregory *Ibid.* Caus. II. Qu. l. c. 15: Whoever does not tolerate the bad is a witness against himself by his own intolerance that he is not good. *Id. Ibid.* c. 74: It were indeed grave and unbecoming to pronounce a certain sentence in a doubtful case. *Id. Ibid.* I. Dist. LXXIV. c. 2; Nicolaus *Ibid.* Caus. XV. Qu. v. c. 2: Let no bishop or priest excommunicate any one until the cause is proven. Eugenius in Decret. Lib. I. Tit. XXXI. c. 2: If a priest knows for certain that any one is guilty of a crime, or if he has confessed and refuses to amend, yet he ought not to charge him by name

which have never ripened into action ([53]) the outer tribunal takes no account, except in the case of heresy ([54]) and simony ([55]); but on the other hand, whenever a wrong act has been done it presumes that it was done with a wrong intention until the contrary appears ([56]). In public discipline, moreover, a person is held responsible for all the consequences of a wrongful act ([57]), whereas in the court of penance he is not

unless he can prove it judicially. . . . But he ought to admonish him not to put himself forward to communicate, because Christ did not repel Judas from communion. Lynd. 233 gives four reasons, quoted note 45, also *ibid.* 311.

([53]). Public discipline does not deal (1) with sins of thought, Gratian Caus. xxxiii. Qu. iii. Dist. 1. c. 14 ; (2) with that which cannot be proved ; (3) with what is not grave ; (4) with what is not completed—a man cannot be charged with murder who has only wounded another ; (5) with acts for which he is not responsible. Rule 22 in Sext. Lib. v. Tit. xii. c. 5: Non debet aliquis alterius odio praegravari. Lynd. 347 : A sin does not merit accusation and punishment except when it has passed into an outward act.

([54]). Const. 3 Arundel, A.D. 1408 : Let no person touch or observe any sort of heresy. . . . Let him incur the sentence of excommunication *ipso facto* who knowingly and pertinaciously attempts the contrary after the publication of these presents.

([55]). See *Excesses*.

([56]). Lynd. 263 : Either a thing is injurious on the face of it or it is indifferent. (1) If it is bad on the face of it, it is so either (*a*) of itself, as beating or slandering, which is presumed to be done with a bad intention unless the contrary appears ; or (*b*) because of some aggravating circumstance, as if a man, knowing that he was about to be served with a process, caused the server to be arrested on a fictitious charge ; or (*c*) it is done *ex officio judicis*, in which case the presumption lies in favour of the judge. (2) If it is indifferent, then by the rule of law the best construction must be put upon it. Lynd. 345 : Malice is presumed unless a just cause is shown.

([57]). Decret. Lib. v. Tit. xxxvi. c. 5 : If a fire spread to stacks of grain or corn, . . . the man who kindled the fire shall recompense the damage. Gregory ix. *Ibid.* c. 9 : If hurt is done or injury inflicted by your fault, or you have assisted others in inflicting it, or it has resulted from your want of skill and negligence, it behoves you to make satisfaction, nor is ignorance an excuse. Lynd. 347 says that a man is responsible for the consequences of his actions, even though these consequences were not what he intended. Lynd. 250 : Negligence is a great sin.

held answerable for unpremeditated results (58). Again, as the rule of charity requires Christians to be slow to believe the report of other men's sins (59), so the rule of the Church requires the strictest interpretation to be put on penal canons (60).

SOLEMN DISCIPLINE.

15. Solemn discipline is discipline which is publicly imposed by the bishop, with the common assent and concurrence of the clergy and people, or, as it is said, *in medio* (61), and is solemnly undergone, whilst public prayers are continually being offered on behalf of the offender. It involves the humiliation of public exposure as a penitent (62), and carries with it the benefit of the united intercessions of the faithful. The first step towards obtaining this benefit is the request for admission to the ranks

---

(58). Lynd. 248 observes that, although *in foro contentioso* a man committing perjury is guilty of all the evils which result therefrom, yet in the court of the soul penance is only imposed for the false witness, although it were aggravated by the results following.

(59). Gregory ap. Gratian I. Dist. LXXXVI. c. 23 and 1; Pseudo-Isidor. *Ibid.* Caus. XXX. Qu. v. c. 6: Let hearsay of evil move no one, nor let any one believe what is currently stated without certain proof; but first let him diligently inquire into what he has heard, lest he should act precipitately. Lynd. 16, 27, 78, 93.

(60). Leo, A.D. 446, ap. Gratian I. Dist. XLV. c. 6; Caus. XXXIII. Qu. III. Dist. l. c. 18: Poenae legum interpretatione molliendae sunt potius quam exasperandae. Rule 49 in Sext. Lib. v. Tit. XII. c. 5: In poenis benignior est interpretatio facienda. Lynd. 15, 27, 78, 52, 127, 144, 151, 155, 171, 219, 240, 296.

(61). St. Paul, in 1 Cor. v., did not himself alone condemn the incestuous Corinthian, but συναχθέντων ὑμῶν καὶ τοῦ ἐμοῦ πνεύματος, so that his action was *in medio*. Cyprian Ep. 25 (Oxf. 31), 6: A great crime must be treated cautiously, with the advice of all the bishops, presbyters, deacons, confessors, and also the laymen who stand [at prayers]. Ep. 30 (Oxf. 33), 5: It is fitting that, an assembly for counsel being gathered together, with bishops, presbyters, deacons, confessors, as well as with the laity who stand [at prayers], we should deal with the case of the lapsed. Ep. 13 (Oxf. 19); Ep. 54 (Oxf. 59), 15: Scarcely do I persuade the people; nay, I extort it from them that they should suffer them to be admitted.

(62). Tertullian de Poenit. c. 9.

of penitents ([63]). In early times admission was not given without difficulty, and sometimes the applicant was given to understand that he must continue a penitent for life ([64]). Applicants for penance were called *Weepers*, because outside the Church-porch, clad in sackcloth and with ashes on their heads, they besought both clergy and people with tears to intercede with God and the bishop on their behalf ([65]).

16. It is a moot point whether there existed in the first ages of the Church any other form of discipline besides solemn discipline ([66]). One thing is, however, clear, that whatever may have been the case with regard to lesser offences of a private character, all the greater offences were originally dealt with by a course of solemn discipline ([67]). The offender was first

(63). Roman clergy to Cyprian, Ep. 30, 6: Let them knock at the doors, but not break them down; let them present themselves at the threshold of the Church, but not leap over it; let them watch at the gates of the heavenly camp, but let them be armed with modesty. Cyprian de Laps. 35: Think you that He will easily have mercy whom you have declared not to be your God? . . . Lying stretched on the ground, ye must cling close to the ashes, be surrounded with sackcloth and filth; after losing the raiment of Christ you must be willing to have no clothing; after the devil's meat you must prefer fasting. Ambros. de Poenit. Lib. I. c. 16; Devoti Lib. II. Tit. II. § 74; Euseb. v. 28 says that Natalius, A.D. 200, putting on sackcloth and covered with ashes, rolled at the feet of both clergy and laity. Concil. Agath. A.D. 506, Can. 15: When penitents ask for penance, let them receive the imposition of hands.

(64). Duchêsne, Origines du Culte Chrétien, p. 420. Concil. Elib. A.D. 305, Can. 3, prescribes this penalty for having after baptism acted as a heathen priest; Can. 13, for a brother marrying two sisters. Concil. Aurel. III. A.D. 538, Can. 25.

(65). Tertullian de Poenit. c. 9: Penitence requires the offender to lie in sackcloth and ashes, to cover his body in mourning . . . to roll before the feet of the presbyters . . . to enjoin on all the brethren to bear his deprecatory supplication before God.

(66). Martène de Ant. Eccles. Rit. Lib. I. c. 6, art. 3; Devoti Lib. II. Tit. II. § 73; Morinus de Poenit. Lib. IV. c. 1, no. 3; Bona Rer. Lit. Lib. I. c. 17, § 3; Craisson, § 3847; Cyprian Ep. 9, 2: In smaller sins offenders do penance for a set time, and, according to the rules of discipline, come to public confession, and by imposition of the hand of the bishop and clergy receive the right of communion.

(67). Iren. Haer. II. 13, 5, relates that women who had been defiled pub-

excluded from Church-fellowship, *i.e.*, from the offering, from Communion, and from participation in the prayers. In this country this was called suspension from entrance to the Church (⁶⁸). Then, when his weeping or application for penance had been successful, he was admitted by the imposition of the bishop's hands (⁶⁹), but not without probation at each successive step, to the several privileges from which his sin had excluded him.

17. In the East very generally but not universally there were, besides the weepers, or those suspended from entrance to the Church, three classes of penitents, called respectively *Hearers, Kneelers,* and *Standers* (⁷⁰); but in this country and in the West commonly there were only two, called respectively

licly confessed the same. *Ibid.* I. 6, 3, and L 13, 5, III. c. 43, that Cerdon, coming frequently into Church and making public confession, remained one time making public confession and then teaching in secret. Tertullian de Poenit. c. 10, says many put off penance because it was public. Theodulf ap. Gratian Caus. XXII. Qu. L c. 171; Morinus de Poenit. V. c. 8; Natalis Alexander Hist. Eccl. Saec. 3, Diss. 6, p. 54. On the other hand, Bellarmine and Sirmond contend that, from the first, discipline was not necessarily public unless the sin was public.

(68). Theodori Poenit. I. v. 10 and 14 in H. and S. III. 181, A.D. 673, calls the lowest class "those extra ecclesiam." For suspension from entrance to the Church, see *Ecclesiastical Severity*, § 4.

(69). Cyprian Ep. 11 (Oxf. 17), 2: No one can come to Communion unless the hands of the bishop and clergy be first imposed upon him. Ep. 9 (Oxf. 16), 2; Ep. 13 (Oxf. 19), 2: When they have made confession, and have received the imposition of hands in acknowledgment of their penitence; Ep. 14 (Oxf. 20), 3. Concil. Agath. A.D. 506, Can. 15: When those who repent ask for penance, let them receive the imposition of hands and have sackcloth placed on their head by the priest (sacerdos), as is everywhere the use. Concil. Barcin. A.D. 540, Can. 8: Those who demand penance in illness and receive it, if they afterwards recover let them lead the life of penitents, excepting the imposition of hands. The Vita Hilarii III. 17 (who died 447) supposes that the bishop addresses the offenders, lays his hands upon them, and recites a prayer over them.

(70). Gregory Thaumaturgos of Neocaesarea in Epist. Can. (Can. ult.), is the first to mention four classes. Also Basil. Epist. 199, Can. ad Amphiloch. 2, Can. 22; Concil. Ancyr. A.D. 314, Can. 6, 16, 17; Concil. Nic. A.D. 325, Can. 11; Concil. Trull. A.D. 692, Can. 87, viz., flentes, audientes, substrati, consistentes.

Discipline Generally.

Penitents and those *Excluded* from offering (⁷¹). Hearers or penitents were allowed to occupy the lower part of the Church, the *narthex* or *ferula*, up to the end of the sermon, when they were dismissed together with the heathen and probationer-catechumens, being required like them to learn again the first principles of the faith.

18. The place above the hearers was occupied by the kneelers. These were placed in Church as high up as the ambon. They remained to the prayers which were made for the approved catechumens, and then were dismissed with the Bishop's collect and imposition of hands (⁷²). In the Western Church, kneelers, if they ever existed as a class, had disappeared before the eighth century (⁷³), and offenders passed at once from the rank of hearers or penitents to that of standers or those excluded from offering (⁷⁴). In this country there is no trace of there having ever been any class of kneelers.

19. The highest place of all was occupied by those called standers, a class who were so called because they stood with the faithful in the prayers of the Church after the dismissal of the catechumens (⁷⁵). They were then themselves usually dismissed. At no time were they allowed to make an offering with the rest (⁷⁶), but some of them were permitted, after a

---

(71). Theodori Poenit. I. v. 10, in H. and S. III. 181, mentions (1) those *extra ecclesiam*, (2) *audientes* or *poenitentes*, and (3) those *extra communionem* [oblationis]. In I. v. 10 the same persons are called auditores, who in I. v. 14, are called poenitentes.

(72). Apost. Const. VIII. 8, 9.

(73). Devoti Lib. II. Tit. II. § 75; Duchêsne (p. 421), however, following Funk Theol. Quartalschrift, 1886, p. 373, states that these four classes never existed in the Latin Rite, and that it may be doubted whether they were of universal observance in the East. Neither the Apostolical Constitutions nor Canons mention them, nor the Council of Antioch, A.D. 341, nor St. Chrysostom. The Constitutions, moreover, II. 16, do not prescribe a term beyond seven weeks—the length of the Oriental Lent.

(74). Devoti, § 76. See previous note.

(75). Apost. Const. VIII. 8.

(76). Concil. Nic. A.D. 325, Can. 11 : For two years let them communicate with the people in prayer without [being admitted to] the oblation.

time, to partake of the hallowed offering made by others ([77]). This position in penitence was often called simply *separation* or *exclusion* ([78]).

20. All who underwent solemn discipline were required to submit to privations of various kinds. They were clothed in sackcloth, and put ashes on their heads ([79]). Men had their hair clipped ([80]), and sometimes women also. The latter wore a penitential veil ([81]). They were forbidden to take part in festivities ([82]), to trade, or to marry ([83]). They fasted and gave alms, knelt whilst others stood at prayers, withdrew themselves

It is not quite clear whether they were placed by themselves, or were intermingled with the faithful in Church.

([77]). Theodori Poenit. I. XII. 4 in H. & S. III. 186 : Penitents, according to the canons, may not communicate until the consummation of penance, but we, out of mercy, allow them to, after a year or six months. *Id.* I. v. 10, *Ibid.* 181 : If one withdraw from the Catholic Church and afterwards repent, let him do penance for twelve years, viz., four years outside the Church, six among the hearers, and two more without communion [in the offering]. The Synod [of Nicaea] says of such that in the tenth year they may receive the communion or oblation. See *Penance*, § 12.

([78]). Theodori Poenit. I. XIV. 2, *Ibid.* 187 : Let them [*i.e.*, newly married people] not be separated [*i.e.*, excluded from offering]. Rabanus, A.D. 849, ap. Gratian Caus. XXX. Qu. 1. c. 5 ; Devoti Lib. II. Tit. II. § 75, and Lib. IV. Tit. XVIII. § 4.

([79]). Cilicium, sack-cloth or hair-cloth, which all monks were required to wear. Ambros. de Laps. Virg. c. 8 no. 35.

([80]). Concil. Agath. A.D. 506, Can. 15, forbids their being admitted to penance unless they have clipped their hair and changed their garments. Concil. Barcin. A.D. 540, Can. 6 : That penitents with clipped hair, wearing the garb of religion, devote their life to prayer. Concil. Tolet. III. A.D. 589, Can. 12 : Whoever applies to a bishop or presbyter for penance, let the bishop or presbyter clip him and then prescribe penance. Devoti Lib. I. Tit. I. § 11. According to Isidor de Eccl. Offic. II. 17, during penance neither hair nor beard were trimmed.

([81]). Optatus Milev. contra Parmenian Lib. II.

([82]). Concil. Barcinon., A.D. 540, Can. 7.

([83]). Concil. Arelat. II. A.D. 443, Can. 21 ; Leo, A.D. 459, ap. Gratian Caus. XXXIII. Qu. II. c. 14 says that if a young man marries whilst undergoing penance, *timens lapsum juvenilis incontinentiae*, he may be held to have committed only a venial offence.

from the public baths and the society of their friends ([84]), and practised conjugal abstinence ([85]).

21. Solemn discipline, as it is met with in the Western Church in the sixth century, was confined to the forty days of Lent in each year ([86]). The subjects of it presented themselves on Ash Wednesday, barefoot and clothed in sackcloth, at the doors of the Church, where, after being admitted and repeating the seven penitential psalms, the bishop sprinkled them with water, laid his hands upon them, and covered their heads with sackcloth; then announcing to them that, as Adam was turned out of Paradise so must they be turned out of Church for their sins, he gave the order for their expulsion ([87]). On Maundy Thursday they were restored by the bishop with equal solemnity ([88]) in order to participate in the Easter Eucharist imperative on all. Solemn discipline was not, however, practised in this country until after the seventh century ([89]). Here, as elsewhere, the substitute for it was seclusion in a monastery for a time or for life ([90]), and in later times the under-

([84]). Martene de Ant. Rit. Lib. I. c. 6, art. 4.
([85]). Hieronym. ap. Gratian Caus. XXXIII. Qu. IV. c. 6.
([86]). Gerbert Disquis v. 458; Lingard's Anglo-Saxon Church I. 329; Egbert's Excerpt. 162: Let him do penance five years or five Lents.
([87]). Concil. Agath. A.D. 506, ap. Gratian I. Dist. l. c. 64; Can. 13 Dunstan, A.D. 963: Every bishop shall be in his episcopal chair on Ash Wednesday. There every one that is defiled with capital crimes shall come to him by day and declare his sins, and then he directs a satisfaction to every one according to the quality of his crimes. Leofric Missal, p. 73, contains an Ordo agentibus publicam poenitentiam, and p. 92 an Ordo ad reconciliandum. Lynd. 336, 340, 352.
([88]). Concil. Carthag. II. A.D. 390, ap. Gratian Caus. XXVI. Qu. VI. c. 1 limits public reconciliation to the bishop. Theodori Poenit. I. XIII. 2 l. c. p. 187: The reconciliation of penitents is only done by the bishop on Maundy Thursday, after penance is over. Concil. Cabil. II. A.D. 813, ap. Gratian III. Dist. II. c. 17, quoted in the *Eucharist*, note 254.
([89]). Theodori Poenit. I. XIII. 4 in H. & S. III. 187: Public [*i.e.*, solemn] reconciliation is not in use in this country, because public [*i.e.*, solemn] penance is not used here.
([90]). Theodori Poenit. I. VII. 1, A.D. 673, in H. & S. III. 182: Let him who is guilty of many crimes—homicide, adultery, unnatural crime, and stealing—enter a monastery and do penance all his life. Gel. Sacr. L 16:

taking a pilgrimage, or practising almsgiving on a large scale ([91]).

22. Solemn discipline requires to be ended by solemn restoration ([92]), except at the point of death. Unless undergone by special desire ([93]), it is only employed for manifest and notorious crimes ([94]), but for some of these it is directed to be imposed ([95]). On the young it may not be imposed because of the frowardness of youth, nor on one of two married persons without the consent of the other ([96]). Women guilty of adultery were also excused from it, because the revelation of the crime might involve them in the death penalty ([97]), and adulterers, unless with consent of their wives ([98]), because solemn discipline necessitated conjugal abstinence ([99]). Those in Holy Orders are not allowed to be the subjects of it ([100]), and when it

Take him on the Wednesday at the head of the fast, cover him with sackcloth, pray for him, and shut him up (inclaudis) until the Lord's Supper day. Duchêsne 423

([91]). Devoti Lib. II. Tit. II. § 79.

([92]). Concil. Carthag. II. Can. 3, A.D. 390, ap. Gratian Caus. XXVI. Qu. VI. c. 1 ; Concil. Carthag. III. Can. 32, A.D. 397, *Ibid.* c. 14.

([93]). Decret. Lib. V. Tit. XXXVIII. c. 7.

([94]). Concil. Carthag. III. Can. 32 l. c. c. 14: Cujuscumque autem poenitentis publicum et vulgatissimum crimen est.

([95]). Const. 7 Peckham, A.D. 1281: Whereas according to the canons greater sins, such as murders, incest, and the like . . . are to be chastised with solemn penance, . . . we charge that such solemn penance be imposed for the future according to the canons.

([96]). Concil. Agath. A.D. 506, Can 15: That no one presume to give the benediction of penance to youthful persons, and certainly not to married persons, except with consent of both, and unless they are of ripe age (aetate plena). Concil. Aurel. III. A.D. 538, Can. 24.

([97]). Basil. in Beveridge Pandect. II. part 1, p. 47; Devoti Lib. II. Tit. II. § 78.

([98]). Concil. Arelat. II. Can. 22, A.D. 443, ap. Gratian Caus. XXXIII. Qu. IV. c. 13.

([99]). Hieronym *Ibid.* Caus. XXXIII. Qu. IV. c. 6.

([100]). Concil. Carthag. V. Can. 11, A.D. 401. *Ibid.* I. Dist. l. c. 65: If either presbyters or deacons are convicted of any greater offence, necessitating their removal from the ministry, hands are not to be laid on such as on penitents, as on faithful laymen, nor are they to be rebaptized and readmitted to the clerical order. Leo Epist. 90, c. 2, A.D. 458, *Ibid.* c. 67:

has once been undergone it may never be undergone a second time ([101]). The mediaeval and modern practice of repeating private confession and absolution can only be justified in the case of lesser offences, on the assumption that the offender is slowly becoming what he ought to be, and that these several acts are moments in one protracted course of discipline akin to solemn discipline ([102]). The term penitents is, however, properly confined to those undergoing solemn discipline publicly ([103]).

It is contrary to ecclesiastical usage that those who have been hallowed to the rank of priesthood or diaconate should by the imposition of hands receive the remedy of penance, which usage doubtless comes from apostolical tradition, because it is written, If a priest shall sin who shall pray for him? Such as have lapsed in this position must privately seek seclusion to deserve God's mercy, where proper satisfaction, when made, may be profitable to them.

([101]). Herm. Sim. III. 9 : For the servants of the Lord there is but one repentance. Tertullian de Poenit. c. 7, quoted *Penance*, note 96. Origen Hom. in Levit. 15, c. 2 (III. 262). Socrates VI. 22 mentions as a complaint against Chrysostom: Whereas by the synod of bishops repentance was accepted but once from those who had sinned after baptism, he did not scruple to say, Approach although you have repented a thousand times. Augustin ap. Gratian I. Dist. 1. c. 62, and Caus. XXXIII. Qu. III. Dist. III. c. 22: Whence careful and healthful provision has been made that room should only once be allowed for that most humiliating penance, lest a too useful medicine should be little esteemed because of its cheapness, yet forgiveness is never denied after penance to those who sin daily. Ambros. *Ibid.* c. 2: Some there are who think repentance may be often undergone and luxuriate in Christ; but if they had true repentance they would know that it must not be repeated, for as there is one baptism so there is one repentance. Concil. Tolet. III. A.D. 589, Can. 11 : Some demand to be reconciled by a priest as often as they sin. Let penance be imposed on such after the ancient form. Lynd. 41, 340.

([102]). Augustin Epist. 265 ad Seleuc.; Serm. 392.

([103]). Augustin ap. Gratian Caus. XXXIII. Qu. III. Dist. 1. c. 81, says there are three kinds of penitence: (1) that which leads to baptism, (2) the life-long penitence of the baptized who look forward to eternal life, and (3) penance such as fasting, almsgiving, and prayer for breaches of the Decalogue. It follows that breaches of the Decalogue should not be allowed to form part of repeated confessions. See *Penance*, note 96.

The Foundation of Discipline—Vows.

23. The foundation of the Church's claim to exercise discipline of any kind is contract originated by a vow. A vow is defined to be a promise made to God in order to obtain some spiritual good. To render it lawful, it must fulfil three conditions: (1) It must have some good object in view ([104]); for nothing that is wrong can be offered to God ([105]). (2) It must be possible of execution by divine aid; for it is mockery to promise what cannot be performed. (3) It must be voluntarily and deliberately made ([106]); for what is done under pressure is not the party's act, and a hasty or thoughtless promise carries with it no stability ([107]). Nevertheless, a vow may sometimes be made on behalf of another, such as the baptismal vow, when its object is to secure some surpassing spiritual good for him ([108]).

24. Vows may be generally divided into two classes: (1) private vows, and (2) public vows. Private vows are either those of a private character affecting the individual only, such as a promise to build a Church, or to undertake a pilgrimage, or to make a gift to God, or to nurse in a contagious hospital,

---

(104). Theodori Poenit. I. XIV. 6 in Haddan and Stubbs III. 188, orders foolish and rash vows to be set aside. Hieronym. ap. Gratian Caus. XXII. Qu. 1. c. 7 and 8, and Concil. Tolet. X. *Ibid.* c. 1, allows a vow to be taken to promote peace. *Ibid.* c. 4 and 5 permit an oath to be taken when required by lawful authority. Lynd. 203.

(105). Concil. Araus. II. A.D. 529, Can. 11: No one can rightly make a vow to God unless he has received from God the power of vowing. Ambros. ap. Gratian Caus. XXII. Qu. IV. c. 8: It is better not to fulfil an oath than to do that which is wrong. Augustin. *Ibid.* c. 20; Syn. VII. A.D. 787; *Ibid.* c. 18.

(106). Gelasius ap. Gratian Caus. XXVII. Qu. 1. c. 42, says, propria voluntate. Concil. Tolet. VI. A.D. 638, Can. 2 *Ibid.* Caus. XX. Qu. III. c. 2 and 4 and 5. Conf. Const. 18 Peckham, A.D. 1281; Lynd. 202.

(107). Concil. Aurel. II. A.D. 533, Can. 12: Let no one make a vow in Church in jest, drink, or wantonness. Alexander III. in Decret. Lib. III. Tit. XXXIV. c. 3.

(108). See *The Sacraments*, § 18; *Baptism*, § 10.

or otherwise public vows which have been taken privately. Of private vows some are approved, others tolerated only, others again forbidden; but the private taking of all vows is discountenanced, (1) because many things may be vowed rashly; (2) because the faithful are thereby deprived of the stimulus of a good example; and (3) because the person who vows loses the help of the corporate sympathy and intercession of others in the communion of saints ([109]).

25. Public vows are vows which admit to a distinct position in the Church, and render those who take them amenable to the special discipline of that position. Such are (1) the baptismal vow, (2) the renewal of vows at confirmation, (3) the ordination vow, (4) the marriage vow, (5) the monastic vow or vow of religion, and (6) the vow of canonical and feudal obedience, which is the basis of the bishop's or abbot's jurisdiction.

26. Every public vow is held to consist of three parts ([110]): (1) the proposal, promise, or simple vow, which is sometimes called the oath, because a Christian man's word should be equivalent to an oath ([111]); (2) the confirmation or profession, called the solemn vow ([112]); and (3) the consummation or

---

(109). Alcuin Ep. in H. and S. III. 471: The Scripture saith: A brother assisted by a brother is like a strong city. See Cavagnis III. 169.

(110). Lynd. 203 calls them Initium, Confirmatio, Consummatio.

(111). Matt. v. 37; James v. 12; Augustin ap. Gratian Caus. XXII. Qu. 1. c. 3. Leo, A.D. 459, *Ibid.* Caus. XX. Qu. 1. c. 8, distinguishes the proposition from the vow.

(112). The Thomists say that a simple vow differs from a solemn vow, as a promise does from a gift. Craisson, § 2479. A second view is that solemnity is the result of a kind of consecration. A third view is that the difference between simple and solemn vows is a purely human distinction, not being earlier than Gratian's time. The difference is, however, substantially there in the Stat. Ant. Eccl. A.D. 505, respecting widows ap. Gratian Caus. XXVII. Qu. 1. c. 1; Concil. Chalcedon A.D. 451, *Ibid.* c. 22; Augustin. *Ibid.* c. 41 and 1 Dist. XXVII. c. 2, and Hieronym. *Ibid.* c. 4, 5, 9. Devoti Lib. II. Tit. II. c. 129; Saunderson, De Jurament. Prael. 1, calls them respectively oath and vow: Per hoc distinguitur jurmmentum a voto. In voto transigitur cum Deo ipso ut cum parte; ast in juramento transigitur cum homine; Deus autem adducitur non ut pars sed ut testis. Hence he argues an oath may be dispensed, but not a vow.

execution. A simple vow is a promise made to or before man of some allowed thing, such as a betrothal or promise of marriage at a future date, or a promise of religion, *i.e.*, a promise to keep the rules of perfection ; and perhaps the baptismal vow, taken by an infant by deputy, may be regarded in the same light. A solemn vow is a vow solemnly made before God and the Church, by one who is conscious of what he is doing ([113]), which irrevocably pledges him who makes it to fulfil it without excuse ([114]), such as the vow renewed at confirmation, the actual contract of marriage, the solemn profession made on taking orders, or on entering the religious life.

27. Simple vows, when once taken, ought to be fulfilled ([115]), and delay in fulfilling them calls for discipline, because of the breach of faith ([116]). Hence, one who has devoted himself to the religious life by a simple vow, and afterwards resumes the secular habit, may not be advanced to any degree of order ([117]), and may even be compelled to take the solemn vow of religion, since by God's grace and the help of a common life its obligations are capable of being fulfilled by all ([118]). There are, how-

(113). Craisson, § 2467.

(114). Augustin ap. Gratian Caus. XVII. Qu. 1. c. 1 : When we have promised a thing to God we are bound of necessity to perform it. Gregory *Ibid.* c. 3 denounces the punishment of Ananias for not performing it. Sext. Lib. III. Tit. xv. ; Suarez ap. Craisson, § 2501.

(115). Apost. Const. III. 1 and IV. 14 : It is better not to vow than to vow and not to pay, repeated by Pseudo-Isidor. ap. Gratian Caus. XII. Qu. 1. c. 9. Other authorities, *Ibid* Caus. XVII. Qu. 1, and Caus. XX. Qu. III. c. 1 and 2 ; Theodori Poenit. II. XIV. 5 in H. and S. III. 202 : Laymen ought not to delay to fulfil their promises, because death is not slow. Concil. Chelsea A.D. 787, Can. 18 ; Alfred's Law 14, A.D. 877 : If one implead another of breach of promise to God, and will accuse him for not having performed that which he had plighted, let him first make oath of it in four Churches ; and the other, if he will justify himself, let him do the same in twelve. See *Discipline of the Religious Life*, § 27.

(116). See *Excesses*.

(117). Theodori Poenit. I. IX. 2 in Haddan and Stubbs III. 185 : If any one who has vowed himself to God has afterwards assumed the secular habit, he ought not to be advanced to any step [of order] at all.

(118). Concil. Tolet. VI. A.D. 638, ap. Gratian Caus. XX. Qu. III. c. 2 ; Const. 18 Peckham, A.D. 1281 : Such nuns as have voluntarily led a regular

ever, cases in which a simple vow may be annulled; but this can only be done with the sanction of the Church, or, as it is said, by dispensation for some good cause ([119]). A simple vow may also by permission be commuted into one of another kind ([120]), and any vow into a vow of religion, even without permission ([121]).

28. A dispensation from a simple vow may be granted by a diocesan bishop ([122]) or the superior of an order ([123]): (1) if change of circumstances renders it impossible to fulfil the vow literally, ([124]) in which case an equivalent ought to be substituted ([125]); or (2) if the person who makes it or the thing vowed is in the power of another, and the other refuses to consent ([126]); —Thus a parent may annul the vow of a child ([127]), the husband

---

life in a college for above a year we declare to be deemed *ipso facto* professed, so as not to be permitted to return to a secular life, though they are to be solemnly consecrated or veiled by the bishop. We give the same judgment as to monks, that if they have for above a year willingly worn the religious habit in a monastery and then, rejecting it, return to a secular life, they be repelled as apostates. Cavagnis III. 169.

(119). Ambros. ap. Gratian Caus. XXII. Qu. IV. c. 2; Cavagnis III. 169; Chap. CLIV. 7.

(120). Alexander III. to Bishop of Exeter in Decret. Lib. III. Tit. XXXIV. c. 1, allows a pilgrimage vow to be commuted. *Id.* to Bishop of Norwich, *Ibid.* c. 2; Innocent III. to Archbishop of Canterbury, *Ibid.* c. 8, 9.

(121). Alexander III. *Ibid.* c. 4.

(122). Theodori Poenit. II. XII. 15 in Haddan and Stubbs III. 200, and Caus. XXVII. Qu. II. c. 23: If any one in the secular habit vows a vow without the bishop's consent, the bishop, if he will, has power to change his sentiment.

(123). Theodori Poenit. II. VI. 9, *Ibid.* p. 195; Lynd. 212.

(124). Alexander III. to Archbishop of Canterbury in Decret. Lib. III. Tit. XXXIV. c. 8.

(125). Theodori Poenit. II. XIV. 6, *Ibid.* p. 203: Similarly cattle [which have been vowed] may be changed for those of equal value in case of necessity.

(126). Theodori Poenit. I. XIV. 7, *Ibid.* p. 188; II. VI. 9, *Ibid.* p. 195; Gratian Caus. XXVII. Qu. II. c. 22: Caus. XX. Qu. II. c. 2; Const. 28 Edmund, A.D. 1236.

(127). Gratian Caus. XXXII. Qu. II. c. 14; and Caus. XXII. Qu. V. c. 15.

the vow of a wife ([128]), an abbot the vow of a monk ([129]);—or (3) if it is a rash vow, or a vow to do evil ([130]). But when the vow is to do some good to a fellow-Christian, no dispensation can take effect without the consent of the person interested. Hence a bishop cannot dispense from the vow to profess the religious life without the consent of the abbot who is interested, nor annul a vow to enter a stricter order ([131]).

29. The effect of a solemn vow, *i.e.*, a vow solemnly professed before God and the Church, is to render all acts done contrary thereto not only irregular, and therefore the subject-matter for discipline ([132]), but also in Christian communities invalid, except a dispensation has been granted ([133]). Hence solemn vows are not allowed to be taken except (1) by persons of full age ([134]), and (2) after previous probation ([135]). Moreover, no dispensation can entirely release from a solemn vow ([136]), the substantial

---

([128]). Theodori Poenit. I. XIV. 7, *Ibid.* p. 188 : A woman may not make a vow without her husband's consent. If she do, the vow may be annulled, and she should do penance as the priest enjoins. Concil. Compend. A.D. 756, ap. Gratian Caus. XXXIII. Qu. V. c. 6.

([129]). Theodori Poenit. II. VI. 9, *Ibid.* p. 195 : A monk may not take a vow without the abbot's consent. If he do, it should be annulled.

([130]). Isidor. ap. Gratian Caus. XXII. Qu. IV. c. 19, quoted note 172.

([131]). See *Discipline of the Religious Life*, § 15.

([132]). Concil. Chalcedon A.D. 451, Can. 7 ap. Gratian Caus. XX. Qu. III. c. 3, anathematises those who give up orders or religion.

([133]). Const. 45 Langton, A.D. 1222, regarding regulars as dead persons, forbids them to make a will. The law of this country considered them dead persons, and they were in consequence not able to sue nor to be sued in a court of law before 31 Hen. VIII. c. 6. Sext. Lib. III. Tit. XV. c. 1.

([134]). Egbert's Excerpt. 91, A.D. 740, says 25. Const. 41 Langton, A.D. 1222.

([135]). Const. 18 Peckham, A.D. 1281, prescribes one year. See *Discipline of the Religious Life*, § 23. Boniface VIII. in Sext. Lib. III. Tit. XIV. c. 3.

([136]). Leo, A.D. 458, ap. Gratian Caus. XX. Qu. III. c. 1 : A monk's vow undertaken voluntarily and of free choice cannot be abandoned without sin. For one ought to pay to God what he has vowed. Egbert's Excerpt. 65, A.D. 740 ; Innocent III. in Decret. Lib. III. Tit. XXXV. c. 6 : The renunciation of property and the preservation of chastity are so bound up with the monastic rule that not even the pope can grant a license to dispense therewith.

Discipline Generally.

obligation of which extends to the end of life ([137]); but it may release from the literal fulfilment of it, by granting exemption from penal discipline in the external tribunal ([138]), and also render acts valid which would otherwise be invalid ([139]).

PRIVILEGES, DISPENSATIONS, AND LICENSES.

30. To prevent the Church's rules or any religious rule or vow from becoming oppressive, and a hindrance to that holiness which they are intended to promote ([140]), two general maxims of practice have been laid down: (1) that all canons made by the Church in restraint of freedom must be construed strictly ([141]); and (2) that for good and sufficient reason privileges, dispensations, and licenses may be granted by proper authority ([142]). And since an obligation or disability may be

([137]). Decret. Lib. III. Tit. XXXIV. c. 10 and 17. See *Order*, § 40.

([138]). This has been done in this country by the general dispensation of the civil power by statutes 33 Hen. VIII. c. 29, and 5 and 6 Ed. VI. c. 13.

([139]). Decret. Lib. III. Tit. XXXIV. c. 10.

([140]). Socrates v. 22: Neither the apostle nor the evangelists have anywhere imposed the yoke of servitude on those who have embraced the Gospel, but have left Easter and every other feast to be honoured by the gratitude of the recipients of grace. . . . The Saviour and His apostles have by no law enjoined us to keep this feast, nor in the New Testament are we threatened with any penalty for the neglect of it. . . . The apostles had no thought of appointing festival days, but of promoting a life of blamelessness and piety. . . . Since no one can produce a written authority, it is evident that the apostles left each one to his own free will in the matter, to the end that the performance of what is good might not be the result of constraint and necessity.

([141]). Sext. Lib. V. Tit. XII. c. 5, Rule 15; Lynd. 40, 75, 76, 171, 253, 268, 283.

([142]). Gelasius, A.D. 494, ap. Gratian Caus. I. Qu. VII. c. 6: We are compelled . . . to reconsider the decrees of the paternal canons, and to measure backwards the precepts of our predecessors, that these rules which the necessity of present times require to be relaxed, we may temper as far as possible by the employment of diligent consideration. Innocent I. *Ibid.* Caus. II. Qu. 1. c. 7: That which has been appointed by way of remedy for a temporal necessity did not exist in primitive times . . . and may also be laid aside when necessity is past. Gregory *Ibid.* Caus. I. Qu. VII. c. 11.

created either by a general rule of law or by the party's own act, so relief may be had from either upon proper cause shown.

31. A privilege may be defined to be a private law conferring some special advantage on a particular place or body of men within the Church, at variance with the generally received law ([143]), which either exists by custom or by some special grant. Such is the privilege enjoyed by certain Churches called peculiars, which was enjoyed by custom until recent times; or that bestowed upon certain monastic houses and orders termed exempt jurisdictions by grant, making them independent of the ordinary territorial relations and self-governing in spirituals. A dispensation is relief from the obligation of obedience to a general rule, or from the obligation incurred by the party's own act, which is granted either in consideration of infirmity or to obtain some greater good, such as dispensation from observing the rule of fasting, or from a disability for ordination, or from fulfiling his own oath ([144]). A faculty or license is a permission to do that which would ordinarily be contrary to rule, which is given by virtue of some written or customary law authorising such permission to be given in certain cases ([145]), such as a permission to be non-resident on a benefice for purposes of study, or a license to marry without banns ([146]).

(143). Gregory ap. Gratian Caus. XVI. Qu. 1. c. 52, mentions the exemption of some bishops from archiepiscopal control. In Decret. Lib. v. Tit. XXXIII. c. 1 complaint is made of the Templars abusing their privileges. Craisson, § 156, defines a privilege as a private law making some special concession contrary to or beyond law.

(144). Iren. Haer. IV. 15, 2: In the New Testament the apostles are found granting certain dispensating precepts in consideration of human infirmity, lest such persons, having grown obdurate and despairing of salvation, should become apostates. . . . In the Old Testament the same God permitted similar indulgences for the benefit of His people. Cyril in Syn. VII. A.D. 787, ap. Gratian Caus. I. Qu. VII. c. 15; Ayliffe 219, 353; Craisson, § 957.

(145). Concil Lat. III. A.D. 1179, Can. 13 in Decret. Lib. III. Tit. IV. c. 3, and Concil. Lat. IV. A.D. 1215, *Ibid.* Tit. V. c. 30, and Const. 14 Langton, A.D. 1222, require personal residence in a benefice-holder. Yet a bishop is authorised to give leave of non-residence for a limited time for a definite cause.

(146). Urban II. A.D. 1083, ap. Gratian Caus. I. Qu. v. c. 3: Let him have

32. A dispensation may be granted (1) at the party's own instance, in the cases allowed by custom, when it is termed a *legitimation* or *justice* (147); or (2) on the spontaneous initiative of the dispensing authority, when it is termed a *grace* or *favour*. Dispensations granted at the party's instance are said to be odious, and are therefore construed strictly (148). Those granted by way of grace or favour may have an extended and favourable construction put upon them (149).

33. To be lawful and valid every dispensation must fulfil three conditions : (1) It must be conceded by competent authority ; (2) it must not be a relief from any obligation created by divine law (150); (3) it must be granted for some good cause. Every dispensation, therefore, should specify the law with which it dispenses, and the cause for which it is granted, and unless it does so, it is accounted null and void (151). It is a matter for the judge's discretion to decide whether the cause is sufficient. A faculty or license, on the other hand, may not be granted or withheld at discretion ; but whenever the circumstances exist in which custom or law authorises the permission to issue, it may be claimed as a right, and any attempt to withhold it may be set aside on appeal as an act of favouritism or prejudice.

34. The competent authority to grant a dispensation is the same by which the rule proposed to be departed from was originally made. Dispensations may therefore be granted (1) by an ecumenical synod ; (2) by a provincial synod or its representative, the metropolitan ; and (3) in some few cases by a territorial bishop. But since no inferior can dispense with the

---

a license by the bishop's leave and the consent of the brethren to discharge the office of a priest there. Const. 1 Reynolds, A.D. 1322 ; Lynd. 48.

(147). Ayliffe 219. This is denied by Devoti Lib. II. Tit. II. § 121, note 2. The recipient of a marriage dispensation is said to be consoled (consolari).

(148). Devoti Lib. I. Tit. VI. § 14.

(149). Ayliffe 220.

(150). Ayliffe 220.

(151). "If contrary to Holy Scriptures and the laws of God"— these are not included in the despensations which 25 Hen. VIII. c. 21 sec. 3 allows the archbishop to grant.

law of a superior (^{152}), unless authorised by the superior so to do, neither a metropolitan can dispense from an ecumenical, nor a bishop from a provincial canon, except in those cases in which they are authorised so to do either by canon or custom (^{153}). Such authorised dispensations are more properly called faculties or licenses.

35. Formerly the power of dispensation was exercised on behalf of the ecumenical synod by the pope or his legates, in some cases by custom (^{154}), in others by express canon (^{155}).

(152). Innocent III. in Decret. Lib. I. Tit. XI. c. 15; Concil. Vien. A.D. 1311, in Clem. Lib. I. Tit. III. c. 2: The law of a superior cannot be abrogated by an inferior. Ayliffe 220: A bishop cannot grant a dispensation contrary to the common law of the Church; for by a dispensation the laws are violated, and it is not lawful to violate the laws of his superior. Concil. Tolet. IV. A.D. 633, ap. Gratian Caus. X. Qu. III. c. 8: Whatever bishop shall presume to act contrary to what we have decreed, the same shall be liable to canonical correction as a transgressor of synodal decrees, and a violator of the rules of the fathers.

(153). Concil. Ancyr. A.D. 314, ap. Gratian I. Dist. l. c. 22, 32: If a priest or deacon have committed sacrilege, he may no longer be retained in the ecclesiastical rank. Yet it may be left to the bishop to determine whether he may be retained or not. Concil. Nic. A.D. 325, Can. 12: The bishop may use some favour towards him. Theodori Poenit. I. IV. 5 in Haddan and Stubbs III. 180: If any one slay a monk or a clerk, let him do penance seven years; it is in the bishop's power [to dispense]. I. XII. 5 *Ibid.* p. 187, *Id.* II. XII. 15, *Ibid.* p. 200: If any one in the secular habit vows a vow, the bishop, if he will, has power to change the vow. Concil. Lat. IV. A.D. 1215, Can. 19, 20, 57, 58, bestow on bishops the power of dispensing in certain cases. Lynd. 240: When any cause concerns the whole province, the archbishop is a competent judge. Ayliffe 220: He that can limit and interpret a law may in a particular case, by way of dispensation, repeal or take away for a season the force of such law, but he cannot do so entirely, though it be on a lawful account. Craisson, § 959-961, 972; Gousset Théol. Moral. I. 306.

(154). Socrates VII. 40 relates that in A.D. 434, Coelestine dispensed with the rule against translations in the case of Proclus. Devoti Lib. I. Tit. III. § 16, gives instances of such dispensations by custom from the fourth century. 25 Hen. VIII. c. 21, sec. 2 and 4, speaks of "dispensations, compositions, faculties, &c., which have been accustomed to be had at the see of Rome." See *Wedlock*, § 16.

(155). Concil. Lat. IV. A.D. 1215, in Decret. Lib. III. Tit. V. c. 28: As

Discipline Generally. 33

The pope or the proper patriarch therefore dispensed with disqualifications for holy orders ([156]). He also dispensed from the obligation of a solemn oath, subject to the consent of any person who would have been injured thereby ([157]), and from the duty of residence on a spiritual cure ([158]). He also granted dispensations to hold two benefices simultaneously ([159]), to contract marriage within the forbidden degrees ([160]), and to appropriate to a nunnery a benefice with cure of souls ([161]). By the Reformation statutes this power was transferred in this

regards high and literate persons, when reason requires, a dispensation may be granted by the Holy See. *Ibid.* c. 29 : Let not a sentence of this kind be relaxed, except by authority of the Roman pontiff or the proper patriarch.

(156). Alexander III. in Decret. Lib. I. Tit. VI. c. 5, allows a bishop converted from schism to be consecrated immediately by virtue of a dispensation. Concil. Lat. IV. A.D. 1215, in Decret. Lib. III. Tit. v. c. 29, says the pope or the proper patriarch may dispense. Const. 37 Edmund, A.D. 1236. Boniface VIII. in Sext. Lib. I. Tit. XI. c. 1, requires the pope's dispensation in all irregularities for holy orders. Lynd. 130, 27, mentions being convicted of perjury.

(157). Therefore not with an oath of allegiance without the consent of the sovereign. Craisson, § 5242.

(158). Syn. VII. A.D. 787, ap. Gratian Caus. XXI. Qu. l. c. 1, only allows this in villages, because of the scarcity of clergy. Const. 1 Peckham, A.D. 1279 ; Const. 24 Peckham, A.D. 1281 : We cannot dispense with pluralities. Lynd. 135, 137, states that where there is no cure of souls a bishop can grant a dispensation to hold two benefices.

(159). Nevertheless a bishop was formerly authorised to grant a license for non-residence for a period not exceeding seven years, whilst the incumbent was qualifying himself at an approved university. Lynd. 238. By Const. 8 Otho, A.D. 1237, and Const. 20 Othobon, A.D. 1268, this period was reduced to five years. Coelestin III and Innocent. III. in Decret. Lib. III. Tit. IV. c. 8 and 9, authorised fresh elections in two cases in which a dean had been non-resident for ten and four years respectively. In this country residence is now regulated by sec. 42 of 1 and 2 Vict. cap. 106. Ayliffe 220.

(160). Pseudo-Gregory, A.D. 601, to Augustin Qu. V. in Baeda L 27 [*i.e.*, Theodore], dispenses with certain forbidden degrees, and Gregory II. did the same for Germany. The earliest personal dispensations are those of Paschal II. to Philip of France, A.D. 1104, and Innocent III. to the Emperor Otho IV., A.D. 1209. See *Wedlock*, note 128.

(161). Hobart 148 ; Gibson 89.

VOL. II.   C

country to the commissary of faculties under the archbishop, but in all unaccustomed cases the archbishop is required to have a special license from the crown ([162]).

36. A dispensation from a canon of a provincial council may be granted by the metropolitan ([163]), and in the cases authorised by law by a provincial bishop ([164]). The latter may therefore dispense with the observance of a fast ([165]) or feast ([166]), the fasting reception of the communion ([167]), the residence of nuns within the convent walls ([168]), the publication of banns of marriage ([169]), an irregularity for minor orders ([170]), a simple vow, so that the dispensation do not prejudice another ([171]), or from an oath to do wrong ([172]). A bishop, and likewise an

---

([162]). 25 Hen. VIII. c. 21, A.D. 1533.

([163]). Lynd. 240, who, however, states, 137, that the archbishop cannot dispense from a decree of a general council.

([164]). The gloss on Decret. Lib. II. Tit. 1. c. 4, has given rise to much controversy. Some contend that a bishop can only dispense in the cases in which he is specially authorised so to do; others that he has an inherent power of dispensation in all, except the cases in which he is specially forbidden to dispense. Bouix de Episcopo II. 96; Stephen's Eccl. Stat. 167. See Devoti in *Wedlock*, note 157.

([165]). Innocent III. A.D. 1206, in Decret. Lib. III. Tit. XCVI. c. 2.

([166]). Lynd. 102, says that in case of necessity a bishop, and even a parochial incumbent, may grant a dispensation to work on Sunday. See *Liturgical Discipline*.

([167]). Theodori Poenit. L. XII. 5, quoted *The Eucharist*, note 269.

([168]). Const. 18 Peckham, A.D. 1281: Bishops for some necessary cause may please to have it otherwise [*i.e.*, allow nuns to be absent for more than six days]. Lynd. 212.

([169]). Const. 8 Mepham. A.D. 1328.

([170]). Lynd. 27.

([171]). Or before it has come to the knowledge of the person to be benefited. Craisson, § 5240.

([172]). Ambros. ap. Gratian Caus. XXII. Qu. IV. c. 2; Concil. Ilerd A.D. 523, Can. 7, requires a year's penance for the perjury in such a case. Isidor. *Ibid.* c. 19: In three cases oaths which have been taken must be cancelled (solvenda): (1) when an oath has been taken to do wrong, (2) when an oath has been taken rashly, and (3) when an oath has been taken by a minor which the parents disavow. Concil. Tolet. VIII. A.D. 653, *Ibid.* c. 14: Stulta vota frangenda sunt. Syn. VII. A.D. 787, *Ibid.* c. 18. Conf.

abbot ([173]), can also in most cases dispense his own subjects from the penalty imposed by a provincial canon ([174]), and, except in the cases reserved to the metropolitan, can substitute one penance for another ([175]). Neither, however, can dispense with the solemn forms required by law to be observed in dealing with ecclesiastical property ([176]).

37. As no human authority can dispense with divine laws, so no dispensation can issue which is either an infringement of natural right ([177]), of a fundamental precept of the Gospel, or of any apostolic rule which is an integral part of the Church's constitution ([178]). If, however, a question arises as to whether

Ibid. I. Dist. XIII. ; Alfred's Law I. A.D. 877 ; Sext. Lib. V. Tit. XII. c. 58 ; Lynd. 117. See above, § 28.

(173). Const. 44 Langton, A.D. 1222, forbids an abbot to dispense with some things. Lynd. 209. See above, § 28.

(174). See above, note 153. Decret. Lib. II. Tit. 1. c. 4 ; Concil. London A.D. 1108, Can. 9 ; Lynd. 264.

(175). Decret. Lib. V. Tit. VIII. c. 2 ; Const. 12 Stratford, A.D. 1343. Lynd. 52, 261, says a pecuniary penance cannot be substituted for a corporal penance except by such authority. A bishop's dispensing powers in all accustomed cases are preserved by sec. 15 of 25 Hen. VIII. c. 21 ; sec. 4 of 13 Eliz. c. 12 ; and, under the general head of jurisdiction, by sec. 1 of 12 Car. II. c. 13.

(176). Const. 33 Langton, A.D. 1222 ; Lynd. 149, 150.

(177). Gratian I. Dist. XIII. Concil. Tolet. VIII. A.D. 653, *Ibid.* c. 1, directs that of two evils the least must be chosen, and that a man had better perjure himself than fulfil a rash vow to injure his neighbour. Alexander III. in Decret. Greg. IX. Lib. V. Tit. XIX. c. 4, says that he cannot give a dispensation to practise usury, because that is forbidden in Holy Writ. Liguori Lib. VI. No. 1119, says : In those matters in which divine right has its origin from human will, such as oaths and vows, the pope can dispense. He does not then take away the divine right, but the foundation of obligation which a man has by his own act imposed on himself. Craisson, § 693.

(178). Egbert's Ans. 13, A.D. 734 : No one acts against the Gospel or the Apostle without punishment, therefore we give no consent to adultery. 25 Hen. VIII. c. 21, § 1, recites that the pope claimed " that he hath power to dispense with all *human* laws, uses, and customs of all realms, in all causes which be called spiritual," and that it has been so used many years by the sufferance of the king and his progenitors. Hobart, p. 146. Sec. 2 limits dispensations to cases not contrary to Holy Scripture.

a particular thing is commanded by divine law or not, it is for the Church, as the interpreter of Holy Writ, to decide it.

38. No dispensation may be granted except for some good cause ([179]), such as the welfare of the Church ([180]) or the helping forward of an individual in the way of holiness; and although a bishop can validly dispense with a statute which is only of authority in the diocese, he cannot regularly do so without some good cause ([181]). Moreover, since the question of the goodness of the cause is one which affects the whole Christian society, the granting of a dispensation is properly a solemn act, for which the people's consent was formerly necessary ([182]). As such it requires judicial or extra-judicial discretion ([183]), and on an allegation of the improper exercise of such discretion, both the validity of one which has been granted may be called in question ([184]), and the refusal of one may be the subject-matter of appeal ([185]).

(179). Ayliffe 219; Craisson, § 970, 4406, 5238.

(180). Urban II. A.D. 1093, ap. Gratian Caus. I. Qu. v. c. 3, says that a dispensation may be granted to one innocently promoted by simony, if the welfare of the Church require it.

(181). Craisson, § 968.

(182). Euseb. VI. 43, relates that the people were unwilling that a dispensation should be granted to ordain Novatus, A.D. 250, who was disqualified because he had received clinical baptism; but that the bishop requested that it should be granted him to ordain only this one. Craisson, § 971, says that now by custom in the Roman Church the bishop uses the power independently of the chapter and clergy, and the chapter does the same *sede vacante*, unless the diocesan law has been confirmed by the pope *in forma specifica*.

(183). Cyril in Syn. VII. A.D. 787, ap. Gratian Caus. I. Qu. VII. c. 16: That we may not be thought to love contention, we embrace the communion of Bishop John, granting him an indulgence, and let him understand that in a cause of a dispensation the matter against him will not be too closely, or severely, or harshly inquired into, as the power of a dispensation is a matter requiring much concern. Judicial discretion takes the place of the consenting obedience of the brethren required by Gratian Caus. I. Qu. v. c. 3, and Ayliffe 219.

(184). 25 Hen. VIII. c. 21, § 17, authorises an appeal to the Lord Chancellor from the archbishop's refusal.

(185). Benedict XIV. *Ad apostolicæ:* Expressio et causarum earumque verificatio ad substantiam et validitatem dispensationis pertinet.

39. Absolute necessity is held to be a good cause of dispensation from almost every canonical rule ([186]). Thus to avoid starvation it is a venial offence to steal the necessaries of life ([187]). In a bad season servile work may be done on Sunday ([188]). When no presbyter may be had, a deacon may baptize ([189]), and also a layman ([190]). Confession can be made in an emergency to any priest ([191]), and a marriage may be contracted in infancy ([192]). In danger of death ([193]) confession may be made to a layman ([194]), a deacon may give penance ([195]), a priest may absolve from a reserved crime ([196]) and give the

---

(186). Egbert's Answer, 13 A.D. 734 : Necessity often breaks a law. The rule of law as laid down in Decret. Lib. v. Tit. XLI. c. 4, and Lib. III. Tit. v. c. 33, and Lib. I. Tit. IV. c. 4 : On account of necessity the unlawful becomes lawful. Lynd. 205 and 233. Lynd. 209 : A monk who has nothing to give of his own may practise charity at the expense of his order to save a man from perishing of starvation. Lynd. 38, 233 : Necessitas facit licitum quod alias foret illicitum.

(187). Augustin ap. Gratian L Dist. VIII. c. 1 ; Decret. Lib. v. Tit. XVIII. c. 3 ; Lynd. 58.

(188). Alexander III. in Decret. Lib. II. Tit. IX. c. 3, and Baeda *Ibid.* Lib. v. Tit. XLI. c. 4 ; Lynd. 102.

(189). Gelasius ap. Gratian I. Dist. XCIII. c. 13 ; Const. 10 Edmund, A.D. 1236 ; Lynd. 63, 243, 98. See *Baptism*, note 106.

(190). John VIII. A.D. 879, ap. Gratian Caus. XXX. Qu. 1. c. 7. See *Baptism*, note 106.

(191). Theodori Poenit. I. VIII. 5 in H. and S. III. 184, and I. IX. 7, *Ibid.* 185, and Gratian III. Dist. IV. c. 22, and Caus. XXVI. Qu. VI. c. 12 ; Const. 1 Peckham, A.D. 1281 ; Lynd. 185, 238. See *Penance*, note 78.

(192). Const. 30 Edmund, A.D. 1236 ; Lynd. 272.

(193). A wide extension is given to this phrase, " in danger of death." It includes going about in fear of a mortal enemy, or being surrounded by enemies, or living in a place constantly exposed to attack, or having to pass through places known to be infested with danger, or being about to undertake a perilous voyage, being about to undergo her first childbirth. Decret. Lib. v. Tit. XXXIX. c. 26 ; Lynd. 355.

(194). Lynd. 164.

(195). Concil. Westminster A.D. 1200, Can. 3 ; Const. 1 Langton, A.D. 1223.

(196). Concil. Carthag. III. A.D. 390, ap. Gratian Caus. XXVI. Qu. VI. c. 14 ; Const. 7 Peckham, A.D. 1281 ; Const. 5 Winch. A.D. 1305.

communion to one solemnly excommunicated (197), and the offices of religion may even be received from a heretic (198).

40. In this country a certain power of dispensation is allowed to the sovereign (199), not only on the ground of necessity, but because of his being consecrated with holy oil (200) to a kind of priestly office (201). In some cases local custom operates as a general dispensation, but such dispensation does not affect strangers coming from elsewhere.

(197). Concil. Nic. A.D. 325, Can. 13; Gratian Caus. XVII. Qu. IV. c. 29; Const. 16 Edmund, A.D. 1236; Sext. Lib. III. Tit. XXIII. c. 3; Const. 7 Mepham, A.D. 1328; Const. 4 Stratford, A.D. 1343; Lynd. 187.

(198). Augustin ap. Gratian Caus. XXIV. Qu. I. c. 40; Lynd. 249.

(199). Concil. Chelsea, A.D. 787, Can. 12; Alfred's Law 6, A.D. 877; Lynd. 126. Henry I. is said to have granted them freely to married clerks after the Council of Westminster in 1127. Hobart 146 says that the Crown still retains this prerogative, notwithstanding sec. 3 of 25 Hen. VIII. c. 21. Stephen's Eccl. Stat. 163.

(200). Concil. Chelsea A.D. 787, Can. 12; Innocent III. A.D. 1204, in Decret. Lib. I. Tit. XVI. § 5, says that a bishop is anointed with chrism on the head to express his authority and dignity, but a sovereign is anointed with oil on the arm to show his power.

(201). Augustin contr. Petilian II. 112: David honoured Saul alive and avenged him dead, because of the sacred unction. For Saul had not innocence, but he had sanctity, not of life but of God's sacrament. Leo Ep. 24, 115, 155, ascribes to the emperor "a sacerdotal energy" and "a sacerdotal mind." Gregor. Expos. Lib. I. Reg. c. 10: Because this unction is a sacrament, he who is advanced is rightly anointed without, that within he may be strengthened by the power of the sacramental sign. The term "Christus Domini" is used of a temporal sovereign by Gratian Caus. XXII. Qu. V. c. 19, as well as of a bishop or presbyter. *Ibid.* Caus. XXIV. Qu. III. c. 22. "Sacring" was originally confined to the kings of England, Jerusalem, France, and Sicily. See *Baptism*, § 35, note 297.

II.

EXCESSES.

Subject-Matter of Personal Discipline.

1. The foundation of the personal discipline of the Church is the baptismal contract or vow. Any act or contemplated act ([1]) which is done or intended in violation of this vow, either by the transgressor himself or by one who is privy to it ([2]), is called generically an excess ([3]), or, according to its nature and gravity,

(1). Tertullian de Idol. c. 23 : Sins are committed in the mind and in the conscience. Origen Hom. 2 in Jud. § 5 ; Hippol. x. 29 : Evil is not consummated unless you actually commit some wickedness. But it is in regard of desiring anything that is wicked or meditating upon it that it is called sin. Chrysostom ap. Gratian Caus. XXXII. Qu. v. c. 2 ; There is no sin without intention. Augustin *Ibid.* Caus. XXXIII. Qu. III, Dist. II. c. 21 : There are three kinds of sins—those of intention, of act, and of habit, . . . which three kinds of dead persons Christ raised. *Ibid.* Caus. XXII. Qu. v. c. 13 : He who is prepared to commit perjury is perjured before he swears, because God judges not by actions but by the heart and intentions. Lynd. 337.

(2). Cyprian Ep. 30, 3 : He is not guiltless of wickedness who has bidden it be done ; nor is he unconcerned in the crime with whose consent it is publicly spoken of, although it was not committed by him. Ep. 67, 9 ; Augustin ap. Gratian Caus. XXXIII. Qu. III. Dist. l. c. 23 ; Caus. XI. Qu. III. c. 100 : Let him who consents to sinners, and defends another who is at fault, be visited with severest punishment. *Ibid.* Qu. l. c. 22 : Not only conspirators but they who consent to them are guilty of the same crime. John VIII. *Ibid.* I. Dist. LXXXVI. c. 3 ; Edgar's Law 7, A.D. 960 ; Alexander III. to Bishop of London in Decret. Lib. I. Tit. XXIX. c. 1 : Agentes et consentientes pari poena scripturae testimonio puniuntur. Lynd. 263, 338, 343, 270, 276, 314. Devoti Lib. IV. Tit. II. § 3.

(3). Gratian I. Dist. XXV. c. 3, Pars. III., gives three definitions of *crimina*, showing that he uses *crimina* in the sense of excesses : (1) all evil deeds, whether intentional or unintentional ; (2) all evil deeds done with intention ; and (3) those evil deeds which cause obloquy. Lynd. 347 ; Devoti Lib. IV. Tit. II. § 1, also uses *delictum* and *crimen* interchangeably. Const. 26, Langton, A.D. 1222, and English Constitutions generally use the

a crime, a sin (*peccatum*), a fault or trespass (*delictum*) (⁴), and becomes as such the subject-matter of personal discipline. A crime is defined to be any open and manifest excess which calls for condemnation and punishment in the public interest (⁵). A sin is an excess either of act or intention (⁶), which not being outwardly seen, or at least if seen not causing public scandal, requires discipline in the inner rather than in the outer tribunal (⁷). The term fault or trespass is applied to lesser shortcomings.

2. The obligation to fulfil the requirements of the baptismal contract or vow is held to belong to different positions in the

term excess to express all crimes and faults which may be dealt with in the outer forum.

(4). Cyprian Ep. 11 (Oxf. 17), 2, distinguishes (1) smaller, and (2) the gravest and extremest sins: In smaller sins, which are not committed against God, penance may be performed in a set time: . . . how much more ought this to be observed in the gravest and extremest sins. Euseb. VI. 46 says that Dionysius of Alexandria, in 256 A.D., wrote a book on the degrees of faults. Concil. Laodic. A.D. 363, Can. 2 ap. Gratian Caus. XXVI. Qu. VII. c. 4 : The time of penance must be awarded according to the quality of the crime, because of God's mercy and goodness. Apost. Const. II. 48 : Distinguish all the several sorts of excesses with much prudence, the great from the little. Treat a wicked action after one manner, and a wicked word after another, a base intention still otherwise. Gratian Caus. XXXIII. Qu. III. Dist. 1. c. 19 : Either acts are punished as robbery and murder, or words as slanders, or writings as libels, or intentions as conspiracies. Egbert's Poenit. in Haddan and Stubbs III. 418 divides all excesses into (1) *capitalia*, (2) *minora*, (3) *minuta*. Lynd. 347 distinguishes greater crimes, which may be the subject of solemn discipline, and intermediate crimes, which call for public discipline, and 93, 174, 248, 250, 297, calls them *crimina, peccata, delicta*.

(5). Innocent ap. Gratian Caus. XXXII. Qu. v. c. 23.

(6). Iren. IV. 16, 5 : We shall give account to God not of deeds only as slaves, but of words and thoughts, as those who have received the power of liberty. 1 Pet. II. 16 ; Syn. Rom. A.D. 502, ap. Gratian I. Dist. XCV. c. 1 ; Const. 26 Langton, A.D. 1222. See above, note 1.

(7). Tertullian de Poenit. c. 3 : Human incapacity (*mediocritas*) judges only sins of deed, because it is not equal to pierce the lurking-places of the will. Augustin ap. Gratian 1 Dist. LXXXI. c. 1 ; Lynd. 93, 347 : Sin does not merit [outward] accusation and punishment, except it proceeds to external action.

Excesses.

Church in different degrees : (1) Upon those who have been admitted to the Church in unconscious infancy ([8]) or by force ([9]) the obligation is held to rest most lightly, as being a simple vow, and from them the minimum only is expected, unless they would forfeit altogether their claim to receive the life of Christ through the sacraments. (2) Upon those who, by their own act and of deliberate choice, have become members of the Church, the obligation rests as a solemn vow, and requires to be fulfilled more strictly, without the same allowances being made as for the former class. This is the position held in ancient times by all converts, in modern times by the clergy. (3) Those who to the baptismal vow have added the vow to live the life of perfection ([10]), reproducing the communistic life of the Church of Jerusalem before the dispersion, and cultivating the martyr spirit in will if not in act ([11]), are held to the strictest fulfilment of it, as being honoured among their fellows for having voluntarily adopted the highest kind of life ([12]). Such

---

([8]). Innocent III. in Decret. Lib. III. Tit. XLIII. c. 3.

([9]). Concil. Tolet. IV. A.D. 633, Can. 28 ap. Gratian I. Dist. XLV. c. 5 : Jews must not be saved against their will, but voluntarily, that the form of justice may be perfect. For as man obeyed the serpent by the free choice of his own will, so by the conversion of his own mind at the call of God's grace each one is saved by believing. . . . But it behoves such as have been compelled to embrace Christianity, because they have been associated with the divine sacraments, . . . to retain the faith they have been compelled to hold, that the name of God be not blasphemed, and that the faith be not held cheap or vile.

([10]). Matt. v. 48 : Be ye perfect, even as your Father which is in heaven is perfect. XIX. 21 : If thou wilt be perfect, go sell all that thou hast.

([11]). Basil Hom. in XL. Martyr. speaks of "those who are desirous of being martyrs in will if not in act."

([12]). In Acts v. 4, St. Peter, addressing Ananias, says, Οὐχὶ μένον σοὶ ἔμενε, καὶ πραθὲν ἐν τῇ σῇ ἐξουσίᾳ ὑπῆρχε, showing that there was no necessity, even at Jerusalem, to join the communistic society. Urban II. A.D. 1096, ap. Gratian Caus. XIX. Qu. II. c. 2 : There are two laws, one private, the other public [in the sense of applying to all]. The public law is that which is laid down by the holy fathers in their writings, and is the canon law introduced because of transgressions. . . . The private law is that which is written in the heart by the action of the Holy Spirit. . . . If any one who has a cure of souls in a church under a bishop, and lives

were the hermits and ascetics in early times, and all who now embrace the monastic or religious life. Of these three classes the two last constitute the estate known as the *spirituality* ([13]) or ecclesiastical persons ([14]), and are alone qualified to legislate upon disciplinary matters. The anointed sovereign is deemed, by virtue of the unction, to belong to this estate; and since he also, as head of the state, belongs to the temporal estate, he is usually described as a mixed person (*persona mixta*).

3. In accordance with this difference of obligation there is a difference of criminality or sinfulness in different persons in regard to excesses ([15]). The same excess is a greater sin in one person than another—in one of the clergy, for instance, than in a layman, in a monk than in one living in the world ([16]), just as the same drug is death to one person and hardly injurious to another ([17]). Some excesses are in themselves greater, such as simony and heresy ([18]). Some are relatively greater, because

after the fashion of the world, under the Holy Spirit's influence is led to seek salvation in some monastery or under a canonical rule, because he is led by private law, there is no reason why he should be restrained by the public law.

(13). Thus 24 Hen. VIII. c. 12: This realm is an empire . . . governed by one supreme head and king . . . unto whom a body politick compact of all sorts and degrees of people, divided in terms and by names of spirituality and temporality ben bounden and owen to bere next to God a natural and humble obedience.

(14). See *Duties of Order*, § 54.

(15). Gratian Caus. XXXII. Qu. II. c. 11; Ayliffe 450: One sin is greater than another in several respects, as (1) in respect of a lapse or fall from a greater good; (2) in respect of the measure and bulk of the punishment assigned to it; (3) in respect of the example which it gives to others; (4) in respect of its condition, place, time, and person; (5) in respect of the turpitude and gravity thereof; and (6) in respect of the repetition of it.

(16). Baedae Poenit. in Haddan and Stubbs III. 327; Egbert's Poenit. *Ibid.* 417: All must not therefore be weighed in the same balance, though they be guilty of the same wrong, but a distinction must be made between the rich and the poor, the free and the slave, the infant, boy, youth, young or old man, the infirm or ignorant, laymen, clerks, monks, bishops, priests, deacons. . . . See *Penance*, § 4.

(17). Augustin ap. Gratian Caus. XXIII. Qu. IV. c. 22; Lynd. 266.

(18). Gratian Caus. I. Qu. VII. c. 27; Augustin *Ibid.* Caus. XXII. Qu. II. c. 8.

Excesses. 43

of the horror and disgust they create ([19]), such as murder ([20]), and sins against nature ([21]). Some are greater because they are evidence of innate corruption ([22]), and others because of their effect upon society, such as adultery ([23]).

4. By the baptismal vow all Christians are pledged to three things ([24]) : (1) to dissociate themselves from the devil and the indulgence of the lower animal nature, which brought death into the world ; (2) to associate themselves with their fellow-Christians in the sacrament of unity ([25]) to be the light of the world by doing good to all and not invading the rights of any ; (3) to consecrate themselves as a royal priesthood to a life of communion with God. All the various excesses which discipline is intended to restrain will be found to be violations of one or other of these obligations, and may be fitly grouped under the three heads of adultery, murder, and idolatry ([26]).

5. Under the head of idolatry may be grouped all crimes which are defections from the allegiance due to God and interrupt communion with Him, of which idolatry, or spiritual fornication, is the type ([27]). Such are apostasy, blasphemy,

---

([19]). Gratian I. Dist. l. c. 4 ; Caus. XXXIII. Qu. II. c. 8.

([20]). Gratian Caus. XXXIII. Qu. II. c. 8 ; Const. 7 Peckham, A.D. 1281, requires such to be visited with solemn discipline. Lynd. 339.

([21]). Gratian Caus. XXXII. Qu. VII. c. 11 and 13.

([22]). *Ibid.* Caus. I. Qu. I. c. 21.

([23]). Lynd. 316.

([24]). See *Baptism*, § 29.

([25]). Cyprian de Unit. Eccl. c. 6.

([26]). Titus II. 12 : ἵνα [1] σωφρόνως καὶ [2] δικαίως καὶ [3] εὐσεβῶς ζήσωμεν. Pacian of Barcelona Paraenesis ad Poenit. c. 4 : There are three mortal sins—idolatry, murder, adultery. Const. 4 Thorsby, A.D. 1363, enumerates thirty-six greater crimes which it reserves to the archbishop, of which nine are crimes against God, nine crimes against fellow-men, four crimes against the body of Christ, and fourteen are ecclesiastical crimes. It adds, as a thirty-seventh, any notorious crime which shocks a whole neighbourhood. Ayliffe 238, divides them into (1) *impietas*, or acts contrary to piety to God ; (2) *facinora*, acts contrary to justice to neighbours ; and (3) *flagitia*, acts contrary to sobriety towards ourselves.

([27]). 2 Chron. XXI. 11 ; Ps. LXXIII. 27 ; Tertullian de Idol. c. 1 ; Clem.

here y, schism, simony, and sacrilege. Under the head of murder may be placed all crimes which are invasions of other men's rights and violations of natural justice, of which murder is a type. Such are homicide and the cognate crimes of strife and conspiracy, robbery and theft, arson, deceit, and usury. Under the head of adultery may be grouped all crimes which are indulgences of the lower animal nature, and dishonouring to the body redeemed by Christ ([28]), of which adultery is the type ([29]). Such are adultery, rape, incest, and unnatural crime.

6. In each of these classes the excesses which fall short of the enormity of a greater crime, but nevertheless obscure the Church's light in the world by causing scandal and offence, may be termed intermediate, and require discipline, but in a lower degree. Such are simple incontinency ([30]), stealing ([31]), judicial calumniation ([32]), falsehood ([33]), excess in eating ([34]) or drink-

Strom. VII. 14: He who conducts himself heathenishly in the Church, commits fornication in reference to the Church. Augustin ap. Gratian Caus. XXVIII. Qu. 1. c. 5: Idolatry and every hurtful superstition is fornication. Apost. Const. II. 23: There is no sin more grievous than idolatry. Isidor. *Ibid*. Caus. XXXII. Qu. VII. c. 15; Lynd. 334.

(28). 1 Cor. VI. 15; Hieronym. ap. Gratian Caus. XXXII. Qu. IV. c. 12.

(29). Augustin *Ibid*. c. 11, says that all adultery is fornication, but all fornication (for instance that of the unmarried) is not adultery. Yet the term adultery is used generically to express all illicit concubinage and unlawful use of the organs of procreation.

(30). Gratian Caus. XXXVI. Qu. I. and II.; Caus. XXXII. Qu. IV. c. 4; Theodori Poenit. I. II. 1 in Haddan and Stubbs III. 178, prescribes one year's penance for fornication, four for adultery. Const. 16 Edmund, A.D. 1236; Const. 7 Peckham, A.D. 1281; Const. 10 Stratford, A.D. 1342; 1 Hen. VII. c. 4, and 32 Hen. VIII. c. 10, give to ordinaries power to punish clerks for incontinency. See *Wilson* v. *Hancock*, No. 66; *Dargavell* v. *Langdon*, No. 67; *Harris* v. *Twittey*, No. 102; *Watson* v. *Thorpe*, No. 184; *Burgoyne* v. *Free*, No. 187 in Rothery's Report.

(31). See below, § 24.

(32). Gratian Caus. II. Qu. III. c. 8.

(33). See below, § 25.

(34). Gregory ap. Gratian III. Dist. v. c. 22: Vitium gulae nos tentat quinque modis. Const. 9 Peckham, A.D. 1281; Lynd. 62.

ing ([35]). Those which are excesses of thought only do not come within the range of public discipline ([36]).

CRIMES AGAINST GOD.

7. Of all crimes the greatest are those which are defections from the allegiance due to God, and interruptions of that communion with Him to re-establish which Christ came into the world. They are of two kinds: (1) those which are open and avowed defections from the allegiance to God, such as apostasy and blasphemy; and (2) those which are unavowed, but none the less real defections from that allegiance, resulting from self-will, such as heresy, schism, simony, and sacrilege.

8. Open and avowed defection from the allegiance due to God, when it is complete and entire, is termed apostasy ([37]), and of it there are three kinds: (1) the abandonment of the faith by one who has been baptized, in order to embrace heathenism or Judaism ([38]), or the abandonment of the faith

---

([35]). Hieronym. ap. Gratian Caus. xv. Qu. 1. c. 7; Concil. Andegav. A.D. 453, Can. 3: Ut a violentia et crimine perpotationis abstineatur. Concil. Venet. A.D. 465, Can. 13; Theodori Poenit. I. 1 in Haddan and Stubbs, III. 177; Baedae Poenit. *Ibid.* 331; Boniface, A.D. 746, *Ibid.* 382: This is the special vice of pagans and of our nation. Neither Franks, Gauls, Lombards, Romans, or Greeks give way to drunkenness. Concil. Agath. A.D. 506, ap. Gratian I. Dist. xxxv. c. 9, orders a drunken priest to be suspended for thirty days. Concil. Clovesho A.D. 747, Can. 21; Const. 6 Edmund, A.D. 1236; Const. 2 Langham, A.D. 1367; Lynd. 119.

([36]). See above, note 7.

([37]). Cyprian de Laps. c. 7, calls it dissolving the allegiance to Christ (*sacramentum Christi*).

([38]). Cyprian de Laps. c. 8: Could a servant of God renounce Christ when he had already renounced the devil and the world? There were three kinds of this apostasy: (1) Some wholly abjured Christianity and relapsed into Judaism, like Aquila, who, being excommunicated because of his study of astrology, joined the Jews and published a new version of the Bible. Epiphanius de Pond. et Mens. 15, Tom. II.; Devoti, Lib. IV. Tit. III. § 2. (2) Others combined circumcision and Jewish rites with Christianity, such as the Coelicolae, Cerinthians, Ebionites, Nazarenes, and Elcesaites. Gal. v. 4 calls such persons "fallen from grace." (3) Others followed Jewish observances in lesser matters. Devoti l. c. § 3. Concil.

without embracing any religion at all (³⁹); (2) the abandonment by clergy of the clerical life; and (3) the abandonment by regulars of the religious life. Christians forsaking their allegiance to Christ under stress of persecution were anciently called the *lapsed*, but there were several degrees recognised in their crime. Those who voluntarily burnt incense before idols were termed the *thurificati;* those who took part in heathen sacrifices the *sacrificati* (⁴⁰); those who purchased exemption from the penalty of being a Christian by promising to take part in the sacrifice, or by getting a friend to take part in their place, or by paying for a certificate (*libelli*) of having taken part, the *libellatici* (⁴¹).

9. By ancient custom apostates actually guilty of idolatry were not only excommunicated, but, if they had done so spontaneously, remained excommunicate for life (⁴²). In some parts of the Church they were not even allowed the *viaticum* at the hour of death (⁴³). Regulars who apostatised by forsaking the vow of religion were excluded from communion (⁴⁴), and were

Lat. IV. A.D. 1215, Can. 70 in Decret. Lib. v. Tit. IX. c. 4, condemns the mingling of Christianity with heathenism.

(39). Concil. Tolet. IV. A.D. 633, Can. 63 ap. Gratian Caus. II. Qu. VII. c. 24: He cannot be true to men who is false to God. Lynd. 306; Ayliffe 85.

(40). Cyprian Ep. 14 ad Cler. Rom., 3, and Ep. 51 ad Antonian, 14; Augustin ap. Gratian Caus. XI. Qu. III. c. 85.

(41). Cyprian Ep. ad Antonian 51, 14; de Laps. 27.

(42). Cyprian Ep. 51, 13 : If any such are seized with sickness, help is given to them in danger.

(43). Concil. Elib. A.D. 305, Can. 1; Concil. Arelat. A.D. 314, Can. 22 : Apostates who never come to Church or ask for penance, and afterwards, when taken ill, seek communion, should not be allowed it, except they recover and have done proper penance. Concil. Nic. A.D. 325, Can. 13, requires the *viaticum* to be given to all who desire it at the hour of death. Const. 16 Edmund, A.D. 1236 : At the hour of death absolution is to be denied to none.

(44). Concil. Chalcedon, A.D. 451, Can. 7 ap. Gratian Caus. XX. Qu. III. c. 3 : Concil. Turon. A.D. 460, Can. 6 ; Leo A.D. 458, *Ibid.* c. 1 ; Concil. Tolet. VI. A.D. 638, Can. 6, *Ibid.* c. 2 ; Egbert's Excerpt. 65 ; Cnut's Law 4, A.D. 1018 : We command that apostates and outlaws be gone off the land. Concil. Winton. A.D. 1071, Can. 12 : That monks who have thrown off

Excesses. 47

ordered to be imprisoned for life ([45]). Clergy who apostatised by abandoning their order were declared excommunicate *ipso facto* ([46]), were accounted infamous ([47]), and forbidden any future exercise of their calling ([48]).

10. Blasphemy is open and avowed defection from the faith which is confined to words only. It includes (1) profane swearing, or taking God's name in vain ([49]); (2) cursing, or direct malediction of God and Christ; and (3) taking rash and improper vows which cannot be kept ([50]). Of all blasphemies that against the Holy Ghost is the worst, as being the unpardonable sin ([51]).

---

their habit be deemed excommunicate. Honorius III. in Decret. Lib. III. Tit. XXXI. c. 22 and 9; Const. 18 Peckham, A.D. 1281; Boniface VIII. in Sext. Lib. III. Tit. XXIV. c. 2.

(45). Honorius III. in Decret. Lib. III. Tit. XXXI. c. 5.

(46). Concil. Chalcedon. Can. 7, l. c.; Concil. Turon. A.D. 460, Can. 5; Egbert's Excerpt. 60; Concil. Westminster, A.D. 1102, Can. 11; Alexander III. in Decret. Lib. v. Tit. IX. c. 1: Clerks who, giving up the clerical order and habit, live like laymen, are in apostasy. Clem. Lib. IV. See *Order*, § 40.

(47). Gratian Caus. III. Qu. IV. c. 2: All who spontaneously transgress their own rules are called apostates, and no apostate can be received in accusation.

(48). Honorius III. in Decret. Lib. v. Tit. IX. c. 6. See *Order*, § 40.

(49). Exod. XX. 7; Matt. XXIII. 16–22; 1 Tim. I. 20; James II. 7; Rev. XIII. 6; Gratian Caus. XXII. Qu. 1. c. 10, calls it blasphemy to swear by the head or hair of God. Tertullian de Idol. c. 11: Of false swearing I am silent, since even swearing is not lawful; c. 23: Christ prescribes that there is to be no swearing.

(50). Cyprian de Laps. c. 6: They swear not only rashly, but falsely. Hieronym. ap. Gratian Caus. XXII. Qu. II. c. 2: Every oath requires three things—truth, judgment, justice. If these are wanting it is not an oath, but perjury. *Isidor. Ibid.* Qu. IV. c. 19: In three cases oaths which have been taken must be broken: (1) if it is an oath to do wrong; (2) if it is a rash oath; (3) if it is an oath taken by those in the power of another which the latter disavow. Concil. Ilerd. A.D. 523, Can. 7, directs one who has sworn eternal feud to come quickly to charity, and to be excommunicated for a year.

(51). Matt. XII. 31, 32; Mark III. 28, 29; Cyprian Ep. 9, 2, considers it the sin of apostasy. Athanasius deems it to be the sin of denying that Christ is God. Ambros. de Spiritu l. c. 3, and Epiphanius Haer. 75, consider it the crime of denying the work of the Spirit, or, as we might say,

Cursing God ([52]) or Christ ([53]) is a form of apostasy for which the same course of discipline is prescribed as for idolatry ([54]). Rash and improper vows are ordered not to be kept, but penance to be done for breaking them ([55]).

11. Among unavowed defections from the faith the first place is occupied by heresy in a general sense, or the crime of self-will ([56]), which has been likened to a plunge into the stormy ocean in religious matters ([57]). It includes (1) doctrinal self-will, technically called heresy and forbidden association with heretics; (2) sacramental self-will or schism; and (3) that particular form of covetous self-will known as simony, which for the sake of gain treats sacred things as unsacred. Doctrinal self-will, or heresy properly so called, consists in choosing for oneself what to believe in regard to the faith once for all delivered to the saints, wilfully departing from what has been settled by competent synodal authority ([58]), or even unneces-

---

attributing the work of the Holy Ghost to Satanic agency. Chrysostom Hom. 41 in Math.; Pseudo-Damasus ap. Gratian Caus. xxv. Qu. l. c. 5.

(52). Job II. 9.

(53). Pliny Epist. x. 96, relates that the apostate Christians venerated the emperor's image and cursed Christ (Christo maledixerunt). Euseb. IV. 15: The governor said to Polycarp: Swear, and I will dismiss you; curse Christ. Polycarp replied: Eighty and six years have I served Him, and He never did me wrong. How can I now blaspheme my King that has saved me?

(54). Gregory IX. in Decret. Lib. v. Tit. xxvi. c. 2

(55). Ambros. ap. Gratian Caus. xxii. Qu. iv. c. 8 and 12; Concil. Ilerd. A.D. 546, *Ibid.* c. 11, orders one year's penance. Baeda *Ibid.* c. 6; Syn. VII. A.D. 787, *Ibid.* c. 18: A mendacious oath must be dissolved. See *Discipline Generally*, notes 172 and 177.

(56). Cyprian de Unit. Eccl. c. 19: [Schism] is a worse crime than that into which the lapsed have fallen, who nevertheless standing as penitents beseech God with full satisfaction. In their case the Church is sought after and entreated, in schism the Church is resisted. Here it is possible that there may have been necessity; then the will is engaged in the wickedness. Concil. Laodic. A.D. 363, Can. 32 ap. Gratian Caus. I. Qu. I. c. 66; Hieronym. *Ibid.* c. 60; Innocent *Ibid.* c. 73; Leo *Ibid.* c. 69; Concil. Brac. II. A.D. 572, Can. 70, *Ibid.* c. 68.

(57). Hippolyt. Haer. VII. 1.

(58). 1 Tim. VI. 2, 3, calls it ἑτεροδιδασκαλία, which Ayliffe 288 renders

Excesses.

sarily throwing doubts upon it (⁵⁹). This is called lying in doctrine (⁶⁰), and may be condemned after death (⁶¹); but holding wrong views through ignorance or traditionally is not formal heresy (⁶²). Forbidden association with heretics includes (1) aiding, abetting, or associating with those known to be wilful heretics (⁶³); (2) ecclesiastical tolerance (⁶⁴), or communicating with heretics, on the ground that definiteness in doctrine is of no importance (⁶⁵); and (3) reading

"pertinacious teaching of false doctrine." 2 Pet. II. 1; Jude 5; Cyprian Ep. 71 (Oxf. 72), 2, says of heresy: What stain can be more odious than to have stood in opposition to Christ? Hieronym. ap. Gratian Caus. XXIV. Qu. III. c. 27: Heresy is the Greek for choice, because a heretic chooses a discipline which he thinks best for himself. Whoever, therefore, interprets Scripture otherwise than the mind of the Holy Spirit, by whom it was written, requires, although he does not depart from the Church, is nevertheless a heretic, because he chooses what is worse. As Devoti Lib. IV. Tit. IV. § 2 observes: The faith is the faith of the whole Church, not of a section only. Christ promised that He would be with His Church [not with a section] to the end of time, that it might be built on a rock, and its members not tossed about by every wind of doctrine (Eph. IV. 14). Const. 9 Peckham, A.D. 1281; Gelasius *Ibid.* Qu. 1. c. 1 and 2. A list of eighty-eight heresies is given *Ibid.* Caus. XXIV. Qu. III. c. 39.

(59). Decret. Lib. V. Tit. VII. c. 1: Dubius in fide infidelis est.

(60). Augustin ap. Gratian Caus. XXII. Qu. II. c. 8.

(61). Syn. V. A.D. 553, *Ibid.* Caus. XXIV. Qu. II. c. 6.

(62). Augustin Ep. 162: Those who cling to their opinion, although false and perverted, not from obstinate animosity . . . and seek after truth with cautious care, ready to embrace it when they have found it, can by no means be accounted among heretics.

(63). Ignat. ad Smyrn. c. 4: From these beasts in the shape of men you must turn away; c. 7: Keep aloof from such heretics. Polycarp ad Phil. 6: Keeping ourselves from false brethren. Ambros. ap. Gratian Caus. XXIV. Qu. 1. c. 26; Pelagius *Ibid.* c. 34; Baeda *Ibid.* c. 24; Augustin *Ibid.* Caus. XXIII. Qu. IV. c. 6: To associate with evil-doers is to do evil with them or to help them in evil-doing. Const. 4 Thorsby, A.D. 1363.

(64). This must not be confounded with civil tolerance. Devoti Lib. IV. Tit. VI. § 4. Julius ap. Gratian Caus. XXIV. Qu. 1. c. 41 prescribes a year's penance. Gregory *Ibid.* 42.

(65). This was the heresy of Apelles, according to Euseb. V. 13: He also said that one ought not to examine doctrine, but that each one should continue as he believed; for those who trusted in Him that was crucified would be saved if they were only found engaged in good works. Devoti

books condemned as contrary to the faith without good cause ([66]).

12. Schism is self-will in regard to the sacraments, and consists in violating the sacrament of unity ([67]), either by setting up altar against altar or by withdrawing from communion for no adequate cause ([68]). If persisted in, it becomes heresy, because it ignores the Church's note of unity, and it generally ends by inventing some new teaching to justify the separation ([69]). The setting up of altar against altar or the withdrawal

Lib. IV. Tit. VL. § 1. On the other hand, 2 John v. 10; Titus III. 10; Rom. XVI. 17. Euseb. IV. 14 relates how St. John fled out of the bath to avoid Cerinthus. Apost. Can. 45: Let a bishop, presbyter, or deacon who only prays with heretics be suspended, but if he permit him to perform any part of the office of a clergyman, let him be deprived.

(66). Heathens burnt the books of their opponents. Acts XIX. 19 relates that many brought their books and burnt them. Apost. Can. 60: If any one reads the spurious books of the ungodly, let him be deprived. Socrates I. 9 relates that the Council of Nicaea condemned Arius' book called Thalia; and I. 36 that Marcellus promised to burn his book, and was deposed for not doing so. Hieronym. ap. Gratian L. Dist. XXXVII. c. 5; Stat. Eccl. Ant. *Ibid.* c. 1: Let not a bishop read the books of the heathen; those of the heretics he may in case of necessity. Rabanus *Ibid.* c. 7. Books have been condemned in three ways: (1) by condemning certain propositions as false without regard to their author; (2) by condemning the propositions made by a certain author as false; and (3) by condemning the propositions contained in a certain book. The first and last involve questions of fact, and do not necessarily condemn the author, (1) because he may not have made them, (2) because they may not be contained in his book. Gregory in Decret. Lib. v. Tit. VII. c. 4: Since Coelestinus and Pelagius were condemned in the synod of Ephesus, how can those propositions be received whose authors have been condemned? Devoti Lib. IV. Tit. VII. § 6.

(67). Cyprian Ep. 41 (Oxf. 45), 14; Ep. 75 (Oxf. 69), 6; de Unit. Eccl. c. 7 and 23.

(68). Devoti Lib. IV. Tit. v. § 2.

(69). Hieronym. in cap. 3 Ep. in Titum. ap. Gratian Caus. XXIV. Qu. III. c. 26: Between heresy and schism there is this difference, that heresy involves perverse teaching, whereas schism also causes separation from the Church, because of some episcopal dispute. But this must be understood at the beginning, for no schism goes on for long without inventing some heresy to justify its separation from the Church.

of one part of the Church from communion with the universal Church is termed *external* schism (⁷⁰); the refusal of an individual to hold communion with his own proper bishop or incumbent *internal* schism (⁷¹).

13. Heretics and those who create schisms in the Church are directed to be excommunicated if they do not repent after a first and second admonition (⁷²); and if they die excommunicate, to be deprived of Christian burial (⁷³). Those who withdraw from the communion of their bishop (⁷⁴), unless the bishop's heresy, apostasy, or schism was the cause (⁷⁵), and

---

(70). Cyprian ap. Gratian Caus. XXIV. Qu. 1. c. 19. Apost. Can. 32: If any presbyter despises his own bishop, and assembles separately, and fixes another altar when he has nothing to condemn in his bishop, either as to piety or righteousness, let him be deprived ... and let the laity be suspended. Concil. Carthag. II. A.D. 390, Can. 8, anathematises a priest who sets up another Eucharist apart from his bishop.

(71). Concil. Afric. Can. 99 ap. Gratian Caus. VI. Qu. II. c. 3: If a bishop declares he has scruples of conscience in communicating with any one, so long as the bishop refuses to communicate with him, so long let other bishops refuse to communicate with that bishop, that a bishop may take care not to bring a charge against any one which he cannot establish by proof. Hincmar, A.D. 866, *Ibid.* Caus. XXIV. Qu. III. c. 6: Let no bishop or priest excommunicate another before his cause has been proved.

(72). Titus III. 10: A man that is an heretic after a first and second admonition avoid. Iren. Haer. I. 16, 3 ap. Gratian Caus. XXIV. Qu. III. c. 13: We have learnt from apostolical authority that the spirits of those who err and cause others to err, should be delivered to Satan, that they may learn not to blaspheme. Concil. Lat. III. A.D. 1179, Can. 27, in Decret. Lib. V. Tit. VII. c. 8, orders heretics, their defenders, and harbourers, to be anathematised, and " we forbid under pain of anathema that any one presume to receive them into his house or to have any dealings with them ;" and if he should die in heresy forbids the oblation being made for him or his receiving Christian burial. Lucius III. *Ibid.* c. 9; Concil. Lat. IV. A.D. 1215, Can. 3, *Ibid.* c. 13; Lynd. 290, 293; Const. Chichele, A.D. 1416, reserves cognisance of heresy to the archbishop.

(73). Concil. Lat. III. A.D. 1179, Can. 27, l. c.; Alexander IV. in Sext. Lib. V. Tit. II. c. 2.

(74). Apost. Can. 32.

(75). Cyprian Ep. 67, 3: A people obedient to the Lord's precepts and fearing God ought to separate themselves from a sinful prelate. Syn. VII. A.D. 787, ap. Gratian Caus. I. Qu. VII. c. 15.

bishops who refuse to communicate with their clergy or subjects for no proved cause ([76]), and those who persist in associating with heretics ([77]), are directed to be excommunicated also.

14. Severer penalties were at one time prescribed for obstinate heretics, and the temporal power was appealed to to put these penalties in force ([78]). Their property was ordered to be confiscated ([79]); advocates were forbidden to defend them when accused ([80]); if clergy, they were ordered to be degraded ([81]) and handed over to the secular arm ([82]); those who relapsed to be imprisoned for life ([83]), and to be thankful to be admitted to communion and penance ([84]). On the other hand, those who spontaneously renounce their heresy are directed to be received to communion ([85]); and such as have been baptized and brought up in heresy to be reconciled with the imposition of hands ([86]), or by anointing with chrism if they have not been anointed before ([87]).

(76). Concil. Afric. ap. Gratian Caus. VI. Qu. II. c. 3, quoted above, note 71.

(77). Concil. Lat. III. A.D. 1179, l. c. Euseb. VI. 2 relates that Origen would never associate in prayer with the heretic Paul, observing even when a boy that rule of the Church. Devoti Lib. IV. Tit. VI.

(78). 25 Hen. VIII. c. 14 ; 1 Eliz. c. 1, sec. 36 ; Lynd. 284.

(79). Innocent III. A.D. 1199, in Decret. Lib. v. Tit. VII. c. 10 ; Boniface VIII. in Sext. Lib. v. Tit. II. c. 19 makes the confiscation *ipso jure.*

(80). Innocent *Ibid.* c. 11.

(81). Gregory IX. *Ibid.* c. 15.

(82). Pelagius ap. Gratian Caus. XXIII. Qu. v. c. 43 : Those who cause rents in Holy Church should be restrained not only by exile, but also by proscription of goods and durance vile at the hands of public authorities. Paschal *Ibid.* Caus. I. Qu. VII. c. 27 : Heretics, if they do not repent when admonished, should be suppressed by external powers. Gregory IX. in Decret. Lib. v. Tit. VII. c. 15 ; Boniface VIII. in Sext. Lib. v. Tit. II. c. 18, forbids secular authorities to oppose inquisitors, and calls on them to assist them.

(83). Gelasius ap. Gratian Caus. XXIV. Qu. l. c. 1 ; Gregory IX. l. c.

(84). Alexander IV. in Sext. Lib. v. Tit. II. c. 4.

(85). Concil. Aurel. IV. A.D. 541, Can. 8.

(86). Leo A.D. 458, ap. Gratian. III. Dist. IV. c. 38 ; Gregory *Ibid.* c. 44.

(87). Concil. Constant. A.D. 382, Can. 7 ; Gregory l. c. See *Baptism,* notes 136, 137.

Excesses. 53

15. In the thirteenth century the practice was introduced in the West of appointing delegates to search out and bring to trial those suspected of heresy ([88]). These delegates soon became permanent officials, under the title of the Holy Office or Inquisition ([89]), and were invested with full powers to try and punish heresy, without reference to a council or the bishop ([90]). They were generally chosen from the Dominicans or Franciscans, and having to do with the most important of all subjects, they were placed under a congregation of cardinals at Rome, presided over by the pope ([91]). The procedure of their tribunals was summary and secret ([92]), which afforded great opportunity for abuses ([93]), and led to many charges being made against them; and to them was also entrusted the delicate task of dealing with priests charged with having abused their position in the confessional ([94]).

([88]). Concil. Verona A.D. 1185, in Decret. Lib. v. Tit. VII. c. 9, orders bishops, not only themselves but by their commissaries, to make inquiries into cases of heresy. Innocent III. in 1198 despatched Rainer and Guido into the province of Narbonne as delegates for this purpose. Devoti Lib. IV. Tit. VIII. § 3. This was an innovation. See *Ordinaries*.

([89]). It is generally stated that the Cistercian monks, Arnald, Peter of Castronovo, and Rodolph, were the first permanent officials appointed by Innocent III. in 1204 (Annal. Cisterc. III. 420), but the title of Inquisitors was first given to the Dominican officials appointed by Gregory IX., A.D. 1231 (Echardi Script. Ord. Praed. I. 88). It is also clear that the Dominican, John of Marburg, was appointed substantially an inquisitor in 1227 by Gregory IX. (Bullar. Ord. Praed. I. 20, Const. 7), and, in the same year also, John of Salerno (Annal. Ord. Praed. 203, note).

([90]). Concil. Lat. IV. Can. 3, A.D. 1215, in Decret. Lib. v. Tit. VII. c. 13, gives cognisance of heresy to archbishops and bishops. Const. Courtney, A.D. 1391, and Const. 1 Arundel, A.D. 1408; Boniface VIII. in Sext. Lib. v. Tit. II. c. 17, committed it equally to inquisitors, authorising them to act either separately or in conjunction with the bishops. Concil. Vien. A.D. 1311, in Clem. Lib. v. Tit. III. c. 1.

([91]). Urban IV. A.D. 1273, appointed the Cardinal of St. Nicolas in carcere Tulliano chief inquisitor. Nicolaus III. appointed Cardinal Ursinius; Clement IV. Cardinal William of Toulouse. Devoti Lib. IV. Tit. VIII. § 3.

([92]). Boniface VIII. in Sext. Lib. v. Tit. II. c. 20.

([93]). Concil. Vien. A.D. 1311, in Clem. l. c.

([94]). Either by soliciting to evil, or inquiring the names of accomplices. Devoti Lib. IV. Tit. VIII. § 16.

16. Simony is a special form of covetous self-will or heresy ([95]), in which money or anything of value is demanded, given, or received, directly or indirectly ([96]), (1) for any spiritual gift, such as absolution ([97]), ordination ([98]), the consecration of a Church ([99]), the election ([100]) or benediction ([101]) of a bishop or abbot, the chrism ([102]), or the administration of a sacrament ([103]); and

(95). Gratian Caus. I. Qu. 1. c. 3, 11, 13, 20, 21, 28, 105, 117; and Qu. VII. c. 27. Augustin *Ibid.* Caus. XXII. Qu. II. c. 8, accounts it the greatest of crimes.

(96). Leo ap. Gratian Caus. I. Qu. 1. c. 1 : Grace, unless it is given and received freely, is not grace. Simoniacs do not receive freely, therefore they do not receive grace, which is chiefly operative in ecclesiastical orders. Gelasius, A.D. 494, *Ibid.* c. 6 : The damnation of Simon involves the giver equally with the receiver. Concil. Brac. II. A.D. 572, Can. 3; *Ibid.* c. 22.

(97). Alexander III. in Decret. l. c. c. 14, says that it is simony for a priest to receive a reward from a public sinner to pass over the sin, or to reconcile one not truly penitent, or to refuse to reconcile one who is penitent. *Ibid.* c. 24.

(98). Gregory ap. Gratian Caus. I. Qu. II. c. 4 : The bishop may not sell the hand which ordains (quam imponit). Baeda *Ibid.* Qu. III. c. 11 ; Alexander II. A.D. 1068, *Ibid.* c. 9; Concil. Winton. A.D. 1071, Can. 2 : That no one be ordained by means of simoniacal heresy. Decret. Lib. v. Tit. III. c. 1.

(99). Concil. Brac. II. A.D. 572, Can. 5 ap. Gratian Caus. I. Qu. II. c. 1 and Qu. IV. c. 11; Concil. London A.D. 1126, Can. 3; Alexander III. in Decret. Lib. v. Tit. III. c. 10.

(100). Gregory ap. Gratian Caus. I. Qu. VI. c. 3 ; Concil. Lat. III. A.D. 1179, Can. 7 in Decret. Lib. v. Tit. III. c. 9.

(101). Concil. London A.D. 1126, Can. 3 : That at the consecrating of bishops, blessing of abbots . . . [nothing] be demanded.

(102). Egbert's Excerpt. 12 ; Elfric Can. 27, A.D. 957 ; Concil. London A.D. 1126, Can. 2 : We charge that no price be demanded for chrism, oil, baptism, visiting or anointing the sick, for the communion of the Body of Christ, or for burial. Concil. Westminster A.D. 1138, adds to the above, penance, espousals of women, and makes excommunication the penalty. Alexander III. in Decret. Lib. v. Tit. III. c. 8, 16, 21 ; Concil. London A.D. 1175, Can. 7 ; Concil. Westminster A.D. 1200, Can. 8 ; Concil. Lat. IV. A.D. 1215, Can. 66 in Decret. l. c. c. 42 ; Const. 27 Langton, A.D. 1222 : To demand anything for chrism or the holy oil we judge to be unreasonable. See *The Sacraments*, note 79.

(103). Concil. Elib. A.D. 305, Can. 48 ap. Gratian Caus. I. Qu. l. c. 104 ; Gelasius, A.D. 494, *Ibid.* c. 99 : Let priests ask no price from those about to

Excesses. 55

(2) in a secondary sense for any spiritual office ([104]), the presentation ([105]) or institution ([106]) to a benefice, any position of jurisdiction ([107]) or teaching in the Church ([108]), or by rendering temporal homage for spiritual things ([109]). It is so called from Simon Magus, who offered money to the apostles that he might receive at their hands the spiritual gift of the Holy Ghost ([110]).

17. There are usually said to be three kinds of simony ([111]):

be baptized or confirmed. Concil. Brac. II. A.D. 572, Can. 4 and 7, *Ibid.* 102, 103; Concil. Tolet. XI. A.D. 675, Can. 8, *Ibid.* c. 101; Syn. Trull. A.D. 692, Can. 23, *Ibid.* c. 100: Let no bishop, priest, or deacon who dispenses the Holy Communion ask any price from him who receives the benefit. Egbert's Excerpt. 40; Concil. Tribur. A.D. 895, *Ibid.* c. 105; Concil. Cabilon. A.D. 813, Can. 16, *Ibid.* c. 100; Innocent III. in Decret. Lib. v. Tit. III. c. 29; Const. 4 Otho, A.D. 1237, and Const. 2 Othobon, A.D. 1268, forbid money payments for penance. Lynd. 74, 278.

(104). Paschal, *Ibid.* Qu. II. c. 7: If any one says he does not buy the consecration, but only the profits which accrue after consecration, he seems to talk nonsense. For since the bodily Church, bishop, or abbot is of no avail without his bodily belongings, and since the soul has no mortal existence without the body, so he who buys one of these things without which the other does not exist leaves neither unbought. Urban II. *Ibid.* c. 8; Alexander III. in Decret. Lib. v. Tit. III. c. 8.

(105). Syn. Rom. A.D. 1078, ap. Gratian Caus. I. Qu. III. c. 3: Let a bishop who sells prebends, archdeaconries, provostships, or other ecclesiastical offices for money be suspended. Urban II. *Ibid.* c. 4; Concil. Westminster A.D. 1127, Can. 1: We forbid churches, benefices, and dignities to be in any wise sold or bought. Lynd. 109. 31 Eliz. c. 6 enforced the prohibition by adding temporal penalties. Hobart. 167; Stephen's Eccl. Stat. 450. In this country, simony is a common law as well as an ecclesiastical crime.

(106). Innocent III. to Archbishop of Canterbury, in Decret. Lib. v. Tit. III. c. 36, and Concil. Lat. IV. A.D. 1215, Can. 65, *Ibid.* c. 41.

(107). Innocent. III. l. c. c. 38, applies this to a vicar-generalship or any ecclesiastical administration.

(108). Decret. Lib. v. Tit. v. c. 1, 2, and 3.

(109). Alexander III. in Decret. Lib. v. Tit. III. c. 17, but Const. 12 Clarendon, A.D. 1164, requires homage in respect of the temporal barony.

(110). Acts VIII. 18.

(111). Nicolaus II. A.D. 1059, ap. Gratian Caus. I. Qu. I. c. 107, distinguishes (1) simony in which both parties are guilty; (2) simony in which the person ordained, but not the ordainer, is guilty; and (3) simony

(1) *true*, (2) *conventional*, and (3) *confidential*. In true simony, both he who gives and he who receives anything of value for a spiritual gift or office are equally guilty. So, too, are all who take part, directly or indirectly, as intermediaries. Conventional simony consists in a promise to give when no money passes, or in a giving and receiving by one of the parties only, to which the other is not privy, as when a gift is made by a friend ([112]), or money or anything of value is given to one who will have influence with a bishop or patron ([113]). Confidential simony consists in accepting a benefice to hold for the use of another, or under a secret promise to resign, or in resigning a benefice in consideration of money, a pension, or some other benefit ([114]). Either true or conventional simony may be committed ([115]) (1) by hand, or direct payment; (2) by laying another under an obligation ([116]), or indirect payment; and (3) by making interest on behalf of an unworthy candidate, or corrupt payment ([117]).

18. By ancient rule the penalty for obtaining orders by simony is perpetual deposition ([118]), and relegation to a mona-

in which the ordainer, but not the ordained, is guilty. The two latter are forms of conventional simony. Urban II. *Ibid.* Qu. v. c. 3, allows some consideration to be shown in the second case, and Nicolaus II. *Ibid.* l. c., allows it generally in the third; but Innocent III. to the Prior of Canterbury, in Decret. Lib. v. Tit. III. c. 35, forbids any one to receive orders from one whom he believes to be a simoniac. Devoti Lib. IV. Tit. IX. § 2.

(112). Alexander III. in Decret. Lib. v. Tit. III. c. 23, advises a man to resign in such a case.

(113). Urban II. ap. Gratian Caus. I. Qu. v. c. 3.

(114). Alexander III. to bishops of Exeter and Worcester, in Decret. Lib. I. Tit. XXXV. c. 4.

(115). Gregory ap. Gratian Caus. I. Qu. l. c. 114.

(116). Alexander III. to Archbishop of York, in Decret. Lib. v. Tit. III. c. 12.

(117). Gregory ap. Gratian Caus. I. Qu. l. c. 120; Paschal II. *Ibid.* c. 125; Concil. Tolet. X. A.D. 656 *Ibid.* I Dist. LXXXIX. c. 6, forbids a bishop to exercise favouritism.

(118). Concil. Chalcedon, A.D. 651, Can. 2 ap. Gratian Caus. I Qu. l. c. 8: If any bishop shall ordain for money, and bring down to sale the grace which cannot be sold, . . . let him who is convicted of having attempted this forfeit his own degree, and let him who has been ordained benefit

Excesses. 57

stery for life ([119]). The penalties originally prescribed for obtaining orders by simony were afterwards extended to obtaining offices by simony, but not without some relaxation of their severity ([120]). An office or benefice obtained by true simony is held to be absolutely void ([121]), and if the simony is known the guilty party is bound to avoid it ([122]). Where, however, there has only been conventional simony, he may be dispensed with ([123]), if either (1) such simony has been perpe-

nothing by the ordination. Syn. VII. A.D. 787, *Ibid.* c. 2 ; Syn. VIII. A.D. 869, *Ibid.* c. 9 ; Gregory *Ibid.* c. 12 ; Urban II. A.D. 1095, *Ibid.* c. 110 ; Lucius III. in Decret. Lib. v. Tit. III. c. 6 ; Alexander III. *Ibid.* c. 11, 13.

(119). Ambros. ap Gratian Caus. I. Qu. l. c. 7.

(120). Concil. Lat. I. A.D. 1123, ap. Gratian Caus. I. Qu. l. c. 10 ; Concil. Westminster A.D. 1127, Can. 1 : We forbid churches, benefices, or dignities to be in any case sold or bought. If the offender be a clergyman, let him be degraded ; if a layman, outlawed and excommunicated. Concil. London A.D. 1175, Can. 9 ; Alexander III. to Bishop of Worcester in Decret. Lib. v. Tit. III. c. 15. Const. 12 Langton, A.D. 1222, forbids a man to resign and accept the vicarage afterwards, "because in this case some unlawful bargain may be suspected." Const. 18 Langton, and Const. 24 Edmund, A.D. 1236, require an oath against simony from presentees. Const. 12 Otho, A.D. 1237 ; Const. 33 Othobon, A.D. 1268 : Because a presentee often agrees with a patron to pay him a certain annuity, we, intending to obviate this simony, do wholly revoke all such promises and contracts. Boniface VIII. in Sext. Lib. III. Tit. VII. c. 2 ; Const. 1 Reynolds, A.D. 1322 ; Const. Courtney, A.D. 1391 : That all presentees to ecclesiastical benefices make oath that they have not given or promised, directly or indirectly, by themselves or others in their employ, for the presentation to the presenter, or to any other persons whatever. 31 Eliz. c. 6 visited simony with legal penalties.

(121). Concil. Placent. A.D. 1095, ap. Gratian Caus. I. Qu. III. c. 5 : Whatever in the way of holy orders or ecclesiastical property has been acquired by gifts or promises of money, we declare to be null, and never to have any force. Concil. Lat. II. A.D. 1139, *Ibid.* c. 15.

(122). Alexander III. in Decret. Lib. v. Tit. III. c. 20 ; Innocent III. *Ibid.* c. 33.

(123). Gelasius ap. Gratian Caus. I. Qu. VII. c. 15 ; Leo IV. *Ibid.* c. 6 ; Nicolaus II. *Ibid.* Qu. l. c. 114, says if he was not party to it ; because Augustin *Ibid.* Qu. IV. c. 1, says : No one's crime taints him who is ignorant of it. Lucius III. in Decret. Lib. v. Tit. III. c. 22 ; Gregory IX. *Ibid.* c. 46.

trated by a third party to avoid his election ([124]), or (2) if it has been done against his prohibition ([125]). But so strict is the law against the semblance of simony, that even for ordaining any one on condition that he shall support himself, a bishop is ordered to be suspended for three years ([126]).

19. It is also accounted simony, but not of equal gravity, for any one to pay money, or to enter into any agreement ([127]), in order to be allowed to make the profession of religion or to be enrolled among the members of any religious house or corporation ([128]). One who has been guilty of this offence is required to embrace a stricter rule ([129]), or to be deposed from his position, unless he is otherwise a man of approved life ([130]), and the house or corporation taking the gift to be suspended ([131]). Nuns are, nevertheless, allowed to give a dower to their convent ([132]), but canons are forbidden upon election to forego their right to fruits and distributions, even for a limited period ([133]).

20. In general the treatment of sacred persons and things as unsacred, or the attributing of sanctity to profane persons and things, constitutes the crime of sacrilege ([134]). It is sacrilege

([124]). Coelestin III. in Decret. Lib. v. Tit. III. c. 27.
([125]). Innocent III. *Ibid.* c. 33.
([126]). Honorius III. *Ibid.* c. 45.
([127]). Urban III. in Decret. Lib. III. Tit. XIX. c. 5.
([128]). Concil. Westminster A.D. 1127, Can. 3 : We condemn all demands of money for admitting monks, canons, or nuns.
([129]). Clemens III. in Decret. Lib. v. Tit. III. c. 25 ; Concil. Lat. IV. A.D. 1215, Can. 64, *Ibid.* c. 40.
([130]). Urban II. A.D. 1095, ap. Gratian Caus. I. Qu. v. c. 2.
([131]). Alexander III. in Decret. Lib. v. Tit. III. c. 19.
([132]). Devoti Lib. IV. Tit. IX. § 14.
([133]). Gregory IX. in Decret. Lib v. Tit. III. c. 44, says, not although there be a custom so to do.
([134]). Hieronym. ap. Gratian Caus. XI. Qu. III. c. 57 : He who calls that which is holy unholy and that which is unholy holy is abominable in God's sight. Ambros. *Ibid.* c. 58 : If any one believing a man to be holy who is not holy joins him to the Body of Christ, he violates Christ, of Whose body we all are members. Pseudo-Gregory III.'s Poenitent. Can. 2 in Wasserschsleben, p. 538 : He is called sacrilegious who treats sacred things as unsacred (qui violat sacra) or steals sacred things. And this is

Excesses. 59

against persons (1) to use violence to one in holy orders or to one who has embraced the religious life ([135]) otherwise than in self-defence ([136]); (2) to violate the person of a nun ([137]); or (3) to abuse a position of hallowed authority or obedience for selfish ends, as for a subject to violate the allegiance due to an anointed sovereign or to a superior in religion ([138]), or for a liege-lord to abuse his relations to a liege-man ([139]), or for a

the greatest crime of all. Const. 4 Thorsby, A.D. 1363; Lynd. 256, 258, 315. Devoti Lib. IV. Tit. XI. § 1 distinguishes three kinds of sacrilege—*personal, local,* and *real;* but local sacrilege is only one form of sacrilege against things.

(135). Laws of Satisfaction, A.D. 725; Syn. VIII. A.D. 869, Can. 3 ap. Gratian Caus. XVII. Qu. IV. c. 22: If any one seizes or strikes a bishop, unless he [the bishop] has been canonically condemned, . . . let him be anathematised. If he treats a presbyter or any other clerk so let him do penance and be deposed. Concil. Mogunt. A.D. 847, *Ibid.* c. 24; Concil. Troslei A.D. 909, *Ibid.* Caus. XXII. Qu. III. c. 22: Whoever by stealth uplifts his hand against the Lord's anointed, *i.e.,* a bishop or presbyter, because this is a grave sacrilege, and if any one destroys, damages, or burns a church, because this is the greatest sacrilege, the holy synod decrees that all his goods be confiscated and himself be confined in a monastery all the days of his life. Can. 38 Dunstan, A.D. 963; Concil. Westminster A.D. 1138, Can. 10: Let him be struck with anathema that kills a clerk, monk, or nun, or lays wicked hands on such. 9 Ed. II. St. I. c. 6; Alexander III. in Decret. Lib. V. Tit. XXXIX. c. 5.

(136). Alexander III. in Decret. Lib. V. Tit. XXXIX. c. 3 and 4; Clemens III. *Ibid.* c. 24.

(137). Concil. Trull. A.D. 692, ap. Gratian Caus. XXVII. Qu. 1. c. 6; Gregory *Ibid.* c. 29. Cap. Franc. *Ibid.* c. 37; Alfred's Law 6, A.D. 877: If a man take a nun out of a convent . . . let him pay 120 shillings, half to the king, and half to the bishop and the lord of the church to whom the nun belonged. Concil. Westminster A.D. 1138, Can. 10; Concil. Lat. II. A.D. 1139, *Ibid.* Qu. IV. c. 29.

(138). Gratian Caus. XXII. Qu. V. c. 12: If any layman profanes the oath of allegiance to his king and lord by violating it, and afterwards perversely and treasonably assails his kingdom, because he commits sacrilege by raising his hand against the Lord's anointed (in Christum Domini Caus. XI. Qu. III. c. 11, 13, 14, 27), let him be anathema. *Id.* Caus. XXIV. Qu. III. c. 22 says the same of a bishop or priest. Alexander III. in Decret. Lib. I. Tit. III. c. 5; 25 Ed. III. St. V. c. 2, A.D. 1350: To his prelate a man oweth faith and obedience. See *The Diocese.* Honorius III. quoted below, note 284; Lynd. 11.

(139). Fulbert ap. Gratian Caus. XXII. Qu. V. c. 18: The lord also must

superior in religion to impose an excessive spiritual punishment to further his own private objects ([140]). This kind of sacrilege was formerly visited with excommunication *ipso facto* ([141]) in addition to other penalties ([142]), and absolution from it was reserved to the pope only ([143]).

21. Sacrilege against things is committed (1) by treating sacred things as unsacred ([144]), as by reiterating the sacrament of baptism, confirmation, or order ([145]), converting consecrated property to ordinary uses ([146]), violating ecclesiastical liber-

in all such matters do his duty towards his liege-man. Otherwise he commits a breach of faith.

(140). Concil. Agath. A.D. 506, Can. 3 ap. Gratian Caus. XI. Qu. III. c. 8: If bishops, in neglect of priestly moderation, presume to excommunicate the innocent or those guilty of trifling offences, let them be admonished in writing by neighbouring bishops of the same province, and if they refuse to obey, be put out of communion until next synod-time. Gregory *Ibid.* c. 60: He forfeits the power of binding and loosing who exercises it [to suit] his own will, and not according to his subject's deserts. *Id. Ibid.* 1. Dist. CXXIV. c. 2; Isidor. *Ibid.* 1. Dist. XLV. c. 2. Rabanus *Ibid.* Caus. XXIV. Qu. III. c. 5: Many bishops (sacerdotes) say that they punish faults out of zeal for God. But when this is done without discrimination it is a kind of sacrilege, and whilst they rush headlong to amend others they themselves are guilty of a deeper fault. Even nowadays it is not quite an unknown thing for a prelate to abuse his claim to obedience to protect his own purse; and in one case one who was guilty of so doing did not scruple afterwards to defend his conduct against a simple claim for justice by proclaiming a reluctant act of obedience to be an acknowledgment of a non-existing crime.

(141). Nicolaus ap. Gratian Caus. XXII. Qu. IV. c. 23 prescribes excommunication after the third warning; but Syn. VIII. A.D. 869, *Ibid.* c. 22 prescribes the anathema. Const. 1 Langton, A.D. 1222, makes it *ipso facto*.

(142). Gratian Caus. XXII. Qu. IV. c. 21 and 26.

(143). Concil. Westminster A.D. 1138, Can. 10: Let none but the pope give him penance at the last, unless in extreme danger of death. Concil. Lat. II. A.D. 1139, *Ibid.* Caus. XVII. Qu. IV. c. 29; Clemens III. in Decret. Lib. V. Tit. XXXIX. c. 19.

(144). Synod. Rom. A.D. 878, ap. Gratian Caus. XVII. Qu. IV. c. 21, enumerates (1) violating the precincts of a church, (2) carrying away holy things, or (3) things placed for safe keeping in holy places.

(145). Augustin ap. Gratian Caus. I. Qu. 1. c. 97; Alexander III. in Decret. Lib. V. Tit. IX. c. 2.

(146). Apost. Const. 73; Concil. Ancyran. A.D. 314, ap. Gratian I. Dist.

Excesses.   61

ties (¹⁴⁷) or immunities, or entrusting Church offices to Jews
and unbelievers (¹⁴⁸). It is committed (2) by treating profane
things as sacred, as by practising divination or soothsaying (¹⁴⁹),
either by lots (¹⁵⁰), observation of the stars (¹⁵¹), the flight of
birds, intestines, or the palms of the hands (¹⁵²); keeping lucky

l. c. 22; Ambros. *Ibid.* Caus. XVII. Qu. IV. c. 3: Some who have given property to a church under a fervid impulse and not a lasting judgment afterwards wish to have it back. In their case neither the first nor the second gift is valid, the first because it was done thoughtlessly, the second because it was done sacrilegiously. Gregory *Ibid.* c. 4; Pseudo-Isidor. *Ibid.* Caus. XII. Qu. II. c. 5.

(147). Const. 1 Langton, A.D. 1222; Boniface, A.D. 1253, confirmed by 38 Hen. III. A.D. 1254, and 21 Boniface, A.D. 1261; Const. 3 Peckham, A.D. 1279, and Const. 10 Peckham, A.D. 1281; Const. Winchelsea, A.D. 1298; Const. 3 Mepham, A.D. 1328; Const. 1 Stratford, A.D. 1342; Const. 14 Stratford, A.D. 1343; Const. Chichele, A.D. 1430 and A.D. 1434; Ayliffe 85, 239.

(148). Concil. Tolet. III. A.D. 589, ap. Gratian. 1 Dist. LIV. c. 14; Concil. Tolet. IV. A.D. 633, Can. 64, *Ibid.* Caus. XVII. Qu. IV. c. 31; Gregory in Decret. Lib. V. Tit. VI. c. 18; Concil. Lat. IV. A.D. 1215, *Ibid.* c. 16.

(149). Apost. Const. VIII. 32; Concil. Ancyran. A.D. 314, Can. 24; Innocent ap. Gratian Caus. I. Qu. 1. c. 24; Concil. Narbon. A.D. 589, Can. 14; Concil. Agath. A.D. 506, *Ibid.* Caus. XXVI. Qu. V. c. 6; Isidor. *Ibid.* c. 1 defines soothsaying, sortilegium, as the practice of divination by the lots of the saints or the inspection of writings. Concil. Aurel. I. A.D. 511, *Ibid.* c. 9; Concil. Martini A.D. 572, Can. 71; Gregory *Ibid.* c. 10; Leo IV. A.D. 850, to the English bishops, *Ibid.* c. 7; Alexander IV. in Sext. Lib. V. Tit. II. c. 8 directs inquisitors not to meddle with these subjects.

(150). Hieronym. ap. Gratian Caus. XXVI. Qu. II. c. 2 objects to casting lots, as was done in the case of Matthias, because "the privileges of individuals cannot make a common law." Also Augustin *Ibid.* c. 3, 5: Baeda *Ibid.* c. 4; Theodore in Decret. Lib. V. Tit. XXI. c. 1; Honorius III. *Ibid.* c. 3 declares an election void because lots had been cast.

(151). Apost. Const. VIII. 32; Augustin ap. Gratian Caus. XXVI. Qu. II. c. 8 calls star-gazers planetarios. Hieronym. *Ibid.* c. 9; *Id. Ibid.* Qu. III. c. 1 calls them astrologi and mathematici. Alexander III. in Decret. Lib. V. Tit. XXI. c. 2 suspends a priest for a year who had looked at an astrolabe with a view of recovering what had been stolen from a church.

(152). Διδαχή III. 4: Be not thou an observer of birds, for it leadeth to idolatry; nor a charmer, nor an astrologer, nor a user of purifications, for from these things is generated idolatry. The several kinds of divination by earth, air, fire, and water, the flight of birds, the inspection of entrails,

or unlucky days ([153]), practising magic, spells, incantations ([154]), sorcery ([155]), witchcraft, or the dark art ([156]), and worshipping fountains, stones, or dead bodies ([157]). This

the casting horoscopes, and dancing, are enumerated by Augustin ap. Gratian Caus. xxvi. Qu. iii. c. 1 and Qu. v. c. 14, and condemned by Gregory ii. A.D. 721, *Ibid.* Qu. v. c. 1 ; Concil. Autissiodor. A.D. 578, Can. 4.

(153). Augustin *Ibid.* Caus. xxvi. Qu. vii. c. 17 ; Concil. Martini A.D. 572, Can. 72.

(154). Concil. Laodic. A.D. 363, Can. 36 ; Augustin *Ibid.* c. 15 ; Iren. Haer. ii. 32, 5 : Let priests teach men that magic and incantations cannot benefit infirmities. Stat. Eccl. Ant. *Ibid.* Qu. v. c. 11 ; Gregory *Ibid.* c. 8 ; Concil. Martini. A.D. 572, Can. 59 : Clergy may not practise enchantment and spells, because this is a binding of souls. Concil. Rothomag. A.D. 650, Can. 4.

(155). Cap. Reg. Franc. *Ibid.* Qu. v. c. 12.

(156). Concil. Tolet. xiii. A.D. 683, *Ibid.* c. 13 : Whatever priest or deacon under the influence of grief or resentment shall hereafter presume to strip the divine altar of its holy coverings, or surround it with any other gloomy covering, or even withdraw from the temple of God the accustomed service of holy lights, . . . let him know that he is deprived of the dignity and honour of his place. . . . For very many priests wounded with the fraud of hatred lay themselves out to say with deceitful intention a Mass appointed for the repose of the dead, for no other purpose but that he for whom the sacrifice is offered may by the intervention of the most holy libation incur the danger of death. Cnut's Law 5, A.D. 1018. We forbid all heathenism . . . or to practise witchcraft or to contrive any private murder, either by lots or by fear. Ethelstan's Law 3, A.D. 925 : Concerning witchcraft, magical medicines, and secret arts of murder, if one have been slain and the man cannot deny it let him forfeit his life.

(157). Augustin ap. Gratian Caus. xxvi. Qu. ii. c. 6 ; Concil. Chelsea A.D. 787, Can. 19 ; Alfred and Guthrum's Law 2, A.D. 878 ; Egbert's Excerpt. 146-148 ; Concil. Tolet. xii. A.D. 681, Can. 11 ; Law's Northumbrian Priests, 47, 56, A.D. 950 ; Edgar's Law 16, A.D. 960 : That every priest forbid the worship of fountains, and witchcraft, and auguries, and spells, and soothsaying, and the worship of dead bodies and palmistry, which carry men into various impostures, and to groves, and ellens and many trees of divers sorts, and stones. Cnut's Law 5, A.D. 1018 : We strictly forbid all heathenism. It is heathenism to worship idols, *i.e.*, the heathen gods, the sun or moon, fire or river, water, wells, or tall stones [maen-hirs], or any kind of tree, or to practise witchcraft, or to contrive any private murder by lots or firebrands. Concil. London A.D. 1075, Can. 8 : That the bones of dead animals be not hung up to drive away pestilence from cattle. Concil. Westminster A.D. 1102, Can. 26 ; Concil. Winton A.D. 1308.

Excesses. 63

kind of sacrilege is visited with excommunication *ipso jure* ([158]).

CRIMES AGAINST FELLOW-MEN.

22. On a very different level from crimes which are defections from allegiance to God are those which are invasions of other men's rights, or crimes against fellow-men. These include homicide, strife, and conspiracy, robbery, arson, and the crime of deceit and usury. Nearly all of these, as being offences against civil order ([159]), are in civilised communities punished in secular courts; but they also render those guilty of them liable to spiritual censures and penances ([160]), and in Christian countries the religious aspect of them has influenced to a large extent the view taken of them by civil tribunals.

23. Homicide consists in intentionally taking the life of another ([161]), or doing so unintentionally and accidentally, if the act was the result of carelessness ([162]) or of doing any

---

(158). Concil. Ancyran. A.D. 314, Can. 23 ap. Gratian Caus. XXVI. Qu. V. c. 2, punishes divination and sorcery with five years' excommunication. Theodor. Poenit. I. XV. 4 in Haddan and Stubbs III. 190; Concil. London A.D. 1076, Can. 8; Concil. London A.D. 1127, Can. 15; Clemens III. in Decret. Lib. V. Tit. XXXIX. c. 22 reserves this crime to the pope.

(159). Ayliffe 238.

(160). Concil. Aurel. IV. A.D. 541, Can. 28: Whoever has voluntarily murdered an innocent man, although he has obtained acquittance from the prince or the dead man's relatives, must remain liable to do penance at the bishop's hands. In such a case, according to Lucius III. in Decret. Lib. II. Tit. II. c. 8, and Bracton, a man may be twice tried and twice punished. 9 Ed. II. St. I. c. 6, A.D. 1315. Remigius ap. Gratian Caus. XXIII. Qu. V. c. 39, says that enormous crimes are better left to secular courts.

(161). Augustin ap. Gratian Caus. XXIII. Qu. VIII. c. 33; Caus. XXXIII. Qu. II. c. 819; Const. 7 and 9 Peckham, A.D. 1281; Const. 4 Thoresby, A.D. 1363; Decret. Lib. V. Tit. XII. c. 1; Lynd. 339.

(162). Concil. Elib. A.D. 305, Can. 5: If a woman in a fit of anger strike her maid so that she die within three days, it being uncertain whether it was intentional or accidental, let her do penance for seven years if it was intentional, or five years if it was accidental. Decret. Lib. V. Tit. XII. c. 7 and 12.

other criminal act (¹⁶³). It includes aiding and abetting in murder (¹⁶⁴), or not interposing when interposition might have prevented it (¹⁶⁵), killing an adulterous wife (¹⁶⁶), overlaying an infant (¹⁶⁷), procuring abortion (¹⁶⁸) or taking drugs for that purpose (¹⁶⁹), self-murder (¹⁷⁰), and spiritual murder (¹⁷¹). Closely allied to homicide is strife (¹⁷²), and the crime to which it gives rise, conspiracy (¹⁷³). It is, however, not homicide when an-

(163). Gratian I. Dist. 1. c. 47 ; Decret. Lib. v. Tit. XII. c. 8.

(164). Augustin ap. Gratian Caus. XXXIII. Qu. III. Dist. 1. c. 23 ; Hieronym. *Ibid.* c. 25.

(165). Ambros. *Ibid.* Caus. XXIII. Qu. III. c. 7 ; Augustin *Ibid.* c. 11.

(166). Augustin *Ibid.* Caus. XXXIII. Qu. II. c. 9 ; Nicolaus *Ibid.* c. 5.

(167). Dunstan Can. 52. A.D. 963 ; Const. 15 Edmund. A.D. 1236 ; Const. 2 Zouche, A.D. 1347 ; Const. 4 Thorsby, A.D. 1363.

(168). Διδαχή II. 2 ; Athenag. Apol. c. 35 ; Augustin ap. Gratian Caus. XXXII. Qu. II. c. 8, says, after quickening, not before. Concil. Ilerd. A.D. 523, Can. 2, excludes them from communion for seven years. Theodori Poenit. I. XIV. 24, in Haddan & Stubbs III. 189 ; Innocent III. in Decret. Lib. v. Tit. XII. c. 20 ; Tertullian Apol. c. 9 : In our case we may not even destroy the fœtus in the womb.

(169). Concil. Guarmarcia in Decret. Lib. v. Tit. XII. c. 5 ; Concil. Elib. A.D. 305, Can. 63, forbids communion to be given in extremis to an adulterous wife who had killed her offspring to conceal her liaison.

(170). Augustin ap. Gratian Caus. XXIII. Qu. v. c. 10 : Concil. Brac. 1, A.D. 561, *Ibid.* c. 12.

(171). Augustin *Ibid.* Caus. XXII. Qu. v. c. 5, says that homicide of the soul is worse than homicide of the body. Concil. Tolet. VIII. A.D. 653, *Ibid.* Qu. IV. c. 1, speaks of "slaying a father's soul" (jugulare animam patris). Theodori Poenit. I. VIII. 5, *Ibid.* Caus. XXVI. Qu. VI. c. 12, and Haddan & Stubbs III. 184 ; I. IX. 7, *Ibid.* p. 185 ; L XIV. 28, *Ibid.* p. 189, and Gratian III. Dist. IV. c. 22 ; Lynd. 58.

(172). Διδαχή III. 2 : Be not soon angry, nor given to party spirit nor contentions . . . for from all these are generated murders. Cyprian ap. Gratian I. Dist. XC. c. 3 ; Stat. Eccl. Ant. *Ibid.* c. 2, forbids the offerings of such to be received. Concil. Lat. II. A.D. 1139, *Ibid.* c. 11.

(173). Διδαχή II. 6 : Thou shalt not take evil counsel against thy neighbour. Concil. Chalcedon A.D. 451, Can. 18 ap Gratian Caus. XI. Qu. I. c. 22 : If clergy or monks are found conspiring or banding together, or laying snares against their bishop or fellow-clergy, let them be deposed from their proper rank. Concil. Aurel III. A.D. 538, Can. 21, *Ibid.* c. 25 ; Concil. Narbon. A.D. 589, Can. 5, forbids concinnabula vel conjurationes clericorum sub patrocinio laicorum. Caus. III. Qu. IV. c. 4, 5 ; Decret. Lib. II.

Excesses.

other is accidentally killed, through no fault of the slayer's, whilst doing a lawful act ([174]), nor if he was killed by a dependent against his master's prohibition ([175]), nor if he was killed in lawful warfare ([176]), or by an official at the command of a superior ([177]), or in necessary self-defence ([178]), nor if a woman commits suicide to escape dishonour ([179]). The discipline awarded for homicide depends upon circumstances ([180]), and it is more leniently dealt with when committed by an avenger of blood or in anger than under other circumstances ([181]).

Tit. I. c. 19; 3 Ed. I. c. 28, and 13 Ed. I. St. l. c. 49, forbid clerks committing maintenance of any matter pending in the King's court. Const. 1 Stratford, A.D. 1343; Const. 4 Thorsby, A.D. 1363; Lynd. 11, 254.

(174). Alexander III. to Bishop of Exeter in Decret. Lib. v. Tit. XII. c. 9; Innocentius. III. *Ibid.* c. 13; Honorius III. to Archbishop of York, *Ibid.* c. 22 and 23. (1) If a schoolmaster chastises a pupil reasonably, and the pupil dies in consequence, *Ibid.* c. 7; (2) if a boy is killed by an ungovernable horse, *Ibid.* c. 13; or (3) by a dog known to be ferocious and let loose, but not if the dog has accidentally broken his chain; (4) by a mason accidentally dropping a stone or tile without calling out; (5) if a patient dies from a drug which it is the usual custom to administer. Clement III. in Decret. Lib. I. Tit. XIV. c 7; Craisson, § 1828.

(175). *Ibid.* Lib. v. Tit. XII. c. 17.

(176). Augustin ap. Gratian Caus. XXIII. Qu. v. c. 9; Hieronym. *Ibid.* c. 25, Qu. I.; Leo IV. *Ibid.* Qu. VIII. c. 9; Theodori Poenit. I. IV. 6, in Haddan & Stubbs III. 180: One who has killed another by order of his lord, let him keep from church for forty days; one who has done so in public warfare, let him do penance forty days. Urban II. ap. Gratian Caus. XXIII. Qu. v. c. 47; Soldiers' Penances, A.D. 1072.

(177). Innocent ap. Gratian Caus. XXIII. Qu. IV. c. 45, 46; Hieronym. *Ibid.* Qu. v. c. 31; Augustin *Ibid.* c. 41, and Qu. VIII. c. 33; Theodori Poenit. I. IV. 6 l. c.

(178). Decret. Lib v. Tit. XII. c. 2.

(179). Hieronym. ap. Gratian Caus. XXIII. Qu. IV. c. 11; Eusebius VIII. 12 and 14, commends a Christian woman for committing suicide to escape dishonour.

(180). Theodori Poenit. I. IV. 7, l. c. p. 180: If homicide is the result of anger, let him do penance three years; if of accident, one year; if effected by drugs or art, four years or more; if the result of strife, ten years. Gregory ap. Gratian Caus. XXIII. Qu. v. c. 7; Nicolaus *Ibid.* Caus. XXXIII. Qu. II. c. 15, prescribes twelve years for a matricide. Alexander III. to Bishop of Exeter, in Decret Lib. v. Tit. XII. c. 6.

(181). Theodori Poenit. I. IV. 1.

Clergy guilty of it, either directly or indirectly ([182]), are for ever after forbidden the exercise of their order ([183]). Strife and conspiracy are both visited with excommunication.

24. Robbery is of two kinds: (1) robbery with violence, and (2) larceny or stealing ([184]). Robbery with violence, and arson or incendiarism rank together as two of the most atrocious crimes against fellow-men ([185]), and as such may be punished anywhere, regardless of where they have been committed ([186]); and to those guilty of them Christian burial was formerly denied ([187]). Larceny is a less serious crime, but one who shares the proceeds of larceny is deemed as guilty as the thief ([188]); and because the earth is the Lord's and the fulness thereof, it is held to be venial larceny to take the necessaries of life to avoid starvation ([189]). A more lenient discipline is also imposed on those who make restitution after stealing ([190])

(182). Innocent ap. Gratian Caus. XXIII. Qu. VIII. c. 2; Ambros. *Ibid.* c. 3; Concil. Tolet. IV. A.D. 633, *Ibid.* c. 5; Concil. Melden. A.D. 845, *Ibid.* c. 6; Lynd. 29.

(183). Concil. Ilerd. A.D. 523, Can. 1, says, if they have borne arms during a siege; Decret. Lib. V. Tit. XII. c. 10, 11; 18, 24, 25 names other cases; *Ibid.* c. 19, if death supervenes after performing a surgical operation; *Ibid.* Tit. XXV. c. 3 and 4, if they have been concerned in a *mêlée* in which any one has been killed.

(184). Lynd. 58 says that to invade another's right is a mortal sin; to defend one's own right is not a venial sin, p. 112.

(185). Eutychianus ap. Gratian Caus. XXIII. Qu. VIII. c. 31; Concil. Lat. II. A.D. 1139, *Ibid.* c. 32; Decret. Lib. V. Tit. XXIX. c. 19, and Tit. XVII. c. 5; Const. 4 Thorsby, A.D. 1363; Lynd. 329.

(186). Concil. Lat. III. A.D. 1179, in Decret. Lib. V. Tit. XVII. c. 3.

(187). Eugenius III. and Alexander III. *Ibid.* c. 2 and 5.

(188). *Ibid.* Lib. V. Tit. XVIII. c. 4.

(189). Διδαχή I. 5: Woe to him that stealeth; for if, indeed, any one having need stealeth, he shall be guiltless; but he that hath not need shall give account. Augustin ap. Gratian I. Dist. VIII. c. 1; Decret. Lib. V. Tit. XVIII. c. 3: If any one pressed by hunger and nakedness has taken food or clothing, let him do penance three weeks, and if he make restitution, let him be excused fasting. Lynd. 58.

(190). Theodori Poenit. I. III. 3, in Haddan & Stubbs III. 179, quoted *Penance*, note 157; Augustin ap. Gratian Caus. XIV. Qu. V. c. 14 and 15; Gregory *Ibid.* Qu. VI. c. 3.

than to others, and a private thief who has made restitution is even allowed to be advanced to holy orders ([191]). To retain the property of another to satisfy a counter-claim which is made against him is not accounted stealing at all ([192]).

25. The crime of deceit ([193]) consists in stating what is false or concealing what is true ([194]), either in word or in writing. It includes (1) judicial perjury ([195]), or subornation of perjury ([196]), or attempted perjury ([197]) for the purpose of depriving another of his lawful rights ([198]); (2) defamation of the good ([199]), with which is closely allied the recommendation of the bad ([200]);

([191]). Decret. Lib. v. Tit. XVIII. 5.
([192]). Iren. Haer. IV. 30, 2 on Exod. III. 22.
([193]). Διδαχή II. 3: Thou shalt not forswear thyself, thou shalt not bear false witness, thou shalt not bear malice. Thou shalt not be double-minded nor double-tongued. . . . Thy speech shall not be false or vain, but filled by deed. Crimen falsi in Decret. Lib. v. Tit. XX.
([194]). Augustin ap. Gratian Caus. XI. Qu. III. c. 80, and Decret. Lib. v. Tit. XX. c. 1: Both are equally guilty, he who conceals the truth and he who utters a falsehood, because the one does not wish to do good and the other intends to do harm. Baeda *Ibid.* c. 83. Augustin *Ibid.* Caus. XXII. Qu. II. c. 7 enumerates eight different kinds of falsehood. Hieronym. *Ibid.* c. 1; Lynd. 58, 59 defines lying as using words in a false sense with intent to deceive, 304 as knowingly and fraudulently saying what is false and concealing what is true. Ayliffe 419.
([195]). Concil. Agath. A.D. 506, ap. Gratian I. Dist. l. c. 7; Isidor. *Ibid.* Caus. XXII. Qu. V. c. 9 says that it is a double crime—(1) taking God's name in vain, and (2) wronging a neighbour. Pseudo-Isidor. *Ibid.* Caus. VI. Qu. l. c. 18; Cap. 26 Theodulf, A.D. 994; Concil. Ebor. A.D. 1195, Can. 17; Const. 9 Peckham, A.D. 1281; Const. 4 Thorsby, A.D. 1363. Perjury may be said to include (1) renunciation of vows to God, apostasy; (2) breach of the same, sacrilege; (3) rash swearing, blasphemy; and (4) judicial perjury or false witness.
([196]). Gelasius ap. Gratian Caus. XXII. Qu. V. c. 4; Augustin *Ibid.* c. 5; Concil. Matiscon. I. A.D. 581, Can. 17, *Ibid.* c. 7.
([197]). Gregory *Ibid.* Qu. V. c. 18; Concil. Matiscon. Can. 17.
([198]). Const. 6 Boniface, A.D. 1261; Const. 1 Langton, A.D. 1222; Lynd. 315.
([199]). Syn. VIII. A.D. 869, ap. Gratian Caus. XI. Qu. III. c. 77; Const. 1, 21, 24 Langton, A.D. 1222; Const. 5 Boniface, A.D. 1261; Const. 3 Peckham, A.D. 1279; *Fletcher* v. *Harpur*, No. 51; *Jackson* v. *Hobday*, No. 54 in Rothery's Ecclesiastical Appeals.
([200]). Const. 9 Peckham, A.D. 1281.

(3) falsification or forgery of instruments ([201]); and (4) falsely pretending to be in holy orders, or acting as one who is in holy orders without being so ([202]).

26. In the crime of deceit there are many degrees of criminality ([203]). Judicial perjury renders those guilty of it infamous ([204]), disqualifies them from acting as witnesses in future ([205]) or holding benefices ([206]), excludes from Christian burial ([207]), and is otherwise placed on a par with homicide ([208]). Defamation of the good stands on a level with sacrilege and violation of ecclesiastical liberties ([209]); forgery is treated like heresy ([210]); and falsely pretending to be in holy orders is visited with perpetual suspension ([211]). It is, however, excusable falsehood

([201]). Concil. Agath. A.D. 506, ap. Gratian I. Dist. 1, c. 7; Lucius III. to Bishop of Worcester in Decret. Lib. V. Tit. XX. c. 2 directs a sentence obtained by a forged instrument not to be ordered for execution. Innocent III. Ibid. c. 5 specifies nine ways of falsifying papal bulla. Const. 1 Reynolds, A.D. 1322; Const. 4 Thorsby, A.D. 1363; Lynd. 33.

([202]). Decret. Lib. V. Tit. XXVIII. c. 2; Const. 4 Thorsby, A.D. 1363.

([203]). Augustin ap. Gratian Caus. XXII. Qu. II. c. 12: There is a great difference with what mind or as to what things a lie is uttered. The sin is not so great when it is done to help another as when it is done to hurt another, nor is he equally guilty who misleads a traveller as he who misleads another in the way of life.

([204]). Gratian Caus. III. Qu. V. c. 9, and Caus. VI. Qu. VII. c. 17.

([205]). Ethelstan's Law 7, A.D. 925: Let him that takes a false oath never be held worthy to swear afterwards. Eugenius III. to Bishop of Hereford in Decret. Lib. II. Tit. XX. c. 7, and Gregory IX. Ibid. c. 54.

([206]). Lucius III. to Bishop of Norwich in Decret. Lib. II. Tit. XXIV. c. 11.

([207]). Ethelstan's Law 7, A.D. 925.

([208]). Concil. Agath. A.D. 506, Can. 37 ap. Gratian Caus. XXIV. Qu. III. c. 20; Eutychianus Ibid. Caus. XXII. Qu. 1. c. 17; Theodori Poenit. I. VI. in Haddan and Stubbs III. 182: Let him who commits perjury in a church do penance eleven years; he who does so under necessity, three Lents; he who commits perjury in the hand of bishop, priest, or deacon, or a consecrated cross, three years; if the cross was unconsecrated, one year.

([209]). Const. 1 Langton, A.D. 1222.

([210]). Innocent III. in Decret. Lib. V. Tit. XX. c. 7, decrees that all forgers of papal bulls, their aiders and abettors, be excommunicated, degraded, and delivered over to the secular arm, and all clergy using them be deprived of office and benefice. Const. 4 Thorsby, A.D. 1363.

([211]). Id. Ibid.

Excesses. 69

to say what is false, believing it to be true at the time [212], or in jest [213], or when lawfully pledged to secrecy [214], or to a person not entitled to ask for information, when it is done to avoid a greater wrong [215].

27. Usury is the making unlawful profit out of a thing lent [216], and the crime of it consists in the covetousness which would take advantage of another's need to inflict on him loss for selfish gain [217]. Forbidden usury, therefore, presupposes: (1) that the thing lent is not necessary to the lender as a means of livelihood, and is of less value to him than the amount asked from the borrower; (2) that the amount asked is not a payment to ensure the lender being in the same position when the thing lent is repaid as he was in before he lent it; and (3) that it is not a payment for some service rendered.

28. It is not usury to receive payment for the loan of that which is a means of livelihood to the lender, as rent for a farm, which in return produces a livelihood to him who pays the rent [218]. It is not usury to receive repayment of a larger sum than that originally lent either, (1) to secure to the lender the same purchasing power if things are likely to increase in price [219], provided he do not make a profit out of the trans-

[212]. Augustin ap. Gratian Caus. XXII. Qu. II. c. 3 and 4.
[213]. Augustin *Ibid.* c. 18.
[214]. See *Penance*, note 85.
[215]. Hieronym. *Ibid.* c. 21.
[216]. Alexander III. in Decret. Lib. v. Tit. XIX. c. 1.
[217]. Eph. v. 5 calls covetousness idolatry. Col. III. 5, 6; Cyprian Ep. 51 (Oxf. 55), 27; Ambros. ap. Gratian I. Dist. XLVII. c. 8: When you came into the world, what did you bring with you? . . . Let no one call his own that which belongs to all. That which has been taken in excess of what would suffice has been violently taken. . . . It is not a less crime to take from him that hath than, having and abounding, to refuse to them that want. Augustin *Ibid.* Caus. XIV. Qu. IV. c. 11: Which is the more cruel, he who deprives and plunders the rich or he who oppresses the poor by usury? Labour, says Leo XIII.'s Encyclical, 1891, p. 13, 14, differs from any other commodity, because to-day's labour cannot be sold after to-day. To make one's profit out of the need of another is condemned by all laws, human and divine.
[218]. Innocent III. in Decret. Lib. v. Tit. XIX. c. 16.
[219]. Alexander III. *Ibid.* c. 6.

action ([220]); or (2) to compensate the lender for loss sustained by delay in repayment ([221]); or (3) to cover risk of loss altogether through the borrower's inability to repay ([222]). It is not usury to receive repayment of a larger sum than that lent when the excess is paid for some service rendered, such as taking care of an object left in pawn ([223]), changing money, or giving a bill of exchange ([224]). Neither is the purchase of perpetual rent-charges, or fee-farm rents ([225]), or life annuities forbidden usury ([226]).

29. To the Jews of old ([227]), and to Christians in early times ([228]), all usury was forbidden which exceeded the bounds of fraternal assistance, and to the clergy any and every kind of usury, because it savoured of the nature of trade ([229]). In

([220]). Urban III. *Ibid.* c. 10.

([221]). *Lucrum cessans.* To constitute a *lucrum cessans* three things are requisite according to Paul de Castro: (1) the money lent must not be useless to the lender, (2) he must be in a position to use it profitably, (3) he must have sustained actual loss by non-payment. A mortgage was therefore usually drawn repayable after six months, a stipulation being added that if the money were not then repaid the loss to the lender should be represented by an agreed sum yearly. Devoti Lib. IV. Tit. XVI. § 6–10.

([222]). *Damnum eveniens.* Gregory IX. in Decret. Lib. V. Tit. XIX. c. 19 calls this presumptive usury (est censendus usuarius). Devoti l. c. § 11.

([223]). *Commissoria lex.* Devoti, § 16, 17.

([224]). *Ibid.* § 26.

([225]). *Census.* Martin V. in Extrav. Com. Lib. III. Tit. V. c. 1. Devoti § 19.

([226]). *Census vitalicius.* Concil. Vien. A.D. 1311, in Clem. Lib. III. Tit. IV., forbids monasteries to sell such annuities except for necessity or evident utility.

([227]). Exod. XXII. 25; Deut. XXIII. 19; Lev. XXV. 36; Ps. XV. 5; Luke VI. 34, 35.

([228]). Leo, A.D. 444, ap. Gratian Caus. XIV. Qu. IV. c. 7; Gregory *Ibid.* I. Dist. XXXIII. c. 2; Concil. Chelsea A.D. 787, Can. 20: We have also forbidden usury. Where there is gain there is loss; gain in the coffers, loss in the conscience. Const. 4 Thoresby, A.D. 1363; Lynd. 160.

([229]). Can. Apost. Can. 44 ap. Gratian I Dist. XLVII. c. 1: Let a bishop, priest, or deacon who requires usury of those to whom he lends, either leave off or be deprived. Concil. Elib. A.D. 305, Can. 20, *Ibid.* c. 5; Concil. Nic. A.D. 325, Can. 17, *Ibid.* c. 2; Concil. Arelat. A.D. 314, *Ibid.* Caus. XIV.

Excesses.

mediaeval times this prohibition was extended to the laity, owing to the abuses and oppression connected with usury wherever it was practised ([230]); and it was provided by stringent laws that those guilty of it should be excommunicated and deprived of Christian burial unless they came to repentance ([231]), that they should be held infamous ([232]) and compelled to restore their unlawful gains ([233]), and the secular arm was invoked to compel them so to do ([234]).

CRIMES AGAINST BODILY HOLINESS AND REDEEMED HUMAN NATURE.

30. Crimes against the humanity redeemed by Christ are all carnal indulgences which offend against sobriety and bring dishonour on the body, and through it on the body of Christ ([235]),

Qu. IV. c. 1; Concil. Laodic. A.D. 363, *Ibid.* I. Dist. XLVI. c. 9: Ministers of the altar may not practise usury. Leo, A.D. 443, *Ibid.* c. 10, says, neither in their own names nor in the names of others. Concil. Carthag. III. A.D. 397, Can. 16, *Ibid.* Caus. XIV. Qu. IV. c. 6: Let no one of the clergy receive from any one more than he lent; if money, money; if kind, kind; what he gave that let him receive. Gelasius, A.D. 494, *Ibid.* c. 1; Concil. Tarracon. A.D. 516, Can. 2, *Ibid.* c. 3.

(230). In the twelfth century the usual charge is stated to have been 100 per cent. Const. 18 Edmund, A.D. 1236: We forbid a man to detain a pledge after he has received the principal out of the profits, after a deduction of expenses.

(231). Concil. Turon. A.D. 1163, in Decret. Lib. V. Tit. XIX. c. 1; Alexander III. to Archbishop of Canterbury, *Ibid.* c. 2; Concil. Lat. III. A.D. 1179, *Ibid.* c. 3; Sext. Lib. V. Tit. V. c. 1 and 2; Concil. Vien. A.D. 1311, in Clem. Lib. V. Tit. V. c. 1.

(232). Gratian Caus. III. Qu. VII. c. 2.

(233). Alexander III. in Decret. Lib. V. Tit. XIX. c. 5 and 9; Innocent III. *Ibid.* c. 13, 14; Concil. Lat. IV. A.D. 1215, Can. 67, *Ibid.* c. 18, extends this even to Jews.

(234). Innocent III. l. c. c. 12.

(235). 1 Thess. IV. 5; Διδαχή III. 3: Be not lustful, for lust leadeth to fornication, neither be a filthy talker nor a lifter up of the eyes, for from all these are generated adulteries. Hieronym. ap. Gratian Caus. XXVI. Qu. II. c. 9: He who is guilty of fornication sins against his own body, not that body only which has been made a temple of the Holy Ghost, but that which is also called the Body, because the whole Church is the Body

such as gluttony, drunkenness, and adultery in all its forms. Gluttony and drunkenness are the opposites of that abstemiousness in eating and drinking the climax of which is fasting. Adultery is used in a wide sense to express—(1) generally any illicit or forbidden intercourse between the sexes ([236]), and (2) specifically the violation of wedlock ([237]).

31. In a wide sense adultery includes ([238]) (1) any natural intercourse between the sexes which is not explicitly sanctioned by the Church, such as simple incontinence, concubinage, and promiscuous fornication; (2) any natural intercourse between those to whom it is forbidden by vows or divine law, such as the violation of wedlock, incest, or sacrilege; and (3) intercourse coupled with violence, or contrary to nature, such as rape, sodomy ([239]), and bestiality ([240]). The first of

of Christ, and he who defiles his body sins against the whole Church, because by means of one member the spot spreads over the whole.

(236). Apost. Const. VI. 28; Augustin ap. Gratian Caus. XXXII. Qu. IV. c. 11: Under the name of adultery must be understood all illicit intercourse, and the non-legitimate or forbidden use of those organs. Hieronym. *Ibid.* c. 14; *Id. Ibid.* Caus. XXXII. Qu. II. c. 2: Not all matrimony in which a wife is joined to a husband otherwise than according to the precepts of Christ can be properly called lawful wedlock, but rather adultery. Isidor. *Ibid.* Caus. XXXII. Qu. V. c. 15: Let no one outside the marital bond have intercourse with other women to gratify lust. Gregory *Ibid.* Qu. V. c. 13, says that adultery is committed when an unmarried girl is unlawfully desired. Lynd. 314.

(237). Pseudo-Gregory III.'s Poenit. Can. 4, in Wasserschleben, p. 538; Adultery is violating the wife of another or a consecrated virgin. Cap. 26 Theodulf, A.D. 994; Const. 10 Stratford, A.D. 1342; Const. 4 Thorsby, A.D. 1363; Lynd. 58.

(238). Augustin *Ibid.* c. 11: The evil of adultery surpasses fornication, and is surpassed by incest. For it is worse to have intercourse with a mother than with any other woman. But the worst of all is that which is contrary to nature. . . . In things allowed for use, an excessive use is far more tolerable than a single or rare giving way in a fashion that is not allowed.

(239). Devoti Lib. IV. Tit. XV.: Sodomia est conjunctio duarum personarum ejusdem sexûs, quae sodomia perfecta dicitur; eam vero proxime sequitur sodomia imperfecta quam admittunt duae personae dissimilis sexûs, quae corporum copulatione violarunt ordinem naturae. Rom. I. 26, 27; Augustin l. c. c. 11 and 13.

(240). Theodori Poenit. I. II. 3, in Haddan & Stubbs III. 178.

these are called excesses, the second crimes, the last monstrosities ([241]).

32. Simple incontinence is voluntary indulgence of sexual desires ([242]) between two persons who are under no disability to marry one another ([243]). Concubinage is a habit of such indulgence which stops short of wedlock to avoid the obligation of mutual fidelity ([244]). Promiscuous fornication (stuprum) is the degradation of the human body to promiscuous embraces for purposes of lust ([245]). Simple incontinence and concubinage are accounted lesser crimes ([246]), because they are strictly according to nature, and are visited with suspension for a year and doing penance during the forty days of Lent ([247]). Promiscuous fornication was formerly visited with suspension for ten or seven, but the time has been reduced to three years, because of human infirmity ([248]).

([241]). Tertullian de Pud. c. 4: All other frenzies of passions impious both to the body and the sex beyond the laws of nature, we banish from all shelter of the Church, because they are not sins, but monstrosities.

([242]). Greg. Nyss. Ep. Can. II. p. 118: πορνεία ἐστὶν ἡ χωρὶς ἀδικίας ἑτέρου γενομένη τισὶ τῆς ἐπιθυμίας ἐκπλήρωσις. Ambros. ap. Gratian Caus. XXXII. Qu. v. c. 2: There is no real corruption of the flesh unless there has first been a corruption of the mind. Augustin *Ibid.* c. 4–7; Chrysostom *Ibid.* c. 10, says fornication can be committed by the will alone.

([243]). Tertullian de Pud. c. 4: Among us secret connections not first professed in presence of the Church run risk of being adjudged akin to adultery and fornication. Augustin l. c. c. 4, 5. See *Wedlock*, § 9.

([244]). Apost. Can. 67: If any one has had connection with a virgin not betrothed and keeps her, let him be suspended [from offering]. Decret. Lib. v. Tit. XVI. c. 1: If a man lie with a maid, let him endow her and take her to wife.

([245]). 1 Cor. VI. 15 defines the sin as making the members of a temple of the Holy Ghost the members of a harlot. Hieronym. ap. Gratian Caus. XXXII. Qu. v. c. 12.

([246]). Alexander III. in Decret. Lib. II. Tit. l. c. 4.

([247]). Theodori Poenit. I. II. 1, in H. and S. III. 178: Si quis fornicaverit eum virgine uno anno peniteat; si cum marita quatuor annos. I. XIV. 10, *Ibid.* p. 188. Baedae Poenit. III. 1, *Ibid.* p. 327: Adolescens si cum virgine peccaverit, annum unum poeniteat; si semel et fortuitu, levigetur etiam ad annum plenum.

([248]). Theodori Poenit. I. II. 18, in H. and S. III. 179; Baedae Poenit. III. 27, *Ibid.* 328.

33. Any natural intercourse between those to whom marriage is forbidden is a greater crime ([249]), because it involves the violation of a vow or of some relation having the divine sanction. Such is adultery, which involves a breach of the marriage vow ([250]); incest, which is a violation of the family relation ([251]); sacrilegious incontinence, sometimes called incest, which involves the breach of a vow of chastity ([252]); and spiritual fornication, which is lewdness between persons spiritually related, as between a godparent and godchild ([253]), or an incumbent and a member of his flock ([254]). Adultery and sacrilegious inconti-

([249]). Theodori Poenit. l. c. III. 178; Alexander III. in Decret. Lib. IL. Tit. l. c. 4; Const. 10 Stratford, A.D. 1342; Lynd. 212.

([250]). So defined by Cyprian Ep. 51 (Oxf. 55), 26; Augustin ap. Gratian Caus. XXXII. Qu. V. c. 16: He is an adulterer who, either when his wife is long ill, or long absent, or is desirous of living continently, has intercourse with another woman. Innocent *Ibid.* c. 23.

([251]). Concil. Agath. A.D. 506, Can. 61: We call it incest if one take his brother's wife, who was almost the same as a sister, or if a brother take his wife's sister. If one wed his mother-in-law or first cousin (consobrina), or his maternal uncle's widow or daughter, or his paternal uncle's daughter or step-daughter, or has defiled one akin to himself or the wife of one akin. Concil. Paris. V. A.D. 615, Can. 14; Pseudo-Isidor. ap. Gratian Caus. III. Qu. IV. c. 4; *Ibid.* Caus. XXXIII. Qu. II. c. 17; Const. 17 Peckham, A.D. 1281; Decret. Lib. IV. Tit. XII.; Const. 4 Thorsby, A.D. 1363. See *Wedlock*, § 22.

([252]). Hieronym. ap. Gratian I. Dist. XXVII. c. 9: Virgins who have married after they have been consecrated are guilty not so much of adultery as of incontinence. Siricius, A.D. 385, and Concil. Tribur. A.D. 895, *Ibid.* Caus. XXVII. Qu. l. c. 14: We hear that some have associated themselves to sacred virgins, and have entered into incestuous and sacrilegious relations with them after their making a solemn vow to God. See *Discipline of the Religious Life*, § 36; *Privileges of Order*, § 50.

([253]). Gratian Caus. XXXIII. Qu. II. c. 18 mentions a man and his godmother. Caus. XXX. Qu. l. c. 8 a child and a godfather.

([254]). Gratian Caus. XXX. Qu. l. c. 8: All whom we receive in penance are as much our spiritual children as those whom the water of baptism regenerates, either when held by us or dipped by us. Sylvester, therefore, admonishes every priest never to approach in fornication his penitential child. *Ibid.* c. 9: Let a priest know that if he has been guilty of incontinence with a spiritual daughter, he has committed grave adultery. *Ibid.* c. 10: Neither bishop nor priest ought to have intercourse with those who have confessed their sins to him.

nence were formerly visited with three and four years' exclusion from communion and severe penance ([255]), incest and spiritual fornication with seven years ([256]).

34. The greatest crimes of this class are rape and unnatural offences. Rape consists in forcibly abducting or criminally assaulting an innocent girl against her will without any arrangement of marriage ([257]). It is not, therefore, deemed to have been committed if both parties afterwards are prepared to marry one another ([258]). It is usually dealt with as a civil crime because of the assault ([259]), and in that case the ecclesiatical discipline is made lighter. Unnatural crimes ([260]) are visited with exclusion from communion for from seven to fifteen years, because of the horror and disgust they create ([261]), and are mostly punished by civil tribunals ([262]).

35. In early days the contracting of a second marriage was altogether forbidden by the Church. Under the relaxed rule of the fourth century second marriages were tolerated except among the clergy, as being according to nature but a concession to human infirmity, provided those who entered upon them

---

([255]). Theodori Poenit. I. XIV. 9 and 11 in H. and S. III. 178. Baedae Poenit. III. 7, *Ibid.* p. 328, but Theodori Poenit. I. II. 1 says four years.

([256]). Baedae Poenit. III. 9, 11, 17, 18, *Ibid.* 328.

([257]). Gelasius, A.D. 494, ap. Gratian Caus. XXXVI. Qu. 1. c. 2: Rape is said to be committed when a girl, without any arrangement of marriage, is violently carried off. Caus. III. Qu. IV. c. 4; Const. 16 Edmund, A.D. 1236: Const. 4 Thorsby, A.D. 1363.

([258]). Lucius III. in Decret. Lib. V. Tit. XVII. c. 6.

([259]). Alexander III. in Decret. Lib. V. Tit. XVII. c. 4, says that by leave of the prince spiritual judges may take cognisance of rape.

([260]). Pseudo-Gregory III.'s Poenit. Can. 11 in Wasserschleben, p. 538: Incesti qui proprie illicitam commixtionem perpetrant.

([261]). Ambros. ap. Gratian Caus. XXXII. Qu. VII. c. 12: Minus est secundum naturam coire quam adversus naturam delinquere. Theodori Poenit. I. II. 3–6 in H. and S. III. 178; Const. 16 Edmund, A.D. 1236.

([262]). Remigius *Ibid.* Caus. XXIII. Qu. V. c. 39: There are some enormous crimes which are better judged by secular judges than by priests and governors of churches. . . . Princes of this world are principally constituted because of robbers, homicides, those guilty of rape. . . . Concil. Turon. III. A.D. 813, *Ibid.* c. 22, mentions incestuous persons, parricides, homicides as of civil cognisance.

underwent the discipline due to simple incontinence, and were suspended from communion for a time ([263]). By mediaeval rule clergy guilty of simple incontinence or concubinage who had not taken a vow of chastity were ordered to be suspended from office for forty days, and to undergo discipline in the bishop's discretion, after which they might be dispensed with, provided they had not intermeddled meanwhile with spiritual things ([264]). Such, however, as persisted in concubinage after being warned were ordered to be deprived ([265]); those guilty of adultery to be suspended for five or seven years ([266]); and those guilty of sacrilegious incest ([267]), spiritual fornication ([268]), or unnatural crime ([269]), to be imprisoned in a monastery for life. A pres-

(263). Apost. Const. 48 : If a layman marries a second wife or a divorced woman, let him be suspended. Theodori Poenit. I. XIV. 2 in H. and S. III. 187 : Digamus peniteat unum annum. See *Wedlock*, note 71.

(264). Concil. London A.D. 1108, Can. 9 : Priests who choose to leave their women and to serve God and His holy altars shall have vicars to officiate for them during the forty days in which they are to desist from their office, and are to have penance enjoined them at the bishop's discretion. Concil. Lat. IV. A.D. 1215, Can. 14 in Decret. Lib. III. Tit. l. c. 13 ; Const. 3 Edmund, A.D. 1236 ; Const. 16 Otho, A.D. 1237 : That those in holy orders keeping concubines do wholly discard them within a month. Const. 8 Othobon, A.D. 1268. See *Privileges of Order*, § 13.

(265). Alexander II. A.D. 1065 ap. Gratian I. Dist. LXXXI. c. 16 : Should any bishop, priest, or deacon hereafter take a woman or keep one, let him be deprived till he come to satisfaction, and neither remain in the choir of singers nor receive any portion from the things of the Church. Concil. London A.D. 1175, Can. 1 : If a priest publicly keeps a concubine and does not dismiss her upon a third admonition, let him be deprived. Concil. Lat. III. A.D. 1179, Can. 11 in Decret. Lib. V. Tit. XXXI. c. 4; Concil. Westminster A.D. 1200, Can. 10 ; Const. 31 Langton, A.D. 1222 : Let clergymen [keeping concubines] after admonition be restrained by subtraction of their benefice. Const. 5 Peckham, A.D. 1279, directs the reading of Othobon's Constitution to be looked upon as a monition. Lynd. 10.

(266). Concil. Aurel. III. A.D. 538, Can. 7 ap. Gratian I. Dist. LXXXI. c. 10 prescribes imprisonment in a monastery for life ; but Isidor. *Ibid.* Caus. XXXIII. Qu. II. c. 11, and Decret. Lib. V. Tit. XVI. c. 5 are more lenient.

(267). Concil. Aurel. III. A.D. 538, Can. 16.
(268). Gratian Caus. XXX. Qu. 1. c. 9.
(269). Concil. Elib. A.D. 305, Can. 7 ; Concil. Tolet. XVI. A.D. 691, Can.

Excesses.

byter accidentally guilty of drunkenness is ordered to be suspended for thirty days ([270]), and an habitual drunkard till he comes to satisfaction ([271]); a layman for a shorter time, according to circumstances ([272]).

EXCESSES PECULIAR TO SPECIAL POSITIONS IN THE CHURCH.

36. In addition to the above, there are excesses peculiar to particular ranks in the Church, the criminality of which consists in their being violations of specially undertaken obligations, or of disciplinary rules made by competent authority for those to whom they apply ([273]). From the clergy the Church expects obedience to all her laws ([274]), unless the same are dispensed with by local custom ([275]), and to them many things are forbidden which are tolerated in other Christians, who are

---

3, forbids those guilty of such offences to receive communion even at the hour of death. Concil. Westminster A.D. 1102, Can. 28 : Profligate obstinate sodomites were struck with anathema till by confession and penance they deserve absolution. If any ecclesiastical person be guilty of this crime, let him never be admitted to any higher order, and be degraded from that he holds. Theodori Poenit. I. II. in Haddan and Stubbs III. 178 ; Concil. Lat. III. A.D. 1179 in Decret. Lib. v. Tit. XXXI. c. 4 ; Const. 4 Thorsby, A.D. 1363.

(270). Concil. Agath. A.D. 506, Can. 41, prescribes either corporal punishment or thirty days' suspension. Const. 6 Edmund, A.D. 1236, forbids drinking bouts. See *Privileges of Order*, note 57.

(271). Apost. Can. 42 : Let a bishop, presbyter, or deacon who indulges in dice or drinking either leave off or be deprived. Theodori Poenit. L. I. 1 in H. and S. III. 177: If a bishop or any one in orders is an habitual drunkard, either let him desist or be deposed from his place. Baedae Poenit. VI. 1, *Ibid.* 331 : He who vomits from drunkenness, if a presbyter or deacon, [let him do penance] for forty days, a monk for thirty, a layman for twelve. Concil. Lat. IV. A.D. 1215, in Decret. Lib. III. Tit. l. c. 14.

(272). Theodori Poenit. I. I. 5 in H. and S. III. 177 ; Baedae Poenit. *Ibid.* p. 331.

(273). Cyprian, Testimonies against the Jews, III. 66 : The discipline of God is to be observed in Church precepts.

(274). Egbert's Excerpt. ; Const. 12 Wethershed, A.D. 1229 : Such as disobey are called transgressors. Lynd. 38, 316, 330.

(275). Augustin ap. Gratian Caus. XXXII. Qu. IV. c. 7 : Jacob had four wives, but because it was the custom it was not a crime.

not such by choice but by early initiation. Elsewhere their special duties have been set forth ([276]), any violation of which is accounted an excess. Clergy are also enjoined, under pain of deposition, not to plot or conspire against brother-clergy ([277]); not to disobey their bishop ([278]), save when he wantonly ([279]) invades a right ([280]); not to expose his wrong-doing before the world ([281]); and to respect ecclesiastical sentences, even when unjust ([282]).

37. Among excesses which are accounted particularly criminous for clergy may be mentioned bigamy ([283]), suing for spiritual matters before secular judges ([284]), contu-

(276). *Duties of Order*, § 10.

(277). See above, § 23.

(278). See *Ordinaries*.

(279). Gratian Caus. xv. Qu. 1. c. 2 ; Lynd. 263 : The presumption is in favour of a judge unless the contrary is shown ; but Lynd. 345 : Malice is presumed unless a just cause appears. *Id.* 15, 76.

(280). Concil. Aurel. A.D. 511, ap. Gratian Caus. II. Qu. VII. c. 20 : Should any one think to reclaim anything from his bishop, either in right of his Church or of his own right, let him not be removed from communion simply for convening him, so that he do not charge him with wrong-doing or crime. Decret. Lib. I. Tit. XXXIII. c. 8, and Lib. V. Tit. XXXI. c. 5.

(281). Apost. Const. II. 31 : He that casts reproach on his bishop by word or deed opposes God, not considering what He saith, Thou shalt not speak evil of the gods [Exod. XXII. 28]. Theodori Poenit. II. II. 9, in Haddan and Stubbs III. 191 : A priest may not expose the wrong-doing of his bishop, because the bishop is over him. See last note.

(282). Concil. Antioch. A.D. 341, ap. Gratian Caus. XI. Qu. III. c. 6 : If a bishop condemned by a synod, or a priest or deacon by his bishop, intermeddle with his ministry . . . let him never hope for restitution, or have opportunity of satisfaction in any other synod. Chrysost. *Ibid.* c. 30 and 31 ; Gregory *Ibid.* I. Dist. CI. c. 8 ; Alexander III. in Decret. Lib. II. Tit. XIV c. 2 ; Innocent III. *Ibid.* c. 6.

(283). Bigamy includes (1) marrying more than one wife, either successively or cotemporaneously, and (2) marrying a widow, a divorced, or a defiled woman. Apost. Const. III. 2 ; Elfric's Can. 9, A.D. 957. See *Order*, § 47.

(284). In addition to the authorities quoted, *Duties of Order*, note 12, may be added Concil. Arelat. II. A.D. 443, Can. 31 : If any clergyman presume to bring spiritual matters before secular judges, leaving the synod, let him be excommunicated by all. Concil. Autissiodor. A.D. 578, Can. 35 ; Concil.

Excesses.

macy (285), obtaining orders improperly, as by stealth, at a bound, out of the Embertides, when excommunicate, or for the second time (286), and neglecting clerical studies whilst holding a cure of souls (287). Should they be found to have offended in any of these matters, they should be visited with discipline regularly in consistory (288).

Tolet. III. A.D. 589 Can. 13 in Labbé VI. 700; Concil. Paris v. A.D. 675, Can. 3, *Ibid.* VL 1389; Concil. Cabilon. A.D. 649, Can. 11, *Ibid.* VII. 397; Pseudo-Isidor. ap. Gratian Caus. XI. Qu. 1. c. 10, 13, 14; Law 5, Northumbrian Priests, A.D. 950; Honorius III. in Decret. Lib. v. Tit. XXXI. c. 15, orders an archdeacon to be excommunicated for having, contrary to his oath of homage, and in violation of due reverence, raised a question with his bishop, touching a spiritual matter, in a court of law. Const. 1 and 5 Boniface, A.D. 1261: Even the writ called *juris utrum*, for trying the validity of an alienation of ecclesiastical property, did not issue in this country before the statutes 13 Ed. I. St. I. c. 24, A.D. 1285, and 14 Ed. III. St. I. c. 17, A.D. 1340; Const. 12 Stratford, A.D. 1343. For the cases in which a temporal court may be appealed to, see *Ordinaries.* Lynd. 93, 261, 146.

(285). Apost. Can. 29: If any bishop, or presbyter, or deacon, who is deprived justly for manifest crimes, does venture to meddle with that ministration which was once entrusted to him, let the same person be entirely cut off from the Church. Concil. Lat. IV. Can. 14, A.D. 1215, in Decret. Lib. III. Tit. l. c. 13, reproduced in Const. 3 Edmund, A.D. 1236: Those who, being suspended, do yet presume to officiate, are ordered not only to be deprived of their benefices, but to be for ever deposed for their double crime. Concil. Agath. A.D. 506, ap. Gratian I. Dist. l. c. 21. See chapter on *Ordinaries.* Const. 4 Boniface, A.D. 1261, says that contumacy is either simple or pregnant, and that simple contumacy merits excommunication. Const. 4 Thorsby mentions—(1) officiating whilst suspended, (2) whilst excommunicate, (3) communicating in crime with one excommunicate, (4) communicating with an excommunicate in divinis as instances of contumacy.

(286). Const. 4 Thorsby, A.D. 1363. *Havers* v. *Bp. of London,* No. 69 in Rothery's Report. See *Order,* § 40.

(287). Const. 4 Thorsby, A.D. 1363; Decret. Lib. III. Tit. L.

(288). Innocent ap. Gratian I. Dist. LXXXI. c. 6: Those priests who are said to have done such things you shall order to be summoned before all (in medio collocari), and upon hearing the charges made against them, if they are found guilty, to be removed from clerical office. Stat. Eccl. Ant. A.D. 505, *Ibid.* L Dist. XC. c. 1: Let the bishop reduce discordant clergy to reason, and the synod condemn the disobedient.

III.
DISCIPLINE OF THE RELIGIOUS LIFE.

THE RELIGIOUS LIFE.

1. The religious life has been defined to be "a systematised form of life according to the Gospel counsels, existing for its own sake, as a full expression of the Church's true and perfect life" ([1]). By early writers it was spoken of as "the angelic life," the heavenly citizenship, the apostolic life, the highest or the divine philosophy ([2]). Of it there are three varieties, viz. (1) the religious life in isolation, (2) the religious life in association, and (3) the religious life in common ([3]). The discipline of the religious life is the discipline imposed by rule on those who have embraced any one of these three forms.

2. Previously to the third century the religious life was chiefly pursued by isolated effort. Those who looked upon this world and the next as enemies ([4]) withdrew from their surroundings to cultivate asceticism in solitude ([5]), and for so doing the Church honoured them highly ([6]). Paul of Thebes.

(1). Gasquet, in Introduction to Montalembert's Monks of the West; Concil. Aurel. I. A.D. 511, Can. 11; Concil. Paris V. A.D. 615, Can. 13; Concil. Tolet. IV. A.D. 633, Can. 55; Concil. Tolet. X. A.D. 656, Can. 6; Const. 21 Peckham, A.D. 1281: The name of religious is by us appropriated to the monastic life.

(2). Epiphan. Haer. LXI. 4 calls it ὁ τῶν ἀγγέλων βίος. τὰ οὐράνια πολιτεύματα. ἀποστολικὸς βίος. Gregor. Nyss. Orat. Catech. c. 18: ἡ ὑψηλὴ φιλοσοφία ἔργῳ μᾶλλον ἢ λόγῳ κατορθουμένη. Nilus de Monast. Exercit. c. 8: ἡ κατὰ θεὸν φιλοσοφία.

(3). Isidor. de Orig. Offic. 16, 3: There are three kinds of monks—[1] anchorites (*i.e.*, solitaries), [2] eremites (desert-dwellers in associations), and [3] coenobites (those leading a common life).

(4). Clem. 2 Ep. ad Rom. c. 6.

(5). Devoti Inst. Lib. I. Tit. IX. § 2. See note 10.

(6). Apost. Const. VIII. 13 directs the ascetics to be communicated after the singers and before the deaconesses. Socrates VII. 17 relates that the

in the Decian persecution, and Antony in the following century, are usually spoken of as the pioneers of solitary asceticism [7], but it had its votaries before among those less known to fame [8]. In the pillar-saints of the fifth century it received its extreme development. Those who supported themselves whilst leading it were generally called *anchorites* [9] or *monks* [10], those whom others supported, *recluses*. In mediaeval times in the West none were allowed to become recluses without the bishop's or abbot's permission [11].

3. Religious life in association is said to have been introduced in the fourth century, in the Thebaid, by St. Pachomius [12]

Novatians made Paul the ascetic their bishop. See Chrysostom, Against the Opponents of Monastic Life, II. 4.

(7). Hieronym. Ep. 22 ad Eustoch. c. 36, calls Paul the founder, and Antony the illustrator, of anchorite life. Socrates I. 21. Paul died A.D. 340.

(8). Curzon, Monasteries of the East, relates that Fronto, with seventy brethren, is said to have retired to the villages on the natron lakes about 150 A.D. Simeon Stylites stood on a pillar in the neighbourhood of Antioch from A.D. 420 for more than forty years.

(9). ἀνωχωρῆται = retirers.

(10). An unknown author ap. Gratian Caus. XVI. Qu. 1. c. 8 : Let a monk know his name, for μόνος is Greek for *alone* (unus), and ἄχος is Greek for *sad* (tristis). Monk he is called because he is solitary and sad. Hieronym. *Ibid.* c. 5 : If you wish to be what you are called, a monk, *i.e.*, a solitary one (solus), what are you doing in cities, which are not abodes of solitary ones, but of crowds ?

(11). Concil. Venet. A.D. 465, Can. 7, forbids a monk to withdraw to a solitary cell without the abbot's leave. Concil. Agath. A.D. 506, Can. 58 ap. Gratian Caus. XVIII. Qu. IL. c. 13 : We forbid new hermitages (cellulas) or small congregations of monks to be established without the bishop's knowledge. Concil. Aurel. L A.D. 511, Can. 24, *Ibid.* c. 14 : Let no monk leaving the congregation of the monastery presume to erect a hermitage for purposes of ambition and vain-glory, without the bishop's permission and the will of the abbot. Bridgett's Hist. of the Eucharist, II. 181, gives a graphic account of the walling up of a recluse. Const. 31 Edmund, A.D. 1236, forbids men or women to be made close recluses without the bishop's license. Const. 9 Mepham, A.D. 1330 ; Lynd. 269.

(12). Pachomius, born 292, established, in A.D. 325, on the island of Tabennae, in the Nile, in Upper Egypt, a society, κοινόβιον, μάνδρα, or claustrum, which at the time of his death consisted of eight or nine mona-

and St. Macarius (¹³), and by St. Basil in Pontus and Cappadocia (¹⁴). Those who adopted it were called *hermits* (¹⁵). In that and the following centuries, notwithstanding the measures taken by the Emperor Valens to restrain it (¹⁶), the deserts of Egypt and Nitria swarmed with societies of associated hermits. As St. Basil is often spoken of as the founder of associated asceticism in the East, so St. Athanasius is in the West (¹⁷). St. Ambrose established a monastery at Milan (¹⁸). At the same time convents for both sexes were founded in Rome, notwithstanding the ill-will of the people (¹⁹). The small

steries, and contained 5000 monks, according to Sozomen III. 14, and a century later, 50,000. Socrates IV. 23, gives a list of holy monks. On the ground stated by Cassian de Inst. Coenob. x. 23, that "a working monk is plagued by one devil, whereas an idle one is torn to pieces by innumerable evil spirits," St. Pachomius' monks united agriculture, boat-building, basket-making, and mat-weaving with their spiritual exercises, and not only supported themselves thereby, but also the poor and the sick. They were divided into twenty-four classes, named after the letters of the alphabet, lived three in a cell, ate in common, kept strict silence, with the face covered, and made known their wants by signs.

(13). Macarius of Alexandria, chief of the recluses of Nitria, where were afterwards fifty monasteries (Sozomen VI. 37), retired into the Thebaid A.D. 335, established himself in the desert of Scetis A.D. 373, and died A.D. 394.

(14). St. Basil, born in 328 A.D., established a monastery at Pontus, 358, and was elected Bishop of Caesarea A.D. 370. His improved rule was accepted by 80,000 monks before his death in 379, and was translated by Rufinus for Western use.

(15). ἐρημῖται, from ἔρημος = desert-dwellers.

(16). Cod. Theodos. XII. I. 63 A.D. 365: Some partisans of idleness, leaving the duties of the community, take to solitudes and secret places, and, under pretence of the religious life, associate themselves with troops of Amazons. These and all such, when caught in Egypt, we have ordered to be ferreted out from their hiding-places by the Governor of the East, and to be compelled to discharge their duties towards their country.

(17). He introduced it in 340 A.D., when exiled.

(18). Augustin Confess. VIII. c. 6: There was a monastery at Milan, full of good brethren, outside the walls of the city, under Ambrose as its supporter. *Id.* de Moribus Eccles. Cath. I. 33: I have seen a place of entertainment for the saints at Milan, in number not a few, over whom one presbyter presided, a most excellent and learned man. Ambrose Ep. 5, 19.

(19). Hieronym. Ep. 96 de Laudibus Marcellae, A.D. 412; *Id.* Epist. 54

islands on the west coast of Italy([20]), and the islands on the Dalmatian coast ([21]), became important monastic seats. St. Martin first established in Gaul a monastery at Poitou ([22]), and afterwards, when he became Bishop of Tours, another in that city ([23]). Honoratus founded the celebrated monastery on the island of Lerina, now St. Honorat, about the year 400 A.D. ([24]). Others rose on the island of Lero or St. Marguerite, and the Stoechades on the south coast of France. John Cassian, who was educated among the Egyptian monks, founded two at Marseilles about 414 A.D. ([25]). Monasteries of hermits appear to have been numerous in the early Welsh, Irish, and Scottish Churches before they came under the influence of St. Benedict ([26]), the most celebrated being the two Bangor monasteries in Wales ([27]), and the Irish Bangor on the southern shore of the Belfast Lough.

ad Pammachium, A.D. 398 ; Augustin de Mor. Eccl. Cath. I. 33, A.D. 388 : I know of many places of entertainment for saints at Rome . . . where, not to be burdensome to any one, after the Eastern fashion and St. Paul's precept, they labour with their hands. I understand they practise almost incredible fastings, not refreshing the body once a day at nightfall, as is the most common custom, but going for three days or more without food or drink. Hieronym. Ep. 22 (al. 25) ad Paulam, relates that at the burying of a young nun supposed to have died of over-fasting, Blaesilla, a daughter of Paula, the people cried out, How long shall this detestable race of monks go without being expelled from the city ? Why are they not stoned or drowned ?

(20). Ambrose Hexaemeron III. c. 5 ; Hieronym. Ep. 84 (al. 30) de Morte Fabiolae, A.D. 400. Such were Gallinaria, now Galinara ; Gorgon, now Gorgona ; Capraria, now Capraia ; Palmaria, now Palmarola.

(21). Hieronym. Ep. 92 ad Julianum : You build monasteries, and a vast number of the saints are supported by you in the islands of Dalmatia.

(22). Monasterium Locociagense. See Severi Sulpicii Vita Martini and Gregory of Tours de Miraculis St. Martin IV. 30

(23). Majus Monasterium, corrupted into Marmoutier.

(24). Acta Sanctorum ad 16 Jan. Pliny, Nat. Hist. III. 5, calls the island Lerina, and the other island Lero. Sidonius, Carm. XVI. 104, calls it Lerinus, whence it is often abbreviated into Lerina.

(25). Cassian de Inst. Coenob. II. c. 2. He died after 432 A.D.

(26). Baeda II. 2 ; Haddan and Stubbs I. 122, and II. 142.

(27). Warren Leofric Missal IX. says that Bangor Fawr or Bangor

4. Already in the fifth century the irregular monastic life as then observed was becoming discredited, and the wandering of monks from place to place was condemned by conciliar authority (²⁸). In this country wandering was also discountenanced in the seventh century (²⁹). Monasteries were then founded in which the monks led a common life. One of the most celebrated of these monasteries was that of the Sleepless (ἀκοίμητοι), founded at Constantinople by Studius in the year 460 A.D. (³⁰). Throughout the West the rule of St. Basil gradually made way for the rule of St. Benedict, and religious life in common took the place of religious life in association. The rule of St. Basil continued to have adherents in some parts of Spain, Italy, Germany, and Sarmatia, but in this country only a few isolated societies of women survived the tenth century.

5. The extension of religious life in common, after the fashion of the early Church of Jerusalem, to the clergy, is usually referred to Eusebius of Vercellae, about 365 A.D., who required his clergy to live together under a common roof (³¹). His

Deiniol, in Carnarvonshire, was founded by Bishop Deiniol, circa 510 A.D.; Bangor Iscoed, in the valley of the Dee, in Flintshire, was founded somewhat earlier by Dunawd, father of Bishop Deiniol.

(28). Augustin de Opere Monach. c. 28, complains of monks wandering about from sheer love of idleness. Sozomen I. 12. *Id.* VI. 33, says that wandering monks were called βόσκοι, also Evagrius I. 21. See note 38. Concil. Chalcedon A.D. 451, Can. 23, forbids wandering; also Pelagius ap. Gratian Caus. XVI. Qu. l. c. 18. Justinian c. 51, C. de Epis. et Cler. *Ibid.* c. 40: Those monks shall enjoy the privilege of exemption who continue to dwell in monasteries, not those who wander about (*divagantes*).

(29). Wihtraed's Law 7, A.D. 693, in Haddan and Stubbs III. 234: If a shorn man [= a monk] go wandering about for hospitality, let it be given him once; and unless he have leave let it not be that any one entertain him longer.

(30). Nicephor, Hist. Eccl. XV. 23.

(31). Ambros. Ep. 63 ad Vercellenses, § 66: In the West, Eusebius of holy memory first combined these two distinct things; living in the city he clung to the regulation of monks, and governed the Church with the sobriety of fasting. Maximus, Bishop of Turin, circa 422 A.D., Serm. IX. de Eusebio in Muratorii Anecdot. Tom. iv. p. 88: That he might exhibit himself to all his clergy as a heavenly mirror of spiritual institutions,

Discipline of the Religious Life. 85

example was followed by St. Augustin of Hippo, whence a clergy-house was often called a monastery ([32]). The practice was introduced among the Franks by Chrodegang, Bishop of Metz, in the eighth century, and an improved rule drawn up for such communities by Amalarius was sanctioned by the Council of Aix, in 816 A.D. ([33]); but vows appear not to have been taken by clergy living in community before the eleventh century ([34]). Those who then took them were called regulars and Augustinian canons, because the rule they observed was based on the directions given by St. Augustine in his letter *ad sanctimoniales* ([35]).

6. In the eleventh century two well-established varieties of coenobites are found existing in the Western Church, viz. (1) lay-coenobites, generally called *monks*, who followed simply or with additions the rule either of St. Benedict or St. Basil, and (2) clerical coenobites or *canons regular*, who followed the rule of St. Augustin ([36]). Each of these rules had communities of

he gathered them all together under the enclosure of one roof, that they whose religious vow was one and undivided might lead a common life, and have a common table. Concil. Turon. II. A.D. 567, Can. 14, requires clergy and monks to have a common school and dormitory. Lingard's Anglo-Saxon Church, I. 150.

(32). Ambros. Serm. 355, Possidio Vit. Augustini, c. 5: Having been ordained presbyter, he quickly erected a clergy-house (monasterium) within the Church precincts, *Ibid.* c. 11; Augustin Sermones duo de Moribus Clericorum. Hieronym. ap. Gratian Caus. XII. Qu. 1. c. 5 and 7; Gregory *Ibid.* c. 8, say that clergy [*i.e.*, regular clergy] may possess nothing. Hist. Monast. de Abbendon II. 28, calls a country rectory monasterium.

(33). See *The Diocese*. Concil. Ensham A.D. 1009, Can. 1, requires canons to have a common dormitory and refectory. Const. 44 Langton, A.D. 1222, does the same.

(34). Warren's Leofric Missal, p. xxvi.; Haddan and Stubbs III. 461, say that "the first use of the word *canonici* in the sense of canons living in community, but without monastic vows, that occurs in English history" is in the legatine synod of Chelsea, A.D. 787.

(35). Ep. 109. See Augustin ap. Gratian Caus. XII. Qu. 1. c. 10, 11.

(36). Const. 40 Langton, A.D. 1222: That monks, canons regular, and nuns eat in one refectory. Concil. Educ. ap. Gratian Caus. XIX. Qu. III. c. 1, forbids monks to draw off canons regular from their own rule to monasticism. See *Religious Orders*, § 8.

women as well as of men ([37]). The professed members of a lay-society were called cloistered *monks* or *minikins*, and were restricted to the cloister-walls ([38]), those of a clerical society *canons regular* or *canonesses*. Nunneries where minikins dwelt were directed to be placed under the protection of monasteries ([39]), but at some distance from them, because of the wiles of the devil and the tongues of men ([40]). In many places there existed double monasteries ([41]), and in this country some monasteries were under a lady-abbess ([42]).

7. As the northern nations for the most part first became acquainted with Christianity through the teaching of monastic missionaries, so the common form of the religious life was the one which commended itself most to their sympathies, besides being in itself best adapted to a northern climate and the prevailing system of agriculture. Under the conviction of its truth, thousands of men and women—the noblest, the wisest, the best, and the most cultured—turned their backs on the world, overcame

(37). Concil. Lat. II. A.D. 1139, Can. 26 ap. Gratian Caus. XVIII. Qu. II. c. 25 : We desire that the pernicious and detestable custom of certain women be abolished who desire to be looked upon as minikins, although they conform neither to the rule of St. Basil, Benedict, or Augustin. Lynd. 213.

(38). Alexander II. ap. Gratian Caus. XVI. Qu. 1. c. 11 ; Concil. Ebor. A.D. 1195, Can. 14 : That all opportunity of wandering may be taken away, we forbid [monks, canons regular, and nuns] to take to farm *Obediences*, or to take long travels, or go out of their monasteries without some certain reasonable cause. Can. 15 : That nuns do not go out of the verge of their monastery but in the company of their abbess or prioress.

(39). Concil. Hispal. II. A.D. 619, Can. 11 ap. Gratian Caus. XVIII. Qu. II. c. 24.

(40). Concil. Agath. A.D. 506, Can. 28, *Ibid.* c. 23. Concil. Augustodun. A.D. 670, Can. 10. Baeda IV. 25, relates the disgrace of the nuns of Coldingham, A.D. 684, which called forth canons of Clovesho, A.D. 747.

(41). Double monasteries existed at Whitby, Wimborne, Barking (Baeda IV. 7) and Coldingham. See notes 81, 216, 254.

(42). Theodori Poenit. II. VII. 8, in Haddan and Stubbs III. 195, condemns but tolerates the practice. Syn. VII. A.D. 787, Can. 20 ap. Gratian Caus. XVIII. Qu. II. c. 21, also condemns it. Lingard's Anglo-Saxon Church I. 212, 227. Nevertheless double monasteries were not unknown in this country in later foundations. See *Religious Orders*, § 11.

the fervid impulses of youth, and abandoned all that seemed fairest and most attractive in life, in order to present themselves to God a living sacrifice, and to serve Him with undistracted mind. Can it be wondered at that, when in the sixteenth century the monasteries were blackened by the calumnies of sacrilege and oppression, the religious life of the people was for a time brought to a standstill?

GILDS, CONFRATERNITIES, SOCIETIES, CONGREGATIONS.

8. The simplest form of voluntary association for a united purpose is that of a religious gild or confraternity. A religious *gild* has been defined to be an association of Christians directed by spiritual authority, having for its object the performance of some special work of piety or philanthropy ([43]). It is distinguished from a confraternity in that a gild aims at fulfilling something more than the minimum of Christian duty by a simple promise or vow to do some particular works of piety ([44]), whereas a *confraternity* is an association in which the whole life is devoted to some religious or philanthropic work, and

---

([43]). Theodorus a Spiritu Sancto Pars. II. c. II. art. 2 § 1 : Confraternitates fidelium sunt congregationes in unum quandoque convenientium ad quaedam pietatis officia obeunda, ecclesiastica auctoritate institutae. See Béringer, Les Indulgences, 1890, vol. II. p. 2. Craisson, § 4654, says: Fidelium congregationes ad exercenda pia opera auctoritate ecclesiastica institutae. Hatch, Bampton Lectures, p. 26, traces the origin of the Church to a series of gilds whose essential feature was poverty. *Ibid.* 35.

([44]). Toulmin Smith, in his Introduction to English Gilds (Early English Text Society, No. 40): "The gilds were lay bodies, and existed for lay purposes, and the better to enable those who belong to them rightly and understandingly to fulfil their neighbourly duties as freemen in a free state." The Cambridge gild in Kemble's Saxons I. 513 recites: In this writ is the notification which the brotherhood hath made at the thanes' gild of Grantabyrig. That is, that each give oath upon the relics to the rest that he would hold true brotherhood for God and for the world, and all the brotherhood to support him that hath the best right. If any gild brother die, all the gildship is to bring him where he desired to lie, . . . and let each brother contribute 2d. to the alms, and out of this sum let what is fitting be taken to St Ethelthryth. . . .

is initiated by a solemn vow. A gild becomes a *society* or corporation when its members adopt for certain purposes a common life, or acquire collectively some foundation property (⁴⁵), although the members are not thereby withdrawn from their own family life, and do not part with their own private property. A confraternity becomes a *congregation* when a common life is part of the rule (⁴⁶), coupled with solemn admission, a novitiate, and a special habit.

9. There existed in former times numerous religious gilds and societies in nearly every town and parish in this country (⁴⁷), the objects of which were invariably threefold, viz.—(1) some particular form of charity or temporal good to others; (2) some work of piety or spiritual good; and (3) some kind of social entertainment for mutual benefit (⁴⁸).

10. As a work of temporal charity some undertook the care of the sick, the aged, and the unfortunate through fire or shipwreck (⁴⁹); others helped prisoners or pilgrims, or contributed funds to redeem captives from the infidels, like the celebrated gild of the Gonfalonieri. Others made it their

---

(45). The term foundation includes (1) fundatio incipiens, or the act of incorporation, and (2) fundatio perficiens, or the dotation. He who makes the first dotation is the founder in law. Stephens' Eccl. Stat. 471, who observes, p. 88, that prior to the statute 15 Ric. II. c. 5, A.D. 1391, restrictions in mortmain did not extend to lands purchased for gilds or fraternities, but only to those purchased for the religious.

(46). Lynd. 151. Congregations existed as corporations aggregate (1) by common consent or repute, as well as (2) by explicit foundation, before the statute 23 Hen. VIII. c. 12. That statute forbad corporations to take property to *religious* uses for more than twenty years, but left unimpaired their power of taking property to charitable uses. The statute 1 Ed. VI. c. 14, took away the property from all. Corporations for charitable purposes were made legal by 14 Eliz. c. 14, and 43 Eliz. c. 4 (Stephens' Eccl. Stat. 494), and hospitals by 39 Eliz. c. 5, A.D. 1597.

(47). Taylor's Index Monasticus gives a list of 909 in the county of Norfolk only.

(48). The ἀγαπή is the association-meal in the great gild of the Church.

(49). Exeter Gild in Kemble's Saxons in England I. 512: At a house-burning let each man contribute one penny. Gild of Wigendale in Toulmin Smith, p. 117.

Discipline of the Religious Life. 89

business to keep highways, bridges, and city walls in repair; others, again, to build churches, or to supply vestments and chalices to those that required them; others supported schools. These religious gilds must not be confounded either with the *frith-gilds* ([50]), the object of which was the preservation of the king's peace, the protection of life, and the prosecution of thieves; nor yet with the *hansas* or *merchant-gilds*, the object of which was the promotion of trade ([51]).

11. Together with works of temporal charity were combined works of spiritual piety, such as the comfort of the dying, the burial of the dead ([52]), praying for the souls of gild-members alive or dead, the provision of devotional lights in churches ([53]), the ringing of church bells. And to these were

(50). Lingard's Anglo-Saxon Church II. 62; Stubbs' Const. Hist. I. 413.

(51). Stubbs, p. 414. J. Brooking Rowe in Trans. Devon. Assoc. VIII. 821, states that in 1236 A.D. the abbot and monks of Bucfast became members of the Merchants' Gild at Totnes.

(52). Exeter Gild in Kemble, p. 512: The Assembly was collected in Exeter for the love of God and for our soul's need, both in regard to our health of life here, and to the after-days which we desire for ourselves by God's doom. We have agreed that our meeting shall be thrice in the 12 months—(1) at Michaelmas; (2) at St. Mary's mass after midwinter [2 Feb.]; and (3) at All Hallows' mass. And let the mass priest at each of our meetings sing two masses—one for the living friends, the other for the dead; and let each brother of common condition sing two psalters of Psalms, one for the living and one for the dead; and at the death of a brother each man 6 masses or 6 psalters; and at a death each man 5 pence. Abbotsbury gild in Monast. Angl. I. 278. Judicia civitatis Londin. in Kemble I. 243: And we have ordained respecting every man who has given his wed [contract] in our gildship, if he should die that each gild brother should give a gesuful loaf (*i.e.*, an ubble) for his soul, and sing 50 (psalms) or get them sung within 30 days.

(53). Gild of Wigendale in Toulmin Smith, p. 117: Also, if a gild-fellow die, *i.e.*, perish by water or by land, then shall the gild brethren go seek him 3 mile about and bring him to Christian burial, and the light before him to dirge and church, *i.e.*, a torch that shall burn at the elevation of the mass every Sunday. And when the brethren and sistern be gathered at their general day what good man come to our fraternity, he shall have meat and drink while it will last. Stratford-on-Avon gild, *Ibid.* p. 25, requires payments to be made four times a year, and from this fund one wax-taper to be kept up. "And the taper shall be kept alight every day

added festal celebrations or gatherings for social entertainment on stated days, when, under the management of the steward and caterers, the gild-members met for mutual benefit to both body and soul, and invited others also to partake of their hospitality ([54]).

12. Among religious gilds the associations of the secular clergy for mutual instruction and the observance of a common rule, after the fashion of the frith-gilds or lay-tithings ([55]), have had a lasting effect, and have developed into the institution of rural-deaneries. The members of these gilds were pledged to stand by one another for satisfaction ([56]) if a gild-member were wronged ([57]), to act as compurgators, to the required number of six or twelve ([58]) if a member were falsely accused, to abstain from meddling with the gild-relations of outsiders ([59]),

throughout the year at every mass in the Church before the blessed cross, so that God, and the Blessed Virgin, and the venerable Cross may keep all the brethren and sistern from ill."

(54). Judicia civitatis Londin. in Kemble I. 242 : That we gather to us once in every month if we can have leisure. . . . And let the 12 men have their refection together, and feed themselves as they think right, and deal the remains of the meal for the love of God.

(55). Kemble's Saxons I. 238, 250 ; Stubbs' Const. Hist. L 414 ; Brown in St. Paul's Eccl. Society III. 239.

(56). Laws of Satisfaction 7, A.D. 725 : Of satisfaction made for violation of orders one share belongs to the bishop, a second to the altar, a third to the fraternity.

(57). Laws of Northumbrian Priests 1, A.D. 950 : If any wrong be offered to a priest, let all his mates, with the help of the bishop, be very zealous for satisfaction.

(58). Law 5 Cnut, A.D. 1017 : If it happen that a priest who lives regularly be impleaded for crimes and want of skill, and he knows himself to be clear, let him make his purgation by himself alone if it be a single accusation [i.e., made by three men]. If the accusation be double [i.e., made by four men] let him purge himself together with two of the same order with him. If he be impleaded by a triple accusation [made by six], let him take six of the same order. Law 19 Cnut, A.D. 1018 ; Concil. London A.D. 1108, Can. 4 : Let him make his purgation by six witnesses. Can. 12 Westminster, A.D. 1200 ; Const. 10 Stratford, A.D. 1342.

(59). Edgar's Law 9, A.D. 960.

Discipline of the Religious Life. 91

and on the death of a member to say each one a trental of psalms for the repose of his soul ([60]).

13. For the establishment of a frith-gild or a merchant-gild no religious recognition is necessary. For the establishment of a religious gild the sanction of the incumbent who has the cure of souls is requisite, and also that of the bishop for any self-governing congregation ([61]). This sanction carries with it three things: (1) the rule is thereby admitted to be an allowed rule of the Church; (2) the cure of souls of the members is committed to the head of the congregation; and (3) the congregation becomes extra-parochial and extra-diocesan to the extent that all monastic institutions are ([62]).

14. A congregation which exists for a philanthropic purpose is called a *hospital* ([63]); one which exists for educational

[60]. Concil. London A.D. 940.

[61]. Concil. Agath. A.D. 506, Can. 27 ap. Gratian Caus. XVIII. Qu. II. c. 12: Let no one presume to found a new monastery without the bishop's permission or approval. Concil. Chalcedon A.D. 457, Can. 4: That no one anywhere build or establish a monastery contrary to the will of the diocesans. Concil. Montpellier A.D. 1215: Non fiant de caetero confratriae nisi accedente episcoporum auctoritate. Const. 31 Edmund, A.D. 1236; Lynd. 157, 166, 214; Béringer, Les Indulgences II. 8.

[62]. Concil. Tolet. IV. A.D. 633, Can. 50 ap. Gratian Caus. XVIII. Qu. II. c. 1: Let bishops (sacerdotes) claim no more authority over a monastery than the canons allow them, viz. [1] to exhort monks to a holy conversation, [2] to institute abbots and other offices, and [3] to correct breaches of rule. Craisson, § 4663. See note 83.

[63]. Some hospitals, says Coke 342, (a), are [1] corporations aggregate of many, as of master or warden and his confrères; some [2] where the master or warden hath alone the estate or inheritance in him, and the brethren or sisters have power of consent, having a college or common seal. It has been held that only hospitals founded for superstitious purposes (to which the statute 2 Hen. V. St. I. c. 1, A.D. 1414 refers) were included in the statute 31 Hen. VIII. c. 13, which abolished monasteries and abbeys, that act applying only to regular and not to secular foundations. Stephens 239, *Id.* 470, observes that hospitals at which [3] the master or warden "hath the estate in view, but they have no college or common seal," cannot be deemed incorporations, the master or warden being merely a trustee for the house.

purposes a *college* (⁶⁴); one whose sole aim is the religious life a *convent* (⁶⁵). At the beginning of the thirteenth century the Fourth Lateran Council forbad the establishment of any new congregations for the religious life, except upon one of the three existing rules of St. Basil, St. Benedict, or St. Augustin (⁶⁶). In this country all congregations for the exercise of the religious life were abolished by Henry VIII. (⁶⁷); and by Edward VI. all the property of "colleges, free-chapels, chantries, hospitals, brotherhoods, and gilds," except those existing for trading purposes, was forfeited to the Crown (⁶⁸).

Religious Societies or Houses.

15. In its origin a religious house is an associated monastic household, consisting of members who have renounced the world in order the better to devote themselves to God's service by a systematised course of life, but still are free to come and to go and to place themselves in some other household as they find most conducive to holiness. When the inmates live apart in separate cells, the association is called a *laura* (⁶⁹); when they lead a common life, and have all things in common, a *convent*. The household belongs to the abbot, called ἀββᾶς, ἡγούμενος, or

(64). The two universities and their colleges were refounded by 13 Eliz. c. 29, A.D. 1570, because they were included in sec. 9 of 1 Ed. VI. c. 14.
(65). Honorius III. in Decret. Lib. V. Tit. XXXI. c. 14, says that private persons "associating themselves together cannot regularly constitute a college unless it is specially conceded to them." This must be understood in a religious sense. Otherwise it was not the law here. See note 46.
(66). Can. 13 in Decret. Lib. III. Tit. XXXV. c. 9; Const. 31 Edmund, A.D. 1236: Because diversity of religion brings confusion into the Church, we charge that they who will found a new religious house or hospital take from us the rule and institution of it. Concil. Lugdun. II. A.D. 1274, in Sext. Lib. III. Tit. XVII. c. 1; Concil. Vien. A.D. 1311, in Clem. Lib. III. Tit. XL. c. 1, condemns the Beguins.
(67). See Gasquet's Henry VIII. and the English Monasteries.
(68). 37 Hen. VIII. c. 4, A.D. 1545, and 1 Ed. VI. c. 14. The last acts were so general that the colleges of Oxford and Cambridge, Winchester and Eton had to purchase mercy. Only trading gilds were exempt.
(69). Evagrius I. 21.

ἀρχιμανδρίτης, who presides over it in temporal concerns, and makes rules affecting the inmates, to which all are subject as long as they continue inmates; but originally the abbot had no rule over the members in spiritual matters.

16. A new departure was taken in the sixth century in the West by the rule of St. Benedict, which substituted religious life in common for associated religious life, and to the customary ascetic vows of poverty and chastity added a further one, that of permanent obedience to the abbot. Thereby, in accordance with the then customary feudal ideas, the monk became the abbot's man, and the latter could reclaim him as such [70], just as a bishop could reclaim a runaway clerk [71]. The legal possession of whatever property belonged to the house, and the sole disposal of it, lay with the abbot as the only person competent to own property, all monks being accounted dead men in law [72]. In the use, nevertheless, which he made of it he was called upon to consider the purposes for which it had been given, to treat his monks as his children, to provide them with necessaries to the utmost of his ability [73]; not to waste the estate [74], or to grant leases of it, or to alienate it without the consent of the family [75] and the bishop [76], and

---

[70]. Concil. Aurel I. A.D. 511, Can. 19: Those who have wandered away when found shall be recalled to custody by the help of the bishop. Gregory IX. in Decret. Lib. III. Tit. XXXI. c. 24: Let abbots and priors every year carefully seek out those who have deserted or been ejected from their monasteries, and excommunicate them if they refuse to return. Ayliffe 13.

[71]. Concil. Arelat. IV. A.D. 524, Can. 4.

[72]. Innocent III. in Decret. Lib. I. Tit. III. c. 21, states that abbots are *ex officio* bound to act as proctors in the affairs of their congregations. Coke I. Inst. sec. 133: Abbots, priors, and other religious and secular persons are dead persons in law, and have capacity to have lands and goods only for the benefit of the house, and cannot make any testament. Ayliffe 11; 52 Hen. III. c. 28, A.D. 1267, and Stephens' Eccl. Stat. 5. See note 195.

[73]. Concil. Cloveaho A.D. 747, Can. 4.

[74]. *Ibid.*

[75]. Concil. Chelsea A.D. 816, Can. 7, says for not more than one life. Honorius III. in Decret. Lib. III. Tit. XXXV. c. 8.

[76]. Concil. Agath. A.D. 506, ap. Gratian Caus. XVII. Qu. IV. c. 40; Gre-

not to admit more members than the estate could support ([77]). An abbot was, moreover, forbidden to convert an exempt into a non-exempt monastery, or to unite a church which belonged to himself in full right (*pleno jure*) ([78]) without the consent of the brethren.

17. At first the abbot was regarded as the lay-lord only of the house, and had no cure of souls ([79]). He was himself a layman ([80]), and according to English use often a lay-woman ([81]). The Celtic monasteries of associated hermits had their own bishop, who was under the abbot, but there were in Saxon times abbeys which had no presbyters among their members ([82]). The Gallican and the Roman rule made the abbot subject to the bishop's visitation ([83]); the old English rule placed him

gory *Ibid.* c. 41; Concil. Epaon. A.D. 517, Can. 8; Const. Kempe, A.D. 1444.

(77). Concil. Clovesho A.D. 747, Can. 28.

(78). Coelestin. in Decret. Lib. v. Tit. XXXI. c. 8.

(79). Gregory Ep. 11, A.D. 594, ap. Gratian Caus. XVI. Qu. I. c. 38: They who as presbyters, deacons, or other clergy of whatever order, in any way discharge the active service of a Church (ecclesiis militant), you cannot allow to be abbots over monasteries.

(80). Wihtraed's Dooms, A.D. 696, Can. 18; Egbert's Answers 7, 11, and 12; Gregory ap. Gratian Caus. XVI. Qu. l. c. 2: No one can preside over the government of a monastery whilst daily obliged to continue in the service of the Church.

(81). Gregory ap. Gratian Caus. XVIII. Qu. II. c. 20, forbids women to have the run of monasteries, or monks to employ them to manage their households (commatres). Theodori Poenit. II. VI. 8 in Haddan and Stubbs III. 195: Men may not preside over women monks, nor women over men; yet we do not destroy the custom which prevails in this land. In 700 A.D., four out of the eight monasteries in Kent are found governed by abbesses. H. and S. III. 242.

(82). Concil. Clovesho A.D. 747, Can. 5; Ayliffe 12.

(83). Concil. Aurel. I. A.D. 511, Can. 19 ap. Gratian Caus. XVIII. Qu. II. c. 16; Concil. Arelat. v. Can. 2, A.D. 554, *Ibid.* c. 17; Gregory *Ibid.* c. 19 and 23; Concil. Rothomag. A.D. 650, *Ibid.* c. 29: Not once but often in the year let bishops visit monasteries, and if aught be amiss, let it be amended. Egbert's Excerpt. 62, A.D. 740: Let abbots continue under the power of the bishop, and if they transgress their rule let the bishops correct them. Concil. Autissiodor. A.D. 578, Can. 23, directs an abbot to be sent to another monastery to do penance who fails to inform the bishop or archdeacon of

Discipline of the Religious Life. 95

under the archbishop ([84]); and to preserve the ancient freedom of monks to place themselves under whom they pleased, the rule of St. Benedict gave to the community the power of electing their abbot with the bishop's assistance ([85]), and required him when elected to be admitted to office by the bishop's benediction ([86]). By the rule of the ninth century the abbot was himself required to be in Holy Orders ([87]); and then, under the influence of the same causes which perfected the parochial system in the eleventh century, the household became a recognised centre of religious ministrations, of which the abbot was deemed to have the cure of souls ([88]). He then nominated to the bishop those who were required to be ordained for the

the offences of a monk. Concil. Lat. III. A.D. 1179, in Decret. Lib. v. Tit. XXXI. c. 5, authorises abbots to refuse more than canonical obedience. Innocent III. *Ibid.* Lib. III. Tit. XXXV. c. 8; Honorius III. *Ibid.* Lib. v. Tit. III. c. 43, requires Cistercian abbots to take an oath of canonical obedience to the bishop.

(84). Wihobaed's privilege, A.D. 692, Can. 3: When an abbot departs this life let it be notified to the archbishop, and let such an one as is worthy be chosen with his advice and consent.

(85). Gregory ap. Gratian Caus. XVIII. Qu. II. c. 3 and 4; Theodori Poenit. II. VI. 3, A.D. 680, in Haddan and Stubbs III. 195: The congregation ought to choose for themselves an abbot after a death. Concil. Chelsea A.D. 787, Can. 5: If an abbot departs this life, let religious pastors of approved life be chosen from among themselves in the Lord, with the advice of the bishop within whose parish the monastery is situate. Concil. Chelsea A.D. 816, Can. 4.

(86). Boniface, writing to Cuthbert, A.D. 746, in Haddan and Stubbs III. 381, calls those robbers and sacrilegious persons who intrude themselves into monasteries without the bishop. Concil. Chelsea A.D. 816, Can. 8; Concil. London A.D. 1126, Can. 3: That at the blessing of abbots a cope, a carpet, a towel, a basin be not demanded. Concil. Westminster A.D. 1138, Can. 3; Alexander IV. in Sext. Lib. v. Tit. VII. c. 3; Chron. Monast. de Abbendon II. 281, relates that when Siward, who was elected abbot in 1034 A.D., received the benediction, to all the customary interrogatories he answered No, but when asked if he wished to be blessed, replied, I desire to have God's blessing and yours.

(87). Concil. Clovesho A.D. 803, in Haddan and Stubbs III. 545, forbids the future appointment of laymen and seculars as abbots.

(88). Concil. Westminster A.D. 1102, Can. 18.

spiritual needs of his household ([89]), and appointed confessors for his monks ([90]). His jurisdiction thus extending over clergy as well as over laity, he was accounted a prelate ([91]), in token whereof he used a pastoral staff ([92]), and had a seal of office ([93]). If he had been blessed he was allowed to bestow minor orders upon his subjects ([94]), and to give the solemn benediction to the people in Churches belonging to himself in full right (*pleno jure*) ([95]).

18. As being the head of a religious household ([96]), an abbot was always required to be of approved life ([97]), and by mediaeval rule might not be admitted to office until he had himself made the profession of a monk ([98]). That he might have abundant evidence of his own holy life, he was directed to change his chaplain every year ([99]). It was declared to be his duty to see that his subjects were regular in their conversation ([100]), and that they applied themselves to reading and study ([101]); but his authority was strictly confined to his own subjects ([102]).

([89]). Const. I. Reynolds, A.D. 1322: We enjoin abbots and priors not to cause their monks and canons to be ordained by any bishop except the diocesan.

([90]). Concil. Westminster A.D. 1102, Can. 18: That monks enjoin penance to none without their abbot's consent.

([91]). Ayliffe 6; Const. 35 Langton, A.D. 1222.

([92]). Chron. Monast. de Abbendon II. 286, relates that when Faritius was appointed abbot in 1102 A.D., he placed his pastoral staff above the altar directly after mass, because Archbishop Anselm was then in exile.

([93]). Const. 28 Otho, A.D. 1237.

([94]). Innocent III. A.D. 1210, to the Archbishop of Rouen, in Decret. Lib. I. Tit. XIV. c. 11; Alexander IV. in Sext. Lib. V. Tit. VII. c. 3.

([95]). Alexander IV. l. c.

([96]). Alexander IV. in Sext. Lib. v. Tit. VII. c. 3.

([97]). Gregory ap. Gratian Caus. XVIII. Qu. II. c. 3 and 4; Wihtraed's Privilege, A.D. 692, Can. 3: Let such an one as is worthy be chosen. Concil. Chelsea A.D. 787, Can. 5.

([98]). Const. 19 Otho, A.D. 1237.

([99]). Const. 37 Langton, A.D. 1222.

([100]). Concil. Clovesho A.D. 747, Can. 4.

([101]). *Ibid.* I. Can. 7.

([102]). Theodori Poenit. II. VI. 16, in Haddan and Stubbs III. 196: A monastery has no power of imposing penance on seculars, because that is

Even when by special privilege he had peculiar jurisdiction over the parishioners of his own churches, he could not conclude in matrimonial causes, enjoin public penance, nor grant indulgences without the bishop's sanction ([103]).

19. When the abbot had thus acquired a quasi-episcopal position, the cure of souls of the community was usually exercised under him by the prior and sub-prior, and the care of the temporal concerns by other officers, called obedientials. A prior is the acting head in spirituals of a religious house; the sub-prior is his deputy. Priors are, however, said to be of three kinds ([104]), viz. (1) *claustral*, (2) *conventual*, and (3) *secular*. A claustral prior is the abbot's deputy in spirituals, where there is an abbot ([105]). A conventual prior is the actual, as well as the acting, head of a smaller religious house, where there is no abbot. He has therefore charge of the temporalities as well as the spiritualities, and as such is called *provost* ([106]). A secular prior is the head of a body of secular clergy having the cure

---

proper to the clergy. Concil. Westminster A.D. 1102, Can. 18: That abbots give no license to enjoin penance to any but such whose souls are entrusted to their care.

([103]). Paschal II. ap. Gratian Caus. XVI. Qu. 1. c. 9 : It has reached our ears that certain monks and abbots arrogantly assume in your diocese episcopal rights and offices contrary to the decrees of the holy fathers, to wit, penance, the remission of sins, and reconciliation, tithes, and churches—this we entirely forbid. Ayliffe 13.

([104]). Concil. Lat. III. A.D. 1179, in Decret. Lib. III. Tit. XXXV. c. 2, names claustral and conventual priors; Honorius III. *Ibid.* Tit. XXXVII. c. 3 and 4, conventual priors; Clement V. in Clem. Lib. I. Tit. II. c. 2, claustral priors.

([105]). Concil. London A.D. 1126, Can. 7: That none be promoted to a deanery or priory save a presbyter. Innocent III. in Decret. Lib. III. Tit. XXXV. c. 6: But let the prior next after the abbot be powerful before the rest in deed and discourse, so that he may be able both to teach the brethren by example of life and word of doctrine, and also to reclaim them from evil; having a conscientious zeal for religion, so that he may upbraid and correct offenders, but cherish and comfort the dutiful.

([106]). Concil. Vien. A.D. 1311, in Clem. Lib. III. Tit. x. c. 1, § 7: Let no conventual priory be given to any one unless he has attained his twenty-fifth year.

of souls of a collegiate church ([107]). The two latter have a perpetual office, and are dignitaries, but a claustral prior is not ([108]).

20. Those who take charge of the temporal concerns of a religious house under an abbot are termed *obedientials*. Such are the chamberlain, the kitchener, the cellarer, the refectioner, the infirmarer, the hosteller or dispenser, and the hayward ([109]). All these are required to render up their accounts twice or four times a year before the community according to custom, but this rule does not apply to any private estates which they may hold as a benefice of office distinct from those of the convent ([110]). By the rule of the thirteenth century, obediences or benefices of office were forbidden to be granted as freeholds ([111]). Both priories and obediences were also forbidden to be given for money ([112]), but those who hold them are permitted to farm manors or tithes belonging to their own monasteries ([113]).

([107]). Innocent III. in Decret. Lib. III. Tit. xxxv. c. 5, and Tit. xxxvi. c. 5. Ayliffe 7.

([108]). Concil. Lat. III. A.D. 1179, Can. 10, in Decret. Lib. III. Tit. xxxv. c. 2; Concil. Westminster A.D. 1200, Can. 15: Let not priors once appointed be removed except for dilapidations, incontinence, or some manifest cause.

([109]). Hist. Monast. de Abbendon II. 384 enumerates the above, A.D. 1230. Berkshire Domesday mentions the kitchener as holding an estate of the abbey of Abingdon.

([110]). Const. 35 Langton, A.D. 1222: That the obedientials of monasteries, as well as the greater prelates, do twice or four times in the year yield up their accounts before the brethren, or before their superiors, according to the custom of the monastery. Such prelates as have estates distinct from those of the monks are not bound by this constitution.

([111]). Innocent III. in Decret. Lib. III. Tit. xxxv. c. 6: Nor let any benefice of office (obedientia) be given to any one to be held by him as a perpetuity for life. Ayliffe 6.

([112]). Concil. Lat. III. A.D. 1179, Can. 10 in Decret. Lib. III. Tit. xxxv. c. 2; Concil. Ebor. A.D. 1195, Can. 14: We forbid monks to take to farm such places as are called obediences. Concil. Westminster A.D. 1200, Can. 15.

([113]). Const. 46 Langton, A.D. 1222: Let neither a canon regular nor monk take any church [rights to tithes] or manor to farm that belongs to

21. When a religious house has once been established, and become (as it could not fail to become in a heathen country) the centre of the religious life of a neighbourhood, it may not be removed elsewhere without the consent of the bishop and the congregation, and in every case of transfer a priest must be left behind to care for the religious needs of the people ([114]).

ADMISSION TO THE RELIGIOUS LIFE.

22. The religious life may be entered upon in one of two ways ([115]): (1) by being dedicated to it in childhood, which is equivalent to a tacit profession ([116]); and (2) by voluntarily undertaking its vows, which is an express profession. As all public vows admit of two degrees ([117]), so there are two degrees in the profession of religion: (1) a lower degree, of those who have expressed a desire to enter it, and are called the converted ones (*conversi*) ([118])—postulants, petitioners or novices; and (2)

his own Church, nor have any manor committed to his custody, unless he be an obediential. Hist. Monast. de Abbendon II. 299, A.D. 1188: The chamberlain ought to hold [Welford and Chieveley] as freely and independently as the abbot holds his.

(114). Theodori Poenit. II. VI. 7 in Haddan and Stubbs III. 195; Gratian Caus. XVI. Qu. VII. c. 41; Concil. Lugdun. A.D. 1274, in Sext. Lib. III. Tit. XVII. c. 1, requires Papal consent. Const. 2 Kempe, A.D. 1444.

(115). Concil. Tolet. IV. A.D. 633, ap. Gratian Caus. XX. Qu. III. c. 2, and Qu. I. c. 3: A monk becomes such either by his father's dedication of him, or by his own profession. Whichever it be, when it is concluded, it will be binding on him (alligatum tenebit). Gregory II. A.D. 726, *Ibid.* c. 2: If a father or mother have placed a son or daughter within the bounds of a monastery in years of infancy under a regular rule ... such ought not when they have grown up to go forth and indulge in matrimony.

(116). Devoti Lib. I. Tit. IX. § 13.

(117). See *Discipline Generally*, § 26.

(118). Concil. Aurel. I. A.D. 511, Can. 21, speaks of monks either (1) conversi, or (2) qui acceperunt pallium; Gregory, A.D. 599, ap. Gratian Caus. XIX. Qu. III. c. 7, speaks of Ingredientes monasterium convertendi gratia, *Id. Ibid.* c. 6: Miles si converti voluerit. Hieronym. *Ibid.* Caus. XII. Qu. I. c. 7: Ut sunt clerici et Deo devoti videlicet conversi. Alexander III. in Decret. Lib. III. Tit. XXXI. c. 7, also speaks of monachos vel con-

a higher degree, of those who have taken the solemn vow, and are called the religious ([119])—professed monks and nuns. In later times the term "converted ones" was usually applied to the lay brethren who did the menial work of the monastery, and they among the Carthusians occupied a position very much below that of professed monks.

23. Children may be dedicated to the religious life by their parents, provided this is done before boys are fourteen ([120]), and before girls are twelve years of age ([121]). Such dedication should take place before witnesses ([122]). By Gallican usage the dedicated child (*oblatus*) was presented to the abbot by his next-of-kin, wrapped in an altar-cloth ([123]), as an offering to the Church ([124]), and the abbot's blessing was deemed equivalent

versos. Lynd. 152: The converted and others aforesaid who are devoted to divine office, although they are not ordained, nevertheless, by reason of their profession and habit, differ from laymen.

(119). Concil. Lat. IV. A.D. 1215, in Decret. Lib. III. Tit. XXXVI. c. 9; Const. 45 Langton, A.D. 1222: Since religious persons have no property. Const. 31 Edmund, A.D. 1236: Because too great diversity of religions [*i.e.*, rules of profession] brings confusion. Const. 18, 19, 20 Peckham, A.D. 1281.

(120). Concil. Tolet. X. A.D. 656, Can. 6 ap. Gratian Caus. XX. Qu. III. c. 1; Theodori Poenit. II. XIV. 5 in Haddan and Stubbs III. 202: One infant may be given to a monastery to God instead of another which he had vowed to give; yet it were better to fulfil the vow. Egbert's Excerpt. 92.

(121). Concil. Tribur. A.D. 895, Can. 2 ap. Gratian, *Ibid.* c. 2; Clemens III. in Decret. Lib. III. Tit. XXXI. c. 12.

(122). Gratian *Ibid.* c. 4; Egbert's Excerpt. 92.

(123). Objection was raised ap. Gratian Caus. XX. Qu. III. c. 1, that Lambert was not a monk—(1) because he had professed no rule; (2) his father had never offered him pallio altaris indutum; and (3) he had never received the abbot's benediction. Nicolaus *Ibid.* c. 4, speaks of a monk being presented pallio altaris indutum (alias palla). *Ibid.* III. Dist. I. c. 40, contains a direction not to wrap the dead in an altar-cloth, nor for the deacon to cover his shoulders with it. Concil. Tolet. X. A.D. 656, *Ibid.* Caus. XXVII. Qu. 1. c. 36: Women coming to religion cover their heads with a cloth (pallio). Concil. Aurel. I. Can. 26, quoted note 118, uses pallium accipere, as equivalent to making his profession.

(124). Such offerings were made at other times. Concil. London A.D. 1126, Can. 3: That at the consecration of bishops, blessing of abbots,

Discipline of the Religious Life. 101

to co-optation by the brethren. When he attained his fourteenth year he could, if he wished, depart within twelve months ([125]), and, according to St. Basil, might marry before his sixteenth year, if such a course were necessary; but in that case he had to submit to penance ([126]).

24. When the religious life is adopted voluntarily, boys must be fifteen and girls sixteen or seventeen before being allowed to adopt it ([127]). They must also go through a period of probation ([128]); and by English rule, and that of other places wherever the rule is a severe one, they must be eighteen before making their profession ([129]), or it is not binding ([130]). By the rule of St. Pachomius ([131]), which was also for a time followed in the West, three years were required for the probation ([132]). In St. Gregory's time the three years were generally abbreviated to two ([133]). Subsequently one year was held to be

---

dedication of churches, a cope, a carpet, a towel, a basin be not demanded by force, nor taken unless freely offered. Concil. Westminster A.D. 1138, Can. 3.

(125). Coelestin III. in Decret. Lib. III. Tit. XXXI. c. 14, and Concil. Lugdun. I. A.D. 1234, in Sext. Lib. III. Tit. XIV. c. 1.

(126). Theodori Poenit. I. VIII. 14 in Haddan and Stubbs III. 184: Basil held that a boy might be allowed to marry, if he could not contain, before his sixteenth year, although he had previously been a monk, but in that case he should rank among bigamists and do penance.

(127). Theodori Poenit. II. XII. 6 in Haddan and Stubbs III. 201.

(128). Gregory, ap. Gratian I. Dist. LIII.; Concil. Clovesho A.D. 747 Can. 24: That rectors of monasteries examine every one whilst he is in the lay habit, before his conversion to the monastic life.

(129). Gregory Lib. I. Epist. 48 ap. Gratian Caus. XX. Qu. l. c. 5: Because the rule (congregatio) of the monks in the islands is a hard one, we forbid youths being received in the said monasteries under eighteen years of age. Const. 41 Langton, A.D. 1222: That none be admitted monks under eighteen years of age, unless evident utility or necessity require.

(130). Alexander III. in Decret. Lib. III. Tit. XXXI. c. 8. See *Discipline Generally*, § 28.

(131). Regula Pachomii ed. Vallarsi II. 50.

(132). Nov. 115, c. 55 ap. Gratian Caus. XVII. Qu. II. c. 3.

(133). Gregory *Ibid.* Caus. XIX. Qu. III. c. 6: Let no monasteries by any means dare to give the tonsure to such as they have received for conver-

sufficient ([134]), and even less than a year, except in the case of friars ([135]). Such, however, as had taken a vow to enter religion ([136]), or had worn the habit of professed monks for above a year, were held in the thirteenth century to be tacitly professed, and if they declined to make an explicit profession afterwards, were ordered to be treated as apostates ([137]).

25. With the exception of children dedicated in infancy, the profession of religion must always be made, (1) of free choice ([138]); (2) by those capable of making it—not, therefore, by a slave against his master's will ([139]), nor by a bishop without

sion before they have fulfilled two years in novitiate (conversatione, for which others read conversione).

([134]). Decret. Lib. III. Tit. XXXI. c. 16: The regular institution forbids any one becoming a monk before one year. Sext. Lib. III. Tit. XIV. c. 1 and 3.

([135]). Boniface VIII. in Sext. Lib. I. c 3: The constitution of Innocent [IV. *Ibid.* c. 1] which forbids the profession of the converted to be received before the year of probation is ended, our predecessor, Alexander [IV. *Ibid.* c. 2], extended to the orders of Preachers and Minorites. We, led by similar considerations, extend the same declaration to the other mendicant orders. In other religious rules profession may be lawfully made expressly or tacitly within the year. If made expressly, it strictly binds to the form of religion which is professed, even though the habit be not changed. If it is tacitly made within the year of probation by taking the habit which is only given to those professing, it does not pledge the recipient specially to that religion to which the habit belongs, but generally to some form of religion, *i.e.*, supposing him to be of sufficient age, to have assumed it knowingly and voluntarily, and to have continued to wear it three years.

([136]). Innocent III. A.D. 1198, in Decret. Lib. III. Tit. XXXI. c. 13 and 17.

([137]). Alexander III. to Bishop of Ely, *Ibid.* c. 9, says if they only wear the novice's habit they may return to the world; Innocent III. A.D. 1204, *Ibid.* c. 20, that they may return to the world within a year; and *Id.* A.D. 1212, *Ibid.* c. 21, that they are not thereby disqualified for orders or holding a benefice. Honorius III. *Ibid.* c. 22, says that if they wear the habit for more than a year they are to be deemed professed. Both statements are repeated by Gregory IX. *Ibid.* c. 23, and embodied in Const. 18 Peckham, A.D. 1281.

([138]). Alexander III. in Decret. Lib. I. Tit. XL. c. 1. See *Discipline Generally*, § 23.

([139]). Concil. Chalcedon A.D. 451, Can. 4: Boniface ap. Gratian Caus. XVII. Qu. II. c. 3.

the consent of his metropolitan ([140]), nor by a married man without his wife's consent ([141]); and (3) it must be made before the proper persons ([142]). No one may under any circumstances be admitted to a monastery for a pecuniary consideration ([143]). One who has been induced to enter by fraud should remain, but the monastery should not have the benefit of his property ([144]); or the vow may be set aside ([145]), provided application is made for that purpose within five years ([146]). One who is forcibly detained should be unconditionally set free ([147]).

26. When a monk is received or makes his profession ([148]), he puts on the habit of a professed monk, if it is different from the novice's habit ([149]), receives the tonsure ([150]), and solemnly vows to keep the rule ([151]). The abbot then offers the Eucharist, and repeats over him three prayers ([152]), which are

[140]. Innocent III. in Decret. Lib. I. Tit. IX. c. 10, and Lib. III. Tit. XXXI. c. 18.

[141]. Coelestin. III. l. c. Lib. III. Tit. XXXII. c. 12: See *Discipline Generally*, § 28; *Wedlock*, § 21.

[142]. Innocent III. A.D. 1198, l. c. Lib. III. Tit. XXXI. c. 16.

[143]. Concil. Westminster A.D. 1127, Can. 3: We condemn all demands of money for admitting of monks, canons, or nuns. Concil. London A.D. 1175, Can. 8: Let no prelate exact or take, by way of bargain, any price for the reception of any monk, canon, or nun who enters a religious life, under pain of anathema. Concil. Westminster A.D. 1200, Can. 15; Const. 39 Langton, A.D. 1222: That nothing be demanded for the reception of any one into a religious house.

[144]. Concil. Cabilon. II. A.D. 813, ap. Gratian Caus. XX. Qu. III. c. 5.

[145]. Nicolaus, *Ibid.* c. 4.

[146]. Devoti Lib. I. Tit. IX. § 15.

[147]. Eugenii Synod. A.D. 826, ap. Gratian Caus. XX. Qu. 1. c. 9; Nicolaus *Ibid.* Qu. III. c. 4.

[148]. Theodori Poenit. II. III. 3 in Haddan and Stubbs III. 192, calls it *ordinatio monachi*. For a description of the Benedictine form of admission, see Lingard's Anglo-Saxon Church I. 204. See Dionysius de Eccles. Hier. c. 6, quoted note 172.

[149]. Decret. Lib. III. Tit. XXXI. c. 13 and 22.

[150]. Gregory ap. Gratian Caus. XIX. Qu. III. c. 6; Concil. Clovesho A.D. 747, Can. 24.

[151]. Clemens III. in Decret. Lib. III. Tit. XXXI. c. 13.

[152]. Theodori Poenit. II. III. 3 l. c. A detailed account of the admission of a professed monk is given in Hist. Monast. de Abbendon II. 318.

termed the benediction ([153]). He thereupon covers him with a cowl, which he removes after seven days ([154]). The solemn profession of religion is deemed equivalent to a second baptism ([155]). The house in which it is made is ever afterwards the monk's home ([156]), and he is the abbot's man, and cannot remove to another house ([157]) without the abbot's leave, except to follow a stricter rule ([158]).

27. Admission to religion did not in early days admit to the privileges or duties of order ([159]); nay, more, the observance of the monastic rule was at first considered incompatible with the exercise of order ([160]). In the fourth century, however, clerical monks began to be allowed to continue to exercise their office ([161]), and next the practice was introduced of ordain-

(153). Nicolaus l. c. says benedictione percepta.

(154). Theodori Poenit. II. III. 3 l. c.

(155). Hieronym. Ep. 22 ad Paulam, says "to enter upon a monk's life is to wash oneself with a second baptism of a vow." Dionysius de Ecclea. Hier. c. 6 calls monastic consecration a sacrament ($\mu\nu\sigma\tau\acute{\eta}\rho\iota\sigma\nu$). Theodore l. c.: On the seventh day the abbot should remove the covering, as the priest in baptism removes the veil of infants; . . . because it is a second baptism, according to the judgment of the fathers, whereby all sins are forgiven, as in baptism.

(156). Concil. Agath. A.D. 506, Can. 27 ap. Gratian Caus. XX. Qu. IV. c. 3: Concil. Hertford A.D. 673, Can. 4: That monks continue in that obedience which they promised at the time of their conversion. Concil. Clovesho A.D. 747, Can. 24: Let them not by any means rashly expel him.

(157). Odo, Can. 6, A.D. 943; Urban II. ap. Gratian Caus. XIX. Qu. III. c. 3. See § 4, note 28.

(158). Decret. Lib. III. Tit. XXXI. c. 10, 18.

(159). Hieronym. Epist. XIV. c. 8: The case of monks is one, the case of clergy another. See note 172.

(160). Cassian de Inst. Coenob. XI. 17 says that the old rule of the Fathers was that a monk ought carefully to avoid a woman and a bishop, for neither of them would let him attend to the quiet of his cell, or give his mind to divine contemplation. Gregory ap. Gratian Caus. XVI. Qu. l. c. 2: No one can simultaneously attend to ecclesiastical duties and strictly follow the rule of a monk. Boniface ap. Gratian Ibid. c. 25, objects that those who are dead to the world cannot exercise the power of the keys.

(161). Unknown author ap. Gratian Caus. XVI. Qu. l. c. 21: We approve of learned and devout monks, who have been dedicated with the

ing monks ([162]), to obtain which the leave and request of the abbot was then necessary ([163]). By ordination they were not emancipated from the observance of their rule ([164]), but were placed in a position to be of service to others. Ordained monks are not therefore allowed to officiate, even in their own monasteries, without the bishop's leave ([165]), nor outside them without their abbot's leave also ([166]). If, with the abbot's leave, they at any time minister outside them, they are required to be wholly under the bishop ([167]).

28. When a vow of religion has once been taken, even in simple form, it ought to be fulfilled. Hence all who forsake the cloister for military or married life ([168]), before taking the

honour of the priesthood, being allowed to baptize, to preach, to give penance, and to forgive the debts (debita) of the poor. Other authorities *Ibid.* c. 22-25. The practice is stated to have been introduced by St. Athanasius.

([162]). Hieronym. ad Rusticum, A.D. 402, *Ibid.* c. 26: So live in the monastery as to deserve the clerical office. If the people or the bishop choose you to such office, do the duties of it. Gelasius, A.D. 494, *Ibid.* c. 28, and I. Dist. LV. c. 1, permits monks to be ordained to parishes where secular clergy cannot be had. Concil. Ilerd. A.D. 523, Can. 3, *Ibid.* c. 34; Gregory *Ibid.* Caus. XVI. Qu. 1. c. 32.

([163]). Concil. Agath. A.D. 506, Can. 27 ap. Gratian Caus. XVI. Qu. 1. c. 33'; Concil. Ilerd. A.D. 523, Can. 3, *Ibid.* c. 34; Gregory *Ibid.* I. Dist. LVIII. c. 1.

([164]). Innocent, A.D. 404, ap. Gratian Caus. XVI. Qu. 1. c. 3; Theodori Poenit. II. VI. 12 in Haddan and Stubbs III. 195: If the congregation have elected a monk to be ordained for them to the degree of presbyter, he ought not to intermit his former conversation. Concil. London A.D. 1138, Can. 14: That monks who have been long in a monastery ought not to recede from their former way of living when they become clerks.

([165]). Gregory ap. Gratian Caus. XVI. Qu. 1. c. 13, to the bishop of the city: The abbot of St. Gregory's complains to us that you forbid the celebration of mass and the burial of the dead in his monastery. We entreat you to desist from such inhumanity.

([166]). Gelasius ap. Gratian Caus. XVI. Qu. 1. c. 28; Concil. Agath. A.D. 506, Can. 27, *Ibid.* c. 33; Concil. Tarracon. A.D. 516, Can. 11, *Ibid.* c. 35: We forbid monks to leave their abbey and discharge any ecclesiastical function, except by command of the abbot.

([167]). Gelasius l. c.; Innocent III. A.D. 1209, in Decret. Lib. III. Tit. XXXVI. c. 7, *Id.* A.D. 1198, *Ibid.* c. 8.

([168]). Augustin ap. Gratian Caus. XXVII. Qu. 1. c. 41, says that a marriag

solemn vow, are required to do penance for the transgression ([169]), and can never afterwards be admitted to orders ([170]). Those who violate the solemn vow by renouncing the monastic life, and refuse to return to it when pressed, are ordered to be excommunicated as apostates ([171]).

DUTIES OF THE RELIGIOUS LIFE.

29. The order of monkhood, although not, like the presbyterate, an order endowed with a special spiritual gift ([172]), is yet

concluded after a [simple] vow cannot be dissolved. Also Caus. XXVII. Qu. II. c. 20–26: Alexander III. in Decret. Lib. III. Tit. XXXI. c. 1 and 2; Innocent III. *Ibid.* c. XIX.; Devoti Lib. II. Tit. II. § 129.

(169). Leo ap. Gratian Caus. XX. Qu. III. c. 1 : One who deserts the profession of a single life for military service or marriage must be purified with the satisfaction of public penance, because, although military service is innocent and marriage honourable, still it is a transgression to have deserted the choice of better things. Apost. Const. III. 1. and IV. 14 ; Concil. Arelat. II. A.D. 460, *Ibid.* I. Dist. L. c. 69 ; Theodori Poenit. I. XIV. 5 in Haddan and Stubbs III. 188, and ap. Gratian I. Dist. XXVII. c. 3, and Caus. XXVII. Qu. l. c. 43 : If any man having a simple vow of chastity marries a wife, let him not put her away, but do penance for three years. *Id.* I. VIII. 12, *Ibid.* p. 174 : If any one renounces the world, and then resumes the secular habit . . . let him do penance for ten years, and after the first three the bishop may deal mercifully with him. Egbert's Excerpt. 65. See *Discipline Generally*, § 27.

(170). Concil. Arelat. II. A.D. 460, ap. Gratian Caus. XX. Qu. III. c. 1 ; Concil. Aurel. I. A.D. 511, Can. 23, *Ibid.* Caus. XXVII. Qu. l. c. 32 ; Theodori Poenit. I. IX. 2 in Haddan and Stubbs III. 185. But see note 137.

(171). Concil. Chalcedon, Can. 7 ap. Gratian Caus. XX. Qu. III. c. 2 and 16, *Ibid.* Caus. XXVII. Qu. l. c. 22 ; Concil. Turon. II. A.D. 567, Can. 15, excommunicates professed monks who marry, and separates them from their wives. Concil. Tribur. A.D. 895, *Ibid.* c. 2 ; Gregory *Ibid.* c. 39 ; Concil. Winton A.D. 1071, Can. 12 ; Concil. Westminster A.D. 1102, Can. 11 : That monks or clergymen who have forsaken their order do either return or be excommunicate. Concil. Lat. II. Can. 7, A.D. 1139, *Ibid.* c. 40 ; Alexander III. to Bishop of Ely, in Decret. Lib. III. Tit. XXXI. c. 9, and c. 13 and 17 ; Const. 19 Peckham, A.D. 1281 : These cannot desert their religious habit, but must at least continue in a laxer state of religion.

(172). Dionysius de Ecclea. Hier. c. 6 : The order higher than all the initiated is the sacred order of the monks. . . . Wherefore the divine insti-

under the same obligation with it to devote to God's service in prayer, praise, and contemplation the life redeemed by Christ; and by doing what is just before men, living regularly and interceding for all ([173]), to be perpetually pointing to higher things ([174]). Since the fourth century laymen in general have to a great extent shaken off these obligations, or contented themselves with fulfilling them by deputy ([175]); but upon monks they are held to be binding to the fullest extent, as those who have voluntarily bowed their neck to the yoke of Christian vows, and undertaken to give full expression to the Church's true and perfect life.

tution accorded them a perfecting grace, and deemed them worthy of a certain invocation for their consecration—not of sacred government, for that is confined to the sacerdotal orders—but of sacred action, as being hallowed by the hierarchical consecration in the second degree. Elfric Can. 18 A.D. 957: There is no order appointed by ecclesiastical institution but these seven. Monkship and abbotship are of another sort, and are not to be reckoned in their number.

(173). Justin I. Apol. c. 10: God accepts those who imitate the excellences which reside in Him, viz., temperance, justice, and kindness. Concil. Augustodun. A.D. 670, Can. 15: Let all monks be in every way obedient, distinguished for frugality, fervent in the work of God, persevering in charity, lest through negligence and disobedience they become a prey to the enemy who goeth about roaring and seeking whom he may devour. Concil. Gall. A.D. 616, Can. 4: That monks live according to rule. Syn. Rom. A.D. 826, ap. Gratian Caus. v. Qu. III. c. 3; Concil. Ensham. A.D. 1009, Can. 1: That men of every order do in earnest submit themselves every one to that law which concerns them both in regard to God and the world; and specially that God's servants, the bishops and abbots, the monks and minikins, canons and nuns, betake themselves to what is right, and live regularly, and earnestly intercede for all Christian people.

(174). Gasquet, in Montalembert's Monks of the West. The perpetual round of prayer and praise is something more than an intercessory power. It, rightly understood, is the medium of intercourse between the monastic body and the people in the midst of which it dwells. No one is so dull that he cannot understand the faith in the unseen, the hope of another world, and the burning love of God, which are manifested in the perennial sacrifice and song of praise of the monastic choir. . . . The choir of the monastery is the monk's real pulpit, and the daily office his most efficacious sermon.

(175). Lynd. 44.

30. In the first ages of the Church ([176]) the higher ascetic life was undoubtedly optional, and a counsel of perfection; nay, more, the particular manner of pursuing it was also optional. In time, however, various rules or systematised forms of life, called religions ([177]), commended themselves by experience as better suited than others for the purpose; some rules containing fixed and written directions, others leaving everything to the abbot's discretion ([178]). All agree in making poverty ([179]), temperance, and chastity ([180]) the initial requirement of monastic discipline, and where there is a common life there must of necessity be obedience ([181]).

31. Foremost among the counsels of perfection is the renunciation of property in every form or shape ([182]). The young

([176]). Acts v. 4: St. Peter says to Ananias, who wished to rank as a member of the communistic brotherhood at Jerusalem, without bringing all that he possessed into the common fund: Whiles it remained, was it not thine own? And after it was sold, was it not in thine power? ... Thou hast not lied unto men, but unto God. See *Excesses*, note 12.

([177]). Concil. Lat. IV. in Decret. Lib. III. Tit. XXXVI. c. 9; Const. 31 Edmund, A.D. 1236, quoted note 119.

([178]). Cassian de Inst. Coenob. Lib. II. c. 2; Mabillon in Praefat. ad Annales Benedict I. XXXIV. points out that sometimes more than one rule was followed under the same roof.

([179]). Matt. XIX. 21, 27-29; Luke XVIII. 28-30; Concil. London A.D. 1075, Can. 2; Const. 45 Langton, A.D. 1222.

([180]). Matt. XIX. 11-13; 1 Cor. VII. 37, 38; Ambros. ap. Gratian Caus. XXXII. Qu. 1. c. 13 declares chastity to be a counsel of perfection. Innocent III. in Decret. Lib. III. Tit. XXXV. c. 6: The renunciation of property and the preservation of chastity are so bound up with the monastic life that not even the Pope can grant a license to dispense therewith.

([181]). Hieronym. ad Eustoch. Ep. 22, c. 35; The confederation was that they should obey their superiors, and do everything they were ordered to do. Theodori Poenit. II. VI. 13 in Haddan and Stubbs III. 195: If a monk, after being ordained, prove proud, or disobedient, or vicious, . . . let him be deposed. Alcuin Epist. *Ibid.* 470, 510.

([182]). Eusebius VII. 32 relates that Pierius was celebrated for his voluntary poverty. Augustin ap. Gratian Caus. XII. Qu. 1. c. 11: Call nothing your own, but let all things be in common. Concil. Autissiodor. A.D. 578, Can. 23; Concil. Gall. A.D. 616, Can. 3; Gregory in Decret. Lib. III. Tit. XXXI. c. 5: Nor do you allow any monk to have anything of his own (peculiare). Concil. Augustodun. A.D. 670, Can. 1; Concil. London A.D.

Discipline of the Religious Life. 109

man who, desiring to be perfect, was told by Christ to sell all that he had ([183]), and the Christians of Jerusalem having all things in common ([184]), are the types for this life. Those who have food and raiment are bidden therewith to be content ([185]). Religious persons are not therefore allowed to trade ([186]), or to have any dealings involving money, except as obedientials in their own monasteries ([187]). They may not act as executors ([188]), or as bishop's officials ([189]), or farm benefices ([190]). They may not even have private property in clothing ([191]), a separate room ([192]), or a separate table, except they are sick or

1075, Can. 2 : If any monks without license are found to have anything of their own, and do not with repentance confess and discard it before they die, let not the bells be tolled nor the salutary sacrifice be offered for such an one. Concil. Lat. III. A.D. 1179, in Decret. Lib. III. Tit. XXXV. c. 2 ; Concil. Westminster A.D. 1200, Can. 15 : Let not monks have any property. Clemens III. *Ibid.* c. 4, extended the same rule to canons regular.

(183). Matt. XIX. 21.

(184). Acts IV. 32 ; Διδαχή IV. 8 : Thou shalt share all things with thy brother, and shalt not call them thine own ; for if ye are fellow-sharers in that which is imperishable, how much more in perishable things ? Augustin ap. Gratian I. Dist. VIII. c. 1 ; Gregory Caus. XII. Qu. L c. 8 in Baeda I. 27 ; Pseudo-Isidor. *Ibid.* c. 2 : The common life is necessary for all, and chiefly to those who desire to serve God free from blame. Concil. Paris A.D. 829, *Ibid.* c. 16 ; Concil. Aurel. A.D. 511, *Ibid.* Caus. XVIII. Qu. II. c. 16 ; Egbert's Excerpt. 62 ; Concil. London A.D. 1075, Can. 2 ; Baeda IV. 23, A.D. 731, says that in Hilda's monastery, "after the example of the primitive Church, no person was rich and none poor." Concil. Westminster A.D. 1200, Can. 15.

(185). 1 Tim. vi. 18 ; Hieronym. ap. Gratian Caus. XII. Qu. L c. 8.

(186). Concil. London A.D. 1175, Can. 10 : We forbid, under terror of anathema, monks or clerks to trade for gain.

(187). Const. 46 Langton, A.D. 1222.

(188). Const. 15 Boniface, A.D. 1261 ; Const. 20 Peckham, A.D. 1281 ; Const. 7 Stratford, A.D. 1343.

(189). Unknown author ap. Gratian Caus. XVI. Qu. 1. c. 20.

(190). Concil. London A.D. 1175, Can. 10 ; Const. 46 Langton, A.D. 1222.

(191). Const. 40 Langton.

(192). Concil. Agath. A.D. 506, Can. 24 ap. Gratian Caus. XX. Qu. IV. c. 3 : It should also be a rule that monks be not allowed to leave the congregation for solitary cells, unless they be approved monks after completed labours, or those for whom, because of their infirmity, the severity of the

infirm ([193]). All, as being dead to this world, are accounted dead persons in law, and could formerly in this country neither own property ([194]) nor dispose of anything by will ([195]).

32. To ensure greater earnestness in and to give greater effect to their prayers ([196]), the diet of monks is ordered to be spare ([197]), and they are required to observe the regular fasts ([198]). The use of flesh is at all times forbidden except to the sick and infirm ([199]). They are prohibited from dining

rule is relaxed by the abbot's permission. In that case, let them, whilst remaining within the cloister walls, and under the abbot's rule, be permitted to have separate rooms. An abbot, also, may not have several different rooms or several different monasteries. Concil. Lat. II. A.D. 1139, Can. 26 ap. Gratian Caus. xxviii. Qu. ii. c. 25.

(193). Const. 44 Langton, A.D. 1222. Let the fare of all in the refectory be the same. The head of the house may have such provision prepared for him as he sees proper for the relief of the sickly.

(194). Const. 46 Langton, A.D. 1222. 31 Hen. viii. c. 6 first enabled a monk to sue and be sued in a court of law. It was confirmed by 33 Hen. viii. c. 29, and explained by 5 and 6 Ed. vi. c. 13. See note 72.

(195). Gregory ap. Gratian Caus. xix. Qu. iii. c. 7: It is laid down by clear title of law, that those who enter a monastery have no power of bequest. What they possess belongs to the monastery. Leo iii. in Decret. Lib. iii. Tit. xxxviii. c. 2 directs that one-half the property of one who embraces religion shall go to the Church to which the monk belongs; but Alexander iii. *Ibid.* c. 4 restricts this rule to cases in which a person embraces religion when taken suddenly ill. In other cases the monk carries with him to the monastery his whole property. Const. 45 Langton, A.D. 1222.

(196). See *Baptism*, § 13, 21; *The Eucharist*, § 7.

(197). Concil. Chelsea A.D. 787, Can. 4: That monks and nuns behave themselves regularly both as to diet and apparel.

(198). Concil. Turon II. A.D. 567, Can. 17: From Easter until Pentecost, excepting the three rogation days, the brethren may dine. After Pentecost let them live on dry meats for a week, and then fast three days a week to the 1st August. In August, because saints' days occur daily, let them dine. In the whole of September, October, and November let them fast three days a week, and every day from December to Christmas. From Christmas day to Epiphany, because saints' days occur daily, let them dine, excepting the three days on which litanies are said for the extirpation of paganism. From Epiphany to Lent let them fast three times a week.

(199). Egbert's Excerpt. 69: Let monks never have flesh in commons.

before the high noon office has been said (^{200}), and are enjoined always to say grace before meals, and to give thanks afterwards (^{201}). In the East, fasting was carried on with much greater severity than in the West (^{202}).

33. In respect of dress they are directed to wear a distinctive habit (^{203}), differing from that of secular clergy both in shape and colour (^{204}). Neither monks nor canons regular may wear linen shirts (^{205}), nor an outer garment of shaded brown (^{206}), nor girdles of silk, nor gold or silver ornaments (^{207}), nor caps (^{208}). Each one's habit must be proportioned to his height (^{209}). Whereas secular clergy may wear any colour

Animals, either young or full-grown, may never be served up at the table in the congregation. They may be provided and eaten by them that are infirm only. Const. 19 Otho, A.D. 1237: According to the rule of St. Benedict, monks ought to abstain from eating flesh excepting the weak and infirm.

(200). Martin Brac. ap. Gratian I. Dist. XLIV. c. 12 : Nec oportet clericos vel laicos religiosos ante sacram diei horam tertiam inire convivia. Concil. Clovesho A.D. 747, Can. 21.

(201). Martin Brac. l. c.

(202). See note 19.

(203). Concil. Aurel. A.D. 511, Can. 20, forbids monks to wear a stole (orarium) or beaked shoes, called tzangae, zancae, chyncae, ciangae. Concil. Clovesho A.D. 747, Can. 19 : Let them not use gorgeous apparel or such as savours of vainglory, like seculars, but a simple habit, and such as agrees with their profession. Can. 28 : Let them use the accustomed apparel. Concil. Ensham A.D. 1009, Can. 1 ; Clemens III. in Decret. Lib. III. Tit. XXXI. c. 13 : The habit does not make the monk, but a regular profession. Const. 40 and 44 Langton, A.D. 1222.

(204). Concil. Clovesho A.D. 787, Can. 4 in H. and S. III. 450 : Let the monks use the habit that the Easterns [monks of Italy and Germany, Stubbs III. 460] do, and the canons also, and not garments dyed with Indian tinctures or costly. Elfric's Can. 36, A.D. 957 : Let every one wear what belongs to his order, the priest that to which he was ordained, and let him not wear a monk's shroud, nor that which belongs to laymen.

(205). Innocent III. in Decret. Lib. III. Tit. XXXV. c. 6.

(206). Const. 36 Langton, A.D. 1222 : Let neither monks nor canons regular use burnet nor any irregular cloth.

(207). Const. 36 Langton, A.D. 1222.

(208). Concil. Westminster, A.D. 1200, Can. 15.

(209). Const. 36 Langton, A.D. 1222.

excepting red, green, or purple ([210]), monks are, by English rule, confined to a black or a white habit, with black or white facings either of cats' skins, lambs' skins, or foxes' skins ([211]), and a monk discarding his habit is ordered to be treated as one excommunicate ([212]).

34. By the vow of chastity monks are pledged not merely to live a temperate life, but for the kingdom of heaven's sake to refrain from marriage altogether ([213]). To avoid temptation they are forbidden to employ women to manage their households ([214]), to go out alone ([215]), or after dark without a light ([216]), to wander about ([217]) or frequent

([210]). Concil. Lat. IV. Can. 16 in Decret. Lib. I. Tit. XV. See *Duties of Order*, § 8.

([211]). Concil. Westminster, A.D. 1200, Can. 15; Eunapius in Vita Aedesii says that: Every man who then [in the fifth century] wore a black garment [*i.e.*, a monk] exercised a tyrannical authority.

([212]). Concil. Winton A.D. 1071, Can. 12: That monks who have thrown off their habit be neither admitted into the army nor into any convent of clerks, but be esteemed excommunicate.

([213]). Matt. XIX. 13; Concil. Ensham A.D. 1009, Can. 1: Let the monk that hath no monastery engage himself before God and man to observe three things, at least for the time to come, *i.e.*, his chastity, the wearing of the monastic habit, and the serving the Lord in the best manner that he can. Const. 11 Peckham, A.D. 1279: That friars and nuns rigidly preserve their chastity.

([214]). Concil. Turon. II. A.D. 567, Can. 16, forbids women to enter a monastery, and excommunicates an abbot or provost who permits this rule to be infringed. Gregory ap. Gratian Caus. XVIII. Qu. II. c. 20. See notes 42 and 81.

([215]). Const. 43 Langton, A.D. 1222: Nor may the religious go out except leave be given for some reasonable cause, nor even visit their parents unless they are such as are liable to no just suspicion, and not even then without a mate.

([216]). Concil. London A.D. 1075, Can. 2: That all of them carry lights by night.

([217]). Concil. Chalcedon A.D. 451, Can. 23 ap. Gratian Caus. XVI. Qu. I. c. 17; Pelagius *Ibid.* c. 18; Wihtraed's Dooms 8, A.D. 696: If a shorn man irregularly wander about, entertainment may be given him for once, but let him not be entertained for any long time unless he have a license. Can. 6 Odo, A.D. 943: Let monks not be strollers and saunterers. Alexander II. ap. Gratian Caus. XVI. Qu. l. c. 11.

Discipline of the Religious Life. 113

towns (²¹⁸) or attend wedding-feasts (²¹⁹), to be placed singly in charge of parishes (²²⁰), to visit nunneries except for necessary business (²²¹), or stay at laymen's houses (²²²), or to act as god-parents (²²³).

35. Originally monks were the voluntary subjects of the abbot in whose monastery they were staying (²²⁴), and took no vow of obedience. In the fifth and following centuries wandering monks were looked upon with disfavour (²²⁵). St. Benedict's rule required a vow of obedience. It gave to monks in return the power of electing their abbot (²²⁶), but did not empower them to dismiss him (²²⁷). Obedience was held to extend to all matters (²²⁸) short of transgressing a divine

(218). Hieronym. ap. Gratian Caus. xvi. Qu. l. c. 5 : If you wish to be what you are called—a monk, what have you to do in towns? Concil. Augustodun. A.D. 670, Can. 6.

(219). Concil. Autissiodor. A.D. 578, Can. 24.

(220). Concil. Lat. III. A.D. 1179, in Decret. Lib. III. Tit. xxxv. c. 2, and Tit. xxxvii. c. 3 and 4 ; Concil. Westminster A.D. 1200, Can. 5 ; Innocent III. *Ibid.* Tit. xxxv. c. 5 ; Honorius III. *Ibid.* Tit. xxxvii. c. 3 and 4.

(221). Concil. Clovesho A.D. 747, Can. 20 ; Syn. VII. A.D. 787, Can. 20 ap. Gratian Caus. xviii. Qu. II. c. 21 : Let not a monk sleep in a nunnery nor have a meal alone with a nun ; and when the necessaries of life are carried to the nuns by men, let the abbess receive them outside the gate, together with some very ancient woman. Const. 42 Langton, A.D. 1222.

(222). Concil. Clovesho A.D. 747, Can. 29 : That monks and nuns may not dwell in the houses of seculars with laymen.

(223). Concil. Autissiodor. A.D. 578, Can. 25 ; Concil. Augustodun. A.D. 670, Can. 5 ; Concil. Westminster A.D. 1102, Can. 19.

(224). Lingard's Anglo-Saxon Church I. 149. See § 15.

(225). Concil. Venet. A.D. 465, Can. 5, forbids them to wander without letters, testimonials. Concil. Agath. A.D. 506, Can. 38 ; Concil. Aurel. A.D. 511, Can. 19 ; Wihtraed's Dooms 8, A.D. 696 ; Concil. Ensham. A.D. 1009, Can. 1.

(226). Lingard I. 209 ; Concil. London A.D. 1075, Can. 2 : That monks observe their order according to the rule of Benedict. See note 85.

(227). Pelagius ap. Gratian Caus. xviii. Qu. II. c. 9.

(228). Concil. Aurel. A.D. 511, Can. 19 ; Concil. Augustodun. A.D. 670, Can. 8 ; Concil. Hertford A.D. 673, Can. 4 ; Egbert's Excerpt. 62 : Let monks be subject to their abbots with a most devout obedience. Concil. Clovesho A.D. 747, Can. 19 : That monks or nuns be humbly subject to their superior. Odo's Can. 6, A.D. 963 : We exhort monks that in

VOL. II.   H

command ([229]). Monks are also enjoined to observe the rule of silence, according to ancient custom ([230]); silence, or the power to withdraw, being a necessary mark of self-control ([231]).

COMMUNITIES OF RELIGIOUS WOMEN OR NUNS.

36. The term nuns is applied to all religious women who consecrate their lives to the service of Christ by a simple vow of self-dedication, or renounce the world by solemnly undertaking to observe the counsels of perfection ([232]). It includes (1) ordinary nuns or canonesses, who correspond with the widows of ancient times, and (2) cloistered nuns or minikins, who correspond with the consecrated virgins of St. Augustin's and earlier times ([233]). The latter represent the feminine side of monasticism, and follow either the rule of St.

humility and obedience they study night and day to perform their vows. Innocent III. in Decret. Lib. III. Tit. XXXI. c. 16.

(229). Gregory ap. Gratian Caus. II. Qu. VII. c. 57 : That subjects be not obedient beyond what is right (plus quam expedit), lest in studying to be obedient beyond what is necessary they are obsequious to the vices of others.

(230). Innocent III. in Decret. Lib. III. Tit. XXXV. c. 6; Const. 43 Langton, A.D. 1222.

(231). Gasquet in Montalembert's Monks of the West : A life of silence. What a power does this give him [the monk] over the man of the world, who is, perhaps, the very slave of the little pleasures, the frivolous vanities, the busy interests, the all-engrossing ambitions which the monk leaves and ignores. The power to withdraw is a mark of strength, and we worship strength in spite of ourselves. The man who can show himself perfectly independent places himself in a position of superiority.

(232). Nonna in Hieronym. Ep. 18 ad Eustoch. ; νοννίς in Palladii Hist. Lausiaca c. 46, the feminine for Nonnus, according to Arnobius, junr., in Ps. CV. and CXL.=Egyptian for holy ; according to Jablonski, properly Nueneh=not of this world, i.e, one who has renounced the world.

(233). Sanctimoniales or Moniales ap. Gratian Caus. XX. Qu. 1. c. 13, Caus. XXVII. Qu. 1. c. 13 ; Concil. Lat. II. A.D. 1139, *Ibid* Caus. XVIII. Qu. II. c. 25 ; Const. 18 Peckham, A.D. 1281 ; Lingard's Anglo-Saxon Church, I. 215 ; II. 12 ; Devoti Lib. I. Tit. IX. § 17. See *Duties of Order*, § 48.

Discipline of the Religious Life. 115

Benedict or St. Basil. Observers of St. Basil's rule were in this country very rare ([234]).

37. Ordinary nuns or canonesses, whether professed or non-professed, are required to lead a regular life ([235]), like canons regular, and to observe chastity ([236]), as the spouses of Christ ([237]); otherwise they are not confined to their convents ([238]). They are, however, forbidden to wear sables or gaudy apparel ([239]), to let their convents be haunts of laymen ([240]), to occupy private rooms in them ([241]), to walk out alone ([242]) or without

---

([234]). Lynd. 213.

([235]). Concil. Clovesho A.D. 747, Can. 19: That monks and nuns be humbly subject to their superior, and lead a quiet, regular life. Concil. Chelsea A.D. 787, Can. 4: That monks and nuns behave themselves regularly. Concil. Ensham A.D. 1009, Can. 1; Cnut's Law 6, A.D. 1017.

([236]). Const. 11 Peckham, A.D. 1279; Const. 17 Peckham, A.D. 1281.

([237]). Innocent A.D. 404, ap. Gratian Caus. XXVII. Qu. 1. c. 10: Quae Christo spiritualiter nubunt. Concil. Chelsea A.D. 787, Can. 16.

([238]). Concil. Paris A.D. 615, Can. 13 ap. Gratian Caus. XXVII. Qu. l. c. 7, speaks of the assumption of the religious habit *in domibus propriis*. Syn. Rom. A.D. 826, *Ibid.* c. 31: Let women, veiled with a view to religion, either live regularly in a convent or chastely keep the habit they have taken at home.

([239]). Cyprian de Vest. Virg. c. 5: If virginity is destined for the kingdom of God, what have they to do with earthly dress and with ornaments? Concil. Clovesho A.D. 747, Can. 19; Concil. Westminster A.D. 1127, Can. 10: That no abbess or nun use more costly apparel than such as is made of lambs' or cats' skins. Concil. Westminster A.D. 1138, Can. 15: We forbid nuns, under pain of anathema, to use particoloured furs, sable, martin, ermine, beaver, or golden rings, or to wreathe or curiously plat the hair. Concil. Westminster A.D. 1200, Can. 15: Const. 36 Langton, A.D. 1222: We decree that nuns and other religious women wear no silk veils, nor needles of silver or gold in their veils.

([240]). Concil. Rothomag. A.D. 650, Can. 10, forbids any but bishops to be admitted. Concil. Clovesho A.D. 747, Can. 20: Let not nunneries be places of secret meeting for filthy talk, drunkenness, and luxury, but habitations for such as live in continence and sobriety. Can. 29: That nuns may not dwell in the houses of seculars with laymen.

([241]). Concil. Lat. II. A.D. 1139, Can. 26 ap. Gratian Caus. XVIII. Qu. II. c. 25.

([242]). Const. 18 Peckham, A.D. 1281.

the abbess or prioress ([243]), to act as godmothers ([244]), or even to stay for any length of time in the houses of their parents and friends ([245]). If they marry, they are looked upon as incontinent rather than as adulteresses ([246]); and to those offering violence to their persons, Christian burial is denied ([247]).

38. Minikins, as their name implies, are feminine monks ([248]) who are confined to their monasteries ([249]), and called cloistered nuns. Those having houses in a cathedral city are usually

([243]). Concil. Ebor. A.D. 1195, Can. 15: That nuns do not go out of the verge of their convent but in the company of the abbess or prioress.

([244]). Concil. Westminster A.D. 1102, Can. 19.

([245]). Const. 18 Peckham, A.D. 1281: We forbid any nun under pain of excommunication to stay, even in company with a sister nun, much less without it, in the house of her parents or relations . . . above three natural days, for the sake of change, nor above six on any occasion except sickness.

([246]). Hieronym. adv. Jovinian ap. Gratian I. Dist. XXVII. c. 9: Non tam adulterae quam incestae. *Id.* Ep. 97 (al. 8) ad Demetriadem: The holy vow of virgins and the glory of the heavenly and angelic family is disgraced by some who do not conduct themselves properly. Such ought to be told plainly either to marry if they cannot contain, or to contain if they do not wish to marry. Augustin de Bono Viduit. c. 10: They who say that the marriages of such are not marriages but adultery, do not seem to me to consider with sufficient accuracy and care what they say. For no little harm is done by this ill-considered opinion that the marriages of such women as fall away from the holy vow are not marriages, so that they ought to be separated from their husbands as very adulteresses, and not wives; for by separating them they make the husbands real adulterers if they should marry any other women during the lifetime of their first wives. Concil. Chalcedon A.D. 451, Can. 16 forbids a monk or consecrated virgin to marry; but if they do, allows the bishop of the place to be indulgent towards them. Odo's Can. 7, A.D. 943: We forbid all incontinent marriages with nuns . . . for Pope Gregory [II. A.D. 721] . . . ordained, If any one marry a nun, let him be anathema. See *Excesses*, § 33.

([247]). Edmund's Law 4, A.D. 944: Let him that defiles a nun be unworthy of a consecrated burial-place. Concil. Tribur. A.D. 895, ap. Gratian Caus. XXVII. Qu. 1. c. 13, requires him ever to lament it. *Ibid.* c. 37; Can. 23, *Ibid.* c. 17 orders excommunication. Const. 17 Peckham, A.D. 1281.

([248]). Concil. Ensham. A.D. 1009, Can. 1; Cnut's Law 6, A.D. 1017.

([249]). Boniface VIII. in Sext. Lib. III. Tit. XVI. c. 1; Devoti Inst. Lib. I. Tit. IX. § 18.

under the bishop's rule ([250]); those elsewhere are mostly under the rule of some religious house of their own order ([251]). To avoid scandal, they are forbidden to have their convents adjacent to those of men, so as to form double monasteries ([252]), or to sing in the same choir with monks ([253]). Cloistered nuns are allowed to receive the Eucharist in their own oratories on principal festivals, as well as at other times ([254]), and to have a confessor appointed by the bishop ([255]); but neither clergy nor youthful monks, nor others than those of approved life, may be admitted within the convent walls ([256]).

39. Girls placed in a convent by their parents in tender years are at liberty to decide, when they reach their fifteenth year ([257]), whether they will remain or not. A girl under twelve spontaneously taking the veil may not afterwards withdraw ([258]), but she may be withdrawn by her friends, provided this is done within a year ([259]). Should she herself withdraw and marry, she is enjoined to do penance as one guilty of bigamy ([260]);

([250]). Concil. Arelat. V. A.D. 554, Can. 5: That bishops have charge of the monasteries of nuns in this city, and that abbesses have no power of acting contrary to rule.

([251]). Concil. Hispal. II. Can. 11, A.D. 619; Lynd. 212: In England, for the most part, nuns under the rule of the religious are cloistered (inclusae); those which are under the bishop are not cloistered.

([252]). Concil. Agath. A.D. 506, Can. 28 ap. Gratian Caus. XVIII. Qu. II. c. 23, says, "because of the wiles of the devil or the tongues of men." Euseb. II. 17 mentions double monasteries in Egypt, but Syn. VII. A.D. 787, Can. 20, *Ibid.* c. 21, condemned them. See notes 41, 81, 214.

([253]). Concil. Lat. II. A.D. 1139, Can. 27, *Ibid.* c. 25.

([254]). Cap. 45 Theodulf, A.D. 994: We charge men of every rank to frequent the high mass, except the holy maidens only whose custom or manner it is not to go from their own minster.

([255]). Const. 42 Langton, A.D. 1222: Let the nuns make confession to priests appointed by the bishop.

([256]). Concil. Epaon. A.D. 517, Can. 38; Concil. Matiscon. I. A.D. 581, Can. 2; Concil. Rothomag. A.D. 650, Can. 10; Const. 42 Langton, A.D. 1222.

([257]). Concil. Mogunt, A.D. 813, Can. 23 ap. Gratian Caus. XX. Qu. l. c. 10: Gregory, writing to Augustin of Canterbury, *Ibid.* c. 2, held otherwise.

([258]). Leo ap. Gratian Caus. XX. Qu. l. c. 8; Concil. Tolet. VI. A.D. 638, Can. 6, *Ibid.* Qu. III. c. 2.

([259]). Concil. Tribur A.D. 895, Can. 24, *Ibid.* Qu. II. c. 2.

([260]). Syn. Rom. ad Gall. A.D. 384, Can. 2; Innocent ap. Gratian Caus. XXVII. Qu. l. c. 9; Concil. Turon. II. A.D. 567, Can. 20; Can. 36 Dunstan,

and should she withdraw after being solemnly veiled, to be excommunicated (261), as guilty of incest (262). No novice may be received into a religious house for money (263).

40. By the rule of the fourth century a virgin might not be consecrated under twenty-five years of age (264), nor a canoness under forty (265), and an abbess was required to be sixty years of age before appointment (266). The consecration or veiling of a nun should be performed by the bishop (267), or else by a presbyter with his authority, but not by an abbess (268). It should be preceded by a novitiate of one year for a cloistered

A.D. 963: If a religious woman turn herself to secular vanity ... and thinks with her wealth to make satisfaction, this will be vain.

(261). Syn. Rom. ad Gall. Can. 1; Innocent I. ap Gratian l. c. c. 10; Concil. Chalcedon A.D. 451, Can. 16, *Ibid.* c. 26; Concil. Aurel. V. A.D. 541, Can. 19: If afterwards leaving the hallowed precincts they give up their holy purpose from love of the world, or those who at their own homes have either as virgins or widows adopted the habit of conversion, let them be deprived of communion, together with those whom they have married. Concil. Paris III. A.D. 557, Can. 5; Concil. Turon II. A.D. 567, Can. 20; Concil. Martin. Brac. A.D. 572, *Ibid.* c. 26; Concil. Matiscon. I. A.D. 581, Can. 12; Concil. Lugdun. III. A.D. 583, Can. 3; Concil. Paris V. A.D. 615, Can. 13.

(262). Concil. Ancyr. A.D. 314, Can. 18 ap. Gratian l. c. c. 24, *Ibid.* c. 21, says she is worse than an adulteress. Leo, A.D. 459, *Ibid.* Caus. XX. Qu. l. c. 3. See note 246, and *Duties of Order*, notes 320 and 323.

(263). Concil. Westminster A.D. 1127, Can. 3; Concil. London A.D. 1175, Can. 8.

(264). Concil. Carthag. III. A.D. 397, Can. 4 ap. Gratian Caus. XX. Qu. l. c. 14, *Ibid.* c. 15; Concil. Turon. II. A.D. 567, Can. 20; Egbert's Excerpt. 91. See *Duties of Order*, note 321.

(265). Concil. Agath. A.D. 506, *Ibid.* c. 13: This was the rule for deaconesses by Concil. Chalcedon, Can. 15. See *Duties of Order*, § 49.

(266). Gregory *Ibid.* c. 13.

(267). Concil. Carthag. II. A.D. 390, Can. 3 ap. Gratian Caus. XXVI. Qu. VI. c. 1.

(268). Concil. Paris VI. A.D. 829, ap. Gratian Caus. XX. Qu. II. c. 3: If an abbess has the presumption either [to receive] a widow or veil a girl a virgin, let her be subject to canonical judgment until satisfaction. Innocent III. in Decret. Lib. v. Tit. XXXVIII. c. 10: We hear that in some dioceses abbesses bless their own nuns, hear their confessions, read the Gospel, and publicly preach. . . . Forbid its being done in future, for although the blessed Virgin was more honoured than all the apostles, yet to them and not her were given the keys.

nun, and of three years for a canoness (²⁶⁹). In taking the veil the nun is first attired in the habit of her order (²⁷⁰), her head being covered with a large altar-cloth or veil (²⁷¹); a written profession then is handed in by her and laid upon the altar (²⁷²), after which she receives the blessing (²⁷³). In the thirteenth century it was ruled that those who had worn the religious habit for a year should be deemed to be professed, so far at least as to be under all the obligations of the rule (²⁷⁴).

41. The veiling of nuns is directed to take place only at Easter, the Epiphany, or on the festival of some apostle, except by urgent request to avoid dishonour, or when death seems impending (²⁷⁵). Once veiled a nun may not migrate to another house, except to embrace a stricter rule (²⁷⁶). Spanish custom required the queen-dowager, on her husband's death, at once to enter a convent of canonesses (²⁷⁷), and the Gallican rule required the same from the widows of clergy (²⁷⁸).

(269). Concil. Aurel. V. A.D. 541, Can. 19: Let them remain a year in the lay garb, but in monasteries where the nuns are not cloistered three years.

(270). Stat. Eccl. Ant. A.D. 505, Can. 11 ap. Gratian I. Dist. XXIII. c. 24: When a holy virgin is presented to the bishop for consecration, let her be vested in the usual garment suited for her profession and holiness.

(271). Concil. Tolet. X. A.D. 656, Can. 5 ap. Gratian Caus. XXVII. Qu. 1. c. 36: Pallio capita sua contegant, and Caus. XX. Qu. 1. c. 11 and 13. The service of veiling is described in Lingard's Anglo-Saxon Church II. 12. See note 123.

(272). Concil. Tolet. X. A.D. 656, Can. 5.

(273). Cap. Reg. Franc. ap. Gratian Caus. XXVII. Qu. 1. c. 37: Let all know that the bodies of holy women consecrated to God by the vow of their own undertaking and the priest's words [of prayer] are proved by Scripture testimony to be God's temples. Therefore the violators of them are known to be guilty of sacrilege, and to be sons of perdition.

(274). Const. 18 Peckham, A.D. 1281.

(275). Gelasius, A.D. 494, *Ibid.* Caus. XX. Qu. 1. c. 11 and 15; Egbert's Excerpt. 90: The holy veil ought not to be put on virgins [or widows] devoted to God, except on the Epiphany, or Low Sunday, or on the nativity of an apostle, unless they be dangerously sick.

(276). Concil. Tribur. A.D. 895, *Ibid.* Caus. XX. Qu. IV. c. 1.

(277). Concil. Tolet. XIII. A.D. 683, Can. 5; Concil. Caesaraugust. III. A.D. 691, Can. 5.

(278). See *Duties of Order*, § 42; *Wedlock*, § 15.

IV.

RELIGIOUS ORDERS.

Origin of Religious Orders.

1. A religious order is the name applied to a group of associated communities or an aggregate of affiliated congregations, either of monks, regulars, or friars, which are united under a common head and hierarchy of their own, and are exempted from the ordinary territorial jurisdictions, being governed by laws of their own. Since the time of the Fourth Lateran Council, in 1215 A.D., when the consolidation of all the then existing monastic congregations was enjoined (¹), and the establishment of any new rule was forbidden (²), centralised religious orders have succeeded to the place formerly occupied by isolated congregations.

2. The religious orders which are most widespread and best known may be grouped under four different classes, according to the objects which they have primarily set themselves to attain (³),

(1). Decret. Lib. III. Tit. XXXV. c. 7; Const. 16 Peckham, A.D. 1281: We have found that many religious houses of the order of St. Augustin do not meet with the rest in their general chapter held every third year, according to the General Council. Lynd. 213.

(2). Concil. Lat. IV. A.D. 1215, in Decret. Lib. III. Tit. XXXVI. c. 9: Lest a too great diversity of religions [rules for the religious life] should introduce confusion into the Church of God, we forbid that any one in future should invent a new religion, but whoever wishes to be converted to religion, let him embrace one of the approved [rules]. Similarly, he who would in future found a new religious house, let him take the rule and appointment of it from the approved [forms]. We altogether forbid any man having a monk's place in different monasteries, or one abbot presiding over several monasteries. Const. 31 Edmund, A.D. 1236; Const. 9 Mepham. A.D. 1330; Boniface VIII. in Sext. Lib. III. Tit. XV. c. 1.

(3). Lynd. 214: Some religious orders are founded principally for works of the contemplative life, which consists in study and prayer, as the order of the Carthusians. The aim of other orders is to wait on hospitality and the sick, as the Cross-bearers and the brethren of St. Antony of Vienne.

Religious Orders. 121

viz. (1) those whose object is the worship and service of God by the contemplative life, and a closer union with God by knowing Him and forgetting or ignoring themselves([4]), such as the followers of St. Basil and St. Benedict; (2) those whose object is to serve God by active life, by exercising hospitality, caring for the sick and for strangers, and protecting pilgrims, such as the Hospitallers and Templars; (3) those whose object is to deepen and intensify the spiritual life of their brethren living in the world, and to teach them habits of self-denial by precept and example, such as the Friars; and (4) those whose aim is to spread the faith abroad or at home, such as the various missionary orders of mediaeval and post-mediaeval times.

CONTEMPLATIVE ORDERS OF LAYMEN.

3. The parent rule of all contemplative orders is that of St. Basil, but the parent society of all the monastic communities at present existing in the West ([5]) is the congregation founded by St. Benedict of Nursia at Monte Casino, in the year 529 A.D. ([6]). This congregation has, by the foundation of a number of houses which have in the main followed its rule, given rise to a variety of orders, of which the best known are (1) the

Some orders exist for the sake of preaching doctrine and spiritual counsel, such as the Friars-Preachers, Minorites, Augustinian Friars, and Carmelites; other orders for military service, such as the Hospitallers, and formerly the Templars.

(4). John XVII. 3 : This is life eternal, to know Thee the only true God, and Jesus Christ whom Thou hast sent. Cassian Collat. IX. 31 goes so far as to say : Prayer is not perfect in which a monk either understands himself or understands what he prays.

(5). The rule is in seventy-seven chapters, and requires three virtues—silence, humility, obedience, and prescribes three occupations—worship, reading, and manual labour.

(6). Benedict, born at Nursia A.D. 480, retired when seventeen to the desert of Subiaco, and lived for three years in a pit, fed by the monk Romanus. He converted the temple of Apollo at Monte Casino into an oratory, and established a congregation there, A.D. 529, and died 543. Elfric, Can. 34, A.D. 957 : Monks observe the rule of one man, Benedict, and live by his direction. Concil. London A.D. 1075, Can. 2 : That monks observe their order according to the rule of Benedict.

Black monks (⁷), or Benedictines proper; (2) the Cluniacs, Camaldunians, or Romaldeans, and other local orders; (3) the Cistercians; and (4) the Carthusians.

4. From the time of St. Augustin's mission, in 597 A.D., there existed in this country, among the Saxons, monastic houses [8] following a rule sometimes called after St. Gregory the Great, the peculiar features of which are no longer known. There existed also before that time among the Celts, in the western parts of the islands, other religious houses, following an earlier and different rule. Many of these communities appear to have been somewhat secular in their habits, and to have lived an associated rather than a common life [9]. About the year 780 another St. Benedict founded a new monastery at Aniane [10], in which he endeavoured to enforce the strict observance of St. Benedict's rule of a common life, and also to induce neighbouring monasteries to do the same. A century later King Alfred set to work to reform the existing English monasteries upon the new Benedictine pattern, and after him other sovereigns and archbishops attempted the same [11], but success was not permanently assured before the thirteenth century.

(7). Concil. Westminster A.D. 1200, Can. 15.

(8). Theodori Poenit. II. VI. in Haddan and Stubbs III. 195.

(9). Lingard, Anglo-Saxon Church I. 236. In Hist. Monast. de Abbendon II. 277, it is stated that Heane the founder had constructed twelve habitations for monks and twelve chapels; and, p. 272, there are said to have been twelve monks, so that each one had his own house and chapel. Not only the canons of the synods of Clovesho in 747 and 787 A.D., but the Constitutions of Langton seem to show that the inmates of monasteries often lived an associated but not a common life, having rooms of their own, and dressing as they pleased. See *Discipline of the Religious Life*, note 240.

(10). Born A.D. 750, in Languedoc; died A.D. 821, as abbot of Inda near Aix-la-Chapelle.

(11). Dunstan, circa 963 A.D. For instance, Hist. Monast. de Abbendon II. 279 says that in the time of St. Ethelwold, A.D. 1000, the religious life was corrupted by the incursions of the Danes and the austerity of the [new] Benedictine rule, so that hardly any but a poor man could become a monk. Therefore, St. Ethelwold, to attract the rich, did away with all the requirements not contained in St. Benedict's rule. Lanfranc, A.D. 1072, again introduced reform. Const. 19 Otho, A.D. 1237, orders the Benedictines to abstain from eating flesh, in accordance with the decretal of Innocent III. in Decret. Lib. III. Tit. XXXV. c. 6.

5. The order of the Benedictines, or Black monks as they were generally called, has been described as "an organisation diverse, complex, and irregular, rich rather than symmetrical, with many origins and centres and new beginnings, and the action of local influences" ([12]), which insisted upon common rather than associated religious life, combined active labour with prayer and contemplation ([13]), cultivated learning, and insisted upon entire self-surrender and obedience. Wherever the order established itself, it made the wilderness flourish like a garden, and brought untold blessings alike to the bodies and the souls of men. Whatever knowledge of agriculture, science, language, or philosophy the modern world has inherited from the old world, it owes mainly to the labours and industry of the cloistered Benedictines. The great Benedictine abbeys of this country were Westminster, Glastonbury, Bury St. Edmunds, Evesham, and St. Mary of York; and in the West of England, Tavistock and Bucfast ([14]). There were also twelve cathedral priories which were Benedictine foundations, of which Canterbury was the chief ([15]), and many other collegiate priories ([16]), such as Exeter and Crediton, and of later foundation, Ottery St. Mary.

6. The reformed Benedictine rule not being found sufficiently strict to satisfy the religious zeal of all, severer rules were devised for new congregations which sprung up in the tenth and eleventh centuries. Such was (1) the rule of Clugny, a

---

([12]). Newman, quoted by Gasquet in Montalembert's *Monks of the West.*

([13]). Lynd. 214 says that a man must be perfect in active life in order to be perfect in contemplative life. See *Discipline of the Religious Life*, note 12.

([14]). Oliver's Monasticon, p. 90. Bucfast was subsequently refounded as a Cistercian house in 1137 A.D. See J. Brooking Rowe in Trans. Devon. Association VIII. 809.

([15]). Viz., Canterbury, Winchester, Durham, Ely, Worcester, Norwich, Rochester, Bath, Coventry, Peterboro' or Medeshampstead, Gloucester, and Chester.

([16]). There were in Devonshire, Otterton, Totton or Totnes, Pilton, Modbury, Cowick near, and St. Nicolas in Exeter, and Polsloe for nuns. See Dugdale, Monasticon I. 1039.

French congregation established by St. Benno at Clugny, near Mâcon, in the year 909 A.D. ([17]). The Cluniacs, in addition to many other points of discipline, made it a duty to recite psalms whilst they were at work; to keep open hospitality daily for the poor, needy, and travellers; and to make their Churches palaces for the poor. More than 2000 houses were affiliated under this rule before the thirteenth century, amongst those in this country being St. James', Exeter ([18]), St. Mary Magdalen, Barnstaple ([19]), and Carswell Priory in East Devon ([20]). Such was (2) the rule of Camaldoli, an Italian congregation founded at Campo Maldoli, near Florence, by St. Romuald, in 1009 A.D. The Camaldunians, or Romaldeans as they were also called, dwelt in separate cells, and met together only for prayers. Some of them observed an inviolable silence during the two Lents, others during one hundred days in each year. On Sundays and Thursdays their diet consisted of herbs, on other days of bread and water. In the seventeenth century they were divided into five congregations, with about 2000 members ([21]). Outside Italy they had few houses, and in this country none. Such were also the rules of (3) the Cistercians and (4) the Carthusians.

7. The Cistercians ([22]), usually called White monks, because, like the Camaldunians, they wore a white habit with a black

(17). Lorain L'Abbaye de Clugny (Dijon, 1839).
(18). Fehr Geschichte der Mönchsorden I. 68.
(19). Oliver, Monasticon Exoniense 191.
(20). *Ibid.* 196.
(21). *Ibid.* 311.
(22). Alexander III. in Decret. Lib. III. Tit. xxxv. c. 3, complains that many Cistercian foundations, against the rule of their order, possess village lordships (villas), churches, and altars, and undertake liegeships and homages, and hold courts for justice and tribute, . . . and exhorts them to be content with their ancient allowances. *Id. Ibid.* Tit. xxxi. c. 7 forbids Cistercians to be received in other monasteries without the consent of their abbots. Concil. Lat. IV. *Ibid.* Tit. xxxv. c. 37 directs Cistercians, as being experienced in the ordering of congregations, to preside in the general chapters for consolidating monastic congregations. Const. 22 Othobon, A.D. 1268, requires them to appoint perpetual vicars wherever they have Churches.

scapular and hood, were founded by Robert of Molesme, at Citeaux, near Châlons, in 1098 A.D. Their co-founder was the Englishman Stephen Harding, who, in 1119 A.D., devised the rule of the Annual Chapter ([23]), afterwards adopted by all the other orders, and the Chart of Charity. After the election of St. Bernard to the abbacy of Clairvaux, in 1115 A.D., the Cistercians became famous throughout Europe, and within one hundred years had 1800 affiliated houses. They are sometimes called the spoiled children of the Apostolic See. The earliest Cistercian house in this country was founded at Waverley in Surrey, in 1128 A.D., by Walter Giffard, Bishop of Winchester. Others soon followed, and at the time of the dissolution the Cistercians had one hundred and one houses in the kingdom ([24]), amongst others the great houses of Ford ([25]), Dunkeswell ([26]), Newenham ([27]), and Buckland ([28]), in Devon. In sacred things the Cistercians were distinguished for eschewing all colour and ornament; they were also more conservative than others of the traditional forms of service ([29]). A branch of them, of increased severity, was established in 1663 A.D., by the Abbé Armand de Rancé, at La Trappe or the Pond, who take from thence their designation of Trappists.

8. The Carthusians were originally founded at La Chartreuse, in 1086 A.D., by St. Bruno of Cologne, and slowly increased until, in 1258 A.D., they had fifty-six houses. Papal recognition was accorded to them by Alexander III. in 1174 A.D., and

(23). The rule and the Chart of Charity were approved by Calixtus II. in 1139.

(24). 27 Hen. VIII. c. 28 gave to the king all monasteries having lands under £200 a year. 31 Hen. VIII. c. 13 gave him the larger abbeys. See Gasquet's Henry VIII. and the English Monasteries.

(25). Oliver 338 ; Hook's Lives II. 542.

(26). *Ibid.* 393 ; J. Brooking Rowe in Trans. Devon. Assoc. IX. 382.

(27). *Ibid.* 357 ; Trans. Devon. Assoc. IX. 361. Founded 1245, by William de Mohun.

(28). *Ibid.* 330 ; Trans. Devon. Assoc. VII. 329 ; VIII. 797.

(29). Lynd. 9 states that it was the custom of the Cistercians to give the cup to the people in lesser Churches, but, according to ancient custom, first to mix with it unconsecrated wine.

their manner of life was introduced into this country about 1180 by St. Hugh, afterwards Bishop of Lincoln, who established a Carthusian house at Witham, in Somerset[30]. The celebrated Charterhouse in London was founded by Sir William Marney in 1371. At the dissolution the Carthusians had eleven houses in this country, and showed the finest examples of the martyr spirit[31]. Until 1130 A.D. the order had no written rule. Then the fifth prior of the Chartreuse, Guigot by name, compiled the Carthusian Customs (*Consuetudines Cartusiae*), which have since been supplemented by the collected resolutions of general chapters. The peculiarities of the order are (1) the strict separation of the members from each other, to prevent even indirect contact with the world; (2) the separation of the professed brethren from the lay brethren or *conversi*, lay brethren in this rule holding a very inferior position; (3) the separation of each house from all contact with the neighbourhood; and (4) the separation of the order from contact with other monastic orders. For solitude, length of the night office, and scantiness of diet, this is the most austere order.

CONTEMPLATIVE ORDERS OF CLERGY.

9. Canons is the name given to the clergy of a collegiate Church, either because they live according to rule (κανών), or else because they are on the roll of those supported by the Church (ἐν τῷ κανόνι)[32]. Those living a common life under a rule are termed *regular* canons; those only associated in serving the same Church, but not living a common life, secular canons. Although regular canons are met with under that name in the eighth century[33], yet the origin of the order of regular canons

---

(30). Margaret Thompson, History of Somerset Carthusians; Hodges, 1895.

(31). Gasquet's Henry VIII. and the English Monasteries; Froude, Short Studies II. 95.

(32). Concil. Chalcedon A.D. 451, Can. 1.

(33). Concil. Chelsea A.D. 787, Can. 4: That bishops take care that canons live canonically—may refer to secular canons, but Chrodegang's canons at Metz were certainly regular canons.

called after St. Augustin is usually referred to Arnald, Odelo, Pontius, and Durandus, four canons of the Church of Avignon, who, in the year 1038 A.D., obtained permission to withdraw from active clerical work to lead an ascetic and contemplative life in retirement from the world ([34]). The name seems to have been first adopted by them after the Second Lateran Council, in 1139 A.D., to distinguish them from the regular canons of cathedral Churches, who followed Chrodegang's rule. In this country the first congregation of Augustinian canons was established at Colchester in 1105 A.D. Many others followed, and soon the Augustinians became a numerous body ([35]). At the dissolution they had 170 houses, amongst others Hartland Abbey ([36]), Plympton ([37]), Frithelstock ([38]), and Cornworthy ([39]) Priories, besides Canonsleigh Priory for canonesses ([40]). Their dress was a black cassock and white rochet, and over that a black gown and hood.

10. The Praemonstrants or Norbertines were an offshoot from the Augustinians, who followed a somewhat stricter rule. The first monastery of this order was established by St. Norbert, in 1120 A.D., at Prémontré in the Isle of France, and in 1146 their first monastery in this country was erected in Lincolnshire by Peter de Saulia. Their dress was white with a scapulary before the cassock, out of doors a white cloak and hat, and in Church a surplice. In mediaeval times their houses were the great seminaries of the clergy, and they alone among religious orders were eligible to have the charge of secular Churches. In the reign of Edward I. this order had twenty-seven monasteries in this country, amongst others Tor Abbey ([41]) in Devonshire, founded in 1196 A.D., and Dale Abbey in Derbyshire ([42]).

11. Another offshoot of the Augustinian rule were the Gilbertines, founded by St. Gilbert of Sempringham in Lin-

---

([34]). See *Discipline of the Religious Life*, § 5.
([35]). Dugdale's Monasticon VI. 37.
([36]). Oliver's Monasticon Exoniense, 203.
([37]). *Ibid.* 129.   ([38]). *Ibid.* 219.
([39]). *Ibid.* 236.   ([40]). *Ibid.* 224.
([41]). *Ibid.* 169.   ([42]). Dugdale's Monasticon.

colnshire, about the year 1148 A.D. (⁴³). St. Gilbert's original foundation was for poor maidens who were resolved to lead a life of chastity, and made vows of absolute seclusion. They were attended by a few servants, from whom they received all they required through a window. Similar institutions were soon erected in other places, and St. Gilbert requested Pope Eugenius III. to incorporate his foundations with the Cistercians. The scheme not finding favour at Rome, he was obliged to provide for the guidance of his congregations in another way, which he did by attaching a convent of canons to each nunnery, thus after the old English pattern creating double-monasteries— one division for men, the other for women, the two separated by a high wall. The men's monastery consisted of ten canons, together with a number of lay brethren, who followed the rule of Citeaux. The nuns were placed under the rule of St. Benedict; and hospitals for the poor, sick, widows, and orphans were connected with their regular establishments. At the time of the dissolution this order possessed twenty-one houses and eleven double-monasteries, but it was never propagated outside of this country.

CHARITABLE ORDERS.

12. Very different from the contemplative orders are the societies of active charity. Most of these existed as individual congregations, and never grew into distinct orders. Among such may be named the congregation of St. Antony at Vienne, founded by Gaston, in 1095 A.D., for the cure of the sick (⁴⁴); the hospital at Montpellier, founded by Guido in 1173 A.D., and affiliated by Innocent III., in 1204, to the Hospital of the Holy Ghost at Rome (⁴⁵); the order of St. Bridget of Wastena in Sweden (⁴⁶);

---

(43). Holsten. Tom. II.; Hurter Innocenz III. und seine Zeitgenossen IV. 230.

(44). Giesseler III. 219. Lynd. 213 says that there was a house of St. Antony in London, a dependency of the house of St. Antony at Vienne, and that it conformed to the rule of St. Augustine.

(45). Hurter IV. 220.

(46). Lynd. 213 says that Sion House near London was a dependency of

Religious Orders. 129

the Trinitarians, founded in 1198 A.D., at Gerfroi, in the diocese of Meaux, by John de Matha, for the redemption of captives from the hands of the infidels ([47]); the lepers' house at Plympton ([48]), and the hospital of St. John at Exeter for the relief of the poor ([49]). There were nevertheless two which developed into important orders, viz., the Hospitallers and Templars ([50]).

13. The Hospitallers, or Knights of St. John of Jerusalem, were a society of knights who, in 1099 A.D., erected a hospital or guest-house ([51]) at Jerusalem for the reception of pilgrims and the care of the sick. When the kingdom of Jerusalem came to an end in 1291 A.D., they escaped to Cyprus, and afterwards settled in Rhodes. Driven from Rhodes in 1523 A.D., they settled in Malta, and in 1530 A.D. the island was ceded to them by Charles V. The Templars were an order of knights established in 1118 A.D., in the neighbourhood of the Temple at Jerusalem, to preserve the peace in the Holy Land, to protect pilgrims ([52]), and to secure the approaches and public roads from robbers. At the Council of Vienne, in 1311 A.D., the order was suppressed ([53]), on the insinuation that it had misused its

the order of St. Bridget in Sweden, but that it conformed to the Augustinian rule, and that he had himself seen and handled [A.D. 1429] a papal ordination making it independent of the mother-house of Wastena.

(47). Hurter IV. 213.
(48). Oliver Mon. 152.   (49). *Ibid.* Mon. 300.
(50). Concil. Lat. III. A.D. 1179, in Decret. Lib. v. Tit. XXXIII. c. 3; Concil. Westminster A.D. 1200, Can. 14: We decree according to the tenor of the Lateran Council that no brothers Templars, Hospitallers, nor any religious whatsoever do receive tithes, churches, or any ecclesiastical benefices from a lay hand. Lynd. 214. The lands of the Hospitallers in England and Ireland were confiscated by 32 Hen. VIII. c. 24. See 2 Eliz. c. 7.

(51). Syn. Rom. A.D. 826, Can. 24, in Decret. Lib. III. Tit. XXXVI. c. 3, directs guest-houses to be provided by the care of the bishops in whose dioceses they are situated.

(52). Spelman Gloss. says that their vow was ut peregrinis tutum redderent iter Hierosolytanum venientesque exciperent hospitio.

(53). 17 Ed. II. St. III. A.D. 1324, gave their lands to the Hospitallers. Lynd. 352, 221.

VOL. II.   I

position for its own aggrandisement, and that its members had been guilty of horrible crimes. The charges are now generally believed to have been invented as a pretext for despoiling it of its great wealth.

Mendicant Orders.

14. A new class of orders appeared in the thirteenth century, a Western reproduction of the wandering ascetics of the East, with the rule of obedience and subordination to a central authority superadded. Orders of this class go by the name of Mendicant or Begging Orders, or Friars. Intermediate between cloistered monks and laymen, the Friars made it their business to supplement the shortcomings of the parochial clergy as teachers, and to raise the standard of Christian life by example. It was their rule to possess nothing, but to move about from place to place, preaching and teaching, and to be content with whatever might be given them. Two of these orders had the privilege of being allowed to beg conferred upon them [54], viz., the Dominicans or Friars Preachers, and the Franciscans or Minorites [55]; two others were allowed to exercise it because they were already existing before the Lateran decree forbidding new orders was passed [56], viz., the Carmelites and Austin Friars [57].

15. The Dominicans or Preaching Friars, commonly called Black Friars, because, over a white garment and scapular, they wore a black mantle and hood, and in France called Jacobins, because their convent was situated in the Rue St. Jacques, were founded by the Spaniard, St. Dominic, at Toulouse, in 1215.

---

(54). Lynd. 289.

(55). Concil. Lugdun. II. A.D. 1274, in Sext. Lib. III. Tit. XVII. c. 1, § 2, calls them Praedicatorum et Minorum ordines. Alexander IV. *Ibid.* Tit. XIV. c. 2 forbids a shorter novitiate than one year. Lynd. 344.

(56). Concil. Lat. IV. in Decret. Lib. III. Tit. XXXVI. c. 9; Const. 31 Edmund, A.D. 1236.

(57). Concil. Lugdun. II. l. c. calls them Eremitarum sancti Augustini et Carmelitarum ordines.

Their rule was formed by combining the rule of St. Augustine with divers constitutions borrowed from the Carthusians. The aim of the order was the conversion and refutation of heretics by preaching, the pursuit of learning, and austerity of life. In 1221, Gilbert du Fresney, with twelve brethren, founded the first house of the order in this country at Oxford, and soon after another in London. At the house in Holborn two general chapters were held, in 1250 and 1263 A.D., the latter being attended by St. Thomas of Aquinum. In 1276 A.D., the mayor and aldermen of London gave to the order two streets between Ludgate and the Thames, still called after them Blackfriars; and on the site of the present *Times* office their general chapters were held in 1314 A.D. and 1335 A.D. The Dominicans had monasteries at Warwick, Canterbury, Chelmsford, Ipswich, Norwich, Exeter ([58]), and other places, and numbered fifty-two priories and two subsidiary houses in England and Wales at the time of the dissolution.

16. The rivals of the Dominicans in popular esteem were the Franciscans, or Minorites (*fratres minores*) as they were called by their founder. By the public they were called Grey Friars, from the colour of their clothing. As the Dominicans laid themselves out to win the higher and more educated classes, so the Franciscans sought to leaven the masses. To effect this they took a vow of absolute poverty, and then went forth to preach and to beg. The order was founded by St. Francis of Assissi in 1209 A.D., and in 1219 A.D. numbered 5000 members. The rule was approved by Honorius III. in 1223 A.D. There was a second order of nuns, called Poor Ladies or Poor Clares, from Sta. Clara, their first abbess, and sometimes Damiantines, from their first Church, that of St. Damian in Assissi. There was also a third order for those living in the world, called Tertiaries. Brother Angelo of Pisa, with eight companions, introduced the order into this country in 1224 A.D. Their first house was at Canterbury, but they also soon acquired another in London, in the ward of Faringdon Within, on the site now

---

(58). Oliver Monasticon, p. 334, says that this foundation was anterior to 1240.

occupied by Christ's Hospital, and were established in Exeter before the year 1240 A.D. ([59]), and at Plymouth before 1383 A.D. ([60]). The Franciscan province of England was apportioned into seven "custodies" or divisions, and at the dissolution it included sixty-five houses in England and Wales.

17. Almost from the first the Franciscans were divided into two parties—one led by Elias, the third general of the order, who assumed a garb less coarse, built beautiful churches and convents, and cultivated art and learning; these were termed *Brethren of the Community;* the other, led by St. Antony of Padua, who advocated the primitive rigour and called themselves *Spirituals*. St. Bonaventura, who was elected general in 1256 A.D., favoured the latter party, and gradually restored strict discipline; but with the generalship of Matteo di Aquas Spartas the laxer party became predominant, and continued so until the order split into two branches—the *Conventuals*, who followed the mitigated rule ([61]), and the *Observants*, who adhered to the primitive and strict rule. The latter were confirmed by the Council of Constance in 1415 A.D., received permission to hold general chapters of their own, and obtained possession of St. Francis' Portiuncula at Assissi. Henry IV. is said to have introduced the Observants into this country, but no trace of them can be found before Henry VII.'s time, who built two or three houses for them ([62]). The Capuchins are an offshoot of the Observants, who were founded by Matteo di Baschi in 1525 A.D. They were not introduced into this country before 1630 A.D. The Recollets are a French congregation of Observants, founded by the Duke of Nevers in 1592 A.D. The Alcantarines, the strictest branch of Observants, are a Spanish congregation, founded in 1540 A.D. by Peter of Alcantara.

18. There existed on Mount Carmel, from the earliest times,

---

(59). Oliver, *Ibid.* p. 330.

(60). *Ibid.* p. 151.

(61). Extrav. Tit. XIV. c. 1, says that the rule to wear common clothes (vilia indumenta) must be interpreted by the superior.

(62). Gasquet's Henry VIII. and the English Monasteries, 155 note; Tanner, Monasticon VI. 1504.

hermits, to whom John Nepos, Bishop of Jerusalem, gave a rule in the fourth century. After many vicissitudes, Berthold, Count of Limoges, in 1156 A.D., associated them into the order of St. Mary of Carmel, for whom Albert, Patriarch of Jerusalem, in 1209, drew up a rule. They were then called Carmelites or White Friars, and also Barry Friars, from the barred dress which the Saracens compelled them to wear when they took possession of the East. The rule was confirmed by Honorius III. in 1224 A.D. In 1240 A.D. the order was introduced into this country, and a fresh rule given to it by Innocent IV. in 1247. At the time of the dissolution the White Friars had forty houses in England and Wales, amongst others one at Plymouth ([63]), founded in 1314. There are now three branches of Carmelites, known respectively as Calced, Discalced, and Tertiaries. The Tertiaries were established in 1476 A.D. by Sixtus IV. The barefooted or discalced Carmelites were founded by St. Teresa at Avila in 1562.

19. The Augustinians ([64]), or hermits of St. Augustine, commonly called Austin Friars, are the fourth of the Mendicant Orders, and were constituted an order by Alexander IV. in 1256 A.D., by the amalgamation of eight different congregations, among which the John-Bonites, the Brittines, and the Tuscan hermits held the chief place. Each of these congregations followed the so-called rule of St. Augustine, whence they were all called Augustinians or Austin Friars. They were never an important order. At the time of the dissolution they had thirty-two houses in this country, and must be kept entirely distinct from the canons regular of St. Augustine.

LATER MISSIONARY ORDERS.

20. To meet the altered circumstances of more recent times new orders began to appear in the sixteenth century, having for their object the diffusion and spread of the faith at home and abroad. Among these may be mentioned (1) the Jesuits

(63). Oliver, Monasticon 152.
(64). Lynd. 214, quoted note 3.

founded by Ignatius Loyola in 1540 A.D., and distinguished for their moral theology; (2) the Oratorians, a congregation of secular priests without vows, founded in 1575 A D., by St. Philip Neri; (3) the congregation of the Mission, or Vincentians, founded in 1624 by St. Vincent de Paul, for the service of the poor and the improvement of the clergy by missions; (4) the Passionists, founded by St. Paul of the Cross in 1720; and (5) the Redemptorists, founded by St. Alfonso Liguori at Scala, in 1732. The two last-named orders add to the usual vows a vow of perseverance in the order, and the Redemptorists refuse all benefices, dignities, or offices whatsoever.

V.

ECCLESIASTICAL SEVERITY.

Censures, Penances, and Penalties.

1. The various means which are employed for the purpose of enforcing spiritual or ecclesiastical discipline are generally called coercion or severity. They are of three kinds, viz. (1) those which are employed to bring an offender to repentance, termed *censures*; (2) those which are employed to restore him to the lost estate of holiness, called *penances*; and (3) those which are used purely vindictively, called *penalties* ([1]). The power to inflict censures and penances belongs to the Church, as a divine society seeking the salvation of all men. The power to inflict vindictive penalties as such belongs to it as a society entrusted by the civil community with some portion of its temporal government. The term *poena* is used in Latin to express both a penance and a penalty. Hence penal severity includes as well corrective as vindictive severity.

2. It is the contention of many that originally the Church had only one form of severity, viz., exclusion from Church fellowship ([2]). This, however, involved at once both censure

---

([1]). Many canonists make only a two-fold division into (1) *poenae*, and (2) *censurae*. Schmalzgrueber, Jus. Univ. Lib. v. Tit. 37, defines *poenae* as delictorum coercitiones sive vindictae ad disciplinae publicae emendationem institutae. They then distinguish (for instance Craisson § 6302) between (*a*) poenae proprie dictae, *i.e.*, vindictive penalties, and (*b*) opera satisfactoria a confessariis imposita, *i.e.*, private penances.

([2]). Morinus, Petrus de Marca, and others. See *Discipline Generally*, note 34. Devoti Lib. iv. Tit. i. § 6, and Tit. xvii. § 11, clearly shows that penance, the subjective side of severity, was always distinguished from censure, the objective side of it. See Matt. viii. 15. Socrates iv. 23 gives an account of penances undergone by holy monks who were certainly not under censure. Concil. Turon. A.D. 460, Can. 8; Concil. Venet. A.D. 465, Can. 3 and 13; Concil. Agath. A.D. 506, ap. Gratian i. Dist. xxxv. c. 9,

and punishment. For when, by exclusion from the covenant of grace, the use of the ordinary means of grace was withdrawn from an offender, Satan recovered his lost power over the human body. Suffering followed in consequence—either sickness of mind, or sickness of body, or both (³), and thus exclusion from communion became highly penal. The object of the exclusion being nevertheless to bring the offender to repentance, "that the soul might be saved in the day of the Lord" (⁴), the recovery of the offender from the power of the arch-foe by means of the prayers of the Church, and the substitution of voluntarily undertaken penances for his cruel buffetings, or, in other words, the substitution of the lesser excommunication coupled with penance, for the greater excommunication (⁵), was a merciful provision for the benefit of offenders. Severity then only became vindictive when it was met in the spirit of obduracy (⁶), but such was not its intention.

3. In mediaeval times, when the Roman pontiffs had become

directs a drunken presbyter either (1) to be removed from communion for thirty days—(a censure)—or (2) to undergo bodily penance. Concil. Epaon. A.D. 517, Can. 5 ; Concil. Matiscon. A.D. 581, Can. 1 ; Ayliffe 155.

(3). See *Penance*, notes 17, 86, 152, and *Discipline Generally*, note 23.

(4). 1 Cor. v. 5, the delivery of the incestuous Corinthian to Satan was εἰς ὄλεθρον τῆς σαρκὸς, that his body might be buffeted by Satan, in order that his spirit might be saved [*i.e.*, presented pure before God, according to Tertullian de Pudic. c. 13]. In 1 Tim. I. 20 Hymenaeus and Alexander were delivered to Satan, in order that they might "learn not to blaspheme." In 1 Cor. xi. 32, St. Paul says: When we are judged we are being chastened by the Lord, in order that we should not be punished with the world. In 2 Cor. xiii. 10, he states that his spiritual weapons are given him for edification, not for destruction.

(5). Offenders who have come to satisfaction are termed penitents—(see *Penance*, notes 66 and 96, and *Discipline Generally*, § 22)—and belong in a sense to the Church. (See *Penance*, notes 97 and 105.) Hence they are allowed to participate up to a certain point in the prayers of the Church (see *Order*, note 4), although excluded from the prayers of the faithful, and from participation in the offering.

(6). Lynd. 264, speaking of obduracy, says : Man may be without grace in two ways, either because he will not receive it, or because God does not give it. But God does not wish man to be without grace, except in so far as being without it is good for him.

Ecclesiastical Severity. 137

temporal sovereigns, and elsewhere bishops and abbots had acquired the rank and privileges of temporal princes and barons, besides imposing public penances for correction and the soul's health, they also imposed public penalties, for the good of the community and the protection of society. Many of the disputes which agitated the world in mediaeval times arose from an attempt to apply papal decrees concerning temporal matters which the Pope had issued to prelates in localities where he possessed temporal sovereignty, to other localities where he possessed no temporal rights [7]. It is, however, well not to forget that from the time of King John's surrender of the kingdom to Innocent III., in the year 1213 [8], until the year 1366, when the surrender was repudiated by Parliament, this country, besides being an integral part of the Western Church, was held as a fief of the Holy See [9], and was therefore subject to such temporal regulations made by the Pope as an over-lord in feudal times had power to make. Here, therefore, as elsewhere, ecclesiastical severity is found in use of three kinds, viz. (1) remedial or medicinal, to bring an offender to repentance; (2) corrective, to restore him to holiness; and

---

[7]. For instance, the dispute about investitures.

[8]. Lingard, vol. II. p. 165, chap. 5: On the 14th day of May, in the Church of the Templars, the king, surrounded by the prelates, barons, and knights, put into the hands of Pandulph a charter, subscribed by himself, one archbishop, one bishop, nine earls, and three barons, declaring . . . that of his own free will, and with the unanimous consent of his barons, he had granted to God, to the holy apostles Peter and Paul, to Pope Innocent, and Innocent's rightful successors, the kingdom of England and the kingdom of Ireland, to be holden by himself and the heirs of his body of the Bishop of Rome, in fee by the annual rent (*census*) of 1000 marks, reserving to himself the administration of justice and of all the rights of the crown.

[9]. According to Lingard, vol. III. p. 126, chap. 3: The rent or *census* was intermittently paid for nearly a century. On the death of Edward I. seventeen years' arrears were due, which Edward II. discharged, and the rent was faithfully paid by Edward III. up to the year 1333, when the war with France began. On the return of peace, Urban V., in 1366, demanded the thirty-three years' rent in arrear. Edward consulted his Parliament, with the result that Parliament declared King John's act *ultra vires*.

(3) vindictive, to warn others for the public good. The two former are forms of spiritual severity, the last-named is ecclesiastical rather than spiritual.

Remedial Severity, Censures.

4. A censure is defined to be a form of remedial severity ([10]) whereby a baptized person is deprived of some spiritual privilege, such as the use of the sacraments, participation in the suffrages and charitable works of the Church, the exercise of sacred functions either for a fixed time or indefinitely, because of some offence or act of disobedience on his part, in order to bring him to repentance. In itself it is not penal, but it quickly becomes such if it fails in its object of bringing the offender to repentance, and is often spoken of as the spiritual ([11]) or the bishop's sword ([12]). There are generally said to be three kinds of it, viz., suspension, excommunication, and the interdict ([13]).

(10). Innocent III. in Decret. Lib. I. Tit. II. c. 11 : He who is deprived of communion because of contumacy, should be restored as soon as he has made fitting satisfaction. Concil. Lugdun. A.D. 1245, in Sext. Lib. V. Tit. XI. c. 1 : Since excommunication is medicinal, not penal (mortalis), its aim being to discipline, not to destroy (eradicans), provided the subject of it does not meet it with contempt. Const. 28 Othobon, A.D. 1268 : Ecclesiastical censures . . . are . . . a medicine intended for the cure of the party coerced.

(11). Const. 4 Boniface, A.D. 1261. The two swords are distinguished by Concil. Lugdun. A.D. 1245, in Sext. Lib. V. Tit. XI. c. 6 ; Lynd. 127 ; 9 Ed. II. St. I. c. 6, A.D. 1315 ; 31 Eliz. c. 6, sec. 9 ; Lynd. 256.

(12). Gratian Caus. XVI. Qu. II. c. 1 ; Innocent III. in Decret. Lib. V. Tit. XXXIII. c. 11 ; Const. 31 Langton, A.D. 1222 ; Const. 7 Stratford, A.D. 1343 ; Lynd. 176, 196 ; Devoti Lib. IV. Tit. XVIII.

(13). Matt. XVIII. 17 ; 1 Cor. V. 11, 13 ; 2 Thess. III. 14, are instances of the three. Concil. Ilerd. A.D. 523, Can. 6, speaks of (1) separation from communion, and (2) from consorting with the faithful. John VIII. A.D. 868, ap. Gratian Caus. III. Qu. IV. c. 12. The three are enumerated by Innocent III. in Decret. Lib. V. Tit. XL. c. 20, and Const. 28 Othobon, A.D. 1268 ; Lynd. 9, 143, 110, 196, 199, 256. The interdict dates from the twelfth century.

Ecclesiastical Severity. 139

The three kinds have many points in common (14), but in many respects they differ (15).

5. Suspension, called also abstention (16), medicinal repulsion (17), simple separation (18), or the lesser excommuni-

(14). Lynd. 349 states that they have ten points in common: (1) They require the same forms to be followed, Sext. Lib. v. Tit. xi. c. 1; (2) an appeal precedent suspends their operation, but not an appeal subsequent, Decret. Lib. ii. Tit. xxviii. c. 53; (3) they exclude those involved in them from taking part in divine service, Decret. Lib. v. Tit. xxvii. c. 7; (4) each must be preceded by monition, Decret. Lib. ii. Tit. xxviii. c. 26; (5) absolution may be preceded by an oath to stand to satisfaction, and may be granted *ad cautelam*, Decret. Lib. v. Tit. xxxix. c. 52; (6) each must be respected by superiors, *Ibid.* Lib. i. Tit. xxxi. 3; (7) during their existence the party is incapable of promotion, *Ibid.* Lib. i. Tit. iv. c. 8; (8) none of them can be inflicted without a citation, Sext. Lib. ii. Tit. xv. c. 3; (9) the special sons of the Apostolic See claim exemption, Sext. Lib. v. Tit. xii. c. 1; (10) all of them are included in the term ecclesiastical censure, Decret. Lib. v. Tit. xx. c. 20.

(15). Lynd. 349 enumerates: (1) Participation is permitted with one suspended and interdicted, but not with one excommunicated. (2) Excommunication and suspension apply to persons, the interdict to places. (3) The effect of an excommunication when pronounced cannot be suspended; the effect of the two others can. (4) There can be no relaxation of an interdict *ad cautelam*, but there can be of the other two. (5) A bishop is bound by a sentence of excommunication, although not named therein, but not by an interdict of suspension. (6) A corporation cannot be excommunicated, but may be interdicted. (7) Excommunicates are not admitted to penance except *in articulo mortis*, whereas those suspended or interdicted are. (8) On certain festivals the interdicted are admitted to church, but not the excommunicated. (9) Excommunication is never inflicted for the fault of another—Augustin ap. Gratian Caus. xxiv. Qu. iii. c. 1—whereas suspension and the interdict are. *Id. Ibid.* Caus. xvii. Qu. iv. c. 8.

(16). ἀφορισμός. Cyprian Ep. 66 (Oxf. 78), A.D. 254, ad. Steph.; Concil. Elib. A.D. 305, Can. 79: Placuit eum abstineri. Concil. Tolet. A.D. 400, Can. 13, ap. Gratian iii. Dist. ii. c. 18; Pseudo-Isidor. *Ibid.* Caus. vi. Qu. l. c. 3. Theodori Poenit. i. i. 1 in H. and S. iii. 137: Abstineant se ab ecclesia.

(17). Augustin Serm. 351; *Ibid.* Caus. ii. Qu. l. c. 1: We may not repel any one from communion (although such repulsion be not mortal, but medicinal) unless he either confesses himself guilty or is proved guilty. Concil. Lugdun. A.D. 1245, in Sext. Lib. v. Tit. xi. c. 1.

(18). Theodori Poenit. i. xiv. 2 in H. and S. 187: Non separentur.

cation ([19]), and occasionally a personal interdict ([20]), consists in being excluded from offering and participation in the sacred rites of the Church, whilst still being allowed to participate in the prayers. In mediaeval terminology it is described as separation from passive communion, or the receiving of the sacraments whilst still being allowed active communion, or the administration of them to others ([21]). A graver form of it is exclusion from participation in the prayers of the faithful; but this is no longer used as a distinct form of public censure. A graver form still is exclusion from all association with the faithful, or, as it is said, from entrance to the Church ([22]). The last named is termed the greater excommunication.

6. The greater excommunication ([23]), which is generally understood when excommunication is prescribed ([24]), called also complete separation ([25]), or mortal repulsion ([26]), involves not only exclusion from passive communion in the sacraments, but also exclusion from active communion in them, and from all association with the faithful ([27]). With one thus excommunicated

---

(19). Gratian Caus III. Qu. IV. c. 12. Law's Forms, 67.
(20). Const. 10 Clarendon, A.D. 1164; Lynd. 94, 110.
(21). Law's Forms, p. 124.
(22). Gregory VII. ap. Gratian I. Dist. LXXXI. c. 15 : We forbid them entrance to the Church till they come to satisfaction. Concil. Lat. IV. A.D. 1215, Can. 47 in Decret. Lib. v. Tit. XXXIX. c. 48; Const. 17 Boniface, A.D. 1261; Const. 21 Peckham, A.D. 1281; Boniface VIII. in Sext. Lib. V. Tit. XI. c. 20; Const. 7 Stratford, A.D. 1342; Lynd. 99, 110; Morinus de Poenit. Lib. VI. c. 25.
(23). Apost. Const. II. 40 : But do not thou, O bishop, presently abhor any person who has fallen into one or two offences, nor exclude him from the word of the Lord, nor reject him from common intercourse. Const. 31 Langton, A.D. 1222; Const. 20 Edmund, A.D. 1236; Const. 1 Stratford, A.D. 1343; Const. 1 Arundel, A.D. 1408; Lynd. 127.
(24). Gregory IX. in Decret. Lib. v. Tit. XXXIX. c. 59; Lynd. 78.
(25). ἀφορισμὸς παντελής, omnimoda separatio. Concil. Tolet. I. A.D. 400, Can. 15 : If any one is found to speak or eat with one who is separated, let him be separated himself (ipse abstineatur).
(26). Augustin ap. Gratian Caus. II. Qu. 1. c. 1, quoted above, note 17.
(27). Law's Forms, p. 124.

and denounced by name ([28]) no layman, under pain of the lesser excommunication, nor clergyman, under pain of suspension from office, may have relations ([29]), either in food, drink, prayer, or the kiss of peace ([30]). Because of its temporal consequences, this censure is termed animadversion ([31]), or the temporal sword ([32]), and ought never to be imposed without the advice of other skilful physicians ([33]).

7. Excommunication may be awarded either (1) solemnly, *i.e.*, by the Christian body acting collectively, or (2) non-solemnly, by those having jurisdiction to act on its behalf ([34]), as by a

---

([28]). Craisson, § 6493, 6501, 6561, states that this is the rule since the time of the Council of Constance.

([29]). Innocent III. *Ibid.* c. 29 ; Gregory IX. *Ibid.* c. 55.

([30]). Rom. XVI. 17: ἐκκλίνατε ἀπ' αὐτῶν. 2 Thess. III. 14 : καὶ μὴ συναμίγνυσθε αὐτῷ. Apost. Can. 11 : If any one prays with a person excommunicated, let him be suspended. Concil. Antioch. A.D. 341, Can. 2 ; Concil. Tolet. I. A.D. 400, Can. 15 ap. Gratian Caus. XI. Qu. III. c. 26 ; Stat. Eccl. Ant. A.D. 505, *Ibid.* c. 19 : He who communicates or prays with one excommunicate, let him be excommunicated if a layman, or deposed if a clergyman. Chrysostom. *Ibid.* c. 24 ; Concil. Brac. II. A.D. 572, Can. 84 ; Gregory *Ibid.* c. 25 ; Zacharias, A.D. 751, *Ibid.* c. 105 ; Boniface *Ibid.* c. 104 ; Nicolaus *Ibid.* 102 ; Pseudo-Isidor. *Ibid.* c. 17 ; Syn. VIII. A.D. 869, *Ibid.* c. 28 ; Concil. Autissiodor. A.D. 578, Can. 39 : If any priest, clerk, or layman knowingly receive, or eat, or converse with one who is excommunicate, without the knowledge of him who excommunicated him, he will be subject to the same sentence. Const. 20 Edmund, A.D. 1236 ; Const. 4 Boniface, A.D. 1261 ; Clemens III. in Decret. Lib. v. Tit. XXXIX. c. 18 ; Const. 13 Stratford, A.D. 1343 ; Lynd. 266, 352 ; Devoti Lib. IV. Tit. XVIII. § 3.

([31]). Gratian Caus. XI. Qu. III. c. 20 ; Clement III. in Decret. Lib. v. Tit. XXXIX. c. 14. See *Discipline Generally*, § 6.

([32]). See above, note 11.

([33]). Apost. Const. II. 41 : If after all that thou hast done the malady spreads, then with much consideration and the advice of others cut off the putrified member, that the whole Church be not corrupted.

([34]). Alexander III. in Decret. Lib. I. Tit. XXXI. c. 3 ; Thom. Aquin. 4, Dist. 18, Qu. 2, Art. 1, c. 1 : In the tribunal of conscience a cause is dealt with between man and God, but in the tribunal of the outer forum a cause is dealt with between man and man ; and, therefore, binding and unbinding, which affects a man in his relation to God, belongs to the court of penance exclusively, but unbinding, which affects a man in relation to his fellow-

bishop or his vicar-general (35), an archdeacon or dean exercising an ordinary jurisdiction by custom, but not by a metropolitan over a mediate subject except in visitation, devolution, or appeal (36), nor by a parochial incumbent (37) except by a special delegation (38), and only by a delegate when it comes within the scope of his commission, or he is authorised to inflict it (39). Whenever it is non-solemnly inflicted, it is usually spoken of as excommunication. Whenever it is solemnly inflicted, it is termed the *anathema* or *execration* (40).

8. Like all other solemn acts, the anathema should be the act of the whole Church. According to mediaeval rule, not fewer than twelve presbyters were required to assist the bishop in pronouncing it, who stood round, holding lighted candles, whilst he read the sentence from a book, so that it might be seen that it was no hasty or ill-considered act. Meantime the bell was tolled. No sooner had the sentence been concluded than all dashed their candles to the ground, to symbolise the extinction of light in the soul of the anathematised one (41).

men, belongs to the court of the outer forum ; and, because excommunication separates from the communion of the faithful, therefore it belongs to the outer forum, and those alone can excommunicate who have jurisdiction in the outer forum, *i.e.*, the bishop and greater prelates.

(35). Concil. Lugdun. A.D. 1245, in Sext. Lib. II. Tit. XV. c. 3.
(36). Concil. Lugdun. *Ibid.* Lib. V. Tit. XI. c. 7.
(37). Innocent III. to Bishop of Ely, A.D. 1204, in Lib. I. Tit. XXIX. c. 28 ; Lynd. 17, 338, 344. See *The Parish*.
(38). According to Ecclesiastical Courts Commission Report, when such a sentence had to be pronounced on a clerk in holy orders in the Arches Court, a presbyter was called in by the Dean of Arches to pronounce it, under a special commission from the archbishop.
(39). Alexander III. in Decret. Lib. I. Tit. XXIX. c. 5 ; Devoti Lib. IV. Tit. XVIII. § 12.
(40). Concil. Clovesho. A.D. 747, Can. 29 and preface ; Concil. Chelsea A.D. 787, Can. 15 ; Concil. Westminster A.D. 1102, Can. 28, quoted *Excesses*, note 269 ; Gratian Caus. XXIII. Qu. IV. c. 30 ; Decret. Lib. II. Tit. I. c. 10 ; Const. 21 and 27 Langton, A.D. 1222 ; Const. 10, 13, 17, and 20 Peckham, A.D. 1281 ; Lynd. 169, 196, 279, 322, 259, 51, 77, 121 ; Van Espen. Tract. de Caus. Eccl. Tom. IV. p. 9.
(41). Gratian Caus. XI. Qu. III. c. 106 ; Concil. Winton. A.D. 1143, Can. 2. An early form of the anathema is given by Johnson under Can. 17 of

The anathema was therefore popularly spoken of as excommunication by book, bell, and candle.

9. When not solemnly inflicted, a censure may be awarded either (1) by sentence of a judge ([42]), or (2) by sentence of law ([43]). A censure awarded by sentence of a judge is one not prescribed by any canon, but imposed by a judge in the exercise of the discretion committed to him by the Church. A censure awarded by sentence of law is one prescribed by the Church, with a view to the future enforcement of some law

---

Concil. Ebor. A.D. 1195 : By authority of Almighty God, Father, Son, and Holy Ghost, and St. Mary, mother of our Lord, and St. Michael the Archangel, and St. Peter the prime apostle, and St. Nicolas and the blessed Augustin, and all Christ's saints, let the men be excommunicated and damned that committed this theft . . . and let them be separated from entering into Holy Church, and from the fraternity of God's elect. Moreover, let them have their portion of punishment with Judas, our Lord's disciple, and with them that said to our Lord, Depart from us. . . . Let them be accursed eating and drinking, walking and sitting, speaking and holding their peace, waking and sleeping, rowing and riding. . . . Cursed be their head and their thoughts, their eyes and their ears, their tongues and their lips, their teeth and their throats, their feet and their legs. . . . And just as this candle is deprived of its present light, so let them be deprived of their souls in hell. Let all the people say, So be it. Const. 2 and 4 Winch. A.D. 1298 ; Const. 13 Stratford, A.D. 1343 ; Lynd. 350.

(42). Lynd. 39.

(43). These sentences are sometimes stated to have been introduced in the twelfth century. But in Gal. I. 8, St. Paul declares that if an angel from heaven proclaim any other Gospel, let him be anathema. Titus III. 10, 11, that a heretic who refuses to reform after two warnings has turned aside (ἐξέστραπται) and is self-condemned (αὐτοκατάκριτος). Jude 19 : Οὗτοί εἰσιν οἱ ἀποδιορίζοντες ἑαυτούς (who excommunicate themselves). Cyprian Ep. 51, 24, ad Antonian. Augustin ap. Gratian Caus. XXIV. Qu. III. c. 29 ; Paulinus Vita Ambrosii in Migne XIV. 31, relates that when the soldiers surrounded the Church of Milan, in 385, St. Ambrose declared that all who invaded the Church would be excommunicate. Gregory *Ibid.* Caus. V. Qu. 1. c. 2 declares the unknown slanderer of his notary excommunicate. Pseudo-Isidor. A.D. 850, *Ibid.* Caus. XVII. Qu. IV. c. 5, declares robbers of Churches anathema. Concil. Trecass. A.D. 878, *Ibid.* c. 21 : Let [a violator of Churches] know that he is deprived of communion until, admonished in the assembly, he has made satisfaction. Concil. Westminster A.D. 1200, Can. 7 ; Ayliffe 156.

or general rule. Such censures, again, are either censures of law already passed (*sententiae latae*), or censures of law to be passed (*sententiae ferendae*) (44). The latter are called comminatory censures. A canon which declares that certain offenders are *ipso facto* or *ipso jure* excommunicate is a censure of law already passed (45). A canon which directs excommuni-

(44). Lynd. 13, 15, 147, 170, 187, 197.

(45). Sentence of *ipso facto* excommunication is ordered by English constitutions in the following cases: By Const. 5 Peckham, A.D. 1279, on a rural dean for not reading Othobon's Constitution de Concubinariis ; by Const. 16 Stratford, A.D. 1343, for maliciously indicting innocent persons ; by Const. 13 Peckham, A.D. 1281, on an already disqualified official acting fraudulently ; by Const. 5 Boniface, A.D. 1261, on lay judges presuming to condemn clerks ; by Const. 15 Stratford, A.D. 1343, for violating a sequestration ; by Const. 2 Chichele, A.D. 1415, on laymen exercising spiritual jurisdiction ; by Const. 1 Peckham, A.D. 1279, for holding pluralities contrary to the canon of the Council of Lyons ; by Const. 12 Stratford, A.D. 1342, and Const. 3 Boniface, A.D. 1261, for intruding into a benefice imperfectly vacant ; by Const. 9 Stratford, A.D. 1342, for fraudulent alienation of goods ; by Const. 7 Stratford, A.D. 1343, for hindering the execution of a testament ; by Const. 7. Mephum, A.D. 1328, Const. 4 Stratford, A.D. 1343, and Const. 1 Winchelsea, A.D. 1305, for obstructing the payment of tithes and offerings ; by Const. 5 Winchelsea, A.D. 1305, on a stipendiary priest taking offerings or fees without the rector's permission ; by Const. 1 Sudbury, A.D. 1378, on a mass priest demanding from his rector more than his allotted stipend ; by Const. 9 Boniface, A.D. 1261, for invading ecclesiastical property or rights ; by Const. 11 Boniface, for the king's bailiff acting oppressively during the vacancy of a see ; by Const. 12 Stratford, A.D. 1343, for hindering the lawful proceedings of an ecclesiastical judge ; by Const. 13 Stratford, for wrongfully setting at large one imprisoned by an ecclesiastical judge ; by Const. 14 Stratford, for usurping the herbage and trees in holy places ; by Const. 11 Stratford, for unlawfully celebrating prohibited marriages ; by Const. 6 Arundel, A.D. 1408, for publishing unauthorised translations of the Bible ; by Const. 1, 3, and 10 Arundel, for preaching otherwise than allowed by the canon ; by Const. 17 Peckham, A.D. 1281, also Const. 3 Peckham, A.D. 1279, for committing incest with nuns—in all twenty-two, which cover sixty different cases. Lynd. 355 says that besides these the Bishop of Ostia enumerates thirty-three cases, collected from the decrees and decretals ; and John Andrew of Bologna mentions thirty-two more, besides fifty collected from the Clementines, in commenting on Clem. Lib. v. Tit. x. c. 1, making altogether 175 cases, exclusive of those provided for in the constitutions

cation to be awarded as the punishment for certain offences is a censure of law to be passed. The difference between the two will be more fully considered under the subject of sentences ([46]).

10. The effects of a sentence of excommunication, as laid down by mediaeval constitutions, are the following: (1) All persons suspended or excommunicated are forbidden the reception of all sacraments, including order ([47]), and are also forbidden the administration of them ([48]), except in cases of emergency. (2) They are excluded from participating in the intercessions, suffrages, or favours of the Church, and from being commemorated in the public prayers ([49]). (3) They are disqualified from holding benefices ([50]), or taking any active part in judicial proceedings ([51]). (4) They forfeit the benefit of any rescript of favour or justice ([52]). If excommunicated with the greater excommunication, and denounced by name, they are, moreover, (5) forbidden the exercise of jurisdiction ([53]), and (6) are cut off from intercourse with the faithful in life ([54]), and from Christian burial when dead ([55]). The only exceptions allowed to the

of Otho and Othobon. Lynd. 18, 77, 122, 258 ; Cave, Primitive Christianity III. 5 ; Bingham XVI. 3 ; Devoti Lib. IV. Tit. XVIII. § 8 ; Ayliffe 156.

(46). See *The Conclusion of a Cause*, § 12.

(47). Innocent III. in Decret. Lib. V. Tit. XXXIX. c. 32 ; Craisson, § 6510.

(48). Alexander III. to Bishop of London, *Ibid.* Lib. V. Tit. XXVII. c. 3.

(49). Gratian Caus. XI. Qu. III. c. 20 ; Clement III. in Decret. Lib. V. Tit. XXXIX. c. 14. See *Ecclesiastical Sacraments*, § 9.

(50). Innocent III. in Decret. Lib. V. Tit. XXVII. c. 7.

(51). Concil. Lugdun. A.D. 1245, in Sext. Lib. II. Tit. XII. c. 1, except proceedings to prove the injustice of his sentence. Innocent III. in Decret. Lib. I. Tit. XXIX. c. 36.

(52). Innocent III. in Decret. Lib. I. Tit. III. c. 26 ; Gregory IX. in Sext. Lib. I. Tit. IIL c. 1 : It is therefore usual to add an absolution from censures to any grant of indulgence or favour.

(53). Gratian Caus. XXIV. Qu. L c. 3, and 36–42 ; Innocent III. in Decret. Lib. IL Tit. XXVII. c. 24.

(54). Busenbaum ap. Liguori. Lib. VII. 188, sums them up in the line—

Os, orare, vale, communio, mensa negatur.

(55). Concil. Vien. A.D. 1311, in Clem. Lib. III. Tit. VII. c. 1 ; Const. 4 Sudbury, A.D. 1378.

last-named rule are that intercourse is permitted with a husband, wife, or dependent ([56]), with others only in case of necessity ([57]), or when some good purpose may be served, or when the intercourse takes place in ignorance ([58]). In this country, however, by civil legislation of recent times, no civil penalty or incapacity whatever is now incurred by excommunication, except liability to imprisonment for a period not exceeding six months ([59]).

11. The suspension or excommunication of one in orders necessarily carries with it suspension from office, and renders the offender irregular if he officiates before it is relaxed. Even a sentence of the lesser excommunication makes one liable to deprivation who officiates after warning not to do so ([60]), and one who officiates whilst under a sentence of the greater excommunication is deprived *ipso jure* or *ipso facto* for his contumacy ([61]). An unjust excommunication, though it cannot do spiritual harm ([62]), must nevertheless be observed ([63]), until it is set aside on appeal ([64]). Neither a corporate body ([65]), nor one who has not been baptized ([66]), nor a dead person ([67]),

(56). Gregory VII. ap. Gratian Caus. XI. Qu. III. c. 103; Innocent III. in Decret. Lib. v. Tit. XXXIX. c. 31.

(57). Innocent III. l. c. c. 34.

(58). Gregory VII. l. c.

(59). By 53 Geo. III. c. 127.

(60). Alexander III. to Bishop of London in Decret. Lib. v. Tit. XXVII. c. 3; to Bishop of Toledo, *Ibid.* c. 4.

(61). Apost. Can. 29: If one suspended for crime ventures to meddle with the administration formerly entrusted to him, let him be entirely cut off from the Church. Innocent III. l. c. c. 6.

(62). Augustin ap. Gratian Caus. XI. Qu. III. c. 87; Gelasius *Ibid.* c. 46: An unjust sentence can hurt no one before God.

(63). Urban ap. Gratian Caus. XI. Qu. III. c. 27 and 1.

(64). Stat. Eccl. Ant. A.D. 505, Can. 66; *Ibid.* c. 30; c. 34, 36.

(65). Concil. Lugdun. I. A.D. 1245, in Sext. Lib. v. Tit. XL c. 5: We forbid a sentence of excommunication to go forth against a university or college, because it often happens that the innocent may be involved in such a sentence.

(66). 1 Cor. v. 12: τί γάρ μοι καὶ τοὺς ἔξω κρίνειν;

(67). Gelasius, A.D. 494, ap. Gratian Caus. XXIV. Qu. II. c. 2; Innocent III. in Decret. Lib. v. Tit. XXXIX. c. 28.

nor one who is not actually or constructively contumacious ([68]) may be excommunicated. A dead person may nevertheless have his name removed from the diptychs of the Church ([69]), and so be no longer remembered in the Eucharistic prayers. By English constitutions, the names of all persons under a sentence of the greater excommunication are required to be publicly denounced four times a year ([70]).

12. As being the gravest form of spiritual censure ([71]), excommunication may not be awarded (1) for trifling matters, but only for manifest and certain excesses ([72]), or for contumacy in refusing to appear to a citation, or to obey a monition, or for going away before a cause is concluded ([73]); (2) never without monition ([74]), except in the cases prescribed by the canons ([75]), but by mediaeval rule a single peremptory monition suffices ([76]); (3) it may not be awarded without a citation; (4) it must always be drawn up in writing, in a document setting forth the excess for which it is awarded ([77]), unless it is a

---

[68]. Hence a sentence of excommunication given without warning is void and a nullity. Concil. Lat. III. A.D. 1179, in Decret. Lib. II. Tit. XXVIII. c. 26; Concil. Lugdun. A.D. 1245, in Sext. Lib. V. Tit. XI. c. 2; Concil. Lugdun. II. A.D. 1275, *Ibid.* c. 9.

[69]. Syn. V. A.D. 553, ap. Gratian Caus. XXIV. Qu. II. c. 6; Innocent III. l. c. c. 28. In Harduin III. 126, this council at its fifth session removed the name of Theodore from the diptychs of Mopsuestia, replacing it by Cyril of Alexandria. This was done at the instance of the Emperor Justinian.

[70]. Const. 12 Stratford, A.D. 1343; Lynd. 27.

[71]. Augustin ap. Gratian Caus. XXIV. Qu. III. c. 17.

[72]. Concil. Meldens. A.D. 845, *Ibid.* Caus. XI. Qu. III. c. 41; Const. 26 Langton, A.D. 1222.

[73]. Concil. Tribur. A.D. 895, *Ibid.* c. 43. In this country excommunication is, by 53 Geo. III. c. 127, no longer allowed to be awarded for such contumacy. Law's Forms, 125.

[74]. See note 68, and *Discipline Generally*, notes 13 and 15.

[75]. *Discipline Generally*, § 6.

[76]. Concil. Lugdun. A.D. 1274, in Sext. Lib. V. Tit. XI. c. 9, allows a peremptory monition to do duty for three monitions, but requires an interval of time to elapse equal to that required for three ordinary monitions, *i.e.*, six days, since an ordinary monition requires three days. Craisson, § 6112. See *Canonical Procedure*, § 27.

[77]. Concil. Lugdun. A.D. 1245, in Sext. Lib. V. Tit. XI. c. 1;

solemn repetition of a previous excommunication [78]; and (5) it cannot be awarded as a sentence already past for future offences [79] by any ordinary or delegate, but only by a canon of the Church. Moreover, the anathema may not be pronounced without the consent of the metropolitan or the comprovincial bishops [80].

13. Because of the solidarity of the Church, an excommunication pronounced by one bishop, or in one part of the Church, takes effect and must be observed in all other parts of it [81]. Bishops are therefore directed to communicate such sentences to one another [82]. For the same reason, an excommunication can only be withdrawn by the prelate who pronounced it [83], and

---

Const. 4 Boniface, A.D. 1261 ; Lynd. 350.   See the *Conclusion of a Cause*, § 9.

(78). Lynd. 350.

(79). Concil. Lugdun. A.D. 1245, in Sext. Lib. v. Tit. XL c. 5 ; 38 Hen. III. A.D. 1254 ; Const. 1 Langton, A.D. 1222 ; Const. 21 Boniface, A.D. 1261 ; Const. 3 Peckham, A.D. 1279 ; Const. 10 Peckham, A.D. 1281 ; Const. 4 Winchel. A.D. 1298 ; Const. 3 Mepham. A.D. 1328 ; Const. 14 Stratford, A.D. 1343 ; Const. Chichele, A.D. 1434 ; Lynd. 315, 345, 353 ; Craisson, § 6405.

(80). Concil. Melden. A.D. 845, Can. 56 ap. Gratian Caus. XL Qu. III. c. 41 : Let a bishop place no one under anathema without the privity of the archbishop or his fellow-bishops, except in accordance with canonical authority, because anathema is condemnation to eternal death, and ought not to be imposed save for a mortal crime, which cannot in any other way be corrected.

(81). Apost. Can. 13 : If a clergyman or layman who is suspended goes away, and is received in another city without commendatory letters, let both those who received him and him that was received be suspended. Can. 33 : If any presbyter or deacon be suspended by his bishop, it is not lawful for any other to receive him . . . unless he who suspended him dies. Concil. Arelat. II. A.D. 443, Can. 8, calls him who admits one excommunicated by another an offender against the Christian brotherhood (reum fraternitatis). Concil. Paris III. A.D. 615, Can. 7 ; Concil. Lugdun. II. A.D. 567, Can. 4 ; Concil. Rothomag. A.D. 650, Can. 6 ; Innocent III. A.D. 1199, in Decret. Lib. v. Tit. XXXIX. c. 39.

(82). Gratian Caus. XL Qu. III. c. 20 ; Const. 4 Boniface, A.D. 1261 ; Lynd. 350.

(83). Concil. Nic. A.D. 325, Can. 5 ; Concil. Arelat. I. A.D. 314, Can. 16 ; Concil. Antioch A.D. 341, Can. 6 ap Gratian Caus. XL Qu. III. c. 2 and 3,

a solemn sentence only in the same solemn manner in which it was pronounced ([84]). A prelate can, however, be compelled to withdraw a sentence on appeal, if he has pronounced it for no adequate cause ([85]); and if he refuses so to do, it can be withdrawn by his superior ([86]). No bishop should in any case venture to pronounce a sentence of excommunication in a case in which he himself has an interest ([87]).

The Interdict.

14. The interdict is a form of censure of mediaeval origin, wherein all the offices of religion, including Christian burial, are forbidden to be celebrated in certain places or before certain people, with the view of producing the reform of some offender ([88]). It is usually resorted to to influence those towards whom direct censure has been employed in vain, and it presupposes the existence of a powerful spirit of clanship among those to whom it is applied, which, it is presumed, will be able to bring effective pressure to bear on the erring one. In practice it works great injustice, since it too often causes those to suffer who have little power of influencing the guilty ([89]); and it has also been greatly abused

---

7-10; Concil. Taurin. A.D. 401, Can. 5; Concil. Lugdun. A.D. 1245, Can. 4 in Sext. Lib. v. Tit. xi. c. 5.

(84). Gratian Caus. xl. Qu. iii. c. 108; Const. 28 Othobon, A.D. 1268.

(85). Concil. Afric. ap. Gratian Caus. vi. Qu. ii. c. 3; Stat. Eccl. Ant. Ibid. c. 1; Concil. Agath. A.D. 506, Can. 3: Bishops who excommunicate for trivial matters, and refuse to receive those returning to grace, should be exhorted by neighbouring bishops to relent, and if they refuse, [those excommunicated] may receive communion from others until the synod meets. See *Excesses*, note 140.

(86). Jul. Ep. Nov. ap. Gratian Caus. ii. Qu. l. c. 11; Concil. Lat. iv. A.D. 1215, Can. 47 in Decret. Lib. v. Tit. xxxix. c. 48.

(87). Ambros. ap. Gratian Caus. xxiii. Qu. iv. c. 27.

(88). Const. 7 Clarendon, A.D. 1164, forbids an interdict being laid on the king's estate till application has been made to him. Const. 1 Otho, A.D. 1237; Const. 3, 7, and 9 Boniface, A.D. 1261; Const. 4 Winchelsea, A.D. 1298; Const. 1 Arundel, A.D. 1408; Lynd. 320, 258; Devoti Lib. iv. Tit. xix.

(89). Lynd. 308.

as a political weapon. Interdicts are of two kinds, (1) local and (2) personal; but both a local and a personal interdict may be general or particular.

15. In a *local* interdict ([90]), the offices of religion are forbidden to be celebrated within a certain district; but the persons living within the district are not thereby debarred from receiving them elsewhere ([91]). A local interdict is *general* when it includes a whole nation, province, or diocese; *particular* when it is confined to a single place or parish in a diocese, or to a particular Church in a parish. An interdict laid on any place, parish, or diocese extends to all the buildings, chapels, and cemeteries appurtenant to it ([92]).

16. In a *personal* interdict, the offices of religion are forbidden to be celebrated by or before one or more or a whole class of persons ([93]). If such an interdict is laid on the clergy ([94]), it does not extend to the laity. If laid on the laity, it does not apply to the clergy, unless they are specially named in it ([95]). When it is laid on the whole clergy or the whole people of any locality, it is called general. When it is confined to certain individuals who are mentioned by name, it is particular. A particular personal interdict is the same thing as the lesser excommunication ([96]) or suspension.

([90]). Lynd. 94, 110.

([91]). This is denied by Stremler, des Peines Ecclésiastiques 343, and Liguori Lib. VII. 332.

([92]). Concil. Lugdun. A.D. 1274, in Sext. Lib. V. Tit. XI. c. 10; Boniface VIII. *Ibid.* c. 17; *Id. Ibid.* Lib. III. Tit. XXI. c. 1.

([93]). Alexander III. in Decret. Lib. I. Tit. XXIX. c. 11, says that a rebellious bishop may be interdicted entrance to the Church or the exercise of his office.

([94]). Apost. Can. 37: If a bishop-elect is not received . . . because of the people's ill-will, let him continue bishop, but let the clergy be suspended because they have not taught their disobedient people better. Concil. Mogunt. A.D. 851, Can. 8 in Decret. Lib. V. Tit. XXXIV. c. 2, calls an oath under pain of interdict the coercion of Christianity (bannus Christianitatis). Concil. Tribur. A.D. 895, Can. 8, calls it bannus episcopalis.

([95]). Boniface VIII. in Sext. Lib. V. Tit. XI. c. 16.

([96]). Const. 10 Clarendon, A.D. 1164: Bishops may lawfully put under an interdict one who will not make satisfaction upon their summons, but

17. The severity of the interdict, as at first employed, was, after the twelfth century, gradually toned down by the invention of a distinction between *complete* and *partial* interdicts. In a partial interdict, permission was first given to baptize infants, and to give penance to the dying ([97]); next, the permission was extended to allow preaching and confirmation ([98]); afterwards, Communion might be given to the dying, and Christian burial to the clergy ([99]). Still later, the Eucharist was allowed to be celebrated privately once a week, provided this were done in an undertone, without bell-ringing and with closed doors ([100]); and ultimately penance was allowed to be given to all, the Eucharist to be celebrated every day in Churches not specially interdicted, and solemnly at Christmas, Easter, Pentecost, and the Assumption, provided those who were the cause of the interdict were not permitted to approach the altar ([101]).

18. An interdict is forbidden to be imposed except for some very grave crime. When imposed it does not extend to bishops and greater prelates, unless they are specially named in it ([102]); but an interdict imposed by a bishop is held to include exempt regulars ([103]). If it is incurred *ipso facto*, as by bloodshed or adultery committed in a Church ([104]), or by harbouring a convicted heretic ([105]), clergy violating it are not

they ought not to excommunicate him. Craisson, § 6606, holds that the interdict includes much more than the lesser excommunication, quoting Boniface VIII. in Sext. Lib. v. Tit. XI. c. 18; Suarez thinks otherwise, quoting Gratian Caus. XXXIII. Qu. II. c. 15.

(97). Alexander III. in Decret. Lib. IV. Tit. l. c. 11.
(98). Innocent III. A.D. 1206, *Ibid.* Lib. v. Tit. XXXIX. c. 43.
(99). Innocent III. A.D. 1212, *Ibid.* Tit. XXXVIII. c. 11.
(100). Gregory IX. A.D. 1234, *Ibid.* Tit. XXXIX. c. 57.
(101). Boniface VIII. A.D. 1298, in Sext. Lib. v. Tit. XI. c. 24.
(102). Concil. Lat. IV. A.D. 1215, in Decret. Lib. v. Tit. XXXIII. c. 25; Concil. Lugdun. A.D. 1274, in Sext. Lib. v. Tit. XI. c. 4.
(103). Concil. Vien. A.D. 1311, in Clem. Lib. v. Tit. X. c. 1.
(104). Boniface VIII. in Sext. Lib. v. Tit. XI. c. 18, and Lib. III. Tit. XXI. c. 1.
(105). Boniface VIII. in Sext. Lib. III. Tit. XX. c. 4; Const. 1 Arundel, A.D. 1408; Lynd. 294.

guilty of an irregularity, although they are guilty of an offence. If it has been imposed by sentence, they are guilty of an irregularity, from which they can only be relieved by the spokesman of conciliar authority ([106]). Regulars violating it are ordered to be excommunicated ([107]), and also clergy who, during its continuance, bury the non-privileged dead ([108]).

Corrective Severity—Penances.

19. As the severity which is exercised to bring an offender to repentance is termed censure, so that which is either voluntarily undertaken or submitted to, to do away with the effects of sin, is termed penance. Censure and penance borne unsubmissively or without recognition of their justice are deadly, and become vindictive punishments, but the spirit of humility and obedience makes them remedial and purificatory.

20. A penance may be defined to be a form of hardship inflicted on one who has offended against the rule of holiness, in place of leaving him to the tender mercies of the foe of mankind, in order to intensify inward repentance, and to make outward amends for the temporal effects of sin ([109]). It is not, therefore, a vindictive punishment or penalty, but rather a substitute for it; and it is (1) remedial in the inner forum ([110]), in that it enables the sinner to obtain the benefit of the satisfaction made to God by Christ, or, in other words, qualifies him

---

(106). Boniface VIII. *Ibid.* Lib. v. Tit. XI. c. 18.
(107). Concil. Vien. in Clem. l. c.
(108). Concil. Vien. *Ibid.* Lib. III. Tit. VII. c. 1.
(109). Concil. Clovesho A.D. 747, Can. 27 : A man should punish sin at present in proportion to its guilt, if he desire not to be punished hereafter by the eternal Judge. Penance is submission to punishment, and ever punishing oneself (poenam tenere) to avenge sin which has been committed. Ayliffe 420 : Penance is an act of punishment or vengeance whereby the party offending is punished in the ecclesiastical court, or, repenting thereof, afflicts and punishes himself. See *Penance*, note 153. Loening Kirchengeschichte I. 260.
(110). Gregory in Decret. Lib. v. Tit. XXXVIII. c. 1 : Manifest crimes may not be purged by secret correction.

Ecclesiastical Severity. 153

for reconciliation with God([111]); and (2) penal in the outer tribunal, in that it makes amends to the Christian society for the injury done to holiness([112]), or, in other words, qualifies the offender for restoration to corporate communion with the Church. It may be either (1) public or (2) private, but public penance is not necessary where there has been no public offence against holiness([113]).

21. Penances are usually said to be of three kinds, viz. (1) spiritual or devotional, (2) bodily, and (3) pecuniary([114]). Devotional penances, which act as stimulating influences on the

([111]). Clem. Strom. VII. 7 : God ministers eternal salvation to those who co-operate for the attainment of knowledge and good conduct. Cyprian Ep. 54, 13 ad Corn. speaks of penance satisfying an indignant God, redeeming sins, and washing away wounds. De Laps. 17 : The Lord must be appeased by our atonement. *Ibid.* c. 35 : And yet they were not redeeming sins of such a character as lapse. Ad Antonian. Ep. 51, 20 ; Ayliffe 155. The effect of temporal penances is held to be this—(1) that to one who is in a state of grace they are satisfactions to God, in that they apply to the individual the satisfactions made by Christ, through whose merits alone the penitential works are accepted as satisfactory ; and (2) that penitential works done by one who is not in a state of grace are satisfactions *de congruo*, in that they impetrate and dispose towards a state of grace wherein real satisfaction may be made. Hurter's Theol. Dogm. III. 553. Concil. Ilerd. A.D. 523, Can. 1, says "that they may be purified (expientur) by vigils, fastings, prayers, and almsgiving." Hormisdas ap. Gratian I. Dist. L. c. 29 ; Concil. Tolet. XIII. A.D. 683, Can. 10 : Penitentia ad hoc suscipitur ut et peccatum diluat et peccati sordes hominem iterare non sinat, quoted note 145. Durandus in III. Sent. Dist. 19, Qu. 1 : The passion of Christ is the universal cause of the remission of sins, which must needs be applied to individuals, in order to obtain effect in them.

([112]). Cyprian de Laps. c. 23 : Some are punished in the meantime that others may be corrected. Schmalzgrueber Jus. Univ. Lib. v. Tit. 37, defines poenae as delictorum coercitiones sive vindictae ad disciplinae publicae emendationem institutae. Lynd. 265 : If any one has been excommunicated for an offence or sin, if it is only an offence against God, then he may be absolved on repentance, although he has not done penance for it. But when he is excommunicated for some injury done to another, then proper satisfaction must precede.

([113]). See *Penance*, § 3.

([114]). See *Penance*, note 86.

life of holiness, include such spiritual exercises as keeping vigils, saying prescribed prayers ([115]), more particularly the Lord's Prayer ([116]), and reciting the Psalter or parts of it, such as the 119th Psalm, called *Beati*, the 51st, called *Miserere*. Bodily penances, which are also of use by intensifying the command over the senses, and as visible tokens of submission to punishment, include fasting and abstinence ([117]), whipping when given to young people ([118]), and seclusion in a monastery when substituted for solemn discipline ([119]). Pecuniary penances, in so far as they involve personal self-denial, are only a particular form of bodily penances; but in so far as they are relaxations of, or substitutes for, bodily penances, permitted because of the greater good thereby accruing to others—and in

([115]). Concil. Ilerd. A.D. 523, Can. 1, quoted above, note 111.

([116]). Gratian 1 Dist. LXXXI. c. 5; Theodori Poenit. I. VII. 5 in Haddan & Stubbs III. 185: Theodore approved of twelve triduans (three days' fasting and prayer), being equivalent to a year of penance. Baeda x. 1, *Ibid.* 333: Twelve triduans, with three complete psalteries and 300 beads of *Paternosters*, are a substitute for a year of penance. Dunstan's Can. 72, A.D. 963.

([117]). Leo de Pass. XIX. 5: Wise souls mortify their bodies and crucify their senses, and therein set before themselves God's will, loving themselves the more in proportion as for the love of God they love [*i.e.*, spare] not themselves. Ayliffe 279: I will not deny fasting to be a kind of penance for sin.

([118]). Augustin ap. Gratian Caus. XXIII. Qu. v. c. 1: Whipping with a birch (verbera virgarum) is a mode of coercion employed not only by masters of liberal arts but by parents, and also by bishops in their tribunals. Gregory *Ibid.* I. Dist. XLV. c. 1: What shall be said of bishops who make themselves feared by giving blows? Theodori Poenit. I. II. 11 in H. & S. III. 178: Pueri qui fornicantur vapulentur.

([119]). Ambros. ap. Gratian Caus. I. Qu. l. c. 7; Concil. Agath. A.D. 506, *Ibid.* I. Dist. L. c. 7; Concil. Narbon. A.D. 589, Can. 6, directs an abbot to treat a clerk or other great person relegated to a monastery according to the bishop's direction, or otherwise to be suspended, because the offender is there for discipline, not for feasting. Eugenius *Ibid.* I. Dist. LXXXI. c. 7; Gregory *Ibid.* Caus. XVI. Qu. VI. c. 5: Seek out regular monasteries, and in them place presbyters who have gone wrong to do penance. Concil. Trosslei *Ibid.* Caus. XXIV. Qu. III. c. 22, and Caus. XXII. Qu. v. c. 19; Decret. Lib. v. Tit. XXXI. c. 4.

this case they are legally enforceable ([120])—they stand on a lower level ([121]). Hence pecuniary penances are not allowed at all after two relapses ([122]), nor in the reserved cases ([123]), nor may the money obtained from them be applied by spiritual judges to their own uses ([124]), but only in almsgiving ([125]), founding or endowing Churches or hospitals, and in purchasing the freedom of captives.

VINDICTIVE SEVERITY—PENALTIES AND ANIMADVERSION.

22. Vindictive severity is punishment inflicted on an unwilling subject as an act of public vengeance for the good of others, which cannot be relaxed upon repentance, and leaves a permanent stigma behind it. Such severity is of two kinds—

([120]). 13 Ed. L St. IV. c. 1, A.D. 1284 ; 9 Ed. II. St. 1, c. 2 ; Lynd. 96, 154.
([121]). Isidor. ap. Gratian. Caus. XI. Qu. III. c. 72. Lynd. 261 : Qui non luit in corpore luit in bursa.
([122]). Const. 9 Stratford, A.D. 1342.
([123]). Const. 5 Thorsby, A.D. 1363 : The priest is to make no abatement of the penance, nor to convert it into a pecuniary penance, if perchance it be corporeal.
([124]). Concil. Ensham A.D. 1009 : If any money arise on account of divine satisfaction, according as the wise men of the world have fixed the rule, that is to be applied, at the bishop's command, to purchasing prayers, to the relief of the poor, to the reparation of Churches, to the instructing, clothing, and feeding of them that serve God, and the purchasing of bells, books, and Church vestments. Alexander III. to Archbishop of Canterbury in Decret. Lib. V. Tit. XXXVII. c. 3 ; Concil. Lat. IV. A.D. 1215, *Ibid*. Lib. I. Tit. XXXI. c. 13 ; Const. 19 Othobon, A.D. 1268 ; Const. 12 Stratford, A.D. 1343, orders the money to be applied to the cathedral fabric.
([125]). Clem. Epist. 2 ad Rom. c. 16 : Almsgiving lightens the weight of sin. Cyprian de Vest. Virg. c. 11 : Every man in proportion to his wealth ought by his patrimony to redeem his transgressions. De Laps. c. 35 : By the use of wealth the crime and faults may be redeemed. *Id.* ap. Gratian Caus. XXXIII. Qu. III. Dist. 1. c. 57 ; Augustin *Ibid.* c. 63 ; Ambros. *Ibid.* c. 76. Ambros. *Ibid.* I. Dist. LXXXVI. c. 13, says that almsgiving must begin with those of the household of faith. *Ibid.* c. 16 and 20, that it ought to be practised to relatives before others. Aug. Enchir. 72 : There are many kinds of almsgiving, in practising which we are ourselves assisted (adjuvamur). Concil. Cloresho A.D. 747, Can. 30. See *Ecclesiastical Sacraments*, § 2.

(1) temporal, and (2) spiritual. The power to inflict temporal penalties for vindictive purposes is no part of the Church's office as a divine society ([126]), but is a civil and imperial duty, which formerly belonged to the head of the Roman Church in places where he was temporal sovereign, and has at times been held by other prelates of the Church in different localities, in varying degree ([127]). It is otherwise with spiritual punishments which, directly or indirectly, have vindictive consequences. These the Church has divine authority to impose to maintain its own note of holiness; but because of their vindictive effects it is not called upon, or even justified, in imposing them without clear demonstration of their being deserved.

23. Among temporal punishments which have at one time or other been within the power of the prelates of the Church to inflict may be enumerated ([128])—(1) branding, the punishment of slaves and of clerks guilty of forgery ([129]); (2) reduction to slavery ([130]), the punishment of insolvency, of not paying a

[126]. Rom. xii. 19: Vengeance is Mine. I will repay, saith the Lord. The punishment of Ananias and Sapphira, in Acts. v. 5, was the act of God, not the sentence of St. Peter, who only spoke prophetically.

[127]. Thus the Archbishops of Cologne, Mainz, and Triers were princes of the Empire, and had sovereign rights under the emperor. The Bishop of Durham was prince of the County Palatine of Durham, and had as such power of life and death. The Bishop of Sodor and Man had jurisdiction in the recovery of debts from the estates of deceased persons, in affiliation and maintenance cases, and the guardianship of minors under fourteen. See Ecclesiastical Courts Commission ii. 322. And all bishops in this country, and many other spiritual bodies, for instance, the College of Vicars Choral at Easter, had, together with certain lords of manors, jurisdiction in probate and administration cases.

[128]. Lynd. 261 enumerates deprivation of food (inedia Gratian i. Dist. xc. c. 10), flogging, reduction to slavery, forfeiture of effects, transportation, imprisonment, and, p. 321, solitary confinement, and branding.

[129]. Urban iii. in Decret. Lib. v. Tit. xx. c. 3. Ecclesiastical Courts Commission, A.D. 1883, vol. i. p. 52: In A.D. 1166, in a council at Oxford, certain heretics were tried, convicted, excommunicated, branded on the face, and expelled the kingdom.

[130]. Concil. Aurel. 1 A.D. 511, Can. 4 ap. Gratian Caus. xxxvi. Qu. l. c. 3: Let one guilty of rape, who has fled to a Church . . . be reduced to

wer-gild (¹³¹), and certain other offences (¹³²); (3) perpetual exile (¹³³); (4) imprisonment (¹³⁴) in a monastery (¹³⁵) or elsewhere; (5) flogging, the punishment of false accusers (¹³⁶); and

slavery, or have power to buy himself off. Urban II. A.D. 1089, *Ibid.* I. Dist. XXXII. c. 10; Concil. London A.D. 1108, Can. 10: Bishops ... shall have their adulterous concubines [as slaves].

(131). Laws of Satisfaction 8, A.D. 725, decree that for violation of orders one share of the fine is to be paid to the bishop, one to the altar, and one to the murdered clerk's gild-clergy. Alfred's Laws, A.D. 877, Pref.; Concil. Tribur. A.D. 895, in Decret. Lib. v. Tit. XXXVIII. c. 2: Let the composition-money for a murdered priest be paid to the bishop to whose diocese he belonged, so that the bishop apply one-half of his wer-gild to the parish over which he presided, and the other half in alms to himself.

(132). Baeda Poenit. III. 3, in H. & S. III. 327: If a girl under twenty and a young man have been incontinent, let them do penance for three Lents and the weekly fast days. If because of this sin they have been reduced to slavery, then forty days only. Concil. London A.D. 1108, Can. 16: The bishops shall take away all the movable goods of such [clergy] as shall offend herein, and also their concubines with their goods.

(133). Leo ap. Gratian L Dist. LXIII. c. 23: Any one contravening this rule we order to be excommunicated, and, unless he repent, to be consigned to perpetual exile. Alfred's Law 12, A.D. 877; Decret. Lib. v. Tit. XXVII. c. 2, and Coelestin. III. *Ibid.* Lib. II. Tit. 1. c. 10, leaves this to the temporal power. Edward's Law 7, A.D. 1064.

(134). Alexander III. to Bishop of London in Decret. Lib. III. Tit. XVI. c. 1: If it be necessary, let them imprison and afflict him, that he may be compelled to restore the stolen money. *Id.* to Bishop of London *Ibid.* Lib. v. Tit. XXXIX. c. 35, directs the incarceration of a clergyman who would escape from a monastery. Honorius III. *Ibid.* Tit. XI. c. 5: Such persons, if you think well, you must imprison in durance vile. Const. 21 Boniface, A.D. 1261: Let every bishop have one or two prisons in his bishopric for the safe-keeping of clerks, according to canonical censure. Const. 1 Islep, A.D. 1351. According to Lingard, vol. iii. p. 126, chap. 3 Edward III. in 1344 A.D., granted that clerks convicted of any other capital crime than treason should be delivered to their ordinaries, to be condemned by them to perpetual imprisonment and penance.

(135). Concil. Aurel. III. A.D. 538, Can. 7 ap. Gratian I. Dist. LXXXI. c. 10: Let a clerk guilty of adultery be placed in a monastery for the rest of his days. Concil. Lat. III. A.D. 1179, Can. 11, in Decret. Lib. v. Tit. XXXI. c. 4, prescribes it as a punishment for unnatural offences.

(136). Hadrian ap. Gratian Caus. v. Qu. 1. c. 1.

(6) forfeiture of goods and chattels ([137]). In the States of the Church, prelates, as being representatives of the Pontiff who had sovereign rights, could inflict all these penalties. In this country, bishops had of old the same power when they sat in judgment with the sheriff in the Hundred Court ([138]); but since the Conquest their power to inflict temporal penalties has been confined to those in their *mund* or protection, including (1) their own lay dependents, where they possess the privileges of *sac, soc, toll, team,* and *infangthef* ([139]); and (2) their clerical dependents, *i.e.*, the clergy within their jurisdiction ([140]).

24. The only spiritual punishment which is directly vindictive, if degradation and the anathema are excepted, is the incapacity to receive or exercise order set up by irregularity, whether the irregularity arises from the iteration of the sacrament of baptism, confirmation, or order, or from the infamy due to the party's own crime ([141]). This incapacity is not relaxed upon repentance, and can only be got rid of by means of dispensation. Several forms of spiritual severity, nevertheless, lead to consequences which are of a vindictive nature, because they do not benefit the individual, but have only the public good in view. These are usually spoken of as animadversion. Such is (1) the greater excommunication, the sequel

---

([137]). Gratian I. Dist. LXIII. c. 22: Let all who act contrary to this decree be involved in anathema, and their goods be confiscated, unless they repent. Alfred's Law 12, A.D. 877; Concil. London A.D. 1108, Can. 10, directs the chattels of presbyters who refuse to separate from their wives to be forfeited to the bishop.

([138]). See *Spiritual Courts*, § 6.

([139]). Edward's Law 14, A.D. 1064: Let archbishops, bishops, earls, barons, and all that have sac and soc, toll, team, and infangthef, have their knights and proper servants.... And if they incur any forfeiture, and a complaint of the neighbourhood rise against them, they should oblige them to what is right in their own court; they, I say, who have sac, soc, toll, team, and infangthef.

([140]). Because ordination formerly changed the ordinand's allegiance, villagers were not allowed, by Const. 16 Clarendon, A.D. 1164, to be ordained without the lord's consent,—see *Order*, note 289,—nor in France any one without the king's leave.

([141]). See *Order*, § 52.

Ecclesiastical Severity. 159

to which, if it fails to bring the offender to satisfaction, is by the law of this country imprisonment, but the imprisonment is now limited to six months ([142]). Such is (2) condemnation for heresy, the sequel to which, unless there is recantation, was in former times delivery to the secular arm to be burnt ([143]). This consequence has now also been abolished ([144]). Such is (3) the public suspension or deprivation of clergy, which deprives them of the right to receive the offerings of the people, and in this country may, if the judge so order, deprive them of the enjoyment of a foundation benefice. Such is also (4) degradation, the solemn act of deposition, which deprives them of all clerical position and privileges.

25. The rule of the Church, as has been already seen, forbids clergy to undergo penance otherwise than in private ([145]), requiring, instead, that such clergy as are found to be guilty of offences calling for discipline, should be removed from their position and from participation in clerical offices for a season, during which they should do penance in private. This removal was formerly called deposition ([146]), occasionally degrada-

---

[142]. 53 Geo. III. c. 127.
[143]. 2 Hen. IV. c. 15, A.D. 1400; 2 Hen. V. c. 7, A.D. 1414.
[144]. 25 Hen. VIII. c. 14.
[145]. Concil. Carthag. V. A.D. 401, Can. 11: If presbyters or deacons are convicted of any grave fault requiring their removal (eos removeri) from the ministry, let not hands be laid on them, as on penitents or faithful laymen. Gratian L. Dist. L. c. 65, 66; Concil. Araus. A.D. 441, Can. 4, and Concil. Arelat. II. A.D. 443, Can. 29, allow private penance to be given to a cleric upon request. Concil. Tolet. 13, A.D. 683, Can. 10: Penance is undertaken as a remedy against sin, but the priesthood is retained, because of cleansing, that it may flourish by the good conduct of the priest and the fruit of good works, whereby he extinguishes in himself the motions of sin, and potentially destroys the reign of sin in others by his preaching. What, then, shall prevent a priest living thus, as we have premised, from offering the bread of propitiation at the divine altar, after submitting to the rules of penance? Leofric Missal, p. 240, forbids hands to be laid on a presbyter as a penitent. Clemens III. in Decret. Lib. v. Tit. XXXVIII. c. 7.
[146]. Socrates I. 24, and the Apost. Canons 25, 29, 52, mention deposition as the clerical equivalent of lay suspension. Theodori Poenit. I. VI. in Haddan and Stubbs III. 180: If any one has been ordained by heretics, and is found free from blame, he ought to be reappointed (iterum ordinari).

tion ([147]), and is of three degrees, which are now called respectively (1) suspension, (2) deprivation, and (3) deposition or degradation.

26. Suspension ([148]), called also sometimes deprivation, because it is a form of deprivation ([149]), or reduction to strangers' communion ([150]), and also temporary deposition, consists in removal from the clerical office and clerical duties in the part of the Church to which the offender belongs, because of some public offence ([151]). When it is a removal from the clerical office for a time only, it is technically called *suspension;* when a removal from some clerical duties, *regradation*, or going back in order ([152]). Regradation is the mildest form of clerical punishment, and of it there are several kinds, such as (1) being deprived of the exercise of order, whilst allowed to retain the honour and dignity of it in the Church ([153]); (2) being deprived

Otherwise let him be put out of the ministry (deponi oportet). *Id.* L IX. 1, *Ibid*, p. 184 : Bishops, priests, and deacons guilty of fornication ought to be deposed from office, and do penance according to the bishop's ruling; yet let them not be excluded from communion. Egbert's Ans. XV. A.D. 734.

(147). Concil. Elib. A.D. 305, Can. 20 ap. Gratian I. Dist. XLVII. c. 5 : Placuit eum degradari et abstineri. Stat. Eccl. Ant. A.D. 505, Can. 56, 57 : If he will not ask pardon, degradetur, nor let him be restored to office without satisfaction. Theodori Poenit. I. IX. 1 l. c. : Degradari debent. Rabanus ap. Gratian I. Dist. L. c. 34 : A proprio gradu decidant. Stremler des Peines Ecclés, p. 38 ; Craisson, § 6346.

(148). Concil. Ilerd. A.D. 523, ap. Gratian I. Dist. L. c. 52.

(149). Lynd. 99, 127, 195: In the phrase, When proceedings are taken for deprivation, deprivation means the particular degree of suspension required by the laws ecclesiastical.

(150). Apost. Can. 34 orders the wants of strange clergy to be supplied, but themselves not to be received to Communion unless they have commendatory letters. Strangers' Communion is mentioned by Concil. Agath. A.D. 506, Can. 2 ; conf. Euseb. VI. 43 ; Bona Rer. Lit. Lib. II. c. 19, § 6 ; Bingham Lib. VII. c. 3, § 7 ; Devoti Lib. I. Tit. VIII. § 19.

(151). Hieronym ap. Gratian L Dist. L. c. 15, 19, 20 ; Gregory *Ibid.* c. 16 ; Pseudo-Isidor. *Ibid.* c. 14 ; Egbert's Poenit. V. in Haddan and Stubbs. III. 421 : Lynd. 340 ; Devoti Lib. IV. Tit. XX.

(152). Concil. Tolet. I. A.D. 400, Can. 4 ; Concil. Aurel. III. A.D. 538, Can. 27 ; Concil. Matiscon I. A.D. 581, Can. 10 and 19.

(153). Concil. Ancyr. A.D. 314, ap. Gratian I. Dist. L. c. 32, allows priests

Ecclesiastical Severity. 161

of the discharge of some duties belonging to order, but not of all ([154]), as for a presbyter to be limited to discharging the deacon's duties, or for a deacon to be confined to discharging those of the sub-diaconate ([155]); (3) being deprived of rights of seniority in the same order ([156]); and (4) being deprived of all hope of advancement, without being reduced in rank ([157]).

27. When suspension amounts to more than regradation, it may be either (1) suspension from order only and the power of offering ([158]), or (2) from office also or the charge of a cure of

and deacons who have sacrificed, and afterwards given proof of a good fight, to retain their honour and dignity in the Church, but forbids such priests to offer, to preach, or to do any other priestly office, and such deacons to give the Lord's body or the cup, or to read the Gospel. Concil. Nic. A.D. 325, Can. 8, allows the Novatian clergy to remain in the same order; but if there is already a Catholic bishop, the Novatian bishop shall have the honour of a bishop. The synod, in Socrat. I. 9, permitted Meletius to remain in his own city, but decreed that he should exercise no authority to ordain or to nominate for ordination. Concil. Agath. A.D. 506, Can. 43; Concil. Epaon. A.D. 517, Can. 2; Concil. Trull. A.D. 691, Can. 26.

(154). Concil. Neocaesar. A.D. 314, Can. 9; Stat. Eccl. Ant. A.D. 505, Can. 68.

(155). Concil. Neocaesar. A.D. 314, Can. 10, ordered an incontinent deacon to be reduced to the rank of a sub-deacon. Also Concil. Tolet 1, A.D. 400, ap. Gratian I. Dist. L. c. 68. The same council, Can. 4, *Ibid.* I. Dist. XXXIV. c. 17, ordered a sub-deacon who had married again to be reduced to the rank of a reader or door-keeper.

(156). Socrates I. 9, relates that the Nicene Council directed that the clergy who supported Meletius should continue to hold their rank and ministry, but regard themselves as inferior to all who had been previously ordained in every place and Church by Bishop Alexander. Concil. Turon. 1, A.D. 461, Can. 4; Concil. Trull. A.D. 692, Can. 7; Coucil. Nic. A.D. 787, Can. 5.

(157). Concil. Taurin. A.D. 401, Can. 8; Concil. Tolet. 1, A.D. 400, c. 1; Concil. Araur. 1, c. 24; Concil. Andegav. A.D. 453, Can. 54.

(158). Concil. Neocaes. A.D. 314, Can. 1, mentions suspension from offering, but not from other functions. Also Innocent I. A.D. 404, ap. Gratian 1 Dist. LXXXI. c. 6. Gregory of Tours Hist. Franc. VIII. c. 20, relates that Bishop Urssacius was suspended from his episcopal order, but that nevertheless the administration of his Church was left to him. Concil. Carthag. V. A.D. 401, in Codex Eccles. Afric. Can. 76, directs that a bishop

souls ([159]), and it may (3) include in addition suspension from benefice ([160]); but being the clerical substitute for simple excommunication it does not usually entail exclusion from communion ([161]). Its effect is not to take away the capacity to minister ([162]), but to make acts of ministration unlawful, and the person who performs them irregular if it is a suspension from order, and acts of jurisdiction nullities if it is a suspension from office ([163]).

28. A suspended clerk is disabled by the suspension from receiving the tithes and spiritual offerings of the people ([164]),

who without adequate cause fails to appear at a synod shall be content with the communion of his Church [*i.e.*, shall be excluded from offering].

(159). Concil. Aurel. 1, A.D. 511, Can. 9 ap. Gratian 1 Dist. LXXXI. c. 14, directs a presbyter or deacon to be deprived of his office and a share [in the distributions], but permits him to minister by request. Gregory *Ibid.* 1 Dist. L. c. 10: Ab officii honore depositus laicam tantummodo communionem accipiat. Alexander II. A.D. 1065, *Ibid.* 1 Dist. LXXXI. c. 16, and Urban II. A.D. 1095, *Ibid.* Caus. I. Qu. v. c. 3, mention both order and office. Lynd. 39 says there are twenty-four different kinds of suspension, and that unless expressly named the least penal is always to be understood.

(160). Cyprian Ep. 27, 3: In the meantime let [the accused clergy] abstain from the monthly division. Concil. Aurel. III. A.D. 538, Can. 7; Concil. Narbon, A.D. 589, Can. 11 and 13.

(161). Cyprian Ep. 48 (Oxf. 52), says that Evaristus, from being a bishop, has not even remained in lay communion. *Ibid.* 3, that the crimes of Novatus were so great that it was certain he would not only be turned out of the presbytery, but also restrained from communion. Apost. Can. 23 ap. Gratian 1 Dist. LXXXI. c. 12: Let a bishop, presbyter, or deacon who is taken in fornication, or perjury, or stealing be deposed but not separated from communion; for the Scripture saith: Thou shalt not avenge twice for the same offence. *Ibid.* Can. 15: Let him receive lay-communion. Theodori Poenit. I. IX. 1 in H. and S. III.; Egbert's Poenit. v. 1 *Ibid.* III. 421.

(162). Concil. Aurel. A.D. 511, Can. 12, says that clergy whilst doing penance may lawfully baptize in case of necessity. Gregory IX. Decret. Lib. v. Tit. XXVII. c. 10; Lynd. 12.

(163). Ayliffe 241; Craisson, § 6584.

(164). Alexander II. ap. Gratian 1 Dist. LXXXI. c. 16: Nec in choro psallentium maneat, nec aliquam portionem de rebus ecclesiasticis habeat. Const. 21 Peckham, A.D. 1281; Lynd. 120, 163, 182; Ayliffe 221.

but he is not excluded from the simple benefice or foundation endowment unless he is expressly excluded therefrom by one who has power to exclude him, as a visitor in spirituals ([165]). What is sometimes spoken of as suspension from benefice only is not properly suspension at all, but subtraction of the fruits of an endowment ([166]); and although in this country it extends to tithes because tithes form part of the foundation endowment, it does not disable from participating in offerings and distributions ([167]).

29. The period of time for which temporary suspension is imposed varies according to the nature of the offence and the custom of the country ([168]). In this country it was usually the same as the layman's period of suspension from entrance to the Church, but the penitential period for remedial purposes was considerably longer ([169]). When laymen were allowed to be restored to communion after a short period of exclusion, clergy were also allowed to be restored to their office after a short suspension therefrom. In the seventh century the customary period of suspension from entrance to the Church was one-third of the canonical time of penance ([170]), and the same

---

([165]). Lynd. 113 : When the fee is involved it is true what is said, that the discussion of it ought to be before the lord, otherwise it ought to be before the ordinary. Ayliffe 222 : A person who is deprived of his distributions on the score of crime is not for that reason deemed to be deprived of the fruits of his prebend or benefice. In depriving *ab officio* the bishop *acts as* president of the local Church. To deprive *a beneficio*, the bishop must be the visitor of the parochial foundation or benefice, and his office as such must be promoted. Law's Forms 60 ; Craisson, § 6533. According to Ecclesiastical Courts Commission, 1883, in France a curé may be suspended from office and from the right to wear the clerical garb, but this does not deprive him of his benefice.

([166]). Const. 19 Peckham, A.D. 1281 ; Const. 4 Stratford, A.D. 1342 ; Lynd. 306, 134.

([167]). Craisson § 6577.

([168]). Authorities ap. Gratian Caus. XXVI. Qu. VII.

([169]). Thus Egbert's Poenitential in Haddan and Stubbs III. 419, prescribes for capital crimes that a layman shall do penance four years, a clerk five, a sub-deacon six, a deacon seven, a presbyter ten, a bishop twelve years.

([170]). Thus when the penance was fixed at one year, the suspension

rule appears to have obtained for the time of suspension from office of clergy ([171]). Subsequently, when laymen were restored to communion so soon as they had come to satisfaction, a like indulgence was extended to clergy other than those guilty of public or notorious crimes, who (unless they had been guilty of irregularity by officiating) were only suspended until they made satisfaction and undertook to do penance privately for the remainder ([172]).

30. Under the parochial system the duties of an incumbent whilst he is suspended from the discharge of his office are performed by a temporary vicar ([173]); and since by English Constitutions temporary vicars may not be appointed for a longer period than five years without the bishop's special leave ([174]), and in no case for a longer period than seven

from entrance to the Church was for one Lent of forty days, which counted as a third of a year. See Theodori Poenit. I. II. 8 in Haddan and Stubbs III. 178; *Id.* XIV. 24, *Ibid.* 189; I. XV. 4, and Baedae Poenit. *Ibid.* 327. For an offence for which three years was the ordinary time of penance, the period of suspension was one year. For an offence for which seven years was the period of penance, the period of suspension was two to three years. For offences which required fifteen or twenty years of penance, the term of suspension was five to seven years. Theodori Poenit. L. II. 1 prescribes a year's penance for simple fornication; and Concil. London A.D. 1108, Can. 9, orders that priests who choose to leave their women and to serve God shall have vicars to officiate for them during the forty days in which they are to desist from their office. Theodore I. v. 10 prescribes a penance of twelve years, of which four are to be extra ecclesiam, and I. v. 14 another penance of twelve years, of which three are to be extra ecclesiam; I. VIII. 12 a penance of ten years, but provides that after three years, if he has given proof of true repentance, the bishop may treat him with leniency.

(171). Egbert's Poenit. v. 2 imposes twelve years' penance on a bishop guilty of simple fornication, but allows an abatement after three or four years. Lynd. 11, 39, 281.

(172). Alexander II. ap. Gratian I. Dist. LXXXI. c. 16: Decidat proprio gradu usque dum ad satisfactionem veniat. Concil. London A.D. 1108, Can. 9, and Alexander III. in Decret. Lib. I. Tit. XI. c. 4, impose on him some suitable penance, and direct him when part of the penance has been performed to use his order.

(173). Innocent III. A.D. 1199, in Decret. Lib. I. Tit. XXXIV. c. 10.

(174). Const. 7 and Otho, A.D. 1237; Const. 20 Othobon, A.D. 1268;

Ecclesiastical Severity. 165

years ([175]), a suspension for more than five years renders the office itself liable to forfeiture, and a suspension for more than seven years necessarily forfeits it. This degree of suspension is ordinarily termed deprivation.

31. Suspension, like excommunication, may not be imposed without a previous monition ([176]), except in cases in which the canons dispense with warning or in the case of open offences ([177]), nor may it be imposed on a bishop unless the canon which orders it specially makes bishops subject to its provisions ([178]). Simple suspension is incurred, *ipso facto*, by burying an excommunicated usurer ([179]), marrying those related within the forbidden degrees ([180]), electing a disqualified person as bishop ([181]), or being an habitual drunkard ([182]). A suspended clerk who meddles with the duties of his office without a dispensation becomes irregular ([183]).

32. The cases in which suspension extends to complete deprivation are: (1) when an excess has been committed of such a nature as to call for suspension for a longer period than five or seven years, in the former case in the bishop's discretion, in the latter by sentence of law; (2) when one who is sus-

---

Const. 3 Stratford, A.D. 1343. Concil. Worms. A.D. 868, Can. 10 ap. Gratian Caus. II. Qu. v. c. 26, had prescribed five years' suspension for a bishop or priest guilty of homicide, adultery, theft, or fraud. According to Concil. Meldens. A.D. 845, *Ibid.* Caus. x. Qu. II. c. 5, five years was the usual time for a precaria.

(175). Lynd. 238. See *The Parish*.
(176). Concil. Lat. III. A.D. 1179, Can. 6 in Decret. Lib. II. Tit. XXVIII. c. 26; Const. 15 and 26 Langton, A.D. 1222; Sext. Lib. v. Tit. XI. c. 13; Lynd. 13, 18, 127.
(177). Const. 5 Peckham, A.D. 1279; Lynd. 15. See *Discipline Generally*, § 6.
(178). Concil. Lugdun. A.D. 1245, in Sext. Lib. v. Tit. XI. c. 4.
(179). Concil. Lat. III. A.D. 1179, in Decret. Lib. v. Tit. XIX. c. 3.
(180). Concil. Lat. IV. A.D. 1215; *Ibid.* Lib. IV. Tit. III. c. 3.
(181). Concil. Lat. III. *Ibid.* Lib. I. Tit. VI. c. 7, § 3; Innocent II. to convent of Winchester, A.D. 1205, *Ibid.* c. 25; Concil. Lat. IV. *Ibid.* c. 43, 44.
(182). Concil. Lat. IV. *Ibid.* Lib. III. Tit. 1. c. 14.
(183). Concil. Lugdun. A.D. 1274, in Sext. Lib. v. Tit. XI. c. 1; Const. 1 Peckham, A.D. 1279.

pended ([184]), or excommunicated ([185]), has intermeddled with sacred offices or been disobedient to a judicial ruling or monition ([186]); (3) when it is expressly ordered by sentence of law, as for simony ([187]), heresy ([188]), sacrilege ([189]), homicide ([190]), self-mutilation ([191]), falsification of ecclesiastical documents ([192]), intrusion into another's benefice ([193]), holding two benefices at once without a dispensation ([194]), unnatural crime ([195]), and incest ([196]). In all these cases, however, a declaratory sentence

(184). Apost. Can. 29, quoted above, note 61; Gregory ap. Gratian I. Dist. L. c. 10: It has reached our ears that after being deposed from the priestly rank for a criminal offence he has presumed to fulfil the ministry of the priesthood. . . . If such be the case . . . let him be deprived of communion and reduced to penance. Concil. Antioch. A.D. 341, Can. 4, *Ibid.* Caus. XI. Qu. III. c. 6; Decret. Lib. V. Tit. XXVII. c. 3.

(185). Syn. Rom. A.D. 878, ap. Gratian Caus. XI. Qu. III. c. 109: Those priests who, having been excommunicated in the time of our predecessor Nicolaus, have presumed to meddle with the holy ministry, have brought on themselves the sentence of damnation. Decret. Lib. V. Tit. XXVII. c. 6.

(186). Concil. Agath. A.D. 506, Can. 2 ap. Gratian I. Dist. L. c. 21; Innocent III. in Decret. Lib. V. Tit. XXXVII. c. 11.

(187). Cap. 16 Theodulf, A.D. 994.; Urban II. A.D. 1095, ap. Gratian Caus. I. Qu. V. c. 3; Const. 1 Reynolds, A.D. 1322; Lynd. 33.

(188). Leo ap. Gratian Caus. I. Qu. l. c. 42; Innocent *Ibid.* c. 73.

(189). Const. 1 Reynolds, A.D. 1322; Lynd. 33.

(190). Martin. Brac. ap. Gratian I. Dist. L. c. 8; Theodori. Poenit. I. IX. 8 in Haddan & Stubbs III. 185; Decret. Lib. V. Tit. XII. c. 6.

(191). Concil. Nic. A.D. 325, Can. 1.

(192). Concil. Agath. A.D. 506, Can. 50 ap. Gratian I. Dist. l. c. 7; Decret. Lib. V. Tit. XX.; Const. 1 Reynolds, A.D. 1322; Lynd. 33.

(193). Northumbrian Priests, Can. 2, A.D. 950; Conf. Edgar's Law 10, A.D. 960; Cap. 14 & 15 Theodolf, A.D. 994; Gratian Caus. II. Qu. l. c. 7; Concil. London A.D. 1175, Can. 12; Const. 1 Langton, A.D. 1222; Decret. Lib. V. Tit. XXXI. c. 6, and Lib. III. Tit. VIII. c. 1; Const. 5 Winchel. A.D. 1305; Const. 11 Otho, A.D. 1237; Const. 10 Othobon, A.D. 1268; Lynd. 233, 237, 319.

(194). Concil. Lat. III. A.D. 1179, Can. 29 in Decret. Lib. III. Tit. V. c. 5; Concil. Lat. IV. A.D. 1215, *Ibid.* c. 28; *Discipline Generally*, note 158.

(195). Concil. Westminster A.D. 1102, Can. 28; Concil. Lat. III. A.D. 1179, in Decret. Lib. V. Tit. XXXI. c. 4.

(196). Gratian I. Dist. XXVII. c. 9; Augustin *Ibid.* Caus. XXXII. Qu. VII. c. 11; Const. 17 Peckham, A.D. 1281; spiritual incest a fortiori, *Ibid.* Caus. XXX. Qu. l. c. 8-10, and *Excesses*, § 33.

Ecclesiastical Severity. 167

is necessary by a spiritual judge before the office is vacant *de facto* ([197]), because doubt may otherwise be felt as to the existence of the crime ([198]). In all cases of deprivation, moreover, the bishop is required to make some provision for the temporal needs of the deprived person ([199]), since the mendicancy of the clergy is the bishop's disgrace ([200]).

33. Deposition ([201]), formerly called deposition for ever ([202]), or deposition without hope of restitution ([203]), or dejection ([204]), is not merely suspension from the exercise of order and office in some particular part of the Church to which the offender is attached, but the total removal from the ranks of order and from the enjoyment of all clerical privileges ([205]). Like the greater

---

([197]). Const. 20 Edmund, A.D. 1236 ; Const. 5 Boniface, A.D. 1261; Const. 3 Winchel. A.D. 1298 ; Const. 3 Mepham. A.D. 1328 ; Lynd, 13, 15, 16, 77, 136.

([198]). Decret. Lib. v. Tit. xxxix. c. 26 ; Lynd. 16, 308.

([199]). Syn. Rom. A.D. 826, Can. 14 ap. Gratian I. Dist. LXXXI. c. 7 : Let a priest or any other member of the ecclesiastical order, if found guilty of such an offence as to necessitate his being deprived, be deposed and be provided for by the care of the bishop. Gregory *Ibid.* Caus. xvi. Qu. vi. c. 5 : A sufficient stipend ought to be provided for those who are consigned to penance. In early times this was usually done by placing them in a monastery. Ambros. *Ibid.* Caus. I. Qu. l. c. 7 orders this for one simoniacally ordained. Concil. Trosslei *Ibid.* Caus. xxiv. Qu. III. c. 2 ; Pseudo-Augustin *Ibid.* Caus. xxii. Qu. v. c. 19 ; 1 Dist. L. c. 7 and 58 ; 1 Dist. LXXXI. c. 8 ; Decret. Lib. v. Tit. xxxi c. 4. *White* v. *Baldwin*, No. 92, in Rothery's Report ; Stremmler des Peines Eccles. p. 33 ; Craisson, § 6336.

([200]). Apost. Can. 59 ; Hieronym. ap. Gratian I. Dist. xcii. c. 23.

([201]). Sometimes degredari, more often omnino deponi, or omnino de proprio gradu dejici, deordinari, ab ordine cleri amoveri. Pseudo-Isidor. ap. Gratian Caus. xi. Qu. l. c. 31, a clero cessare. Alexander III. in Decret. Lib. II. Tit. l. c. 4 : Perpetuo removeri a ministerio.

([202]). Const. 3 Edmund, A.D. 1236.

([203]). Concil. Lat. I. A.D. 1123, Can. 10 ap. Gratian I. Dist. LXII. c. 3.

([204]). Concil. Lat. III. A.D. 1179, in Decret. Lib. v. Tit. LXXXI. c. 4.

([205]). Devoti Lib. I. Tit. viii. § 21 shows that up to the end of the 12th century degradation in the sense of handing over to the secular arm was an exceptional proceeding. Innocent III. in Decret. Lib. v. Tit. xx. c. 8 ordered as a punishment for falsification. See Maskell, Mon. Rit. II. p. CLX.; Craisson, § 6337.

excommunication, it may be inflicted either (1) non-solemnly, by a prelate or judge, when it is called *verbal* degradation, or (2) solemnly, as the act of the whole participating Church, when it is called *actual* degradation. In verbal degradation the judge decrees that a clerk be removed from his clerical position and adjudges him to be delivered to the lay forum [206]. Actual degradation is the solemn ceremony in execution of the sentence, wherein the clerk is deprived of the insignia of his order and handed over to the secular arm [207].

34. Formerly twelve bishops were required for the solemn degradation of a bishop, six for that of a presbyter, three for that of a deacon [208], and a smaller number for the degradation of one in minor orders [209]. Mitred abbots, prelates, and dignitaries conversant with the law are now allowed to take the place of bishops [210] provided they are not merely assessors but have a definitive voice [211]. Degradation is only allowed for some enormous crime [212], or for incorrigible miscon-

---

[206]. Coelestin. III. in Decret. Lib. II. Tit. 1. c. 10, directs a clerk to be first deposed, then if contumacious to be excommunicated, if still obstinate to be anathematized, and finally to be handed over to the lay judge for exile. Boniface VIII. in Sext. Lib. V. Tit. IX. c. 2.

[207]. Pseudo-Isidor. ap. Gratian Caus. XI. Qu. 1. c. 31 directs lower clergy who conspire against bishops and priests to be removed from the clergy and handed over to the secular arm. Alexander III. in Decret. Lib. II. Tit. 1. c. 4 declares that it is not every excess which deserves handing over to the secular arm. See the Forma degredandi clericum in Maskell's Monumenta Ritualia II. p. 333, and in Reichel's English Liturgical Vestments 17, note 3.

[208]. Concil. Carthag. I. A.D. 348, Can. 11 ap. Gratian Caus. XV. Qu. VII. c. 5; Concil Carthag. II. A.D. 390, Can. 10, *Ibid.* c. 6; Concil. Carthag. III. A.D. 397, Can. 8, *Ibid.* c. 7; Stat. Eccl. Ant. A.D. 505, Can. 23, *Ibid.* c. 8; Boniface VIII. in Sext. Lib. V. Tit. IX. c. 2.

[209]. Boniface l. c.

[210]. Concil. Trident, Sess. 13, Cap. 4 de Refor.

[211]. Gregory in Decret. Lib. II. Tit. XXVII. c. 3: No one can be removed from the sacerdotal rank except for a just cause by the concordant sentence of the bishops (*sacerdotes*).

[212]. Alfred's Law 12, A.D. 877: If a priest slay another man let all that he possesses and his habit be seized, and let the bishop degrade him. Const. 16 Clarendon, A.D. 1164: The king also decreed that bishops should

duct ([213]), such as heresy and apostasy persisted in ([214]), falsification of apostolical letters ([215]), permeditated homicide ([216]), and the abuse of the confessional for sacrilegious purposes ([217]); but modern English statute law permits one who is in holy orders to degrade himself ([218]).

RELAXATION OF CENSURES—RECONCILIATION OR ABSOLUTION.

35. When a censure has been imposed for a definite period by way of vindictive penalty, such as a suspension from communion or from office for a month, it is relaxed *ipso facto* at the expiration of the time named ([219]), and it may even be so far relaxed, or rather dispensed with, before the time has expired that the offender may be re-admitted to his rank in the Church or the exercise of his order in a place where the cause of the censure is unknown ([220]). A censure, however, imposed indefinitely to bring an offender to repentance, such as excommunication or the interdict, is not relaxed of itself, neither by the death of the offender ([221]), his amendment ([222]), the death of the imposer ([223]), or even by an alteration of the law ([224]),

---

degrade clerks in presence of the king's justice whom they had found guilty of any public crime, and then deliver them to the king's court to be punished. Innocent III. in Decret. Lib. v. Tit. XL. c. 27, and Tit. XXVII. c. 2; Boniface VIII. l. c.; Lynd. 322.

(213). Lynd. 322.
(214). Decret. Lib. v. Tit. VII. c. 9, 15; Boniface VIII. in Sext. Lib. v. Tit. II. c. 1 and 4; Lynd. 296.
(215). Innocent III. in Decret. Lib. v. Tit. XX. c. 7, and Tit. XL. c. 27.
(216). Concil. Lugdun. A.D. 1274, in Sext. Lib. v. Tit. IV. c. 1.
(217). Devoti Lib. I. Tit. VIII. § 23; Craisson, § 6348.
(218). See *Order*, § 40.
(219). Cyprian Ep. 9, 2, quoted *Discipline Generally*, note 66. Craisson, § 6437, 6587.
(220). Lynd. 290 says a suspended clergyman may with permission officiate in another diocese. *Id.* p. 75; Craisson, § 6506, 6449.
(221). Innocent III. in Decret. Lib. v. Tit. XXXIX. c. 28 and 38.
(222). Clement III. *Ibid.* c. 15; Gregory IX. *Ibid.* c. 58.
(223). Innocent III. to Bishop of Ely, *Ibid.* Lib. I. Tit. XXXI. c. 11.
(224). Craisson, § 6436.

but continues in force until it is ended in a regular manner ([225]). In ancient times the ending of a censure was called peace ([226]), relaxation, forgiveness, or communion ([227]). It is now generally called reconciliation or absolution.

36. Reconciliation or absolution appears thus to be spoken of in two senses: (1) to express reconciliation with God, which is called *extra-judicial* ([228]) or sacramental absolution, and is effected in the forum of penance by means of the prayers of the Church upon the sinner's true repentance; and (2) to express reconciliation with the Church, which is called *judicial* or ecclesiastical absolution, and is given by one having jurisdiction in the Church. The latter ought to follow after reconciliation with God, and therefore ought not to be granted too readily ([229]). The two absolutions, though parts of one whole, are distinct from each other. Sacramental absolution unloosens the bond of guilt; ecclesiastical absolution relaxes the bond of censure ([230]).

37. The proper person or authority to relax an ecclesiastical

---

(225). Augustin ap. Gratian I. Dist. L. c. 23 : A priest can well be restored to his honour after penance done, aud c. 28. Socrates II. 8 relates that in 341 A.D. Athanasius was accused of having acted contrary to the canon in resuming his episcopal authority without the license of a general council of bishops; II. 24 relates that Athanasius took care to avoid such a charge afterwards. Concil. Tolet. IV. A.D. 633, ap. Gratian Caus. XI. Qu. III. c. 65 : A bishop, priest, or deacon unjustly deposed, if found innocent in a second synod, cannot regain his lost position unless he receives it back from the bishop's hand. Innocent III. A.D. 1198, in Decret. Lib. V. Tit. XXXIX. c. 39, says excommunication must be held to be in force until it is shown to have been removed.

(226). Cyprian Ep. 18; 32, 2; 16; Ayliffe 20. See *Penance*, § 12.

(227). Socrates I. 26 relates that Arius prayed "to be reunited to our Mother the Church;" II. 24 says that Maximus, Bishop of Jerusalem, calling a council, A.D. 349, restored Athanasius to communion; II. 26, that a synod in Egypt did the same.

(228). Ayliffe 18; Law's Forms, 137.

(229). Ambros. ap. Gratian Caus. XXIII. Qu. IV. c. 33.

(230). Innocent III. A.D. 1199, in Decret Lib. v. Tit. XXXIX. c. 28, says that Christ first raised Lazarus and then told the disciples to unbind him. Ayliffe 18.

Ecclesiastical Severity. 171

censure is the same person or authority who imposed it ([231]), his delegate ([232]), successor ([233]), or superior ([234]). Censures imposed by law or by a general sentence ([235]) may be relaxed by any bishop or presbyter who has jurisdiction ([236]), provided they do not extend to the reserved cases ([237]). An incumbent or any presbyter who has authority to give sacramental absolution can, therefore, relax a sentence of the lesser excommunication ([238]), but not a sentence of clerical suspension or interdict ([239]), because these are reserved to the bishop as belonging to the outer tribunal. At the hour of death every presbyter has the same power ([240]), yet so that if the sick man recovers he is under obligation to report his absolution to the authority which imposed the censure, failing which he relapses into it again ([241]). Women, the aged, children, and the infirm ([242]) are excepted from the rule if they have been absolved by a

---

[231]. Ayliffe 18; Gratian Caus. XXXIII. Qu. III. Dist. VI. c. 1; Innocent III. in Decret. Lib. I. Tit. XXXIII. c. 6.

[232]. Concil. Nic. A.D. 325, Can. 5; Gregory IX. in Decret. Lib. I. Tit. XXXI. c. 20.

[233]. Concil. Epaun. A.D. 517, Can. 28 ap. Gratian Caus. XI. Qu. III. c. 40 : If a bishop is taken away by death before the absolution of one condemned, after correction and penitence his successor may absolve him. Sext. Lib. I. Tit. XVII. c. 1.

[234]. Innocent III. in Decret. Lib. v. Tit. XXXIX. c. 40, and Lib. I. Tit. XXXI. c. 8; Gratian Caus. II. Qu. I. c. 11.

[235]. Craisson, § 6443.

[236]. Innocent III. A.D. 1199, in Decret. Lib. v. Tit. XXXIX. c. 29.

[237]. Clemens III. in Decret. Lib. v. Tit. XXXIX. c. 26; Gregory IX. *Ibid.* c. 58. By 25 Hen. VIII. c. 21 these cases are referred to the archbishop. See *Penance*, § 6.

[238]. Craisson, § 6488.

[239]. Craisson, § 6480.

[240]. Clemens III. in Decret. Lib. v. Tit. XXXIX. c. 26; and Innocent III. to Bishop of Ely, A.D. 1204, *Ibid.* Lib. I. Tit. XXXI. c. 11; Boniface VIII. in Sext. Lib. v. Tit. XI. c. 22.

[241]. Clemens III. in Decret. Lib. v. Tit. XXXIX. c. 13; Concil. Ebor. A.D. 1195, Can. 17; Boniface VIII. in Sext. Lib. v. Tit. XI. c. 22.

[242]. Alexander III. *Ibid.* c. 6; Clement III. *Ibid.* Lib. v. Tit. XXXIX. c. 13, 17, 11, 29.

bishop, and likewise monks if they have been absolved by a bishop or by their own prior ([243]).

38. Besides the regular relaxation of a censure, which is only granted after amendment or imposition of penance, there are two other kinds of ecclesiastical absolution — one which is called precautionary (*ad cautelam*), the other absolution *with reincidence*. Precautionary absolution ([244]), which is stated to have been first introduced by Coelestine III. in the twelfth century, is absolution bestowed for safety's sake to ensure the efficacy of some other grant, which without it would be inoperative, or is bestowed to prevent a possible wrong being done. Of the former kind is the absolution which accompanies every indulgence, since an indulgence is unavailing to one who is out of the communion of saints; of the latter kind the absolution granted when an appeal is pending and there is reason for doubting whether the censure appealed against is deserved ([245]).

39. Absolution with reincidence ([246]) is absolution given as a temporary expedient or with a condition annexed. Such is the absolution given to penitents on Maunday Thursday to enable them to receive the Easter communion, or absolution given on condition that restitution is made within a certain time. In the former case the penitential status revives after the Easter communion has been made, in the latter if restitution has not been made at the end of the time limited.

40. Ordinarily, ecclesiastical absolution can only be given to the living ([247]), but if after death any one is found to have been unjustly censured, he may be declared unbound and his name

---

(243). Alexander III. *Ibid.* c. 2; Honorius III. *Ibid.* c. 50.
(244). Honorius III. *Ibid.* c. 52.
(245). Innocent III. A.D. 1202, *Ibid.* c. 40.
(246). Ad reincidentiam Devoti Lib. IV. Tit. XXI. § 6. Suarez holds that a censure may be suspended and be reimposed. This Liguori denies except for a new fault. Craisson, § 477, says that the non-fulfilment of the condition may be looked on as a new fault.
(247). Ayliffe 19.

Ecclesiastical Severity. 173

entered on the diptychs of the dead ([248]). The same publicity should be given to the termination of a sentence of excommunication, suspension, or the interdict as was given to the original sentence of censure ([249]). A purely vindictive penalty, such as clerical irregularity or loss of reputation, is not, however, got rid of by absolution, but by dispensation from its effects ([250]).

([248]). Syn. V. A.D. 553, ap. Gratian Caus. XXIV. Qu. II. c. 6.
([249]). Const. 28 Othobon, A.D. 1268.
([250]). Stremler des Peines Ecclésiastiques, p. 231 ; Craisson, § 6470.

VI.
SPIRITUAL COURTS.

Disciplinary Procedure.

1. From the two keys—the key of interpretation of the divine law which determines what acts are to be counted excesses and what not, and the key of coercion which determines what means may be employed to restrain excesses and to what extent—we pass to the subject of disciplinary procedure. Disciplinary procedure may be defined to be the method of applying the two keys, so as at once to safeguard the sanctity of the Church, to bring back those who have strayed from the path of holiness, and to prevent injustice being done where there is only the appearance of excess but the existence of it is denied. It involves inquiry into three things: (1) into spiritual courts, their jurisdiction past and present, and their constituent elements; (2) into the several modes of procedure adopted in them for the enforcement of discipline; and (3) into the manner of proceeding in judgment to ascertain disputed facts, including the judge's office in giving sentence, and the execution of sentences unless arrested by appeal.

2. In the administration of discipline in the first days of the Church, the decision of all matters affecting the position of its members was taken solemnly, *i.e.*, with the concurrence of all (¹), or, as it was afterwards said, *in medio*; the bishop was

---

(1). Acts xv. 12: Πᾶν τὸ πλῆθος kept silence whilst the case was presented by St. Peter, St. Barnabas, and St. Paul. Then St. James gave his decision, which (ver. 22) commended itself to the apostles and presbyters, together with the whole Church. See also 1 Cor. v., and *Dicipline Generally*, note 61. Cyprian Ep. 13 (Oxf. 19): This is suitable to modesty and discipline, that the chief officers, meeting with the clergy in presence of the people, . . . may order all things with the righteousness of a common consultation. *Id.* Ep. 27 (Oxf. 34), 3: Let him be expelled from

naturally the president and spokesman, the presbyters aided him with advice, and the people were associated in the rulings of their elders. Matters of less importance were dealt with by the bishop and presbyters without the presence of the people (²), or as it was afterwards said, *in consistory*. And again, matters of small moment, or which only involved the application of principles already laid down, were decided by the bishop alone, or, as it was afterwards said, *in audience*.

Origin of Courts Christian.

3. A spiritual court or court Christian may be defined to be any regularly constituted body of persons in the Church which hears and decides disciplinary matters of spiritual or ecclesiastical cognisance, either extra-judicially or judicially. From what has just been said it thus appears that the earliest spiritual courts were extra-judicial, and consisted either (1) of the whole body of the faithful, when they were called *synods, councils*, or, in later times, *visitation-courts*; or (2) of the bishop and his clergy, or the metropolitan and his clergy, *i.e.*, presbyters and deacons, when they were called *consistories* or *consistorial*

our communion, and plead the cause of his rashness before all of us. Ep. 39 (Oxf. 43), 7; Ep. 51 (Oxf. 55), 5. Ambros. Ep. 5 blames Syagrius, Bishop of Verona, for deciding upon the treatment of an accused person without the advice of any of the brethren. Ayliffe 259.

(2). Tertullian Apol. 39: [In the Church] are exhortations made, rebukes and censures administered. For with great gravity is the work of judging done as before trustworthy (certos) persons deputed from the face of God. Firmilian ad Cyprian Ep. 74 (Oxf. 75), 4, A.D. 256: Year by year we, the elders and prelates assemble to arrange those matters which are committed to our care. Apost. Const. II. 45-53, names Monday as the bishop's judicial day, when he sits, surrounded by presbyters and deacons, to hear the contending parties [*i.e.*, civil matters], and also complaints of unchristian conduct [*i.e.*, criminal matters]. First of all the other clergy attempt to reconcile the parties, and if this fails, the matter comes before the bishop. Concil. Elib. A.D. 305, Can. 74, 75, decrees that he who fails to prove his accusation convento clero (*al.* conventui clericorum) shall be suspended for five years, and he who fails to prove, and cannot prove, a charge against a presbyter or deacon, shall be denied the viaticum.

courts (³); or (3) of the bishop or metropolitan alone, when they were called *audiences* or *domestic courts*.

4. The procedure before all these tribunals appears at first to have been extra-judicial and summary. There was no judge in a technical sense, but the whole body present decided the matter, the members generally having a consultative, the members of the apostolic college a definitive voice (⁴). There were no technical forms of procedure to be gone through, but the action was like that now followed in a visitation court, or in the chapter of a monastic body. Offences against the rule of holiness were either known by the party's confession, by presentment, or by public notoriety (⁵); and what the synod, consistory, or audience did, was to determine how they should be dealt with. In so doing, it had (1) to interpret and decide what the Christian law was in each case as it arose, and (2) to determine how it should be applied under the particular circumstances disclosed.

5. The case became altered when the Christian law had been already determined by councils of the Church, and there was either a dispute as to the facts alleged, or differences arose between Christians in their relations to one another, as was early the case in the Corinthian Church (⁶). In these cases—

(3). Law's Forms, p. 2.

(4). See note 1, and Cardinal de la Luzerne, quoted in Ecclesiastical Courts Commission, vol. II. 228.

(5). 2 Cor. x. 6; 2 Tim. iv. 15; 2 Thess. III. 14; Concil. Nic. A.D. 325, Can. 5; Concil. Carthag. A.D. 347, Can. 10, in Labbé II. 590; Concil. Constant. A.D. 382, Can. 6; Stat. Eccl. Ant. A.D. 505, Can. 23; Concil. Agath. A.D. 506, Can. 32; Concil. Aurel. III. A.D. 538, Can. 32; Stephen v. A.D. 887, ap. Gratian Caus. II. Qu. 1. c. 17: In a manifest and known cause witnesses are not wanted, as St. Ambrose, commenting on the Epistle to the Corinthians, thus gives the Apostle's meaning respecting fornication: A judge may not condemn without an accuser, because our Lord, although he knew that Judas was a thief, did not reject him because no one accused him. . . . The Apostle, however, deemed that [the incestuous Corinthian] should be expelled. For all knew his crime, and he publicly had his mother-in-law to wife. Innocent. I. *Ibid.* Caus. XXXII. Qu. v. c. 23; Lynd. 323, 349.

(6). 1 Cor. VI. 1.

Spiritual Courts.

and they soon became the majority—there was no call for interpretation, but only for ascertaining the facts, and giving a decision upon them according to right. In accordance with the apostle's teaching, disputes between Christians are forbidden to be carried before extraneous tribunals, and are directed to be settled by those deputed by the Church ([7]). To do justice in such cases, it becomes necessary to have some kind of discussion in judgment ([8]), and some settled form of judicial procedure ([9]). Hence, side by side with the original extra-judicial

---

([7]). Joseph. Ant. XIV. 10, 17 ; XVI. 6, states that Jews were accustomed to decide their disputes by arbitrators. 1 Cor. VI. 1 directs Christians to do the same. Augustin in Ps. CXVIII. Serm. 24 : The wicked oppress the weak, and these are compelled to bring their causes before us, and we dare not say to them, Man, who made me a judge and divider among you? For the apostle constituted ecclesiastical judges for such matters, forbidding Christians to agitate their quarrels before temporal courts (in foro). Id. de Oper. Monach. c. 29. Apost. Const. II. 45 : If, by any misadventure or temptation, a dispute arises with any one, let him endeavour that it may be composed, though thereby he is obliged to lose somewhat ; and let it not come before a heathen tribunal. Ibid. c. 46 : Let not the heathen know of your differences. Stat. Eccl. Ant. A.D. 505, Can. 87 ap. Labbé II. 1444 : Let a Catholic who carries his cause, whether just or unjust, before the court of a judge of another faith, be excommunicated. See *Duties of Order*, note 12 ; *Excesses*, note 284.

([8]). Isidor. Etym. XVIII. 15 in Decret. Lib. I. Tit. XL. c. 10, says : It is in judgment when it is discussed ; and elsewhere : To discuss according to law is to judge justly. He further says (what Devoti Lib. III. Tit. I. § 18 repeats) that two disputants, a dispute, and a judge are necessary to constitute a judicial court (*judicium*), and that it is not the less a court because the procedure is summary. Innocent III. in Decret. Lib. I. Tit. IV. c. 3, A.D. 1199, reprobates the practice then prevalent at Poitou, of all the members of the Church, learned and unlearned alike, deciding ecclesiastical matters in court. Law's Forms defines a court as " the jurisdiction of the ordinary in taking cognisance of clerical matters, whether contentious or voluntary," but this definition applies only to a judicial court.

([9]). St. Paul's direction to St. Timothy (1 Tim. v. 19) not to receive an accusation against a presbyter, except at the mouth of two witnesses, is a direction concerning procedure. Cyprian ad Cornelium, 48, 3 : The day of investigation was coming on, on which his cause was to be dealt with before us. Ep. 54, 10 states that he had judicially condemned Privatus and others. According to Socrates L 9, the Nicene fathers, before condemning

tribunals, which gave sentence synodically (*in medio*) (¹⁰), or in audience (¹¹), when the facts were known or the interpretation of the law was involved, there grew up judicial tribunals to decide disputed facts, or to apply the law to particular cases in judgment (*in judicio*) (¹²).

6. The constitution of these judicial courts appears to have

Arius, summoned him to appear, then heard him and his accusers, and ultimately condemned him. Apost. Can. 74 : If a bishop be accused of any crime, it is necessary that he be cited by the bishops. . . . If, when cited, he does not obey, let him be cited a second time by two bishops. Nestorius was thrice cited to appear at Ephesus, because, according to the Relatio Concilii ad Coelestinum in Labbé III. 1190, " it is unseemly to omit any of those things which pertain to ecclesiastical order." Even the synod of the Oak, according to Socrates VI. 15, summoned Chrysostom four times to appear. Eutyches received a threefold citation from the Council of Constantinople, and Dioscoros the like from the Council of Chalcedon, according to Labbé IV. 1778 and 1811. In his dialogue with the Emperor Constantius, in Theodoret II. 16, Pope Liberius says : No man ought to be condemned without being examined.

(10). Innocent I. A.D. 404, ap. Gratian I. Dist. LXXXI. c. 6 ; Syn. Rom. A.D. 502, Can. 1 ; *Ibid.* I. Dist. XCVI. c. 1 : Let it be brought before all (Deferatur in medium). Codex Eccles. Afric. I. 8 : Veniat commonitorium in medium. Lynd. 323.

(11). Valentinian III. in Cod. Theodos. I. 47, A.D. 425 : Clergy we reserve for the bishop's audience. Honorius III. in Decret. Lib. II. Tit. L c. 19, says that a petition was addressed to his audience, whereupon he committed the investigation of the facts to the Bishop of Paris and his fellow-judges. Innocent III. states the same, *Ibid.* Lib. III. Tit. XXX. c. 31, and Lib. I. Tit. XLI. c. 2. Van Espen Pars. I. Tit. l. c. 3, contends that the term audience only applies to arbitration courts. Devoti Lib. III. Tit. I. § 22, shows that audience is applied to public determination of the outer forum.

(12). Devoti Lib. III. Tit. II. § 3 : *Imperium* does not always go together with power of judging. For there are judges who have only power of cognisance, but have no jurisdiction, and these only investigate and decide a disputed matter, but have no *imperium* to pronounce and execute a sentence, and they are said not *jus dicere*, but *judicare*. Ayliffe 23, 350 : A controversy may happen either in or out of judgment. It may be judicial or extra-judicial. For a controversy may be *sine lite*. Stat. Eccl. Ant. A.D. 505, ap. Gratian Caus. XV. Qu. VII. c. 6 : Let the bishop hear the cause of no one without the presence of his clergy. Chrysost. de Sacerd. III. 17 : The part which a bishop has to play in judging begets infinite dislikes and infinite offence. Eccles. Courts Commission, 1883, vol. ii. 264.

varied considerably. In criminal cases they consisted of certain
of the elder presbyters ([13]) or ancients ([14]), the number being
more or less numerous according to the nature of the charge
and the position of the offender ([15]); but in civil cases usually a
single "wise man" was deputed by the bishop to investigate the facts and report to him upon the dispute, called
in later times an auditor ([16]). As was natural, the procedure followed was that customary in the empire in arbitration cases, with this difference, that the referees of the Church,
as being the kingdom of righteousness upon earth, were
more anxious than secular arbitrators to act justly ([17]), and

([13]). Apost. Const. II. 47: Those that have the controversy shall stand
severally in the midst of the court. And when you [presbyters] have
heard them, give your votes boldly, endeavouring to reconcile them before
the bishop's sentence, that sentence against an offender may not go abroad
into the world. Gregory ap. Gratian Caus. XV. Qu. VII. c. 2 calls them
seniores, *i.e.*, presbyters. Isidore *Ibid.* 1 Dist. XXI. c. 1 calls them presbyters.

([14]). Concil. London A.D. 1075, Can. 1, calls them ancients, meaning
thereby clerical canonists. Concil. Lat. IV. A.D. 1215, Can. 8 in Decret.
Lib. V. Tit. 1. c. 24 requires that whenever a prelate of the Church is
defamed the truth of the matter should be inquired into before the elders
of the Church (*coram ecclesiæ senioribus*).

([15]). Socrates I. 6 relates that Bishop Alexander of Alexandria convened
a council of many prelates to condemn Arius, but that was a case of
heresy. According to authorities quoted by Gratian Caus. XV. Qu. III., in
Africa twelve bishops were required for the trial of a bishop, six for that of
a presbyter, three for a deacon; but according to Concil. Matiscon. II. A.D.
585, Can. 6 and 7 in Labbe VI. 676, three were sufficient, except in the
most difficult cases, in the Western Church for a bishop.

([16]). In 1 Cor. VI. 4 St. Paul directs those who are thought nothing of
in the Church to be appointed judges if there is not a single wise man.
Socrates VII. 37 relates that Silvanus, Bishop of Troas, "perceiving that
ecclesiastics made a gain of the contentions of those engaged in lawsuits,
would never nominate any of the clergy as judges, but causing the documents of the litigants to be delivered to himself, committed to some pious
layman the adjudication of the case." Concil. Carthag. V. A.D. 401, ap.
Gratian Caus. II. Qu. VI. c. 38, calls such a judge *præses* or *cognitor*. Innocent III. to Archbishop of Canterbury in Decret. Lib. I. Tit. XXIX. c. 27,
§ 3, calls him *auditor*.

([17]). Apost. Const. II. 37: It is the duty of the bishop to judge righteously.
Ibid. II. 42, 44, Apost. Const. II. 47, calls on the presbyters who are told off

in criminal cases to condemn no one without the clearest proof ([18]).

7. If the decision of the referees was not acquiesced in, the only instrument by which the Church was able to enforce a sentence was by excommunication. Roman law was, however, itself favourable to arbitrations, and to give them effect prescribed a penal clause to be inserted in the agreement referring the matter to arbitration ([19]). On the public recognition of the Church by the empire in the fourth century, the law went further. First it allowed clergy, in accordance with the Church's rule ([20]), to be bound in all cases by the sentence of a spiritual tribunal, and in cases of discipline made them amenable to the rulings of spiritual courts only ([21]). Next it

to determine the merits of a case to give their decision fearlessly and straightforwardly, knowing that the bishop who will be called upon to decide, if they have not decided rightly, "has in the judgment-seat a co-decider and co-investigator of the right, the Christ of God." The synod which condemned Paul of Samosata in 269 A.D., in Euseb. VII. 30, charged him with "exacting and extorting money from the brethren, depressing the injured, and promising to give help for a reward;" with preparing for himself a "$\beta\hat{\eta}\mu\alpha$ and lofty throne," and having a $\sigma\acute{\eta}\kappa\rho\eta\tau o\nu$, or, in other words, for taking upon himself, after the fashion of worldly judges, to decide cases on his own motion, without the concurrence of the Church, and selling justice.

(18). See *Discipline Generally*, note 52 ; *Acts in Judgment*, § 35.

(19). Dig. Lib. IV. Tit. 8.

(20). Concil. Carthag. III. A.D. 397, c. 9 : If any bishop, presbyter, deacon, or one of the lower clergy, when a charge is made against him, or a civil dispute arises, shall leave the ecclesiastical *forum* and attempt to clear himself before secular (publici) courts, even though he win his case let him forfeit his place, *i.e.*, if it be a criminal procedure ; but if it be only a civil matter, let him forfeit what he has won if he wishes to retain his place. Concil. Chalcedon A.D. 451, Can. 9. See *Duties of Order*, note 12 ; *Excesses*, note 284.

(21). Lex Constantii in Cod. Theodos. XVL XI. 12, A.D. 355 : In exercise of our clemency we forbid bishops being accused in [civil] courts. If any one has a complaint against [a bishop], it is seemly that it be investigated before other bishops. Gratian *Ibid.* L 23, A.D. 376 : The rule which obtains in civil causes ought also to obtain in ecclesiastial matters, viz., that if of certain disagreements and light shortcomings any have reference to the observance of religion, they ought to be heard in their proper place, and

gave legal effect to the bishop's decisions on ecclesiastical matters ([22]); and ultimately it allowed bishops to decide civil matters definitively, provided they had been chosen as judges by the parties ([23]). The jurisdiction of spiritual courts, it will be thus seen, extended in the Roman Empire to two classes of subjects: (1) to causes concerning the government of souls and matters of religion by right ([24]), and (2) to civil causes by sufferance with consent of the parties.

by the synods of their dioceses, excepting such as criminal action requires to be heard by ordinary or extraordinary courts or other higher powers. Honorius, *Ibid.* I. 41, A.D. 412: Clergy may not be accused except before their bishops. Valentinian III. *Ibid.* I. 47, A.D. 425: Clergy we reserve to the bishop's audience; for it is not according to piety that ministers of the divine gift should be exposed to the caprice of temporal powers. See note 67.

(22). In Euseb. Vita Const. IV. 24 Constantine says to the bishops: Ye indeed are overseers of those things which are within the Church; I, of those which are without it. Honorius in Cod. Theodos. XVI. XI. 1, A.D. 399: Whenever it is a question of religion it is fitting that bishops should judge. Other causes which belong to commissioners (cognitores), or to the cognisance of public judges, must be determined according to law. Justin Nov. 28: If it be an ecclesiastical offence requiring correction and ecclesiastical punishment, let the bishop beloved of God give sentence thereon.

(23). Euseb. de Vita Const. IV. 27; Sozomen I. 9 says that Constantine allowed litigants to apply to the bishop's judgment if they declined the secular tribunals, and ordered that the bishop's decision should have the same force as if it had been given by the emperor himself. Cod. Justin. I. IV. 8, A.D. 408: Let the bishop's judgment stand (*ratum sit*) for all who have chosen to be heard by bishops; and we command that the same respect be shown to their decision as must be shown to your authority, from which no appeal lies. Let the execution of it also be committed to be carried out (definitioni) by the officers of the judges, so that the bishop's ruling may not be in vain. Augustin in Ps. XXV. § 13, A.D. 415: So much have the princes of this world committed to the Church, that whatever has been there ruled cannot be rescinded. Codex. Eccl. Afric. Can. 104, says that if a bishop applies to the emperor to have his court recognised, no objection can be taken. See note 67.

(24). In Athanas. Hist. of Arians, c. 44; Hosius of Cordova says to Constantine: Do not intrude into ecclesiastical matters. To you God has intrusted the kingdom, to us is committed the Church. See note 157. Valentinian I. refused to judge about bishops, and Ambrose quoted his

8. In this country prior to the Norman Conquest the bishop or archbishop was the sole judge of clergy for all crimes ([25]), and he had also cognisance of certain offences against the rights of the Church and ecclesiastical order ([26]); but as he usually sat with the sheriff in the Hundred Court, "to put in use both God's law and the world's law" ([27]), his spiritual and secular jurisdictions were often exercised simultaneously. Following the example of the Emperor Charles, who in 803 A.D. established courts Christian in the Western Empire, William the Conqueror terminated this mixed administration in 1085 A.D., by forbidding causes which concerned the government of souls to be brought before secular courts, and directing that instead they should be heard and decided (1) in ecclesiastical courts, or courts Christian; (2) at fixed places; and (3) according to the episcopal laws ([28]).

decision to his son, Valentinian II., telling him that it was not for him to judge between bishops. Eccles. Courts Com. 1883, vol. ii. 257.

(25). Wihtraed's Doom 6, A.D. 696, in H. and S. III. 234 : If a priest allow of illicit intercourse . . . or be drunk . . . let him abstain from his ministry until the doom of the bishop. Leg. Sax. 83. For a civil case, Leg. Sax. 51 ; Alfred and Guthrum's Law 3, A.D. 878 : If a man in orders commit a capital crime, let him be reserved to the bishop's doom.

(26). Leg. Sax. 12, 34, 53, 142.

(27). Athelstan's Law 9, A.D. 925 ; Edgar's Law 7, A.D. 958 ; Ecclesiastical Courts Commission Report, 1883, p. xvii.

(28). Lingard vol. i. ch. viii. p. 247. William following Edward's Law 3, A.D. 1064 ruled : I command by royal authority that no bishop nor archdeacon do hereafter hold plea in the Hundred according to the laws episcopal, nor bring those causes before the secular judicature which concern the government of souls. But whoever is impleaded by the laws episcopal for any causes or crime, let him come to the place which the bishop shall choose and name for this purpose, and there make answer concerning his cause and crime ; and that not according to the Hundred [sc. the common law], but according to the canons and the laws episcopal, and let him do right to God and the bishop. But if any one refuse to come to the bishop's court, let him be summoned three several times ; and if by this means he be not brought to obedience, let application be made to the power and court of the king or sheriff; and he who upon summons refuses to come to the episcopal court shall make satisfaction for every summons according to the laws episcopal. This also I absolutely forbid, that any sheriff, reeve, minister of the king, do any ways concern himself with the laws

9. This change necessitated the appointment of regular officers to preside over the newly created courts at fixed centres, and seems to have been the origin not only of the archdeacons' ordinary jurisdiction, but also of the multiplication of archdeaconries ([29]). At the same time the great development of the episcopal laws, henceforth called Canon law, rendered special knowledge necessary both in the archdeacons' courts and in the bishop's own court, which acted as a court of appeal from their decisions. Hence permanent officials were appointed to preside over both, conversant with the law of evidence and learned in the Canon law, the higher ones being invested with an ordinary jurisdiction ([30]) not only to hear and determine disputed facts, but also to give sentence upon the facts thus ascertained according to the existing law ([31]). The courts thus brought into existence were regarded as synods acting by representation or permanent delegation, and whatever was done in them was indiscriminately spoken of as being done in court or done in synod ([32]).

which belong to the bishop, or bring another man to judgment [by ordeal], anywhere but in the bishop's court. And let judgment be nowhere undergone but in the bishop's see or in that place which he appoints for this purpose." They are called ecclesiastical courts by the Second Statute of Westminster 13 Ed. I. St. IV. c. 1, A.D. 1285; 25 Ed. III. St. III. c. 8; 1 Ric. II. c. 8 and 13; 1 Hen. VII. c. 4; 23 Hen. VIII. c. 9; 27 Hen. VIII. c. 20; 2 and 3 Ed. VI. c. 13–15; 4 Jac. I. c. 5; Lynd. 97.

(29). Ecclesiastical Courts Commission Report, 1883, p. xviii.

(30). Thus according to Oughton, quoted in Eccles. Courts Commis. vol. II. p. 82, a sentence of suspension by the Court of Arches was formerly fixed by the judge, but read by a presbyter deputed by the archbishop.

(31). Sidonius Apollin. Lib. II. Ep. 12, and Synesius Epist. 105, require a bishop to be learned in the laws, that he may decide in accordance with the laws. See *Privileges of Order*, note 197. When bishops were not themselves thus conversant with the canons, a vicar-general, official principal, or chancellor, was required to be associated with them, who took their place *in judicio*. Ecclesiastical Courts Commission 1883, p. 26, states that within half a century from the Conquest the official was an ordinary.

(32). Pseudo-Isidor. ap. Gratian Caus. v. Qu. II. c. 1; Vocatio in Synodum canonica. Concil. Chelsea A.D. 816, Can. 6: If any one be summoned to synod by his plaintiffs. Concil. Tribur. A.D. 895, *Ibid*. Caus. II. Qu. v. c. 1, directs an accused person to clear himself in synod. Concil.

10. Under the Conqueror's successors spiritual courts rose in importance, and far from having been abolished by Henry I., as has been sometimes said (³³), they claimed to exercise in this country the same twofold jurisdiction which, by favour of the Roman emperors, they had been allowed to exercise in the empire, and in addition the same rights over the clergy which they exercised in the Papal States, where the pope had sovereign authority, viz., that the clergy should be tried and punished in them for all crimes as well against the state as against the Church (³⁴). The latter claim was resisted by the Norman kings, but the formal rejection of it contemplated by the Constitutions of Clarendon in 1164 A.D. (³⁵), was for a time frustrated by the murder of Thomas à Becket. Henry III. nevertheless succeeded by means of the Writ of Prohibition where Henry II. had failed, and the boundaries of the two judicatures were gradually determined. Except in so far as these boundaries have been altered by subsequent legislation (³⁶),

---

Lat. IV. A.D. 1215, Can. 6, in Decret. Lib. v. Tit. l. c. 25, directs a metropolitan to hold a provincial council and a bishop an episcopal council [or visitation court] for the correction of excesses.

(33). Lingard vol. ii. c. 3, p. 63, shows that the statement is erroneous.

(34). Bright, No. 5417, in Ecclesiastical Courts Commission, vol. ii. p. 256. The justification of this claim, at least in part, may be found in the fact that there existed in Saxon times many *frithburh* jurisdictions (*i.e.*, jurisdictions for guaranteeing the king's peace) independently of the Hundred. Law 14 of the so-called Laws of Edward, A.D. 1064, declares that the knights and servants of archbishops, bishops, earls, barons, and all who have *sac* [or the hearing of causes], *soc* [jurisdiction], *toll*, *teem*, and *infangthef*, as also their esquires, shall be under the frithburh of their lords, who "if they incur forfeiture, shall oblige them to what is right in their own courts." No doubt this would include clergy living within such jurisdictions. See Cnut's Law 13. Becket claimed to extend it to *all* clergy. It was the aim of Henry II. to break down these extra-Hundredal jurisdictions. Hence, as Stubbs Const. Hist. § 129, vol. i. p. 400, observes: It was no small triumph when Henry II. forced them to admit his itinerant justices to exercise jurisdiction in them. See note 71.

(35). A similar enactment in regard to tithe disputes is contained in the Second Statute of Westminster, 13 Ed. I. St. l. c. 5, sec. 4, A.D. 1285, confirmed by 2 and 3 Ed. VI. c. 13, A.D. 1548.

(36). The Act 53 Geo. III. c. 127 forbids ecclesiastical courts to pass sen-

Spiritual Courts. 185

spiritual courts in the form in which they existed under the feudal hierarchy of the 13th century are still allowed to decide all matters as to which they can claim jurisdiction by custom ([37]). In the Isle of Man, which was under sovereigns of its own, the restraining power was much less, and spiritual courts have in consequence a much more extensive jurisdiction there than here over mixed and temporal matters ([38]).

11. The spiritual courts which exist in this country are accordingly of two kinds, (1) extra-judicial and (2) judicial. An extra-judicial court is a court in which a matter or controversy is dealt with by the Church or by its representative *in medio*, such as a visitation court, a consistory, and a prelate's own court of audience; but to constitute a court of audience two canonical witnesses, or one notary or public person at

tences of excommunication, save when such sentences are pronounced as spiritual censures for offences of ecclesiastical cognisance only, and in that case forbids excommunication from being followed by any civil penalty or incapacity beyond a liability to imprisonment for a term not exceeding six months, this imprisonment to be enforced only through the civil authority by means of a writ called *Significavit*. Statute 20 and 21 Vict. c. 85, passed in 1857, withdrew Divorce and Matrimonial causes from the cognisance of spiritual courts; and the statute 20 and 21 Vict. c. 77, amended by 21 and 22 Vict. c. 95, abolished all the powers hitherto exercised by them in the granting Probates of Wills and Letters of Administration. The statute 6 and 7 Will. IV. c. 71 took away from spiritual courts jurisdiction in tithe cases, and gave to tithe-owners a summary remedy by distraint, for which 54 Vict. c. 8, A.D. 1891, has substituted a County Court action.

(37). Their jurisdiction is preserved by sec. 7 of 26 Hen. VIII. c. 3. Coke 4 Inst. p. 321, quotes 25 Hen. VIII. c. 21 as allowing that "the spirituality is also at this hour sufficient and meet of itself without the intermeddling of any *exterior* person or persons to declare and determine of such doubts and to administer all such offices and duties as to their rooms spiritual doth appertain." 13 Car. II. c. 12, sec. 1, A.D. 1661, allows them jurisdiction in all matters allowed to them by custom.

(38). See Stephens' Eccles. Stat. II. 1830. In Eccles. Courts Commission 1883, vol. II. p. 322 an account is given of the subject matter of jurisdiction administered by (1) the Chapter-Court (= Visitation Court or Synod), (2) the Vicar-General's Court, a Court of Summary Jurisdiction (= the Bishop's Audience, and (3) the Consistory, the principal ecclesiastical court, in which written pleadings alone are used.

least, must be present besides the prelate and the parties concerned (39). Every executive act which is of a solemn nature, and requires the ordinary's office as the representative of the synod, must be done in a court of this kind, such as the granting institution to a benefice (40), accepting a resignation (41), a metropolitan's confirmation of a bishop, the constituting of a new parish. Disciplinary causes, when either the facts are notorious (42) or are voluntarily admitted, come properly before, and are terminated in, such a court.

(39). Gregory ap. Gratian Caus. xv. Qu. vii. c. 2, calls them elders; also 1 Dist. xxii. c. 1; xxi. c. 1, § 12; Dist. lxiv. c. 6; Caus. xii. Qu. 1. c. 1; Elfric's Can. 15, A.D. 957; Concil. Winton. A.D. 1071, Can. 1; Const. 48 Langton, A.D. 1222. Lynd. 79 call them testes synodales. Their presence is required by Concil. Lat. iv. A.D. 1215, in Decret. Lib. ii. Tit. xix. c. 11, repeated by Const. 29 Otho, A.D. 1237. Also Can. 123 of 1603 A.D.

(40). Alexander iii. to the English bishops in Decret. Lib. iii. Tit. xxxviii. c. 21, states that some presume to take possession of ecclesiastical benefices without the intervention of the bishop's audience-court. Co. 2 Inst. 651 states that in admitting to a benefice the ordinary acts as a judge and not as a minister. Lynd. 111. Conf. sec. 7 of 26 Hen. viii. c. 3. Lynd. 219 : Institutio præsentati fit cum causæ cognitione.

(41). In Fytche's Case 1783, in Cuningham's Law of Simony, p. 79, the judges declined to say whether the acceptance of a resignation is a judicial act, i.e., in the sense in which judicial is understood by secular courts. In Hesketh v. Gray, Ibid. p. 25, Ryder, C.J., declared that "the ordinary is a judicial officer, and is entrusted with a judicial power to accept or refuse resignation as he thinks proper." Judicial is used in these cases in the sense of discretionary, such discretion being usually exercised extra-judicially, when there is no dispute as to the fact of the resignation being made and the clerk wishing to resign. Lynd. 107 calls acceptance judicis officium. There are many cases of appeals from his discretion in Decret. Lib. l. Tit. ix. and Tit. xl. See also Lord Denman in the Dean of York's case, 1 Ad. and El. N. S. p. 11. Law's Forms 78.

(42). Augustin in Decret Lib. v. Tit. l. c. 10 : An evil deed done in the sight of all requires not the clamour of an accuser. Lucius iii. Ibid. Lib. iii. Tit. ii. c. 7 : Notorious is that for which a presbyter may be condemned. Innocent iii. to Bishop of Exeter, Ibid. c. 8 : If their crime is so public that it has become notorious, in that case neither a witness nor an accuser is necessary, . . . but if the publicity is only by report, and not done in the sight of all, reports are not sufficient to condemn. According to Sext. Lib. ii. Tit. xii. c. 2, a conviction in a court of law consti-

Spiritual Courts.

12. A judicial court consists either of a synodal committee (⁴³) or of a single judge learned in the law (⁴⁴), who acts as the judicial adviser of the synod or its president (⁴⁵); and it is the duty of such a court to inquire judicially into the facts, to indicate the sentence due upon them according to the canons, and if authorised by law or by custom so to do, to pronounce it. Such a judge may represent the bishop's consistory, when he is called the bishop's official or chancellor of the diocese; or the archdeacon's rural consistory, when he is called the archdeacon's official or dean (⁴⁶); or the consistory of the province or archbishop, when he is called the provincial dean or the metropolitan's official principal (⁴⁷).

13. The official of a judicial court may entertain a suit judicially without the presiding prelate being present, except it be a charge of heresy (⁴⁸), because on all questions of procedure

tutes notoriety, and may now be acted upon in this country by 55 and 56 Vict. c. 32. Lynd 323 defines notorious as proof publicly concluded established judicially, or else based on a fact judicially discussed.

(43). Gregory IX. in Decret Lib. II. Tit. v. c. 1, mentions them in the plural as *judices*. See note 168.

(44). 1 Cor. VI. 5 reproaches the Corinthians οὐκ ἔστιν ἐν ὑμῖν σοφός, οὐδὲ εἷς ὃς δυνήσεται διακρῖναι ἀνὰ μέσον τοῦ ἀδελφοῦ αὐτοῦ ; Const. 2 Chichele, A.D. 1415, requires the judge to be a clerk. Lynd, 129. Yet 37 Hen. VIII. c. 17 permits him to be a layman, provided he is a doctor of law.

(45). See *The Diocese*. Conf. Const. 7 Stratford, A.D. 1342. Lynd. 80.

(46). Concil. Westminster, A.D. 1200, Can. 5 : Let archdeacons and their deans presume not to exact anything of their presbyters or clerks. Rural deans were in some places the archdeacon's officials. Syn. Lugdun. A.D. 1245, in Sext. Lib. v. Tit. XI. c. 5, mentions the archdeacon's official.

(47). See *The Province*.

(48). It may be doubted whether a single bishop ever possessed the right of adjudicating upon heresy before the Fourth Lateran Council, A.D. 1215, in Decret. Lib. v. Tit. VII. c. 13, committed to the bishop cognisance of heresy. See note 15. Boniface VIII. in Sext. Lib. v. Tit. II. c. 18, authorised the civil power to punish heretics condemned by the bishop regardless of their appealing (*appellatione postposita*). Lynd. 296, quoted in Eccles. Courts Commission, Vol. II. 263, Qu. 7415 : The cognisance of heresy is by law allowed to two judges only, viz., to the bishop of the place and to an inquisitor of heresy sent from the Apostolic See, as appears from Sext. Lib. v. Tit. II. c. 11, 17, 18, in which mention is made only of

and canon law, but not of theology, he represents the knowledge of the synod or consistory; but a prelate cannot hold an inquiry into disputed facts or execute his own extra-judicial rulings by process without his official ([49]), because, at least since the twelfth century, judicial procedure and execution are held to be matters requiring this official's special knowledge. The consistory or auditory of a synod, of its president, and of the judge who represents him and it, are in all cases deemed to be one and the same ([50]); and since each presides over a tribunal which is supplementary to the tribunals of the others, there can be no appeal from one to the other.

14. The judicial tribunals which in popular esteem monopolise the title of courts are thus seen to be only the handmaids to the extra-judicial tribunals or consistories which date from the earliest days of the Church; and since each represents a

---

diocesans and inquisitors sent from the Apostolic See. So it is also said, *Ibid.* c. 20; Clem. Lib. v. Tit. III. c. 1, where it is clear that such jurisdiction or cognisance belongs to the chapter during the vacancy of the see. For no text can be found which gives this cognisance to one inferior to a bishop or to his official or vicar-general; for the case of heresy is one of the most important cases which belongs to bishops only. The Statute 2 Hen. IV. c. 15, A.D. 1400, *de Haeretico comburendo*, and 2 Hen. v. c. 7, also gave authority to bishops and their commissaries. Yet Const. 16 Chichele, A.D. 1416, reserved to the archbishop in Convocation to pronounce what was heresy. In 1701 Convocation condemned Whiston's Book, and eight judges against four ruled that Convocation had jurisdiction in such cases (Phill. 1934), but according to Phill. 1960 the contrary opinion is now generally held. See Eccles. Courts Com. 1883, Vol. II. 49.

(49). Ayliffe 161: Or as it is often said, "without his court," *i.e.*, the official of his judicial court. Ecclesiastical Courts Commission, 1883, p. XXXVIII. reports that: "It has been affirmed in courts of law that a commission of chancellor or vicar-general cannot be regarded as excluding the archbishop or bishop from sitting in his own court," but they can only say "instances may be quoted in which the power has been exercised *since the Reformation*." And apparently the Statute 3 and 4 Vict. c. 86, first introduced the practice of a bishop sitting as judge to investigate the facts. See Dr. Dean's opinion, *Ibid.* Vol. II. p. 312 and 356, Qu. 7198. If the bishop were to sit, how could he award himself costs? See note 169: The bishop is an extra-judicial judge, his official a judicial judge.

(50). Lynd. 80.

particular department in the exercise of discipline, controversies which are introduced extra-judicially in audience or in synod must be appealed against in audience or in synod; and those introduced in judgment must be appealed against in judgment. Still in whatever way a controversy may be begun, when it reaches the highest tribunal of all, judicial acts are at an end, and it must be dealt with in synod or in audience ([51]).

Jurisdiction of Spiritual Courts in this Country.

15. When courts Christian were first established in this country, no very clear line was for some time drawn between matters of spiritual and matters of lay cognisance. The government of souls is a wide subject, and might be and was construed as placing the determination of all *matters* concerning spiritual persons and of all disputes touching ecclesiastical property in the hands of the Church courts ([52]). Henry II., by the assize of *Darrein presentment*, reclaimed for the secular power the determination of right of advowson, and by the Constitutions of Clarendon, in 1164 A.D., attempted still further to delimit the boundaries of the spiritual and temporal authorities ([53]). Fifty years later the Great Charter secured to the

---

([51]). Law's Forms 60, note.

([52]). Ecclesiastical Courts Commission Report, 1883, p. xxii.

([53]). These Constitutions provide: (1) If controversy arise concerning the patronage of Churches, . . . let it be tried and determined in the king's court. (2) Churches belonging to the fee of our lord the king cannot be appropriated without his grant. (3) Clergy accused of any matter upon summons from the king's judge shall come and make answer there as well as to the ecclesiastical court, and shall be dealt with according to the verdict in the ecclesiastical court. (4) It is not lawful for archbishops, bishops, and parsons of the kingdom to depart the kingdom without the king's license. (5) Excommunicates ought not to give security for all time, or to make oath before they are absolved, but only to give security and pledge for standing to the judgment of the Church. (6) Laymen ought not to be accused before the bishop or archdeacon but by trustworthy lawful men, and in default of an accuser the sheriff may empanel a jury at the bishop's request to try the issue of fact. (7) That none who hold of the king *in capite*, nor the officers upon his demesnes, be excommunicate . . . till application has been made to our lord the king

Church all its rights and liberties (⁵⁴), the nature of which can be best gathered from the sentences of curse pronounced at the

... or his justice. (8) If appeals arise, they ought to proceed from the archdeacon to the bishop, from the bishop to the archbishop, and lastly to the king, ... so that it go no further without the king's consent. (9) ... It shall be determined by the award of 12 lawful men before the king's justice whether the estate be in free alms or in lay fee. If the finding be that it is in free-alms, the plea shall be in the ecclesiastical court; but if in lay fee, then, unless both claim their tenure under the same bishop or baron, the plea shall be in the king's court. (10) If one that is cited for any crime for which he ought to make answer to the archdeacon or bishop will not make satisfaction upon three summonses, they may lawfully put him under interdict, but not excommunicate him till application hath been made to the king's chief officer of the vill. (11) Archbishops and bishops and all the parsons of the kingdom who hold of the king *in capite* are to look on their estates as baronies. ... (12) When an archbishopric, bishopric, abbacy, or priory is vacant, it ought to be in the king's hands, and the vacancy filled up by the election of the chief parsons upon viewing the king's mandate. (13) If any great men of the kingdom do violently oppose the archbishop, bishop, or archdeacon in doing justice to himself in things that properly belong to him, the king ought to vindicate him. ... (14) The chattels of those guilty of capital crimes are not to be kept in the Church and churchyard against the king's justices. ... (15) Pleas of debt are in the king's cognisance, whether upon solemn promise or not. ... (16) The sons of villagers ought not to be ordained without the consent of the lord on whose land they are admitted to have been born. Stubbs in Ecclesiastical Courts Commission, A.D. 1883, p. xxx.: The absolution of Henry II. from the guilt of Becket's murder was granted on the condition of his renouncing the evil customs embodied in the Constitutions of Clarendon; and Henry II. solemnly revoked them in 1173. *Ibid.* Vol. II. 113.

(54). Magna Carta, A.D. 1215: That the English Church shall be free, and enjoy all her rights in their integrity and her liberties untouched. ... No clerk shall be amerced for his lay-tenement except after the manner of the other persons aforesaid, and not according to the value of his ecclesiastical benefice. ... All barons, founders of abbeys by charters of English kings and ancient tenure, shall have the custody of the same during vacancy. ... Wherefore we will and firmly charge that the English Church be free, and that all men in our kingdom have and hold all the aforesaid rights, liberties, and concessions. 14 Ed. III. St. 1. c. 1, A.D. 1340: That holy Church have her liberties in quietness, without interruption or disturbance. 50 Ed. III. c. 1, A.D. 1376, after the feudal sovereignty of the pope had been thrown off in 1366, repeats this; also 1 Ric. II. c. 1, A.D. 1377; 1 Hen. IV. c.

Spiritual Courts. 191

Synod of Oxford, in 1222 A.D., on those who violated them ([55]). These sentences received legal effect from an ordinance of Henry III., made in the year 1253 A.D. ([56]), and were promulgated repeatedly in later times by royal authority up to the time of Archbishop Chichele in 1434 A.D., as sentences already passed ([57]).

1, A.D. 1399; 4 Hen. IV. c. 3, A.D. 1402; 3 Hen. V. St. II. c. 1, A.D. 1415; 2 Hen. VI. c. 1, A.D. 1423.

(55). Const. 1 Langton, A.D. 1222: We excommunicate [1] those who maliciously deprive Churches of their rights and disturb their liberties . . . and all that violate sequestrations of vacant Churches; . . . [10] all that violate sanctuaries; [9] all that seize on the goods of clergy, . . . unjustly, or any ways molest their persons; [2] all thieves, robbers, freebooters, incendiaries, sacrilegious and felonious persons. . . . [3] We excommunicate those who knowingly bear false witness, as also [4] advocates who maliciously lay objection to the consummation of marriages. [5] We excommunicate all who, for lucre, favour, ill-will, or any other cause, maliciously charge with crimes such men as have preserved their reputation; [6] and all those who upon the vacancy of a Church maliciously oppose the inquest concerning the right of patronage, [7] or refuse to execute the king's mandate against excommunicates. . . . Let this general excommunication be published by every parochial incumbent in his holy vestments, with bells tolling and candles lighted, before the whole congregation, in the mother-tongue, on Christmas, Easter, Pentecost, and All Hallows' Day.

(56). 38 Hen. III. A.D. 1253; Const. 1 Boniface, A.D. 1261, in Lynd. 315. According to Stubbs, in Ecclesiastical Courts Commission p. 31, Henry III., in 1246 and 1247, issued ordinances confining the ecclesiastical courts in matters of civil interest to the jurisdiction long established in their hands in testamentary and matrimonial causes. 14 Ed. III. St. I. c. 1, A.D. 1340: Qe seinte eglise eit ses franchises en quiete saunz empechement ou distourbance. 50 Ed. III. c. 1, A.D. 1376; 1 Ric. II. c. 1, A.D. 1377; 1 Hen. IV. c. 1, A.D. 1399; 2 Hen. VI. c. 1, A.D. 1423, are statutes confirming the liberties of the Church.

(57). Const. 36 Edmund, A.D. 1236; Const. 1 and 9 Boniface, A.D. 1261; Const. 3 Peckham, A.D. 1279, excommunicate [1] all who maliciously deprive Churches of their right, . . . who obtain letters from any lay-court to ecclesiastics in such cases as by the sacred canons belong to the ecclesiastical court; [2] all robbers, [3] bearers of false witness, [4] obstructors of marriage, [5] defamers of good men, [6] opposers of inquests of patronage; [7] all who refuse to execute the king's mandate as to excommunicates; [8] all who hinder settlement of disputes; [9] all who invade ecclesiastical property; [10] those who violate sanctuaries; and [11] who transgress the

16. As thus defined, the ancient jurisdiction of courts Christian in this country was always held not to include (1) cases involving life or limb, and (2) cases involving the right to a lay fee or to money. The law of the Church forbad ecclesiastics to meddle with pleas of blood([58]); and the law of the land excepted from their cognisance cases of freehold([59]), including right of advowson ([60]), debt, treason, and covenant ([61]). If doubt arose whether a case came within the jurisdiction of the spiritual court, the right of expounding William's mandate and the liberties conferred by the Great Charter was always

Great Charter. Peckham was obliged to withdraw the 1st, 7th, and 9th, and to order the removal of the Great Charter from the Church doors; but when Edward I. withdrew his opposition, the above sentences were revived in Const. 1 Peckham, A.D. 1281, and ordered to be published in every Church on the four Sundays next after the principal chapters—viz., Sunday after Michaelmas, Mid-Lent Sunday, Trinity Sunday, and Sunday after Christmas. They were republished by Archbishop Winchelsea, A.D. 1298; by Mepham, A.D. 1328; by Stratford, A.D. 1343; and by Chichele, A.D. 1434. Lynd. 352 says that the rights of the Church consist, among other things, in the free exercise of ecclesiastical jurisdiction.

(58). Const. 11 Clarendon, A.D. 1164: [Ecclesiastics may judge] till they come to deprivation of life or member. Concil. London A.D. 1175, Can. 3: Let not a man in holy orders be concerned in judgments concerning blood, nor by himself nor by other inflict deprivation of member. Alexander III. to Archbishop of Canterbury in Decret. Lib. III. Tit. I. c. 5; Concil. Lat IV. A.D. 1215, Can. 18, *Ibid.* c. 9; Const. 9 Langton, A.D. 1222; Const. 7 Othobon, A.D. 1268. See *Order*, notes 277, 278. On this ground the lords spiritual withdrew from Parliament before the statute 11 Ric. II. c. 1 was passed in 1387 A.D., attainting the Archbishop of York.

(59). This applies to a freehold held under a spiritual person, but not to a benefice held in free-alms, by Const. 9 Clarendon, A.D. 1164, and 13 Ed. I. St. I. c. 5, sec. 4, A.D. 1285; and tenure in free-alms is still retained by 12 Car. II. c. 24.

(60). Const. 1 Clarendon, A.D. 1164; Glanvil. XIII. c. 20. Alexander III. in Decret. Lib. II. Tit. 1. c. 3, claimed the cognisance of right of advowson for the Church, but it was not allowed here. Pleas of the Crown, A.D. 1250, in Haddan & Stubbs' Ecclesiastical Documents I. 477; Const. 2, 11, and 16 Boniface, A.D. 1261; Lynd. 217, 281, 316, 352; Devoti Lib. III. Tit. 4, § 5 states that such a withdrawal is lawful either by apostolic privilege or long custom.

(61). 2 Hen. V. St. I. c. 3, A.D. 1414.

held to belong to the secular judge ([62]); and since courts Christian could only proceed in cases concerning the government of souls, (3) they were not allowed to hold plea if either the person to be made defendant had quitted this life ([63]), or if he were himself unbaptized, or a Jew ([64]). Moreover, since it is a rule of justice that no one can be twice punished for the same offence ([65]), (4) whenever pains and penalties had been awarded by a secular judge, a spiritual court was no longer allowed to impose penalties, though it could still impose penances for the soul's health ([66]).

17. Here, as in the Roman Empire ([67]), the Church's juris-

([62]). Const. 9 Clarendon and 13 Ed. I. St. I. c. 5, sec. 4, A.D. 1285; see also 13 Ed. I. c. 24, and 14 Ed. III. c. 17; Lynd. 97.

([63]). Gratian Caus. XXIV. Qu. II. Decret. Lib. v. Tit. XXXIX. The statute 15 Ed. III. c. 5, A.D. 1341, gives to the king and his heirs "the conusance of usures dead, and that the ordinaries of Holy Church have the conusance of usures on life." Co. Lit. 2 Inst. 632 and 344; Brooke Quare Impedit. Pl. 102; Cunningham's Law of Simony, 50; Hobart, p. 165.

([64]). Concil. Tolet. IV. A.D. 633, Can. 56 ap. Gratian I. Dist. XLV. c. 5. This is spoken of as a grievance in Const. 7 Boniface, A.D. 1261, who orders the boycotting of Jews to induce them to answer in the spiritual court. Ayliffe 155: As a heathen or infidel is not a subject of the Church, he cannot be subject to censures inflicted by the Church as a baptized person, who is a member of the Church.

([65]). Cap. Reg. Franc. in Decret. Lib. v. Tit. 1. c. 6: Crimes in respect of which the accused has once been absolved cannot be made the subject-matter of a second accusation. Egbert's Poenitent. v. 1, A.D. 766, in H. & S. III. 421: Let him be deposed, but not deprived of communion; for God does not take double judgment on him.

([66]). 9 Ed. II. St. I. c. 6, A.D. 1315. Boniface VIII. in Sext. Lib. II. Tit. XII. c. 2, in accepting the decisions of temporal courts as matters judicially settled so far as penalties are concerned, excepts them so far as the soul is in peril.

([67]). Constantine's Constitution in Extrav. de Epis. Jud. Cod. Theodos. VI. 339, decreed: That all causes which are disposed of by praetorian or civil law, when disposed of by sentence of bishops, shall be confirmed by the perpetual right of stability; nor may a matter be further reopened which the bishop's sentence has decided. See Eusebii Vita Const. IV. 27, and Sozomen I. 9, quoted above, note 23; Lex Marciani in Leg. 14 Cod. de Episc. Audient. Lex Theodosii in Leg. 47 Cod. Theodosii de Episc.

diction was allowed to include (1) purely spiritual matters, (2) mixed matters, and (3) certain temporal matters ([68]). Over the clergy the Church claimed exclusive jurisdiction, not only in civil matters, but also in crimes against fellow-men ([69]); over laymen in all matters affecting their salvation ([70]), including (1)

(68). Theodori Poenit. II. II. 4 in H. and S. III. 191 : The bishop settles the causes of the poor up to 50s., the king when it is more.

(69). Niceph. Hist. VII. 46 ; Concil. Carthag. III. A.D. 397, Can. 9. It is nevertheless a moot point whether the bishop's criminal jurisdiction over the clergy was confined to lesser crimes, or extended to what the civil law regarded as capital crimes. Many edicts reserve the correction of the clergy to the bishop without any reservation; for instance, Cod. Theodos. de Episc. et Cler. Leg. 41, 42; Cod. Justin. de Episc. et Cler. Leg. 1. Justinian's Novels LXXXIII. 1, however, distinguish between *ecclesiastical* and *civil* transgressions, and acknowledge that the emperor has nothing to do with ecclesiastical transgressions. Still, before the civil judge could punish a civil transgression, the offending clerk had to be degraded by his ecclesiastical superior. If the latter refused to degrade him, the whole matter had to be referred to the emperor. Novell. CXXIII. 21. Hence the rule prevalent in the West, that, whatever the nature of the offence, a clerk is in the first instance only amenable to an ecclesiastical tribunal. Concil. Paris v. Can. 4; Concil. Matiscon. II. A.D. 585, Can. 10; Cap. Reg. Franc. I. 38; V. 378, 390; VII. 347, 422, 436. Law 4 Alfred and Guthrum, A.D. 878 : If a clerk commit a capital crime he is in the bishop's judgment. This principle was contended for by Becket, and it cost him his life. In 1176 A.D. Henry II. agreed that no clerk should henceforth be imprisoned or brought before a secular tribunal for any criminality or trespass, except trespass of the forest and questions of lay fees for which lay service was due. By the same act the murderers of clerks were to incur forfeiture of their inheritance over and above the customary penalties, and the clergy were not to be compelled to ordeal of battle. Eccles. Courts Commis. Rep. p. XXIV. 25 Ed. III. St. III. c. 4, A.D. 1350, enacted that clerks convicted of felony or treason should be delivered to their ordinaries.

(70). Concil. Arelat. A.D. 314, Can. 7 : As touching the faithful who are advanced to judgeships, let them when promoted receive letters of communion ; yet so that in whatever place their office takes them, they shall be under the care of the bishop of that place, and shall be excluded from communion so soon as they begin to act contrary to discipline. The same with those who hold offices of state. Basil Ep. VI. relates that St. Athanasius excommunicated a governor of Libya on account of cruelty and excesses. Synesius, Bishop of Ptolemais, Epist. 58, relates how, because of his cruelty and excesses, he had excommunicated the prefect, Andron-

the correction of immorality, which the law of the state did not touch, and (2) the correction of breaches of faith and offences against character, for which there were remedies provided by the common law, such as breach of contract, perjury, slander, and the like. The claim of exclusive jurisdiction over clergy was so far allowed as to exempt them from the death penalty if found guilty by a temporal court [71], and was generally known as "*benefit of clergy.*" But the claim of jurisdiction over laymen, even in spiritual matters, was constantly resisted. Nevertheless, it was practically maintained until the Reformation, and in some points even to modern times [72].

18. Spiritual causes, which properly belong to the province of courts Christian, are usually said to be of five kinds, viz. (1) those which concern faith and morals [73], such as simony [74],

ieus. Socrates VII. 13 : Orestes [the governor] long regarded with jealousy the power of the bishops, because they claimed to have a far greater rule than those appointed by the king, most of all because [Bishop] Cyril wished to overlook his proceedings. In Augustin Ep. 152, Macedonius, Governor of Africa, writes : You say it is the bishop's office to intercede for the guilty, . . . but I very much doubt whether this claim of yours comes from religion. For if sins are so forbidden by God that there is no room for repentance except once, how can you contend that, as a matter of religion, we [the civil authorities] ought to overlook every crime, whatever it may be ? For, by leaving it unpunished, we should be approving it. See Ecclesiastical Courts Commission Report, p. XXII.

(71). 7 and 8 Georg. IV. c. 28, A.D. 1827 : Be it enacted that benefit of clergy, with respect to persons convicted of felony, shall be abolished.

(72). Eccles. Courts. Commis. Report, p. XXII.

(73). 13 Ed. I. St. IV. c. 1, A.D. 1285 (Circumspecte agatis), in Lynd. 96, directs the king's justices not to grant prohibition "for penance enjoined by prelates for deadly sin, as fornication, adultery, and such like, for the which sometimes corporal penance and sometimes pecuniary is enjoined, if a freeman be convict of such things." 9 Ed. II. St. I. c. 2, A.D. 1315 : If a prelate enjoin a penance pecuniary to a man for his offence, and it be demanded [in a spiritual court], the king's prohibition shall hold place. But if prelates enjoin a penance corporal, and they which be so punished shall redeem upon their own accord such penances by money, if money be demanded before a judge spiritual, the king's prohibition shall hold no place.

(74). In *Mackaller* v. *Todderick*, Cro. Car. 36, simony was stated to be an offence at common law [which is true (see Hobart) if the guilty person is

usury ([75]), heresy ([76]), and the public teaching of religion ([77]); (2) those which concern the sacraments, including wedlock and bigamy ([78]), but not wedlock as a civil contract ([79]); (3) those dead], but this was denied in Moor 564. The statute 31 Eliz. c. 6, which attached temporal penalties to certain forms of simony, was careful to preserve, and therefore to recognise, the spiritual jurisdiction in sec. 9.

(75). 15 Ed. III. c. 5, A.D. 1341 : And that the ordinaries of Holy Church have the conusance of usures on life, as to them appertaineth to make compulsion by the censures of Holy Church for the sin, to make restitution of the usures taken against the laws of Holy Church. 3 Hen. VII. c. 5, A.D. 1486 ; 11 Hen. VII. c. 8, A.D. 1494, to the like effect. By 13 Eliz. c. 8, the only usury with which a spiritual court can deal is letting money out to use on condition of receiving more than 10 per cent. for it. Law's Forms 44.

(76). Heresy is named in 2 Hen. v. St. I. c. 7 ; 26 Hen. VIII. c. 1 ; 1 Eliz. c. 1, sec. 17.

(77). Concil. Westminster A.D. 1138, Can. 17 : If schoolmasters hire out their schools to be governed by others, that they be liable to ecclesiastical punishment. Const. 4 Arundel, A.D. 1408, directs schoolmasters not to teach contrary to the rulings of the Church. See 34 and 35 Hen. VIII. c. 1; 2 Jac. I. c. 4, sec. 9 ; Cox's case in Stephens' Eccl. Stat. 509. *Rutter* v. *Wainwright*, No. 82, in Rothery's Ecclesiastical Appeals, 1868.

(78). 18 Ed. III. St. III. c. 2, allows spiritual courts to deal with bigamy.

(79). Benedict XIV. de Syn. Dioc. Lib. IX. c. 9, § 2, says there are three kinds of matrimonial causes : (1) those which concern the sacramental validity of wedlock—these are purely spiritual ; (2) those which concern wedlock as a civil contract, and separation from bed and board, or the interruption of the civil contract—these are mixed causes ; and (3) those which concern the temporal results of wedlock, such as the legitimacy or bastardy of offspring, and rights of succession to property—these are temporal causes. See *Wedlock*, § 2. Of the first kind was the question as to the sacramental validity of Lothair's marriage with Thietberga. This was first heard in a national council at Aachen, A.D. 860 (Labbé X. 140 and 200). On appeal to Nicolaus I., he ruled that the matter did not concern the lay judge, and referred it to the Council of Metz (Labbé X. 1413). Const. 20 Langton, A.D. 1222, forbids rural deans to meddle with the hearing of such cases. Mixed cases concerning marriage were, like other contracts, also cognisable in the spiritual courts for purposes of discipline. Alexander III. in Decret. Lib. IV. Tit. 1. c. 10, and Tit. XIX. c. 3 ; but from Reynold's Constitution, A.D. 1313, the matter seems to have been considered doubtful. 18 Ed. III. St. III. c. 2 recognised them as being of spiritual cognisance, and also 24 Hen. VIII. c. 12, quoted below, note 83, and so they continued until 1857.

which concern public worship, and the duties of the clergy in relation thereto ([80]); (4) those which concern the discipline of regulars and the religious life ([81]); and (5) those which concern ecclesiastical censures.

19. Mixed causes which were in this country generally allowed to be of spiritual cognisance include ([82]): (1) those relating to spiritual benefices, tithes, and customary offerings ([83]), such as suits for pensions charged on benefices ([84]), for neglect of Church repairs ([85]), dilapida-

---

([80]). In this country, spiritual courts are, in respect of worship, called upon to carry out the Statute of Uniformity, 2 and 3 Ed. VI. A.D. 1549; 5 and 6 Ed. VI.; 13 and 14 Car. II. c. 4, A.D. 1662, and the relaxing statutes; but violations of the Act of Uniformity may also form the subject-matter of indictment in the temporal courts. See Eccles. Courts Com. Report.

([81]). Gregory ap. Gratian Caus. XIX. Qu. III. c. 7. Const. 45 Langton, A.D. 1222: Religious persons have no temporal right. They were in law considered to be dead persons before civil rights were restored to them by 31 Hen. VIII. c. 6; 33 Hen. VIII. c. 29, and 5 and 6 Ed. VI. c. 13. See *Discipline of the Religious Life*, notes 72 and 194.

([82]). Report of Commissioners to inquire into the jurisdiction of ecclesiastical courts, A.D. 1832, pp. 12, 13; Rothery's Ecclesiastical Appeals, IV.

([83]). 9 Ed. II. St. I. c. 1, A.D. 1315: In oblations and obventions the king's prohibition shall hold no place. 2 Hen. V. St. I. c. 3; 24 Hen. VIII. c. 12, sec. 2, recites that all causes testamentary, causes of matrimony and divorce, rights of tithes, oblations, and obventions, the knowledge whereof, by the goodness of princes of this realm, and by the laws and customs of the same, appertain to the spiritual jurisdiction.

([84]). 13 Ed. I. St. IV. c. 1, A.D. 1285 (Circumspecte agatis) forbids prohibition: If a prelate of a Church demand of a parson a pension due to him [such as a cathedraticium or synodaticum]. In *Johnson* v. *Ryson*, 12 Mod. 416, the court, referring to the case of *Hinde* v. *Bishop of Chester*, Cro. Car. 237, observed: Though a writ of annuity may lie for a pension by prescription, and is so recoverable at common law, yet it may be sued for in the spiritual court. Stephen's Eccl. Stat. 128; Ayliffe, 433.

([85]). 13 Ed. I. St. IV. c. 1, A.D. 1285: Also if prelates do punish for leaving the churchyard unenclosed, or for that the Church is uncovered or not conveniently decked, in which cases none other penance can be enjoined but pecuniary. Const. 6 Stratford, A.D. 1342. Cf. Lit. 2 Inst. 489; 3 Blackstone Com. 92. The statute 53 Geo. III. c. 127, sec. 7, gave to magistrates

tions ([86]), spoliation ([87]), the recovery of tithes ([88]), and mor-
the adjudication of Church rate suits when the amount claimed was under
£10. The compulsory Church-rates abolition act, 31 & 32 Vict. c. 109,
A.D. 1868, forbids all suits to compel payment of Church rates.

(86). There were anciently of ecclesiastical cognisance. Stephens' Eccl.
Stat. p. 425. 52 Hen. III. c. 28, A.D. 1267, however, allows the successors of
prelates to have "actions to demand the goods of their Churches out of the
hands of trespassers," and 13 Ed. I. St. I. c. 24, A.D. 1283, confirmed by 14
Ed. III. St. I. c. 17, gives to the successor of a parson right to writs called
Juris utrum and *Quod permittat* to recover alienations made by a predecessor.
Yet 35 Ed. I. St. II. A.D. 1307, and 13 Eliz. c. 10, A.D. 1570, recognise them
as of spiritual cognisance. By the Dilapidations Act, 34 and 35 Vict. c. 43,
and 35 & 36 Vict. c. 96, A.D. 1871, they are recoverable at law only.

(87). Spoliation is not the subtraction of rent or tithes by the tenant of
a spiritual person, but the getting hold of the spiritual income of an
ecclesiastical benefice by one who has no right thereto, as in a case of controversy for the incumbency between two clerks both presented by the same
patron, provided it does not raise the question of advowson. By Edward's
Law 5, A.D. 1064; Concil. Westminster A.D. 1125, Can. 9; Concil. London
A.D. 1126, Can. 9; Concil. London A.D. 1175, Can. 13, such a right was
triable in the spiritual court, but the suit had first to be commenced in the
kings court by Const. 9 Clarendon, A.D. 1164, and sec. 4 of 13 Ed. I. St. I. c.
5, to determine that neither the right of advowson nor the extent of the
parish was in issue. By 9 Ed. II. St. I. c. 9, A.D. 1315, the sheriff was
not allowed to execute distresses "in the ancient fees of the Church," i.e.,
in the lands and benefices held by the Church before the twentieth year of
Edward I., in which year the valuation by Pope Nicolas was made. 18 Ed.
II. St. III. c. 7, A.D. 1344, enacted that writs of *Scire facias* should not issue
"to warn prelates, religious, and other clerks to answer dismes in our
chancery, and to show if they have anything or can anything say wherefore
such dismes ought not to be restored to the said demandants, and answer as
well to us as to the party of such dismes," but "that the process hanging
upon such writs be annulled and repealed, and that the parties be dismissed
from the secular judges of such matters." 25 Ed. III. c. 8, A.D. 1350, enacts
that cognisance of voidance rests with the spiritual judge. See Bracton
vol. vi. 217 (ed. 1878), and the action of Giraldus, elected Bishop of St.
David's A.D. 1199, in Haddan and Stubbs I. 428, and Hook's Lives II. 628.
After the dissolution of monasteries, 32 Hen. VIII. c. 7 sec. 7 was passed,
enabling lay-holders to maintain rights to spiritual tithes and benefices
in secular courts. 12 Car. II. c. 17, sec. 28, authorises the sheriff to give
possession of the benefice of one deprived by that act, showing that he had
ordinarily no such jurisdiction. See *Titchborne* v. *Swale*, No. 25; *Aisgill* v.
Bargrave, No. 30; *Viscount Loftus* v. *Archbishop of Dublin*, No. 44 in
Rothery's Report (1868); *Hill* v. *Barne*, 2 Lev. 250.

Spiritual Courts. 199

tuaries (⁸⁹); (2) causes of contract, constructive contract, tres-

(88). 13 Ed. I. St. IV. c. 1, A.D. 1285 : If a parson demand tithes greater or smaller, so that the fourth part of the value of the benefice be not demanded. Suits for tithes were brought in the spiritual court except in two cases : (1) if the tithes demanded amounted to one-fourth part of the value of the benefice ; and (2) if the demand of tithes involved parish boundaries. The reason for the first exception was that a fourth part of the value or more was usually reserved on a grant of real estate (see 6 Ed. I. c. 4, A.D. 1278, and 13 Ed. I. St. I. c. 41, sec. 3), so that when a demand was made for the fourth part, the presumption was that the claim was for a composition real, and that the revenues of the benefice had been let to farm. 9 Ed. II. St. I. c. 1, A.D. 1315 ; In tithes, &c. . . the king's prohibition shall hold no place, although for the long withholding of the same the money may be esteemed at a sum certain. But if a clerk or a religious man do sell his tithes, being gathered in his barn or otherwise, to any man for money, if the money be demanded before a spiritual judge the king's prohibition shall lie, for by the sale the spiritual goods are made temporal, and the tithes are turned into chattels. Leases of benefices were forbidden by 35 Ed. I. St. I. c. 2 ; 3 Ric. II. c. 2 ; 7 Ric. II. c. 12 ; 13 Eliz. c. 20 ; Co. Inst. 490. The reason for the second exception was that if a parson demanded tithes in what was held to be another's parish, he could be prohibited by a writ of *Indicavit*, pursuant to Const. 9 Clarendon A.D. 1164, and then could not recover them at all before 13 Ed. I. St. I. c. 5, sec. 4 ; Co. Inst. 364. 9 Ed. II. St. I. c. 2 : If debate do arise upon the right of tithes, *having his original from the right of the patronage*, and the quantity of the same tithes do come unto the fourth part of the goods of the church, the king's prohibition shall hold place if the cause come before a judge spiritual [*i.e.*, unless the suit was commenced as required by Const. 9 Clarendon and 13 Ed. I. c. 5 in the king's court]. 45 Ed. III. c. 3, A.D. 1372, directed prohibition to issue if tithes were claimed of timber. Lynd. 109, 281. 32 Hen. VIII. c. 7, confirmed by 2 and 3 Ed. VI. c. 13, orders all tithes to be paid according to custom, and directs the withholder to be convened before the ordinary. 1 Ric. II. c. 14 requires a spiritual person claiming tithes in a secular court to show how they have become a laychattel. 32 Hen. VIII. c. 7, sec. 7, empowered temporal grantees of them to sue for them in secular courts. Suits for tithes of small value have been transferred to the civil magistrates by 7 & 8 Will. III. c. 6, sec. 1, A.D. 1696 ; 53 Geo. III. c. 127, sec. 4, A.D. 1813 ; 5 & 6 Will. IV. c. 74, sec. 1, A.D. 1835 ; and 4 & 5 Vict. c. 30, A.D. 1841. The Tithe Commutation Act, 6 & 7 Will. IV. c. 71, A.D. 1836, made them recoverable by distress, and the Tithe Recovery Act, 54 Vict. c. 8, A.D. 1891, makes them recoverable in the County Court.

(89). 13 Ed. I. St. IV. c. 1 : If a parson demand mortuaries in places

pass, and constructive trespass ([90]), including jactitation of marriage ([91]) and other cases of defamation ([92]), but only when brought for purposes of correction, and not to obtain money; and (3) causes involving assault or violence offered to clerks and religious persons ([93]).

where a mortuary hath been used to be given. 9 Ed. II. St. I. c. 1, A.D. 1315. The payment of mortuaries was limited by 21 Hen. VIII. c. 6.

(90). Alfred's Law 1, A.D. 877 : Let satisfaction be made for breach of suretyship as the law directs, and for breach of covenant as the shrift shall require. Const. 1 and 6 Boniface, A.D. 1261, enumerates contract, quasi-contract, trespass, and quasi-trespass. Lynd. 162; but by Const. 15 Clarendon the jurisdiction of spiritual courts does not apply to debts founded on breaches of covenant except between spiritual persons. 2 Hen. v. St. I. c. 3, A.D. 1414, exempts from the jurisdiction of spiritual courts questions of freehold, debt, trespasses, and covenants. 16 Car. I. c. 11 forbids a spiritual judge to inflict any temporal penalty.

(91). *I.e.*, pretending to a marriage which has no existence in fact. This gave rise to three defences : (1) a denial of the jactitation or malicious boast which rendered it a case of defamation ; (2) admission of the jactitation, but pleading a marriage *de facto*, which was the means of establishing an irregular marriage ; (3) admitting the jactitation without pleading marriage, but pleading a license to assume the character of a wife. See Rogers' Ecclesiastical Law, 572.

(92). Concil. Elib. Can. 52, A.D. 305, ap Gratian Caus. v. Qu. l. c. 3 : Let those be anathematised who have placed defamatory writings before the Church. Pseudo-Isidor. ap. Gratian Caus. II. Qu. III. c. 5 admits that words spoken in anger are not defamation (convicium). Syn. VIII. A.D. 809, *Ibid.* Caus. v. Qu. VI. c. 7: If any one has falsely aspersed the person of the innocent, let him be judged. 38 Hen. III. A.D. 1253, gave legislative sanction to the curses of Const. 1 and 29 Langton, A.D. 1222, of which one cursed those who defamed the good. 13 Ed. I. St. IV. c. 1, A.D. 1285 : In causes of defamation it hath been already granted that it shall be tried in a spiritual court, when money is not demanded but a thing done for punishment of sin. 9 Ed. II. St. I. c. 4; but St. 1 Ed. III. St. II. c. 11, A.D. 1327, allows prohibition if the process is abused. Co. Lit. 2 Inst. 492; Stephens' Eccl. Stat. 44. 18 & 19 Vict. c. 41, A.D. 1855, abolished this jurisdiction, and 23 & 24 Vict. c. 32, A.D. 1860, abolished spiritual suits for brawling.

(93). Cnut's Law 13, A.D. 1018 : If one bind or beat or grievously reproach an ecclesiastical person, let him make satisfaction as right is ; and let the bishop have the satisfaction due to the altar, and let satisfaction be paid to the lord or the king as for a notable breach of his protection.

Spiritual Courts.

20. Temporal causes, the cognisance of which was allowed to spiritual judges, included: (1) proof of testaments and grant of administrations ([94]), at least since the twelfth and thirteenth centuries ([95]); and (2) from Saxon times questions of legitimacy and bastardy ([96]). They were nevertheless required to decide them not according to Roman law, but according to English statutes ([97]).

21. Legal recognition of the authority of spiritual courts was

Concil. Westminster A.D. 1138, Can. 10. 13 Ed. I. St. IV. c. 1 : And for laying violent hands on a clerk . . . it hath been already granted that it shall be tried in a spiritual court. 9 Ed. II. St. I. c. 3, A.D. 1315 ; 50 Ed. III. c. 5, A.D. 1375 ; 1 Ric. II. c. 15 ; 5 & 6 Ed. VI. c. 4, repealed by 9 Geo. IV. c. 31.

(94). Concil. Paris III. A.D. 557, Can. 9, and Concil. Lugdun. II. A.D. 567, Can. 2, order effect to be given to the wishes of the dead. Glanvil VII. c. 6 ; Bracton II. 26 ; Fleta II. 57 speak of this as an ancient right, and as such it is allowed in Magna Carta, A.D. 1215, 13 Ed. I. St. I. c. 19, A.D. 1285 ; 18 Ed. III. St. III. c. 6 ; 31 Ed. III. St. I. c. 4 and 11 ; 3 Hen. V. St. II. c. 8 ; 21 Hen. VIII. c. 5 ; and specially by 24 Hen. VIII. c. 12, quoted above, note 99 ; Stephens' Eccl. Stat. 51. Regulations on this subject are found in Const. 15 Boniface, A.D. 1261 ; Const. 14 Othobon, A.D. 1268 ; Const. 5 Stratford, 1342 ; Const. 7 Stratford, A.D. 1343. Wills and administrations were withdrawn from spiritual cognisance by 20 & 21 Vict. c. 77 & 85, A.D. 1857, and 21 & 22 Vict. c. 95.

(95). Ecclesiastical Courts Commission Report, 1883, p. xxii., states that this was not allowed without a struggle. It is recognised by Article 27 of Magna Carta, which was withdrawn in subsequent issues, but asserted in Const. 15 Boniface, A.D. 1261.

(96). These were claimed to be of spiritual cognisance by Alexander III. to Bishop of Exeter, *Ibid.* Lib. IV. Lit. XVII. c. 4, 5, and 6, and to bishops of London and Worcester, *Ibid.* c. 7, and the claim was never disputed. See Crown Pleas, A.D. 1251, in Haddan and Stubbs I. 478. 25 Ed. III. St. II. A.D. 1350, also says: If it be alleged against any born beyond sea that he is a bastard [in an assize of mort dancestor] in a case where the bishop ought to have cognisance of bastardy, it shall be commanded to the bishop of the place to certify the king's court, as of old hath been used in the case of bastardy alleged against them which were born in England. 9 Hen. VI. c. 11. See Devoti Lib. III. Tit. IV. § 3.

(97). 20 Hen. III. c. 9, A.D. 1235: All the bishops instanted the magnates to consent that those born before matrimony should be held legitimate. But all the earls and barons replied unanimously : We will not change the approved and customary laws of England.

given by the so-called Writ of Consultation, awarded in the reign of Edward I. (⁹⁸), and by statutes passed in that and the two succeeding reigns, whereby (1) prohibition was forbidden to issue from the king's court in cases allowed to be of spiritual cognisance (⁹⁹); (2) secular judges were forbidden to inquire of process awarded by spiritual judges when dealing with matters within their jurisdiction (¹⁰⁰); and (3) prohibition was altogether disallowed after consultation (¹⁰¹). In succeeding reigns the franchises of the Church, which included the jurisdiction of spiritual courts, were confirmed by statutes (¹⁰²), more particularly those of Edward VI. (¹⁰³),

(98). 24 Ed. I. A.D. 1296.

(99). 13 Ed. I. St. IV. c. 1, A.D. 1285; Lynd. 96; 9 Ed. II. St. I. A.D. 1315; 18 Ed. III. St. III. c. 5, A.D. 1344: No prohibition shall be awarded out of the chancery, but in cases where we have the cognisance and of right ought to have. See Law Journal, vol. xxiv. p. 331.

(100). 18 Ed. III. St. III. c. 6: Whereas commissions be newly made to divers justices that they shall make inquiries upon judges of Holy Church whether they made just process or excessive in causes testamentary and other, which notoriously pertaineth to the cognisance of Holy Church, the said justices have inquired and caused to be indicted judges of holy Church in blemishing of the franchise of holy Church; that such commissions be repealed and from henceforth defended, saving the article in *eyre* such as ought to be.

(101). 50 Ed. III. c. 4, A.D. 1376: It is ordained and established of the said assent, that whereas a consultation is once duly granted upon a prohibition made to the judge of the holy Church, that the same judge may proceed in the cause by virtue of the same consultation notwithstanding any other prohibition thereupon to him delivered; provided always that the matter in the libel of the said cause be not engrossed, enlarged, or otherwise changed.

(102). 25 Ed. III. St. III. c. 1, A.D. 1350: That all the privileges and franchises granted heretofore to the said clergy be confirmed and holden in all points. 50 Ed. III. c. 1, A.D. 1370: It is ordained and established that Holy Church have all her liberties and franchises in quietness, without impeachment or other disturbance. 1 Hen. IV. c. 1, A.D. 1399; 4 Hen. IV. c. 3; 3 Hen. V. St. II. c. 1, A.D. 1415; 2 Hen. VI. c. 1, A.D. 1423; Const. Chichele, A.D. 1434.

(103). 2 and 3 Ed. VI. c. 13, sec. 15, declares that the jurisdiction of spiritual courts does not extend to matters excepted therefrom (1) by the statute of Westminster the second, the fifth chapter [*i.e.*, 13 Ed. I. St. I.

Spiritual Courts.

Elizabeth ([104]), and Charles II. ([105]); and a concurrent jurisdiction was bestowed upon them in dealing with the newly created offences against religion by the statutes of Edward VI. ([106]) and Elizabeth ([107]). Effect was, moreover, given to their decisions (1) by the common law practice of imprisoning one who remained excommunicate for more than forty days without coming to satisfaction ([108]), and (2) at one time by statutes authorising the bishops to arrest and imprison offenders in cases of heresy ([109]).

c. 5]; (2) by the statutes of *Articuli cleri* [*i.e.*, 13 Ed. I. St. I.]; (3) by the statute *Circumspecte agatis* [13 Ed. I. St. IV. c. 1]; (4) by the statute of *Sylva caedua* [45 Ed. III. c. 3]; (5) by the treatise *de Regia Prohibitione* [which Lord Coke, 2 Inst. 599a, says is the treatise entitled *Prohibitio Formata super Articulis*]; and (6) by the statute in the first year of Edward III., the tenth chapter [1 Ed. III. St. II. c. 10 forbids grants of corrodies at the king's request; but chapter 11, which appears to be meant, declares: No suit shall be made in the spiritual court against indictors].

(104). 23 Eliz. c. 1, sec. 15, A.D. 1581.

(105). 13 Car. II. c. 12: Archbishops, bishops, or any other persons exercising ecclesiastical jurisdiction may proceed, determine, sentence, execute, and exercise all manner of ecclesiastical jurisdiction . . . in all causes and matters belonging to ecclesiastical jurisdiction, according to the king's majesty's ecclesiastical laws used and practised in this realm, in as ample manner and form as they did and might lawfully have done before the making of the said Act [16 Car. I. c. 11].

(106). 2 and 3 Ed. VI. c. 1, sec. 12.

(107). 1 Eliz. c. 2, sec. 23. In *Britton* v. *Standish*, 6 Mod. 188, prohibition was refused to the spiritual court acting under this statute. Stephens' Eccl. Stat. 367.

(108). Edward's Law 7, A.D. 1064: If any one infringe the Church's protection it concerns the bishop's courts. If the guilty person decline or despise their sentence, let complaint of it be brought to the king after forty days. And the king's court shall put him under security to make satisfaction first to God and then to the king and Church. Law's Forms 129, 135.

(109). Richard II. issued a writ, 12th July 1382, empowering the archbishop and his suffragans to arrest and commit to their own or other prisons persons who preached or maintained the condemned conclusions. Stat. 2 Hen. IV. c. 15, and 2 Hen. v. c. 7, A.D. 1414, gave them a statutory right to decide cases of heresy, but these statutes were repealed in Henry VIII.'s time. See Ecclesiastical Courts Commission Report, 1883, p. 53.

22. On the other hand, the civil courts always took upon themselves to restrain the jurisdiction of spiritual courts to matters allowed to them by law, for which purpose the so-called Writ of Prohibition ([110]) was resorted to. This writ, which was extensively employed in the reign of Henry III., is now by custom limited to three cases: (1) when a spiritual court has proceeded with no original power of jurisdiction ([111]); (2) when incidentally it has exceeded its jurisdiction ([112]); and (3) when it has acted with entire disregard of law and justice ([113]). Usually such writs are applied for and granted before sentence is given in the spiritual court ([114]), yet in some cases they may be

([110]). Geoffry Fitz-Peter, as justiciar, prohibited Hubert Walter as legate from holding pleas. See Stubbs in Ecclesiastical Courts Commission, p. 31. Glanvil and Bracton speak of prohibitions as recognised institutions; but Henry III.'s reign is the great era of them. Prohibition was then granted against spiritual courts for entertaining suits touching freeholds, touching the king's peace, touching debt cognisable at common law, touching tithe of essarts or newly reclaimed land, touching the archbishop's order forbidding the sale of provisions to the canons of St. Oswald, for admission of plea after it had been decided in the king's court. 13 Ed. I. St. IV. c. 1, A.D. 1285, prescribes a number of cases in which they shall not issue. By 8 and 9 Will. III. c. 11, sec. 3, and 1 Will. IV. c. 21, the costs of a successful prohibition fall upon the person prohibited. Ayliffe 435; Stephens' Eccl. Stat. 663 and 1443.

([111]). *Pro defectu jurisdictionis*, either (1) because the suit, not being a matter of spiritual cognisance, no spiritual court can entertain it; or (2) because being of spiritual cognisance, the particular court in which it is brought cannot entertain it. Thus where the lord of a manor has probate of wills, prohibition lies if a spiritual court attempt to grant probate. See Stephens' Eccl. Stat. p. 52, note; Viner's Abr. Prohib. C. a. 1.

([112]). *Pro defectu triationis*, which is not the want of jurisdiction over the subject-matter of the suit, but the cropping up of a matter incidentally over which the court has no jurisdiction. Thus the question of a custom or prescription is not allowed to be tried in a spiritual court. Vin. Abr. Prohib. F. 16. See Tindal, C. J., in *Veley v. Burder*, 12 A. and E. 360, and Stephens' Eccl. Statutes, 1530, note.

([113]). For proceeding as the law does not warrant, as by refusing a legal defence, or not hearing a clerk in self-defence, as in Poole's case, *Reg. v. Archbishop of Canterbury*, 28 L. J. p. 154; or for failure of justice, as laid down in Edward's Law 5, A.D. 1064.

([114]). In *Ricketts v. Bodenham*, 4 A. and E. 433, Lord Denman observed:

had after sentence ([115]). There are nevertheless two cases in which they are not allowed to issue, viz. (1) when a simple disregard of the usual practice is all that is alleged ([116]), and (2) when justice can be properly obtained by appeal in the spiritual court ([117]).

23. The tendency of post-mediaeval legislation has been everywhere to confine spiritual courts to spiritual matters, and even for civil courts to encroach upon spiritual matters under the plea of enforcing a civil contract ([118]). In some countries

And there is no doubt that in the case of prohibitions to be granted for the sake of trial, as distinguished from those which are to be granted upon account of a wrong trial or erroneous judgment, the rule is established that a party neglecting to contest the jurisdiction in the first instance and taking his chance of a favourable decree, shall not be allowed after sentence to allege the want of jurisdiction as a ground of prohibition. Stephens' Eccl. Stat. p. 1058.

([115]). Prohibition after sentence is granted in the following cases: (1) Where there is a defect in the original jurisdiction—Coke 2 Inst. 619; (2) where the spiritual court has proceeded in a way the law does not warrant; (3) where the spiritual court has erred in the construction of an Act of Parliament. In *ex parte Mary Evans*, 2 Dowl. P. C. N. S. 726, Mr. Justice Williams observed on the question whether the application after sentence came too late: Upon that point I entertain no doubt. It seems to me to be clear that the application is not too late if an excess of jurisdiction appears. Stephens' Eccl. Stat. 1443.

([116]). In *Jolly* v. *Barnes*, 12 A. and E. 201, the Court of Queen's Bench refused to enter into questions as to the practice of the ecclesiastical courts, as to whether witnesses in a suit had been examined conformably to a general order of the Court of Arches, although such order was made by virtue of 10 Geo. IV. c. 53, s. 9, Lord Denman stating: that "if it were so, it is a matter of irregularity in practice only, and no ground for this court to interfere by Writ of Prohibition." Stephens' Eccl. Stat. p. 1417, note. See Lord Blackburn in *Maconochie* v. *Lord Penzance*, 6 Ap. Ca. 443; Lynd. p. 266 says the same.

([117]). *Titchmarch* v. *Chapman*, 1 Dowl. and Lowndes 732; Tindal, C. J., in *Veley* v. *Burder*, 12 A. and E. 360, and Stephens' Eccl. Stat. p. 1531, note; *Maconochie* v. *Lord Penzance*, 6 Ap. Ca. p. 443; Stephens' Eccl. Stat. p. 1056.

([118]). In *Brown* v. *Curé*, Law Reports, 6 P. C. 87, the Privy Council decreed the interment of Guibard, who had been excommunicated, in a Roman Catholic cemetery, on the ground that the law of the Canadian Catholics could not be altered without the consent of the government.

this legislation has given rise to much friction ([119]). In this country the change was brought about peaceably, by the entire submission of the clergy, under Henry VIII. By the acts of submission and supremacy, the sovereign was acknowledged to hold the position formerly held by the pope as supreme head ([120]) or governor ([121]) of the English Church; and although these acts were limited in intention to the pope's feudal position in relation to property held in free-alms ([122]), yet by the construction which has since been put upon them in courts of law, courts Christian have been transformed into the ecclesiastical courts of the Crown ([123]), the canon law of the Church

---

([119]). Witness the friction still existing in Italy owing to the pope's loss of temporal power, the Cultur Kampf in Germany, the oppression of the Church in France.

([120]). 25 Hen. VIII. c. 19, A.D. 1533; 28 Hen. VIII. c. 1, A.D. 1534: That the king, our sovereign lord, his heirs and successors, kings of this realm, shall be taken, accepted, and reputed the only supreme head on earth of the Church of England, called Ecclesia Anglicana; and shall have and enjoy, annexed and united to the imperial crown of this realm, as well the title and style thereof, as all honours, dignities, pre-eminences, jurisdictions, privileges, authorities, immunities, profits, and commodities to the said dignity of supreme head of the same Church belonging and appertaining. 35 Hen. VIII. c. 3 gives him the title "of the Church of England, and also of Ireland, on earth supreme Head.

([121]). The oath required by sec. 19 of 1 Eliz. c. 1 is: "that the Queen's highness is the only supreme governour of this realm, and of all other her highness's dominions and countries, as well in all spiritual or ecclesiastical things or causes as temporal." Stephens' Eccl. Stat. 358.

([122]). The First Lateran Council, A.D. 1123, acknowledged the pope as supreme liege lord of the Church, and King John did the same, A.D. 1215. Hen. VIII. by these acts renounced that supremacy, claiming to be himself supreme liege lord, and his country to be an empire; and the clergy assented " so far as the law of Christ allowed."

([123]). Sec. 17 of 1 Eliz. c. 1: That such jurisdictions, privileges, superiorities, and pre-eminences, spiritual and ecclesiastical, as by any spiritual or ecclesiastical power or authority hath heretefore been, or may lawfully be, exercised or used for the visitation of the ecclesiastical state and persons, and for reformation, order, and correction of the same, and of all manner of errors, heresies, schisms, abuses, offences, contempts, and enormities shall for ever, by authority of this present parliament, be united

has made way for the ecclesiastical law of the sovereign ([124]), parliamentary statutes have taken the place of conciliar decrees ([125]), and the Judicial Committee of the Privy Council that of the supreme advising congregations of the Church ([126]).

24. In recent times, the civil disabilities incurred by sentences of ecclesiastical courts have been almost entirely abolished by the enactment (1) that excommunication should no longer be employed as a means of compelling obedience to judicial orders, but only be awarded in a definitive sentence, or in an interlocutory decree having the force and effect of a definitive sentence; (2) that it should no longer be awarded, except as a spiritual censure for offences of ecclesiastical cognisance; and (3) that the only civil effect of excommunication should be such imprisonment, not exceeding six months, as the court pronouncing the sentence or decree should direct ([127]). The

and annexed to the imperial crown of this realm. The king's ecclesiastical court is mentioned 2 and 3 Ed. VI. c. 14.

([124]). 2 & 3 Ed. VI. c. 13, sec. 2: The same to be recovered before the ecclesiastical judge, according to the king's ecclesiastical law. 1 Eliz. c. 2, sec. 23; 13 Car. II. c. 12.

([125]). In the legislation of the last sixty years, archbishops and bishops seem to have competed with statesmen to destroy every organisation designed to carry out the principles of the Church, and to assimilate it to the utilitarian standard of the world.

([126]). In place of appeals to the pope, the statute 25 Hen. VIII. c. 19 permitted appeals from the archbishop's court to the king in chancery, the practice being for the Lord Chancellor on petition to appoint certain delegates to hear the appeal, that body being called the Court of Delegates. Should their decision not be satisfactory, a Commission of Review might be granted under the great seal on petition to the king in council, "to revise, review, and rehear the case." The Act 2 & 3 Will. IV. c. 92 prohibited the granting in future of Commissions of Review, and the Act 3 and 4 Will. IV. c. 41 transferred the powers and jurisdiction of the Court of Delegates to the Judicial Committee of the Privy Council. An entirely new court was thus established as the supreme court of appeal in matters ecclesiastical.

([127]). 53 Geo. III. c. 127, A.D. 1813, enacts: Excommunication, together with all proceedings following thereupon, shall in all cases, save those hereafter to be specified, be discontinued, and that instead thereof the person shall be pronounced contumacious. Sec. 2 provides that sentences of ex-

jurisdiction of ecclesiastical courts has also been abolished in tithe cases ([128]), causes of defamation ([129]), suits against laymen for brawling ([130]), causes of matrimony and divorce ([131]), probate and administration ([132]), suits for Church rates ([133]), and the religious teaching of the young ([134]).

25. The jurisdiction which is still retained by them in this country extends to: (1) disciplinary causes, or causes concerning excesses and irregularities of the clergy ([135]), in respect of faith, morals, public worship ([136]), and the discharge of their official duties; (2) discretionary causes, or causes involving the exercise of discretion by ordinaries, such as admitting or refusing to admit to a benefice ([137]), giving or withholding licenses to clergy ([138]), giving or refusing the sacraments, and dedicating

---

communication may be pronounced "as spiritual censures for offences of ecclesiastical cognisance;" but sec. 3 provides "that no person who shall be so pronounced or declared excommunicate shall incur any civil penalty or incapacity whatever in consequence of such excommunication, save such imprisonment, not exceeding six months, as the court pronouncing or declaring such person excommunicate shall direct." Rothery's Appeals, p. v.

(128). By 6 and 7 Will. IV. c. 71, A.D. 1836.
(129). 18 and 19 Vict. c. 41, A.D. 1855.
(130). 23 and 24 Vict. c. 32, A.D. 1860.
(131). 20 and 21 Vict. c. 85, A.D. 1857.
(132). 20 and 21 Vict. c. 77; 21 and 22 Vict. c. 95.
(133). 31 and 32 Vict. c. 109, A.D. 1868.
(134). Elementary Education Act, A.D. 1870.
(135). Const. 1 Boniface, A.D. 1261; 13 Ed. I. St. IV. c. 1, A.D. 1265.
(136). By the Public Worship Act, 1874, 37 & 38 Vict. c. 85, by sec. 7, the archdeacon of an archdeaconry, the churchwarden of a parish, or any three parishioners of the parish, or, in the case of a cathedral, of the diocese, may complain of any addition or alteration of the services or ornaments, which the bishop may dispose of summarily by consent, or otherwise refer to the parliamentary judge created by the statute, to be decided by him, unless, having regard to all the circumstances of the case, the bishop declines to refer it.
(137). 9 Ed. II. St. I. c. 13, A.D. 1315: Of the ability of a person presented unto the benefice of a Church, the examination belongeth to the spiritual judge, and so it hath been used heretofore, and shall be hereafter. Co. Lit. II. Inst. 631, says: And in this examination he is judge, and not a minister.
(138). The above are enumerated, Const. 1 Boniface, A.D. 1261.

Spiritual Courts. 209

Churches; and (3) causes involving the validity or invalidity of purely spiritual acts, such as baptism (139), ordination (140), institution (141), resignation (142), and excommunication, either on the ground of such acts being original nullities (143), or of their having been revoked before completion (144).

(139). Decret. Greg. IX. Lib. III. Tit. XLII. c. 3; Const. 3 Peckham, A.D. 1281.

(140). Lynd. 309.

(141). Alexander III. to the English bishops in Decret. Greg. IX. Lib. III. Tit. XXXVIII. c. 12; Const. 11 and 10 Othobon, A.D. 1268.

(142). Lynd. 107, 146. 25 Ed. III. St. III. c. 8, A.D. 1350: Whereas the said prelates have shewed and prayed remedy for that the secular justices do accroach to them cognisance of voidance of benefices, which cognisance and the discussing thereof pertaineth to the judges of Holy Church, and not to the lay judge, the king will and granteth that the said justices shall from henceforth receive such challenges, made or to be made, . . . and, moreover, thereof shall do right and reason. Co. Lit. 344 states that whether a Church be full or not shall be tried by the certificate of the bishop, because plenarty is by institution, which is a spiritual matter; but, whether it be void or not, shall be tried by the county [because ecclesiastical courts had no cognisance over the dead]. Suits concerning the possession of a benefice were brought in the court of the province as ordered by Const. 36 Edmund, A.D. 1236, as appears from an ordainment of Reynolds, A.D. 1322 (in Johnson and Sir H. Spelman, p. 487), directed to the officials of Canterbury. See Rothery's Appeals, 1868.

(143). Gratian Caus. XXV. Qu. II. c. 3 says, to one unwilling to receive grace, a sacrament is a nullity. Lynd. 264: The baptism and ordination of an unwilling subject are nullities. Lynd. 309; Decret. Greg. IX. Lib. III. Tit. XLII. c. 3. Institution is a nullity in the cases mentioned in Const. 10 Othobon, A.D. 1268, or whilst a *duplex querela* is pending. Ayliffe 233, 76: Also confirmation of an election without a previous citation. Ayliffe 241; Sext. Decret. Lib. I. Tit. VI. c. 47, and Lib. IV. Tit. XII. c. 64. Excommunication may be a nullity. Decret. Greg. IX. Lib. II. Tit. XIX. c. 7; Sext. Decr. Lib. V. Tit. XI. c. 2; Lynd. 351, 319, 150, 264, 351. But a nullity is not suspended by an appeal until it is pronounced to be such, Ayliffe 74; nor is everything which ought not to be done a nullity. Lynd. 23: Licet aliquid fieri non debeat, factum tamen tenet, 319; for instance, marriage, *Ibid.* 273, 274; the acts of a notary suspended by sentence of law, Lynd. 16. Elections, collations to prebends, and admission of canons are not void because all parties interested have not been summoned. Ayliffe 16.

(144). By the civil law, acts of gift and other similar acts are revocable

SPIRITUAL JUDGES.

26. A spiritual or ecclesiastical judge is one who has lawful authority from the Church to hear and decide spiritual or ecclesiastical causes. There are many varieties of such officers. (1) Some are judges by *divine right*. This is the case of the Church as a body in General Synod assembled; others are of *ecclesiastical appointment*, such as territorial bishops and their officials. (2) Some are *ordinaries*, having by custom and long habit authority to hear and decide cases within the limits defined by custom, such as a metropolitan or his official principal, a bishop or his chancellor; others are *delegates* appointed by an ordinary to deal with some particular matter belonging to his jurisdiction, and to deal with it in a particular way ([145]). (3) Some are judges of *competent jurisdiction*, having authority from the Church not only to hear and decide, but also to pronounce sentence on the matters coming within their province ([146]); others are referees and auditors, having only the power to *inquire* and *report*, or else are arbitrators appointed to decide by the sole will of the parties ([147]). Again (4) some

before they have been acted on. By English law they are not so, but they may be set aside in cases of fraud, compulsion, and the like by action at law, or by the office of the judge. Lynd. p. 163, 332, 107. Until such acts are completed, however, a person may go against his own act in certain cases. Lynd. 150 distinguishes: Either such acts take effect in law, or they do not. (1) If they take effect in law, (a) if a mistake has been made, the doer may correct his mistake, and even (b) if no mistake has been made, he may revoke them until the effect has actually come about, as in the case of a last will or an interlocutory sentence. (2) If they do not take effect in law, (a) a man may impugn his own act as being a nullity, either in the interest of a third party, or in his own interest, provided he do not allege his own wrong-doing; or (b) a man may defend himself against his own act as being a *nudum pactum*.

(145). Law's Forms 16.
(146). See above, note 12.
(147). Gratian Caus. II. Qu. VI. c. 33: Ordinary judges are those who are either appointed by the pope as ecclesiastical judges or by the emperor as secular judges. Arbiters are those who, having no authority of their own, are elected to be judges with consent of the parties.

are judges of *first instance,* and are spoken of as judges from whom (*a quibus*), others are judges of appeal, and are called judges to whom (*ad quos*) an appeal lies.

Judges Ordinary.

27. For any person to be in a position lawfully to hear and determine a cause as judge ordinary, he must be neither (1) naturally disqualified, as by being blind, deaf, or the like; (2) morally disqualified, as by being a woman or a slave; nor (3) legally disqualified, as by having an interest in the case, being an enemy of the accused ([148]), or a person of ill repute ([149]); but there is nothing to prevent a judge being a layman, provided he is an ecclesiastical person ([150]). In early times the judge was required to be approved by the parties ([151]). Hence in North Africa ([152]) and in Southern Europe judges were at one time elected as each case arose ([153]). When, however, the decrees of councils became more numerous, and stricter procedure became requisite in the interests of justice, it was found necessary to have a standing judge or judge ordinary, who was deemed to be generally of competent jurisdiction (1) if he was full twenty-six years of age at the least, (2) was learned in the civil and ecclesiastical laws, (3) had taken the

---

([148]). Socrates I. 31 relates that Athanasius appealed to the Emperor from the Council of Tyre in 335 A.D., because (1) Eusebius and his party who were to judge him were his enemies, and (2) because Ischyras, described as a presbyter in the indictment, was not proved to be one.

([149]). Gratian Caus. III. Qu. VII. c. 1.

([150]). See notes 16 and 192.

([151]). Concil. Chalcedon A.D. 451, Can. 9.

([152]). Concil. Milev. A.D. 416, ap. Gratian Caus. VI. Qu. VI. c. 33; Concil. Carthag. III. A.D. 397, Can. 10, *Ibid.* c. 34: If the judges have been elected by consent of the parties. Concil. Carthag. V. A.D. 401, Can. 5, *Ibid.* c. 39: If there is an appeal, let him who appeals choose his judges.

([153]). Pseudo-Isidor. ap. Gratian Caus. IV. Qu. IV. c. 1; Caus. V. Qu. IV. c. 2 and Qu. III. c. 1; Caus. III. Qu. VIII. c. 1; Egbert's Excerpt. 141.

oath of office ([154]), and (4) no exception were taken to him by the parties as a suspect person ([155]).

28. Although a judge may, by his own qualifications and in relation to the parties, be a judge of competent jurisdiction, yet he may not be competent to hear a particular class of causes ([156]). This disability may arise from one of three causes. Either (1) the subject-matter may be one with which he is not competent to deal. Thus a spiritual judge may not decide causes which belong to the temporal judge ([157]), nor a secular judge spiritual causes. (2) The subject-matter may be one which is excepted from his jurisdiction. Thus a bishop cannot judge his clergy in cases which are reserved to the arch-

(154). Can. 127, 1603: No man shall hereafter be admitted a chancellor, commissary, or official to exercise any ecclesiastical jurisdiction except he be of the full age of twenty-six years at the least, and one who is learned in the civil and ecclesiastical laws, and is at the least a master of arts or bachelor of laws, and is reasonably well practised in the cause thereof, as likewise well affected and zealously bent to religion; touching whose life and manners no evil example is had; and except, before he enter into and execute any such office, he shall take the oath, &c.

(155). Gratian Caus. III. Qu. v. c. 15; Ayliffe 310, 452; Devoti Inst. Lib. III. Tit. x. § 8. See note 164.

(156). Pseudo-Isidor. ap. Gratian Caus. XI. Qn. 1. c. 48; Innocent IV. in Sext. Decret. Lib. II. Tit. II. c. 1.

(157). Thus Hosius of Cordova addressed the emperor in the fourth century in Hist. Arianorum ad Monachos c. 44: To thee God has given the empire, but to us He has entrusted the Church. And as he who withstands your empire opposes the ordainment of God, so beware that you do not incur crime by drawing to yourself matters which belong to the Church. Gratian 1 Dist. xc. c. 11: If the emperor is a Catholic, he is the son not the president of the Church, and so far as pertains to religion he ought to learn and not to teach. He has the privileges of his power which he has divinely obtained for administering public laws, so that not ungrateful for these benefits he may usurp to himself nothing against the disposition of divine rule. Concil. Paris A.D. 615, Can. 6 in Decret. Lib. II. Tit. II. c. 2, directs a secular judge to be excommunicated who takes upon himself to judge a clerk for a spiritual matter. Alexander III. *Ibid.* c. 5, lays it down that for a spiritual matter a layman may be summoned by a spiritual court, which the Statute 18 Ed. I. (*Circumspecte agatis*) allows; but *Ibid.* c. 6 directs that a dispute concerning a lay fee belongs to the lord of the fee.

bishop ([158]). (3) The subject-matter may be one which does not fall within the local limits of his jurisdiction, as if either the parties reside ([159]), or the offence has been committed ([160]), or the obligation contracted, or the matter in dispute is situate outside them ([161]).

29. If a person is cited to appear before a court or a judge which for any of these reasons has no jurisdiction, he may either decline to obey the citation, or he may obey under protest, pointing out that the judge's sentence cannot bind him ([162]). It is therefore of primary importance that spiritual

---

([158]). See *Penance*, § 6.

([159]). Concil. Chalcedon A.D. 451, Can. 9 in Decret. Lib. II. Tit. II. c. 1; Pseudo-Isidor. ap. Gratian Caus. III. Qu. VI. c. 2 : One who is accused may not be judged except in his own proper forum. *Id. Ibid.* c. 4 : Let not liberty to accuse extend beyond the bounds of the province. *Id. Ibid.* c. 17 ; Nicolaus *Ibid.* Caus. VI. Qu. III. c. 3 : [Bishop Suffred] ought to have awaited the judgment of his primate, and not have invited the judgment of other prelates of the diocese. Also Caus. IX. Qu. III. Innocent III. in Decret. Lib. II. Tit. II. c. 13. Lynd. 27, 84, 199, says that the Church where a person attends service and receives the sacraments is his Church. Const. 3 Mepham. A.D. 1320 ; Const. Othobon, A.D. 1268.

([160]). Concil. Afric. in Decret. Lib. II. Tit. II. c. 3 : If the bishops between whom the controversy exists belong to different provinces, let the metropolitan in whose province the place in dispute lies appoint the judges. Pseudo-Isidor. Caus. III. Qu. VI. c. 1 and 18 : There let the cause be gone into where the crime is admitted. The statute 23 Hen. VIII. c. 9 in this country forbids any one to be cited out of his diocese except into the archbishop's court. See *Acts in Judgment*, § 11.

([161]). Cap. Carlomani ap. Gratian Caus. VI. Qu. III. c. 5 : Those who have a benefice or inheritance within a diocese, and are parishioners of another bishop, and commit rapine and depredation, shall be excommunicated where they are. And let their excommunication be signified to their senior and to their proper bishop. Thus exempt monasteries were liable to Church rates for their property within a parish. Const. 4 Stratford, A.D. 1342 ; Lynd. 255. Const. Chichele, A.D. 1439 : We ordain that in causes concerning augmentations rectors be as strictly obliged to appear by virtue of citations publicly and solemnly made in their Churches as if they had been personally served.

([162]). Concil. London A.D. 1126, Can. 10 : No man is bound by a sentence passed by an improper judge. Alexander III. quoted, note 177. See *Acts in Judgment*, note 87.

causes should be undertaken before the proper judge, or that letters of request (*literae remissoriales*) should be presented by him to the judge who has jurisdiction over the defendant to obtain his co-operation. All ordinary judges within the province are required to assist one another upon request ([163]), but the usual course in this country in such a case is to take proceedings in the provincial court, which has jurisdiction over both parties.

30. A judge may nevertheless be disqualified to hear and determine a particular case, because he is what is termed a suspect person ([164]). A judge is held to be a suspect person who is either (1) a close friend ([165]), or akin, or related to the plaintiff or accuser ([166]); or (2) the personal enemy of the defendant or accused ([167]); or (3) has previously given advice upon the case ([168]); or (4) has an interest in it either directly by having received a gift from either of the parties, which is termed baratry ([169]), or indirectly by having himself a similar case pending before another

---

([163]). Const. 8 Othobon, A.D. 1268; Const. 3 Islep A.D. 1328; Const. Islep A.D. 1351; Lynd. 81, 90, 303; Law's Forms 89.

([164]). Gregory, A.D. 601, in Decret. Lib. II. Tit. II. c. 4; Concil. Lat. IV. A.D. 1215, Can. 35, *Ibid.* Lib. II. Tit. XXVIII. c. 61. Ayliffe 452 enumerates fifteen things which make a judge suspect. See *Acts in Judgment*, note 87.

([165]). Nicolaus I. ap. Gratian Caus. IV. Qu. IV. c. 3.

([166]). Lucius III. in Decret. Lib. II. Tit. XXVIII. c. 36.

([167]). Nicolaus ap. Gratian Caus. III. Qu. V. c. 15. Personal ill-will is assumed if the judge has already attempted to deal extra-judicially with the same matter—Ayliffe 314; Law's Forms 14—or has used threats in matters touching his office. Lynd. 115. See note 148.

([168]). Lucius III. in Decret. Lib. II. Tit. XXVIII. c. 36, says, who in the same business has discharged the office of advocate.

([169]). Gregory ap. Gratian Caus. XXIII. Qu. IV. c. 27, says that a bishop cannot excommunicate for a wrong done to himself. *Ibid.* Caus. III. Qu. V. c. 15. It was ruled in ex parte *Medwin v. Hurst*, 1853, 1 Ed. and Bla. 609, that the fact of the Chancellor being able to award a bishop his costs should the decision be given in his favour does not give the bishop such an interest in the case as to disqualify his chancellor from hearing it at the suit of the bishop.

tribunal ([170]); or (5) has shown himself ignorant of the law ([171]).

31. If exception is taken to the judge on the general ground that he has no jurisdiction to hear and determine the cause, the judge is competent himself to hear and decide the validity of the exception. If, on the other hand, a judge otherwise allowed to be of competent jurisdiction is refused on the ground of being suspect, the party refusing him is required first to state the ground of his objection openly before the judge, and then, unless the adversary assents, for each to nominate one commissioner, and the two commissioners a third, who are thereupon to hear and determine the validity of the suspicion without delay ([172]). If the suspicion is upheld, either the bishop must appoint a special commissioner (*executor*) to take the judge's place, or, according to the practice of earlier times, some one to compel the parties to agree upon arbiters ([173]). The refusal to admit an exception of being suspect is a good ground of appeal ([174]).

32. The duties of an ecclesiastical judge are fourfold: (1) to bring sufficient knowledge to bear on the hearing of a cause ([175]);

([170]). Hieronym. ap. Gratian Caus. I. Qu. 1. c. 23 ; Cod. IX. c. 4 to 27, *Ibid.* c. 126 ; Augustin, A.D 414, *Ibid.* Caus. XIV. Qu. v. c. 15 ; Innocent III. A.D. 1198, in Decret. Lib. III. Tit. I. c. 10 ; Boniface VIII. in Sext. Lib. I. Tit. III. c. 11 ; Craisson, § 5563.

([171]). Const. 23 Otho, A.D. 1237: Since discretion and knowledge are required in determining matters, all are to take heed that such a judge or hearer of causes be not deputed as may pass an impudent or unjust sentence through simplicity, unskilfulness, or want of knowledge, so that the guilty be acquitted, the innocent condemned. Const. 29 Otho: Let judges who know not the law, if any doubt arise by which damage may happen to either party, ask the advice of some man of knowledge. Thomas Aquin. II. 2, Qu. 66, art. 2 : A judge lacking in necessary knowledge ought not to be absolved unless he renounces his office. Lynd 4 : Ignorance of matters which any one is required to know by virtue of his office is a sin. *Id.* 80 : A judge must have a competent practical knowledge of law.

([172]). Concil. Lat. IV. A.D. 1215, *Ibid.* Lib. II. Tit. XXVIII. c. 61.

([173]). Gregory, A.D. 601, in Decret. Lib. II. Tit. II. c. 4.

([174]). Innocent III. in Decret. Lib. I. Tit. XXIX. c. 27, § 5.

([175]). See note 171.

(2) to expedite it without delay ([176]), and without fear or favour ([177]); (3) only to accept as facts what have been before himself ([178]) judicially proved to be such ([179]); and (4) as being the guardian, not the critic of the law, to pass sentence according to the law as it stands ([180]), not as he conceives it

([176]). Concil. Ebor. A.D. 1195, Can. 12 ; Concil. Westminster, A.D. 1200, Can. 12 : Let [an inquiry] not be deferred from time to time for the sake of money. Const. 1 Arundel, A.D. 1408 ; Lynd. 29.

([177]). Cyprian ap. Gratian III. Dist. IV. c. 127 ; Hieronym. *Ibid.* Caus. I. Qu. 1. c. 23 and 126 : Augustin *Ibid.* Caus. XIV. Qu. V. c. 15 ; Stat. Eccl. Ant. c. 74, *Ibid.* Caus. XXVI. Qu. VII. c. 6 ; Gregory *Ibid.* Caus. II. Qu. VII. c. 46 ; Boniface VIII. in Sext. Lib. I. Tit. III. c. 11 ; and Rule 12, *Ibid.* Lib. V. Tit. XII. c. 5 ; Lynd. 122.

([178]). Pseudo-Damasus ap. Gratian Caus. XI. Qu. III. c. 76 : It is not lawful to discuss the causes of those who are accused before they have appeared after being canonically cited before the synod, so that present he may learn from one who is present accurately, and understand what are the charges made against him. Synodus VIII. A.D. 869, *Ibid.* Not only is he guilty who states concerning another what is false, but he who too readily listens to accusations. Alexander III. in Decret. Greg. IX. Lib. II. Tit. I. c. 4 : As a sentence passed by a judge without jurisdiction is not binding, so a confession made before such a judge is of no avail. Gratian Caus. XV. Qu. VI. c. 1 ; Lynd. 113, 308, 312.

([179]). Gregory ap. Gratian Caus. XI. Qu. III. c. 74 ; It were grave and unbecoming indeed to give certain sentence in a doubtful matter. Augustinus *Ibid.* c. 75 : Although things may be true, yet no judge must believe them until they are proved by certain evidence. Ethelred's Law 6, A.D. 1014 : Let every man be deemed worthy of common right. Cnut's Law 2 A.D. 1018 : Let him that presides in judgment consider very seriously what he desires of God when he says, Forgive us our trespasses as we forgive them that trespass against us, and that they do not rashly condemn Christian men. Eugenius III. in Decret. Greg. IX. Lib. I. Tit. XXXI. c. 2 : If a priest knows for certain that any one is guilty of a crime, . . . yet ought he not to accuse him of it by name unless he is prepared to prove it judicially, but only indefinitely, as Christ said, One of you shall betray Me. Lynd. 40, 113, 266 ; Const. 13 Stratford, A.D. 1343. See *Discipline Generally*, note 45.

([180]). Concil. Aurel. V. A.D. 549, Can. 2 : That no bishop suspend from communion except for those faults for which the ancient fathers decreed such suspension. Cnut's Law 9, A.D. 1019 : Let satisfaction be always sought for towards God by the canon book. Gratian Caus. XXVI. Qu. VII. A fragment attributed to Innocent *Ibid.* 1 Dist. XX. c. 3 : In cases in which no authority for binding or loosing is to be found in the Book of the Old

ought to be ([181]). If either party in a judicial suit suffers damage through the wrongful neglect of the judge, the latter may be compelled to compensate him for the loss ([182]), and an action may be maintained to oblige him so to do ([183]).

Testament, the four Gospels, and the writings of the apostles, refer to the divine writings in Greek (Apocrypha). If no directions are found there, look to the canons of the Apostolic See. If none are there, go to the Catholic histories of the Catholic Church, written by Catholic doctors. If none are there, carefully look over the examples of the saints. Augustin *Ibid.* Caus. XXIV. Qu. 1. c. 21 : Let us not apply treacherous balances, weighing what we wish, how we wish, at our caprice (pro arbitrio nostro), saying : This is grave, that is light ; but let us apply the divine balance from the Holy Scriptures as from the Lord's treasury, and by that let us weigh what is grave, or rather let us not weigh it, but accept what has been weighed by the Lord. And who can doubt that the graver offence was the one more severely punished. Concil. Clovesho A.D. 747, Can. 24, says that it may not exceed it. Also Alexander III. in Decret. Lib. I. Tit. XXIX. c. 4, and Honorius III. *Ibid.* Tit. XXXVI. c. 11.

(181). Innocent III. to Bishop of Ely, A.D. 1204, *Ibid.* Lib. II. Tit. XXII. c. 8 : A judge ought not to proceed by authority of his own law (juris), but of common law. Const. 21 Peckham, A.D. 1281 ; Lynd. 13, 38, 121, 146, 157, 231 ; Ayliffe 349. Lynd. 231 : Punishment is preserved to the authority of the law, and is not left to the president's discretion. Ayliffe 153 says a suit should be decided in pursuance of such laws as existed at the time the suit was commenced. Craisson, § 5566.

(182). Concil. Tolet. XII. A.D. 680, ap. Gratian Caus. XVII. Qu. IV. c. 35, makes a presbyter responsible for wrongfully delivering a fugitive out of sanctuary, or for allowing one to escape whom he ought to deliver. Concil. Lugdun. A.D. 1274, in Sext. Decr. Lib. III. Tit. XIV. c. 1, pronounces a judge who gives a sentence contrary to justice suspended *ipso facto*, and declares him liable to compensate the injured person. In *Beaurain* v. *Scott*, 3 Cowper 388, an action was sustained against a judge for excommunicating where he had no right so to do. In *Davis* v. *Black*, 1 Q. B. 900, Stephens' Eccl. Stat. 226, an action lay against a priest for not marrying parties who requested him to marry them. Innocent III. A.D. 1204, to Bishop of Ely, in Decret. Lib. III. Tit. XXXVIII. c. 29, makes a bishop liable in damages for maliciously refusing a suitable presentee. Lynd. 257. To be wrongful a thing must be done with a wrong intent *culpa interveniente*, as Lynd. 263 and Gratian Caus. XV. Qu. I. c. 3 express it ; but a man does not do wrong who only uses his own right. Mr. Girdlestone, in Ecclesiastical Courts Commission, vol. II. 186, Qu. 4170, mentioned three cases in which he had been put to expense through neglect of a bishop or his officials, but this was in extra-judicial proceedings under a statute.

(183). Lynd. 278.

Surrogates.

33. Every judge who himself holds an ordinary office as principal (*princeps*) can substitute another to act for him in whole or in part, who is then called a delegate; and every delegate, the terms of whose commission permit him so to do, can appoint a sub-delegate in whole or in part ([184]), provided the persons thus appointed are properly qualified to act. Delegates and sub-delegates are termed surrogates. When several delegates are appointed to deal with a cause, one or more may act without the rest if the cause is committed to them with authority for one or more to deal with it, or as it is said jointly (*in solidum*) ([185]); but if the cause is committed to them in common (*simpliciter*), unless those who are absent authorise their co-delegates to act for them, all proceedings taken in their absence are null and void ([186]). Moreover, whenever the commission is addressed to several in common, the decision must be given by at least a majority of them ([187]). A delegation may also be made to a corporation sole, in which case if the personal name of the holder is omitted it descends to his successor ([188]).

34. The general qualifications of a judge-delegate or surrogate are: (1) he must be a man and not a woman ([189]), full

([184]). Alexander III. to Bishop of London in Decret. Lib. I. Tit. XXIX. c. 3; Innocent III. to Bishop of Ely, *Ibid.* c. 28.

([185]). Innocent III. *Ibid.* c. 23; Boniface VIII. in Sext. Lib. I. Tit. XIV. c. 8, says, If several are appointed so that all or two or one may carry out the apostolic [*i.e.*, the pope's] command. Ayliffe 424.

([186]). Alexander III. to Bishop of Winchester in Decret. Lib. I. Tit. XXIX. c. 6 says that one can sub-delegate his authority to the other. Otherwise, according to *Id.* c. 16, the decision of one will not hold.

([187]). Coelestin III. A.D. 1193, *Ibid.* c. 21, says, because the sacred canons provide that a judgment shall be deemed in force (integrum) which is supported by the opinions of many. Innocent III. *Ibid.* c. 22; Craisson, § 5577.

([188]). Alexander III. *Ibid.* c. 14.

([189]). Isidor. Etym. XVIII. 15 in Decret. Lib. V. Tit. XL. c. 10, requires three things in a witness and a fortiori in a judge, viz., (1) condition, (2) sex, and (3) character. "In respect of condition he must be a free man;

20 years of age ([190]), and not disqualified by blindness or deafness ([191]); (2) he must be a baptized person and a member of the spirituality, or at least an ecclesiastical person ([192]); (3) he must be a free agent ([193]), and therefore not be of servile condition; (4) he must not himself be under censure ([194]) or disqualified by ill-repute. He must, moreover, (5) not be suspect by the parties ([195]). The particular qualifications required by the law of this country are that he must be (6) either a grave minister and a graduate, or a licensed public preacher and a beneficed man, living near the place where the courts are kept, or a bachelor of law, or a master of arts at least; and (7) have some skill in the civil and ecclesiastical law ([196]).

for a slave often suppresses the truth in giving testimony, for fear of his master. In respect of sex (*natura*) he must be a man, not a woman; for a woman's evidence is always shifty and evasive. In respect of character (*rita*) he must be innocent and upright in action; for if he has lost his character, he ceases to be trustworthy. A thoroughly debased (*sceleratus*) man has lost all sense of justice." Honorius III. in Decret. Lib. I. Tit. XXXIII. c. 12 allows an abbess to act as judge, but Craisson, § 6378, explains the passage otherwise.

([190]). Gregory IX. in Decret. Lib. I. Tit. XXIX. c. 41; Craisson, § 313 and 5573.

([191]). Canon 128, A.D. 1603: No chancellor, commissary, archdeacon, official, or any other person exercising ecclesiastical jurisdiction, shall at any time substitute in their absence any to keep any court for them, except he be either a grave minister and a graduate, or a licensed public preacher and a beneficed man, near the place where the courts are kept, or a bachelor of law, or a master of arts at least, who hath some skill in the civil and ecclesiastical law, and is a favourer of true religion, and a man of honest and modest conversation.

([192]). Eugenius III. in Decret. Lib. II. Tit. 1. c. 2.

([193]). Gregory IX. in Decret. Lib. V. Tit. XXXIX. c. 54.

([194]). Concil. Belvac. 1 ap. Gratian Caus. XXIV. Qu. 1. c. 4. According to Gregory IX. in Decret. Lib. V. Tit. 1. c. 26, a suspended bishop, if tolerated, can validly but not lawfully excommunicate. If denounced by name he cannot do so validly, because he has ceased to be the representative of the Church, nor can the official of an excommunicated bishop exercise the latter jurisdiction. Concil. Lugdun. A.D. 1245, in Sext. Lib. I. Tit. XIII. c. 1; Ayliffe 18.

([195]). Alexander III. to the Bishops of Exeter and Winchester in Decret. Lib. I. Tit. XXIX. c. 17. ([196]). Canon 128, A.D. 1603.

35. A judge-delegate can take no action until he has received notice of his commission, since it takes effect not from the date of sealing but of delivery ([197]), nor can he execute it unless he is in a position to prove that it has issued ([198]). He may nevertheless begin to execute it by anticipation, (1) if he is a Papal legate whose word the bishop is willing to accept; or (2) if the delegator is present to confirm the fact that it has issued; or (3) if the parties have already contested suit ([199]).

36. A delegate cannot deal with matters not named in his commission unless they are included in it by implication ([200]), nor may he cite the parties outside the district for which he is deputed to act ([201]), but within it he can compel them to appear ([202]). He can also restrain third parties who would hinder the exercise of his jurisdiction ([203]); can hear and decide objections raised to his jurisdiction ([204]); absolve from a sentence of excommunication passed in the cause with which he is dealing, in order to give either party a *locus standi* in judgment ([205]); can reinstate one dispossessed if the defendant contumaciously fails to appear ([206]); and a Papal legate can either execute his own sentence, provided he does so within a year ([207]), or can

---

([197]). Alexander III. in Decret. Lib. II. Tit. XXVIII. c. 12.
([198]). Innocent III. in Decret. Lib. I. Tit. XXIX. c. 31.
([199]). Lucius III. *Ibid.* c. 19; Craisson, § 5580.
([200]). Alexander III. in Decret. Lib. I. Tit. XXIX. c. 5: So soon as the cause is simply delegated to him he is competent to compel the parties to appear, and to visit the contumacious with ecclesiastical severity, even though his commission does not contain those words, . . . because by the fact that the cause is committed to him he receives full authority over all matters which are known to be pertinent to the cause.
([201]). Boniface VIII. in Sext. Lib. I. Tit. III. c. 11.
([202]). Alexander III. in Decret. Lib. I. Tit. XXIX. c. 4.
([203]). Alexander III. to Bishop of London in Decret. Lib. I. Tit. XXIX. c. 1 and 11; Alexander IV. in Sext. Lib. I. Tit. XIV. c. 2; Innocent IV. *Ibid.* c. 1.
([204]). Alexander IV. to Archbishop of Canterbury in Decret. Lib. I. Tit. III. c. 2. Schmaltzgrueber ap. Bouix de Jud. I. 157.
([205]). Innocent III. *Ibid.* c. 36; Craisson, § 5385.
([206]). Alexander III. in Decret. Lib. I. Tit. XXIX. c. 10.
([207]). Alexander III. to Bishop of Norwich in Decret. Lib. I. Tit. XXIX. c. 7; Innocent III. *Ibid.* c. 26.

commit it to the bishop([208]), or even to the secular power for execution ([209]).

37. A delegate's commission terminates (1) by his own death or the death of his co-delegate if the commission is to them in common (*simpliciter*) ([210]), or by the efflux of the time-limit named in the commission ([211]); (2) by the death of his principal, unless he has already taken some step whereby his own jurisdiction is perpetuated ([212]); (3) by the revocation of his commission at any time if it is a commission from a principal, or if from a delegate before the sub-delegate has begun to act upon it ([213]); (4) by the giving of sentence and ordering it for execution ([214]), or the termination of the controversy in some other way; and (5) by the delegate's interlocutory decision that he has no jurisdiction, or that he cannot exercise it because he is suspect ([215]), or by his committing the entirety to a surrogate ([216]). The appeal from a sub-delegate does not lie to the delegate but to the principal, if the delegation has been of the whole cause ([217]). It is otherwise if the delegation has been of a part only ([218]).

([208]). Alexander III. *Ibid.* c. 11; Craisson, § 5387.
([209]). Concil. Pav. A.D. 877, ap. Gratian Caus. XXIII. Qu. v. c. 26: Let the administrators of secular dignities, ... whenever approached by bishops and ecclesiastical persons, give heed to their complaints, and as necessity requires diligently examine them and set them right.
([210]). Gregory IX. in Decret. Lib. I. Tit. XXIX. c. 42.
([211]). Alexander III. *Ibid.* c. 4; Innocent III. *Ibid.* c. 24.
([212]). Boniface VIII. in Sext. Lib. I. Tit. XIV. c. 6.
([213]). Lucius III. to Archbishop of Canterbury in Decret. Lib. I. Tit. XXIX. c. 19; Urban III. *Ibid.* c. 20; Innocent III. *Ibid.* c. 30.
([214]). Alexander III. *Ibid.* c. 9.
([215]). Boniface VIII. in Sext. l. c. c. 5.
([216]). Innocent III. A.D. 1208, in Decret. Lib. II. Tit. XX. c. 40, requires him to hand his office over to a surrogate in case he has to give evidence in the cause.
([217]). Innocent III. to Archbishop of Canterbury in Decret. Lib. I. Tit. XXIX. c. 27, § 2; Boniface VIII. in Sext. l. c. c. 3.
([218]). Alexander III. *Ibid.* c. 18; Boniface VIII. in Sext. l. c. c. 14.

Plaintiffs and Defendants.

38. Four persons are necessary to constitute a court in every matter of controversy, viz., a lawful judge, a qualified plaintiff or accuser, a defendant, and proper witnesses ([219]). Of these the three former are accounted principals, witnesses being only necessary in judgment as accessories ([220]). The person who introduces a controversy in synod or audience, or sets judicial procedure in motion, is termed the plaintiff (*actor*) in a civil cause, in a criminal cause the accuser or promoter of the judge's office. He who is convened in audience, or against whom judicial procedure is set in motion, is termed the defendant (*reus*) in a civil cause ([221]), in a criminal cause the accused.

39. Not all persons are capable of being plaintiffs or defendants. Some are altogether disqualified in any and every cause; others are disqualified only in a criminal cause. Those who are altogether disqualified are (1) infants, madmen or lunatics; (2) children under fourteen, unless they appear by a curator or next friend ([222]); and (3) those who have taken a vow of religion, except to make charges against their own abbot ([223]).

---

(219). Isidor. Etym. XVIII. 15 in Decret. Lib. v. Tit. XL. c. 10: In every matter of controversy these persons are necessary—a judge, an accuser, a defendant, and three witnesses. Pseudo-Isidor. ap. Gratian Caus. IV. Qu. IV. c. 1; Law's Forms, 61. *Id.* p. 63, observes that sometimes there may be proceedings without a plaintiff, as when a judge of mere office makes inquisition of executors touching a will; or without a defendant, as when a judge makes inquisition of notorious crimes, and denounces, without knowing, who is guilty of them. Eugenius in Decret. Lib. v. Tit. L. c. 9: The manifest appearance of a completed crime requires not the clamour of an accuser. These are, however, properly extra-judicial proceedings. There is no discussion in judgment.

(220). Ayliffe 147.

(221). Isidor. l. c. and Lib. II. Tit. XIX.: *Actor* is so called *ab agendo*, because he acts by invoking the judge; *reus a re* from the matter or thing for the sake of which he is convened.

(222). Boniface VIII. in Sext. Lib. II. Tit. I. c. 3.

(223). Alexander III. to Bishop of Worcester in Decret. Lib. v. Tit. L c. 11: Monks, because they are under obedience and subjection to the abbot, are not to be repelled from accusing him. Nay, more, since they have no

Women also (4) may not be accusers in criminal causes ([224]), except to obtain redress for their own wrongs; nor (5) persons excommunicate, unless they are first absolved by the judge ([225]).

40. No one can be compelled to act as plaintiff or accuser against his will unless (1) he has promoted the judge's office, when in the interest of the accused he may be compelled to go on; or (2) unless he has slandered another, when he can be compelled to prove his words; or (3) unless he is appointed tutor, curator, or proctor, and his client's interest requires him to act. But every one who is cited can be compelled to appear as defendant, or in default the cause may be adjudicated upon as though he were present ([226]). Personal appearance is, however, not necessary to avoid contumacy. It is sufficient to appear by a proctor, but not in a criminal cause until after the matter has been judicially contested ([227]).

property of their own, necessary expenses must be allowed them from the property of the monastery.

([224]). Boniface VIII. in Sext. L c. 2.

([225]). One who is excommunicate and denounced as such may not be plaintiff or accuser, according to Gregory IX. in Decret. Lib. II. Tit. XXV. c. 12, unless it be to prove that his excommunication is *ipso jure* a nullity, not merely that it is unjust, according to Bouix de Judic. I. 174. One who is not denounced may be a plaintiff, but exception may be taken to him by the defendant, when the judge must determine whether to receive him or not. In *Mastin* v. *Escott*, 2 Curt. 692, 4 Moore P.C. 104; 1 Notes of cases 552, and 3 Notes of cases 387, the Privy Council allowed one excommunicate by sentence to be a promoter in a criminal cause. Excommunicates who are denounced can, however, be defendants according to Alexander III. in Decret. Lib. II. Tit. I. c. 7. Conf. Lib. I. Tit. XXVIII. c. 15.

([226]). Apost. Can. 74: If the accused refuses to appear, let the synod pass what sentence they please against him, that he may not appear to gain advantage by avoiding their judgment.

([227]). Pseudo-Isidor. quoting the rule of Civil Law ap Gratian Caus. II. Qu. VI. c. 40: If an appeal is made in a capital cause, it may not be conducted by proctors but in person. *Ibid.* Qu. VIII. c. 5: Let no accuser's evidence be received in writing, but from his own lips, in presence of the accused, because no absent person can either accuse or be accused. Caus. V. Qu. III. c. 2 & 3. Innocent III. in Decret. Lib. V. Tit. I. c. 15: We cannot receive the proctors [of the accused] in a criminal cause. *Id. Ibid.* Lib. I.

Proctors and Advocates.

41. A proctor ([228]), formerly called an answerable person (*responsalis*) ([229]), is one who stands in the place of his principal, having been properly appointed by the principal to act for him ([230]). A proctor may be either (1) general ([231]) or (2) special ([232]); but in either case he must be properly appointed, or he cannot be admitted in the mandatory's name ([233]). A general proctor can undertake and transact all matters (*negotia*), both judicial and extra-judicial, except those which require a special mandate. A special proctor can only represent his principal in the particular business he is empowered to transact, and such is

Tit. xxxviii. c. 5, says that the accuser cannot appear by proctor in a criminal cause, because he has to make an inscription. Ayliffe 424 observes that the defendant must appear personally to answer for a crime, because an absent person cannot be punished corporally; but if the proceedings are only criminal in form, the object being to get him to pay money, he may appear by a proctor.

(228). See Decret. Lib. I. Tit. xxxviii. and Sext. Lib. I. Tit. xix. *de Procuratoribus*. In the Report of the Ecclesiastical Commissioners, 1832, it is said: "Proctors in the ecclesiastical and Admiralty courts discharge duties similar to those of solicitors and attorneys in other courts." According to 2 Dom. 583, Proctors are officers established to represent in judgment the parties who empower them (by warrant under their hands called a *proxy*) to appear for them. 33 & 34 Vict. c. 27 imposes a stamp duty of £25 on admission to office. 53 Geo. III. c. 127 forbids proctors to allow their names to be used by unqualified persons. 10 Geo. IV. c. 7, sec. 16, forbids Roman Catholics from acting as proctors. 33 & 34 Vict. c. 28, sec. 20, enables attorneys or solicitors "to perform all such acts as appertain solely to the office of a proctor in any ecclesiastical court other than the provincial courts of the Archbishops of Canterbury and of York, and the diocesan court of the Bishop of London.

(229). Gregory ap. Gratian Caus. v. Qu. l. c. 2; Alexander III. in Decret. Lib. II. Tit. xxviii. c. 7, and Tit. xiii. c. 7; Innocent III. A.D. 1203, *Ibid.* Lib. I. Tit. vi. c. 22, and Lib. v. Tit. III. c. 12, and Lib. II. Tit. xx. c. 34.

(230). Cicero pro A. Caecina c. 20 calls him *alieni juris vicarius*.

(231). Boniface VIII. in Sext. Decr. Lib. I. Tit. xix. c. 5.

(232). Boniface VIII. *Ibid.* c. 9 states that a special proxy is necessary for entering into a marriage-contract; Lynd. 273 says for resigning a benefice. Lynd. 107.

(233). Decret. Lib. I. Tit. xxxviii. c. 1.

a judicial proctor. Every proctor is strictly bound by the terms of his mandate ([234]), whether it be simple or plenary. If he acts contrary thereto in a judicial proceeding, the matter may be appealed against, even after a year ([235]).

42. Proctors may also be divided into (1) judicial and (2) extra-judicial proctors ([236]). A judicial proctor is one who represents another judicially in a suit (*ad lites*), an extra-judicial proctor one who represents him in business matters (*ad negotia*). A business proctor may make answer in court for his principal, except in a case requiring a special mandate ([237]); but he cannot take an oath, or compound or withdraw from a suit on his behalf, unless he has been entrusted with full administration of effects and causes ([238]).

43. A judicial proctor may be appointed either (1) before the judge in court (*apud acta curiae*), or alternatively (2) by an instrument called a mandate or proxy ([239]), which requires to be attested before two witnesses ([240]) and to be either drawn or executed before a notary or authentic person ([241]). It must also be, at least tacitly, accepted by the person named ([242]). Canons and clergy,

---

([234]). Innocent III. to the bishop, dean, and precentor of Hereford in Decret. Lib. II. Tit. xxviii. c. 48. Concil. Vien. in Sext. Lib. I. Tit. x. c. 3; Clem. Lib. I. Tit. x.; Ayliffe 426.

([235]). Honorius III. in Decret. Lib. II. Tit. xxviii. c. 69.

([236]). Boniface VIII. in Sext. Lib. I. Tit. x. c. 5; Ayliffe 150, 421.

([237]). Boniface VIII. *Ibid.*

([238]). Boniface VIII. *Ibid.* c. 4.

([239]). Innocent III. in Decret. Lib. I. Tit. xxviii. c. 4; Const. 25 Otho, A.D. 1237. Can. 129, A.D. 1603: None shall procure in any cause whatsoever unless he be thereunto constituted and appointed by the party himself, either before the judge and by act of court, or unless in the beginning of the suit he be by a true and sufficient proxy thereunto warranted and enabled. We call that proxy sufficient which is strengthened and confirmed by some authentical seal, the party's approbation, or at least his ratification therewithal concurring. Ayliffe 421; Law's Forms 32 and 122.

([240]). Gregory IX. in Decret. Lib. I. Tit. xxxviii. c. 1; Law's Forms 32.

([241]). Law's Forms 32, 101.

([242]). Boniface VIII. in Sext. Lib. I. Tit. xL. c. 7; Concil. Vien. A.D. 1311, in Clem. Lib. I. Tit. x. c. 1 says that a proctor who receives a proxy without protestation can be compelled to defend the client.

however, do not require such an authority to appear for their own Churches (243).

44. As the proctor is bound by the terms of his mandate, so on the other hand the mandatory is bound by the acts of his proctor (244), unless indeed the mandate was obtained by undue influence (245). If therefore the proctor omits anything which the mandatory ought to have done, the latter is thereby prejudiced (246); but if he omits to do anything which as proctor he ought to have done, the mandatory, although still bound by the consequences, has a remedy against the proctor if the negligence was his fault. Except in a criminal case, a proctor may appoint a substitute before contestation of suit with the mandatory's sanction (247); and in all causes he may do so of his own authority after contestation (248). The substitute appointed by the proctor ceases to hold office if the proctor who appointed him dies, whereas the substitute appointed by the mandatory continues.

45. Several proctors may be constituted simultaneously, either in common (*simpliciter*) or jointly (*in solidum*). If appointed to act in common, all must concur, except in cases of election, postulation, provision, and other ecclesiastical matters requiring prompt decision, when the judge can call upon the one who is best qualified to go through with the matter (249). If they are constituted jointly, either can act without the other,

---

(243). Syn. Rom. A.D. 502, in Decret. Lib. III. Tit. XIII. c. 6; Gregory IX. *Ibid.* Lib. II. Tit. XIII. c. 1.

(244). Gregory IX. in Decret. Lib. I. Tit. XXXVIII. c. 13.

(245). Gregory IX. *Ibid.* c. 10.

(246). Alexander III. to Bishop of Durham, Lib. I. Tit. XXXVI. c. 3, says that the chapter is not bound by a composition effected by the abbot or prior as proctor on its behalf.

(247). Boniface VIII. in Sext. Lib. I. Tit. XL. c. 1. It is, however, stated in Law's Forms, 113, to be doubtful whether in a cause of correction a voluntary promoter can appoint a judicial proctor before contestation of suit. The reason seems to be because the accused may submit to summary correction, and the matter never come into judgment.

(248). Ayliffe 422.

(249). Boniface VIII. in Sext. Lib. I. Tit. X. c. 6, § 2.

but preference is given to him who acts first (²⁵⁰), and after
contestation of suit the other cannot intermeddle, because the
first one has become lord of the suit. The appointment of a
fresh proctor by a subsequent instrument acts as a revocation
of any former mandate (²⁵¹). A principal is not responsible,
however, for his proctor's wrong-doing (²⁵²).

46. Any person, either clerk or layman (²⁵³), may be constituted a proctor, except those who are expressly forbidden to
act as such, viz. (1) excommunicates (²⁵⁴) who cannot even
appear on their own account (²⁵⁵); (2) persons under the age of
twenty-five (²⁵⁶); (3) infamous persons, *i.e.*, persons found guilty
of crime on impeachment (²⁵⁷); (4) women, because of the
modesty of their sex (²⁵⁸); (5) soldiers, because of their military
exercises and duties (²⁵⁹); (6) all who occupy such a high station
in life that their appearance would prejudice the court against
the adverse party (²⁶⁰); (7) those who buy up the interest in
lawsuits, called *litium redemptores* (²⁶¹); and (8) by English
law justices of the peace (²⁶²). Monks and regular canons may
not act, except on behalf of their own monasteries (²⁶³), or other-

---

(250). Gregory IX. in Decret. Lib. I. Tit. XXXVIII. c. 14.
(251). Gregory IX. *Ibid.*
(252). Lynd. 115.
(253). Boniface VIII. in Sext. Lib. I. Tit. X. c. 1.
(254). Concil. Lat. IV. A.D. 1215, Can. 3 in Decret. Lib. V. Tit. VII. c. 13,
§ 5; Innocent III. *Ibid.* Lib. II. Tit. XIX. c. 7; Concil. Lugdun. II. A.D.
1274, in Sext. Lib. II. Tit. XII. c. 1.
(255). Alexander III. in Decret. Lib. II. Tit. I. c. 7.
(256). Boniface VIII. in Sext. Lib. I. Tit. X. c. 5: Although any one may
be lawfully appointed a business proctor after he is seventeen, yet no one
may be appointed a judicial proctor who is not over twenty-five.
(257). Gratian Caus. III. Qu. VII. c. 1 and 2.
(258). *Ibid.*
(259). Law's Forms, p. 29.
(260). Ayliffe 423, 55.
(261). Law's Forms, p. 29.
(262). Stat. 5 Geo. II. c. 18, sec. 2.
(263). Gregory in Decret. Lib. I. Tit. XXXIX. c. 1; Concil. Turon. A.D.
1163; *Ibid.* Lib. III. Tit. L. c. 3; Concil. Vien. A.D. 1311, in Clem. Lib. I.
Tit. X. c. 3.

wise for defendants, and then not without a dispensation ([264]); nor bishops and presbyters ([265]), except on behalf of their Churches, or of widows, orphans, and such as have no other helper ([266]); but clergy in minor orders may ([267]), unless either (1) they hold an ecclesiastical benefice, or (2) are asked to appear against their own Churches, or (3) if it is a cause which may involve bloodshed.

47. Proctors may be constituted in all judicial causes, not excepting criminal causes provided they are prosecuted in civil form ([268]), but they cannot appear for either plaintiff or defendant in a criminal suit voluntarily promoted ([269]) until after contestation of suit. A plaintiff or defendant may either appear in person or employ a proctor in his discretion, but corporate bodies can only appear in judgment by a special kind of proctor, called a syndic ([270]) or steward

(264). Gelasius, A.D. 494, ap. Gratian Caus. XVI. Qu. 1. c. 20.

(265). Concil. Carthag. III. A.D. 397, Can. 15 : That neither bishops, presbyters, deacons, nor clergy act as proctors [sc., before secular judges]. Eugenius III. in Decret. Lib. III. Tit. L. c. 2 ; Concil. Lat. III. A.D. 1179. Can. 12, *Ibid.* c. 4, and Lib. I. Tit. XXXVII. c. 1.

(266). Concil. Mogunt A.D. 813, in Decret. Lib. III. Tit. L. c. 1 ; Concil. Lat. III. A.D. 1179, Can. 12 ; *Ibid.* Lib. I. Tit. XXXIX. c. 1. It must be remembered that in the Roman Empire, Justinian (see Cod. Justin. Lib. I. Tit. IV. de Episcopali Audientia) had entrusted to bishops the care of prisoners, minors, insane persons, foundlings, stolen children, and oppressed women.

(267). Gregory IX. in Decret. Lib. I. Tit. XXXVII. c. 3 ; Craisson, § 5622.

(268). Innocent III. A.D. 1206, in Decret. Lib. I. Tit. XXXVIII. c. 5, says that although a man who charges his wife with adultery before a secular judge, in order that she may receive vindictive punishment, must appear in person, yet if he makes the same charge before a spiritual judge, in order that separation from her may be decreed, he may appear by a proctor, because it is not a criminal suit, but partakes of the nature of both (*mixta inter civilem et criminalem*). *Id. Ibid.* Lib. V. Tit. I. c. 16, A.D. 1202, says that he may appear by a proctor in a case of denunciation, because denunciation is undertaken for correction, not for vengeance. Concil. Lugdun. A.D. 1245, in Sext. Lib. II. Tit. I. c. 1 ; Ayliffe 424.

(269). Pseudo-Isidor. ap. Gratian Caus. V. Qu. III. c. 2. See notes 268 and 247. Craisson, § 5626 ; Ayliffe 254.

(270). Gregory in Decret. Lib. I. Tit. XXXIX. c. 1 ; Innocent III. *Ibid.*

(*oeconomus*) ([271]), elected by the whole body, who when elected is deemed, like a vicar-capitular, to hold a public office. He, therefore, can alone take the oath against vexatious litigation on their behalf, whereas, in other cases, the oath may be tendered indiscriminately to either the proctor or the mandatory ([272]). The syndic of a town is generally called *actor universitatis* ([273]).

48. After the proctor has become master of the suit (*dominus litis*) by contestation ([274]), he can substitute another in his place ([275]), and his proxy can then only be withdrawn for some good cause ([276]), by informing the judge and his opponent of the change ([277]). All steps, nevertheless, taken in the cause until the judge becomes aware of the revocation hold good ([278]). A proctor's office may be determined (1) before contestation of suit by mutual agreement, the revocation of the mandate, the substitution of another proctor ([279]), or the death of the mandatory ([280]); (2) after contestation of suit by the conclusion of the cause or by appeal ([281]), by the death of the proctor, or in a

Lib. I. Tit. XLI. c. 2, and Tit. XXXVIII. c. 7; Gregory IX. *Ibid.* c. 15; Law's Forms, pp. 95, 190, 191.

(271). Eugenius III. in Decret. Lib. II. Tit. VII. c. 4.

(272). *Id. Ibid.* c. 3.

(273). Ayliffe 428.

(274). Boniface VIII. in Sext Lib. I. Tit. X. c. 2; Ayliffe 421; Law's Forms 28, 82, 160.

(275). *Id. Ibid.* c. 1; Law's Forms 35.

(276). *Id. Ibid.* c. 2.

(277). Innocent III. A.D. 1206, in Decret. Lib. I. Tit. XXXVIII. c. 4.

(278). Gregory IX. *Ibid.* c. 13: If a proctor's mandate is revoked after contestation of suit, and this has been done unbeknown to the judge or the opposite party, the judgment which the reputed proctor has subsequently obtained shall hold good.

(279). Clemens III. *Ibid.* c. 3; Innocent III. *Ibid.* c. 4; Gregory IX. *Ibid.* c. 16; Boniface VIII. in Sext. Lib. I. Tit. XIX. c. 2; Ayliffe 428; Law's Forms 36.

(280). By Roman law the death of the mandatory did not terminate the proctor's power to carry on the suit if it had been contested. Concil. Vien. A.D. 1311, in Clem. Lib. I. Tit. X. c. 4, altered the law. Law's Forms 37.

(281). Law's Forms, p. 37; but *Id.* p. 39 states that his proctorship is only placed in abeyance by an interlocutory appeal.

personal action of the mandatory ([282]), or by the mandatory intervening and conducting his own cause in person ([283]), unless he is careful to protest that his intervention is without prejudice to his proctor's proxy ([284]).

49. A proctor differs from a curator or next friend ([285]), because a curator is appointed by the court, and a proctor is constituted by the suitor. He differs also from an advocate or patron, because he conducts a case, whereas an advocate only advises upon it, and speaks to the merits of it in court ([286]). Hence a proctor can take an oath on behalf of his client ([287]), whereas an advocate cannot. Any person may, moreover, act as proctor, but an advocate must be a person learned in the canon and civil law ([288]); and since no one except a bishop or abbot may by English rule speak in a synodical court without the metropolitan's permission ([289]), an advocate can only be admitted to practice in the provincial court by license from him, or by the bishop's license in a diocesan court ([290]).

50. An advocate, sometimes called a defensor ([291]) or

(282). Law's Forms, p. 39.
(283). Boniface VIII. in Sext. Lib. I. Tit. XIX. c. 8.
(284). *Id. Ibid.* Law's Forms, p. 243.
(285). Gratian Caus. III. Qu. VII. c. 2.
(286). A person is said to be client to an advocate, but master and mandator to a proctor.
(287). Eugenius III. in Decret. Lib. II. Tit. XX. c. 3.
(288). According to the Report of the Ecclesiastical Commissioners, 1832: "No person can be admitted a member, or allowed to practise as an advocate in the courts at Doctors' Commons, without having first taken the degree of Doctor of Laws in one of the English Universities." The Stat. 3 and 4 Vict. c. 86, § 7, requires that in criminal proceedings instituted against a clergyman the articles drawn up against him must be signed by an advocate practising in Doctors' Commons. But the College of Advocates having been abolished in 1857, the duties of advocate are now usually discharged by barristers. Ayliffe 53.
(289). Concil. London A.D. 1075, Can. 5. See Ecclesiastical Courts Commission, 1883, vol. II. p. 371. Craisson, § 5644, states that this is a local and not a general rule.
(290). Const. 25 Othobon, A.D. 1268: Let no advocate be allowed to undertake a cause unless he first show the letters of the diocesan.
(291). Ayliffe 421.

Spiritual Courts. 231

patron (^{292}), is a person learned in the civil and canon law, who gives advice upon a controversy out of court, and speaks to its merits in judgment. His duties are fourfold: (1) to bring sufficient knowledge to bear upon the cause; (2) not to prevent or delay justice by suggesting what is false or suppressing what is true (^{293}), and therefore not to undertake a cause which he knows to be bad, though he may always defend the accused in a criminal cause (^{294}); (3) not to disclose his client's affairs to his opponent (^{295}); and (4) not to take more than a fair fee for his assistance (^{296}).

51. No person may act as advocate until he is seventeen years of age (^{297}), and has been first a diligent hearer of the civil and canon law for three years at least (^{298}), or five years if he proposes to practise in the provincial court (^{299}). This he may be required to prove by his own corporal oath, if the same does not appear either by a testimonial from the professor under whom he has studied, or else by evidence of the fact, *i.e.*, by submitting to examination. In this country a doctor's degree is, however, usually considered sufficient. He must also neither be deaf nor blind (^{300}). A woman cannot act as advocate except on her own behalf or on behalf of her infant child (^{301}). Persons who are infamous, or branded with any note of infamy,

---

(292). Gratian Caus. III. Qu. VII. c. 2 ; Const. 29 Otho, A.D. 1237 ; Law's Forms 24.

(293). Const. 29 Otho, A.D. 1237, requires an advocate to make oath that in the causes which he undertakes he will perform the part of a faithful patron. Const. 26 Othobon, A.D. 1268 ; Law's Forms 24, 27.

(294). Liguori Lib. IV. n. 223 says, because even a guilty man need not be publicly punished unless he can be convicted.

(295). Const. 29 Otho, A.D. 1237.

(296). Law's Forms 26, 27 ; Gregory in Decret. Lib. I. Tit. XXXIX. c. 1 ; Engenius, *Ibid.* Lib. II. Tit. XX. c. 4, speak of the fixed salary of a syndic or oeconomus.

(297). Craisson, § 5643; Cardinal Soglia Inst. Jur. Priv. § 207, puts the minimum age at seventeen. Law's Forms 25.

(298). Const. 25 Peckham, A.D. 1281 ; Law's Forms 24.

(299). Lynd. 74, 76 ; Law's Forms 23.

(300). Law's Forms 25.

(301). Gregory IX. in Decret. Lib. II. Tit. XXVIII. c. 67.

or condemned of calumny in any public court of judicature, and persons convicted of any capital crime, are *ipso jure* forbidden to be advocates either for themselves or others ([302]). The same disqualification applies to those who are excommunicated, who can only themselves appear by deputy ([303]), and to clergy in a cause of blood ([304]). Bishops, presbyters, and monks may act for their own Churches or for brother-clergy in the cases in which they might act as proctors, but not otherwise ([305]); and even clergy in minor orders are forbidden to plead before a temporal judge unless they are either prosecuting their own causes or that of their Churches, or acting for those who are too poor to have other assistance ([306]).

(302). 3 Jac. c. 5, § 8, A.D. 1605; Law's Forms 25.
(303). Alexander IV. in Sext. Lib. V. Tit. XI. c. 8; Alexander III. in Decret. Lib. II. Tit. I. c. 7.
(304). Gratian Caus. XXIII. Qu. VIII. c. 30.
(305). Can. 30 Elfric, A.D. 957: Let no priest plead causes.
(306). Law's Forms 25.

VII.

CANONICAL PROCEDURE.

Spiritual Causes.

1. All proceedings in disciplinary matters, and all disputes, when they are propounded for settlement by judicial process, are termed causes (¹), and may be broadly divided into two classes — (1) criminal and (2) civil (²). Criminal causes are those concerned with the administration of discipline, civil causes with the settlement of disputes. Some causes, again, concern spiritual matters, and others temporal matters. They may therefore be crossly divided into (1) spiritual causes and (2) temporal causes. Those which partake of the nature of both are termed (3) mixed causes (³).

2. Any excess against faith, discipline, or morals, which calls for accusation and punishment, is in view of the Church a crime, and any proceeding primarily instituted to punish such excess is a criminal cause. Any dispute between Christians as to the validity of an ecclesiastical act, or as to the rights or duties of one person towards another, is termed a civil cause (⁴).

3. Civil causes include (⁵) — (1) causes merely civil, (2) civil causes which involve private crime, and (3) civil causes which involve public crime. Criminal causes include (1) causes merely criminal, and (2) those called popular causes, in which crime concerns the public interest of the Church, such as benefice causes. Nearly all civil causes are now dealt with by secular courts, excepting those relating to clerical stipends and

---

(1). Ayliffe 147. See *Acts in Judgment*, § 1.
(2). Lynd. 73.
(3). Eccles. Courts Commission, 1883, vol. II. 320, note A.
(4). Lynd. 162   Eccles. Courts Commission, 1883, vol. II. 218.
(5). Lynd. 73.

faculty seats. Popular causes are the only ones which by recent legislation are allowed in this country to be instituted for the sake of the penalty ([6]); all others are only permitted to be conducted in a spiritual court for the soul's health ([7]).

4. A spiritual cause is one concerned with matters merely spiritual, such as faith, the sacraments, divine worship, whether the procedure be civil or criminal. A mixed cause is one concerning a spiritual matter which carries with it temporal rights ([8]), or one which is partly spiritual, partly temporal. A temporal cause is one concerning a temporal matter ([9]). It is not always easy to distinguish between spiritual and mixed causes in practice, since nearly every spiritual act has some effect upon temporal position in the circumstances of modern life ([10]).

5. A temporal cause does not cease to be temporal although spiritual accidents may be annexed thereto. Thus the right of advowson or presentation to a foundation-endowment is a matter of temporal right, although the exercise of it bestows upon the presentee a right to be admitted to a spiritual office. On the other hand, although temporal courts may decide who is entitled to exercise the right of presentation, it is for the spiritual judge to determine whether the right has been exercised in a manner agreeable to the spiritual law, or, as it is

---

([6]). Thus, although the statute 27 Geo. III. c. 44 forbad any suit to be brought in an ecclesiastical court for incontinence after eight months had elapsed, for the soul's health, yet it was ruled by the House of Lords that this did not prevent the ordinary from purging the Church of an incontinent clerk within two years, or by 55 and 56 Vict. c. 32, within five years.

([7]). 13 Ed. I. St. IV. c. 1, A.D. 1285.

([8]). Innocent III. in Decret. Lib. I. Tit. XXXVIII. c. 5.

([9]). Phillipps Ch. IX. §. 10, p. 397, defines a spiritual cause as one the object of which is principally spiritual.

([10]). Benedict XIV. de Syn. Dioec. Lib. IX. c. 9, no. 2 and 12; Suarez de Leg. Lib. IV. c. 11, no. 9; Craisson, § 264. A very different division is given by the Attorney-General of the Isle of Man in Eccles. Courts Commission, 1883, vol. II. p. 329.

said, in favour of a fit person ([11]). Causes concerning covenant, quasi or constructive covenant usually called trust, trespass, and quasi or constructive trespass ([12]), although now regarded as exclusively temporal causes, were before the twelfth century ([13]) treated as spiritual causes, because each of them involved a breach of faith; and they are still spiritual causes in the inner forum.

6. According to the custom of the civil law, causes may be otherwise divided into (1) possessory causes, *i.e.*, causes which concern possession, and (2) proprietory causes, *i.e.*, causes which concern property rights ([14]); into (1) real causes, *i.e.*, causes which have to do with things, and (2) personal causes, which have to do with persons ([15]); or, again, into (1) simple causes, in which one is plaintiff and the other defendant, and (2) double

([11]). 9 Ed. II. St. I. c. 13, A.D. 1315, acknowledges that the bishop may refuse admission on canonical grounds, of which he is the judge, but he cannot refuse admission on the ground that the presentor has not the patronage.

([12]). Quasi-covenant is when a man takes care of the goods of an absent friend, or of the estate of a minor, in which case, though there is no real agreement, the law supposes one. Quasi-trespass (delictum or maleficium) is when a man hires or borrows a horse, and rides it further or keeps it longer than he engaged to do. These four cases are mentioned in Const. 1 Boniface, A.D. 1261; Lynd. 162 and 316.

([13]). Const. 5 Clarendon, A.D. 1164, requires persons to be absolved on giving security that they would stand to the judgment of the Church. If the Church afterwards proceeded to inquire into matters held to be of temporal cognisance, prohibition issued. Innocent III. in Decret. Lib. II. Tit. I. c. 13. See *Spiritual Courts*, note 90, and Eccles. Courts Commission Report, 1883, p. XXII.

([14]). Gregory I. in Decret. Lib. II. Tit. XII. c. 1 calls them *causae possessionis et proprietatis*. Innocent III. *Ibid.* c. 3, *judicium possessorium et petitorium*. Lynd. 146 distinguishes possession of a benefice from property in a benefice. Benedict XIV. de Syn. Dioc. Lib. IX. Tit. 9, § 7, says, by custom secular courts may determine possessory, and spiritual courts proprietory rights in benefice cases. Devoti Lib. III. Tit. II. § 6; Law's Forms 41.

([15]). Ayliffe 152 : In a personal action the proximate cause is the obligation, and the remote cause is the contract. . . . In a real action the proximate cause is the ownership, and the remote cause is the fact whereby such ownership is caused. Devoti Lib. III. Tit. II. § 8.

causes, in which the defendant makes a counter-claim, so that each party is at once plaintiff and defendant ([16]).

Various Modes of Procedure.

7. A cause may be introduced for judicial settlement in one of four different ways, viz. (1) by action, (2) by accusation, (3) by denunciation, or (4) by inquisition ([17]). The first of these actions applies to civil matters, and is the pursuing in a court of competent jurisdiction whatever any one supposes to be properly his due ([18]). It is therefore said to be taken at the instance of a party. The three others are modes of proceeding to enforce the discipline of the Church; and since correction or punishment is the judge's office, in them the judge's office is said to be brought into exercise or promoted ([19]). Actions are accordingly called causes of *instance;* proceedings by accusation, denunciation, or inquisition causes of *office* ([20]). To these modes of procedure a fifth is sometimes added, viz., exception; but this is only a privileged form of accusation allowed to a defendant for self-protection in judgment ([21]).

8. Causes of office may again be instituted in one of two ways, viz., either (1) by a prelate or officer of the Church of his own motion to enforce discipline, when they are said to be instituted by the *mere office* of the judge, or as the civilians say, by the *noble* office of the judge; or (2) at the instance of a private person, when they are said to be instituted by the

---

([16]). Devoti Lib. III. Tit. II. § 8, whence the term *Duplex querela* is applied to an action to obtain institution to a benefice.

([17]). Innocent III. A.D. 1199, in Decret. Lib. v. Tit. III. c. 31; Concil. Lat. IV. A.D. 1215, Can. 8, *Ibid.* Tit. I. c. 24; Ayliffe 152.

([18]). Law's Forms 41; Ayliffe 152, 398.

([19]). *Ibid.* p. 356; Ecclesiastical Courts Commission, 1883, p. 182, and vol. II. 207.

([20]). Innocent III. l. c. and Concil. Lat. IV. A.D. 1215, Can. 8, mention these three modes. Ayliffe 22, 153, 210; Law's Forms 356.

([21]). Innocent III. A.D. 1202, in Decret. Lib. v. Tit. I. c. 16: Crime may be objected [by a private individual] in three ways—[1] by way of presentment, [2] by way of exception, and [3] by accusation. See *Acts in Judgment*, § 29.

Canonical Procedure. 237

judge's *promoted office*, or as the civilians say, by the judge's *mercenary* office (²²). They may also be instituted on account of some breach of discipline or crime actually committed, or on suspicion of some crime which it is in the interest of the Church to clear up and dispose of. As a matter of form the office of the judge is promoted (²³) both when he proceeds of mere office or when he proceeds of his promoted office, at least if the proceeding takes place in judgment; but in a cause of mere office some public person or official takes upon himself to promote his office, who is then called a *necessary promoter*, whereas in a cause of promoted office the private accuser who promotes his office is called a *voluntary promoter* (²⁴).

9. Causes of instance may again be either (1) *summary* or (2) *plenary*. Summary causes are of two kinds, though the distinction has practically become obsolete in this country. Some are summary in the sense that the parties proceed in them without the noise of judicial wrangling (*absque strepitu judicii*), the observance of technical forms (*de simplici*), and the occupation of the seat of judgment by the judge (*de plano*) (²⁵). Such causes might be better called extra-judicial or extraordinary causes, because the judge does not act in them as a judge hearing a discussion in judgment, but as a representative of the Church deciding a matter in synod or audience; and such causes a prelate or judge may hear and decide anywhere. Others in which the judge does act as judge, and occupies the seat of judgment, are really judicial causes, but owing to the absence of the criminal element he is authorised to act with a shortened procedure, as in proving wills and administrations.

(22). Ayliffe, p. 397; Law's Forms 357.

(23). In the former case the cause is described as: The office of the judge against A. B.; in the latter as: The office of the judge promoted by C. D. against A. B.

(24). Law's Forms, p. 112. In France the necessary promoter is called *promotor fiscalis*, because he is paid from the fiscus of the Church, or simply *fiscalis*. See Craisson, § 5767, 5929.

(25). *Ibid.* p. 42; Craisson, § 5486, observes that this distinction which the civil law kept up is now disregarded. § 5882 calls them *judicia extraordinaria*.

In these there is no contestation of suit, nor any term assigned to propound acts or to conclude ([26]), but some forms are nevertheless observed.

10. Plenary causes are those in which all the solemnities of procedure are observed which the wisdom of the Church has devised or adopted as safeguards against fraud, surprise, or injustice in judgment, such as a regular contestation of suit, a proper interval to propound acts, and a term assigned to conclude ([27]). All causes formerly dealt with in the Prerogative Court concerning wills and administrations, causes of contempt, and disciplinary causes, in which the judge proceeds of mere office upon notorious facts, are summary ([28]). All causes of correction, on the other hand, and all temporal causes in which facts are in dispute requiring discussion in judgment, are plenary ([29]). If in a plenary cause any one proceeds sum-

(26). Clemens v. in Clem. Lib. v. Tit. XI. c. 2: It often happens that we commit causes, and in some of them direct that they should be heard *simpliciter* et *de plano ac sine strepitu* et *figura judicii*, as to the meaning of which words opinions differ, and doubts are felt how to proceed. To do away with such doubts, we enjoin by this perpetual constitution that a judge to whom we commit a cause in the manner aforesaid need not necessarily demand a libel nor require contestation of suit; he may also proceed on ferial days because of necessities allowed by law, and strike out all matter causing delays, and shorten the suit as far as possible by refusing the dilatory and frustratory exceptions and appeals of the parties, by checking the wranglings and disputes of advocates and proctors, and the superfluous multitude of witnesses. Still he may not so shorten the suit as to exclude necessary proofs and lawful defences (defensiones). But we do not understand that a commission of this kind dispenses with a citation, or with taking the oath of calumny or malice, or the oath of truth. Since, however, the declaration must accord with the form of the petition, a petition must be made at the very beginning of the suit, either on the part of the plaintiff or of the defendant, if he wishes to make one, either in writing or by word of mouth, and [such petition must] forthwith be inserted in the acts. Concil. Lat. IV. A.D. 1215, in Decret. Lib. v. Tit. I. c. 25, orders this mode of procedure in visitation. Ayliffe 151; Law's Forms 41, 357.

(27). Law's Forms, p. 357.

(28). Law's Forms, p. 42, 55, 59. See *Acts in Judgment*, § 3; Ecclesiastical Courts Commission, 1883, Hist. App. I. 197.

(29). Law's Forms, p. 59, gives a list of plenary causes, viz. (1) all testa-

marily, the proceedings are null and void from the commencement, because it is *ultra vires* for the judge to dispose of them summarily ([30]). If, on the contrary, in summary causes the proceedings are plenary, such proceedings are valid and binding ([31]).

ACTION.

11. Civil actions are of two kinds: (1) those which are brought to ascertain that purely ecclesiastical acts have been properly performed, such as an election, a resignation, a postulation, a vow; and (2) those which are brought to obtain civil redress for a private wrong. The former class of actions may be dealt with in a summary manner ([32]). Not so the latter, unless by consent, since they are either brought by those who are forbidden to litigate in temporal courts, or else are instituted to obtain satisfaction from a wrong-doer by means of spiritual censures. The latter class of actions therefore, although civil in form, involve a criminal element ([33]).

mentary proceedings in solemn form, (2) causes of legacy, (3) defamation, (4), of divorce or separation, (5) of dilapidation, (6) of jactitation of marriage, (7) subtraction of procurations, (8) subtraction of annual pensions, (9) perjury at the instance of parties, (10) simony at the instance of parties, (11) correction by the voluntary promotion of the judge's office, (12) usury at the instance of parties, (13) injection or violence to clergy at the instance of parties, (14) impediments to marriage, (15) seats in Churches; but many of these are no longer the subject-matter of spiritual jurisdiction.

([30]). Innocent III. in Decret. Lib. I. Tit. III. c. 22: The process conducted contrary to the form of our rescript and the order of law we declare to be a nullity (inanem).

([31]). Ayliffe 151; Law's Forms, p. 60.

([32]). Innocent III. in Decret. Lib. II. Tit. VI. c. 5, § 1, says: Lest the Church should suffer injury through a long delay in spirituals and temporals.

([33]). Of such a proceeding Innocent III. in Decret. Lib. v. Tit. I. c. 16 says: Although the action concerns a crime, yet it is not a criminal cause, and may be conducted by a proctor. A civil action was brought before Gregory ap. Gratian Caus. II. Qu. 1. c. 7, petitioning for reinstatement in a benefice on the ground that there was no crime deserving deprivation. See Bartolus in Ayliffe 154.

12. The presence of the criminal element in civil actions instituted before a spiritual judge not only requires (1) plenary procedure to be adopted in all such actions whenever the facts are in dispute, but also (2) greater strictness to be observed in the conduct of them than would be necessary in civil actions before a secular judge, and (3) more perfect proof of the facts. When the procedure is in criminal form this strictness is intensified, since the Church, being before all things the kingdom of righteousness and justice, accounts it preferable that many guilty of private wrong-doing should go unpunished in this world rather than that one who denies his guilt should be punished unjustly ([34]). A private accuser is therefore placed at a great disadvantage, as being one who *prima facie* violates the law of Christian charity by publicly attacking his brother's reputation.

13. As every spiritual cause, civil as well as criminal, has avowedly for its object the peace of the Church and the composing of all differences ([35]), two things are required from every private individual who would set the judge's office in motion in his own interest: (1) he must be able and willing to carry the cause through to a decision, and may be required to find security to that effect ([36]); and (2) he must be prepared to take the so-called oath of calumny ([37]), whereby he pledges himself that he

(34). See *Discipline Generally*, note 52.
(35). Const. 5 Edmund, A.D. 1236.
(36). See *Acts in Judgment*, § 4.
(37). Concil. Tolet. XIII. A.D. 653, Can. 2 ap Gratian Caus. XXII. Qu. l. c. 1 allows oaths to be lawful (1) to make leagues of peace, (2) to cement the good-will of friends, (3) to give credit to the statements of witnesses, and (4) to establish innocence when witnesses are not forthcoming. Law's Forms 282 states that four kinds of oaths are in use in courts Christian: (1) the *oath of truth*, which litigants and witnesses take to answer truly to the best of their knowledge in regard to such things as concern themselves and to the best of their belief as to such things as are not matters of personal knowledge—Const. 17 Boniface, A.D. 1261; (2) the *oath decisory* or *ex officio* or of *purgation*, whereby the principal party either confesses or purges himself. This oath, deprecated by 25 Hen. VIII. c. 14, was abolished by sec. 6 of 13 Car. II. c. 12, so far as the compulsory taking of it is concerned; (3) the *oath of calumny*, or oath against vexatious litigation, a

is not proceeding maliciously or vexatiously ([38]). These things are not required from a public person, because he is presumed to be acting in the interests of the Church.

14. The principal points wherein procedure in a civil cause, if it comes into judgment, differs from the procedure prescribed in a criminal cause are: (1) The libel must specify the remedy which is asked for, whereas in criminal causes this is not necessary; the judge, who is conversant with the law of the Church, will decide as unto law and justice shall appertain. (2) A defendant is not contumacious *ipso facto* by not appearing when cited, but requires to be libelled against or accused of contumacy before he can be punished for it. (3) Peremptory exceptions, such as a plea that the matter has been judicially settled, may be made at once, without waiting for contestation of suit, as in a criminal cause ([39]). (4) The judge may in some cases accept a form of which is the *oath of malice*. This may be administered to both litigants at any stage of the proceedings; and (4) the *oath suppletory*—See Gratian Caus. II. Qu. v.—when the plaintiff has more than half proved his case, and prays that he may be allowed to complete the proof by his own oath. The oath of calumny was required by Justinian's legislation, and is referred to in the law of the Emperor Henry II. A.D. 1047. It is approved of by Honorius IL. in Decret. Lib. II. Tit. VII. c. 1, and Lucius III. to Bishop of Ely and Archdeacon of Norwich, *Ibid.* c. 5. Const. 24 Otho, A.D. 1237, enjoins it. Lynd. 72, 108. As to other oaths, Lynd. 298 mentions the oath of faith against heresy, the oath of canonical obedience, and the oath to pay costs. See *Acts in Judgment*, note 138.

(38). According to Law's Forms 283, in this oath the party states (*a*) that he is persuaded that his cause is just and good, (*b*) that when interrogated he will not deny what he believes to be the truth, (*c*) that he will not knowingly use falsehood in proof, (*d*) that he will not fraudulently seek delay, (*e*) that he has neither given nor offered a bribe to win his case, and (*f*) that he has paid no other fees than those allowed by the canon. These declarations are commemorated in the lines—

> "You this shall swear that this your suit doth seem
> Right just to be, at least in your esteem.
> That you when asked the truth will not deny,
> Nor promise aught; neither that knowingly
> You any false proofs will employ,
> Nor urge delays the other to annoy."

(39). See *Acts in Judgment*, § 30.

single witness or a private instrument as proof, or allow the oath suppletory to be taken by the plaintiff to convert half-proof into full proof. In criminal causes half-proof can only be accepted where it is fortified with other confirmatory evidence or a presumption ([40]). (5) After a conclusion in the cause, witnesses can no longer be admitted.

15. It is a first principle of justice that every cause must be decided in accordance with the laws which were in force at the time the subject-matter of it occurred, and every criminal cause according to those which were in force at the time the instance commenced. A privilege obtained or a law passed during the time that a matter is being judicially contested does not affect the issue retrospectively, unless the law or privilege specially includes pending suits ([41]).

ACCUSATION.

16. Accusation is a mode of proceeding in criminal causes originating extra-judicially, but contemplating also a judicial trial in case the charge is denied, in which one person publicly accuses another of crime, and makes himself responsible, if necessary, to prove the same, not for the sake of his correction, but for public vengeance. It may be made either (1) in synod or (2) in audience; but if the charge is denied, it can only be judicially sustained before a judge.

17. The essential features of procedure by accusation are: (1) It is undertaken for the purpose of public vengeance ([42]); hence the accused must first have been warned ([43]), and without previous warning it ought not to be allowed, except in the case of what are called excepted crimes ([44]), viz., treason,

---

(40). Honorius III. in Decret. Lib. II. Tit. XIX. c. 13; Coelestin. III. *Ibid.* Tit. XX. c. 27; Innocent III. *Ibid.* Lib. III. Tit. XXVII. c. 3.

(41). Ayliffe 152.

(42). Innocent III. in Decret. Lib. v. Tit. I. c. 16: Accusation is instituted for deposition, and denunciation for correction.

(43). Pseudo-Isidor. in Decret. Lib. v. Tit. I. c. 2.

(44). Innocent III. A.D. 1206, *Ibid.* c. 20; Lynd. 73; Craisson, § 5804. See note 112, and *Discipline Generally*, § 6.

simony, sacrilege, homicide, forgery, and embezzlement. (2) It does not apply to cases of notorious crime,—in these the judge proceeds, of mere office, without an accuser ([45])—to cases of heresy, which are established by inquisition, or to matters which are usually dealt with in visitation courts ([46]), but only to crimes known to the accuser which might otherwise have remained unknown. (3) The accuser takes upon himself the onus of proof ([47]); otherwise it would be presentment, not accusation.

18. Procedure by accusation is regarded as specially odious([48]), because it is a breach of charity to expose non-notorious crimes for public punishment ([49]). It is therefore surrounded with several safeguards ([50]): (1) The accuser must be a person lawfully competent to accuse ([51]). (2) The person accused must be one whom he may accuse. (3) An inscription must be solemnly made ([52]). (4) Caution must be given for the judicial

---

(45). Ambros. ap. Gratian Caus. II. Qu. 1. c. 15: Manifest things need no accuser. Eugenius III. in Decret. Lib. v. Tit. I. c. 9: A crime perpetrated in public needs not the voice of an accuser. See notes 125 and 129.

(46). Innocent III. in Decret. l. c. c. 21, nevertheless declares that crimes denounced for correction in visitation may, if grave enough, be dealt with for punishment.

(47). Gregory, A.D. 598, ap. Gratian Caus. VI. Qu. v. c. 1: The onus of proof rests not on you [the accused], but on the accusers. Craisson, § 5800: An accuser who does not undertake to prove his charge is only a denouncer.

(48). Pseudo-Isidor. ap. Gratian Caus. VI. Qu. 1. c. 16: It is the height of iniquity to disparage and accuse brethren.

(49). Augustin ap. Gratian Caus. II. Qu. 1. c. 19: Offences committed before all should be corrected in the sight of all; but secret offences should be secretly corrected. Lynd. 334. See on detraction, Lynd. 61, 71, 78. So Liguori Lib. IV. n. 247: Delinquens jus habet ad servandum suam famam; because an accusation incapacitates for promotion until it is disposed of, according to Gregory in Decret. Lib. v. Tit. I. c. 4 and 16.

(50). Ayliffe 24.

(51). Const. 6 Clarendon, A.D. 1164, requires accusers to be *certi et legales;* Pseudo-Felix II. Ep. I. c. 17 in Decret. Lib. v. Tit. I. c. 1: If there be not a legitimate accuser, let not the accused be called upon to answer (fatigetur).

(52). Cod. Theodos. Lib. II. Tit. 2, c. 1 ap. Gratian Caus. IV. Qu. IV. c. 2,

prosecution of the charge if necessary. (5) In the judicial prosecution the forms of law must be followed most strictly.

19. All persons are not allowed to come forward as accusers. Those who are disqualified are: (1) women and children ([53]); (2) criminous ([54]) or infamous ([55]) persons, including apostates and heretics ([56]); (3) paupers ([57]), and those who are paid to accuse ([58]); (4) avowed enemies ([59]); and (5) persons excommunicate with the greater excommunication ([60]), and generally all who are forbidden to be received as witnesses ([61]). None,

and Caus. II. Qu. III. c. 2; Innocent III. A.D. 1202, in Decret. Lib. v. Tit. c. 16; Concil. Lat. IV. A.D. 1215, Can. 8, *Ibid.* c. 24.

(53). Dig. ap. Gratian Caus. II. Qu. l. c. 14: Some are forbidden to accuse because of sex and age, as women and children; others because of an obligation, as those who are in another's pay. Cod. IX. Tit. I. L 12, *Ibid.* Caus. XV. Qu. III. c. 1: A woman is not allowed to be an accuser of a crime which comes into public judgment, unless she is prosecuting a wrong done to herself or her belongings.

(54). Concil. Const. A.D. 382, Can. 6: That they who have been themselves before accused be not allowed to accuse a bishop or clergyman. Gratian Caus. II. Qu. l. c. 14; Pseudo-Isidor. *Ibid.* Caus. III. Qu. IV. c. 4, mentions incestuous persons. Caus. VI. Qu. l. c. 1, 6, and 17.

(55). Codex Eccles. Afric. 129, and Concil. Carthag. VII. A.D. 419, ap. Gratian Caus. IV. Qu. l. c. 1, excludes from accusing slaves, freedmen, all forbidden by the laws of state, and infamous persons, heretics, pagans, or Jews. Pseudo-Isidor. ap. Gratian Caus. II. Qu. VII. c. 23; also Caus. III. Qu. V. c. 4, 9, 10; Caus. VI. Qu. l. c. 2, 3, 17, enumerates as infamous persons, homicides, perjurers, robbers, poisoners, adulterers, cravens in war, robbers of churches, slanderers of others.

(56). Concil. Const. A.D. 382, Can. 6: That heretics and schismatics may not accuse orthodox bishops. Gratian Caus. II. Qu. VII. c. 23; Caus. III. Qu. IV. c. 1 and 2; Caus. VI. Qu. l. c. 17.

(57). Dig. ap. Gratian Caus. II. Qu. l. c. 14.

(58). *Ibid.*

(59). Pseudo-Isidor. ap. Gratian Caus. III. Qu. IV. c. 10, and Qu. V. c. 2, 3, 4, and 13; Pseudo-Stephen II. Ep. 2 in Decret. Lib. v. Tit. L c. 7; Alexander III. *Ibid.* c. 13; Innocent III. A.D. 1206, *Ibid.* c. 19.

(60). Concil. Carthag. VII. A.D. 419, ap. Gratian Caus. IV. Qu. l. c. 1; Pseudo-Isidor. *Ibid.* Caus. II. Qu. VII. c. 4; Caus. III. Qu. IV. c. 7; Caus. VI. Qu. l. c. 14 and 17.

(61). Gratian Caus. III. Qu. v. c. 517; Caus. VI. Qu. l. c. 5 and 19. See *Acts in Judgment*, § 39.

however, excepting conspirators and persons excommunicate, are excluded from being accusers for wrongs done to themselves ([62]). Presbyters and deacons are forbidden to act as accusers, even in their own causes, and should procure some layman to act for them if necessary ([63]).

20. No one can be lawfully accused by an inferior ([64]), unless the latter is seeking redress for a personal wrong ([65]). Hence a Christian may not be accused by an infidel or Jew ([66]), nor a presbyter by a layman ([67]), nor a bishop by a presbyter ([68]), nor a master by a freedman or servant ([69]). All persons are, however, at liberty to denounce a superior for correction, provided the charges are true ([70]); but this is not accusation, the object of which is vengeance. For the same reason neither the pope nor the sovereign can be accused by any one in the proper sense of the term ([71]), but both may be supplicated for redress in their own courts, and may also be denounced for heresy in an ecumenical synod ([72]).

(62). Concil. Const. A.D. 382, Can. 6 : If any one bring a private or personal accusation . . . no regard shall be had of the person or religion of him who brings it. Codex Eccles. Afric. 129 ; Innocent III. in Decret. Lib. v. Tit. I. c. 20 ; Lynd. 304 ; Ayliffe 24.
(63). Concil. Autissiodor. A.D. 573, Can. 41.
(64). Pseudo-Clemens ap. Gratian Caus. VI. Qu. I. c. 5, requires the accusers of presbyters to be their equals. Caus. VI. Qu. l. c. 2: As superiors cannot be judged by inferiors, no more can they be accused.
(65). Concil. Carthag. III. A.D. 397, ap. Gratian Caus. IV. Qu. VI. c. 1 : If the person of the accuser is reprehensible, let him not be admitted to proof except to maintain his own rights (*causes*), so that they be ecclesiastical or criminal rights. Concil. Carthag. VII. c. 2, A.D. 419, *Ibid.* c. 2 : All to whom accusation is forbidden have a right to accuse in their own causes. See note 59.
(66). Pseudo-Isidor. ap. Gratian Caus. III. Qu. IV. c. 11.
(67). Gratian Caus. II. Qu. VII. c. 1, 2, and 3 ; Alexander III. in Decret. Lib. v. Tit. I. c. 10.
(68). Gratian Caus. III. Qu. IV. c. 8, 9 ; Caus. VI. Qu. l. c. 13.
(69). Gratian Caus. II. Qu. l. c. 14 ; Caus. III. Qu. v. c. 8.
(70). Concil. Epaon. A.D. 517, Can. 24 : We allow laymen, if they have anything criminal to object, to propound it against clergy of any degree, so that what they say is the truth.
(71). Ayliffe 24.   (72). Gratian I. Dist. XL. c. 6.

21. To prevent accusations being maliciously made, no accuser is allowed to attempt judicial proof until he has entered into a bond pledging himself to submit to the same penalty in case of failure which would be inflicted on the accused if the charge should prove true ([73]). This is termed inscription or subscription to the law of retaliation (*lex talionis*) ([74]). An accuser, moreover, who fails on one charge cannot be heard on any other ([75]), because he has thereby become disqualified for being an accuser, and may be excommunicated for slander ([76]). Inscription is not, however, necessary when the crime of apostasy is charged ([77]).

22. Since the effect of accusation is to render the accused incapable of promotion until it is disposed of ([78]), one who objects

([73]). Concil. Const. A.D. 382. Can. 6: Let not informers be permitted to produce their allegations till they have obliged themselves in writing to some equal penalty, if it appear that the information was false. Gregory ap. Gratian Caus. v. Qu. vi. c. 2; Pseudo-Isidor. *Ibid.* Caus. ii. Qu. viii. c. 4: He who objects a crime, let him put in writing that he will prove it. He who fails to prove it, let him bear the penalty which he pressed for. *Ibid.* Caus. ii. Qu. ii. c. 2: Let the false accuser who fails in proof receive the like retribution (*talionem*). Concil. Lat. iv. A.D. 1215, Can. 8, *Ibid.* c. 24: Accusation ought to be preceded by lawful inscription. This is also required by the Bull of Pius v. A.D. 1566, *Cum primum.* See note 47.

([74]). Pseudo-Isidor. ap. Gratian Caus. ii. Qu. iii. c. 2; Innocent iii. in Decret. Lib. v. Tit. i. c. 14; Lynd. 73, 278; Ayliffe 23.

([75]). Concil. Carthag. vii. A.D. 419, Can. 3, in Codex Eccles. Afric. 130; Concil. Rom. A.D. 704, in H. and S. iii. 260.

([76]). Concil. Elib. A.D. 305, Can. 74: If he has failed to prove [his charge] before the assembled clergy, let him be excommunicated (abstineri) for five years. *Ibid.* Can. 75 ap. Gratian Caus. ii. Qu. iv. c. 4: But if any one charges a bishop, presbyter, or deacon with false crimes and cannot prove them, we decree that communion should not be given him, even at the end of life. Stat. Eccl. Ant. Can. 55, A.D. 505: Let the bishop excommunicate accusers of brethren who fail to prove their charges. Hadrian *Ibid.* Caus. v. Qu. l. c. 1, directs a false accuser to be flogged. Gregory, A.D. 594, *Ibid.* Qu. vi. c. 4, orders a false accuser to be excommunicated. Concil. Agath. A.D. 506, Can. 32, *Ibid.* c. 8, directs him to be "kept away from the threshold of the Church and the communion of the faithful."

([77]). Ayliffe 25.

([78]). Gregory in Decret. Lib. v. Tit. i. c. 4.

a crime by way of accusation must also give security that he will persevere in prosecuting it until sentence is given ([79]). A criminal accusation cannot, therefore, be withdrawn or compounded for, when it has once been brought, without leave of the judge ([80]), and even if it is abandoned before inscription, the accuser must be required for ever after to hold his peace, or, as it is said, perpetual silence must be imposed on him ([81]). An accuser who withdraws without leave may be punished for deserting the cause ([82]). Leave is only given to withdraw if (1) the accusation does not seek to establish a greater crime, or (2) the prosecution of it might lead to bloodshed.

23. If an accusation has to be established in judgment, the process is the same as in any other criminal suit. There must be a proper libel in writing ([83]), contestation of suit, exceptions, replications, and proof by witnesses, or by instruments clearer than noon-day ([84]), a term probatory, and a conclusion ([85]), and the cause itself must be determined within two years ([86]).

24. Prior to the eleventh century, procedure by public accusation was the only mode of proceeding for public vengeance open to a private accuser; for proceedings in visitation synods were taken for correction ([87]). Since that time it has

---

([79]). Ayliffe 25.

([80]). Gregory in Decret. Lib. v. Tit. xxii. c. 1, gives as the reason, Lest the agreement should prove not to be the result of charity but of the accuser's having been bought off.

([81]). Innocent III. A.D. 1198, in Decret. Lib. v. Tit. I. c. 14, says that an accuser may withdraw a charge before publicity is given to it, but in that case must be required ever after to hold his peace. Lynd. 73 says that the accused's composition is equivalent to a confession. As to cases which may be settled, see Decret. Lib. I. Tit. xxxvi., and *Acts in Judgment*, § 19.

([82]). Gregory ap. Gratian Caus. v. Qu. vi. c. 4. See also Caus. II. Qu. III. c. 2 and 3.

([83]). Pseudo-Isidor. *Ibid.* Caus. II. Qu. VIII. c. 1; Decret. Lib. II. Tit. III. c. 1.

([84]). Cod. Lib. IV. *Ibid.* Caus. II. Qu. VIII. c. 2; Pseudo-Isidor. *Ibid.* c. 5, requires the chief witnesses to be produced personally.

([85]). Ayliffe 25.

([86]). Ayliffe 153.

([87]). Bouix de Judic. II. 114. See note 91.

gradually become obsolete, partly from regard for the reputation of others ([88]), but still more from fear of the penalties incurred in case of failure ([89]). In most countries spiritual courts are no longer allowed to proceed vindictively, but only for the soul's health. In this country the place of accusation has been taken by judicial denunciation and the promotion of the judge's office when the facts are denied, whereby the accuser attains the same object, provided the judge allows his office to be promoted, and does not expose himself to any risk in case of failure ([90]).

DENUNCIATION OR PRESENTMENT.

25. Denunciation is a mode of procedure in which an individual denounces or presents another's offence to the Church, without undertaking the onus of proof, in order that the offender, as circumstances require, may receive either warning, correction, or punishment ([91]). When the object in making the dresentment is to obtain redress for some private wrong, it is called a complaint (*querela*). When the presentment is of common fame, and not of a fact known to the denouncer, it forms the prelude to inquisition ([92]).

26. Denunciation is said to be of three kinds ([93])—(1) paternal or evangelical, (2) canonical, and (3) judicial. Paternal and canonical denunciation are undertaken wholly or primarily for

(88). Lynd. 332.

(89). Gratian Caus. II. Qu. III. c. 8: If the judge says, You have not proved it, he spares the accuser. But if he says, You have slandered him, he condemns him. Const. 1 Langton pronounces sentence of excommunication on such as slander others. See *Spiritual Courts*, note 55.

(90). Ayliffe 26 ; Ecclesiastical Courts Commission, 1883, II. 207.

(91). Innocent III. A.D. 1202, in Decret. Lib. v. Tit. L c. 16: Accusation is instituted for the purpose of deposition, denunciation for correction. The employment of denunciation for the purpose of deposition is of comparatively late origin, but Innocent III. *Ibid.* c. 21 allows vindictive penalties to be imposed for crimes established by inquisition. See note 46.

(92). Concil. Lat. IV. in Decret. Lib. v. Tit. I. c. 24, quoted note 94.

(93). Ayliffe 210. Innocent III. in Decret. Lib. II. Tit. I. c. 13 mentions two only, paternal and judicial. Lynd. 311.

the amendment of an offender, and, according to the Gospel precept, ought to be preceded by twofold personal warning ([94]). Judicial denunciation, on the other hand, is undertaken to procure the redress of some public or private wrong, and being the mediaeval substitute for accusation, it may be resorted to without previous warning whenever the canons allow it ([95]).

27. Paternal or evangelical denunciation is a reporting to the Church, or to the prelate who represents it, a matter which has already been the subject of two private warnings, in order that by means of a third warning, coming from the prelate as a father, the offender may be brought to repentance. It is called evangelical, because it is made in accordance with the Gospel precept. It may be made by any one, and by whom-

[94]. Matt. XVIII. 15-17; Luke XVII. 3, 4; Concil. Aurel. V. A.D. 541. Can. 17: If any one has a complaint against a bishop, let him first approach him in the spirit of charity, that, warned by friendly intercourse, he may set those matters right which are the cause of complaint. Baeda Poenit. v. 7 in H. & S. III. 331. Concil. Ebor. A.D. 1195, Can. 19: Let him that is suspected of a crime upon common fame be familiarly admonished once, twice, and thrice by the dean of the place to reform himself; which, if he do not, let the dean reprove him, in conjunction with two or three more with whom he hath lost his reputation; if he cannot be reformed by those means, let him tell the Church, *i.e.*, let him be reproved in the chapter, that, upon conviction or confession, he may be canonically punished; or, if he deny it, and cannot be convicted, a canonical purgation may be enjoined him, so that the compurgators do not exceed the number of twelve, and that more or fewer be accepted, according to the quality and circumstances of the person and of the infamy, at the discretion of the judge. Concil. Lat. IV. A.D. 1215, in Decret. Lib. V. Tit. I. c. 24: As lawful accusation must be preceded by inscription, so denunciation must be preceded by charitable warning, and inquisition by the presentment of fame. Innocent III. *Ibid.* Tit. LII. c. 31 repeats these words; also Lib. I. Tit. XXVII. c. 1, and Lib. II. Tit. I. c. 13. Const. 26 Langton, A.D. 1222; Concil. Lugdun II. A.D. 1274, in Sext. Lib. V. Tit. XI. c. 9; Const. 24 Peckham, A.D. 1281; Lynd. 143, 211, 278.

[95]. Const. 5 Peckham, A.D. 1279, and Const. 21 Peckham, A.D. 1281, quoted in *Discipline Generally*, note 17; Const. 1 Winchelsea, A.D. 1305. Const. 2 Stratford, A.D. 1343, orders punishment to be inflicted without warning for neglect of clerical dress. Lynd. 122, 127, 196; Craisson, § 6411.

soever made it should be received by the prelate to whom it is made as a private communication, and may not be made the basis of proceedings in judgment ([96]).

28. Canonical denunciation, on the other hand, is made not only for the good of the offender, but also for the public good, and it is made to the Church publicly and solemnly ([97]). It ought, therefore, always to be contained in articles reciting that the offender has been already twice privately warned, and unless this recital is contained it ought not to be received ([98]). It may be either (1) general or (2) special ([99]). In a general denunciation, one who may not accuse may denounce, and in it the superior does not proceed unless the matter denounced is found to require it. A special canonical denunciation is made by one who has a special interest to serve, as by a patron who desires to have a good incumbent ([100]). If, however, the matter complained of is public, there is no need for proving private warning ([101]).

29. Judicial denunciation is by many considered to be identical with canonical denunciation, and to differ from it only in that it is made for the purpose of judicial proceedings being instituted in the public interest, rather than for the good of the offender. In itself it is not a judicial proceeding, but only a prelude to provoke the exercise of the judge's office, and a species of accusation in which the informant is not made a party in the cause. It should therefore (1) always be made in writing, (2)

---

(96). Stremler des Peines Ecclésiastiques, p. 209; Craisson, § 6413, say this communication must be regarded as private.

(97). Concil. Westminster A.D. 1200, Can. 7 : That prelates do not excommunicate their subjects without canonical warning first given them, except their crimes be such as bring them under a general excommunication. Alexander III. in Decret. Lib. III. Tit. II. c. 4 authorises the Archbishop of Canterbury to depose concubinary clerks if they do not desist after warning. Alexander III. to Bishop of London, *Ibid.* c. 6.

(98). Innocent III. in Decret. Lib. v. Tit. I. c. 20 : If the said bishop has not been warned by them [his accusers] touching the alleged excesses, do you repel them from making presentment. Ayliffe, p. 21.

(99). Ayliffe 210.

(100). Ayliffe 210.

(101). Ayliffe 210.

with the solemnities usual in cases of accusation, excepting the inscription ([102]), and (3) it should name the persons through whom the crime may be proved, because the same exceptions may be taken to the witnesses that might otherwise have been taken to the accuser ([103]). In accusation the third requirement is not necessary, because the accuser takes upon himself the onus of proof. Unless sufficient evidence is indicated to prove the crime, a judicial denunciation should not be received ([104]).

30. Both canonical and judicial denunciation may be made either (1) solemnly ([105]), as in a visitation court, when the people, or their representative synods-men ([106]) are examined upon oath under pain of excommunication, called the oath of Christianity ([107]); or (2) at some other time, publicly or privately. In the first case it is called public, in the two latter private denunciation ([108]).

31. No one is bound to give information of another's offence unless (1) it is a mortal sin ([109]); (2) is certainly known to the

(102). Innocent III. in Decret Lib. v. Tit. I. c. 16.
(103). Innocent. III. *Ibid.* c. 20. Lynd. 278: If a judge, by virtue of a presentment, proceeds to inflict penalties [*i.e.*, not for correction], the accused may take the same exceptions to the denouncer that he might have done to an accuser.
(104). Lynd. 276.
(105). Reiffenstuel Lib. v. Tit. I. No. 89.
(106). Concil. Lat. IV. A.D. 1215, Can. 6 in Decret. Lib. v. Tit. I. c. 25, and Tit. VII. c. 13. Const. 17 Edmund, A.D. 1236: Let there be two or three men in every deanery, who have God before their eyes, to denounce the public excesses of prelates or other clergy, at the command of the archbishop or his official. Lynd. 277.
(107). Concil. Mogunt. A.D. 851, Can. 8, in Decret. Lib. v. Tit. XXXIV. c. 2, quoted note 124; Pseudo-Isidor. ap. Gratian Caus. XXXV. Qu. VI. c. 7. Can. 26 Edgar, A.D. 960, requires the clergy to denounce in synod (*i.e.*, in visitation-court) those whom they cannot bring to satisfaction. Concil. Lat. IV. A.D. 1215, Can. 6 in Decret. Lib. v. Tit. c. 25.
(108). Lynd. 278; Ayliffe 210.
(109). Baedae Poenit. v. 7 in Haddan & Stubbs III. 331: Let him who passes over the mortal sin of another, and does not warn him according to the Gospel rule, do penance for so long as he has failed in his duty. Ayliffe 211; Can. 6 Edgar, A.D. 960; Lynd. 278.

informer ([110]); and (3) unless the giving of information is likely to lead to some spiritual good ([111]). Yet every one is bound to give such information ([112]) if the offence, besides being a mortal sin and known to the informer, is also one which does spiritual harm to the community, or to others ([113]). Among others, however, accomplices are not included ([114]).

32. Certain matters, again, cannot be made the subject of denunciation. Thus no one can be publicly denounced for bygone offences after the period of penance prescribed by the canons has elapsed ([115]). Some offences are therefore barred by an interval of six months, others of a year, others, again, of five years, and all by twenty years ([116]). Instead of varying periods, the statute law of this country has interposed, fixing a time limit for the institution of public proceedings for the correction or punishment of offences, of six or eight months in the case of laymen ([117]),

([110]). Lynd. 311.

([111]). Craisson, § 5836.

([112]). Lynd. 73 says, in cases of adultery, rape, incest, treason, heresy, and excepted crimes, p. 311.

([113]). Baedae Poenit. v. 7 in Haddan and Stubbs III. 331; Craisson, § 5834.

([114]). Alexander III. in Decret. Lib. II. Tit. xx. c. 10.

([115]). Isidor. ap. Gratian Caus. XXXIII. Qu. II. c. 11, assigns seven years as the period of penance for any mortal sin, which period may be abridged for some sins and increased for others of great enormity. The penitential of Theodore gives penances from one day, three days, seven days, up to seven years, ten years, twelve years, and fifteen years. Schmalzgrueber ap. Bouix de Judic. II. 19 says that a bishop may receive an accusation at any time. Innocent III. in Decret. Lib. v. Tit. XXXIV. c. 16 says that a defamed archbishop may be required to clear himself by purgation for the whole time that he has held his archbishopric. See note 156.

([116]). Innocent III. in Decret. Lib. II. Tit. xxv. c. 6.

([117]). The Act 27 Geo. III. c. 44, A.D. 1787, limited the time for commencing proceedings in suits for defamation (which have been since abolished by 18 and 19 Vict. c. 41, A.D. 1855) to six calendar months, and in suits for fornication, incontinence, and brawling (which have been also since abolished by 23 and 24 Vict. c. 32, A.D. 1860) to eight calendar months from the time when such offence shall have been committed, and forbad them altogether for fornication at any time after the parties shall have lawfully intermarried. See *Free* v. *Burgoyne*, No. 187, in Rothery's "Ecclesiastical Appeals."

Canonical Procedure. 253

and of two years ([118]), extended by recent legislation to five years ([119]), in the case of those in Holy Orders. If a conviction in a common law court has at any time been obtained, the time limit for purposes of vengeance is extended to a period of six months by former, and to a period of two years by recent legislation, from the date of the conviction ([120]).

33. When a superior receives a presentment, it is his duty to act wisely, according to the rule of charity ([121]), carefully considering the person and the motives of the informer ([122]), and remembering that an offender's reputation is as necessary to others as his life is to himself ([123]). If it is an official presentment of suspected crime, he should warn in private, then before witnesses, and afterwards admonish in consistory if necessary ([124]). If it is a presentment of notorious crime, he is

---

[118]. By 3 and 4 Vict. c. 86. sec. 20. It has been ruled by the Privy Council that the commencement of the suit dates from the service of the citation upon the accused clerk, and not from the date of the issue of a preliminary commission. *Denison* v. *Ditcher*, Deane and Swabey's Rep. 334 ; 11 Moor. P. C. 324.

[119]. 55 and 56 Vict. c. 32, sec. 5.

[120]. 3 and 4 Vict. c. 86, sec. 20, and 55 and 56 Vict. c. 32, sec. 5. Craisson, § 6407, observes that censure in such cases is not true censure, but only necessary caution for avoiding scandal. Liguori Lib. VII. 49.

[121]. Gratian Caus. XXVI, Qu. VII.

[122]. Pseudo-Isidor. ap. Gratian Caus. II. Qu. VII. c. 17: If any are accusers of bishops and other clergy, it befits not to hear them in judgment before the opinion of their honesty has been weighed [and it has been ascertained], with what object they are thus presumptuous, whether in good faith or temerity . . . for God's sake, or for vainglory, or even for covetousness. *Ibid.* c. 18.

[123]. Augustin ap. Gratian Caus. XI. Qu. III. c. 56 : To ourselves our life is necessary, to others our reputation. Lynd. 73 : In losing reputation, life is worse than death. Causing scandal is itself a ground for punishment. See letter of Charles to Offa in Haddan and Stubbs III. 487. Lynd. 237, 233 says that avoiding scandal is good ground for many otherwise forbidden acts.

[124]. Concil. Mogunt. A.D. 851, in Decret. Lib. V. Tit. XXXIV. c. 2: If any priest, careless of his conduct, has by bad example allowed evil to be suspected of him, and the people, constrained by the bishop under the bann of Christianity, have disclosed his want of reputation, and there are no certain accusers of the crime, let him first be admonished by the bishop

bound at once to proceed of mere office (¹²⁵). If it is a private presentment, he should forbear to proceed judicially, unless (1) the accused is already defamed (¹²⁶), or (2) he has satisfied himself by warning that reform is otherwise not to be hoped for, or (3) unless the offence is so injurious to others that warning is out of the question. Should he act otherwise, he commits a grave breach of charity (¹²⁷), though not such a wrong for which there exists a remedy.

INQUISITION.

34. Whenever presentment is made of common fame only, and not of facts known to the denouncer, or whenever there is grave suspicion of the existence of some crime, a case arises for inquisition (¹²⁸). Inquisition is the judge's act setting inquiry on foot either *ex mero motu*, in the interests of the Church (¹²⁹), to ascertain whether the rules of the Christian life

apart, then in the presence of two or three witnesses, and if he refuse then to amend, let the bishop visit him with public censure in the assembly of the presbyters. If even then he refuse to amend his ways, let him be suspended from office until he come to proper satisfaction, lest the faithful should be scandalised through him. Gregory ap. Gratian. I. Dist. LXXXVI. c. 23 : If anything should come to your ears respecting any cleric, which might justly give you offence, do not believe it too readily, nor let an unknown matter goad you on to vengeance, but, in the presence of the senior presbyters of the Church, let the truth be carefully investigated, and then, if the quality of the charge so requires, let canonical censure visit the delinquent's offence. Concil. Lat. IV. A.D. 1215, Can. 8 in Decret. Lib. V. Tit. I. c. 24, and Lib. III. Tit. II. c. 2 ; Lynd. 211.

(125). Alexander III. to Archbishop of Canterbury in Decret. Lib. III. Tit. II. c. 4 ; the same to the Bishop of London, *Ibid.* c. 6 ; Innocent III. to Bishop of Exeter, *Ibid.* c. 8. Lynd. 323 defines notoriety as proof beyond dispute, needing no further discussion. See note 45.

(126). Concil. Lat. III. A.D. 1179, in Decret. Lib. V. Tit. I. c. 21 and 24; Craisson, § 5827.

(127). Letter of Daniel of Winchester to Boniface, A.D. 740, in Haddan and Stubbs III. 348.

(128). Innocent III. in Decret. Lib. III. Tit. II. c. 8, says that report is no manner of proof, but notoriety is. *Id. Ibid.* Lib. V. Tit. I. c. 21 ; Ayliffe 278, 488.

(129). Ayliffe 152 ; Rothery's Appeals IX.

are being observed, or else as the result of a presentment to ascertain whether a report or suspicion is true. In the former case it is called general inquisition, in the latter particular inquisition. General inquisition is the method anciently and to some extent still practised at a visitation synod, when a number of questions are propounded to be truly answered under pain of excommunication ([130]). Particular inquisition appears to have been introduced after the eleventh century, when the practice of accusation fell into disuse, either for the purpose of correcting the guilty or clearing the innocent.

35. The aim of general inquisition being to ascertain that the rules of Christian life are being faithfully observed, this object is found to be best attained by propounding articles of inquiry in a synod or visitation-court. On the other hand, the aim of particular inquisition being to ascertain whether a particular person is guilty of offences of which he is suspected or denounced ([131]), this object is best secured by direct questions put to him or else by a judicial proceeding. At one time inquisition was largely resorted to for the purpose of suppressing heresy ([132]); now it is almost entirely confined to ascertaining that clergy are conducting themselves as beseems their profession, or are conforming to the rules of the foundations to which they belong.

36. Before particular inquisition is resorted to there should exist (1) either strong grounds for suspecting crime, or the presentment of some informer who is himself above suspicion ([133]);

([130]). For instance, in Hingeston-Randolph's Stapeldon's Register's, p. 130, under Culmstoch, the Visitation, A.D. 1319, reports (1) on the condition of the vestments and furniture of the Church; then (2) the *testes sinodales* report that the vicar is a good-living man and of honest conversation, as also his clerk, and he carefully teaches his parishioners. In visiting the sick, baptizing infants, and in other matters of his office, they know of nothing to complain of, except that it appears to them that on festival days he allows too long a pause between Matins and Mass.

([131]). Innocent III. in Decret. Lib. II. Tit. XIV. c. 8.

([132]). See *Excesses*, § 15.

([133]). Lynd. 278.

and (2) public fame or scandal ([134]). Without ill-fame preceding, particular inquisition ought not to be made, at least publicly ([135]), unless such a crime as apostasy or heresy is charged ([136]), since (1) the rule of charity enjoins respect for another's reputation ([137]), and (2) publicity in such a case may do more harm than good to the Church. Particular inquisition may, however, be made ([138]) privately and preparatorily, or, as it is said, by way of summary information, in order to ascertain (1) whether there exists probable proof of the alleged offence, and (2) whether the accused is defamed in consequence of it. For summary information the presence of the accused is not needed.

37. If the result of private inquisition is to establish a *primâ facie* case against the accused, and also the existence of ill-fame, particular inquiry may be made solemnly in audience or synod, when personal answers may be required upon oath from the suspected person. Should the latter admit the offence, or the same be notorious, he may then be dealt with summarily by

(134). Concil. Lat. IV. A.D. 1215, Can. 8 in Decret. Lib. v. Tit. I. c. 24, requires clamosa insinuatio to precede inquisition. Lynd. 254, 312.

(135). Innocent III. in Decret. Lib. v. Tit. I. c. 19 and 21; Concil. Lat. IV. A.D. 1215, *Ibid.* c. 24: Inquisition ought always to be preceded by ill-fame or rumour; otherwise proceedings ought not to be taken. But Boniface VIII. in Sext. Lib. v. Tit. I. c. 1 and 2, states that if inquisition is held when a person has not previously been defamed, and is submitted to without protest, any crime thus disclosed may be visited with punishment.

(136). Concil. Lat. IV. Can. 3, *Ibid.* Lib. v. Tit. VII. c. 13, § 2: Those who are only noted as suspected of heresy, unless having regard to the suspicion and the quality of the person they have demonstrated their innocence by a suitable purgation, ought to be struck with the sword of anathema. Innocent III. A.D. 1207, *Ibid.* Tit. IX. c. 3: Clergy who are defamed for apostasy because they have abandoned the clerical garb . . . must be restrained by ecclesiastical constraint until, if proof is not forthcoming, they have made their canonical purgation to do away with their ill-fame. See note 44.

(137). *Id. Ibid.* c. 19; Concil. Lat. IV. *Ibid.* c. 24: Ne forte per leve compendium ad grave dispendium veniatur. Boniface VIII. in Sext. Lib. III. Tit. XX. c. 1, § 4; Lynd. 109.

(138). Lynd. 17 says preparatorily or solemnly. *Id.* 109.

Canonical Procedure. 257

the mere office of the judge ([139]). Should he deny it, the matter may be referred for judicial discussion in a plenary proceeding by promoting the judge's office ([140]); and since the oath *ex officio* has in this country been abolished by statute ([141]), and in the case of clergy new modes of procedure have by recent legislation been introduced in place of the canonical methods, a judicial trial is the only available course when the offence is denied.

38. Whenever a judge proceeds of mere office to correct or punish, the necessary promoter ([142]), who undertakes to act for the Church, enjoys several privileges denied to a voluntary promoter. (1) Custom exempts him from the obligation of subscribing to the law of retaliatory punishment or from taking the oath against vexatious litigation ([143]). (2) The judge may require the accused to give an affirmative or negative answer upon oath ([144]). (3) Proofs are not admitted to establish the defendant's good fame. (4) A negative answer holds the place of contestation of suit ([145]). (5) Additional witnesses may be examined after the publication of evidence. On the other hand, the same exceptions may be taken to a voluntary promoter as to an accuser ([146]).

---

(139). Nicolaus ap. Gratian Caus. II. Qu. 1. c. 21 ; Innocent III. in Decret. Lib. v. Tit. xxxiv. c. 15. Innocent IV. in Sext. Lib. III. Tit. xx. c. 1, § 4, says that the ordinary would be wanting in his duty if he failed to punish. Ayliffe 153, 240, 450. See note 45.

(140). By 3 and 4 Vict. c. 86, this is the only method now permitted for the punishment of clerical excesses, even though notorious. To relieve bishops from expense and responsibility 55 and 56 Vict. c. 32 was recently passed, which empowered them to deprive for any moral offence, and threw the onus of declaring the offence proven upon an irresponsible and mixed body of nominees.

(141). 16 Car. I. c. 11, A.D. 1640 ; 13 Car. II. c. 12, sec. 4. Rothery's Ecclesiastical Appeals, p. IX. says that in practice the oath was still taken. See *Acts in Judgment*, notes 150-152.

(142). Ayliffe 274, 397.

(143). *Ibid.* Craisson, § 5931.

(144). Ayliffe, 397. See note 141.

(145). Innocent III. in Decret. Lib. v. Tit. xxxiv. c. 15 ; Ayliffe 397.

(146). Lynd. 279.

39. If as the result of solemn inquisition no adequate proof is forthcoming of the existence of the crime denounced or suspected, it is competent for the prelate or judge to-administer the oath of purgation (¹⁴⁷), and thus establish the innocence of the accused, and to suspend a defamed clerk from office (¹⁴⁸) until he has purged himself. In this country the oath cannot now be compulsorily administered, at least not to

(147). Concil. Agath. A.D. 506, ap. Gratian Caus. II. Qu. v. c. 12: If lawful accusers cannot prove the crimes of a presbyter, and he denies them, then let him, if he be able, purge himself from crime with seven fellows of his own order. If a deacon be accused of the same crime, let him excuse himself with three. Gregory II. A.D. 726, *Ibid.* c. 5: If a presbyter or any priest [*i.e.*, sharer in the official priesthood, bishop, or deacon] be accused by the people, and there are no certain witnesses, . . . let an oath be administered to him in public, and let him call Him to witness the purity of his innocence to Whom all things are naked and open. Concil. Wormac. *Ibid.* c. 26: If a bishop or presbyter is charged with a crime such as manslaughter, adultery, theft, or wrong-doing, let him say mass for each charge, and communicate, and show himself innocent of such imputation. If he fail to do so, let him for five years be removed from his Church. Cnut's Law 5, A.D. 1017: If a priest who lives regularly be impleaded for crimes, and knows himself to be clear, let him say mass if he dare, and make his purgation by himself alone, if it be a single accusation [*i.e.*, made by three men]; if the accusation be triple [*i.e.*, made by six accusers], let him purge himself on the Housel if he dare, together with two of the same order. Concil. Ebor. A.D. 1195, Can. 19, quoted note 94. Alexander III. in Decret. Lib. v. Tit. XXXIV. c. 6, reproduced in Concil. Westminster A.D. 1200, Can. 12: Let such as are publicly defamed or suspected, but cannot be convicted, be thrice admonished to confess and make satisfaction. If they persist in denying the crime, let a purgation be enjoined them. Const. 29 Langton, A.D. 1222; Innocent III. to Patriarch of Aquileia, *Ibid.* c. 5; Gregory IX. *Ibid.* Lib. II. Tit. XXIV. c. 36: The oath of purgation cannot be refused except for a just cause. . . . If the promoter altogether fails in proof, the defendant ought to win, although he has done nothing. But if a presumption is made out for the promoter, the oath ought to be tendered to the defendant, that he may thereby prove his innocence, unless the judge, considering all the circumstances of the case, should think it best to tender it [the oath suppletory] to the promoter. Const. 5 Boniface, A.D. 1261; Const. 10 Peckham, A.D. 1279; Const. 10 Stratford, A.D. 1342; Const. 1 Islep. A.D. 1351; Ayliffe 419. See note 135, and *Acts in Judgment*, note 188.

(148). Innocent III. in Decret. Lib. v. Tit. XXXIV. c. 10.

Canonical Procedure. 259

laymen ([149]), although it may be voluntarily taken; nor could it ever be required unless a person was defamed not only among enemies and malicious persons ([150]), but also among good and grave men ([151]); neither may it be taken when the charge admits of proof ([152]). It may nevertheless be administered upon suspicion of an offence not grave in itself, if the same causes scandal ([153]).

40. In purgation the defamed person appears before the prelate or judge with the prescribed number of compurgators ([154]), two or three, but not more than six, in a case of alleged incontinence or lesser crime; seven or nine, but not more than twelve, in a case of alleged adultery or greater crime ([155]); and

---

(149). By 13 Car. II. c. 12, the oath *ex officio* cannot be required in any case where the party might, by virtue thereof, be compelled to confess, or accuse, or purge himself of any crime or the breach of any penal law. Lynd. 312; Law's Forms 46, 187, 282, notes.

(150). Innocent III. A.D. 1212, in Decret. Lib. v. Tit. I. c. 21.

(151). Const. 29 Langton, A.D. 1222; Ayliffe 449.

(152). Innocent III. A.D. 1208, in Decret. Lib. v. Tit. XXXIV. c. 15.

(153). Ayliffe 450: An enormous crime is said to be that which engenders and begets scandal, though otherwise it be not in itself enormous; for men ought to keep themselves free from all criminal imputations.

(154). Concil. Ilerd. ap. Gratian Caus. II. Qu. v. c. 13: It is a sufficient satisfaction if, according to the canons or at the bishop's will, he joins with himself seven colleagues, and swears upon the Gospel that he has not committed the crime alleged. Concil. Tribur. A.D. 895, *Ibid.* c. 15, requires a nobleman to purge himself with twelve, but "if he has previously been guilty of the same crime, let him not be admitted to the oath." Hincmar, *Ibid.* c. 16, requires a presbyter to purge himself with the required number of neighbouring presbyters (cum denominatis sibi vicinis presbyteris). Innocent III. in Decret. Lib. v. Tit. XXXIV. c. 12 assents to the principle that two bishops and three abbots would be enough for the purgation of a bishop, provided they could be got. Ayliffe 449 says that in this country the number is in the judge's discretion. Muratori Antiq. Diss. 38; Martene de Ant. Rit. Eccl. Lib. III. c. 7, § 3; Devoti Lib. III. Tit. IX. § 26.

(155). Innocent II. ap. Gratian Caus. II. Qu. v. c. 17 directs a bishop to purge himself with seven, viz., three (tertia manu) of his own order and four abbots. Concil. London, A.D. 1108, Can. 4: If any are accused by two or three lawful witnesses, or by public report, to have transgressed this statute [against concubinage], let him, if a priest, make his purgation

swears upon the Gospels not only that he is innocent of the crime alleged, but also that he has not committed it ([156]). His compurgators then declare that they believe that what he says is the truth. As the object of purgation is not merely to show that crime is not proven, but to establish the innocence of the defamed person before all, it should be made in the place where the accused is defamed ([157]).

41. Compurgators ought to be persons of honesty and integrity, or at least persons tolerated by the Church, and not condemned for any crime ([158]), living in the neighbourhood ([159]), and personally acquainted with the defamed person ([160]); but their testimony is confined to stating that they believe his word ([161]). In default of his being able to procure such persons, he may produce as compurgators women and inferior laymen, so that they be tolerated by the Church, or his own kinsfolk ([162]).

by six witnesses, if a deacon by four, if a subdeacon by two. If he fail, let him be deemed a transgressor. Const. 10 Stratford, A.D. 1342 : In enjoining purgations to such as are defamed, let bishops, archdeacons, or other ordinaries impose no more than six compurgators in case of fornication, or any such like crime ; nor above twelve in case of adultery, or other greater crime, under pain of suspension from office.

(156). Innocent III. A.D. 1214, in Decret. Lib. v. Tit. xxxiv. c. 16 : He asks to be allowed to swear that he is innocent of the crimes with which he has been charged, perhaps meaning innocent in the sense that they have been remitted by penance. . . . But if he will and can, let him swear that, according to the ordinary meaning of words, he has not committed those crimes with which he is charged, . . . since his promotion to the archbishopric, and let his compurgators swear that they believe what he says is true.

(157). Const. 10 Stratford, A.D. 1342 : A man ought to make his purgation in the place where he was defamed. . . . Therefore we ordain that such as are defamed for crimes and excesses, but are willing to make their purgation, be not drawn from one deanery to another, or to country-places where necessaries of life are not to be found.

(158). Innocent III. to the Bishop of Winchester in Decret. Lib. v. Tit. xxxiv. c. 9.

(159). *Id.* A.D. 1202, *Ibid.* c. 11. Hincmar quoted, note 154.

(160). *Id. Ibid.* c. 7.

(161). *Id.* A.D., 1199, *Ibid.* c. 13. See note 156.

(162). Cnut's Law 5, A.D. 1017 : If a minister of the altar that hath no friends be impleaded, and has none to support him in his oath, let him go

One who fails in a canonical purgation is deemed a transgressor ([163]), and may be dealt with as such.

to corsned, and be the event as God will, unless he be allowed to make his purgation on the Housel. If a man in orders be impleaded for a mortal feud, . . . let him make purgation with his kindred. Lynd 314; Ayliffe 451.

(163). Concil. London A.D. 1108, Can. 4, quoted note 155. Innocent III. in Decret. Lib. v. Tit. l. c. 23, and Tit. xxxiv. c. 7 and 10: If he fails in purgation, smite him with the sword of ecclesiastical discipline.

VIII.

ACTS IN JUDGMENT.

1. Whenever any matter is submitted to the Church for decision, it is called a matter for settlement (*negotium*); and whenever there is any kind of opposition or difference as to the way in which it is to be settled, it is termed a disputed matter or controversy (*controversia*). A cause (*causa*), on the other hand, is defined to be that very right which is deduced and set forth in a judicial proceeding (¹). Hence a matter for settlement or controversy may be disposed of either extra-judicially in synod or audience, or judicially by a judge; but there is no cause unless the matter is introduced before a judge, either for argument or for proof (²).

2. All the various steps whereby a controversy is discussed in judgment—such as a libel, contestation of suit, exceptions, depositions of witnesses, the assignment of a term (³)—are called the acts and members of the cause, and constitute what is also known as the process (⁴). These acts and members follow for the most part the usages of the civil law, and in this country are allowed to be valid on the ground of long usage

---

(1). Isidore in Decret. Lib. v. Tit. XL. c. 10 : A controversy when propounded is a *cause;* when it is discussed in judgment, a *judicial proceeding* (judicium) ; when it is decided, *justice.* Ayliffe 150. Schmalzgrueber in Craisson, § 5483, says that a controversy before it is propounded is a *question*, and the action whereby a controversy is brought to trial is a *suit*, and the carrying on of the action from contestation to sentence is the *instance.* Ayliffe 151. See *Canonical Procedure*, note 1.

(2). Isidore l. c. : Causa aut argumento aut probatione constat. Ayliffe 150 : A cause is so called before as well as after contestation of suit.

(3). Ayliffe 152 ; Law's Forms 76.

(4). Concil. Lat. IV. A.D. 1215, in Decret. Lib. II. Tit. XIX. c. 11 ; Ayliffe 149 ; Ecclesiastical Courts Commission, 1883, p. 183.

and custom (⁵). They may be arranged in three groups (⁶): (1) those which are concerned with the introduction of a cause while it is still in the stage of a matter for settlement or controversy. These are termed the preparatory acts (⁷), and are said to be in the forefront of judgment (*in principio judicii*) (⁸). (2) Those which are concerned with the instance of a cause when it has passed from the stage of controversy to that of a suit, and become judicial; and (3) those which have to do with the conclusion of a cause, and concern the exercise of the judge's office (⁹), including execution, or the stay of execution by appeal.

(5). See *Spiritual Courts*, § 8.
(6). Ayliffe 152; Devoti. Inst. Lib. III. Tit. XIII. § 4; Law's Forms 355.
(7). Ayliffe 181.
(8). Innocent III. to Archbishop of Canterbury in Decret. Lib. I. Tit. XXIX. c. 27, says a judge must take into consideration all the acts in a cause as well those [1] *in principio*, as [2] those *in medio*, and [3] those *in fine*. Law's Forms 77.
(9). The principal acts in a process are the following:—

THE CAUSE.

A. The preparatory acts, acts in *principio* or *in jure*.
  (1) Petition, or articles containing the libel.
      (a) Nature of a libel.
      (b) Requisites in a libel.
      Summary information before issuing a citation in a criminal cause.
      A civil cause may now be settled out of court by a composition.
  (2) The citation, and the term citatory.
      (a) Nature of a citation.
      (b) Service of a citation.
      (c) Certificate of service.
  (3) Appointment of proctors, and bringing in of the libel or articles.
  (4) Dilatory exceptions, and the term deliberatory.
      (a) Exceptions to the citation.
      (b) Exception to the judge.
      (c) Exceptions to the libel.
  A criminal cause may now be settled by submission to sentence, a civil cause by a *compact* or *transaction*.

B. The suit or discussion in judgment, acts *in medio* or *in judicio*.
  (1) Contestation of suit, and the answer of the principal party.
  (2) Peremptory exceptions.
      At this stage the oath of calumny may be administered.
  (3) Assignment of the term probatory.
  (4) The proofs.
      (a) Degrees of proof.
      (b) Production of witnesses by both parties.
      (c) Publication of the depositions.
      (d) Exceptions to the witnesses or their depositions.

C. The concluding acts or acts *in fine*. The judge's office and appeal.
  (1) Term to propound all acts.
  (2) The sentence and the term definitive.
      (a) Presumptions.
      (b) The facts in evidence.
      The matter judicially settled (*res judicata*).
  (3) Execution, and the term executory.
  (4) Appeal, and the fatal terms.

For a fuller account of all the steps, see Arthur Brown's compendious view of the ecclesiastical law, 1796, and Law's Forms, p. 356.

3. A controversy introduced before a judge may be decided by him sometimes with, at other times without discussion in judgment. When it is decided without discussion in judgment it is said to be dealt with *summarily*, or rather extra-judicially, the procedure being similar to that pursued in an extra-judicial hearing in synod or in audience. By the law of this country there must, however, always be a libel in criminal causes, except in causes of contempt ([10]) or execution ([11]). When a controversy comes up for discussion in judgment, it must ordinarily be dealt with in a plenary manner, unless it is itself what is called a summary cause ([12]), *i.e.*, a cause which a judge is authorised to deal with as though it were a hearing in audience or in synod. Hence all causes, when they come to be dealt with on appeal before the highest court of all, become summary ([13]); for the highest courts, which by interpreting make the law, are not tribunals of judges, but of prelates.

The Introduction of a Cause—The Controversy.

4. To introduce any matter for judicial settlement two things are necessary ([14]): (1) a petition ([15]) or supplicatory libel ([16]), called also an accusatory or criminal libel, and in this country popularly articles in a criminal case, a conventional libel in a

---

(10). Law's Forms 113.

(11). 2 Hen. v. St. I. c. 5, A.D. 1414, re-enacting the old common law rule: At what time the libel is grantable by the [common] law, that it may be granted and delivered to the party without any difficulty [to enable him to apply for prohibition if necessary]. See Ecclesiastical Courts Commission, 1883. Ayliffe 351 says summary proceedings may be taken upon a *viva voce* petition, called a petition *grosso modo*, when the process is *sine figura judicii*, but that some petition or other ought of natural right to be exhibited. See *Canonical Procedure*, note 26.

(12). See *Canonical Procedure*, § 9.

(13). Law's Forms, 42, 59.

(14). Ayliffe 174 calls the introducing of a controversy *editio actionis*.

(15). Gregory, A.D. 600, ap. Gratian Caus. II. Qu. l. c. 7, calls it a *petition*. Ibid. Caus. VII. Qu. l. c. 3; Ayliffe 349.

(16). Ayliffe 346.

civil case ([17]); and (2) a citation by the judge having authority from the Church, calling upon the person cited to make answer to the libel or articles. According to the practice of the civil law there are several other acts which may have a place in the controversy stage ([18]); but of these only (1) contempt ([19]) and contumacy ([20]), (2) re-convention or counter-claim, (3) the administration of interrogatories ([21]), (4) security for proceeding or for costs, and (5) exceptions have place in ecclesiastical procedure.

5. A petition or supplicatory libel is a short and well-ordered writing ([22]), setting forth in a clear manner, as well to the judge as to the defendant, the plaintiff's intention in judgment ([23]). It has been also defined to be a fit conception of words setting forth a specimen of the future suit ([24]). It is the first step and the foundation of every suit, whether criminal or civil, and

([17]). Gregory IX. in Decret. Lib. II. Tit. III. c. 3 ; Law's Forms 148.
([18]). Ayliffe 152.
([19]). Law's Forms 112.
([20]). Law's Forms 121. See note 79.
([21]). In Decret. Lib. II. Tit. VIII. c. 3, the defendants met a claim for payment of a pension which had been paid for three years and *upwards*, by interrogating as to the meaning of *upwards*, and the reply being seven years, asked to have the case adjourned on the ground that this was an alteration of the libel. Honorius III., on appeal, dismissed the defendants' application as frivolous.
([22]). Ayliffe 351 says that the usual practice is for the citation to issue upon the petition, and a copy of the libel in the form of articles to be afterwards given to the defendant. See Law's Forms 154.
([23]). Concil. Constant. A.D. 382, Can. 7, calls it λιβελλοι. Gratian Caus. II. Qu. VII. c. 1. Socrates II. 40 relates that when the Council of Seleucia in 359 A.D., condemned Cyril of Jerusalem *in absentia*, " he sent a written notification to those who had condemned him that he should appeal to a higher jurisdiction." VII. 37 relates that Sylvanus of Troas caused "the documents of the litigants [*i.e.*, the libel] to be delivered to himself." Alexander III. directs the Bishop of Exeter and the chapter of London, in Decret. Lib. II. Tit. I. c. 6, that it is not necessary to describe the particular kind of action, but only to set forth simply the facts of the case and the truth. Innocent III. *Ibid.* Tit. III. c. 2 requires the subject-matter of a real action to be set forth without obscurity or equivocation. Ayliffe 346.
([24]). Law's Forms, p. 147.

is absolutely necessary in every plenary proceeding (25). In a criminal cause it must contain everything which is intended to be afterwards charged in the articles, the libel being interpreted in favour of the accused (26); in a civil cause the libel is interpreted in the plaintiff's favour. A libel is called *simple* when it declares the action in a continued speech, *articulate* when the merits of the cause are propounded in articles (27).

6. To be in proper form a libel must contain (28) (1) the name of the judge before whom the matter is to be brought; (2) the name and description sufficient for purposes of identification of the accuser, promoter, or plaintiff (29); (3) the name of the accused or defendant; (4) the offence charged, or the matter in demand or dispute, termed the *major proposition;* (5) particulars of the facts relied on to support the charge or complaint, called the *narration* (30); and (6) the *conclusion* or prayer. A libel is therefore a judicial syllogism. In a criminal cause there need be no prayer, since it is understood that the judge will decree as unto law and justice shall appertain (31); but in a civil cause the conclusion must state the particular

---

(25). Gratian Caus. II. Qu. VIII. c. 1 ; Concil. Suesson. II. A.D. 853, in Decret. Lib. II. Tit. III. c. 1 ; 2 Hen. V. St. I. c. 3, and 2 and 3 Ed. VI. c. 13-14 require a copy of it to be delivered to the defendant. Law's Forms 150. No libel existing proceedings are rendered null. See *Procedure*, note 25.

(26). Ayliffe 352.

(27). Law's Forms 148 ; Craisson, § 5882.

(28). The five points necessary for every libel are commemorated in the lines from Hostiensis, quoted in Law's Forms 149, and there rendered :—
> The plaintiff's and defendant's name,
> And eke the judge who tries the same ;
> The thing demanded, and the right whereby
> You claim to have it granted instantly—
> He doth a libel right and well compose
> Who forms the same, omitting none of those.

(29). *Griffith* v. *Williams*, No. 177, in Rothery's Ecclesiastical Appeals.

(30). Innocent III. in Decret. Lib. II. Tit. XXVIII. c. 49. Gregory IX. *Ibid.* Tit. III. c. 3 says that unless the ground of the demand as well as the demand is set forth in a civil case, the defendant cannot be called upon to answer. Lynd. 301.

(31). Lynd. 125, 297 : Videbitur expedire. . Ayliffe 349.

Acts in Judgment. 267

remedy or redress asked for to enable the judge to give the proper relief (³²). In so doing it must be careful not to ask for too much, to be too specific (³³), to ask for redress prematurely or at a wrong place (³⁴), and ought to be, as the civilians say, round, dilucid, conclusive; and neither obscure, uncertain, general, or alternative (³⁵). Otherwise the plaintiff may be condemned in costs.

7. In a civil cause, and also in a criminal cause in which the plaintiff is seeking redress for a private wrong (³⁶), the citation ought to issue as a matter of natural right and justice (³⁷), except in appealing against a sentence of excommunication; for in such cases the appellant must first pray for absolution (³⁸). But since it is not incumbent on a judge to allow his office to be promoted for public vengeance without good grounds for

(32). Ayliffe 349.

(33). Gregory IX. in Decret. Lib. II. Tit. XI. says that for asking too much, *i.e.*, twenty shillings when only ten shillings are due, or for asking too specifically (causa), *i.e.*, some specific thing when the mode of performance is in the defendant's choice, or for asking for a debt before the time for payment, the plaintiff should be condemned in costs.

(34). For asking too soon the defendant is allowed additional time, and for asking at the wrong place the defendant is allowed to counterclaim for his loss by the difference by Gregory IX. *Ibid.*

(35). Ayliffe 346 says a libel must avoid five things: Generality, obscurity, ambiguity, conditionality, and disunity. Conset's Practice 402; Law's Forms 148.

(36). Concil. Carthag. III. A.D. 397, Can. 7 ap. Gratian Caus. IV. Qu. VI. c. 1: It is resolved that when any one commences proceedings before the committee of bishops (in judicio episcoporum), if the person of the accuser has been guilty, he be not heard, unless in private causes, not in ecclesiastical or criminal causes. Concil. Carthag. VII. A.D. 419, Can. 2, *Ibid.* c. 2: All who are excluded from accusation must not be prevented from accusing in their own causes. This right seems to be preserved by sec. 19 of 3 & 4 Vict. c. 86.

(37). Before 26 Otho, A.D. 1268, quoted note 67, the plaintiff could himself serve the libel on the defendant without the judge's intervention, and even compel him to appear unless he found bail. See Devoti Lib. III. Tit. V. § 8; Ayliffe 180, 274: To convene and commence a suit against a party ought to be denied to no one.

(38). Innocent III. A.D. 1202, in Decret. Lib. V. Tit. XXXIX. c. 40; Boniface VIII. in Sext. Lib. V. Tit. XL. c. 7; Law's Forms 86.

believing that such promotion will be for the public good, a criminal suit in the interest of the Church cannot be instituted without the judge's consent (³⁹). Before giving such consent it is his business to satisfy himself by summary information (1) that there are *prima facie* grounds for believing the charges made to be true (⁴⁰); and (2) that the accused is publicly defamed (⁴¹). Otherwise the judge is forbidden to allow his office to be promoted (⁴²).

8. A citation is a judicial act whereby a defendant is summoned to appear before a judge, deputed by the Church, on a certain day, to make answer to the plaintiff's or promoter's libel (⁴³). It ought, therefore, to be directed to all who are concerned in the cause as defendants (⁴⁴); but the same citation may not include the names of more than four persons (⁴⁵), and by English rule a separate citation must be issued to each person, or the stamp duty would be evaded (⁴⁶). A citation should contain (1) the name of the judge, and his commission if he be a delegate with special powers; also (2) the style of the court wherein he presides, lest a defendant should be com-

---

(39). By 3 & 4 Vict. c. 86, and the Public Worship Act, 1874, the allowing the promotion of any criminal suit is left in the bishop's discretion. Several witnesses complained before the Ecclesiastical Courts Commission, 1883, vol. II. 62, 171, 235, that this was an injustice, on the ground that to have public worship conducted in the way prescribed by the Act of Uniformity is a private right.

(40). Innocent IV. in Sext Lib. III. Tit. XX. c. 1, § 4, says this of the archbishop when holding a visitation. Lynd. 109, says this informal inquiry is not upon oath.

(41). Innocent III. in Decret. Lib. v. Tit. I. c. 21, § 2, and c. 19; Boniface VIII. in Sext. Lib. v. Tit. I. c. 2.

(42). Innocent III. A.D. 1206, in Decret. Lib. v. Tit. I. c. 19: Unless you find that his reputation has suffered from the above charges, do not hastily proceed to a judicial inquiry into their truth. *Id.* A.D. 1212, *Ibid.* c. 21: No one ought to be [publicly] punished for a crime which has not damaged his reputation. Concil. Lat. IV. A.D. 1215, Can. 8, *Ibid.* c. 24.

(43). Ayliffe 174; Law's Forms 79, 87.

(44). Lynd. 254: All who have an interest must be cited when a matter is raised to their prejudice. Can. 120 of 1603; Gibson's Codex 1009.

(45). Ayliffe 181.

(46). Law's Forms 88.

pelled to appear and plead in more courts than one on the same charge ([47]); (3) the name of the plaintiff or promoter; (4) the name of the defendant or accused; (5) the cause or subject-matter of the suit or complaint; (6) the place where the defendant is to appear, which is required to be some safe place ([48]) within the territorial limits of the citing judge's authority ([49]); and (7) the day of appearance, a competent interval or term being allowed, such as ten days, according to Roman law, for a simple, or thirty days for a peremptory citation ([50]).

9. The day or time of appearance is settled by the judge ([51]) In the time of the Court of Arches it used to be the next court day after the third day for those living in the city of London or suburbs, and after the fourth or sixth day for those living farther off, according to distance ([52]). The judge ought to take care that it is not too short ([53]). When, as is now necessarily

[47]. Law's Forms 87.

[48]. Innocent III. to Bishop of Worcester in Decret. Lib. II. Tit. XXVIII. c. 47. *Id. Ibid.* Tit. VI. c. 4. If it is not a safe place there is ground for appeal, according to Boniface VIII. in Sext. Lib. V. Tit. XL. c. 7.

[49]. Concil. Vien. A.D. 1311, in Clem. Lib. II. Tit. XI. c. 2; Ayliffe 176. By the statute 23 Hen. VIII. c. 9, and 3 & 4 Vict. c. 86, sec. 19, no one may be cited out of his diocese. But during the vacancy of any episcopal see within the province of Canterbury, the Archbishop as ordinary (except in the dioceses of London, Lincoln, Salisbury, and Worcester—*Oughton*) may cite into his court. Law's Forms, p. 54.

[50]. Concil. Carthag. III. Can. 7, A.D. 397, ap. Gratian Caus. IV. Qu. V. c. 1, says one month. Pseudo-Isidor. *Ibid.* Caus. V. Qu. II. c. 2, allows seven days, then another seven, then two, then two more, and a day of grace, after which it allows the defendant to be excommunicated for contumacy. Gratian Caus. III. Qu. III. c. 4, § *Offeratur*, says twenty days. Innocent III. in Decret. Lib. II. Tit. XIV. c. 6; Const. 14 Peckham A.D. 1281; the possessor being first lawfully cited, and so much time allowed him as may be sufficient for consulting with wise men and providing for the defence of his estate Ayliffe 178 states that a citation without assigning a term is valid, the defendant's duty being then to appear so soon as he can.

[51]. Concil. Vien. A.D. 1311, in Clem. Lib. II. Tit. I. c. 1; 3 & 4 Vict. c. 86 allows fourteen days in criminal cases.

[52]. Law's Forms, p. 89.

[53]. Alexander III. to the Archbishop of Canterbury and Bishop of Worcester in Decret. Lib. II. Tit. VIII. c. 1; Innocent III. *Ibid.* Lib. I. Tit. XXIX. c. 24, and Tit. XLI. c. 4.

the custom, a fixed day of appearance is decreed in the provincial court, the citation is called a citatory decree [54]. No citation ought to issue except at the instance of some party as promoter, except the judge is proceeding extra-judicially of mere office [55], nor ought one to be decreed on a principal holiday, though it may be served on one [56]. If it fails in any one of these particulars, exception may be taken to it as invalid.

10. By mediaeval rule a citation may be either (1) simple or (2) peremptory. A simple citation must be thrice repeated before a defendant can be deemed contumacious [57]. In an extra-judicial matter a single citation suffices [58]. A peremptory citation is a form of citation which has been introduced as a substitute for three simple citations. It must therefore (1) express that it is peremptory [59], and (2) must allow an interval of time equal to three simple terms [60], which

[54]. *Ibid.* p. 86, 90.

[55]. Ayliffe 177, 180 says that there are three exceptions: (1) when the party appears without objecting; (2) when the judge perceives that the instance of the party perishes; (3) when the cause concerns the public good.

[56]. Concil. Tarracon. A.D. 516, Can. 4 ap. Gratian Caus. XV. Qu. IV. c. 1, and Labbé v. 698: That no bishop, presbyter, or clerk dare to judge any matter brought before him on the Lord's Day. Gregory IX. in Decret. Lib. II. Tit. IX. c. 5; Ayliffe 178.

[57]. Hincmar of Rheims, A.D. 850, ap. Gratian Caus. XXIV. Qu. III. c. 6, states that Nestorius was thrice cited by Coelestin and the Synod of Ephesus, A.D. 431. See *Spiritual Courts*, note 9. Concil. Milev. A.D. 402, Can. 16, recites that the accusers had been thrice cited, and failed to appear. Concil. Chelsea A.D. 816, Can. 6: If any one be summoned to synod by his plaintiffs, and do not delay to meet them at the first, second, or third call, being ready to give an account of himself, but the plaintiff flinches, . . . let nothing further be done. Concil. Winton A.D. 1076, Can. 4: If laymen are accused of any crime, and will not obey the bishop, let them be summoned three several times. William's mandate, A.D. 1085: If any one refuse to come to the bishop's court, let him be summoned three several times. Innocent III. to Archbishop of Armagh in Decret. Lib. II. Tit. XIV. c. 7; Law's Forms, 91.

[58]. Ayliffe 180.

[59]. Innocent III. in Decret. Lib. II. Tit. XIV. c. 6; Lynd. 82, 114, 218. It is sometimes called an authority.

[60]. Alexander III. to Archbishop of Canterbury in Decret. Lib. II. Tit. VIII. c. 1; Innocent III. *Ibid.* Lib. I. Tit. XXIX. c. 24, and Tit. XLI. c. 4; Ayliffe 179.

is called a term peremptory (⁶¹). According to their subject-matter, citations are also called (1) *peremptory*, when they contain a definite command to appear; (2) *mandatory and inhibitory*, when they forbid a judge to proceed further, or a party in a matrimonial cause to enter into a fresh contract of marriage until the suit is decided; or (3) *mandatory and intimatory*, when they intimate to the parties cited that if they do not appear, proceedings will go on in their absence. They are also called (1) *general*, when they cite to attend the whole course of proceedings; or (2) *special*, when they cite to perform some particular act; or, again, (1) *public*, when they are executed by a public writing in Church; or (2) *private*, when they are verbally executed, or by notice left at the defendant's house; and, lastly, (1) *personal*, when they are directed to persons; or (2) *real*, when they are executed upon specific goods, as upon a ship in a maritime cause (⁶²).

11. By the rule of the Fourth Lateran Council, no one can be cited to appear at a place more than two days' journey beyond the limits of the citing authority's jurisdiction (⁶³); nor, in this country, can any one be cited to appear outside his diocese, except into the provincial court (⁶⁴), and that only (1) during the voidance of an episcopal see of which the archbishop is the superior ordinary (⁶⁵); (2) if a suit is instituted against a bishop, archdeacon, or any official, for an excess committed or a neglect of duty; (3) in a cause of appeal; (4) on complaint of a grievance against the prelate or official before whom a suit is pending; (5) when a bishop or other immediate judge dares not or will not proceed; (6) when an ordinary or judge has, or pretends to have, an interest in the suit; (7) when an ordinary or judge voluntarily renounces his jurisdiction, or passes it on by letters of request; and (8) when the suit relates to some matter

---

(61). Gregory IX. in Decret. Lib. II. Tit. VIII. c. 4; Ayliffe 180.
(62). Law's Forms, p. 80, 89.
(63). Can. 37, A.D. 1215, in Decret. Lib. I. Tit. III. c. 28; Honorius III. *Ibid.* Lib. II. Tit. XXV. c. 7; Ayliffe 181.
(64). 23 Hen. VIII. c. 9; 3 and 4 Vict. c. 86, sec. 19.
(65). Law's Forms 55; see note 49.

which is already being dealt with by a higher court([66]), as a legacy in probate cases.

12. Before any citation can have effect, it must be brought to the knowledge of the person cited, or, as it is said, be served upon him; and its effect dates not from the time of issue, but from the time of service. A citation may not be served by the person at whose instance it was granted, but only by the judge or some official acting for him ([67]). Service may, however, be effected in one of three ways, viz.—(1) personally (*denunciatione*); (2) by a writing (*literis*), in the manner called by ways and means (*viis et modis*); or (3) by proclamation *edicto* ([68]). Personal service is effected by showing the original citation, explaining its contents, and giving the person cited a copy, if he asks for one; or by giving the same to his proctor, or to some member of his family ([69]). When personal service cannot be effected, the judge may decree the citation to be affixed to the door of his house, or to the Church door during the time of divine service, and a copy left there. This is termed service by ways and means (*viis et modis*) ([70]). Citations by proclamation

---

(66). Law's Forms 81.

(67). Const. 26 Otho, A.D. 1237: That letters of summons be not sent by such as obtain them, or by their messengers, but that the judge send them by his own faithful messenger, at the moderate expense of him who obtained them. Const. 25 Othobon, A.D. 1268; Const. 3 Mepham, A.D. 1328; Const. 7 Stratford, A.D. 1342, says citations should be served by officials, deans, apparitors, or other their ministers, but not by rectors, vicars, or parish priests. Lynd. 81, 87.

(68). Devoti Inst. Lib. III. Tit. v. § 13 calls them *denunciatione, literis, edicto*. Law's Forms 89.

(69). Alexander III. to Bishops of Exeter and Winchester in Decret. Lib. II. Tit. XIV. c. 3, says that if a man has left the country the citation may be made on his proctor, or, if he has left no proctor, *denunciationibus ad domum ejus missis*. Law's Forms 91; Craisson, § 5898.

(70). Gregory IX. in Decret. Lib. II. Tit. XIV. c. 10; Const. 26 Otho, A.D. 1237: We hear that men obtaining letters of summons send them forth by three vile messengers, two of whom put up the letters over the altar or in some other place, and the third presently takes them away. Ayliffe 177 states that a citation ought to be served at the place where a person dwells. Law's Forms 97. See *Spiritual Courts*, note 161.

(*citationes edictales*) are those not confined to any one person, but directed to all who have an interest in the cause.

13. Before any proceeding can be founded on the defendant's non-appearance, the service of the citation must be proved ([71]). The proof of service of the citation is the first judicial act in a cause after the citation. So absolutely essential is the citation as the beginning and foundation of every judicial proceeding, that every judicial act exercised against a person not cited, or not cited to answer the particular matter named in it, is null and void *ipso jure* ([72]). On the other hand, the service of the citation at once produces three effects: (1) It pledges the defendant to appear, otherwise he is contumacious ([73]). (2) It perpetuates the jurisdiction of a judge-delegate until he becomes aware of the death of his principal ([74]), or until the suit is disposed of, if contestation of suit has already taken place ([75]). (3) It creates a pending suit ([76]), so far as to prevent the matter in dispute being dealt with in any way ([77]), although it creates no pending suit against the defendant until he contests

---

[71]. Gregory IX. in Decret. Lib. II. Tit. XV. c. 4; Lynd. 200; Ayliffe 160; Law's Forms 99.

[72]. Ayliffe 176.

[73]. Alexander III. to Abbot of Ramsay and Archdeacon of Ely in Decret. Lib. II. Tit. XIV. c. 2.

[74]. Urban III. *Ibid*. Lib. I. Tit. XXIX. c. 20.

[75]. Lucius III. *Ibid*. c. 19 states that the office is not perpetuated until contestation. Ayliffe 155.

[76]. Concil. Vien. A.D. 1311, in Clem. Decret. Lib. II. Tit. V. c. 2; Lynd. 278, 115: There is said to be a judicial proceeding (*judicium*) so soon as the citation has been served. Ayliffe 153: Though it may be styled *lis* or suit before contestation of suit, yet it cannot be said to be *lis mota* or pendency of suit till afterwards. Therefore, before contestation of suit, the defendant is not *in mora*. But a libel offered to the prince effects a pendency of suit. . . . But a pendency of suit in respect of the plaintiff is induced *ex sola commissione*, or by the judge's decree for citing the defendant. *Ray* v. *Sherwood*, 1 Curt. 217, in Stephens' Eccl. Stat. 1651.

[77]. Gelasius A.D. 494, ap. Gratian Caus. XI. Qu. 1. c. 50; Alexander III. to Archbishop of York in Decret. Lib. II. Tit. XVI. c. 1; Innocent III. *Ibid*. c. 2. Honorius III. *Ibid*. Tit. XXVIII. c. 69 allows that for the judge to alter the matter involved in a suit before contestation is a good ground of appeal. Ayliffe 151.

it ([78]), because he may never contest it. In addition, (4) in a civil cause it breaks a prescription. A citation in itself invalid, becomes valid if the defendant appears to it.

14. If the defendant either does not appear to the citation, or appears and goes away before the cause is heard and determined, or is disobedient to a ruling of the judge ([79]), he is said to be contumacious; and unless he is able to excuse his contumacy as being apparent only and not real, he cannot be heard in judgment ([80]). In a criminal cause the evidence may be taken and the defendant condemned in his absence ([81]) after it is shown that he is, and he has been pronounced to be contumaciously absent ([82]). In a civil cause the judge does not pronounce the defendant contumacious except on the petition of the plaintiff ([83]), but he may hear evidence and give a preliminary sentence in the plaintiff's favour, which, unless appealed against, becomes definitive at the end of a year ([84]).

(78). Honorius III. in Decret. Lib. v. Tit. XL. c. 30.

(79). Concil. Milev. A.D. 416, ap. Gratian Caus. II. Qu. VI. c. 19: Whoever contumaciously refuses to obey the judges, after this has been proved to the primate, let him issue letters that no bishop may communicate with him until he obeys. Concil. Tribur. *Ibid*. Caus. XI. Qu. III. c. 43 : For these three crimes any one may be lawfully excommunicated—refusing to come when canonically summoned to synod [*i.e.*, court], or when there refusing to obey sacerdotal precepts, or presuming to leave the synod before the final conclusion of the cause. Alexander III. to Bishops of Exeter and Winchester in Decret. Lib. II. Tit. XIV. c. 3.

(80). Lynd. 114 says that contumacy may be either apparent or real. In both cases the contumacy prevents the defendant being heard by the judge of first instance, but the judge of appeal may hear him for the purpose of deciding that his contumacy was not real. See Gratian Caus. IV. Qu. V. c. 1. If the defendant changes his forum after being served with the citation, he is still liable to answer before the citing judge. Decret. Lib. II. Tit. II. c. 19 ; Innocent III. *Ibid*. Lib. II. Tit. XXVII. c. 18.

(81). Innocent III. in Decret. Lib. II. Tit. XIV. c. 8, and Tit. VI. c. 5, § 8. This is not allowed in a matrimoniul cause when the respondent is not contumacious. *Ibid*. Lib. II. Tit. VI. c. 4 ; Ecclesiastical Courts Commission, 1883, I. 197, and II. 189.

(82). Craisson, § 5903.

(83). Innocent III. A.D. 1203, to the Bishop of Durham, in Decret. Lib. I. Tit. XX. c. 34.

(84). Concil. Lat. IV. A.D. 1215, Can. 40, in Decret. Lib. II. Tit XIV. c. 9,

15. If the defendant appears, he may do so under protest, or to take exception (⁸⁵) either (1) to the citation, as being defective, uncertain, or ambiguous (⁸⁶); (2) to the judge, as not being a judge of competent jurisdiction, or as being suspect (⁸⁷); (3) to the plaintiff, as being disqualified (⁸⁸), or to his proctor as having no sufficient mandate (⁸⁹); or (4) to the admission of the libel in whole or in part—in whole when the facts alleged will not support the conclusion, in part when some of them are irrelevant, or could not be proved by evidence, or involve matter at the time pending before another tribunal (⁹⁰). Such exceptions are called dilatory, because they delay the plaintiff's intention in judgment, and prevent the controversy becoming

directs the plaintiff to be put in possession as custodian for a year, and directs a final judgment to be then passed constituting him true possessor; and Tit. VL c. 5, § 6.

(85). Decret. Lib. II. Tit. XXV. Sext. Lib. II. Tit. XII.; Ayliffe 252; Law's Forms 167 and 69; Apost. Const. II. 49 names some of these exceptions. Ecclesiastical Courts Commission Report, p. 197.

(86). Ayliffe 252, when it is not known who is the person intended to be cited; Ayliffe 176, or for any other defect in the citation. Innocent III. in Decret. Lib. II. Tit. XXVIII. c. 49, says it is good ground for appeal if the defendant's request to have the piece of land demanded in a libel identified is refused.

(87). See above, *Spiritual Courts*, § 29. Socrates I. 31 relates that Athanasius took exception to the jurisdiction of the Council of Tyre in 335 A.D.—(1) on the ground that Eusebius and his party, who sat in it, were his enemies, and (2) that Ischyras his accuser, described in the libel as a presbyter could not be proved to be one; and when the Council disallowed the exceptions he appealed to the Emperor. Concil. Lat. IV. A.D. 1215, in Decret. Lib. II. Tit. XXVIII. c. 61 and 41. According to Alexander III. *Ibid.* c. 6 and 24, exception cannot be taken to a judge because the defendant has in a previous suit appealed from a sentence of his. Ayliffe 252: It is held that a judge can himself decide the question of his jurisdiction, subject of course to appeal, but that he cannot decide the question of being suspect. Craisson, § 5911.

(88). Because of being excommunicated, under age, outlawed, and the like. Devoti of Lib. III. Tit. X. c. 7; Ayliffe 252, 254.

(89). Innocent III. to the bishop, dean, and precentor of Hereford, in Decret. Lib. II. Tit. XXVIII. c. 48.

(90). Law's Forms, 169; Ecclesiastical Courts Commission, 1883, Hist. App. L 197.

a suit ([91]); they form the subject of argument, and the refusal to admit them is good ground of appeal ([92]).

16. All dilatory exceptions, unless it be that of the greater excommunication ([93]), which may be alleged at any time ([94]), ought to be made before contestation of suit ([95]). They may nevertheless be made afterwards if (1) the defendant has reserved his right of making them by protest; (2) if they have since cropped up; or (3) have been since discovered ([96]); but if exception is not taken at once to the judge's jurisdiction, the defendant is deemed to have consented to it ([97]). The first thing, therefore, which the judge has to do when the defendant has appeared, is to fix the term deliberatory, within which dilatory exceptions must be propounded ([98]). At the expiration of this term, if no exceptions have been made or sustained, he decrees the admission of the libel, and the controversy is then ripe for discussion in judgment.

17. Besides taking exception to the libel and citation, the defendant can also, in some cases, protect himself by making a counter-claim (*mutua petitio* or *reconventio*) ([99]). This he may

---

([91]). Gratian Caus. III. Qu. VI. c. 2; Innocent III. to Bishop of Ely in Decret. Lib. II. Tit. XXV. c. 4, and Tit. XXVIII. c. 62; Ayliffe, 252; Law's Forms, 167.

([92]). Innocent III. in Decret. Lib. I. Tit. XXIX. c. 27, § 5, and Lib. II. Tit. XXVIII. c. 48; Ecclesiastical Courts Commission 1883, I. 183.

([93]). Concil. Lugdun. A.D. 1274, in Sext. Lib. II. Tit. XII. c. 1, forbids this exception to be made unless the kind of excommunication is specified and the name of the excommunicating judge, and the same proved within eight days. Innocent III. to the archdeacon of Richmond, *Ibid.* Tit. XXV. c. 2, says that this exception cannot be rebutted by alleging that the defendant has ignored the excommunication.

([94]). Gregory IX. in Decret. Lib. II. Tit. XXV. c. 12; Concil. Lugdun. A.D. 1245, in Sext. Lib. II. Tit. XII. c. 1.

([95]). Innocent III. *Ibid.* Lib. II. Tit. XXVII. c. 20; Ayliffe, 252.

([96]). Innocent III. *Ibid.* Lib. I. Tit. XXIX. c. 21 and 25; *Id.* to the Bishop of Ely, *Ibid.* Lib. II. Tit. XXV. c. 4, quoted note 126.

([97]). See *Spiritual Courts*, § 30.

([98]). Innocent III. to Bishop of Ely, l. c.

([99]). Devoti Lib. III. Tit. XI. § 4, in Decret. Lib. II. Tit. IV.; Sext. Lib. I. Tit. III. c. 3.

do, provided he is not excommunicate ([100]), by reconvening the plaintiff before the same judge, or by separate action if the judge is suspect ([101]). By reconvening him before the same judge, he acquiesces in the judge's jurisdiction, but, on the other hand, he secures the simultaneous settlement of claim and counter-claim ([102]), provided the reconvention or counter-claim is made before, or immediately after, contestation of suit ([103]).

18. As the object of counter-claim is to secure an allowance or compensation ([104]) by way of set-off, reconvention is not possible whenever compensation is not possible. There can therefore be no reconvention (1) in criminal causes ([105]) in which the accused must be acquitted on the ground of his innocence, not on the ground of his being less guilty than his accuser; (2) in prejudicial causes ([106]), because a prejudicial exception perempts the principal matter; (3) in causes of breach of trust ([107]); and (4) in causes of wrongful dispossession ([108]). Moreover, no one can reconvene another who could not support an independent action himself ([109]), nor can one reconvene another before arbitrators ([110]), but a judge delegate can entertain counter-claims ([111]). Reconvention is always made on exactly the same footing as the original action ([112]).

19. Before contestation of suit a controversy may be with-

(100). Innocent III. in Decret. Lib. II. Tit. XXV. c. 5.
(101). Concil. Lugdun. A.D. 1245, in Sext. Lib. I. Tit. III. c. 3.
(102). Alexander III. in Decret. Lib. II. Tit. IV. c. 1.
(103). *Id. Ibid.* Craisson, § 5922.
(104). Devoti Lib. III. Tit. XI. § 4.
(105). Lib. IX. Cod. Tit. 1. c. 19 ap. Gratian Caus. III. Qu. XI. c. 2 and 4.
(106). Clemens III. in Decret. Lib. II. Tit. X. c. 1.
(107). Gregory IX. in Decret. Lib. III. Tit. XVI. c. 2.
(108). Innocent III. in Decret. Lib. II. Tit. X. c. 2. Pseudo-Isidor. ap. Gratian Caus. III. Qu. l. c. 1, 2, 3.
(109). Innocent III. in Decret. Lib. II. Tit. XXV. c. 5.
(110). Innocent III. in Decret. Lib. I. Tit. XLIII. c. 6.
(111). Alexander III. *Ibid.* Lib. II. Tit. IV. c. 1.
(112). Coelestin III. A.D. 1193, in Decret. Lib. II. Tit. IV. c. 2. Thus if the citation is made *appellatione remota*, the reconvention is also *appellatione remota*, although this is not expressed.

drawn from judgment except in a matrimonial cause [113]. The withdrawal from a criminal proceeding is termed *abolitio*, and is not permitted except by leave of the judge, unless it be to avoid bloodshed [114]. Such a withdrawal by the accuser bars him from again raising the same charge [115]. A withdrawal by the accused is equivalent to an admission of guilt, and he may be dealt with accordingly [116]. The withdrawal or settlement of a civil controversy is a thing which a judge is directed to encourage [117]. If made gratuitously, it is termed a *composition* [118]; if made upon terms the value of which has been already ascertained in judgment, a *compact* [119]; if made upon terms the value of which is unascertained, but made with the sanction of the court, a *transaction* [120].

(113). Honorius III. in Decret. Lib. I. Tit. XXXVI. c. 11.

(114). Gratian Caus. II. Qu. 1. c. 7, § 2, *Ibid.* Qu. III. c. 8; says that to make a false charge is called *calumniation*, to conceal the truth *prevarication*, and generally to desist from prosecution *tergiversation*. Lynd. 73. See *Canonical Procedure*, note 81.

(115). Innocent III. in Decret. Lib. v. Tit. I. c. 4.

(116). *Id. Ibid.* If the judge finds that the accused is criminous, and that the withdrawal is made by collusion, let the accused receive the legal punishment.

(117). Pseudo-Isidor. ap. Gratian Caus. II. Qu. VI. c. 18, permits a man to withdraw from a suit. Honorius III. in Decret. Lib. I. Tit. XXXVI. c. 11, urges a judge to use every endeavour to bring about compositions, even abating for that purpose from legal severity, excepting always matrimonial causes, which do not admit of a composition. Const. 28 Langton, A.D. 1222: That archdeacons or their officials give leave to the parties to agree or withdraw by compounding, so that the suit be such as admits of composition. Const. 21 Otho, A.D. 1237.

(118). Alexander III. in Decret. Lib. I. Tit. XXXVI. c. 7.

(119). *Pactum* or *pactio.* Concil. Carthag. I. A.D. 347, in Decret. Greg. IX. Lib. I. Tit. XXXV. c. 1.: Either let compacts be observed, or let the defendant be amenable to ecclesiastical discipline. Alexander III. to Bishops of Exeter and Worcester, *Ibid.* c. 4, forbids a compact for the resignation of a benefice. *Id.* to the Archbishop of York, *Ibid.* c. 5; *Id.* to the Archbishop of Canterbury, *Ibid.* c. 6, forbids a Church to be given under a compact for an increased pension. Coelestin III. to Bishop of Lincoln in Decret. Lib. v. Tit. III. c. 28, also Tit. XL. c. 12; Law's Forms 160.

(120). Gregory, A.D. 599, in Decret. Lib. I. Tit. XXXVI. c. 1. Devoti Inst.

20. A libel may be sometimes changed, as if an estate demanded under a will is demanded under a contract; and sometimes mended or enlarged, as if instead of a debt of £10 one of £20 is claimed. With certain exceptions ([121]) a libel can be changed in a civil cause before contestation of suit, but not in a criminal cause, and by English practice the plaintiff in a testamentary cause is allowed to make three allegations, but not more ([122]). A libel can also be enlarged by the addition of new matter, but substantial matter can only be added before contestation of suit ([123]). Therefore since time and place are considered substantial matters in a criminal cause, the omission of them in a criminal libel cannot be afterwards rectified. On the other hand, the conclusion or petition being accounted the substantial matter in a civil cause, additions are permitted to any part of a civil libel except the conclusion, even after contestation of suit; and in universal actions such as suing for an inheritance, or general actions such as an action for waste, additions may be made in the way of specifying particulars, even up to the time of giving sentence.

21. The period of time which is allowed to intervene, either by law or by the judge's ruling before any judicial act is concluded, is called a delay-term (*dilatio*). Any additional allowance of time at the request of either of the parties is termed an extension of time (*induciae*) ([124]). Terms are allowed by law at each stage of a judicial proceeding, and extensions of time may be had when they are necessary. There

---

Lib. III. Tit. XVIII. says that pactio is the generic term of which transactio is one species. Ulpianus in leg. 1 de Transac.: Qui transigit quasi de re dubia et lite incerta neque finita transigit; qui vero paciscitur donationis causa rem certam et indubitatam liberaliter remittit. Law's Forms 162.

(121). *Ibid.* 166.
(122). Ayliffe 350; Law's Forms 180.
(123). Law's Forms 166. See *Spiritual Courts*, note 101.
(124). Pseudo-Isidor. ap. Gratian Caus. III. Qu. III.; Coelestin III. A.D. 1193, in Decret. Lib. II. Tit. VIII. c. 2; Honorius III. *Ibid.* c. 3, and Tit. XXVIII. c. 62.

280   *Short Manuals of Canon Law.*

are two regular terms in the introduction of a cause, for which a fixed time is set by law or by custom, viz. (1) the term citatory ([125]), or the interval allowed before appearance to the citation becomes obligatory; and (2) the term deliberatory ([126]), or the interval allowed to the defendant after appearing to the citation, to deliberate whether he has any exception to propound before the judge decrees the admission of the libel.

THE INSTANCE OF A CAUSE—THE SUIT.

22. When the judge has decreed the admission of the libel or articles, and the controversy is thereby allowed to be a fit matter for discussion in judgment, the first and necessary act is contestation of suit or joining of issue, and the acts which follow it are called the suit (*lis*) or trial. All the proceedings that took place before were said to be acts in law (*in jure*); all that now take place are said to be acts in judgment (*in judicio*). The suit proper includes three things: (1) contestation of suit or joining of issue; (2) the ordering of the investigation upon the allegations made, and the exceptions pleaded ([127]); and (3)

(125). Alexander III. to the Archbishop of Canterbury and Bishop of Worcester in Decret. Lib. II. Tit. VIII. c. 1, forbids too short a term to be allowed in the citation.

(126). Coelestin III. A.D. 1193, in Decret. Lib. II. Tit. VIII. c. 2. Innocent III. A.D. 1204, to the Bishop of Ely, *Ibid.* Tit. XXV. c. 4: Since the termination of causes is sometimes maliciously delayed, in answer to your inquiry we decree that within a certain time to be assigned by the judge, all dilatory exceptions must be propounded, so that if afterwards they wish to allege them, they shall not be heard unless [1] they had before made protest, unless [2] by chance some new and valid one should arise, or [3] he who wishes to allege one first makes oath that it has subsequently come to his knowledge.

(127). According to Clemens v. in Clem. Lib. v. Tit. XI. c. 2, the original libel should be divided into positions or sections, called *allegations* in a civil cause, *articles* in a criminal cause. In a civil cause the plaintiff *alleges and propounds* what is contained in them, in a criminal cause the judge *articles and objects*. See Ecclesiastical Courts Commission, 1883, vol. II. 207. In a civil cause the plaintiff may put in three allegations or pleadings amending the libel, and the defendant may reply to each. Law's Forms 179.

the judicial production of the evidence in support of the libel and exceptions called the proof.

23. The instance of a suit is said to commence when a controversy is judicially contested, and to last until sentence is given, or till the end of three years ([128](#)). For contestation three things are necessary: (1) There must be an allegation of crime or statement of claim made by an accuser or plaintiff, and an answer or defence made by a defendant or accused person. (2) The allegation must be made by way of petition before a judge, and the answer by way of direct reply to it. (3) The answer must be made with intent to invite a judicial decision ([129](#)). The answer may, however, be (1) simply affirmative, or (2) simply negative, or (3) affirmative or negative with a qualification ([130](#)).

24. Before a suit is contested there can be no judicial examination of witnesses, except in cases where the death of a witness may be apprehended, or else to perpetuate evidence ([131](#)), because

---

(128). Ayliffe 151: The instance of a cause is said to be that judicial process which is made from the contestation of a suit, even to the time of pronouncing sentence in the cause, or till the end of three years. Honorius III. in Decret. Lib. V. Tit. XL. c. 50: Lis dicitur mota cum fuerit contestata Lynd. 162: Res est litigiosa post litem contestatam. Ayliffe 150: A lis or suit is the cause itself deduced in judgment. . . . A *lis* or suit does not commence but from contestation of suit. Devoti Lib. III. Tit. VI. § 3 says that by the civil and canon law the usual time allowed before contestation of suit is twenty days. Lynd. 72 says that it must take place within two months, appealing to Concil. Carthag. III. A.D. 397, Can. 7 ap. Gratian Caus. IV. Qu. V. c. 1, which requires an incriminated bishop to appear within one or two months at the most. Boniface VIII. in Sext. Lib. II. Tit. III. c. 2 says that contestation of suit is not to be delayed because a peremptory exception is propounded. Law's Forms 173. See above, note 76.

(129). Gregory IX. in Decret. Lib. I. Tit. VI. c. 54, § 3, and Lib. II. Tit. V. c. 1: Contestation of suit is not made by positions (or articles), and answers to them, but by a petition propounded in law, and a reply to it [before the judge].

(130). Law's Forms 173, 81.

(131). Innocent III. in Decret. Lib. II. Tit. VI. c. 1 and 5: The same to the Bishop of Durham, *Ibid*. Tit. XX. c. 34 and c. 41. Law's Forms 173 says that the practice, nevertheless, is to administer the oath to witnesses in court by anticipation.

as yet the suit has no existence ([132]); neither can there be any judicial sentence in the cause, but only an extra-judicial ruling on the controversy. Contestation of suit is therefore defined to be the fundamental act and basis (*principium formale*) of all judicial discussion. Accordingly it has no place (1) in summary or extra-judicial causes, (2) in executive and other causes introduced without a libel, (3) in criminal causes where the facts are notorious, and (4) generally in all causes in which a judge is authorised to proceed of mere office without judicial forms ([133]); nor (5) in appeals, because the original contestation applies to these. In certain causes, nevertheless, such as a proceeding for heresy, contumacy in not appearing when cited is deemed equivalent to contestation of suit ([134]), and in summary and executive causes the act which ordinarily follows contestation is held to set up the instance of the cause ([135]).

25. The principal effects which follow upon contestation of suit are the following: (1) With it the judicial suit commences, and the instance begins to run. (2) It breaks a prescription, or from it a prescription may be set up ([136]). (3) It excludes dilatory exceptions, except in the three cases already named ([137]). (4) It perpetuates the decision of a judge-delegate up to the final decision of the suit ([138]). (5) The proctors of both parties are now masters of the suit (*domini litis*).

26. Contestation of suit is followed by the oath against vexatious litigation, called the *oath of calumny* ([139]). In this

---

(132). Innocent III. *Ibid.* Lib. I. Tit. XXXVIII. c. 4; Gregory IX. *Ibid.* Lib. II. Tit. v. c. 1. Law's Forms 172: Contestation of suit is defined to be the *principium formale*, the fundamental judicial act whereby the judge begins to take cognisance of the cause.
(133). See *Canonical Procedure*, § 8.
(134). Lynd. 302.
(135). Ayliffe 151.
(136). Devoti Lib. III. Tit. VII. § 4.
(137). See § 15 and note 126.
(138). Lucius III. to Archbishop of Canterbury in Decret. Lib. I. Tit. XXIX. c. 19.
(139). Devoti Inst. Lib. III. Tit. VII. § 1. Const. 24 Otho, A.D. 1237:

oath the party swears that he believes his cause to be just and good, that he will neither knowingly deny the truth nor use false evidence, and that he will not vexatiously cause delays nor attempt to succeed by bribery. This oath, which was customary among the Romans, was at first administered only to laymen, but afterwards to clergy also, including public bodies and bishops ([140]). By the rule of the thirteenth century it could be required from both plaintiff and defendant ([141]), in causes criminal as well as civil ([142]), on appeal as well as in the first instance ([143]); but by the custom of this country laymen can only be called upon to take it in matrimonial and testamentary causes ([144]) In cases in which it is allowed, a plaintiff refusing to take it is cast in his suit, and a defendant refusing it is treated as one who has confessed the injustice of his defence ([145]). Formerly it could be taken by a proctor on behalf of his principal, but this practice is at least discountenanced here ([146]). A special form of it, called the oath of malice,

---

" We ordain that the oath of calumny, in all ecclesiastical causes whatsoever, and of speaking the truth in spiritual causes [*i.e.*, the oath *ex officio*], be for the future taken in the kingdom of England." The oath may be administered before contestation of suit whenever a dilatory exception is propounded. Sext. Lib. II. Tit. IV. c. 1 ; Ayliffe 138. See *Canonical Procedure*, note 37.

(140). Lucius III. to the Bishop of Ely and the Archdeacon of Norwich in Decret. Lib. II. Tit. VII. c. 5, authorises clergy to take the oath of calumny, and Gregory IX. *Ibid.* c. 7 authorises bishops.

(141). Lucius III. to the Bishop of Ely and Archdeacon of Norwich in Decret. Lib. II. Tit. VII. c. 5.

(142). Honorius II. in Decret. Lib. II. Tit. VII. c. 2 states that it was not the Roman custom to administer it in causes concerning churches, tithes, and spiritual causes ; but Boniface VIII. in Sext. Lib. II. Tit. IV. c. 1 ordered it to be taken in these. Ayliffe 139 ; Lynd. 111.

(143). Sext. Decret. Lib. II. Tit. IV. c. 2.

(144). The act 2 Hen. IV. c. 15, which at one time allowed it, was repealed by 1 Eliz. c. 1. Ayliffe 138 ; Law's Forms 281.

(145). Gregory IX. in Decret. Lib. II. Tit. VII. c. 7 ; Athon. 60 ; Law's Forms 256, 283.

(146). This is sanctioned by Eugenius III. in Decret. Lib. II. Tit. VII. c. 3 and 4, also Sext. Lib. II. Tit. IV. c. 3, but forbidden in this country by Can. 132 of 1603.

may be administered by the judge to either of the parties as often as he sees fit ([147]).

27. Before the question of proof is gone into an important part of every suit is the so-called personal decree ([148]). By this decree, which is issued by the judge at the plaintiff's instance, the defendant is required to make answer upon oath to certain positions extracted from the libel and propounded to him in judgment, called interrogatories ([149]). In all civil causes interrogatories may be administered to the defendant, and personal answers may be required from him, except when they suggest matter which might incriminate him ([150]). In criminal causes personal answers may not be required from the defendant ([151]) when the judge's office is promoted at the instance of a voluntary promoter; but when the judge proceeds of mere office, or, in other words extra-judicially, the so-called *ex officio* oath compelling him to answer to the criminal charge could formerly be administered to him in synod or audience. This has now been made illegal in this country by secular legislation ([152]); but if he

([147]). Law's Forms 257, 281, 284.

([148]). Law's Forms 183.

([149]). Gregory IX. quoted note 129; Boniface VIII. in Decret. Lib. II. Tit. IX. c. 2; Ayliffe 65; Eccles. Courts Commission, 1883, Hist. App. I. 182.

([150]). Law's Forms 189 says not in cases of defamation, correction, and perjury. Boniface in Decret. Lib. II. Tit. x. c. 2 requires public bodies to make answer to interrogatories through their syndic.

([151]). Ayliffe 65, 397; Law's Forms 177 and 190: In criminal charges the party is not bound to answer on his oath; but the position is admissible as far as regards the proof. Sir John Nicoll's decree in the case of *Schultz v. Hodgson*, Addam's Reports I. 113, has confirmed this practice, and it is now fully understood that in criminal charges the defendant cannot be required to return any personal answer on oath. But see note 151.

([152]). Const. 25 Otho, A.D. 1237, introduced the oath of truth or oath *ex officio*, as well as the oath of *calumny*, into this country. The act 25 Hen. VIII. c. 14, since repealed, recited that it standeth not with the right order of justice or equity that any person should be convicted or put to the loss of his life, good name, or goods, unless it were by due accusation and witnesses, or by presentment, verdict, confession, or process of outlawry. 13 Car. II. c. 12, sec. 4, forbids the oath *ex officio*. Stephen's Eccl. Stat. 149; Ecclesiastical Courts Commission, 1883, Hist. App. I. 182, II. 207, 239; Law's Forms 189. See *Canonical Procedure*, notes 141 and 149.

tendered himself as a witness in a judicial proceeding it was usual to examine him as to the existence of fame or scandal respecting the matter charged ([153]).

28. If the plaintiff's case is established by the defendant's admissions, he may proceed to the conclusion and to sentence without proof by witnesses; or if any portion only is established he may produce witnesses in confirmation of the remaining articles only ([154]). It is for the judge to determine the proper order of the investigation ([155]). In doing so he has to consider three things: (1) the nature of the defendant's exceptions, (2) the existence or absence of a counter-claim, and (3) the style or custom of the court ([156]). It must, however, be remembered that by recent secular legislation in this country three different styles are in use in ecclesiastical courts, according to the nature of the cause, viz. (1) the old canonical mode of procedure, which is still followed in faculty cases; (2) the mode of procedure introduced by the Church Discipline Acts of 1841 and 1892, for the public discipline of clergy; and (3) the mode of procedure prescribed by the Public Worship Act, 1874, for restraining deviations from the forms sanctioned by the Act of Uniformity. The two last are statutory modes of procedure, differing in many respects from that prescribed by the Canon Law.

29. The term exception is applied to any allegation in the nature of a defence which delays or defeats the plaintiff's intention in judgment ([157]). The general effect of alleging an

---

([153]). Ecclesiastical Courts Commission Report, 1883, p. 4, states that the effect of 17 and 18 Vict. c. 47 is to render the parties to an ecclesiastical cause, including the defendant in a criminal suit, competent and compellable witnesses. See also Hist. App. I. 191. Paschal II. quoted note 201, declared him a competent witness.

([154]). Law's Forms 183.

([155]). Ordo cognitionum in Decret. Lib. II. Tit. X.; Devoti. Lib. III. Tit. XL.

([156]). Ayliffe [193].

([157]). Concil. Lugdun. A.D. 1245, in Sext. Lib. II. Tit. III. c. 1, calls a peremptory exception a defence. Boniface VIII. *Ibid.* c. 2 states that it does not effect a contestation of suit. Devoti Lib. III. Tit. X. c. 1.

exception is to introduce a new question, and to change the position of the parties until it is disposed of by casting the burden of proof upon its propounder ([158]). The plaintiff may meet this by himself excepting to the defendant's exception, whereby the burden of proof is thrown back upon him ([159]). This is termed a replication or reply, and other exceptions for and against may follow in like manner ([160]). An exception is called (1) criminal when it alleges a crime which would disqualify the adverse party from appearing in judgment, or (2) civil when it alleges some ground or reason which strikes at the root of a cause. One who alleges crime by way of exception is allowed two advantages, because he is acting in self-defence: (1) He is not required to subscribe to the law of retribution before proceeding to proof. (2) He is not liable to an action for defamation if he proves his exception ([161]), nor by the custom of France if he fails in proving it ([162]),

30. Exceptions are usually divided into (1) dilatory and (2) peremptory. Any defence which delays the plaintiff's intention in judgment but does not perempt it by going to the root of the matter, is termed a dilatory exception ([163]). One which defeats and perempts the suit itself is called a peremptory ([164]) or incident ([165]) exception. Dilatory exceptions have place when a cause is first introduced before contestation of suit ([166]), and if

(158). Ayliffe 251; Devoti Lib. III. Tit. x. § 11.
(159). Innocent III. to Archdeacon of Richmond in Decret. Lib. II. Tit. xxv. c. 2.
(160). They are termed duplications, triplications, quadruplications, or rejoinders, surrejoinders, and rebutters. Ayliffe 251; Devoti, § 12.
(161). Ayliffe 254.
(162). *Ibid.* Craisson, § 5873; Law's Forms 177. See *Canonical Procedure*, note 76.
(163). See § 15.
(164). Innocent III. in Decret. Lib. II. Tit. xx. c. 29, says that a witness called to prove a dilatory exception cannot be examined respecting the principal matter, but a witness called to prove a peremptory exception can. Concil. Lugdun. A.D. 1245, in Sext. Lib. II. Tit. III. c. 1.
(165). Ayliffe 253: Every peremptory exception is styled an incidental exception, quasi incidens seu perimens ipsum negotium principale.
(166). Ayliffe 252. See § 15 and note 87.

not then made are ordinarily taken to be waived. Peremptory
exceptions may be propounded at any time, but, to be decisive
of the suit, they cannot be propounded until by contestation
the cause has become a suit. Some peremptory exceptions
are called *merely peremptory*, because they dispose of the suit
but do not destroy its instance, such as prescription or fraud,
and these may be propounded at any time before sentence,
but not afterwards ([167]). Others are called exceptions conclusive of a suit (*litis finitae*) ([168]), because they destroy the
instance, such as that the matter has been already judicially
settled (*res judicata*), or that it has been settled by a composition out of court. These may be alleged at any time, even
after sentence in bar of execution ([169]).

31. The various incidental questions which are thus raised
by way of exception may be grouped in three classes, having
regard to their bearing on the main issue, viz. (1) those called
prejudicial ([170]), (2) those called *preparatory*, and (3) those called
collateral ([171]). A prejudicial question is one which carries with
it the decision of the main issue. Thus a decision that there
never has been a valid marriage is a prejudicial decision which
disposes of a suit for the restitution of conjugal rights ([172]). A
preparatory question is one without the decision of which the
main question cannot be decided, but which does not in itself

---

([167]). Ayliffe 252, 255; Devoti, § 4.

([168]). Innocent III. A.D. 1198, to the Archbishops of Armagh and Cashel, in Decret. Lib. II. Tit. XIV. c. 7. Gregory IX. *Ibid*. Tit. XXV. c. 13 calls them res judicatae. Devoti Lib. III. Tit. X. § 2 calls them peremptoriae litis finitae. Ayliffe 253. Boniface VIII. in Sext. Lib. II. Tit. XII. c. 2 directs secular judges to receive a plea of *res judicata* from spiritual judges, and *vice versâ*.

([169]). Ayliffe 252.

([170]). Boniface VIII. in Sext. Lib. II. Tit. XV. c. 12 : Although no appeal was made from an interlocutory ruling prejudicial to the principal matter, yet if a definitive sentence is [successfully] appealed against, the grievance inflicted by the interlocutory ruling may be lawfully set right by the judge of appeal.

([171]). Devoti Lib. III. Tit. XI. § 1.

([172]). Clemens III. in Decret. Lib. II. Tit. X. c. 1; Honorius III. A.D. 1224, *Ibid*. c. 3.

settle the main question. Thus, if a bishop is called to account for the acts of his official which are said to be illegal, and denies that he is responsible for them, a decision that he is responsible does not dispose of the main issue unless the official's acts are shown to be illegal. A collateral question is one the decision of which does not affect the main issue.

32. The order in which exceptions are admitted to proof depends on their nature. Those involving prejudicial questions should be first taken, because they dispose of the whole cause ([173]); next those involving preparatory questions, and lastly those involving collateral questions. When several exceptions of equal relevance are propounded, those which raise criminal suggestions should have precedence of those raising civil suggestions ([174]). An exception of wrongful dispossession takes precedence of all others, because no one who has been wrongfully dispossessed can be required to answer to the party who has dispossessed him ([175]). The judge determines the order, and assigns to each party a time within which his proofs are to be made. This is called the term probatory ([176]), and is the most important term in the suit.

---

[173]. Clemens III. *Ibid.* c. 1: When by the proof of the exception the principal question is disposed of, the exception itself ought first to be inquired into.

[174]. Devoti, § 5.

[175]. Pseudo-Isidor. ap. Gratian Caus. III. Qu. 1. c. 1, 2, 3, and Qu. II. c. 2; Caus. v. Qu. II. c. 4; Innocent III. A.D. 1204, in Decret. Lib. II. Tit. X. c. 2; Gregory IX. *Ibid.* c. 4. Spoliation presupposes (1) possession, (2) dispossession (*dejectio*). Alexander III. in Decret. Lib. I. Tit. XXIX. c. 10, and Lib. II. Tit. XIII. c. 17; Innocent III. to the Bishops of Rochester and London, *Ibid.* Tit. XXVIII. c. 51. Alexander III. to Bishop of Worcester, *Ibid.* Lib. II. Tit. XIII. c. 2, states that a resignation of a benefice is void if the resigner has been previously dispossessed. The same to the Bishop of Exeter, *Ibid.* c. 6, says that a charge of crime cannot be allowed as a defence to a petition for restitution to a benefice. The same to the Archbishop of Canterbury, *Ibid.* c. 7, directs a clerk to be first restored, and then the criminal charge against him to be ventilated.

[176]. Pelagius I. ap. Gratian Caus. III. Qu. IX. c. 20 directs a judge to assign a competent term for law and truth. Ecclesiastical Courts Commission, 1883, Hist. App. I. 197. The introduction of *viva voce* evidence

Proof.

33. It is the business of the plaintiff or accuser to prove his libel, of the defendant or accused to prove his exceptions, and for each one to do so within the term assigned him (¹⁷⁷). Unless the defendant's exception perempts the whole libel, each one must further prove his several allegations, or they cannot be received in judgment. If the defendant fails to prove his exception, the plaintiff is not thereby relieved from proving his libel; but if the plaintiff or accuser fails to prove his libel, the defendant is under no obligation to prove a negative (¹⁷⁸), except in some few cases in which the presumption of law is against him (¹⁷⁹).

34. Proof is defined to be the establishment by evidence or demonstration of a doubtful or disputed matter in judgment, in order to enable a judge to determine a controversy pending between two parties (¹⁸⁰). It includes (1) producing proper and trustworthy evidence, (2) meeting or rebutting all exceptions taken to the evidence, and (3) the publication of sufficient evidence before the judge. By the last-named act it becomes

before the judge in court by 14 and 15 Vict. c. 99, has practically abolished the term probatory.

(177). Ayliffe 151 : If no sentence is pronounced in a civil cause within three years, or in a criminal cause within two years, the instance is said to be perempted. *Id.* 154 says by English usage there is no certain time. Law's Forms 202, 214.

(178). Gregory ap. Gratian Caus. VI. Qu. v. c. 1, quoted in *Canonical Procedure*, note 47, and Caus. II. Qu. v. c. 11. Innocent III. in Decret. Lib. II. Tit. XII. c. 3 : If the plaintiff proves nothing, the defendant wins, although he does nothing. Ayliffe 444 ; Honorius III. in Decret. Lib. II. Tit. XIX. c. 12. Lord Selborne in *Leonard v. Ellis*, 26 Ch. D. 204 : No one is bound to prove a negative.

(179). Boniface VIII. in Sext. Lib. II. Tit. v. c. 2, says that the presumption of law is against a man who claims tithes in another's parish, and Concil. Lugdun. A.D. 1274, *Ibid.* Tit. IX. c. 1. See *Canonical Procedure*, note 147.

(180). Isidor. in Decret. Lib. v. Tit. XL. c. 10 ; Devoti Inst. Lib. III. Tit. IX. § 1 ; Ayliffe 442, 275 ; Law's Forms 200.

VOL. II.   T

judicial proof. Judicial proof is nevertheless of two degrees, viz. (1) full and complete, and (2) half or incomplete ([181]).

35. Full proof is made (1) by evidence of the fact, or (2) by the confession of the opposite party, or (3) by the deposition of two or more credible witnesses touching the same matter, or as it is said by the living voice (*viva voce*), or (4) by a public instrument ([182]) called the dead voice (*mortua voce*) ([183]). Its effect is threefold: (1) it determines the sentence; (2) it prevents the plaintiff being required to prove his intention by an oath, which if tendered to him he is justified in refusing ([184]); (3) in a criminal cause the oath of purgation can no longer be tendered to the accused, because purgation is allowed only to those suspected, not to those convicted. In all criminal causes full proof is imperative ([185]).

36. The deposition of a single witness, or of several doubtful witnesses, or a private writing, or in some cases a strong presumption or common fame, constitutes half proof. In civil causes half proof may sometimes suffice, as when private accounts are allowed to prove a debt ([186]), or common fame is allowed to prove parish boundaries ([187]). In other cases half proof may be converted into full proof by means of an oath, called the necessary oath or oath suppletory ([188]), and in criminal causes it may be rebutted by the defendant's oath of purgation ([189]). In all

---

([181]). Ayliffe 444; Devoti, § 3.

([182]). Innocent III. in Decret. Lib. II. Tit. XIII. c. 15.

([183]). Law's Forms 264.

([184]). Alexander III. in Decret. Lib. II. Tit. XIX. c. 2.

([185]). Gratian Caus. II. Qu. VIII. c. 2: In crimes the evidence ought to be clearer than noon-day. Concil. Brac. II. A.D. 572, *Ibid.* Caus. II. Qu. IV. c. 1. Alexander III. in Decret. Lib. II. Tit. XX. c. 10: The testimony of one is not sufficient to condemn any one. Innocent III. *Ibid.* c. 23, 28: The same to the Bishop of Exeter. *Ibid.* Lib. III. Tit. II. c. 8: Fame is not sufficient evidence in a criminal case. Lynd. 296, 304; Ayliffe 448; Stephens' Eccl. Stat. 557.

([186]). Law's Forms 201. See *Canonical Procedure*, note 40.

([187]). Honorius III. in Decret. Lib. II. Tit. XIX. c. 13; Ayliffe 275, 277.

([188]). Alexander III. in Decret. Lib. II. Tit. XIX. c. 2; Devoti Lib. III. Tit. IX. § 25; Law's Forms 284.

([189]). Alexander III. in Decret. Lib. V. Tit. I. c. 10, directs it to be taken

Acts in Judgment. 291

criminal causes, when the matter is left doubtful by the evidence, the rule of charity requires the best construction to be put on the appearances([190]), and the oath of purgation to be administered to the defendant, unless there is a strong presumption against him ([191]).

37. Evidence of a fact is such evidence as is either (1) notorious or most evident ([192]), (2) manifest or more evident, or simply (3) clear (*liquida*) ([193]). Notorious evidence is that which is known to all men, as that St. Paul's Church stands in London ([194]), or which can be proved to the judge by ocular demonstration ([195]), as that a person alleged to be dead is alive and present in court. Manifest evidence is that which has been openly done, and can be proved by any number of witnesses, although it is not known to all men, as when a criminal has been caught in the act of committing a crime ([196]).

in a case of alleged simony. Innocent III. *Ibid.* Tit. IX. c. 5 directs it to be administered to a presbyter charged with apostasy. *Id. Ibid.* Tit XII. c. 14 prescribes it in a case of alleged homicide. *Id.* to Bishop of Exeter, *Ibid.* Lib. III. Tit. II. c. 8, in a case of alleged concubinage. Clement III. *Ibid.* Lib. II. Tit. XVIII. c. I, in a case of alleged abetting of murder. Other cases, *Ibid.* Lib. V. Tit. II. c. 2, and Tit. I. c. 19. See *Canonical Procedure*, note 151 : Administering the oath of purgation properly belongs to the judge's noble or extra-judicial office.

(190). Baeda in Decret. Lib. V. Tit. XLI. c. 2 : Those things as to which it is doubtful with what intent they are done should have the best explanation put upon them. Lucius III. *Ibid.* Lib. II. Tit. XIX. c. 3 : If the witnesses of both parties are equally worthy of credit (idonei), let the witnesses of him who is in possession be preferred, because principles of right (jura) are more ready to absolve than to condemn. Innocent III. *Ibid.* c. 9.

(191). Law's Forms 284. See the *Conclusion of a Cause*, § 4.

(192). *Ibid.* 201.

(193). Ayliffe, 443, 447.

(194). Innocent III. to Bishop of Exeter in Decret. Lib. III. Tit. II. c. 8. In a case of notoriety neither witness nor accuser is necessary, evidently referring to Eugenius III., *Ibid.* Lib. V. Tit. I. c. 9. Innocent III. *Ibid.* c. 7, says that notoriety which cannot be refuted constitutes proof. Lynd. 323, defines notoriety as proof beyond dispute wanting no further discussion. Ayliffe 448.

(195). Gregory IX. in Decret. Lib. II. Tit. XIX. c. 4.

(196). Ayliffe 443.

Clear evidence is that which is neither notorious nor manifest as regards the public at large, but yet to the judge is equally clear, such as an act of court ([197]).

38. The best kind and the queen of proofs is held to be the confession of the adverse party ([198]). A confession may, however, be made: (1) either discreetly ([199]), as when it refers to the pending controversy, or indiscreetly, when it is made in connection with some other matter; (2) simply or qualifiedly, as when the fact is admitted, but a different version is given of the attendant circumstances; (3) judicially, when made before a judge, or extra-judicially, when made elsewhere; (4) explicitly, when made in express words, or tacitly, as when it may be inferred from flight or contumacy, or from refusing to answer interrogatories ([200]).

39. To constitute proof, a confession must be made (1) judicially, *i.e.*, before the proper judge ([201]), (2) freely and without constraint ([202]), and (3) in the adversary's presence ([203]). If not made spontaneously, it may be withdrawn ([204]). A tacit confession only amounts to half proof, unless it be a refusal to answer interrogatories ([205]); but no value attaches in a criminal

---

([197]). *Liquido constat*, by Innocent III. in Decret. Lib. II. Tit. XII. c. 3.
([198]). Lucius III. in Decret. Lib. III. Tit. II. c. 7: When he does not deny a notorious crime, or when he has been publicly condemned for it.
([199]). Craisson, § 5708 ; Law's Forms, p. 174.
([200]). Boniface, A.D. 419, ap. Gratian Caus. III. Qu. IX. c. 10; Boniface VIII. in Sext. Lib. II. Tit. IX. c. 2.
([201]). Alexander III. in Decret. Lib. II. Tit. I. c. 4 ; quoted *Spiritual Courts*, note 178.
([202]). Pascal II. in Decret. Lib. II. Tit. XX. c. 4: In every matter the principal person may be admitted as a witness.
([203]). Gregory in Decret. Lib. II. Tit. XX. c. 2: Evidence not taken in the other party's presence is not available. Pseudo-Isidor. ap. Gratian Caus. III. Qu. XI. c. 3 ; Nicolaus, A.D. 864, *Ibid.* Caus. XV. Qu. VI. c. 1; Devoti Lib. III. Tit. IX. § 4 and 18; Ayliffe 545.
([204]). Gregory IX. in Decret. Lib. II. Tit. XVIII. c. 3 ; Law's Forms 190, 194.
([205]). Boniface VIII. in Sext. Lib. II. Tit. IX. c. 2: If the defendant or his proctor, after taking the oath of truth or calumny, without reasonable cause refuses to answer to the interrogatory positions propounded by his

Acts in Judgment. 293

cause to an extorted confession([206](#)), to the confession of an accomplice, unless it discloses the crime of treason ([207](#)) or simony ([208](#)) ; nor is any confession evidence against third parties ([209](#)).

40. To make proof by witnesses, (1) fit and proper persons must be produced, (2) in sufficient number to comply with the canon, and (3) they must give unequivocal evidence upon oath, in presence of the opposite party ([210](#)). An exception may be taken to the evidence of any witness who fails to fulfil these conditions, and, if sustained, the evidence cannot be admitted ([211](#)). Such exception may be either (1) general or (2) specific ([212](#)). An exception is said to be general when it is made by word of mouth, and neither specifies time, place, nor mode of proceeding; special when it is made in writing, and specifically states the cause why such and such a person's evidence ought not to be received ([213](#)). Sometimes exception is made against the persons of the witnesses, as that they are evil reported of, criminal, or worthless; at other times against their depositions, as that they are ambiguous, contradictory, or irrelevant ([214](#)), and such exceptions may be advanced both before and after the publication of the depositions ([215](#)). A general exception may be met by

adversary, or contumaciously fails to do so, he shall be deemed to have confessed to the contents of the interrogatories.

(206). Nicolaus ap. Gratian Caus. xv. Qu. v. c. 2.

(207). Cod. Theodos. *Ibid.* Caus. xv. Qu. III. c. 5; Clemens III. in Decret. Lib. II. Tit. XVIII. c. 1.

(208). Innocent III. *Ibid.* c. 2.

(209). Pseudo-Isidor. ap. Gratian Caus. III. Qu. XI. c. 3. Alexander III. in Decret. Lib. II. Tit. XX. c. 10.: No one who testifies against himself can be trusted testifying against another in the same matter. Clemens III. *Ibid.* Lib. II. Tit. XVIII. c. 1.

(210). Gregory, A.D. 594, in Decret. Lib. II. Tit. XX. c. 2; Pseudo-Isidor. ap. Gratian Caus. III. Qu. X. c. 15.

(211). Alexander III. to Archbishop of Canterbury in Decret. Lib. II. Tit. XX. c. 13.

(212). Law's Forms 256.

(213). *Ibid.* 255, 258.

(214). *Ibid.*

(215). *Ibid.*

tendering the oath of calumny to the objector, or an oath of malice in substitution for it ([216]). A specific exception must be proved within an assigned term, or it cannot be allowed. The refusal to admit an exception is a good ground of appeal ([217]).

41. Fit and proper witnesses are upright and honest men, who depose to what is matter of their own knowledge and belief ([218]), preference being given to those who are themselves Christians ([219]). Unfit persons are (1) slaves and dependents, clothed and paid by the party producing them ([220]), except in causes of adultery, non-payment of rent, or treason ([221]); (2) children under fourteen years of age ([222]); (3) persons of ill-repute, perjured ([223]), and criminous persons ([224]); (4) those who have an interest in the cause ([225]), or who may be suspected of having an interest, such as paupers ([226]); and (5) all who are excommunicate ([227]). If they are denounced persons, they

(216). Law's Forms 257, 281.
(217). Alexander III. to Bishop of Hereford in Decret. Lib. II. Tit. XX. c. 7; *Id. Ibid.* Tit. XXVII. c. 22.
(218). Pseudo-Isidor. ap. Gratian Caus. III. Qu. IX. c. 15, 16; Caus. IV. Qu. II. c. 3; Ayliffe 65, 446. Law's Forms 187: On those points which relate to actions done by yourself, you shall answer according to your knowledge, and, with relation to the actions of others, according to your belief.
(219). Concil. Lat. III. A.D. 1179, in Decret. Lib. II. Tit. XX. c. 21.
(220). Pseudo-Isidor. ap. Gratian Caus. III. Qu. V. c. 8. Alexander III. in Decret. Lib. II. Tit. XX. c. 24: Those are not fit witnesses whom the plaintiff produces from among his dependents (de familia sua). Ayliffe 536.
(221). Cod. Lib. IX. Tit. de Quaest. ap. Gratian Caus. XII. Qu. II. c. 59.
(222). Concil. Carthag. VII. A.D. 419, ap. Gratian Caus. IV. Qu. II. c. 1: Let not those be admitted to give testimony who are under fourteen. Cap. Franc. *Ibid.* Caus. XXII. Qu. V. c. 14.
(223). Halitgar ap. Gratian Caus. VI. Qu. 1. c. 18; Concil. Matiscon. I. Can. 17, A.D. 581, *Ibid.* Caus. XXII. Qu. V. c. 7; Cap. Franc. *Ibid.* c. 14.
(224). Pseudo-Isidor. *Ibid.* Caus. II. Qu. VII. c. 39. Alexander III. to Archbishop of Canterbury in Decret. Lib. II. Tit. XX. c. 13, says that if they have not been previously convicted of crime: but the exception is now sustained, they ought not to be admitted as witnesses.
(225). Alexander III. in Decret. Lib. II. Tit. XX. c. 9.
(226). Law's Forms 255.
(227). Concil. Carthag. VII. A.D. 419, Can. 1 in Codex Eccles. Afric. 128; Pseudo-Isidor. ap. Gratian Caus. III. Qu. IV. c. 6.

should be repelled by the judge, otherwise it is for the adverse party to take exception to them ([228]). In causes concerning their Churches, nevertheless, clergy are not disqualified from being witnesses simply on the ground that they are interested ([229])

42. In criminal causes, avowed enemies ([230]), those who are guilty of the same offence ([231]), unless they have purged their crime ([232]), accomplices ([233]), children under twenty years of age ([234]), renegade Jews ([235]), and women, unless in matters concerning themselves ([236]), are also excluded. In the three excepted crimes of treason, heresy, and simony, all persons may be admitted as witnesses, except accomplices and avowed enemies ([237]). Laymen cannot be witnesses against clergy in

([228]). Gregory IX. in Decret. Lib. II. Tit. XXV. c. 12; Alexander IV. in Sext. Lib. V. Tit. XI. c. 8.

([229]). Alexander III. to Archbishop of Canterbury in Decret. Lib. II. Tit. XX. c. 12 and 6.

([230]). Socrates VI. 17 relates that Chrysostom took exception to his accusers on the ground that they were avowed enemies. I. 31 says that Athanasius did the same. See *Spiritual Courts*, note 148. Pseudo-Isidor. ap. Gratian Caus. III. Qu. V. c. 2, 4, 10, 11, 13; Nicolaus I. A.D. 864, *Ibid.* c. 15; Pseudo-Stephen in Decret. Lib. V. Tit. I. c. 7 also excludes those living under the same roof as enemies. Innocent III. *Ibid.* c. 19; Sext. Lib. V. Tit. II. c. 5; Lynd. 304.

([231]). Alexander III. to Bishop of Norwich in Decret. Lib. II. Tit. XX. c. 20.

([232]). Cod. Val. ap. Gratian Caus. III. Qu. XI. c. 2 and 3; Coelestin III. in Decret. Lib. II. Tit. XXV. c. 1, and Innocent III. Tit. XX. c. 54; Lib. V. Tit. III. c. 32.

([233]). Pseudo-Isidor. ap. Gratian Caus. III. Qu. IV. c. 5; Caus. XV. Qu. III. c. 5; Caus. III. Qu. XI. c. 3; Clemens III. in Decret. Lib. II. Tit. XVIII. c. 1; Alexander III. *Ibid.* Tit. XX. c. 10; Ayliffe 536.

([234]). Ayliffe 536.

([235]). Concil. Carthag. VII. A.D. 419, ap. Gratian Caus. IV. Qu. l. c. 1; Concil. Tolet. IV. A.D. 633, says renegade Jews. *Ibid.* Caus. II. Qu. VII. c. 24.

([236]). Gregory in Decret. Lib. II. Tit. XX. c. 3, A.D. 593, directs that the evidence of women, with whom he is said to have been too familiar, should be received against a presbyter. Alexander III. *Ibid.* c. 22 says that a mother's evidence is suspect when she would wed her daughter to a man much older than herself. Devoti Inst. Lib. III. Tit. IX. § 14.

([237]). Concil. Tolet. VI. A.D. 639, ap. Gratian Caus. III. Qu. IX. c. 9;

criminal causes unless they have an interest in them ([238]), nor proctors nor advocates in causes which they are defending ([239]), nor a judge in a cause which he has to decide, without previously delegating it to another ([240]); but both laymen and women are competent to prove the disqualification of one elected for promotion ([241]).

43. In criminal causes requiring full proof, two witnesses at the least are necessary ([242]), and in some cases more ([243]); but more than forty may not be produced in any case ([244]). A witness

---

Deusdedit in Decret. Lib. v. Tit. III. c. 7; Innocent. III. A.D. 1199, *Ibid.* c. 31. Alexander III. *Ibid.* Lib. II. Tit. xx. c. 10 forbids accomplices to be received as witnesses in cases of simony. Gregory IX. *Ibid.* c. 56 forbids an accused person to be a witness, except in the excepted crimes. Innocent III. *Ibid.* Lib. v. Tit. III. c. 31 excludes enemies and accomplices in a case of simony. Concil. Lugdun. I. A.D. 1245, in Sext. Lib. II. Tit. x. c. 1, allows an accomplice to give evidence in a case of simony if the proceedings are in civil form. Alexander IV. *Ibid.* Lib. v. Tit. II. c. 5, allows accomplices to give evidence against heretics.

(238). Alexander III. *Ibid.* Lib. v. Tit. I. c. 10, and Innocent III. *Ibid.* Lib. II. Tit. xx. c. 14.

(239). Eugenius. III. *Ibid.* Lib. II. Tit. xx. c. 6; Concil. Lugdun. II. A.D. 1274, in Sext. Lib. II. Tit. x. c. 3.

(240). Concil. Carthag. V. A.D. 401, Can. 1 ap. Gratian Caus. II. Qu. VI. c. 38; Innocent III. in Decret. Lib. II. Tit. xx. c. 40.

(241). Innocent III. *Ibid.* c. 33.

(242). Hist. Susannah v. 48; Deut. XIX. 15; John VIII. 7. Apost. Const. II. 21: Do not admit less evidence to convict any one than that of three witnesses, and those of known reputation. IL. 37, 49; Apost. Can. 75: Do not receive an heretic in a testimony against a bishop, nor a Christian if he be a solitary witness, for the law saith, In the mouth of two or three witnesses every word shall be established. Concil. Ilerd. A.D. 546, ap. Gratian Caus. xxxv. Qu. VI. c. 11; Egbert's Dial. 4, A.D. 734; Concil. Brac. II. Can. 8, A.D. 572, ap. Gratian Caus. II. Qu. IV. c. 1; Paschal II. in Decret. Lib. II. Tit. xx. c. 4; Innocent III. *Ibid.* c. 23.

(243). Pseudo-Silvester ap. Gratian Caus. II. Qu. IV. c. 2, prescribes seventy-two for a bishop, forty-four for a cardinal, twenty-seven for a cardinal-deacon, seven for a subdeacon, collet, &c. Leo IV. A.D. 850, *Ibid.* c. 3, says that a bishop can only be condemned by twelve bishops upon the evidence of seventy-two witnesses. Devoti Inst. Lib. III .Tit. IX. § 9.

(244). Innocent III. A.D. 1206, in Decret. Lib. II. Tit. xx. c. 37.

Acts in Judgment.

may be compelled (²⁴⁵), by a compulsory decree (²⁴⁶) and ecclesiastical censures (²⁴⁷), even though residing out of the jurisdiction (²⁴⁸), to give evidence, and to give it upon oath (²⁴⁹). The oath usually administered is to the effect that, setting aside favour and affection, malice and prejudice against either of the litigants, he will testify the truth, and the whole truth, so far as his knowledge extends (²⁵⁰), and beyond that his belief; and that he has not been bribed, nor has any pecuniary interest in the cause. A witness is also enjoined to give his testimony fasting (²⁵¹), and to give it simply and unequivocally (²⁵²). Monks and religious persons are not exempt from taking the oath before giving evidence, except by consent of the parties (²⁵³). The oath must be administered to the witness in court in presence of the adverse party, but the depositions are usually taken either before the judge or before a commissioner deputed to act for him, called an examiner (²⁵⁴), and, when

---

(245). Alexander III. in Decret. Lib. II. Tit. XXI. c. 1 and 2; Innocent III. *Ibid.* c. 8, 9. Honorius III. *Ibid.* c. 11 says that accomplices can be compelled. Const. 17 Boniface, A.D. 1261; Lynd. 109.

(246). Alexander III. to Bishop of Exeter in Decret. Lib. II. Tit. XX. c. 18. Law's Forms 210, 240.

(247). Alexander III. in Decret. Lib. II. Tit. XXI. c. 2 says that if the evidence is necessary, a clergyman may be suspended, and a layman excommunicated, to make him give evidence. Innocent III. A.D. 1213, *Ibid.* Tit. XX. c. 45.

(248). Law's Forms 209, 236, 248, says by the judges directing a requisition *sub mutuae vicissitudinis obtentu*, to the ordinary under whose jurisdiction they live, committing to him the examination, in order that when completed he may transmit the depositions.

(249). Honorius III. in Decret. Lib. II. Tit. XX. c. 51.

(250). Gratian Caus. III. Qu. IX. c. 20; Eugenius III. in Decret. Lib. II. Tit. XX. c. 5; Lynd. 254, 299; Law's Forms 215.

(251). Cap. Reg. Franc. ap. Gratian Caus. IV. Qu. II. c. 2, and Decret. Lib. II. Tit. XX. c. 1; Devoti Lib. III. Tit. IX. § 12.

(252). Ambros. ap. Gratian Caus. III. Qu. IX. c. 17, says, Pura et simplex testimonii series. Gregory IX. in Decret. Lib. II. Tit. XX. c. 53.

(253). Innocent III. A.D. 1208, *Ibid.* c. 39 and 51.

(254). Eugenius III. to Bishops of Exeter and Worcester, in Decret. Lib. II. Tit. XX. c. 8; Honorius III. *Ibid.* c. 52. The usual practice here was for the registrar to take the witness' depositions, which were read over

taken, are kept from the knowledge of both parties until published. By modern practice they are taken by word of mouth in court, as in a summary proceeding.

44. In all causes, civil as well as criminal, three productions of witnesses are allowed ([255]), but not more, except by special leave of the judge ([256]); viz. (1) by the plaintiff, to prove his libel, called probatory witnesses; (2) by the defendant, to make his exceptions as well against their depositions as against their persons, called reprobatory witnesses ([257]); and (3) by the plaintiff, to except against the depositions and the persons of the defendants' reprobatory witnesses, called reprobatory of the reprobatory witnesses. They may also be produced to corroborate the evidence already given in a matrimonial cause ([258]), or if the existence of additional necessary witnesses has subsequently come to the plaintiff's knowledge ([259]), or if the witnesses first produced have been confuted ([260]), or to prove new matter ([261]). The defendant may also administer interrogatories to the plaintiff's witnesses ([262]), without waiving his right to take exception to their fitness ([263]), provided he protests against their being received as witnesses at the time ([264]).

45. A public instrument, or document to constitute proof,

to him before the judge. Reading over before the judge was discontinued in the seventeenth century, except by request. Law's Forms 236.

(255). Alexander III. in Decret. Lib. II. Tit. xx. c. 15; Honorius III. *Ibid.* c. 29. The rule quoted in Law's Forms 255 is, In testem testes et in hos, sed non datur ultra.

(256). Alexander III. *Ibid.* c. 15; Innocent III. *Ibid.* c. 36 and 46; Gregory IX. *Ibid.* c. 55; Law's Forms 261.

(257). Clemens III. in Decret. Lib. II. Tit. xx. c. 26. Innocent III. *Ibid.* c. 35 allows this even after publication.

(258). Innocent III. A.D. 1212, in Decret. Lib. II. Tit. xx. c. 44.

(259). Law's Forms 218 calls it the production of witnesses after publication upon the first interrogatories; also 289.

(260). *Ibid.* 220.

(261). Alexander III. in Decret. Lib. II. Tit. xx. c. 19; Urban III. *Ibid.* c. 25; Innocent III. *Ibid.* c. 35 and 42.

(262). Boniface VIII. in Sext. Lib. II. Tit. x. c. 2; Law's Forms 216, 223.

(263). Law's Forms 216.

(264). Innocent III. in Decret. Lib. II. Tit. xx. c. 31; Law's Forms 224.

must be either (1) an instrument drawn by a public hand, such as a notary, and bearing his seal ([265]), or else (2) one executed by the party before witnesses, and countersealed upon his request ([266]) by a notary or other authentic person in his presence ([267]). The latter is usually called an authentic instrument. A copy of such an instrument is not evidence unless the same has been made by a public person ([268]); nor are instruments evidence which contradict one another ([269]), or have important erasures ([270]), or are illegible or unintelligible ([271]), or have been obtained by fraud ([272]); but the absence of a letter or two does not vitiate an instrument ([273]). In case of doubtful authenticity, the judge should consult his superior ([274]).

([265]). Alexander III. in Decret. Lib. II. Tit. XXII. c. 2, refuses to allow a public instrument if the witnesses are dead, unless it was made by a public hand or bears an authentic seal. Innocent III. *Ibid.* c. 6.

([266]). Const. 27 Otho, A.D. 1237: We hear letters are drawn and sealed in which it is stated that such a man made a contract who yet was not present nor anywhere to be found, nay, perhaps was then in another province or diocese. Now, since such writings do plainly imply forgery, we strictly forbid the drawing of them. Law's Forms 101: The official should specify that he has attached such seal at the special request of the mandatory, otherwise the certificate is of no avail.

([267]). Const. 28 Otho, A.D. 1237: Because notaries public are not used in England, and therefore there is more frequent occasion for authentic seals, we ordain that not only archbishops and bishops but their officials, also abbots, priors, deans, archdeacons, and their officials, and deans rural, as also cathedral chapters and all colleges and convents, have a seal.

([268]). Gregory, A.D. 593, in Decret. Lib. II. Tit. XXII. c. 1, and Gregorius IX. *Ibid.* c. 16.

([269]). Gregory IX. in Decret. Lib. II. Tit. XXII. c. 13.

([270]). Alexander III. *Ibid.* c. 3; Innocent III. A.D. 1199, *Ibid.* c. 6, and Lib. III. Tit. XXXVI. c. 7; *Ibid.* Lib. V. Tit. XXXIII. c. 14, and Tit. XX. c. 9.

([271]). Innocent III. in Decret. Lib. II. Tit. XXII. c. 6.

([272]). Innocent III. to Archbishop of Canterbury in Decret. Lib. II. Tit. XXII. c. 7.

([273]). Honorius III. *Ibid.* c. 11, mentions *e* written in place of *ed* (*h* for *her*).

([274]). Innocent III. to Bishop of Ely, A.D. 1204, in Decret. Lib. II. Tit. XXII. c. 8: When a decretal is alleged, the authenticity of which the judge has doubts of, if it is in accordance with common law, let him not fear to base his decision upon it; . . . but if it is at variance with common law, let him base no decision upon it without consulting his superior.

46. An exception lies against a public instrument on the ground of forgery ([275]), and may be supported or rebutted by the inspection of the adverse party and experts ([276]), or by witnesses ([277]); but the party taking exception cannot claim to inspect other parts of the same instrument not pertinent to the matter in dispute ([278]). If upon request, inspection, or a copy of an instrument which is pertinent is refused by the judge, it is a good ground of appeal ([279]). Instruments may be put in evidence after the publication of witnesses, up to the very conclusion of a cause ([280]).

47. At any time after the expiration of the term probatory the judge, at the instance of either of the litigants, but not of a third party ([281]), may appoint a term for the publication of the depositions. By publication they become judicial evidence taken in the presence of the parties ([282]), and may now be used as subject-matter for argument on both sides ([283]). It is then ordinarily too late to take exception to a witness ([284]), or to re-examine him upon the matter on which he has already given

---

([275]). Innocent III. in Decret. Lib. II. Tit. XXII. c. 10, says this may be proved by witnesses.

([276]). Alexander III. to Archbishop of York, in a cause between the Archbishop of Canterbury and the Abbot of St. Augustine's, Canterbury, in Decret. Lib. II. Tit. XXII. c. 1 ; Law's Forms 270.

([277]). Innocent III. in Decret. Lib. II. Tit. XXII. c. 10.

([278]). Coelestin III. in Decret. Lib. II. Tit. XXII. c. 5.

([279]). Gregory IX. Ibid. c. 12.

([280]). Innocent III. Ibid. c. 9.

([281]). Innocent III. to Bishop of Ely in Decret. Lib. II. Tit. XX. c. 30; Law's Forms 251.

([282]). Gregory in Decret. Lib. II. Tit. XX. c. 2, requires the evidence to be taken in the presence of the adverse party. This requirement was ordinarily fulfilled by (1) administering the oath to the witness in his presence, and then (2) by publishing the evidence before him. Ibid. c. 41 ; Law's Forms 280.

([283]). Alexander III. Ibid. c. 15.

([284]). Innocent III. in Decret. Lib. II. Tit. XX. c. 31, allows exception to be taken to the witnesses after publication in three cases: (1) if he make oath that he is not doing it vexatiously; or (2) if he protested before; or (3) if the objections have only come to his knowledge since publication.

Acts in Judgment.

evidence([285]); but his evidence may be taken on other articles to which his previous depositions did not apply ([286]). Evidence allowed in proof before one judge is evidence before another judge in the same cause and between the same parties ([287]); but evidence given in a summary proceeding cannot be admitted as evidence in a plenary one ([288]).

(285). Urban III. in Decret. Lib. II. Tit. xx. c. 25.
(286). Alexander III. *Ibid.* c. 19 ; Innocent III. *Ibid.* c. 42 ; Honorius III. *Ibid.* c. 48.
(287). Alexander III. *Ibid.* c. 11 ; Honorius III. *Ibid.* c. 50 ; Gregory IX. *Ibid.* Tit. XIX. c. 15.
(288). Innocent III. *Ibid.* Tit. xx. c. 38, 44.

IX.
THE CONCLUSION OF A CAUSE.

THE JUDGE'S OFFICE.

1. When all the evidence and exceptions have been exhausted, the suit is ripe for the judge's intervention. This, and the acts which immediately lead up to it, constitute the third and final stage in judgment, and are called the conclusion of the cause. The term conclusion of the cause is, however, a wide one, and is used in three senses—(1) to express all the concluding acts, *i.e.*, not only the judge's determination of a suit by sentence, but also the execution of the sentence, or the suspension of the sentence or stay of execution by appeal; (2) to express the concluding acts of the suit only; and (3) to express one of these concluding acts, which is technically called the conclusion or the second assignation, whereby the suit is concluded so far as the action of the parties is concerned, and there is no place for further discussion in judgment.

2. The concluding acts of the suit, each one of which is taken at the instance of one or other of the parties, consist of the following: (1) the assignment of a term to propound all acts, or, if the cause is summary, the assignment of a term to hear sentence on the first assignation ([1]). On the day assigned to propound all acts, if any exceptive or defensive matter is given in by the defendant and admitted by the judge, the conclusion is thereby rescinded ([2]). Otherwise there follows (2) the assignment of a term to conclude, or, in summary causes, of a term to hear sentence on the second assignation. This is technically called the conclusion, because it precludes further discussion by the parties. Then follows (3) the assignment of a day to hear

---

(1). Law's Forms 291.
(2). *Ibid.* 291 and 299.

The Conclusion of a Cause. 303

informations, on which the judge is first informed by the advocates of the facts of the case, and then of the law which applies to them (³), the latter information being sometimes protracted over several court days. And lastly (4) the assignment of a term to hear sentence, which is called the *final* or *definitory* term (⁴). By the practice of the Arches Court as it formerly existed, one and the same term was usually assigned to hear sentence and to inform; and if the informations were not completed on that day, an assignation was made to inform on another day, and so on until the judge's mind was fully satisfied (⁵).

3. The judge's duty in dealing with a cause extends to three things—cognisance, determination, and execution (⁶). In exercising each he is bidden to remember that he is the representative of the Church, God's minister upon earth; and that his judgment is deemed to proceed from the face of God (⁷), who is before all things a God of righteousness and mercy (⁸). Hence (1), in taking cognisance of a cause, he is warned not to act rashly (⁹), nor to give way to anger (¹⁰), but carefully to

---

(3). Law's Forms 294; Innocent III. in Decret. Lib. II. Tit. XXVIII. c. 44.

(4). Innocent III. to the Bishop of Durham, A.D. 1203, in Decret. Lib. II. Tit. XX. c. 34, requires a judge to fix a peremptory term for the appearance of the parties to hear sentence. Ayliffe 446; Law's Forms 301.

(5). Law's Forms 308.

(6). Ayliffe 396.

(7). Tertullian Apol. 39: For [with us] judgment is conducted with the utmost care (cum pondere), as before tried men [certos] deputed from God's presence [de Dei conspectu]. Ayliffe 314.

(8). Ps. XL. 7; XLVIII. 10; LXXXV. 13; John XVI. 18; Jer. IX. 24; Rom. III. 5, 21; Neh. IX. 17; Exod. XXXIV. 7; Deut. VII. 9; 2 Sam. VII. 15; Ps. LXII. 12; LXXXVI. 5; 1 Tim. I. 2.

(9). Apost. Const. II. 51: Gratian Caus. II. Qu. 1. c. 20; Caus. XI. Qu. III. c. 45–64 and 66–72. Augustin *Ibid.* c. 49: A rash judgment generally does not hurt him who is rashly condemned, but it must needs hurt him who judges rashly. Ambros. *Ibid.* Caus. III. Qu. VII. c. 4.

(10). Apost. Const. II. 37: It is the duty of a bishop to judge rightly. ... For some, through passion or envy, do insist on a false accusation against a brother, as did the two elders in the case of Susanna in Babylon, and the Egyptian woman in the case of Joseph; therefore, receive not

investigate every matter, sparing no pains to arrive at truth ([11]);
(2) in receiving informations, to weigh conscientiously all the evidence and the arguments placed before him ([12]), taking into

rashly such accusations, lest thou take away the innocent and slay the righteous. Augustin ap. Gratian Caus. I. Qu. 1. c. 82 : He is not outside the Church, and not of the body of the Church, who is excluded by the prejudice of the shepherd. Concil. Hispal. II. A.D. 619, Ibid. Caus. xv. Qu. VII. c. 1 : Many there are who condemn with tyrannical power, and not with canonical authority, those whom they have not heard ; and, as they exalt some by favour, so they cast down others out of hatred and ill-will, condemning upon the light breath of opinion those against whom they cannot prove crime. Ibid. Caus. XI. Qu. III. c. 76 ; Nicolaus, A.D. 866, Ibid. Caus. xv. Qu. VIII. c. 5 : Holy Scripture saith [Eccles. XL. 7] : Blame not before thou hast examined the truth, and before proof of an accusation suspend no one from communion ; for a man is not guilty simply because he is accused, but he is criminous who is proved to be such. Egbert's Excerpt. 49. Stevenson's Chronicle of the Abbey of Abingdon, II. XLIX : For centuries the clergy were the only representatives of the principle now so generally acknowledged, that until a man has been proved to be guilty he shall be held to be innocent. They went a step further, and declared that no man should be accuser, witness, advocate, judge, and executioner in his own cause.

(11). See *Spiritual Courts*, § 32. Pseudo-Isidor. ap. Gratian Caus. XII. Qu. v. c. 11 : A judge ought to investigate everything, and spare no pains to get at the right of things ; patiently listening to interrogations, answers, and objections, that the fullest light may be thrown on the action of both parties ; nor ought the judge to obtrude his sentence on litigants until they themselves have exhaustively gone into everything, the action being kept going until he has got at the truth of the matter. Innocent III. to Archbishop of Canterbury in Decret. Lib. I. Tit. XXIX. c. 27 : A judge ought himself carefully to investigate all the steps which have been taken in judgment, as well those in the forefront as those in the middle and end, before giving sentence.

(12). Pseudo-Isidor. ap. Gratian Caus. II. Qu. 1. c. 13 : Judge no one by suspicion, but first prove and then give a charitable sentence, and do not to others what ye would not have done to yourselves. Id. Ibid. Caus. III. Qu. v. c. 10 : We ought to condemn no one before a true and just proof, according to the apostle's words : Who art thou, O man, that judgest another ? Innocent III. in Decret. Lib. II. Tit. XXVII. c. 18, rescinded a. sentence, "because the judge had received the attestations of one party only."

account in so doing presumptions as well as direct proof ([13]); and (3) in giving sentence, to combine mercy with justice ([14]).

PRESUMPTIONS.

4. A presumption is such a strong suspicion as carries with it conviction in default of absolute proof ([15]), but yet a suspicion which may nearly always be rebutted by evidence. It may be either (1) legal or (2) personal. A legal presumption is a strong suspicion, which the law allows to turn the scale of proof, and to convert half-proof into full proof. A personal presumption is a presumption with regard to an individual which a prudent man cannot overlook. Still, neither personal nor legal presumptions taken alone are sufficient to constitute proof in a criminal cause ([16]).

(13). Clemens III. in Decret. Lib. I. Tit. IX. c. 6 : A judge need not always fix his mind to one kind of proof, but may fashion the direction of his mind by confessions, depositions, allegations, and other matters done in his presence. See *Discipline Generally*, note 45. Ayliffe 314 says he may consider other things besides the *allegata atque probata*. *Id.* 446 : All proofs are arbitrary and left to the judge's discretion, yet the judge's discretion ought to be consonant to law and equity. The judge may give credit to proofs that arise from single witnesses, or from presumptions and conjectures in some particular cases. Law's Forms 14.

(14). Honorius III. in Decret. Lib. I. Tit. XXXVI. c. 11 : You should proceed according to the canonical and lawful rulings ; . . . sometimes, also, an abatement may be made in severity, as may seem expedient, considering the state of the empire, and the number guilty of the same offence. . . . In those matters in which the law contains no direction, you must act with equity, always swerving to the side of mercy, according as persons and causes, places and times, seem to require. See *Spiritual Courts*, note 180.

(15). Ayliffe 276 says suspicions are of three kinds—(1) rash, (2) probable, (3) strong. The first deserve no credit, the second create a presumption, the third a legal presumption. Coelestin III in Decret. Lib. II. Tit. XX. c. 27 says carnal copulation may be proved (1) by witnesses who depose to having seen, or (2) by witnesses who depose to having heard of it, if consentient fame supplies a strong presumption, and there are other confirmatory circumstances.

(16). Innocent III. in Decret. Lib. II. Tit. XXIII. c. 14 : On account of

5. Legal presumptions are of two kinds—(1) those termed simple presumptions of law, and (2) those termed necessary presumptions of law. Simple presumptions of law may be rebutted by proper evidence, whereas necessary presumptions, called also presumptions of law by law, allow of no rebutting ([17]). That an evil deed is done with an evil intent, or that one who flees from justice is guilty ([18]), are simple presumptions of law; but it used to be held, until the law was changed by the Council of Trent, and in this country by secular legislation ([19]), that it was a necessary presumption of law, against which no proof could be admitted, that consummation following upon a promise of marriage proved the consent necessary to establish wedlock ([20]).

6. Among personal presumptions may be included such inferences as to guilt or innocence as may be drawn from a successful or unsuccessful submission to ordeal, the ordeal being accepted as the judgment of God ([21]). Various kinds of ordeal

suspicion alone, however strong, we will not have any one condemned of so grave a crime [as heresy]. *Id.* to Bishop of Exeter, *Ibid.* Lib. III. Tit. II. c. 8 ; Ayliffe 277.

(17). According to Hieron. in Decret. Lib. II. Tit. XXIII. c. 3 and 9, youthful conduct is a presumption as to conduct in old age. Gregory *Ibid.* c. 6, *Id. Ibid.* c. 5 : He who denies one only of two things admits the other. *Id. Ibid.* c. 7, 8 : What is known abroad is presumed to be known at home. Alexander III. *Ibid.* c. 10 : Stricter proof is required to prove an improbability. *Id. Ibid.* c. 12 : Immorality is presumed, si testes deponant se vidisse aliquem solum cum sola nudum cum nuda in eodem lecto jacentem. Innocent III. *Ibid.* c. 16 : Fitness is presumed for an ordinary position, not so for an extraordinary one. Lynd. 238, 152; Concil. Vas. A.D. 442, Can. 2 : Where a man is known, the good do not so much want a testimonial, as the bad to be exposed. Sext. Lib. V. Tit. XII. c. 5 : Every one is presumed to be good until he is shown to be bad. *Ibid.* : Doubtful facts ought to be interpreted charitably. Boniface VIII. *Ibid.* Lib. II. Tit. XIII. c. 1 says the presumption is against a person who claims what is contrary to common law. Lynd. 263, 108 ; Craisson, § 5740.

(18). Boniface in Decret. Lib. II. Tit. XXIII. c. 4.

(19). See *Wedlock*, § 5.

(20). Innocent III. in Decret. Lib. IV. Tit. V. c. 6 ; Gregory IX. *Ibid.* Tit. I. c. 30 ; Clemens III. *Ibid.* Tit. XVIII. c. 4 ; Ayliffe 276.

(21). Concil. Seligenstadt, Can. 14, A.D. 1022, ap. Gratian Caus. II. Qu. V. c. 25.

were formerly in use—that of the boiling water, that of the red-hot iron ([22]), another the ordeal of single combat ([23]), or that called *corsned*, or the dry-bread ordeal ([24]). Although ordeals were reprobated in the seventh century ([25]), yet they continued for long to be the sole data upon which judges decided doubtful cases ([26]), unless the position of the parties was such as to entitle them to clear themselves by compurgation ([27]).

(22). Gregory, A.D. 603, ap. Gratian Caus. II. Qu. v. c. 7 ; Concil. Tribur. A.D. 895, *Ibid.* c. 15 allows them. Athelstan's Law 5, A.D. 925 : If any one make a promise or ordeal, let him come three nights before to the mass-priest who is to hallow it, and live on bread and water, and let him stand at his masses these three days, and make his offering, and go to housel the same day that he goes to ordeal, and take an oath that he is not guilty. . . . And if it be water ordeal, let the rope go 2½ ells below the surface. If it be iron ordeal, let it be three nights before the hand be undone. Law 8 : We charge that no one go into the Church, after the carrying in of the fire with which the ordeal is to be heated, but the priest and the person to be tried ; and let 9 feet be measured from the stake to the mark ; . . . and if it be water ordeal, let it be heated till it boils. If it be a single accusation, let the hand be dipped to the fist only, to take out the stone ; but if the accusation be threefold, then let it be dipped to the elbow. Alfred and Guthrum's Law 9, A.D. 878, forbids ordeals on feast or fast days.

(23). Nicolaus I. A.D. 867, ap. Gratian Caus. II. Qu. v. c. 22.

(24). Cnut's Law 5, A.D. 1017, quoted by Kemble, Saxons in England, I. 259 : If a minister of the altar that has no friends be |impleaded, let him clear himself with his kinsmen. And if he have no kin, let him clear himself with his associates, or fast for the ordeal by bread (corsned), and so fare as God may ordain.

(25). Gregory, A.D. 603, ap. Gratian Caus. II. Qu. v. c. 7 ; Stephen V. *Ibid.* c. 20 ; Lucius III. in Decret. Greg. IX. Lib. v. Tit. XXXIV. c. 8.

(26). Edward's Law 10, A.D. 1064 : On the day that there is to be an ordeal, let the bishop's minister, with his clerks, come thither, and likewise the king's justice, with lawful men of the province, to see and hear that all be done with equity ; and let those whom the Lord is willing to save by mercy, not by merits, be acquitted and depart in peace.

(27). Edgar's Law 62, A.D. 960 ; Cnut's Law 5, A.D. 1017, speak of them as allowed only to those who could not canonically purge themselves. Edward's Law 2, A.D. 1065 : If any one be impeached for breaking a monastery, and was never defamed in times past, let him make his purgation with twelve lawful men, his own hand being the twelfth. If he have been defamed before, let him make his purgation with a triple number, *i.e.*, thirty-six lawful men. If he cannot have so many, let him

SENTENCES AND MATTERS JUDICIALLY SETTLED.

7. A sentence is the judge's pronouncement which either settles some disputed matter or disposes of a suit ([28]). One which settles a disputed matter arising in the course of a suit is termed an interlocutory sentence ([29]), such as a sentence decreeing the admission or amendment of a libel, or granting or refusing some delay term. One which disposes of the whole suit is termed a definitive or final sentence. There are, nevertheless, some interlocutory decrees which have the force of definitive sentences, and, by disposing of a disputed matter, settle the whole controversy ([30]); as, for instance, when exception is taken to the admission of the libel, the judge's decree ruling that it is inadmissible.

8. Interlocutory sentences differ from final sentences, and from interlocutory decrees having the force of final sentences in several points. (1) They may be revoked by the judge, because he has still authority in the cause; whereas final sentences may not, because the judge is then discharged of his office ([31]). (2) They may be given orally, whereas final sentences

go to the triple fire ordeal; and if he have in time past made satisfaction for theft, let him go to the water ordeal. Kemble, Saxons in England, I. 249, n. 2, after quoting Ethelred's Law 1, § 1: *Let every freeman have a true borh* (person responsible for his keeping the peace), who may present him to every right should he be accused, adds: *The stranger or friendless man who has no borh, . . . instead of clearing himself by the oath of his friends, must run the risk and endure the pain of the ordeal.* See *Discipline of the Religious Life*, note 58.

(28). Ayliffe 468.

(29). Ayliffe 487; Devoti Inst. Lib. III. Tit. XIV. § 2: An interlocutory sentence may, however, have the force of a definitive sentence if it ends the case. Law's Forms 302.

(30). Law's Forms 303.

(31). Nicolaus I. A.D. 864, ap. Gratian Caus. VI. Qu. IV. c. 6: What has once been definitively settled and deliberated upon upon sworn evidence, may not be altered by any rehearing, except by a superior authority. Ayliffe 486: Although a judge cannot alter his sentence, yet an ordinary judge may declare it to be a nullity. Craisson, § 5962.

The Conclusion of a Cause. 309

must always be in writing ([32]) (3) By the civil law there is no appeal from them, except in cases where they cannot be set right by the definitive sentence; whereas all final sentences may be appealed from within the prescribed time ([33]). By the canon law, however, interlocutory as well as final sentences may be the subject-matter of appeal, lest oppression should be practised under specious pretences ([34]).

9. To be canonically valid, a definitive sentence must fulfil the following conditions: (1) It must be drawn up in writing ([35]), unless it is given in audience, either by a bishop in person ([36]), or by the guardian of the spiritualities during the vacancy of the see ([37]). (2) It must be pronounced and read ([38]). And (3) the judge must be seated at the time, otherwise it is not a formal or *ex cathedrâ* judgment. These requirements do not, however, apply to summary causes ([39]). Further,

---

[32]. Ayliffe 487.

[33]. *Ibid.* 487.

[34]. Const. 6 Mepham, A.D. 1328 : A certain statute is said to have been made [viz., the rule of the civil law], in which it is forbidden to appeal from any judicial grievance before definitive sentence. . . . Now we do wholly lay aside this statute, and whatever has been done in consequence of it, as being made for depriving the oppressed of the remedy of appeal, though covered over with specious pretences. See *Acts in Judgment*, notes 80, 92, 217.

[35]. Cod. ap. Gratian Caus. II. Qu. 1. c. 8 and 9; Boniface VIII. in Sext. Lib. II. Tit. XIV. c. 5, says that a sentence which is (1) not in writing, or (2) is not read out by the judge, or (3) is not read by the judge seated, is an absolute nullity. The sentence is usually drawn up by the proctor of the plaintiff, the judge inserting the word "justice" in his own handwriting, but by custom it is drawn up by the registrar of the Court of Arches. Laws Forms 309.

[36]. Cod. ap. Gratian Caus. XI. Qu. 1. c. 45; Sext. Decr. Lib. II. Tit. XIV. c. 5.

[37]. Innocent III. in Decret. Lib. II. Tit. XX. c. 45.

[38]. Sext. Lib. II. Tit. XIV. c. 5; Ayliffe 488. The sentence is said to be read ex periculo = ex libello. Devoti Inst. Lib. III. Tit. XIV. § 7, or ex breviculo.

[39]. The judge, when judging in the tribunal, which was an elevated place, is described as qui tribunali praeest, qui pro tribunali cognoscit. Causes which were not disposed of by the judge from the elevated tribunal,

(4) it must be given in accordance with elementary justice ([40]), therefore not through fear or favour ([41]), and be in agreement with the canons ([42]). (5) It must be given in presence of the parties, or, at least, they must have been cited to hear it ([43]). (6) The defendant must be amenable to the jurisdiction ([44]). (7) It must be so framed that it corresponds with the libel ([45]); and, lastly, (8) it must be given in the presence

were said to be disposed of on a level (*de plano*), which is the term applied to summary procedure. Devoti Inst. Lib. III. Tit. XIV. § 4. Hence Boniface VIII. in Sext. Lib. II. Tit. XIV. c. 5, declares a sentence a nullity not given by a judge sitting. The bishop's seat is the sign of the bishop's jurisdiction. See *The Diocese*, § 3; *Canonical Procedure*, § 9.

(40). Alexander III. in Decret. Lib. II. Tit. XXVII. c. 22 declares the sentence void if the process in a cause is null and void, or if a sentence is pronounced for money or other consideration, or if a sentence is pronounced against a contumacious person before the return of contumacy has been received. *Id. Ibid.* c. 28: If the proper order of proceeding has been disregarded.

(41). Pseudo-Isidor. ap. Gratian Caus. XI. Qu. III. c. 89: An unjust judgment, or an unjust definition, given through fear, or by command of a king, or any bishop or powerful man, does not hold good. Gregory *Ibid.* c. 66: Even a just sentence must not be given for reward.

(42). Gregory, A.D. 593, in Decret. Lib. II. Tit. XXVII. c. 1: A sentence contrary to the laws and canons is *ipso jure* void, even though it be not suspended by appeal. Alexander III. to the Archbishop of York, *Ibid.* c. 9: When a cause is committed without appeal, and an iniquitous sentence is passed, it should be rendered void. Innocent III. *Ibid.* c. 13, however, says that if the procedure has otherwise been regular, this only applies when the sentence is contrary to the [definite] right of a constitution, not simply contrary to the [indefinite] rights of a litigant. *Ibid.* c. 21; Lynd. 76: Nor ought penalties to exceed the requirements of a case. *Ibid.* 73; Ayliffe 310.

(43). Stat. Eccl. Ant. A.D. 505, Can. 30: Let judges of the Church take care not to give sentence in the absence of him whose cause is being inquired into, because such a sentence is void. Clemens III. in Decret. Lib. II. Tit. XXVII. c. 10; Innocent III. *Ibid.* c. 18; Sext. Decr. Lib. II. Tit. XIV. c. 5. Since Const. 25 Otho, A.D. 1237, this is covered by the original citation whenever a proctor has been appointed. Lynd. 292; Law's Forms 304.

(44). Alexander III. in Decret. Lib. II. Tit. I. c. 4; Innocent III. *Ibid.* Lib. Tit. IV. c. 3.

(45). Concil. Lat. IV. A.D. 1215, Can. 8, in Decret. Lib. V. Tit. I. c. 24:

of witnesses who may be able if necessary to prove it (⁴⁶). A sentence which fails to fulfil these conditions is a nullity *ipso jure* (⁴⁷); nevertheless, a sentence is presumed to be good until it is shown to be bad (⁴⁸), at least, if it has been allowed to become a matter judicially settled (*res judicata*) (⁴⁹).

10. The office of an ordinary judge, in giving sentence in a criminal cause, usually includes three things, viz. (1) the act of the judge in determining the facts, and herein he acts as *cognitor* or *auditor* (⁵⁰); (2) the act of the judge in determining the punishment, and herein he acts as *assessor* (⁵¹), representing the canonical knowledge of the synod; and (3) the act of the judge in declaring the sentence, and herein he acts as the representative of authority in the Church, either by commission or by custom (⁵²). In delegation, each of these functions may be separately committed to a different person, or to a different group of persons.

According to the form of the judgment (libel), let the form of the sentence also be regulated. Lynd. 122; Ayliffe 488; Craisson, § 5952.

(46). Innocent III. in Decret. Lib. III. Tit. xx. c. 28, says that neither the single judge's word, nor yet his writing, can be accepted as worthy of credit, unless attested by two or three witnesses. Law's Forms 78, who states that in some foreign countries it is unusual to have it attested.

(47). Sext. Lib. II. Tit. xiv. c. 5; Lynd. 351: A sentence is a nullity if passed in the absence [other than contumacious] of the principal party, or if the witnesses produced have not been admitted [being unexceptionable], or if witnesses have been improperly received, or, in a plenary cause, if judgment has been given without contestation of suit. In any such cause, the defendant, being called upon to show cause why the sentence should not be ordered for execution, may allege the nullity of the same, and specify particulars. Lynd. 265; Stephen's Eccl. Stat. 133. An appeal on the ground of nullity may be made at any time within thirty years.

(48). Innocent III. in Decret. Lib. II. Tit. xxvII. c. 16; Lib. I. Tit. Ix. c. 6; Lynd. 266, 263.

(49). Innocent III. in Decret. Lib. II. Tit. xxvII. c. 13.

(50). See *Spiritual Courts*, note 16; Craisson, § 5758.

(51). Craisson, § 5766: It is the business of an assessor to watch over the investigation, to keep the judge informed as to the law, and to see that the judge's rescripts do not violate it. For these acts he is held responsible, unless he publicly protests.

(52). See *Ecclesiastical Severity*, note 38.

11. In determining the facts, it is a rule of law that in criminal causes, before a judge can condemn and punish, the evidence ought to be clearer than noonday ([53]). In civil causes, where less evidence suffices, should the depositions of the plaintiff's and defendant's witnesses contradict one another, preference should be given to those witnesses who are more worthy of credit, or who depose to what is more probable ([54]). As a general rule, where the rights of the parties are equally balanced, the decision ought to be given in favour of the defendant ([55]) or possessor ([56]); and in causes concerning matrimony, freedom, dowry, and wills, the presumption is in favour of their validity ([57]).

12. When the punishment is prescribed by a canon, the sentence is said to be a *sentence of law*. When it is left to the judge's discretion, it is said to be *the judge's sentence*. When a sentence of law is prescribed by a canon as a sentence *to be passed* (*sententia ferenda*), it is said to be *awarded* by the judge. On the other hand, when it is prescribed by a canon as a sentence *already* passed (*sententia lata*), it is said to be declared by the judge ([58]).

13. A sentence of law already passed takes effect *ipso jure*, without any other sentence of a judge ([59]), so that, directly the forbidden act is done, the offender, as regards himself and in *foro interno*, is *ipso facto* affected by it. So far as others are concerned, however, and in *foro externo*, it savours of commination, and is not *ipso facto* incurred before the judge's declaratory sentence or denunciation by name ([60]), unless the

---

(53). See *Acts in Judgment*, note 185.

(54). Cap. Reg. Franc. ap. Gratian Caus. IV. Qu. II. c. 3 ; Innocent III. to Bishops of London and Ely in Decret. Lib. II. Tit. XX. c. 32.

(55). Rule of Law 11 in Sext. Lib. V. Tit. XII. c. 5.

(56). Rule of Law 15, *Ibid.* Lucius III. quoted *Acts in Judgment*, note 190.

(57). Gregory IX. in Decret. Lib. II. Tit. XXVII. c. 26.

(58). See *Ecclesiastical Severity*, § 9.

(59). Boniface VIII. in Sext. Lib. V. Tit. II. c. 19 ; Const. 6 Peckham, A.D. 1281 ; Lynd. 143, 144, 217, 254, 258, p. 146, distinguishes a benefice vacant *de jure* and *de facto*. Const. 5 Boniface, A.D. 1261.

(60). Urban II. A.D. 1095, ap. Gratian Caus. IX. Qu. l. c. 5, mentions

crime is notorious ([61]). Meantime, the offender is called a *tolerated* person, his ecclesiastical acts being valid in relation to others, but unlawful as regards himself ([62]). He need not, therefore, if it is a sentence of *ipso jure* excommunication, be shunned as one excommunicate; but any one who is cognisant of his offence is justified in treating him as such ([63]).

14. Doubts sometimes arise as to whether a sentence prescribed by a canon is a sentence already passed, or a sentence to be passed. As a general rule, a sentence already passed is understood (1) if the words *ipso jure* or *ipso facto* are contained in the canon; or (2) if such words as *forthwith, immediately*, are used; or (3) if the present or the past tense is used, as *He is excommunicated*, or *Let him know that he is excommunicated;* and sometimes (4) if the imperative is used. On the other hand, when (1) simply minatory words are employed, as *We command under pain of excommunication;* or (2) when words denoting the future are used, as, *If he shall offend again, let*

those excommunicate, but not *nominatim*. Concil. Westminster A.D. 1200, Can. 14: We ordain that such as are excommunicate by name be avoided by all. Decret. Lib. I. Tit. XXXI. c. 2 directs that a man shall not be warned by name not to communicate, unless the party is able to prove a good cause. Innocent III. *Ibid*. Lib. II. Tit. XXVIII. c. 53 says denunciation does not bind the person excommunicated more than he was bound before. Lib. v. Tit. XXXIX. c. 29, and Lib. II. Tit. XXVIII. c. 53 ; Const. 20 Edmund, A.D. 1236; Boniface VIII. in Sext. Lib. v. Tit. II. c. 19: We declare the goods of these heretics confiscated *ipso jure*, but the execution of a confiscation of this kind ought not to take place before a sentence has been promulgated by the bishop of the place, or some other ecclesiastical person. Conf. Augustin ap. Gratian Caus. XXIII. Qu. IV. c. 24 ; Const. 3 Winchelsea, A.D. 1298; Const. 10 Arundel, A.D. 1408: A declaratory sentence requires to be preceded by a citation, and, in cases required by law, by a monition. Const. 11 Boniface, A.D. 1261; Const. 12 Stratford, A.D. 1342; Lynd. 260, 264. In many cases the publication of the law acts as a monition, and the disregard of it, after publication, is contumacy. Lynd. 264, 268, 13, 74, 94, 107; Law's Forms 124.

(61). Lynd. 147, 187, 224.

(62). Nicolaus, A.D. 866, ap. Gratian Caus. XV. Qu. VIII. c. 5: Communion must be received from a criminous priest until he is condemned by the judgment of the bishops.

(63). Craisson, § 6497, 6505. See *The Sacraments Generally*, note 60.

him be excommunicated; or (3) if doubt exists as to which of the two kinds of sentence is intended, the sentence is understood as one to be passed.

15. Whenever the judge has a discretion in awarding punishment[64], he is required to bring two qualifications to the exercise of it, viz., (1) justice, to make the penalty proportionate to the offence[65], and (2) mercy, to make it accord with the

[64]. Augustin ap. Gratian Caus. XXIII. Qu. IV. c. 25; Ambros. *Ibid.* Caus. XI. Qu. III. c. 68; Gregory *Ibid.* c. 70; Hieronym. *Ibid.* c. 79; Isidor. Sext. III. 52, 4: Every one who judges rightly, holds the balance in his hand, and carries in his thought both justice and mercy. Concil. Chelsea A.D. 787, Can. 13. Ethelred's Law 8, A.D. 1014 (in Hook's Lives I. 477): A judge ought to acquit himself in all respects, both as to mercy and judgment, so as to decree satisfaction in proportion to the crime, according to right knowledge, and yet to do so in measure for mercy's sake. Some crimes are deemed by good judges to be satisfied according to strict right, others to be pardoned for the mercy of God. Judgment ought to be without respect of persons, that they may not spare to pronounce common right against rich and poor, against friend and enemy. He who oppresses the innocent and acquits the guilty for money, love, or hatred, or out of faction, shall be oppressed by the Almighty. ... Wicked judges do often pervert judgment, and not finish a cause till their own desires are satisfied; and when they judge not deeds, but study for bribes, they are like greedy wolves in the evening, which leave nothing until the morning. ... An angry judge cannot attend to the just satisfaction of the doom book, for, through the blindness of his fury, he cannot discern the right, though never so clear. Const. 24 Othobon, A.D. 1268, says that a man of eminent station and large estate may more safely take truth for his guide than another man. Const. 1 Peckham, A.D. 1279; Honorius III. in Decret. Lib. I. Tit. XXXVI. c. 11; Clem. Lib. II. Tit. I. and Lib. V. Tit. VIII. c. 1; Lynd. 136, 153, 232, 250.

[65]. Gregory in Decret. Lib. II. Tit. XXVII. c. 1: A sentence contrary to law and the canons is *ipso jure* invalid. Concil. Ensham. Can. 7 and 32, A.D. 1009: Let every fact be cautiously scanned, and let judgment be according to the fact, and moderation according to the quality, so that it may be gentle in relation to God, tolerable in relation to the world; and let him that judges others consider what he requests for himself when he says: Forgive us our trespasses. Const. 10 Stratford, A.D. 1342; Const. 5 Thorsby, A.D. 1363; Augustin ap. Gratian Caus. XXIV. Qu. I. c. 21; Lynd. 212, 261, 286, 343. Leo ap. Gratian Caus. XXV. Qu. I. c. 16: We ought on no account to exceed the punishments which our ancestors have prescribed, either in holy canons or in the world's laws.

circumstances of the offender ([66]). On the one hand, it is sacrilege to award an excessive penalty ([67]), and the judge who is guilty of so doing is *ipso facto* suspended for a year ([68]). On the other hand, where severity is needed, the judge is not to be blamed for using it ([69]). Still, since the judge's discretion should be the discretion of a good and righteous man, it should, if anything, err on the side of mercy ([70]). If it fails to do so, it may be reviewed on appeal by the synodal superior ([71]). To justify his sentence before the Church, and to show "that he does not make the suit his own" ([72]), a judge usually states his reasons in judgment, but the only part of the judgment which is binding is the decision ([73])

16. If no appeal is lodged within the time allowed for appealing ([74]), the controversy becomes at its expiration a *judicially settled* matter (*res judicata*), and cannot again be disputed in

---

([66]). Honorius III. in Decret. Greg. IX. Lib. I. Tit. XXXVI. c. 11: In those matters which are not provided for by law expressly, do you proceed according to equity, always inclining to the side of humanity. Lynd. 261, 276; Alexander III. to Bishop of Exeter, *Ibid.* Lib. V. Tit. XII. c. 6.

([67]). Hieronym. ap. Gratian Caus. XXIV. Qu. III. c. 4: Should any one be repelled by a wrongful judgment of those who preside over a Church, ... he suffers no damage thereby. Rabanus, *Ibid.* c. 5, quoted *Excesses*, note 140. Hieronym. ap. Gratian Caus. XI. Qu. III. c. 57: If any one calls right wrong and wrong right, both alike are an abomination before God. See *Excesses*, § 20.

([68]). Concil. Lugdun. A.D. 1245, in Sext. Lib. II. Tit. XIV. c. 1.

([69]). Augustin ap. Gratian Caus. XXIII. Qu. IV. c. 38–42.

([70]). Justinian *Ibid.* Caus. II. Qu. VI. c. 28; Alexander III. in Decret. Lib. I. Tit. XXIX. c. 4; Lynd. 274, 290, 293.

([71]). Lynd. 125, 134, 208, 254 says that his discretion must be that of a good man, and his synodal superior is the judge of its goodness.

([72]). Ayliffe 312. But Innocent III. in Decret. Lib. II. Tit. XXVII. c. 6 says: It is usual for a judge not to express in his judgment all the considerations which moved him thereto.

([73]). Ecclesiastical Courts Commission, 1883, vol. II. 337, 365.

([74]). Innocent III. A.D. 1208, in Decret. Lib. I. Tit. VI. c. 32: It has become a judicially settled matter (transiit in rem judicatam), not having been suspended by legitimate appeal for ten days. Innocent III. A.D. 1199, *Ibid.* Lib. II. Tit. XXVII. c. 15, says that it becomes a judicially settled matter if notice of appeal is not lodged within ten days.

judgment. The effects of a cause becoming a judicially settled matter are (75): (1) the sentence may be made the ground of an action for execution, or of an exception in a subsequent action (76); (2) it decides the rights of the parties between themselves, even though it is founded upon error (77); (3) it is taken for judicial truth, so that it decides the rights of third parties who are privy to the same suit, or derive their rights from one of the litigants (78). If, however, new facts are forthcoming to show that the decision was given in error (79), redress may be had in the form of a fresh action praying for restitution (80). This action, it is said, may be brought at any time within thirty years, and is allowed even against a papal sentence (81); but in this country such an action seems to be

(75). Ayliffe 489: The judicially settled matter (*res judicata*) is one thing, the judicial settling (*res judicans*) another. For the judicial settling is the sentence itself, and this puts an end to the controversy. But the judicially settled matter is the cause, which, by the sentence, receives an end of being controverted any further. Devoti Lib. II. Tit. XIV. § 12.

(76). Boniface VIII. in Sext. Lib. II. Tit. XII. c. 2.

(77). Hilary, A.D. 465, ap. Gratian Caus. XXXV. Qu. IX. c. 3: In future sentences, causes, and subscriptions, that in presence of a synodal judgment there may be no opening for fraud. Gregory *Ibid.* c. 5: Things which have been reasonably disposed of and decided ought not afterwards to be disturbed. Lynd. 275: A judicially settled matter is taken for truth. Hobart 144.

(78). Innocent III. in Decret. Lib. II. Tit. XXVII. c. 13; Ayliffe 253; Devoti Lib. III. Tit. X. § 2; Craisson, § 5953.

(79). Innocent III. in Decret. Lib. II. Tit. XXVIII. c. 46.

(80). Leg. 4 Cod. de Re. Judic. c. 21 de Sentent.; Pseudo-Isidor. ap Gratian Caus. II. Qu. VI. c. 10: Wherefore to this Holy See the aforesaid privileges have been specially conceded, . . . so that from it the oppressed may receive succour, and those unjustly condemned, restitution. Innocent III. to Bishops of Ely and Rochester, in Decret. Lib. I. Tit. XLI. c. 3, says that a Church injured in a suit through an omission of necessary proofs, may seek to be restored to its former position. Ayliffe 270: A sentence may be demanded to execution which is not suspended by an appeal, or by a suit of *restitutio in integrum*.

(81). Gregory ap. Gratian Caus. XXXV. Qu. IX. c. 4: The sentence of the Apostolic See is always drawn with such moderation . . . that it does not require retractation, nor is it necessary that it should be altered, unless, perchance, it has been so given that it may be retracted or changed

The Conclusion of a Cause. 317

now barred, as well by statutes of limitations as by special legislation ([82]).

17. Certain sentences never become matters judicially settled ([83]). Such are (1) sentences in matrimonial causes, which are never final during the lifetime of the parties ([84]); (2) sentences given by fraud or mistake ([85]), by judges possessed of no jurisdiction ([86]), or contrary to elementary justice ([87]), which are null and void *ipso jure;* and (3) sentences in criminal causes, based on an erroneous statement of the facts ([88]).

according to the tenor of the previous condition. Innocent III. in Decret. Lib. I. Tit. XLI. c. 5 permits a sentence of his predecessor, Eugenius, to be called in question thus indirectly.

(82). 2 and 3 Gul. IV. c. 92 prohibited the granting in future of commissions of review, which appear to include *restitutiones in integrum.* See below, § 39 and note 47.

(83). Schmalzgrueber and Craisson, § 5960, enumerate six cases: (1) when the sentence is a nullity itself, because given contrary to natural justice, as without a hearing; (2) matrimonial cases; (3) in benefice cases, when there are any new grounds (Decret. Lib. II. Tit. XXVIII. c. 46); (4) when an unjust censure has been pronounced in alleging reasons for its removal (Innocent III. in Decret. Lib. I. Tit. XXIX. c. 36; Honorius III. *Ibid.* Lib. V. Tit. XXXVII. c. 13; Concil. Lat. IV. A.D. 1213, Can. 47; *Ibid.* Lib. V. Tit. XXXIX. c. 48); (5) if the sentence is based on false witness; or (6) depends on the party's necessary, not his voluntary oath.

(84). Alexander III. to Bishop and Archdeacon of Norwich in Decret. Lib. II. Tit. XXVII. c. 7; Clemens III. *Ibid.* c. 9. See the arguments in the Duchess of Kingston's case, XX. State Trials, 443. Ayliffe 492; Devoti Lib. II. Tit. II. § 156.

(85). Alexander III. in Decret. Lib. II. Tit. XXVII. c. 22 says if the witnesses are conspirators, who were allowed against the defendant's protest. *Id. Ibid.* Tit. XX. c. 9 says if it is shown that the witnesses had been bribed. Innocent III. *Ibid.* Tit. XXV. c. 6 says that exception may be taken to a judgment based on a forged instrument twenty years afterwards.

(86). For instance, by a judge excommunicate. Decret. Lib. II. Tit. XXVII. c. 24; Concil. Lat. IV. Can. 3, A.D. 1215; *Ibid.* Lib. V. Tit. VII. c. 13; Ayliffe 271.

(87). Such as a judgment given for money (Gregory ap. Gratian Caus. XI. Qu. III. c. 66), or given in the absence of the party, or without a hearing (Decret. Lib. II. Tit. XXVII. c. 24). Ayliffe 492; A sentence never passes in rem judicatam when there is a constat by an evidence of fact touching the iniquity of such sentence. Ayliffe 84.

(88). Augustin ap. Gratian Caus. XI. Qu. III. c. 50: How can it damage

EXECUTION.

18. Sentence having been given, and the time allowed for appealing having expired ([89]), it is open to the successful litigant to apply for the sentence to be ordered for execution ([90]), or, otherwise, for it to be signified to the civil power, without which his intention in judgment would be frustrated. Some sentences execute themselves, being rather acts than sentences, such as a sentence of excommunication ([91]), which, when publicly declared, excludes from the communion of the Church everywhere ([92]). Others require the judge's intervention, which may be obtained either (1) by action, or (2) by imploring his office ([93]). The latter is the usual method in this country.

a man if human ignorance will not allow his name to be read out from the book [of diptychs], if an iniquitous conscience does not delete his name from the book of life? Stat. Eccl. Ant. A.D. 505, Can. 28; *Ibid.* c. 35: The unjust condemnation of bishops is a nullity, and must be revoked by the synod. Concil. Tolet. IV. A.D. 633, *Ibid.* c. 65: A bishop, priest, or deacon unjustly deposed [by one synod] may be found innocent in a second synod. Innocent I. *Ibid.* Caus. XXXV. Qu. IX. c. 5, A.D. 414, rescinds sentences of condemnation pronounced by his predecessors, because they were based on false evidence as to the facts. Nicolaus I. A.D. 862, *Ibid.* c. 6: We do not dispute that the sentence of the Roman See may be changed for the better, if it has been based on anything surreptitious. Innocent III. A.D. 1198, in Decret. Lib. II. Tit. XXVII. c. 12, repeats the above. Devoti Lib. III. Tit. XIV. § 13; Ayliffe 491. In this country, commissions of review are now forbidden. See below, § 39.

(89). Lynd. 107; Ayliffe 270.

(90). Law's Forms 313 says that the practice of ordering a sentence for execution has grown rare in the now defunct Court of Arches.

(91). Innocent. III. to Bishop of Ely in Decret. Lib. II. Tit. XXVIII. c. 53.

(92). Concil. Nic. A.D. 325, Can. 5: Let sentence according to canon prevail, that clergymen or laymen, being excommunicated by some, be not received by others. Apost. Can. 11: If any one prays with a person excommunicated, let him be suspended. Apost. Can. 13, quoted *Ecclesiastical Severity*, note 81.

(93). Lynd. 107, 94, 351; Law's Forms 312, 313. Ayliffe 272 says that the judge's intervention by office is preferable, because it requires no libel, and is the only kind practised in this country, but that a citation is always required, if either the judge's successor or the defendant's successor is concerned.

Action requires a libel; but in either case the application may be met by an exception of fraud ([94]) or nullity ([95]). Others, again, require to be signified to the temporal authorities, such as excommunication and contumacy, if outward coercion is to be employed to give them effect.

19. Although as a general rule no inferior judge can call in question the acts of his superior, yet, if in a cause pending before an inferior judge any sentence or act of a superior judge is objected by the defendant, and the nullity of such act is alleged by the plaintiff, the inferior judge may indirectly admit the nullity if it is proved before him, by giving sentence, or ordering the sentence for execution, as though such null sentence or null act had never been exhibited ([96]). The term for execution is called the term executory ([97]). In criminal causes, execution follows at the expiration of the fatal term. In civil cases, four months are usually allowed ([98]), unless a shorter time is prescribed by the judge ([99]). If the sentence is not voluntarily obeyed ([100]), and execution becomes necessary, it is the duty of the ordinary to assist a judge dele-

---

([94]). Alexander III. to Archbishop of York in Decret. Lib. II. Tit. XXVII. c. 5.

([95]). Alexander III. to Archbishop of York, *Ibid.* Lib. II. Tit. XXVII. c. 9, says it is a nullity if manifestly unjust. Lynd. 157 : Things which are done contrary to law are taken for things not done. The exception to the sentence may be made on the ground that it is a nullity, because it is contrary to a previous sentence. Law's Forms 313, 311, 106, 79 ; Ayliffe 273 says that the exception of nullity propounded before a judge inferior to him who pronounced the sentence does not hinder the execution.

([96]). Law's Forms 312. In a recent case (in 1896) a secular judge declined to pronounce a sentence of nullity of marriage between a woman and a man whom she had married whilst her first husband was living, although the first husband was produced in court, on the ground that a jury had found that the first husband was dead when she married the second one.

([97]). Innocent III. in Decret. Lib. II. Tit. XXVII. c. 15 ; Ayliffe 27.

([98]). Devoti Inst. Lib. III. Tit. XIII. § 4.

([99]). Innocent III. in Decret. Lib. II. Tit. XXVII. c. 15.

([100]). Coelestin III. in Decret. Lib. II. Tit. I. c. 10.

gate by lending his office for that purpose (¹⁰¹), and of all other ordinaries to assist him in like manner (¹⁰²). A delegate can only order his sentence for execution when he has been authorised to execute the sentence, as well as to decide.

20. As every one who fails in a suit, or who fails to sustain an exception made in a suit, is deemed to have in that respect acted unjustly, the loser in a dilatory or peremptory exception is ordinarily punished by being condemned in the costs connected therewith (¹⁰³), and the loser in the principal cause or main issue, in the costs of the suit (¹⁰⁴), unless it appears to have been vexatiously brought or defended. Payment of costs may be obtained by means of the judge's office, if they have been already taxed, or the loser may be convened by action (¹⁰⁵). Expenses incurred before the suit was judicially contested cannot, however, be recovered as a matter of course, because the suit is only set up by contestation, but they may be recovered by request made to the judge. Those incurred after contestation he may award without request (¹⁰⁶), and may compel their payment by ecclesiastical censures (¹⁰⁷). A judge who omits or refuses to award costs, if a party has moved for them, may be required to pay them himself (¹⁰⁸).

21. When spiritual coercion is lawfully employed in the maintenance of discipline, any disregard of it is called contumacy (¹⁰⁹),

(101). Alexander III. to Bishop of Norwich in Decret. Lib. I. Tit. XXIX. c. 7; Ayliffe 271. See *Acts in Judgment*, note 248.
(102). See *Spiritual Courts*, note 163.
(103). Innocent III. in Decret. Lib. II. Tit. XIV. c. 5, 6.
(104). Gregory IX. in Decret. Lib. I. Tit. XXXIV. c. 17.
(105). Ayliffe 273.
(106). Ayliffe 274.
(107). Law's Forms 320.
(108). Ayliffe 274.
(109). Luke X. 16; Matt. XVIII. 15; 1 Cor. v.; 1 Tim. I. 20; 2 Tim. IV. 13; 2 Thess. III. 14; Concil. Agath. A.D. 506, Can. 2 ap. Gratian I Dist. L. c. 21 : Let contumacious clergy, so far as the degree of their rank (dignitatis ordo) permits, be corrected by the bishops. Stat. Eccl. Ant. A.D. 505, *Ibid.* I. Dist. XC. c. 1 : Let the bishop reduce discordant clergy to harmony. Such as disobey, let the synod condemn. Socrates II. 40 says that the synod of Selucia, A.D. 359, deposed Bishop Patrophilus for contumacy, in

or contempt of the keys ([110]), and such contumacy, if persisted in, becomes obduracy ([111]). Thus, it is contumacy not to appear to a citation when lawfully convened ([112]), and also to disregard a judicial sentence. By the canon law, the usual mode of punishing contumacy is by excommunication ([113]), in a civil case sometimes by sequestration ([114]), and, when the contumacy is that of not appearing to a citation, by proceeding to sentence ([115]) or by interdict ([116]). In this country, a person excommunicated, and continuing for forty days excommunicate without coming to satisfaction, is held to display obduracy, or contempt of the keys, to such an extent as to constitute a civil offence, which renders him liable to imprisonment ([117]); but in

not presenting himself to answer a charge made against him by a presbyter. Concil. Ilerd. A.D. 523, Can. 10: Those who, when excommunicated for any fault, refuse to go out of the Church for the offence of contumacy, ought to be more tardily admitted to pardon. Gregory *Ibid.* I. Dist. LXXXI. c. 29: Unless [the archdeacon] obeys your command, we will that he be deprived of his order.

(110). Honorius III. in Decret. Lib. V. Tit. XXXVII. c. 13; Gregory IX. *Ibid.* Tit. XXVII. c. 10.

(111). Lynd. 264 says obduracy is the act of a will resisting monitions, or resisting grace; that sometimes obduracy is a punishment by which a man is not a fit subject for grace. Law's Forms 128.

(112). See *Acts in Judgment*, § 14.

(113). Concil. Milev. A.D. 418, ap. Gratian Caus. II. Qu. VI. c. 19, directs a man to be excommunicated who contumaciously refuses to obey a citation. Ayliffe [190]. By 53 Geo. III. c. 127, excommunication is now forbidden to be awarded for obduracy. Instead thereof, after forty days the contumacious person may be imprisoned. Laws Forms, p. 129.

(114). Alexander III. to the Abbot of Remess and the Archdeacon of Ely in Decret. Lib. II. Tit. XIV. c. 2.

(115). Alexander III. to Bishops of Exeter and Winchester and the Abbot of Ford in Decret. Lib. II. Tit. XIV. c. 3; Urban III. *Ibid.* c. 4.

(116). Alexander III. in Decret. Lib. I. Tit. XXIX. c. 11.

(117). Cnut's Law 4, A.D. 1018: We command that apostates, and such as are outlawed by God and man, be gone off the land, unless they will submit and make deep satisfaction. Edward's Law 7, A.D. 1064: If the guilty person decline, or contumaciously despise the sentence of the bishop's court, let complaint of it be brought to the king after forty days. Const. 4 Boniface, A.D. 1261: If the customary writ de excommunicato capiendo be denied when it is required in a case where it ought to be

such a case imprisonment can now only be inflicted for a period not exceeding six months, by application to the civil authorities, or, as it is said, by signifying the sentence to them; and no ordinary below the degree of a bishop is competent to make such signification ([118]). Excommunication is also forbidden to be awarded as the punishment of contumacy ([119]).

APPEALS.

22. To prevent injustice being done by hasty or ill-considered sentences, or by the prejudice and imperfect knowledge of a judge, the remedy of appeal is provided ([120]). In the first three centuries, what would be properly called an appeal was unknown. There were no regularly constituted courts; Christian principles had not as yet settled down into uniform laws; and the practice of different Churches varied. Some bishops then made an excessive use of excommunication, with the result that application was made to neighbouring bishops to procure a rectification of their sentences ([121]). Thus was established a kind of informal appeal from the individual bishop to the Church of the province.

23. When, on the conversion of the Empire, the Church was permitted to decide civil matters, arrangements became necessary for dealing with such matters on appeal. Regulations were accordingly made for that object by the Councils of Con-

granted according to the approved custom. 9 Ed. II. St. 1, c. 12, A.D. 1315, mentions forty days. Const. 13 Stratford, A.D. 1343; 5 Eliz. c. 23, sec. 10, saved and reserved to all " having authority to certify any person excommunicated, like authority to accept and receive the submission," &c. 2 and 3 Will. IV. c. 93; Lynd. 264, 348.

(118). Lynd. 350; Law's Forms, p. 135.
(119). See *Spiritual Courts*, note 127.
(120). Pseudo-Isidor. ap. Gratian Caus. II. Qu. VI. c. 1 : It is lawful for an appellant to assist a damaged cause by the remedy of appeal. *Ibid.* 7, 8, 9, 10, 12; Ayliffe 72; Devoti Inst. Lib. III. Tit. XV. § 1.
(121). Concil. Chalcedon A.D. 451, Can. 23; Van Espen Pars. III. Tit. X. c. 1, sec. 5. See *Excesses*, note 140; Ecclesiastical [Courts Commission, 1883, vol. II. 127.

stantinople ([122]) and Chalcedon ([123]). Ultimately, by the Code of Justinian, a civil sanction was given to appeals from the bishop to the metropolitan, and from the metropolitan to the patriarch, with ultimate recourse to the emperor himself ([124]). The place of the emperor was, however, soon taken in the West by the pope, partly owing to the fact that after 476 A.D. there was no longer a Western emperor, partly owing to the preference among Christians for a spiritual to a temporal judge.

24. In its widest sense an appeal may be defined to be a provocation from the decision or action of the authorities of some limited portion of the Church to the decision or action of the authorities of a larger section of the same, with a view to obtain redress for some grievance sustained, or to prevent the infliction of one which is apprehended. A grievance, nevertheless, may be sustained in two ways—either by a judicial sentence or by an official act. Hence appeals are of two kinds —(1) those called judicial, and (2) those called extra-judicial ([125]). A judicial appeal is an appeal from a judicial sentence which has actually been passed, not merely from a sentence which is anticipated. An extra-judicial appeal is an appeal from some official act, which may be either an act done or an act anticipated ([126]), such as an election, a postulation, a provision ([127]).

[122]. Can. 6.
[123]. Can. 17.
[124]. Cod. I. 1 Tit. IV. De episcopali audientia.
[125]. Concil. Nic. A.D. 325, Can. 5 sanctions an extra-judicial appeal from the bishop's excommunication. Alexander III. in Decret. Lib. II. Tit. XXVIII. c. 5: The sacred canons permit appeals out of judgment. Alexander III. Ibid. c. 12 says appeals may be made as well before as after contestation. Clemens III. Ibid. c. 38 directs appeals not to be received except (1) either from a grievance, or (2) from an unjust condemnation. 23 Hen. VIII. c. 9 allows extra-judicial appeals. Stephen's Eccl. Stat. 411.
[126]. Innocent III. to Bishops of Rochester and London in Decret. Lib. II. Tit. XXVIII. c. 51 mentions an appeal by the Abbot of Canterbury to prevent his being molested in the possession of a Church. Boniface VIII. in Sext. Lib. II. Tit. XV. c. 8; Concil. Vien. A.D. 131, in Clem. Decr. Lib. II. Tit. XII. c. 3. Lynd. 106 mentions the issue of a decree of sequestration without a citation. Craisson, § 5974.
[127]. Boniface VIII. in Sext. Lib. II. Tit. XV. c. 8; Innocent III. in

An extra-judicial appeal is, therefore, rather of the nature of a motion introducing a cause than of an appeal ([128]), and has place where no controversy has been introduced before a judge.

25. Judicial appeals are allowed on three grounds: (1) to correct the unfairness of an unjust judge ([129]); (2) to set right a judge's sentence which exceeds the law of the Church ([130]); and (3) to enable one who through ignorance has not had justice done to his cause in the first instance to obtain justice by a second instance ([131]). An appeal is, therefore, open not only to the party cast in a suit, but to all and any who have an interest in it ([132]); but when several persons have a like interest, the appeal of one settles the rights of the others ([133]).

26. By mediaeval practice, appeals are allowed on technical as well as on substantial grounds ([134]), and a judge is bound to respect even what seems to him frivolous appeals ([135]); but appeals are not allowed (1) when the party defeated has in any way acquiesced in the sentence ([136]), or has undertaken to acquiesce in it ([137]); (2) in disciplinary causes, when crime is

Decret. Lib. I. Tit. VI. c. 21; Concil. Lugdun. A.D. 1274, in Sext. Lib. I. Tit. VI. c. 1; Boniface VIII. *Ibid.* c. 19, 30.

(128). Alexander III. in Decret. Lib. II. Tit. XXVIII. c. 5 calls them provocationes ad causas, potius quam appellationes.

(129). Concil. Carthag. III. A.D. 397, Can. 10 ap. Gratian Caus. II. Qu. VI. c. 37; Pseudo-Isidor. *Ibid.* c. 21; Lynd. 290, 133, 124, 208; Ayliffe 76.

(130). Alexander III. to Archbishop of Canterbury in Decret. Lib. II. Tit. XXVIII. c. 20.

(131). Ayliffe 76.

(132). Gratian Caus. II. Qu. VI. c. 30; Ayliffe 73; Innocent III. in Decret. Lib. I. Tit. VI. c. 16 forbids one elected, who has renounced his own election, afterwards to appeal to prevent another's election.

(133). Gregory IX. in Decret. Lib. II. Tit. XXVIII. c. 72.

(134). Alexander III. in Decret. Lib. II. Tit. XXVIII. c. 11.

(135). Alexander III. *Ibid.* c. 19.

(136). As by continuing to litigate before the same judge, which is equivalent to renouncing the appeal, according to Urban III. in Decret. Lib. I. Tit. XXIX. c. 20; Innocent III. *Ibid.* c. 54; Boniface VIII. in Sext. Lib. II. Tit. XV. c. 8; Ayliffe 84.

(137). Alexander III. to Archbishop of Canterbury in Decret. Lib. II. Tit. XXVIII. c. 20.

notorious ([138]), or has been confessed ([139]), or when the appeal is made for the sole purpose of gaining delay ([140]); but they are allowed to correct an unjust condemnation, or a sentence of excessive punishment ([141]). They are also not allowed ([142]) in executory causes, except to remedy an excess committed in the execution itself. They are, however, permitted in causes which have been committed, as it is said, *appellatione remota* ([143]), or *appellatione postposita* ([144]), *i.e.*, without regard for appeal ([145]),

(138). Alexander III. *Ibid.* c. 13 and 14, but warns the Archbishop of Toledo not to accept things as notorious which are not notorious. *Id.* A.D. 1169, *Ibid.* c. 32.

(139). Alexander III. in Decret. Lib. II. Tit. XXVIII. c. 5; *Id. Ibid.* c. 13; *Id. Ibid.* c. 3: Since the remedy of appeal is not designed to assist those who transgress the rule of religion and order, . . . do not on that account hesitate to correct and chastise him. *Id.* to the Bishop of Winchester c. 22; Concil. Lat. III. A.D. 1179, *Ibid.* c. 26: Let not subjects, when corrected, break out into the voice of appeal. Alexander III. A.D. 1169, *Ibid.* c. 32: Let not abbots who have been publicly convicted, and then, when pressed in chapter, refuse to resign, be allowed to appeal. Concil. Lat. IV. A.D. 1215, *Ibid.* c. 61.

(140). Concil. Milev. A.D. 416, ap. Gratian Caus. II. Qu. VI. c. 35; Concil. Afric. *Ibid.* c. 39. Pseudo-Isidor. *Ibid.*: Also in criminal causes there may be an appeal, nor may the voice of appeal be denied to one who lies under sentence of punishment. Alexander III. in Decret. Lib. II. Tit. XXVIII. c. 3; Concil. Lat. III. A.D. 1179, Can. 6, *Ibid.* c. 26: Let not subjects break forth into the voice of appeal against ecclesiastical discipline. But if any one believes that necessity obliges him to appeal, let a competent term be assigned him to prosecute his appeal. Clemens III. *Ibid.* c. 38; Stephen's Eccl. Stat. 146 observes that the archbishop's inhibition to the inferior judge was a frequent ground of complaint in such cases.

(141). Alexander III. in Decret. Lib. II. Tit. XXVIII. c. 29.

(142). Innocent III. in Decret. Lib. II. Tit. XXVIII. c. 43: There lies no appeal from execution agents unless they exceed the proper limit in execution; and Tit. XXVII. c. 15; Ayliffe 84.

(143). Alexander III. to Bishop of Worcester, *Ibid.* Lib. II. Tit. XXVIII. c. 9; Lucius III. to Walter, Bishop of Lincoln, *Ibid.* c. 36; Innocent III. to Bishop of Ely, A.D. 1204, *Ibid.* c. 53, says the phrase *appellatione remota* excludes every kind of appeal except what is specially allowed by law. Gregory IX. *Ibid.* c. 71.

(144). Innocent III. A.D. 1204, *Ibid.* Lib. III. Tit. XXIV. c. 6.

(145). Lucius III. to Bishop of Lincoln, *Ibid.* Lib. II. Tit. XXVIII. c. 36; Gregory IX. *Ibid.* c. 71; Eccles. Courts Commission, 1883, vol. II. p. 95.

the effect of the clause being not to prevent an appeal by way of devolution, but' to prevent an appeal having a suspensory effect on the sentence ([146]).

27. Judicial appeals may be made either (1) before final sentence, when they are termed appeals from a judicial grievance or ruling ([147]); or (2) after final sentence, when they are termed appeals in the principal cause ([148]). Before final sentence they may be made (1) from a judicial grievance either sustained or threatened, but not when there is only a surmise that one is likely to happen, unless it is one which cannot be redressed by sentence ([149]); or (2) from an interlocutory sentence deciding some preliminary or incidental matter in a cause. Appeals made after final sentence must always be from the sentence itself, but such appeals may be made implicitly as well as explicitly ([150]). They may, moreover, be made from any and every judge, excepting (1) the highest of all, and excepting (2) arbitrators selected by both parties of free choice ([151]).

(146). Innocent III. to Bishop of Ely *Ibid.* c. 53 ; Craisson, § 657.

(147). Alexander III. in Decret. Lib. II. Tit. XXVIII. c. 12; Concil. Lugdun. A.D. 1245, in Sext. Lib. II. Tit. XV. c. 1, says super interlocutoria vel gravamine aliquo. Boniface VIII. *Ibid.* Tit. VI. c. 1. The term *oppressi*, ap. Gratian Caus. II. Qu. VI. c. 3 and 17, is explained to refer to appeals before sentence. Const. 6 Mepham. A.D. 1328 : A statute is said to have been made forbidding appeals from judicial grievances before final sentence [no such statute exists, but such was the rule of the civil law, and a constitution of Archbishop Winchelsea, 2 Spelman, p. 419, forbids appeals in causes of correction, except from a definitive sentence]. We wholly forbid this statute, as being made for depriving the oppressed of the remedy of appeal. Lynd. 115 ; Ayliffe 74.

(148). Ecclesiastical Courts Commission Report, 1883, p. 183.

(149). Alexander III. to Archbishop of Canterbury and Bishop of Worcester in Decret. Lib. II. Tit. VIII. c. 1, allows an appeal because the citatory term was too short. Innocent III. *Ibid.* Tit. XXVIII. c. 49, because the citation was too uncertain.

(150). As when a priest put himself under the protection of the metropolitan without specifically using the word appeal in Decret. Lib. II. Tit. XXVIII. c. 39, or undertook a mission to the pope, *Ibid.* c. 52, addressed to the monks of Canterbury, or by a protest if he fears to appeal. Gregory IX. *Ibid.* c. 73.

(151). Craisson, § 658.

28. To render an appeal before final sentence admissible ([152]), there must (1) be a lawful and specific ground of grievance, such as the threat of a judge ([153]) or his refusal to receive an exception ([154]); (2) the appeal must be made in writing, setting forth specifically the grievance which is the subject of appeal ([155]). A general appeal from all grievances without naming them is not admissible ([156]). (3) The appeal must be made within the ten or fifteen days allowed by law ([157]), and letters dimissory must be demanded within thirty days ([158]). Before contestation of suit such an appeal can only be allowed for a reasonable cause ([159]), and the cause, which must be stated to the judge appealed from, must be proved before the judge of appeal ([160]). If the ground of appeal is found to be untenable, the cause is sent back to the judge appealed from ([161]). One who is dispossessed after appealing must be restored to possession before the adversary can be heard against the appeal ([162]).

29. Appeals from interlocutory sentences differ in many respects from appeals made from final sentences. (1) They

[152]. Concil. Lat. IV. A.D. 1215, in Decret. Lib. II. Tit. XXVIII. c. 59.
[153]. Concil. Vien. A.D. 1311, in Clem. Lib. II. Tit. XII. c. 3; Lynd. 115.
[154]. Alexander III. Ibid. c. 10; Innocent III. to the bishop, dean, and precentor of Hereford, Ibid. c. 48; Concil. Lat. IV. Ibid. c. 59; Gregory IX. Ibid. c. 70. See *Acts in Judgment*, notes 92, 217, and 279.
[155]. Honorius III. Ibid. c. 63; Gregory IX. Ibid. c. 70; Ayliffe 83.
[156]. Alexander III. Ibid. c. 18.
[157]. Boniface VIII. in Sext. Lib. II. Tit. XV. c. 8: Desiring to put an end to a long-standing controversy we decree that from elections, postulations, provisions, and other extra-judicial acts whatsoever, in which an appeal is allowed, whoever believing himself aggrieved by such acts, wishes to have the grievance remedied by way of appeal, must appeal within ten days, if he wishes to appeal, from the time when he became aware of it. 24 Hen. VIII. c. 12, allows fifteen days in this country.
[158]. Dig. Lib. 49, Tit. VI. ap. Gratian Caus. II. Qu. VI. c. 31.
[159]. Concil. Lat. IV. A.D. 1215, Can. 35, Ibid. c. 59. See note 167.
[160]. Gregory IX. Ibid. c. 70, § 3.
[161]. Clemens III. in Decret. Lib. II. Tit. XXVIII. c. 38; Clemens IV. in Sext. Lib. II. Tit. XV. c. 5.
[162]. Innocent III. to Bishops of Rochester and London, A.D. 1205, in Decret. Lib. II. Tit. XXVIII. c. 51.

do not suspend the jurisdiction of the judge appealed from unless the superior grants an inhibition, whereas appeals from final sentences do ([163]); nor is inhibition granted in such cases as a matter of course, but only if good ground for it is shown ([164]). (2) They expire naturally if the judge alters his interlocutory ruling ([165]), whereas a judge cannot alter a final sentence. (3) They must always be in writing, and specify the precise ground of appeal ([166]), whereas appeals from final sentences may be made orally in court, and need specify no grounds. (4) They cannot be sustained at the hearing on any other ground than that named in the appeal ([167]), whereas appeals from final sentences may allege new grounds, and justify them with fresh proofs ([168]).

30. The effect of an appeal from a judicial sentence is threefold: (1) It suspends the operation of the sentence appealed from, and does away with the presumption in its favour ([169]),

---

([163]). Boniface VIII. in Sext. Lib. II. Tit. xv. c. 7; Devoti Lib. III. Tit. xv. § 3.

([164]). Alexander III. in Decret. Lib. II. Tit. xxviii. c. 3; Sext. Lib. II. Tit. xv. c. 5.

([165]). Concil. Lat. IV. A.D. 1215, in Decret. Lib. II. Tit. xxviii. c. 60.

([166]). Gonzalez states that before the time of Innocent III. interlocutory and all other appeals might be freely made by virtue of Pseudo-Isidor. ap. Gratian Caus. II. Qu. VI. c. 3: Omnis oppressus libere sacerdotum appellet judicium, but that the Fourth Lateran Council, A.D. 1215, in Decret. Lib. II. Tit. xxviii. c. 61, limited them to cases in which there was probabilis causa appellationis; and that Concil. Lugdun. A.D. 1245, in Sext. Decr. Lib. II. Tit. xv. c. 1, required them to be in writing and to specify the ground.

([167]). Clem. Decr. Lib. II. Tit. xii. c. 5.

([168]). Alexander III. to Archbishop of York in Decret. Lib. VI. Tit. xxviii. c. 16; Ayliffe 85.

([169]). Alexander III. to Bishop of Exeter and Dean of London, *Ibid.* c. 1; *Id.* to Bishop of Norwich, *Ibid.* c. 4; S. Leo *Ibid.* c. 17, authorises the Archbishop of Canterbury to reinstate one who has been disturbed from his benefice pending an appeal. Devoti Inst. Lib. III. Tit. xv. § 15; Ayliffe 73. Lynd. 106 says that if an appeal is abandoned the sentence revives from the date when it was passed. If the sentence is confirmed on appeal, it takes effect from the time of confirmation. *Ibid.* 107.

unless it be a summary sentence given in visitation ([170]), or a declaratory sentence of excommunication or interdict already incurred *ipso jure* ([171]), or a sentence in a cause which has been committed without regard for appeal (*appellatione remota*). (2) It terminates the jurisdiction of the judge appealed from, either by the judge's own issue of letters dimissory, or by the superior's inhibition, so that any act attempted by him in the interval is of no force ([172]); but it does not prevent the same person being punished by the same judge for offences subsequently committed ([173]). (3) It causes a devolution of the cause ([174]), so that the future decision and execution of the sentence rests with the superior judge, except by consent of the parties ([175]). Hence, although a sentence which is a nullity in itself requires no appeal, yet by means of the appeal the superior judge is enabled to judicially declare it to be a nullity ([176]).

31. An appeal must always be made and followed up within the time allowed by law. This is represented by four periods, called the four fatal days or terms ([177]). The first fatal is the

(170). Alexander III. in Decret. Greg. IX. Lib. I. Tit. XXXI. c. 3 ; Craisson, § 650, 655.

(171). Alexander III. to Bishop of Norwich in Decret. Lib. II. Tit. XXVIII. c. 37. *Id.* to Archbishop of York *Ibid.* c. 16, and to Archbishop of Canterbury *Ibid.* c. 25, allows one excommunicate to be meantime absolved *ad cautelam*. Coelestin III. *Ibid.* c. 40, states that a conditional sentence of excommunication is suspended by the appeal.

(172). Innocent III. *Ibid.* c. 55, 56 ; Boniface VIII. in Sext. Lib. II. Tit. XV. c. 7.

(173). Alexander III. to Bishop of Winchester, *Ibid.* c. 22.

(174). Gregory IV. A.D. 832, ap. Gratian. Caus. II. Qu. VI. c. 11 ; Pseudo-Isidor. *Ibid.* c. 12 ; Nicolaus I. A.D. 865, *Ibid.* c. 13 ; Innocent III. in Decret. Lib. II. Tit. XXIV. c. 19 ; Coelestin III. *Ibid.* Tit. XXVIII. c. 42 and 58, but not if the appeal is made *omisso medio*. Honorius III. *Ibid.* c. 66.

(175). Alexander III. in Decret. Lib. II. Tit. XXVIII. c. 35.

(176). An appeal may be brought from a nullity at any time within thirty years, and although it is not necessary to appeal from a nullity, yet by not appealing explicitly, or implicitly by protesting, a *gravamen facti* may be established. Ayliffe 84.

(177). The term is used in Leg. 31 C. de Appellat. Gratian Caus. II. Qu. VI. c. 41 ; Devoti Inst. Lib. III. Tit. XV. § 8.

time within which notice must be given of appeal. The second, the time within which letters dimissory, or letters of despatch, called *apostles*, must be obtained. The third, the time within which the appeal must be introduced before the judge of appeal; and the fourth fatal, the time within which it must be followed up and prosecuted to a conclusion.

32. Notice of appeal from a final sentence may be given either by word of mouth, whilst the judge is sitting in court, or afterwards by means of a public instrument executed before a notary or authentic person ([178]). It is sufficient to hand in to the judge a notice of appeal, without reading it out before him ([179]). Formerly notice of appeal was required to be given within two days ([180]). The time was afterwards extended to ten days ([181]), but by English custom and statute fifteen days are allowed ([182]). Time begins to count from the publication of the sentence ([183]), or from the date of the grievance complained of, if the appeal is from a grievance ([184]); but if the latter is a continuing grievance, the right of appeal continues to run ([185]).

33. Formerly the appellant was allowed five days ([186]) within

([178]). Gratian Caus. II. Qu. VI. c. 31 gives the form.
([179]). Ayliffe 83; Boniface VIII. in Sext. Lib. II. Tit. xv. c. 9.
([180]). This was the rule of the civil law before Justinian. Leg. 1, § 3, 6, 11; Gratian Caus. II. Qu. VI. c. 28.
([181]). Justinian Novel 23, c. 1, ap. Gratian Caus. II. Qu. VI. c. 28; Innocent III. in Decret. Greg. IX. Lib. II. Tit. XXVII. c. 15; Ayliffe 80.
([182]). 24 Hen. VIII. c. 12, sec. 6, allows an appeal "if a matter be commenced before the bishop diocesan or his commissary, from the bishop diocesan or his commissary, within fifteen days next ensuing the judgment or sentence thereof there given to the archbishop." In case the matter were commenced before the archdeacon of any archbishop or his commissary, sec. 7 gives the aggrieved party an appeal to the Court of Arches, or Audience of the same bishop, within fifteen days, and from the Court of the Arches or Audience within fifteen days to the archbishop of the same province.
([183]). Devoti Inst. Lib. III. Tit. xv. § 9; Gratian Caus. II. Qu. VI. c. 29.
([184]). Concil. Vien. in Clem. Lib. II. Tit. XII. c. 3.
([185]). Ayliffe 80.
([186]). Gratian Caus. II. Qu. VI. c. 22; c. 24: Let letters of despatch (dimissoriae), which are popularly called "apostles" [letters of despatch from

which to obtain from the judge letters of despatch ([187]), commonly called apostles ([188]). The time was afterwards extended to thirty days ([189]), which constitute the second fatal term. As the judge who is appealed from is bound to give such letters without being asked for them on receiving notice of appeal, it suffices to have asked for them instantly ([190]). These letters, if issued with the judge's approval, are called letters *dimissory;* if given from respect for a superior, letters *deferential* ([191]); if given contrary to the judge's opinion, letters *refutatory;* if given by a judge with an open mind, letters *testimonial;* and if given by the express wish of both parties, letters *conventional* ([192]).

34. When an appeal has been interposed, it must next be brought to the knowledge of the judge of appeal. This is termed the introduction of the appeal, and is effected by presenting the libel to the judge of appeal, together with a petition that it may be received, that the opponent may be cited to appear to it, and that the inferior judge may be inhibited from proceeding further in the cause. No definite time is prescribed for introducing an appeal, but a time is generally named by the party appellant ([193]), or by the judge appealed from ([194]), at the expiration of which he will resume his office, if the appeal has not been introduced ([195]). This is called the third fatal term.

ἀποστέλλω, I send], be sent by the judge appealed from to the judge who will hear the appeal, the demand and acceptance of which must be had within five days.

(187). Gratian Caus. II. Qu. VI. c. 24; c. 31 gives the form for them. Concil. Vien. A.D. 1311, in Clem. Decret. Lib. II. Tit. XII. c. 1; Lynd. 115; Sext. Decret. Lib. II. Tit. XV. c. 6.

(188). Concil. Lugdun. A.D. 1245, in Sext. Lib. II. Tit. XV. c. 1 and 4.

(189). Boniface VIII. in Sext. Lib. II. Tit. XV. c. 6.

(190). Gratian Caus. II. Qu. VI. c. 31; Boniface VIII. in Sext. Lib. II. Tit. XV. c. 6; Concil. Vien. A.D. 1311, in Clem. Decr. Lib. II. Tit. XII. c. 2.

(191). Concil. Lugdun. A.D. 1245, in Sext. Lib. II. Tit. XV. c. 1, says ex superioris reverentia.

(192). Devoti Inst. Lib. III. Tit. XV. § 10.

(193). Alexander III. to Bishop of Norwich in Decret. Greg. IX. Lib. II. Tit. XXVIII. c. 4; Innocent III. *Ibid.* c. 57, 64.

(194). Alexander III. *Ibid.* c. 4, 33, 44.

(195). Alexander III. *Ibid.* c. 27, 28, says that the judge's jurisdiction revives if the appeal is deserted. *Id. Ibid.* c. 33; Ayliffe 80.

35. The fourth fatal term is the period allowed to the appellant to follow up and finish his appeal. For this one year ([196]) is usually allowed, but a second year may be allowed for good cause ([197]), counting from the day of the interposition of the appeal inclusive ([198]); and in an urgent case the term may be abbreviated by the judge ([199]). In fixing the term the judge appealed from has no voice ([200]); this rests with the judge appealed to. The term fixed counts, nevertheless, as a term peremptory, so that if either party fails to appear, proceedings may go forward in his absence, as though he had been peremptorily cited ([201]).

36. All appeals ought to proceed regularly, *i.e.*, from each jurisdiction to the one next above it, without the omission of any ([202]), unless there is a custom to the contrary ([203]). Thus an appeal goes regularly from the archdeacon to the bishop, from the bishop to the metropolitan ([204]), from the metropolitan

---

[196]. Concil. Carthag. v. Can. 12, A.D. 401, ap. Gratian Caus. XI. Qu. III. c. 36, requires clergy to prosecute an appeal against all unjust accusations within a year. Gelasius, A.D. 494, *Ibid.* c. 37; Authen. *Ibid.* c. 41; Alexander III. in Decret. Lib. II. Tit. XXVIII. c. 5; Concil. Vien. A.D. 311, in Clem. Lib. II. Tit. XII. c. 3; Lynd. 106.

[197]. Authen. ap. Gratian Caus. II. Qu. VI. c. 41; Alexander III. in Decret. Lib. II. Tit. XXVIII. c. 5 and 8; Innocent III. *Ibid.* c. 57.

[198]. Alexander III. in Decret. Lib. II. Tit. XXVIII. c. 8; Ayliffe 82.

[199]. Innocent III. A.D. 1209, *Ibid.* c. 57.

[200]. Innocent III. to Bishop of Evreux, *Ibid.* c. 50.

[201]. Innocent III. *Ibid.* c. 44 and 58.

[202]. As early as the ninth century, the popes claimed to receive appeals direct (*omissis mediis*). Nicolaus I. A.D. 865, ap. Gratian Caus. II. Qu. VI. c. 13, censures Hincmar of Rheims for hearing the case of Bishop Rothard, who had appealed directly to the pope. Devoti Inst. Lib. III. Tit. XV. § 24 states that the only person over bishops, by divine appointment, is the pope; patriarchs, primates, and metropolitans, being his officers; therefore, appeals may be made to him direct.

[203]. Concil. Lugdun. A.D. 1245, in Sext. Lib. II. Tit. XV. c. 3.

[204]. Const. 8 Clarendon, A.D. 1164: If appeals arise, they ought to proceed from the archdeacon to the bishop, from the bishop to the archbishop, and lastly to the king (if the archbishop fail in doing justice), so that the controversy be ended in the archbishop's court by a precept from the king, and so that it go no further without the king's consent. 24 Hen. VIII. c. 12 sec. 5.

to the exarch of the greater administrative district, or primate, as he is termed in the West; from the primate to the patriarch ([205]), and from the patriarch to an œcumenical council, or the pope ([206]). In this country, no appeals are allowed by the law of the land to be taken out of the country in mixed or ecclesiastical causes, without the leave of the crown ([207]).

37. The Act of Supremacy, 26 Henry VIII. c. 1, which substituted the sovereign for the pope as Supreme Head of the Church in this country, without supplying him with the necessary ecclesiastical machinery, practically exempted the bishops of the two English provinces from the supervision of the collective episcopate, which had heretofore, in the intervals between general councils, been exercised by the pope, as representative of the whole episcopal body and president of a permanent committee of revision of the whole Church.

38. In place of appeals to the pope, the statute 25 Henry VIII. c. 19 permitted appeals from the archbishop's court to the king in Chancery, the practice being for the Lord Chancellor, on petition, to appoint certain delegates to hear the

---

(205). Concil. Chalcedon. A.D. 451, Can. 9: If any clergyman has a suit against another clergyman, let him not leave his own bishop and run to the secular courts of justice, but let him first try the question before his own bishop, or with the consent of the bishop, before those persons whom both parties shall choose to have the hearing of the cause. . . . But if a clergyman has any matter against his own bishop, let it be decided by the synod of the province; but if any bishop or clergyman has a controversy against the metropolitan, let him have recourse either to the exarch of the administrative district [primate], or to the [patriarchal] throne of the imperial city of Constantinople.

(206). On the disputed question whether an appeal lies from the pope to a general council, see Devoti Inst. Lib. III. Tit. XV. § 18.

(207). Const. 8 Clarendon, A.D. 1164; 24 Hen. VIII. c. 12 directs that all appeals in "all causes testamentary, causes of matrimony and divorces, rights of tithes, oblations, and obventions" shall be definitively or finally ordered in the archbishop's court. This statute was amended by 25 Hen. VIII. c. 19 in two ways: (1) By sec. 5 these provisions were extended to "any manner of appeals, of what nature or condition whatsoever they be of." (2) Sec. 4 provided an appeal from the archbishop's court, for lack of justice, "to the king's majesty in the king's court of chancery," whereby the jurisdiction of the court of delegates was first créated.

appeal, who were called the Court of Delegates. If their decision did not give satisfaction, a commission of review might be granted under the great seal, on petition to the king in council, "to revise, review, and rehear the case."

39. The Act 2 and 3 William IV. c. 92, having in view the settlement of disputes rather than the conscientious desire of the Church to do justice to all men, prohibited the granting in future of commissions of review, and the Act 3 and 4 William IV. c. 41 transferred the powers and jurisdiction of the Court of Delegates to the Judicial Committee of the Privy Council. An entirely new lay court was thus established as the supreme court of appeal in matters ecclesiastical in this country, *i.e.*, in matters concerning spiritual foundations, and the rights and duties of their members, which followed the received principles of the secular courts, designed to promote the convenience of the public and promptness of decision, rather than the long-suffering and charitable discipline of the Church, which aims at reproducing upon earth the everlasting justice and mercy of heaven.

INDEX.

This Index does not pretend to contain an exhaustive list of the authorities quoted in the notes, to most of which only one reference is given to fix their date.

'Aββᾶs, 92
Abbot, 92; his position under St. Benedict's rule, 93; by Roman and Gallican rule, 94; by English, 95; his authority over monks, 95, 113; election of, 95, 113; required to be in holy orders, 95; a prelate, 96; pastoral staff of, 96; quasi-episcopal position of, 97; cannot give public penance, 97
Abortion, procuring, 64
Abbotsbury gild, 89 note 52
Abingdon, Chronicle of Abbey of, 95 note 86
Abolitio, the withdrawal of a criminal charge, 278
Absolution, 169; of two kinds, 170; precautionary (*ad cautelam*), 139 note 15, 172, 329 note 171; with reincidence, 172. See *Reconciliation*
Abstention, 139. See *Excommunication*
Accusation, 236; defined, 242; private, 240; essential features of, 242; onus of proof on the accuser, 243; specially odious, 243; does not apply to the Pope, 245; or to the sovereign, 245; disqualifies for promotion, 246; withdrawal of, 246, 278; effect of withdrawal, 247; when allowed, 247; disused since 11th century, 247; its place taken by denunciation, 248
Accusers who are disqualified, 243, 244
Actor, 222; *universitatis*, 229
ACTS IN JUDGMENT, chap. viii., p. 262 seq.

Administrations, 185 note 36, 201, 208
Adultery, 44 note 29; term used in two senses, 72; specific, 74; punishment of, 76
Advocates, 224, 230; required to be licensed by archbishop, 230; duties of, 231; qualifications of, 231; disqualified persons, 232
Accessories in judgment, 222
Africa, judges elected in, 211
African Council, A.D. 419, 14 note 52; rule as to constitution of courts, 179 note 15
'Αγαπή, 88 note 48
Agde, Council of, A.D. 506, 18 note 69, —a suffragan's see of Narbonne which has ceased to exist [Brown in St. Paul's Ecclesiological Society, vol. iii. p. 236-240]
Aix, Council of, A.D. 816, 85
'Ακοίμητοι, monastery of, 84
Albert, patriarch of Jerusalem, 133
Alcantarines, a branch of Franciscans, 132
Alcuin, 735-804, A.D., a native of Yorkshire and founder of schools in France, 25 note 109
Alexander, Bishop of Alexandria, A.D. 312-326; condemns Arius, 179 note 15
Alexander II., Pope, A.D. 1061-1073, 54 note 98
——— III., Pope, A.D. 1159-1181, 5 note 13; recognises the Carthusians, A.D. 1174, 125
——— IV., Pope, A.D. 1254-1261, 51 note

73 ; constituted the Austin Friars, 133
Alfred, King, 122
Allegations, 280 note 127
Amalarius, presbyter of Metz in 9th century, draws up a rule for canons, 85
Amazons, 82 note 16
Ambon, the, in Church, 19
Ambrose, Bishop of Milan, A.D. 374–397, 5 note 13 ; introduces monasticism, 82
Ananias, 108 note 176
Anathema, 142
Anchorites, 81
Ancients of the Church, 179
Ancyra, Council of, A.D. 314, 18 note 70
Andreae, John, canonist of Bologna, A.D. 1272–1348, 144 note 45
Angelo of Pisa, a Franciscan, 131
Angers, Council of, A.D. 453, 45 note 35
Animadversion defined, 6, 141
Anointing of a sovereign, its effect, 38, 42, 59 notes 135 and 138
Answers, decree for personal, 284
Antioch, Council of, A.D. 341, 78 note 282
Antony, Congregation of St., at Vienne, 128
Antony of Padua, 132
Antony the recluse, 81
Apelles, heresy of, 49 note 65
'Ἀφορισμός, 139 note 16, 140 note 25
Apocrypha, 217 note 180
Apostasy, 43 ; defined, 45 ; three kinds of, 45 ; desertion of the religious life, 45, 106
Apostles, or letters of despatch, 331
Apostolical Constitutions, A.D. 365, 19 note 72
Appeal, 322 ; origin of, 322 ; to the Pope, 323, 333 ; suspends a proctor's powers, 229 note 281 ; from a grievance or extra-judicial, 323 ; judicial, 324 ; interlocutory, 326, 327 ; from refusal to admit an exception, 276, 294 ; from refusal to give a copy of an instrument, 300 ; from ordinary's discretion, 36 ; final, 326 ; effects of, 328 ; notice of, 330 ; time for, 330 ; to proceed regularly, 332 ; disregarding, 187 note 48, 310 note 42 ; no contestation in, 282 ; allowed on technical grounds, 324 ; when not allowed, 326, 327
Appelatione remota, 277 note 112, 325
Aquila, 45 note 38
Aquinum, 131
Arbitration favoured by Roman law, 179
Archdeacon, ordinary jurisdiction of, 183 ; appeal from, 332
Archdeaconries, multiplication of, 183
Arches, Court of, 303
Archimandrite, 93
Arius, 50 note 66, 192 note 15
Arles, Council of, A.D. 314, 46 note 43 ; collection of canons, called Second Council of, A.D. 443, 20 note 83 ; statutes of the ancient Church of, A.D. 505, 25 note 112 ; Fourth Council of, A.D. 524, 93 note 71 ; Fifth Council of, A.D. 554, 94 note 83
Armand de Rancé, 125
Arnald, 127
Arson, 44, 63, 66
Articles, 280 note 127
Arnald the Cistercian, 53 note 89
Arundel, Thomas, Archbishop of Canterbury, A.D. 1396–1414, 15 note 54
Ascetic life, a counsel of perfection, 108. See *Religious Life*
Ash-Wednesday, beginning of solemn discipline, 21
Assignation, the first in the conclusion of a cause, 302 ; the second, 302
Assisi, home of St. Francis, 131
Athanasius, A.D. 296–373, Bishop of Alexandria, introduces monasticism in the West, 82 ; appeals to the emperor, 211 note 148, 275 note 87, 295 note 230
Athelstan, 182 note 27
Athenagoras, a philosopher of Athens, *circa* 177 A.D., 64 note 168
Audience, acts done in, defined, 175, 262 ; Court of, 185 ; in the Isle of Man, 185 note 38
Auditor, a judge to ascertain facts, 179, 210, 311
Augustin, Archbishop of Canterbury, A.D. 597–604, 122

Index. 337

Augustin, Bishop of Hippo, 395-430 A.D., 3 note 8; establishes a clergy-house, 85
Augustinian canons, 85; their origin, 127
Austin Friars, 133
Autun, Council of, A.D. 670, 86 note 40
Authentic instrument defined, 299
Auxerre, Council of, A.D. 578, 62 note 152
Avignon, 127
Avila, 133
Ayliffe, Fellow of New College, author of Parergon, published 1734, 97 note 130

BAEDA, 672-735 A.D., monk of Wearmouth, 5 note 13
Bangor, monasteries of, 83
Banishment, 157
Banns of marriage, dispensation from publishing, 34
BAPTISM, vol. i. chap. ii. p. 23
Baratry, 214
Barcelona, Council of, A.D. 540, 18 note 69
Barking, double monastery at, 86 note 41
Barnstaple St. Mary Magdalen, a Cluniac foundation, 124
Basil, elected Bishop of Caesarea, A.D. 370, died 379, 18 note 70, 82 note 14; rule of, 82, 121; its adherents in Europe, 84; allows one dedicated to the religious life to marry, 101
Bastardy, 201
Beati, 154
Beauvais, Council of, 219 note 194
Becket, Thomas à, Archbishop of Canterbury, A.D. 1162-1170, 184, 194 note 69
Begging Friars, 130
Belfast Lough, 83
Bellarmine, a Jesuit librarian of the Vatican, A.D. 1542-1621, 18 note 67
Benedict of Aniane, A.D. 750-821, 122
Benedict of Nursia, A.D. 480-543, founder of Western monasticism, 121; his rule, 85, 121; substitutes common for associated life, 93, 122; places monks under the abbot, 95, 113
Benedict XIV., Pope, A.D. 1740-1758,

author of De Synodo Dioecesana, 36 note 185; on matrimonial causes, 196 note 79
Benedictines, 122; form of admission, 103 note 148
Benediction of a monk, 104
Benefice causes, 197
Benefit of clergy, 195
Benno, St., founder of the Cluniacs, A.D. 909, 124
Beringer, Les Indulgences, 1890, 87 note 43
Bernard of Clairveaux, A.D. 1091-1152, 125
Berthold, Count of Limoges, 133
Bestiality, 72, 151
Beveridge, Bishop of St. Asaph, A.D. 1704-1708, 22 note 97
Bigamy, 78; a spiritual cause, 196
Bishop's wrongdoing not to be exposed, 78; appeal from, 332. See *Judge* and *Ordinary*
Black Friars, 131. See *Dominicans*
Black Monks—Benedictines, 122
Blaesilla, 83 note 19
Blasphemy, 43; defined, 47; against the Holy Ghost, 47 note 51
Bonaventura, 766; the Seraphic Doctor, A.D. 1221-1274, a Franciscan, Cardinal-bishop of Albano, 132
Boniface I., Pope, A.D. 418-422, 45 note 35
—— VIII., Pope, A.D. 1294-1303, 28 note 135
Boniface, Archbishop of Canterbury, A.D. 1245-1273, his constitutions, A.D. 1261, 61 note 147
Boniface, Archbishop of Mainz, A.D. 723-755, 95 note 86
Books, reading forbidden, 49
βόσσοι, 84 note 28
Bouix, 34 note 164
Bracton, 63 note 160
Braga, Council of, A.D. 561, 64 note 170; Second, A.D. 572, 11 note 42
Branding, a temporal penalty, 156
Brawling, 208
Brethren of the Community, 132
Breviculum, 309 note 38
Bridget, Order of St., 128
Bridgett, History of the Eucharist, 81 note 11

VOL. II. Y

Bright, Professor of Ecclesiastical History, Oxford, 184 note 34
Brittines, 133
Brooke, 193 note 63
Bucfast Abbey, 89 note 51, 123
Buckland Abbey, 125
Bury St. Edmund's Abbey, 123
Busenbaum, 145 note 54

CALIXTUS II., Pope, A.D. 1119–1124, 12 note 43
Calumniation, 44; defined, 278 note 114
Calumny, oath of, 240 note 37, 228 note 36, 282; what it is, 283; of whom required, 283; when may be tendered, 294
Camaldoli, rule of, 124
Camaldunians, 122, 124
Cambray, Council of, 9 note 34
Cambridge, colleges of, 92 note 68
Canon law, development of, in 11th century, 183
Canonesses, 86, 114, 115; not confined to their cloisters, 115; queen-dowager in Spain required to become, 119; widows of clergy in Gaul, 119
CANONICAL PROCEDURE, chap. vii. p. 233 seq.
Canons in restraint of freedom to be construed strictly, 29
Canons regular, 85, 126; of St. Augustin, 127. See *Augustinians*
Canons secular, 97, 126
Canonsleigh Priory, 127
Canterbury, a Benedictine priory, 123; Dominicans at, 131
Cappadocia, monks in, 82
Capraia, 83 note 20
Capuchins, a branch of Franciscans, 132
Carmelites, one of the four orders of friars, 121 note 3, 132
Carswell Priory, 124
Carthage, First Council of, A.D. 347, 278 note 119; Second, A.D. 390, 11 note 42; Third, A.D. 397, 12 note 43; Fourth, 318 note 88 (see *Statutes of Ancient Church*, A.D. 505); Fifth, A.D. 401, 22 note 100; Seventh, A.D. 419, 245 note 65
Carthusians, 122, 124; position of conversi amongst, 100
Casino, Monte, 121

Cassian, John, monk of Marseilles, died A.D. 432, 83
Catechumens, probationer, 19; approved, 19
Cathedraticum, 197 note 94
Causes defined, 234, 262; spiritual, 233; temporal, 233, 234; mixed, 233, 234; civil, 233; criminal, 233; possessory, 235; proprietory, 235; real, 235; personal, 235; simple, 235; double, 235; involving the validity of spiritual acts, 209; of instance, 236, 237; of office, 236
Cautelam, absolution *ad*, 139 note 15, 329 note 171
Caution = security, 243
Cave, A.D. 1637–1713, vicar of Isleworth, his Primitive Christianity, 145 note 45
Cellarer, a monastic, 98
Celtic monasteries, 94. See *Monasteries*
Censures, 185; defined, 138; their object to bring to repentance, 138; three kinds of 139; suspension, 139; excommunication, 140; the interdict by sentence of a judge or sentence of law, 143
Census, 70 note 225; *vitalicius*, 70 note, 226
Cerinthians, 45 note 38
Cerinthus, 50 note 65
Chalcedon, Council of, A.D. 451, 46 note 44; makes provision for appeals, 323
Châlons, 125; Council of, A.D. 649; Second Council of, A.D. 813, 6 note 20
Chamberlain, a monastic, 98
Chapter Court in the Isle of Man, 185 note 38
Charles, A.D. 800–814, the emperor, establishes spiritual courts, 182
Charles II., King of England, A.D. 1660–1685, 203
Charles V., emperor, A.D. 1520–1558, 129
Charter, the Great, secures the liberties of the Church, 190; expounded by king's judges, 192
Chart of Charity, 125
Charterhouse, 126
Chartreuse, La, 125

Chastity, monastic pursuit of, 93
Chelmsford, Dominicans at, 131
Chichele, Henry, Archbishop of Canterbury, A.D. 1414–1443, constitutions of, A.D. 1416, 51 note 72; A.D. 1434, 191
Children may not be judges, 211; nor plaintiffs, 222; nor proctors, 227; nor advocates, 231; nor accusers, 244
Christ's Hospital, a Franciscan house, 132
Chrodegang, Bishop of Metz, died A.D. 766, 85; rule of, 126 note 33, 127
Chrysostom, John, Bishop of Constantinople, A.D. 397–401, 78 note 282, 295 note 230
Church rates, 208
Chyncse, 111 note 203
Ciancae, 111 note 203
Circumspecte agatis, statute of, 195 note 73, 197 note 84
Cistercians, a branch of cloistered Benedictines, 95; abbots required to take oath of obedience to bishops, 95 note 83
Citation, 263, 267; when a matter of natural right, 267; requisites in, 268; simple, 270; peremptory, 270, 271; mandatory and inhibitory, 271; intimatory, 271; general, 271; special, 271; public, 271; private, 271; personal, 271; real, 271; limits of, 271; when permitted outside the diocese, 271; service of, 263, 272; made in three ways, 272; personally, 272; by ways and means, 213 note 161, 272; by proclamation, 272; proof of, 273; effects of, 273
Citationes edictales, 273
Citeaux, 125
Civil causes, 233; procedure wherein different from criminal, 241
Clairveaux, 125
Clarendon, Constitutions of, A.D. 1164, 55 note 109, 140 note 20, 184, 189 note 53; revoked in 1173 A.D., 190 note 53
Clares, Poor, 137
Clement of Alexandria, A.D. 160–215, author of Stromata (note), 44 note 27

Clement III., Pope, A.D. 1188–1191, 58 note 129
—— IV., Pope, A.D. 1265–1269, 53 note 91
—— V., Pope, A.D. 1305–1314, 97 note 104
Clugny, 123, 124
Cluniacs, 122, 124; their rule, 124
Coelestin, Pope, A.D. 422–432, 11 note 42
—— III., Pope, A.D. 1191–1198, 101 note 125
Coelicolae, 45 note 38
Coercion, the key of, 3; means employed for, 6
Cognitor, a judge, 179 note 16
Coke, institutes, 91 note 63, 93 note 72
Colchester Priory, 127
Coldingham, double monastery at, 86 note 41
Collateral questions, 286
College = a congregation existing for an educational purpose, 92
Cologne, Archbishop of, 156 note 127
Commissions of review, 317 note 82, 318 note 88, 332, 333. See *Review*
Common, in. See *Simpliciter*
Communion, dispensation from fasting, 34; active and passive, 140
Compact, 263 note 278, 279 note 120
Compiègne, Council of, A.D. 756, 28 note 128
Composition, 263 note 9, 278, 307
Compulsory decree, 297
Compurgators, 249 note 94, 259; number of, 259; must be honest persons, 260
CONCLUSION OF A CAUSE, chap. ix. 302 *seq.*; used in three senses, 302; technically, 247, 263, 302
Concubinage, 72, 73, 76
Confession, judicial, 292; discreet or indiscreet, 293; simple or qualified, 293; explicit or tacit, 293; not evidence against third parties, 293
Confraternity, 87
Congregation, monastic, 88, 128
Congregation of the Holy Office, 53
Consistory, acts done in, defined, 175, 185, 187, 188; court in Isle of Man, 185 note 38

Conspiracy, 44, 63, 66; a special offence in clergy, 78
Conspirators may not be accusers for wrongs done to themselves, 245
Constance, Council of, A.D. 1414, 132
Constantinople, Council of, A.D. 381, makes provision for appeals, 323; Fifth, A.D. 553, 147 note 69; monasteries at, 84
Constantine, Emperor, A.D. 323-337, 181 note 23
Constantius, Emperor, A.D. 337-361, 180 note 21
Consultation, writ of, 202
Contempt of the keys, 138 note 10, 265; causes of, 264, 282. See *Contumacy*
Contestation of suit, 229, 247, 280; dilatory exceptions to precede, 276; a controversy may be withdrawn before, 277; in what it consists, 281; defined, 282; no examination of witnesses before, 281; effects of, 282
Contract, 199
Controversy defined, 262; may be withdrawn, 277
Contumacy, 79, 265, 273; defined, 274, 320; simple, 79 note 285; pregnant, 79 note 285, 138 note 10; following upon excommunication a ground for deprivation, 166; is not set up *ipso facto* by disobedience to a civil citation, 241, 274; real and apparent, 274 note 80; mode of punishing, 321
Convent, a congregation pursuing the religious life, 92; having all things in common, 94
Conventuals, a branch of Franciscans, 132
Conversion = the adoption of the religious life. See *Religious Life*
Converted persons, those who have taken the initial step towards the religious life, 99; a name for serving brethren among the Carthusians, 100
Convocation judges in determining what is heresy, 188 note 48
Corinthian, the incestuous, 6 note 23, 16 note 61, 136 note 4

Cornworthy Priory, 127
Correction, 2, 4; causes of, when plenary, 239 note 29. See *Remedial Discipline*
Corsned, 307
Costs, 320
Counterclaim, 265, 276; object of, 277; may be made before a delegate, 277
Court, the, of the soul, 10; of penance, 10, 11, 170
Courts Christian, 175; defined, 177 note 8; extra-judicial, 175, 185; judicial, 175, 185, 187; ancillary to extra-judicial, 188; jurisdiction of, 189; does not extend to life and limb, 192; to lay fees, 192; to dead persons, 193; or to inflict penalties, 193; African rule as to institution of, 179 note 15
Courtney, William, Archbishop of Canterbury, A.D. 1381-1396, his chop-church constitution, A.D. 1391, 57 note 120
Covenant, 199
Crediton Minster, a Benedictine foundation, 123
Crimes defined, 39; excepted, 242; notorious, 243
Criminal causes, 233
Criminous persons may not be judges, 219; nor proctors, 227; nor advocates, 232; nor accusers, 244
Crown lease, 201 note 96
Culmstoch, 255 note 130
Cunningham's Law of Simony, 193
Curator, or next friend, 230
Curzon, Monasteries of the East, 1836, 81 note 8
Custodies, the Franciscan, 132
Cuthbert, Archbishop of Canterbury, A.D. 741-759, 95 note 86
Cyprian, Bishop of Carthage, A.D. 248-258, 2 note 4, 46 note 41
Cyprus, home of the Knights of St. John, 129
Cyril, Bishop of Jerusalem, A.D. 350-386, 265 note 23
Cyril, A.D. 787, 30 note 144

DALE ABBEY, 127
Dalmatia, home of monasticism, 83

Index.   341

Damasus, Pseudo-, 48 note 51
Damiantines, 131
Damnum eveniens, 70 note 222
Dark art, 62
Darrein presentment, a writ whereby right of advowson is tried before the king's judges, 189
Deacon, when allowed to baptize, 37; to give penance, 37; may not be accusers, 245
Deceit, 44, 63, 67
Decian persecution, 81
Decisory oath, 240 note 87
Decree, citatory, 270; personal, 284
Defamation, 67, 208; causes of, 239 note 29
Defendants, 222
Defensor, the name for an advocate, 230
Degradation, or solemn deposition, 160, 168; number of participants required to effect, 168; when allowed, 169
Delay term, 279
Delegates, 210, 218; qualifications of, 218; commencement of commission, 220; termination of, 221; jurisdiction of perpetuated, 273; can entertain counterclaims, 277; court of, 333
Deliberatory term, 276
Denunciation, 236; of three kinds, 248; paternal, 249; canonical, 250; judicial, 249, 250; general, 250; special, 250; solemn, 251; private, 251; who may make, 251; matters excluded, 252. See *Presentment*
Denunciation by name, 312, 313 note 60
Deposition, 160; a removal from the ranks of order, 167; non-solemn or verbal, 168; actual or ceremonial, 168
Deprivation, 160; two degrees of, 160; the result of suspension exceeding seven years, 165; cases of, 165; when ordered by sentence of law, 166
Devoti, John, Bishop of Anagni, and afterwards titular Archbishop of Carthage, author of the 'Institutes of Canon Law,' published 1781, 17 note 66

Διδαχή, an early Ebionite work, *circa*, 98 A.D., 61 note 152
Dignitaries, persons who have jurisdiction over clergy, 98
Dilatio, 279
Dilapidations, 197; causes of plenary, 239 note 29
Dilatory exceptions, 275; should be made before contestation, 276; excluded by contestation, 282
Diocese, citations forbidden out of, 269 note 49
Dionysius, Bishop of Alexandria, A.D. 249–265, 40 note 4
Dionysius the Areopagite, alleged work of, A.D. 532, 106 note 172
Dioscorus, cited by the Council of Chalcedon, A.D. 451, 178 note 9
Diptycha, reading of names from, 318 note 88
DISCIPLINE GENERALLY, chap. i. p. 1; nature and object of, 1; defined, 1; personal, 3; liturgical, 4; remedial, 4, 138; penal, 4, 135, 152; vindictive, 4, 135, 155; public, or of the outer tribunal, 112; rules of, 12; subject matter of, 15; private, or of the inner tribunal, 9, 13; solemn, 10, 16; sacramental, 10; non-sacramental, 10
DISCIPLINE OF THE RELIGIOUS LIFE, chap. iii. p. 80 *seq*.
Disciplinary procedure, 174; causes, 208
Discretion, exercise of, by an ordinary a matter of appeal, 36, 315
Discretionary causes, 208
Disobedience, 78. See *Contumacy*
Dispensation defined, 29, 30; under what circumstances allowed, 31; conditions precedent, 31; by whom granted, 31; those granted by patriarchs, 33; by metropolitans, 34; by bishops, 34; and abbots, 35; sovereign's power, 38; when may not be granted, 35; can only be granted for good cause, 36
Dispossession, 277, 288. See *Spoliation*
Divination, 61
Divorce, 208; causes plenary, 239 note 29; causes, 185 note 36

Domesday Book for Berkshire, 98 note 109
Dominicans, order of, 130; inquisitors, 53
Dominic, St., 130
Dominus litis, 229, 282
Double causes, 235
Dower, presumption in favour of, 312
Drunkenness, 45, 72; punishment of, 77; habitual, a cause of *ipso facto* suspension, 165
Du Pin, A.D. 1657-1719, ecclesiastical historian, 9 note 34
Dugdale, author of Monasticon, 127 note 35
Dunkeswell Abbey, 125
Dunstan, Archbishop of Canterbury, A.D. 960-988, 11 note 39
Duplex querela, 209 note 143. See *Double Causes*
Duplications, 286 note 160
Durand, Canon of Avignon, 127
Durand, Bishop of Mende, A.D. 1286-1296, 153 note 111
Durham, a county palatine, 156 note 127

EASTER, time for veiling nuns, 119
Ebionites, 45 note 38
Ecclesiastical Courts Commission Report, A.D. 1883, 201 note 95
ECCLESIASTICAL SACRAMENTS, vol. i. chap. viii. 371 *seq.*
ECCLESIASTICAL SEVERITY, chap. v. 135 *seq.*
Edgar, King, the Peaceable, A.D. 957-975, laws of, A.D. 960, 90 note 59
Edmund Rich, Archbishop of Canterbury, A.D. 1234-1245, 4 note 10
Edward I., King of England, A.D. 1272-1307, 202
—— VI., King of England, A.D. 1547-1553, appropriates gild property, 92, 203
Egbert, Archbishop of York, A.D. 732-766, 28 note 134
Ἡγούμενος, 92
Egypt, the cradle of monasticism, 82
Elbel, a Franciscan canonist, 10 note 37
Elcesaites, 45 note 38
Electing a disqualified person as bishop, a cause of *ipso facto* suspension, 165

Election of judges, 211 note 152
Elias, a Franciscan, 132
Elizabeth, 203
Elvira (Eliberis), Council of, A.D. 305, 7 note 26
England, a fief of the Roman See, A.D. 1213-1366, 187
Epiphanius, Bishop of Salamis, A.D. 367-403, 80 note 2
Epiphany, a time for veiling nuns, 119
Episcopal laws, 183. See *Canon Law*
Ἐρημῖται, 82 note 15
ἑτεροδιδασκαλία, 48 note 58
Eton College, 92 note 68
EUCHARIST, THE, vol. i. chap. iii. p. 80
Eugenius III., Pope, A.D. 1145-1153, 66 note 187, 128
Eusebius, Bishop of Caesarea, A.D. 313-340, 7 note 27, 275 note 87
Eusebius, Bishop of Vercellae, A.D. 340-371, 84
Eutyches cited before the Council, 178 note 9
Eutychian, Bishop of Rome, A.D. 275-283, 66 note 185
Evagrius the Scholastic, A.D 536-596, 92 note 69
Evaristus, Pope, A.D. 100-108, 12 note 45
Evesham Abbey, 123
Evidence of the fact, 290; notorious, 291; manifest, 291; clear, 291, 292; what admissible, 301
Exarch or primate, appeal from, 333
Excepted crimes, 242
Exception, 247; defined, 285; effect of alleging, 286; dilatory, 275, 286; peremptory, 286; of two kinds, 287; may be made at once in a civil cause, 241; criminal, 286; a mode of objecting crime, 236 note 21; privileges of, 286; have precedence of civil, 288; civil, 286; to witnesses, 293; general, 293; specific, 293
EXCESSES, chap. ii. 39 *seq.;* degrees of, 40, 42; of different positions in the Church, 41; of three kinds, 43: against God, 43, 45; against fellow-men, 43, 44; against redeemed human nature, 43, 44
Exclusion or separation, 20
Excommunicates may not be judges,

211; proctors, 227; advocates, 231; nor accusers, 244, 245
Excommunication a censure, 138; the lesser, 139; the greater, 140; when vindictive, 159, 321; solemn, 142; *ipso facto* or *ipso jure*, 144, 146; effects of, 145; of one in orders, 146; persons exempt from, 146; requirements previous to, 147; of universal observance, 148; by whom withdrawn, 148; when forbidden by law, 207; exception of, 276 note 93; the punishment of contumacy, 321; forbidden in this country, 322
Execration, 142
Execution, 318; may be obtained by action, 318; or imploring the judge's office, 318; or signification to the temporal power, 319; arrest of, 319
Executive causes, 264, 282
Executor, a special commissioner, 215
Executory term, 319; causes, no appeals in, 325
Exeter gild, 88 note 49, 89 note 52
Exeter Minster, a Benedictine foundation, 123; St. Nicolas' priory in, 123 note 16; St. James', a Cluniac foundation, 124; Dominicans at, 131; Franciscans at, 132
Exeter, Vicars-choral of, 156 note 127
Exile, perpetual, 157
Extension of time, 279
Extra-judicial or summary, 237, 264; appeals, 323

FACULTY, a, defined, 29, 30; not withheld or granted at discretion, 31
Falsehood, 44; excusable, 69. See *Deceit*
Falsification, 68
Faringdon Within, 131
Fast, dispensation from observing, 34
Fasting, a penance, 154
Fatal terms, 329
Feast, dispensation from observing, 34
Fehr, author of *Geschichte der Mönchsorden*, 124 note 18
Ferraris, Lucius, a Minorite, editor of *Bibliotheca Juridica Canonum*, died 1760, 10 note 37
Ferula, the, or antechapel, 19

Fiscalis, the French name for a necessary promoter, 237 note 24
Fleta, 201 note 94
Flogging, a punishment, 157
Ford Abbey, 125
Forefront of judgment, 263
Forfeiture of goods and chattels, 158
Forgery, 68, 300
Fornication, 72, 73; spiritual, 74
Foundation, meaning of, 88 note 45
France, no liability in, by failing to prove an exception, 286
Francis, St., 131
Franciscans, 130, 131
Freedom, presumption in favour of, 312; inquisitors', 53
Fresney, Gilbert du, 131
Friars-preachers or Dominicans, 121 note 3, 130
Friars, non-cloistered religious persons, 121; begging, 130; Austin, 121 note 3, 130; Grey, 131; White, 133; Barry, 133
Frithelstock, Priory, 127
Fulbert, Bishop of Chartres, A.D. 1007-1029, 59 note 139
Fytche's case, 186 note 41

GALLICAN COUNCIL, A.D. 616, 108 note 182; custom requires widows of clergy to become canonesses, 119
Gallinaria, 83 note 20
Gasquet's definition of religious life, 80; Henry VIII. and English monasteries, 92 note 67
Gaston, founder of Congregation of St. Antony at Vienne, 128
Gelasius, Bishop of Rome, A.D. 492-496, 4 note 10
Geoffry Fitz-Peter, justiciary, 204 note 110
Gerbert, 21 note 86
Gerfroi, 129
Giffard, Walter, Bishop of Winchester, 125
Gilbert of Fresney, introducer of Dominicans, 131
Gilbert of Sempringham, founder of Gilbertines, 127
Gilds, 87; religious, 88, 89, 91; frith, 89, 91; merchant, 89, 91; sanction

of incumbent required for a religious, 91; brethren, 157 note 131
Glanvil, 192 note 60
Glastonbury Abbey, 123
Gluttony, 72
God-parents, monks forbidden to be, 113; nuns forbidden to be, 116
Gonfalonieri, 88
Gonzalez, 328 note 166
Gorgon, 83 note 20
Gousset, 32 note 155
Gratian, Emperor, A.D. 367–379, 180 note 21
Gratian, monk of Bologna, author of *Concordia Discordantum Canonum*, circa 1144 A.D., introduced into this country circa 1150 A.D., 3 note 9
Gregory I., Bishop of Rome, A.D. 590–604, 4 note 10; the noviciate in time of, 101; monastic rule of, 122
—— II., Pope, A.D. 715–731, 99 note 115
—— IV., Pope, A.D. 828–844, 4 note 12
—— VII., Pope (Hildebrand), A.D. 1073–1085, 5 note 15
—— IX., Pope, A.D. 1227–1241, 15 note 57
Gregory, Bishop of Nyssa, A.D. 372–400, 73 note 242
Gregory Thaumatourgos, a pupil of Origen, A.D. 234, afterwards Bishop of Neocaesarea, where he died A.D. 266, 18 note 70
Grievance, appeal from, 323
Grosso modo, a petition, 264 note 11
Guarmarcia, Council of, 64 note 169
Guido, 53 note 88
Guigot the Carthusian, 126

HALITGAR, Bishop of Cambray, his Penitential was made in A.D. 925, 294 note 223
Hansas or merchant gilds, 89
Harding, Stephen, 125
Hartland Abbey, 127
Hayward, a monastic, 98
Hearers, a class of penitents, 18
Henry I., King of England, A.D. 1100–1135, 184
—— II., King of England, A.D. 1154–1189, 184, 189, 194 note 69

Henry III., King of England, A.D. 1216–1272, 184, 191, 204
—— IV., King of England, A.D. 1399–1413, 132
—— V., King of England, A.D. 1413–1422, statute against heretics, 188 note 48
—— VII., King of England, A.D. 1485–1509, 132
—— VIII., King of England, A.D. 1509–1547, abolishes monasteries, 92; submission of clergy to, 206
Henry II., Emperor of Germany (the Saint), A.D. 999–1024, 241 note 37
Heresy, 44; defined, 48; a spiritual cause, 195; procedure in, by inquisition, 243; delegates for punishing, 53; material, 49; treatment of, 52; punishment of, 51; temporal penalties for, 52, 159; definition of, reserved to archbishop, 188 note 48
Heretics, association with, forbidden, 49; statutes authorising the burning of, 188 note 48
Hermas, circa A.D. 150, 23 note 101
Hermits, 82
Hincmar, Bishop of Rheims, A.D. 845–882, 51 note 71
Hingeston-Randolph, 255 note 130
Hippo, the see of Augustin, 85
Hippolytus, a bishop near Rome, circa A.D. 160–235, 2 note 4
Hobart, 193 note 63
Holborn, 131
Holsten, a native of Hamburg, born 1596, canon of St. Peter's and librarian of the Vatican, died 1661, 128 note 43
Holy Office, the, 53
Homicide, 63; defined, 63; when excusable, 65
Honoratus, 83
Honorius, Emperor, A.D. 395–424, 181 note 21
Honorius II., Pope, A.D. 1124–1130, 241 note 37
—— III., Pope, A.D. 1216–1227, 5 note 13; approves Franciscans, 131
Hook, author of Lives of the Archbishops of Canterbury, Dean of Chichester, 125 note 25
Hosius, Bishop of Cordova, died A.D. 359, 181 note 24; 212 note 157

Hospital, a congregation existing for a philanthropic purpose, 91; of Montpellier, 128; of the Holy Ghost, at Rome, 128; of St. John, at Exeter, 129
Hospitallers, Order of, 129
Hosteller, a monastic, 98
Hostiensis, Henry, of Segusia, A.D. 1225-1271, the canonist, Bishop of Ostia 144 note 45
Hugh, Bishop of Lincoln, introduces the Carthusians, A.D. 1180, 126
Hundred Court, bishop sat in, 158, 182
Hurter, author of *Innocenz III. und seine Zeitgenossen*, 128 note 43

IDOLATRY, 43; forms of, 46
Ignatius, Bishop of Antioch, A.D. 70-115, 49 note 63
Ignatius Loyola, A.D. 1491-1556, founder of the Jesuits, 134
Impediments to marriage, 239 note 29
Imperium, 178 note 12
Imposition of hands used in admitting to each grade of penitents, 18
Imprisonment, 157; in a monastery, 154, 157; a substitute for solemn discipline, 154
Incantations, 62
Incest, 44, 72
Incontinency, 44, 72, 73, 76; sacrilegious, 72, 74
Indicavit, writ of, 199 note 88
Induciæ, 279
Infamous persons. See *Criminous*
Infangthef, the right of trying thieves within the jurisdiction, 158
Infidels may not accuse Christians, 245
Infirmarer, a monastic, 98
Information, summary, 256
Injection or violence to clergy, 239 note 29
Innocent I., Bishop of Rome, A.D. 402-417, 14 note 51
—— II., Pope, A.D. 1130-1143, 259 note 155
—— III., Pope, A.D. 1198-1216, 27 note 120
—— IV., Pope, A.D. 1243-1254, 257 note 139
Instance, causes of, 236, 237; of a cause, 263, 281

Instruments, proof by, 290; exceptions to, 300
Inquisition, 53; 'defined, 254; employed to establish heresy, 243; general, 255; particular, 255; private, 256; solemn, 256
Inscription or subscription to the law of retaliation, 243, 246; what necessary to a necessary promoter, 257
Interdict, a form of censure, 138; defined, 149; personal, 140, 139 note 15, 150; local, 150; complete, 151; partial, 151; when forbidden, 151; who are included 151
Interlocutory, appeals from sentences, 326
Interpretation, key of, 3
Interrogatories, 265; defined, 284; may be put to witnesses, 298
Ipso facto excommunication, offences visited with, 144 note 45; suspension the result of certain offences, 165; sentences, 313
Ipso jure excommunication, 144; sentences, 313
Ipswich, Dominicans at, 131
Ireland, land of Templars in, 129 note 50
Irenaeus, A.D. 133-195, 17 note 67
Irregularity, dispensation from, 34, 158; a spiritual penalty, 158; caused by violating a suspension, 162, 165
Ischyras, 211 note 148; 275 note 87
Isidore, Bishop of Seville (Hispaliensis), A.D. 618-636, 7 note 27
Isle of France, 127
Islep, Simon, Archbishop of Canterbury, A.D. 1349-1366, his constitutions, A.D. 1351, 157 note 134
Italy, introduction of monasticism in, 83
Iteration of a sacrament, 60

JACOBINS, 130
Jactitation of marriage, 200; causes of plenary, 239 note 29
Jerome, a Roman presbyter, A.D. 345-420, 9 note 34
Jerusalem, community of life at, 109; Knights of St. John of, 129
Jesuits, founded A.D. 1540, 133
Jews may not accuse Christians, 245

John VIII., Pope, A.D. 872-882, 37 note 190
John, King of England, A.D. 1199-1216, 137
John, St., of Jerusalem, Knights of, 129
John of Marburg, a Dominican, A.D. 1227, 53 note 89
John Nepos, Bishop of Jerusalem, 133
John of Salerno, 53 note 89
John-Bonites, 133
Jointly. See *Solidum*
Josephus, "Antiquities of the Jews," 177 note 7
Judges, spiritual, 187, 210; various kinds of, 178 note 12, 210; ordinary, 211; delegate, 218, 220; by divine right, 210; of ecclesiastical appointment, 210; of competent jurisdiction, 210; of first instance, 211; of appeal, 211; qualifications, 211, 218; approved by the parties, 211; disqualified, 212, 214, 275; duties of, 215; sentence of, 144; liable for neglect, 217; appointed jointly, 218; appointed in common, 218; office, 302; includes cognisance, 303; determination, 303; execution, 303
Judgment, meaning of, 177 note 8, 178; discussion in, 177, 264; Acts in, 262; what part of, binding, 316
JUDGMENT, ACTS IN, chap. viii. p. 262
Judicia civitatis Londinensis, a collection of ordinances which the bishops and the reeves belonging to London ordained in the time of King Athelstan, A.D. 930, 89 note 52, 90 note 54
Judicial committee, 207; proceeding, 262 note 1, 273 note 76
Judicial courts, ancient constitution of, 179; appeals, 324; in what sense, 186 note 41
Judicial settlements, 286, 311, 315; effects of, 316; what sentences never become, 318
Judicia, acts *in*, 280
Julius, Bishop of Rome, A.D. 336-352, 7 note 28
Jure, acts *in*, 280
Juris utrum, writ of, 198 note 86
Jurisdiction of spiritual courts in the Empire, 180

Justice, or a legitimation, 31, 262 note 1; written by a judge on the sentence, 309 note 35
Justinian, Eastern Emperor, A.D. 527-565, 84 note 28, 241 note 37; sanctions appeals, 323

KEMBLE, Saxons in England, 1846, 87 note 44
Kempe, John, Archbishop of York, A.D. 1426-1452; of Canterbury, A.D. 1452-1454; constitutions of, A.D. 1444, 99 note 114
Keys, power of, 2; two keys, 2; key of interpretation, 2, 40 *seq.*; of coercion, 3, 135 *seq.*
Kitchener, a monastic, 98
Kneelers, a class of penitents, 18, 19

LANGTON, STEPHEN, Archbishop of Canterbury, A.D. 1207-1229, constitutions of, A.D. 1222, 5 note 16
Laodicea, Council of, A.D. 363, 40 note 4
Lapsed, the, 46
Larceny, 66. See *Stealing*
Lateran Council, A.D. 1123, 57 note 120; Second, A.D. 1139, 57 note 121; Third, A.D. 1179, 30 note 145; Fourth, A.D. 1215, 30 note 145; forbids establishment of any new congregation, 92
Laura, an association of members living apart, 92
Laymen may be ministers of baptism, 37
Law, J. T., author of Forms of Ecclesiastical Law, London, 1844, 321 note 111
Law, sentences of, 144
Laws in force, 242
Legitimacy, 201
Legitimation, 31
Lent, the season for solemn discipline, 21
Leo I., Pope, A.D. 440-461, 4 note 10
—— IV., Pope, A.D. 847-855, 57 note 123
—— XIII., Pope, A.D. 1878, 69 note 217
Lerida, Council of, A.D. 523 or A.D. 542, 34 note 172
Lerina, island of, 83

Index. 347

Lero, island of, 83
Letters of request, 214, 297 note 248, 320 note 101; of despatch, 331; dimissory, 331; deferential, 331; refutatory, 331; testimonial, 331; conventional, 331
Lex talionis, 246. See *Inscription*
Libel, what it is, 264, 265; nature of, 263; necessity of, 263, 265; simple, 266; articulate, 266; in civil procedure, 241, 265, 267; in a criminal cause, 247, 264, 266; contents of, 266; exceptions to, 275; when it may be changed, 279; or enlarged, 279
Libellatici, 46
Liberties, violating ecclesiastical, 60; of the Church, as understood in this country, 190
License defined, 29, 30
Liguori, Alfonzo Maria de, born at Naples A.D. 1696, founder of the Order of Redemptorists, A.D. 1749, died 1787, 134, 35 note 177
Lingard's Anglo-Saxon Church, 85 note 31
Liquido constat, 292 note 197
Lis mota, 273 note 76, 281 note 128
Literae remissoriales, 214
Litis dominus, 229, 282; redemptor, 227
Litis finitae, exception of, 287
Locociagense, 83 note 22
Loening, author of Kirchengeschichte, 152 note 109
London, Dominicans in, 131; Franciscans in, 131
Lorain, author of L'Abbaye de Clugny, Dijon, 1839, 124 note 17
Lothair, 196 note 79
Lucius III., Pope, A.D. 1181-1185, 51 note 72
Lucky and unlucky days, 61
Lucrum cessans, 70 note 221
Ludgate, 131
Lyndwood, William, Bishop of St. David's, A.D. 1434-1446, author of Provinciale, A.D. 1429, 3 note 9
Lyons, Third Council of, A.D. 583, 118 note 261; Council of, A.D. 1245, 5 note 15; Council of, A.D. 1274, 5 note 15

MABILLON, Jean, Benedictine preacher, born A.D. 1632, author of *Acta Sanctorum*, A.D. 1702; *Museum Italicum*, A.D. 1689; *Liturgia Gallicana*, A.D. 1685; *Annales Ordinis S. Benedicti*, A.D. 1703-1713, 108 note 178
Macarius, chief of the recluses of Nitria, A.D. 385, died A.D. 394, 82
Mâcon, Council of, A.D. 581, 67 note 196
Magic, 62
Mainz, Council of, A.D. 813, 117 note 257; A.D. 847, 59 note 135; Archbishop of, 156 note 127
Malice, 283, 294. See *Calumny*
Malta ceded to Knights of St. John, 129
Man, spiritual courts in Isle of, 185
Mandate, 225; by whom not required, 226; manifest evidence, 291
Marcellus, 50 note 66
Marguérite, island of, 83
Marmoutier = *majus monasterium*, 83 note 23
Marnay, Sir William, founder of Charterhouse, 126
Marriage dispensation, when forbidden, 33; when may be contracted in infancy, 37; second, forbidden, 75
Marrying persons related within forbidden degrees, a cause of *ipso facto* suspension, 165
Marseilles, monasteries of, 83
Martene, Edmund, born A.D. 1654, a Benedictine monk of St. Maur, died A.D. 1739, author of Commentary on St. Benedict's Rule, A.D. 1690; On the Ancient Usages of Monks, A.D. 1690, 17 note 66
Martin, a native of Pannonia, Archbishop of Braga, A.D. 560-583; Council of, A.D. 572, 61 note 149
Martin of Pannonia, A.D. 316, Bishop of Tours, A.D. 370-396, introduces monasticism at Poitou and Tours, 83
Matha, John of, born at Faucon in Provence, A.D. 1154, founder of the Order of Trinitarians, A.D. 1199, died at Rome, A.D. 1213, 129
Matrimonial causes, 185 note 36, 208; sentences never final in, 317; presumption in favour of validity of marriage in, 312

348 Index.

Matteo di Aquas Spartas, 132
Matteo di Baschi, 132
Maunday Thursday, reconciliation-day, 21, 172
Maximus, born in fourth century, made Bishop of Turin in fifth, signed the acts of the Synod of Rome, A.D. 465, 84 note 30
Meaux, Council of, A.D. 845, 66 note 182; diocese of, 129
Medio, in, i.e., synodically, 16, 174, 178, 185
Mendicants or Friars, 130
Mepham, Simon, Archbishop of Canterbury, A.D. 1328-1833; his constitutions, A.D. 1328, 10 note 36
Mercenary office, 236
Mere office, 236, 243, 254, 282; privileges in proceedings by, 257
Metropolitan, appeal from, 332
Metz, 85, 126 note 33
Milan, monasticism introduced at, 82
Milevis, Council of, A.D. 416, 274 note 79
Minikins, female monks, 86, 114, 116; in towns under the Bishop, 117; in the country under monasteries, 117
Minorites, Order of, 102 note 135, 121 note 3, 130. See *Franciscans*
Miserere, 154
Mixed causes, 194, 197, 228 note 268, 233, 234; person, 42
Monasteries, Welsh, 83; Irish, 83; Scottish, 83; Celtic, 94; name of a clergy-house, 85; double, 86, 94, 117
Monastery, seclusion in a, substituted for solemn penance, 21
Moniales, 114 note 233
Monks, 81, 86, 107 (see *Religious Life*); clerical, 105; may accuse their abbot, 222 note 223
Montpellier, hospital of, 128; Council of, A.D. 1215, 91 note 61
Morin, John, an Oratorian, died 1659, 9 note 34
Mora, in, 273 note 76
Mortgage, 72 note 221
Mortua voce proof, 290
Mortuaries, 199
Mund the bishop's, 158
Muratori, 259 note 154
Murder, 64. See *Homicide*.
Mutua petitio, 265, 276

NARBONNE, Council of, A.D. 589, 61 note 149; province of, 53 note 88
Narthex or antechapel, 79
Natalis, Alexander, 18 note 67
Nazarenes, 45 note 88
Necessary promoter, 237
Necessity a good cause of dispensation, 37
Negotium, 262
Nestorius cited, 270 note 57
Nevers, Duke of, 132
Newenham Abbey, 125
Nicaea, Synod of, A.D. 325, 7 note 28
Nicephorus, 84 note 30
Nicolas I., Pope, A.D. 858-867, 6 note 20
—— II., Pope, A.D. 1058-1061, 55 note 111
—— III., Pope, A.D. 1277-1281, 53 note 91
Nilus the monk, 80 note 2
Nitria, the home of hermits, 82
Noble office, 236
Norbert, founder of Praemonstants, A.D. 1120, 127
Norman Conquest, 182
Northumbrian priests, laws of, 90 note 57
Norwich, Dominicans at, 131
Notorious defined, 186 note 42, 243, 253, 254 note 125, 257 note 139, 291 note 194; causes, 282
Novatus, schism of, 7; ordination of, 36 note 182
Novices, 99, 117; not to be received for money, 118
Noviciate, length of, 102, 118. See *Religious Life*
Nullity of sentence, 319; established by appeal, 329
Nuns, 114; two kinds of, 114; ordinary, or canonesses, 114, 115; cloistered, 114 (see *Minikins*, 116); admission of, 118; dispensation from convent residence, 34
Nursia, birthplace of St. Benedict, 121

OAK, Synod of, 178 note 9
Oath, four kinds of, 240 note 37; may be taken by a proctor for a principal, 229, 230, 283; of calumny, 283; of malice, 283; of truth, 240 note 37, 297; suppletory, 241 note 37, 242,

290; dispensation from, 34; of purgation, 258. See *Purgation*
Obduracy, 136, 321. See *Contumacy*
Obedience, a counsel of perfection, 95, 113; required by St. Benedict's rule, 93, 113
Obediences, farming, of forbidden, 86 note 38, 98; not to be granted as freeholds, 98
Obedientials, 97, 98, 109
Oblatus, a child dedicated to the religious life, 100
Observants, a branch of Franciscans, 132
Odelo, canon of Avignon, 127
Odo, Archbishop of Canterbury, A.D. 942-959, 3 note 9
Offerings, customary, 197
Office, causes of, 236; mere or noble, 236 (see *Mere*); promoted or mercenary, 237; promotion of, 248
Official, the judge of a judicial court, 187
Officio oath, *ex*, 240 note 37; abolished in this country, 257, 284 note 152
Oliver, author of *Monasticon Exoniense*, 124 note 19
Omisso medio appeals, 329 note 174, 332
Oppressi, 326 note 147
Oratorians, 134
Orange, Second Council of A.D. 529, 24 note 105
Ordeals, 307; when required, 307
ORDER, vol. i. chap. v. 178 *seq.*
Order distinct from monkhood, 104, 106
Order of the investigation, 280, 285, 288
ORDERS, PRIVILEGES AND DUTIES OF, vol. i. chap. vi. p. 252 *seq.*
Orders, falsely claiming, 68; obtaining, improperly, 79
Ordinaries, 210; duty of, to assist one another, 297 note 248, 320 note 101
Origen, presbyter of Alexandria, A.D. 185-245, 11 note 39, 52 note 77
Orleans, Council of, A.D. 511, 61 note 149; Second Council of, A.D. 533, 8 note 30; Third Council of, A.D. 538, 17 note 64; Fourth Council of, 52 note 85
Otho, Cardinal-deacon and legate of Gregory IX., his constitutions, A.D. 1237, 6 note 17
Otho IV., Emperor, A.D. 1208-1212, 33 note 160
Othoboni, Cardinal-deacon of St. Adrian, and legate of Clement IV., his constitutions, A.D. 1268, 6 note 22
Ottery St. Mary, a Benedictine foundation, 123
Oughton, author of Ordo Judiciorum, 183 note 30
Oxford, colleges of, 92 note 68; Dominicans at, 131; Franciscans at, 131; Synod of, A.D. 1222, 191

PACHOMIUS the hermit, 81; requires a noviciate of three years, 201
Pacian of Barcelona, *circa* 370 A.D., author of Paraenesis ad Poenitentiam, 2 note 6, 43 note 26
Pactum, 278 notes 119 and 120
Padua, 132
Palmaria, 83 note 20
Palmistry, 61
Pandulph, legate of Innocent III., 137 note 8
Papal States, 184. See *States of the Church*
Paris, Third Council of, A.D. 557, 118 note 261; Fifth Council of, A.D. 615, 74 note 251; Sixth Council of, A.D. 829, 109 note 184
Paschal II., Pope, A.D. 1099-1118, 33 note 160
Passionists, 134
Patriarch's power of granting dispensations, 33
Patron, an advocate, 221
Paul of Samosata, 180 note 17
Paul of Thebes, died A.D. 340, 80
Paul of the Cross, founder of Passionists, 134
Paul the heretic, 52 note 77
Paula, 83 note 19
Paulinus, author of Vita Ambrosii, 143, note 43
Paupers disqualified from being accusers, 244
Peace, a name for reconciliation or absolution, 159
Peckham, John, Archbishop of Canterbury, A.D. 1279-1294; his constitu-

tions at Reading, A.D. 1279, 6 note 17; constitutions at Lambeth, A.D. 1281, 26 note 118

Pelagius, Pope, A.D. 555-560, 3 note 8; 49 note 63

Penal discipline, 4

Penalties, 135, 155; power to inflict, an imperial duty, 156; temporal, 156; spiritual, 158; punishments indirectly, 159

PENANCE, vol. I. chap. iv. p. 138; not to be undergone solemnly more than once, 23; change of, 35

Penances, corrective, 135, 152; defined, 152; public, 153; private, 153; of three kinds, 153; spiritual or devotional, 153; bodily, 154; pecuniary, 154

Penitents, a term applied to those undergoing solemn penance, 23; called also hearers, 19

Pensions charged on benefices, 197; causes of subtraction of, 239 note 29

Peremptory citation, 270; exception, 241

Periculum, 309 note 38

Perjury, 67 (see *Deceit*); causes of plenary, 239 note 29

Perpetuation of jurisdiction, 273, 282

Personal causes, 235; decree, 284

Peter of Castronovo, 53 note 89

Peter de Saulia, 127

Petition or libel, 264; *grosso modo*, 264 note 11

Petitioners for the religious life, 99

Philip of France, 33 note 160

Philip of Neri, 134

Piacenza, Council of, A.D. 1095, 57 note 121

Pisa, 131

Pliny's letter, A.D. 112, 48 note 53

Plaintiff, 222; persons disqualified to be, 222, 275; compellable, 223

Plenary causes, 237, 238; list of, 239 note 29

Plurality, dispensations for, by whom granted, 33

Plymouth, Franciscans at, 132; Carmelites at, 133

Plympton Priory, 127; lepers' house at, 129

Poitou, monasticism introduced at, 83

Polycarp, Bishop of Smyrna, A.D. 115-155, 49 note 63

Pontius, canon of Avignon, 127

Pontus, monks of, 82

Pope not a subject of accusation, 245; appeals to, 333; abolished in this country, 333; appeals from, 333 note 206

Portiuncula at Assissi, 132

Positions or articles, 281 note 129, 280 note 127; to be answered, 284

Possessory causes, 235

Possessors to be preferred in doubtful cases, 291 note 190

Possidio, Bishop of Calamis, *circa* 440 A.D., author of a Life of Augustin of Hippo, 85 note 32

Postulants for the religious life, 99

Praemonstrants, a branch of Augustinians, 127

Praeses, the name of a judge, 179

Preachers, Order of, 102 note 135. See *Dominicans*

Prejudicial causes, 277; exceptions, 277, 287, 288

Preparatory questions, 286

Prerogative court, 288

Prescription, 274, 282

Presentment, 236 note 21, 254 (see *Denunciation*); of fame, 252. See *Inquisition*

Presumptions, 305; legal, 306; personal, 306; insufficient to constitute proof, 305

Prevarication, 278 note 114

Principals in judgment, 218, 222

Priors, 97; of three kinds, 97; claustral, 97; conventual, 97; secular, 97

Privilege defined, 29, 30; not retrospective, 242

Probate of wills, 185 note 36, 208. See *Wills*

Probatory term, 247, 288

Procedure, disciplinary, 174; solemn, the original form, 174; said to be *in medio*, 174; canonical, 233, 285; statutory, 285

Process, 262

Proctors, 224; judicial, 225; how appointed, 225; obligations and powers of, 226; one or more, 226; qualified persons, 227; when they may be

appointed, 228; when not, 226 note
247, 228 note 268, 275, 228 note
268, 239 note 33
Procurations, subtraction of, 239 note
29
Profession of religious life, 100, 229;
an extrajudicial act, 225
Prohibition, writ of, 184, 202; allowed
in three cases, 204; when not allowed,
205
Promoted office, 237
Promoter necessary, 237; privileges of,
257; voluntary, 237
Proof, 281; defined, 289; what it includes, 289; of two degrees, 290;
full, 290; half, 242, 290; full, required in criminal causes, 290; cannot be made by presumptions only,
305
Property, forms in dealing with, may
not be dispensed with, 35; renunciation of, by monks, 93
Proprietory, 235, 275
Protest, appearance under, 275
Provincial canons, dispensation from,
35
Provost, office of, 97
Proxy, 225; revocation of, 229
Publication of depositions constitutes
evidence, 300
Purgation, 259, 307 note 27; failure in,
equivalent to pleading guilty, 26;
when directed to be taken, 290 note
189; when forbidden, 290; oath of,
240 note 37, 258; may not be compulsorily administered in this country,
258; nor administered to a person
not defamed, 259; manner of taking,
260

QUADRUPLICATIONS, 286 note 160
Quasi-contract, 199
Querela, 248
Question, 262 note 1
Quod permittat, writ of, 198 note 86

RABAN MAUR, Abbot of Fulda, died A.D.
856, 8 note 31
Rainer, 53 note 88
Rape, 44, 72, 75
Reading forbidden books, 49
Real causes, 235

Rebutters, 286 note 160
Recluse, 81; none may become without
bishop's leave, 81
Recollets, a branch of Franciscans, 132
Reconciliation, the ending of a censure
in a regular manner, 169; two kinds
of, 170; extra-judicial, 170; judicial,
170; who may give, 171; precautionary, 172; with reincidence, 172;
confined to the living, 172
Reconvention, 265, 276; when not
possible, 277
Redemptionists, 134
Refectioner, a monastic, 98
Regradation, 160; the mildest form of
clerical punishment, 160; several
kinds of, 160
Regular canons. See *Canons*
Rejoinders, 286 note 160
Religions = forms of the religious life,
108, 120
Religious house defined, 92; not to
be removed without proper consent,
99
Religious life, 80; three varieties of,
80; distinct from order, 104, 106;
in isolation, 80 (see *Solitaries*); in
association, 81, 122 (see *Hermits*);
in common, 84 (see *Coenobites*); extension of, to clergy, 84, 126; admission to, 99; tacit profession of, 99,
102; express profession of, 99; dedication of children to, 100, 117;
voluntary profession of, 101; age
required, 101, 118; noviciate, 102,
118 (see *Noviciate*); not to be
allowed for money, 102, 118; manner
of professing, 103, 119; time for,
119; profession of, equivalent to a
second baptism, 104; duties of, 106;
a spiritual cause, 197; poverty, 108;
chastity, 108, 112; regulations to
secure, 112; obedience, 108, 113;
silence, 114; desertion of, apostasy,
45, 106; among the Saxons, 122;
among the Celts, 122; persons dead
in law, 93, 110, 197 note 81
RELIGIOUS ORDERS, chap. iv. p. 120
seq.; defined, 120; rise of, in 13th
century, 120; contemplative, 121;
of clergy, 126; active charitable, 121,
128; spiritual, 121; missionary, 121

Religious women, 14. See *Nuns*
Remigius, 63 note 160
Remissoriales literae, 214
Repairs of churches, 197
Replications, 247
Residence, dispensation from, 33
Res judicata, 286. See *Judicial Settlement*
Restitutio in integrum, 316
Responsalis, name for a proctor, 224
Reus, 222
Review, commissions of, 317 note 82
Reynolds, Walter, Archbishop of Canterbury, A.D. 1313–1328, 31 note 146
Rhodes, home of Knights of St. John, 129
Robbery, 44, 63; of two kinds, 66
Robert of Molesme, founder of Cistercians, A.D. 1098, 125
Rodolph, 53 note 89
Rogers' Ecclesiastical Law, 200 note 91
Romaldesns or Camaldunians, 124
Roman Church, leniency of, 7; head of a temporal sovereign, 156
Roman Empire, jurisdiction of courts spiritual in, 193
Roman pontiffs, temporal sovereigns, 137
Roman Synod to the Gauls, A.D. 384, 117 note 260; A.D. 826, 103 note 147; A.D. 680, 6 note 20; A.D. 878, 60 note 144; A.D. 1078, 55 note 105
Roman law favourable to arbitration, 180
Rome, introduction of monasticism at, 82
Romuald, founder of the Camaldunians, A.D. 1009, 124
Rothery, appeal causes reprinted in Ecclestical Courts Commission, 1883, 44 note 30
Rouen, Council of, A.D. 650, 62 note 154, 115 note 240
Rowe, J. Brooking, 89 note 51

Sac, from Sache = a cause, the right of hearing causes, 158
SACRAMENTS GENERALLY, vol. I. chap. i. 1
Sacrilege, 44; defined, 58; personal, 59; real, 60, 315

Sacring, 38 note 201
Sanctimoniales, 114 note 233
Saracens, 133
Sardica, Council of, A.D. 347, 7 note 26
Satan's power over the body, 136
Satisfactions not to be capricious or arbitrary, 216 note 180
Saulis, Peter of, 127
Scala, La, 134
Schism, 44; defined, 50; external, 51; internal, 51; leads to heresy, 50 note 69
Schmalzgrueber, author of *Jus Universum*, 135 note 1; on sentences, 317 note 83
Scire facias, writ of, 198 note 86
Sects in churches, 239 note 29
Secular canons. See *Canons*
Secular courts, litigation in, 78
Security for prosecuting, 247, 265. See *Caution*
Selborne, Lord, 289 note 178
Seligenstadt, Council of, A.D. 1022, 306 note 21
Sempringham, 127
Sentences, 308; of two kinds, 308; interlocutory, 308; final, 308, 309; involve three things, 311; ought to combine justice with mercy, 305, 314; of law, 144, 312; of a judge, 144, 312; passed and to be passed, 144, 312; *ipso jure* and *ipso facto*, 144, 313
Separation or exclusion, 20; simple, 139; complete, 140 = excommunication
Settlement, matter for, 262 (see *Negotium*); judicial, 311. See *Judicial*
Severity defined, 6; ecclesiastical, 135; of three kinds, 135; remedial, 135, 136; penal, 135; vindictive, 135
Seville, Second Council of, A.D. 619, 86 note 39
Sidonius Apollinaris, 183 note 31
Significavit, a writ whereby a contumacious person is imprisoned, 185 note 36, 322
Silence required from monks, 114
Silvanus, Bishop of Troas, 179 note 16
Simeon Stylites, 81 note 8
Simon Magus, 55

Index. 353

Simony, 44; defined, 54; in obtaining orders, 54; in obtaining benefices, 57; of three kinds, 54; true, 56; conventional, 56; confidential, 56; penalties of, 57; in admission to a monastery, 58; a spiritual cause, 195; plenary, 239 note 29
Simple causes, 235
Simpliciter, 218, 221, 226
Sins, 39, 40
Sion house, 128 note 46
Siricius, Pope, A.D. 384–398, 74 note 252
Sirmond, Jacob, a Jesuit author, died A.D. 1651, 18 note 67
Sixtus IV, Pope, A.D. 1471–1484, 133
Slavery, reduction to, 156
Slaves may not be judges, 211; proctors, 227; advocates, 231; accusers, 245
Smith, Toulmin, English gilds, 87 note 44
Soc, an area of jurisdiction, 158
Socrates, A.D. 380–445, the Church historian, 23 note 101
Society, 88
Sodomy, 72, 75
Sodor and Man, Bishop of, 156 note 127
Solemn discipline, 10, 16, 17, 21; ceremonies at beginning of, 21; restoration at close of, 22; voluntarily submitted to, 22; imposed for public crimes, 22; persons exempt from it, 22
Solidum, in, 218, 226
Sorcery, 62
Spanish custom requires the queen-dowager to become a canoness, 119
Spellman's Glossary, 129 note 52
Spells, 62
Spiritual causes, 194, 233; of five kinds, 195
SPIRITUAL COURTS, chap. vi. 174 *seq.*; their jurisdiction under the Empire; 181; in this country, 182; subject-matter of, 189; in the Isle of Man, 185
Spirituals a branch of Franciscans, 132
Spoliation, 198, 277, 288 note 175
Stamp duties, 224 note 228
Stapeldon, Bishop of Exeter, 255 note 130

Standers, 16 note 61; a class of penitents, 18, 19
State trials, 317 note 84
States of the Church, 158. See *Papal States*
Statutes of the ancient Church, 62 note 154. See *Arles* and *Carthage*
Stephens' Ecclesiastical Statutes, 91 note 63
Stealing, 44, 66; venial, 66
Stevenson, editor of the Chronicles of the Abbey of Abingdon, 304 note 10
Stoechades Islands, 83
Stratford, John, Archbishop of Canterbury, A.D. 1333–1349, his constitutions, A.D. 1342, 61 note 147; his constitutions, A.D. 1343, 35 note 175
Stratford-on-Avon gild, 89 note 53
Strife, 44, 63, 66
Studies, neglecting clerical, 79
Studius, founder of a monastery at Constantinople, 84
Style or custom of the court, 285
Stylites. See *Simeon*
Suarez, 26 note 114
Sub-prior, 97
Suffred, Bishop, 213 note 159
Suit, 262 note 1; pendency of, 273
Summary causes, 237, 264; two kinds of, 237; no contestation of suit in, 282; all become before the highest court, 264; causes allowed to be, 238; information, 256, 263 note 9, 268; sentences in, 309 note 39
Suppletory oath, 241 note 37, 242, 290
Supremacy, Act of, 333
Surfeiting, 44
Surrejoinders, 286 note 160
Surrogates, 218
Suspension, or the lesser excommunication, 138; of clergy, 162; a form of deprivation, 160; from order, 161; from office, 162; from benefice, 162, 163; effect of, 162; duration of, 163; to be preceded by warning, 165; incurred *ipso facto*, 165; violation of, causes irregularity, 165; from entrance to the Church, 18
Suspicions, 305 note 15
Sweden, 129 note 46
Sword, the spiritual, 138; the temporal, 141

Sylvanus, Bishop of Troas, 265 note 23
Syndic, 228, 229
Synesius, Bishop of Ptolemais, 194 note 70
Synod, 262
Synodaticum, 197 note 84

TABENNAE, 81 note 12
Tanner, author of Monasticon, 132 note 62
Tarracon, Council of, A.D. 516, 71 note 229
Tavistock Abbey, 123
Taylor, Index Monasticus, 88 note 47
Team, 158
Templars, 30 note 143, 129; dissolution of, 129
Temporal causes, 194, 201, 233, 234
Teresa, St., 133
Tergiversation, 278 note 114
Term, 229; deliberatory, 276, 280; citatory, 280; probatory, 247, 288; for the publication of depositions, 300; to conclude, 302; to hear sentence, 302; final or definitory, 303; executory, 319; fatal, 319, 329
Tertiaries, a branch of Carmelites, 133
Tertullian, a presbyter who became a Montanist, *circa* 200 A.D., 7 note 29
Testamentary causes, 201; when plenary, 239 note 29
Testaments, 201. See *Wills*
Thalia, a book written by Arius, 50 note 66
Thames, 131
Thebaid, the home of associated religious life, 81
Theft, 44. See *Stealing*
Theodore of Tarsus, Archbishop of Canterbury, A.D. 668-690, 7 note 28
Theodore of the Holy Spirit, 87 note 43
Theodosian Code, 180 note 21
Theodulf, Bishop of Orleans, died A.D. 881, 8 note 31; his capitularies authorised in this country, A.D. 994
Thietberga, 196 note 79
Thomas, born at Aquino, A.D. 1227, educated at Monte Casino, became a Dominican A.D. 1243; studied at Paris and Cologne under Albert the Great, called the Angelic Doctor after 1257; repaired to Naples, A.D. 1272, and died at Fossa-Nova A.D. 1274, on his way to the Council of Lyons; was present at the Dominican Chapter in London, 131
Thompson, Margaret, history of Somerset Carthusians, London, 1895, 126 note 30
Thorsby, John, Archbishop of York, A.D. 1353-1374, constitutions of, A.D. 1363, 49 note 63
Thurificati, 46
Times, The, 131
Tithe causes, 197, 198, 208
Toledo, Third Council of, A.D. 589, 23 note 101; Fourth, A.D. 633, 32 note 152; Sixth, A.D. 638, 26 note 118; Eighth, A.D. 653, 34 note 172; Tenth, A.D. 656, 24 note 104; Eleventh, A.D. 675, 55 note 103; Twelfth, A.D. 681, 62 note 157; Thirteenth, A.D. 683, 62 note 156; Sixteenth, A.D. 691, 76 note 269
Tolerance, ecclesiastical, 49
Tolerated person, 313
Toll, the right of levying dues, 158
Tor Abbey, 127
Toulouse, 130
Tours, Council of, A.D. 460, 46 note 44; Second, A.D. 567, 106 note 171; Third, A.D. 813, 75 note 262; A.D. 1163, 71 note 231; introduction of monasticism at, 83
Transaction, 263 note 9; 278, 279 note 120
Trappe, La, 125
Trappists, 125
Trecasso, Council of, A.D. 878, 143 note 43
Trent, Council of, changed the law of marriage, 306
Trespass, 200
Tribur, Council of, A.D. 895, 55 note 103
Triers, Archbishop of, 156 note 127
Trinitarians, 129
Triplications, 286 note 160
Troslei, Council of, A.D. 909, 59 note 135, 154 note 119
Trullan Council, A.D. 692, 18 note 70

Truth, oath of, 240 note 37; what it is, 297
Tsangae, 111 note 203
Tuscan hermits, 133
Tyre, Council of, A.D. 335; condemns Athanasius, 275 note 87

UNIFORMITY, Act of, 179 note 80
Unnatural crime, 44, 72, 75
Urban II., Pope, A.D. 1088-1099, 14 note 51
—— III., Pope, A.D. 1185-1187, 273 note 74
—— IV., Pope, A.D. 1261-1265, 53 note 91
Ursinius, Cardinal, inquisitor, 53 note 91
Usury, 44, 63; defined, 69; how far permitted, 69; a spiritual cause, 196; when plenary, 239 note 29

VALENS, the Emperor, A.D. 364-367; opposed to monasticism, 82
Valentia, Council of, A.D. 374, 7 note 26
Valentinian II., Emperor, A.D. 375-379, 182 note 24
—— III., Emperor, A.D. 424-455, 178 note 11
Van Espen, Dutch canonist, 9 note 34
Vannes, Council of, A.D. 465, 45 note 35
Vengeance contemplated by accusation, 242. See *Vindictive*
Verona, Council of, A.D. 1185, 53 note 88
Vicar-General's Court in Isle of Man, 185 note 38
Vicars, temporary, 164
Vienne, Council of, A.D. 1311, 32 note 152; dissolves the Templars, 129; St. Antony of, 128
Vincent, St., de Paul, 134
Vincentians, 134
Vindictive discipline, 4, 6; practically abolished, 9; punishments, 135, 155; temporal, 156; spiritual, 158; degradation, 158, 168; anathema, 142, 158; irregularity, 158; indirectly vindictive, called animadversion, 158

Visitation-courts, or synods transacting non-contentious business, 175, 185, 243, 251; held for correction, 247
Viva voce proof, 290
Voluntary promoter, 237
Vow, definition of, 24; three conditions of, 24; private, 24; public, 24, 25; three parts of, 25; simple, 25, 26; annulling of, 27; profession or solemn, 25, 26; dispensation from, 28, 34; consummation or execution, 26; of religion ought to be fulfilled, 105

WARNING, necessity for, 4; when it may be dispensed with, 5
Warren Leofric Missal edited for Henry Bradshaw Society, 83 note 27
Warwick, Dominicans at, 131, 58 note 134, 72 note 237, 75 note 260
Wasserscheleben, 68
Wastena in Sweden, 128
Waverley, 125
WEDLOCK, vol. i. chap. vii. p. 329 *seq.*; violation of, 72, 74; a spiritual cause, 196
Weepers, a class of penitents, 17
Westminster, 123
Wethershed, *alias* Richard Grant, Archbishop of Canterbury, A.D. 1229-1231, constitutions of, A.D. 1229, 77 note 274
Whipping a penance, 154
Whitby (Streaneshalch), double monastery of, 86 note 41
White Friars or Carmelites, 133
White Monks or Cistercians, 124
Wigendale, gild of, 88 note 49, 89 note 53
Wihtraed's laws, A.D. 693, 84 note 29, or A.D. 696, 94 note 80; privilege of, A.D. 692, 95 note 84
Will, presumption in favour of, 312. See *Testaments*
William the Conqueror sets up spiritual courts, 182
William of Toulouse, 53 note 91
William of Mohun, 125 note 27
Wimborne, double monastry at, 86 note 41
Winchelsea, Archbishop of Canterbury, A.D. 1294-1313, 37 note 196

Winchester College, 92 note 68

Witchcraft, 62

Witham, a Carthusian house, 126

Withdrawal of a controversy, 278

Witnesses, two or three required in criminal causes, 290, 296; one may suffice in a civil cause, 242, 290; not more than forty allowed, 296; may not be examined before contestation, 281; fit and proper, 293, 294; disqualified, 294, 295; compellable, 297; to give evidence fasting, 298; may not be produced after the conclusion in a civil cause, 242; when they may in a criminal cause, 257; monks as, 297; three productions of, allowed, 298

Women may not be judges, 211; nor proctors, 227; nor advocates, 231; nor accusers, except for their own wrongs, 244

Worms, Council of, A.D. 868, 165 note 174, 258 note 147

Worship of fountains, stones, elmen, and other trees, 62; public, a spiritual cause, 197

YORK, St. Mary's Abbey, 123

ZACHARIAS, Pope, A.D. 741-752, 141 note 30

Zancae, 111 note 203

Zouche, William la, Archbishop of York, A.D. 1340-1353, constitutions of, A.D. 1347, 64 note 167

THE END.

Printed by BALLANTYNE, HANSON & CO.
Edinburgh and London

The Catholic Standard Library

Under this title is now issuing a series of Standard Works, consisting of Foreign Translations, Original Works, and Reprints, printed in the best style of the typographic art, bound in cloth, in demy 8vo, of from 450 to 600 pages, and issued at short intervals, price 12s. each Volume, net; post free to any part of the world. Twelve Vols. may be selected for £5, 5s.

The Great Commentary on the Gospels of Cornelius à Lapide. Translated and Edited by the Rev. T. W. Mossman, D.D., assisted by various Scholars.

SS. Matthew and Mark's Gospels. 3 Vols. Fourth Edition.
S. John's Gospel and Three Epistles. 2 Vols. Third Edition.
S. Luke's Gospel. 1 Vol. Third Edition.

The six vols., bound by Zaensdorf, half antique calf, £5, 5s., or in whole calf extra, £6, 6s., much used as an Ordination Present.

A New Edition in Monthly Shilling Parts is now being issued. Parts I. to VI. ready.

The Acts of the Apostles to Revelations, completing the New Testament, in about four volumes, will now be issued at short intervals.

"It would indeed be gilding the finest gold to bestow praise on the great Commentary of à Lapide. It is a work of unequalled—we should say unapproached—value. We specially entreat the clergy not to neglect obtaining so vast a treasure of saintly wisdom, even if, in so doing, they are obliged to sacrifice many volumes far inferior to it in real helpfulness."—*John Bull.*

"Mr. Mossman has done his part as an able and sympathetic scholar might be expected to do it, and the volumes, both in translation and execution, are worthy of their author."—*Saturday Review.*

"It is the most erudite, the richest, and altogether the completest Commentary on the Holy Scriptures that has ever been written, and our best thanks are due to Mr. Mossman for having given us, in clear, terse, and vigorous English, the invaluable work of the Prince of Scripture Commentators."—*Dublin Review.*

"Really the Editor has succeeded in presenting the public with a charming book. We have been accustomed to regard à Lapide for consultation rather than to be read. But in the compressed form, clear and easy style, and excellent type in which it now appears, it is a book we can sit down to and enjoy."—*The Month.*

"We set a high store upon this Commentary. There is about it a clearness of thought, a many-sided method of looking at truth, an insight into the deeper meaning, and a fearless devotion which lend a peculiar charm to all that he writes. The great value which his commentaries have for Bible students is in the fact that nowhere else can they find so great a store of patristic and scholastic exegesis."—*Literary World.*

Henry VIII. and the English Monasteries.

An Attempt to Illustrate the History of their Suppression, with an Appendix and Maps showing the Situation of the Religious Houses at the time of their Dissolution. By FRANCIS AIDAN GASQUET, D.D., O.S.B. 2 Vols. Sixth Edition.

"We may say in brief, if what we have already said is not sufficient to show it, that a very important chapter of English history is here treated with a fulness, minuteness, and lucidity which will not be found in previous accounts, and we sincerely congratulate Dr. Gasquet on having made such an important contribution to English historical literature."—*Athenæum*.

"A learned, careful, and successful vindication of the personal character of the monks.... In Mr. Gasquet's skilful hands the dissolution of the monasteries assumes the proportions of a Greek tragedy."—*Guardian*.

May also be had in 2 Vols., with 34 Page Illustrations and 5 Maps, Half bound in Persian Morocco, Top Edge Gilt, Price 30s.; in the best whole Morocco or Calf, £2, 2s.; Half Calf, £1, 14s.; in Quires for Binding, £1, 2s.

The ILLUSTRATIONS may be had separately. Price 5s., Post Free.

The SIXTH EDITION is now being issued in Monthly Shilling Parts. Parts I. to X. ready.

Edward VI. and the Book of Common Prayer.

Its Origin Illustrated by hitherto Unpublished Documents. With Four Facsimile Pages of the MS. By FRANCIS AIDAN GASQUET, O.S.B., and EDMUND BISHOP. *Third Thousand.*

"A more accurate history of the changes of religion and the motives of the statesmen of the reign of Henry VI. than has ever before appeared; and as regards the antecedents and the compilation of the Prayer Book, we have no hesitation in saying this volume is the most valuable contribution to its history that has appeared since the time of Dr. Cardwell."—*Athenæum*.

"We cannot refrain from expressing our admiration of the method in which the author has conducted his whole inquiry. It ought to have a large circulation, for it contains by far the best account we have ever seen of the changes introduced in Edward VI.'s reign."—*Guardian*.

"This book will occupy a place of special importance in the library of every liturgical student."—*Saturday Review*.

"We may say, without hesitation, that the second, third, and fourth appendices are the most valuable contributions to the early history of the Prayer Book that has yet appeared."—*Church Quarterly Review*.

"This volume is one of the most interesting and valuable contributions to the study of the Reformation in England that has appeared for many a day."—*Academy*.

"The book deserves great praise for its learning and fairness."—*Spectator*.

"We gladly acknowledge our gratitude to its authors, and willingly bespeak for their labours the earnest attention of every priest and layman."—*Church Times*.

Historical Portraits of the Tudor Dynasty
and the Reformation Period. By S. HUBERT BURKE. 4 Vols. Second Edition. "Time unveils all Truth."

May also be had in half calf or morocco, £3, 3s.; in whole calf or morocco, £4, 4s.

"I have read the work with great interest, and I subscribe without hesitation to the eulogy passed on it by the *Daily Chronicle*, as making, as far as I know, a distinct and valuable addition to our knowledge of a remarkable period."—*From a Letter by* Mr. GLADSTONE.

"We do not hesitate to avow that, in his estimate of character and events, Mr. Burke is seldom wrong. . . . We heartily wish it a large sale and an extensive circulation."—*The Academy.* Signed, NICHOLAS POCOCK.

"They are full-length portraits, often so life-like, that when placed beside each other, we feel no difficulty in realising the relations which Mr. Burke aims at establishing between them."—*Annual Register.*

"The author writes history as it should be written. The men and women that pass before us in these portraits are no hard lifeless outlines, but beings of flesh and blood, in whom, and in whose fate, we feel a keen and absorbing interest."—*Tablet.*

"We attach great importance to Mr. Burke's work, as it is, we believe, the first attempt on any considerable scale to collect and arrange in a living picture the men and women who made the England of to-day. . . . This effort, seriously and conscientiously undertaken, and aided by a graphic and attractive style, must do immense good."—*Dublin Review.*

"No honest student of a most memorable period can afford to neglect the aid of Mr. Burke's long and laborious researches, while the general public will find in his pages all the interest of a romance, and all the charm of novelty, about events more than three centuries old. He is also what is rare—an historian of absolute impartiality."—*Life.*

The History of the Popes, from the Close of
the Middle Ages. Drawn from the Secret Archives of the Vatican and other Original Sources. By Dr. L. PASTOR, Professor of History in the University of Innsbruck. Translated from the German and Edited by FREDERICK ANTROBUS, of the London Oratory. Vols. I. and II.

"It would be difficult to name any great historical work written with so obvious an anxiety to tell the truth and nothing but the truth, and should these volumes not meet with a favourable reception, we should regard the event as little short of a literary calamity."—*Daily Chronicle.*

"It is no exaggeration to say that this work is one of the most important historical studies of the present century."—*Tablet.*

A History of the Somerset Carthusians.
By MARGARET E. THOMPSON.

This Vol. has Sixteen Page Illustrations of Hinton Charter-House, Witham Friary, &c., by the Author's sister, Miss L. B. THOMPSON, and will prove an interesting work to antiquarians, especially of Somersetshire and the West of England generally.

The Hierurgia; or, The Holy Sacrifice of the Mass. With Notes and Dissertations elucidating its Doctrines and Ceremonies. By Dr. DANIEL ROCK. 2 Vols. A New and thoroughly Revised Edition, with many new Illustrations. Edited, with a Preface, by W. H. JAMES WEALE.

The Editor (whose qualifications for his office are well known) has spared no efforts in making the book perfect; and as he has had much additional matter unknown to the learned author, his success has been assured.

A Large Paper Edition, limited to 250 copies, printed on fine laid paper, with red rubric lines, price £2, 10s., to secure copies of which immediate application is necessary.

"We cordially welcome this excellently printed edition of Dr. Rock's well-known work. The name of Mr. Weale on the title-page is a guarantee that the work of editing has been carefully and conscientiously performed. An examination of the vols. now issued and a comparison of the first edition has convinced us, that so far from this being a mere reprint, there is hardly a page which does not manifest the work of the present Editor."—*Tablet.*

Piconio (Bernardine a). Exposition on St. Paul's Epistles. Translated and Edited by A. H. PRITCHARD, B.A., Merton College, Oxford. 3 Vols.

"The learning, the piety, the spiritual-mindedness and loving charity of the author, which deservedly earned for him a high reputation in France, are everywhere conspicuous, and there is a freshness in the mode in which he presents much that is suggestive, hopeful, and beautiful."—*National Church.*

"We desire to recommend this book to all. Of course to the priesthood any commendation of it is unnecessary; but among the laity there are many souls one of whose greatest drawbacks in the spiritual life is unfamiliarity with the Word of God. Let them read the Scriptures daily, if only for a few minutes, let them bear along with them such guides as Piconio, and the Spirit of God will illumine their minds and inflame their hearts with a freshness and vigour of Divine life altogether peculiar."—*New York Catholic World.*

The Relation of the Church to Society. A Series of Essays by EDMUND J. O'REILLY, S.J. Edited, with a Biographical Notice, by the Rev. MATTHEW RUSSELL.

"Among the many interesting chapters of this book, perhaps the most interesting is that entitled 'The Clergy and the Law of Elections.' Here the author discusses, with clearness and ability, the somewhat vexed question concerning the part that priests may take in politics and public elections. There are many other topics treated in this volume which will well repay the trouble of careful reading."—*Dublin Review.*

The Complete Works of St. Bernard, Abbot of Clairvaux.
Translated into English from the Edition of DOM JOANNES MABILLON, of the Benedictine Congregation of St. Maur (Paris, 1690), and Edited by SAMUEL J. EALES, D.C.L., some time Principal of St. Boniface College, Warminster. Vols. I. and II., containing the Letters of St. Bernard. *Vol. III. Just Ready.*

"In his writings great natural powers shine forth resplendently, an intellect more than that of the subtle Abelard, an eloquence that was irresistible, an imagination like a poet, and a simplicity that wins the admiration of all. Priests will find it a most valuable book for spiritual reading and sermons. The printing and binding of the work are superb."—*Catholic World* (New York).

"We wish Dr. Eales and his publisher all success in what may be called a noble undertaking."—*Church Quarterly Review.*

"No writer of the Middle Ages is so fruitful of moral inspiration as St. Bernard, no character is more beautiful, and no man in any age whatever so faithfully represented all that was best in the impulses of his time, or exercised so powerful an influence upon it. . . . There is no man whose letters cover so many subjects of abiding interest, or whose influence was so widely spread."—*Athenæum.*

"It is not a little strange that a man of intellect so powerful and character so noble and self-denying should have had to wait seven centuries for his works to be rendered into English. . . . The letters are of great historic interest, and many of them most touching. The simple earnestness of the man, and his utter freedom from ambition, strike us on almost every page."—*Notes and Queries.*

"We congratulate both the publisher and the editor upon the issue of these volumes, which we predict will be warmly appreciated by English readers, and which we can thoroughly recommend."—*Literary Churchman.*

"The task which Mr. Eales has undertaken of bringing out an English edition of Bernard's works is one that is deserving of every praise, and we hope that it may be carried to completion by the appearance of the remaining volumes without undue delay."—*Literary World.*

"English readers of every class and creed owe a debt of gratitude to Dr. Eales for the great and useful work which he has undertaken. It is strange that now for the first time has such a task been even, as far as we are aware, approached. . . . In this the earliest complete English edition of Bernard's works, a reparation, tardy indeed, but ample, is about to be made for the neglect or indifference of so many bygone generations of the English-speaking race. . . . We have indeed much to be grateful for to the first English translator of S. Bernard's works."—*The Month.*

The History and Fate of Sacrilege.
By Sir HENRY SPELMAN, Kt. Edited, in part from two MSS., Revised and Corrected. With a Continuation, large Additions, and an Introductory Essay. By Two Priests of the Church of England. New Edition, with an Appendix, bringing the work up to the present date, by the Rev. S. F. WARREN, M.A.

"All who are interested in Church endowments and property should get this work, which will be found to be a mine of information on the point with which it deals."—*Newbery House Magazine.*

The Dark Ages: A Series of Essays illustrating the State of Religion and Literature in the Ninth, Tenth, Eleventh, and Twelfth Centuries. By the late Dr. MAITLAND. Keeper of the MSS. at Lambeth. Fifth Edition, with an Introduction by FREDERICK STOKES, M.A.

"The Essays as a whole are delightful; although they are full of learning, no one can find them dull or heavy; they abound in well-told stories, amusing quotations, and clever sarcasm. Whatever the previous knowledge of a reader may be, he will be stirred up by these essays to learn more of a subject they treat so pleasantly."—*Saturday Review.*

"No task could be more worthy of a scholar and divine so eminently distinguished as the author of this volume, than a vindication of institutions which had been misrepresented for centuries, and a defence of men who had been maligned by those to whom they had been generous benefactors. We have read this work both with pleasure and profit."—*Athenæum.*

Cogitationes Concionales. Being 216 Short Sermon Reflections (Four for each Sunday) on the Gospels for the Church's Year, founded upon Selected Readings from the "Summa Theologica" of St. THOMAS AQUINAS. By JOHN M. ASHLEY, B.C.L., Rector of Fewston, Author of "A Promptuary for Preachers," &c. May also be had in 13 Parts, 1s. each.

A Commentary on the Holy Gospels. In 4 Vols. By JOHN MALDONATUS, S.J. Translated and Edited from the Original Latin by GEORGE J. DAVIE, M.A., Exeter College, Oxford, one of the Translators of the Library of the Fathers. Vols. I. and II. (St. Matthew's Gospel).

"I have often consulted Maldonatus in the original with advantage, and I am glad to see it in English."—W. E. GLADSTONE.

"Maldonatus is as yet but little known to English readers, yet he was a man of far more ability than à Lapide, and is far more original in his remarks and explanations."—*Month.*

"To those who may not with facility be able to read the Latin, this English version will be a great boon. The Commentary is certainly one with which a Biblical student should make himself acquainted."—*Guardian.*

The Life of Edmund Campion. By RICHARD SIMPSON.

This valuable book having been out of print many years, has become very scarce, second hand copies when met with realising fancy prices, it is now reprinted from a corrected copy, made by the learned Author for a new edition before his death. *Just Ready.*

A Complete Manual of Canon Law. By OSWALD J. REICHEL, B.C.L., M.A., F.S.A., sometime Vice-Principal of Cuddesdon College. May also be had in 25 Parts, 1s. each.

    Vol. I. THE SACRAMENTS.
    Vol. II. LITURGICAL DISCIPLINE.
    Vol. III. CHURCH GOVERNMENT. *In the Press.*
    Vol. IV. THE PAROCHIAL SYSTEM. *Preparing.*

"That it is the work of a scholar of very wide reading, the mass of evidence, historical and liturgical, with which the pages are almost overcrowded, amply proves."—*Tablet.*

"It is of the highest value to one entering upon the study of its subject, and likely also to prove of great service to advanced canonists for purposes of reference."—*Scotsman.*

"It is difficult to conceive a work more acceptable to Churchmen. It is a most learned work—learned, indeed, beyond the dreams of the most pedantic."—*Law Times.*

"Written in a style clear and precise. By his accurate and methodical researches the author has rendered a true service to careful studies."—*La Civiltà Cattolica.*

"Supplies a very urgent need which is very widely felt now that the study of Canon Law is being revived in the English Church."—*Church Times.*

"A monument of erudition. The library of no ecclesiastical lawyer, or student of ecclesiastical history, will be complete without it."—*Law Journal.*

THE GREAT COMMENTARY OF CORNELIUS À LAPIDE.

The Acts of the Apostles and The Epistle to the Romans. 2 Vols. Translated and Edited by GEORGE J. DAVIE, M.A., Editor of "Maldonatus' Commentary on the Holy Gospels." *Vol. I. Nearly Ready.*

The First Epistle to the Corinthians. Translated and Edited by W. F. COBB, D.D. 1 *Vol. Nearly Ready.*

The Life of Jesus Christ our Redeemer derived from the Evangelist and the Holy Fathers. By LUDOLF OF SAXONY.

"Ludolf of Saxony, Author of the 'Life of Christ,' Dominican A.D. 1300; Carthusian, A.D. 1338. His work has been one of the most popular for above 500 years, as appears from the multitude of the MSS. and editions, and from the early translations."—*Pusey's Eirenicon,* p. 281.

    Translated and Edited by JOHN M. ASHLEY, B.C.L., Author of "Cogitationes Concionales," &c. *Preparing.*

A History of the Somerset Carthusians.
By MARGARET E. THOMPSON, of Frome and the Record Office. *Now Ready.*

This Vol. has 16 page-illustrations of Hinton Charter House, Witham Friary, &c., by the Author's sister, Miss L. B. THOMPSON, and will prove an interesting work to antiquarians, especially of Somersetshire and the West of England generally.

"This book shows in every page the great zeal of the authoress, and her manifest desire to provide for her readers the fullest and best information."—*Guardian.*

The Reformation in England: A SERIES OF ESSAYS.
By the late Dr. MAITLAND, Keeper of the MSS. at Lambeth, Author of "The Dark Ages," &c. *In the Press.*

This volume is being issued at the special request of many readers of "The Dark Ages," to which it forms an admirable companion.

The Life of St. Jerome.
By Father JOSEPH of Siquenza. Translated from the Spanish by MARIANA MONTEIRO, Author of "Basque Legends," "History of Portugal," &c. *Preparing.*

Saints of the Order of St. Benedict.
From the Latin of F. ÆGIDIUS RANBECK, O.S.B. Adapted and Translated by Professor MOLOHAN of Downside College, and Edited by the Very Rev. JOHN A. MORVALL, O.S.B., Sub-Prior of S. Gregory's Monastery, Downside. [*Vol. I.*

This remarkable work was first published in 1677 at the cost of the great Bavarian Monastery in Augsburg. The Life of a Benedictine Saint is given for every day in the year. The great merit of the work, however, consists in the beautiful engravings which illustrate the lives, and which, in this edition, have been most effectively reproduced.

This work is being issued in parts, each part containing the calendar for one month. Price 3s. 6d. each. *Parts I., II., and III. Ready.*

The Church of our Fathers,
AS SEEN IN ST. OSMUND'S RITE FOR THE CATHEDRAL OF SALISBURY. By the late Rev. Dr. ROCK. A New and Revised Edition by the Benedictines of Downside. 4 vols.

JOHN HODGES, BEDFORD STREET, STRAND, W.C.

www.ingramcontent.com/pod-product-compliance
Lightning Source LLC
Chambersburg PA
CBHW030347230426
43664CB00007BB/568